Data Structures
with Java™

Data Structures
with Java™

John R. Hubbard
Anita Huray
University of Richmond

PEARSON

Prentice
Hall

Upper Saddle River, NJ 07458

Library of Congress Cataloging-in-Publication Data

CIP data on file

Vice President and Editorial Director, ECS: *Marcia Horton*
Senior Acquisitions Editor: *Kate Hargett*
Assistant Editor: *Sarah E. Parker*
Editorial Assistant: *Michael Giacobbe*
Vice President and Director of Production and Manufacturing, ESM: *David W. Riccardi*
Executive Managing Editor: *Vince O'Brien*
Assistant Managing Editor: *Camille Trentacoste*
Production Editor: *Lakshmi Balasubramanian*
Director of Creative Services: *Paul Belfanti*
Art Director: *Jayne Conte*
Cover Designer: *Bruce Kenselaar*
Art Editor: *Connie Long*
Manufacturing Manager: *Trudy Pisciotti*
Manufacturing Buyer: *Lisa McDowell*
Marketing Manager: *Pamela Shaffer*
Marketing Assistant: *Barrie Reinhold*

©2004 by Pearson Education Inc.
Pearson Prentice Hall
Pearson Education Inc.
Upper Saddle River, NJ 07458

The author and publisher of this book have used their best efforts in preparing this book. These efforts include the
development, research, and testing of the theories and programs to determine their effectiveness. The author and
publisher make no warranty of any kind, expressed or implied, with regard to these programs or the documentation
contained in this book. The author and publisher shall not be liable in any event for incidental or consequential damages
in connection with, or arising out of, the furnishing, performance, or use of these programs.

Printed in the United States of America
10 9 8 7 6 5 4 3 2 1

ISBN 0-13-093374-0

Pearson Education Ltd., *London*
Pearson Education Australia Pty. Ltd., *Sydney*
Pearson Education Singapore, Pte. Ltd.
Pearson Education North Asia Ltd., *Hong Kong*
Pearson Education Canada, Inc., *Toronto*
Pearson Educación de Mexico, S.A. de C.V.
Pearson Education—Japan, *Tokyo*
Pearson Education Malaysia, Pte. Ltd.
Pearson Education, Inc., *Upper Saddle River, New Jersey*

Dedicated to our big brothers

William J. Hubbard
and
Paul G. Huray

who helped us discover the joy of learning.

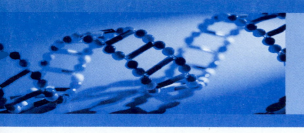

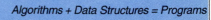

Algorithms + Data Structures = Programs

— Niklaus Wirth, 1976

Preface

This book is intended to be used as a textbook for a university course in data structures, the standard CS2 course offered in American universities. It assumes that the student has completed an elementary course in computer programming with Java. A summary of Java fundamentals is provided in Appendix B for students who need to review the language.

The book covers all the classical data structures topics: basic concepts in Chapters 1–3, linear data structures (stacks, queues, lists, and tables) in Chapters 4–9, nonlinear data structures (trees and graphs) in Chapters 10–14 and 16, and a substantial treatment of ten sorting algorithms in Chapter 15. It is flexible enough to be used either for a one-semester course in data structures or for a two-semester course in data structures and algorithms.

Algorithms are presented explicitly throughout the book. They are introduced in Section 1.5 at a simple level and then studied at progressively deeper levels in later chapters. Complexity analysis is introduced in Section 3.6 and then applied later in chapters 9–16. Loop invariants are finally introduced in Chapter 15 to establish the correctness of the sorting algorithms. Some of these advanced topics can easily be omitted in a one-semester CS2 course.

The chart on the next page shows the chapter dependencies. It shows that the book is flexible enough to support a reordering of some topics. For example, recursion could be done near the beginning of the course, and hash tables could be done at the end of the course.

We use the spiral approach on difficult topics. For example, linked structures are introduced in Chapter 4 as a variant of indirect arrays, and then gradually developed through Chapters 5–8.

The book emphasizes the important distinction between abstract data types (ADTs) and their underlying data structures. ADTs are represented by UML diagrams and realized as Java interfaces. Specific data structures, such as arrays and linked lists, are seen as backing structures for alternative implementations of a given ADT. This important separation of design from implementation is embodied throughout the Java Collections Framework (JCF), which is thoroughly covered in Chapter 7 and Appendix D. Not only does the JCF clarify the value of abstraction, but it also provides the student with many exemplary programming strategies.

Although this is a textbook about data structures, the authors are well aware that students in this course are still learning fundamental programming concepts and Java techniques. Accordingly, we have included many examples and explanations of topics such as polymorphism, simulation, abstract classes, inner classes, and reflection.

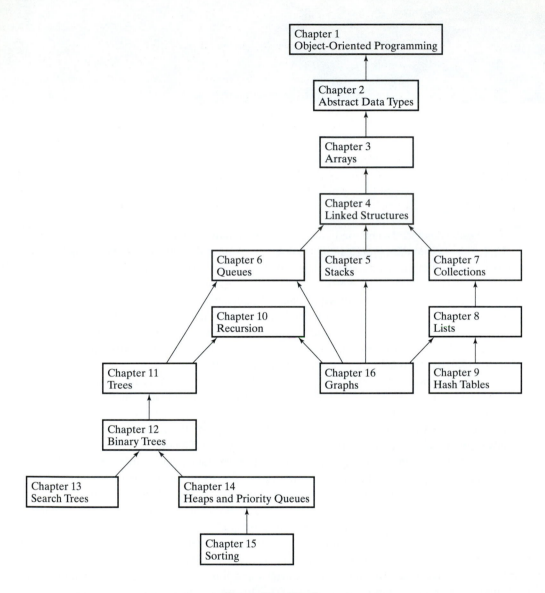

Chapter Dependencies

We are firm believers in the old adage, "A picture is worth 1024 words." So you will find extensive illustrations throughout the book. It contains over 350 figures. It could be subtitled "Visual Data Structures."

We have also tried to make the book as current as possible. It uses Java 1.4, including new features such as the `assert` statement in Chapter 2 and the new `LinkedHash` classes in Appendix D. It also uses Unified Modeling Language (UML) diagrams to summarize class definitions and their relationships.

The companion website for this book is:

`www.prenhall.com/hubbard/`

It contains an on-line study guide and Java source code for all the examples in the book.

An Instructor's Resource CD is also available. It contains Power Point slides, a test bank for each chapter, and solutions to all the exercises and programming problems in the book.

We are grateful for the assistance we have received on this work from our friends at Prentice-Hall and at the University of Richmond. In particular, we wish to thank Matthew Albin, Rom Chan, Natalie Goldberg, Dan Katz, Andrew Lobo, and Molly McCann at Richmond, and Lakshmi Balasubramanian, Petra Recter, and Camille Trentacoste at Prentice-Hall. We also appreciate the suggestions and insights provided by reviewers Benjamin Shults at Western Carolina University, Ted Pawlicki at the University of Rochester, Simon Gray at Ashland University, Frank Coyle at Southern Methodist University, and Bina Ramamurthy at SUNY Buffalo. Finally, we thank our students who used the pre-publication versions in our Data Structures course.

JOHN R. HUBBARD
ANITA HURAY

Table of Contents

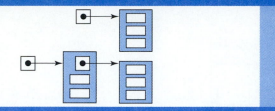

Deep in unfathomable mines
Of never failing skill
He treasurers up his bright designs,
And works his sovereign will.

—William Cowper, *Olney Hymns*

Chapter 1

Object-Oriented Programming

How do you write a computer program? If you are like most beginners, you write the code, run the program, and then spend the rest of your time fixing the mistakes. That may work for small programs. But for substantial production software it can lead to disaster.

Successful modern program development is based on a set of principles that have evolved over the past 50 years. The practice of these principles is called *software engineering*. These principles include top-down design, modularization, and information hiding. A more recent idea, which has now become one of the standard principles of software development, is called *object-oriented programming* (*OOP*). It takes the view that a program is an assembly of interacting objects. The "objects" are abstract representations of real things such as a windows and people.

We begin our study of data structures with a review of object-oriented programming in the Java environment. For a review of the fundamentals of programming with Java, see Appendix B.

1.1 Problem Solving

Commercial software vendors often refer to a computer program as a "solution." This suggests that there is a problem to be solved and that their program solves it. For example, you probably have on your computer a solution that works like an electronic calculator. If you are using Microsoft Windows, you can launch **Programs > Accessories > Calculator** from the **Start** key. This solution solves the problem of error-free, high-precision arithmetic. (See Figure 1.1.)

A good software solution is not produced simply by writing and compiling code. The general process of software development has been widely studied. Researchers have identified a sequence of distinct events in the life of a software solution. These steps are summarized in Figure 1.2 on page 2. In most cases, each step is performed by a separate team of professionals. The diagram is a time line, suggesting that each task is completed before the next one begins.

FIGURE 1.1   The Calculator application.

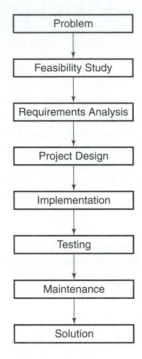

FIGURE 1.2   The stages in the life of a software solution.

The life of a software solution begins when an organization recognizes that there is a problem to be solved. This organization is called the "client," which could be a team of marketing analysts who see a demand for the product, or an engineering department that needs a particular solution to a technical problem. In any case, we assume that the client who poses the problem is separate from the software organization that will solve it.

The first task is a *feasibility study*, which produces a precise statement of the problem and an analysis of the potential profitability of its solution. This requires estimating the resources needed to solve the problem, a time frame for developing the solution, and the benefits expected from its success. The study could discover that another solution already exists and abandon the project.

The next critical stage in the development of a software solution is its *requirements analysis*, which usually results in a document that precisely defines what the end product must do. It includes criteria that the testing team will use later to determine whether the software works correctly. This is also the stage at which a draft of the *user manual* is written.

The *project design* team determines the overall structure of the software system. This includes identifying the individual components and specifying what they will do.

The *implementation* phase produces executable code for each component, ensuring that they work independently of the whole.

The components are assembled in the *testing* stage of the project. Then, the entire system is thoroughly tested against the requirements specification before it is delivered to the client.

Long-term *maintenance* includes user support, patches ("service packs"), and revisions. This long-term phase could involve (from sale or corporate merger) transferring the responsibility of the product from the developer to another company or organization that did not even exist when the software was first developed.

Note the important separation of *what* the solution is required to do from *how* the solution will be designed and implemented. The requirements analysis completely specifies what the system will do before the product design team begins outlining the structure of the software. This separation is an example of *abstraction*, the separation of the "what" from the "how." This important idea is examined in more detail in Chapter 2.

Although this sequence of steps appears to be a linear process, in practice there are usually several repetitions involved. For example, after implementing and testing a product, the decision might be made to add some more features to it. That would take it back to a rewriting of its requirements, as indicated by the loop shown in Figure 1.3.

This description of professional problem solving is only a rough outline of the complete process. If you take a full course in *software engineering* later in your academic career, you will study each of these development stages in greater detail.

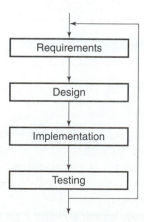

FIGURE 1.3 Software stages.

▼ EXAMPLE 1.1: A Temperature Scale Converter

Suppose that your friend, who will be studying in Europe next semester, says to you, "I wish I had a little program that would convert Celsius to Fahrenheit that I could use over there." This gives you a *problem* to solve for a client.

During your *feasibility study*, you decide to produce a program that will not only convert Celsius to Fahrenheit, but also *vice versa*. You agree that "this afternoon" is a reasonable time frame to complete the solution, and that your compensation will be a souvenir from Europe.

Proceeding immediately to your *requirements* analysis, you adhere to the time-honored *k.i.s.s.* ("keep it simple, stupid") *principle* and decide that your solution will be a simple Java program that reads its input and prints its output in a console window, like the DOS Command Prompt window shown in Figure 1.4. This means that the input values will be string elements of the args[] array.

As the sample run in the figure shows, the user will enter a string in the form java Convert <number> <scale> at the command line, where <number> is a number such as 25, and <scale> is either C for Celsius or F for Fahrenheit. Then the output will be a single line such as

    25.0 C = 77.0 F

which shows the equivalent temperature value in the other scale.

Part of the requirements stage usually involves the production of a user manual that describes how to use the program and gives examples to show how it works. Figure 1.5 shows a user manual for our temperature conversion solution.

This document is brief because the product is simple and the client is your friend. In a larger enterprise, the manual would be much more extensive.

As you can imagine, the team for each stage of the development process is not even formed until after the previous team has completed its work. For example, the design team is assembled after the requirements team has completed its requirements document, and the implementation team is formed after the design is completed.

```
Command Prompt                                                    _ □ ×
C:\>a:

A:\>dir *.java
 Volume in drive A has no label.
 Volume Serial Number is 0000-0000

 Directory of A:\

03/06/2003   04:58p                 695 Temperature.java
03/06/2003   04:59p                 909 Convert.java
03/06/2003   05:00p                 945 MyTemperature.java
               3 File(s)          2,549 bytes
               0 Dir(s)       1,445,376 bytes free

A:\>javac *.java

A:\>java Convert 25 C
25.0 C = 77.0 F

A:\>
```

FIGURE 1.4   Testing the Convert program.

```
                        User Manual
Enter the string: java Convert <number> <scale>
at the command line, where <number> is a number that
represents the temperature in the given <scale>. The output
will be the temperature in both scales.
Examples:
        1. Input:    java Convert 25 C
           Output:   25.0 C = 77.0 F
        2. Input:    java Convert 75 F
           Output:   23.9 C = 75.0 F
Nearly any integer or decimal number, positive or negative,
can be entered.
```

FIGURE 1.5   A User Manual for the Temperature Conversion Solution.

1.2 Object-Oriented Design

The design of a software system begins by identifying the primary parts of the system. In an object-oriented system, those parts will be objects. If Java is used, then the design also will specify the classes that the objects instantiate as well as the interfaces that those classes implement.

The Java programming language has a huge standard library.[1] This provides a wealth of "off-the-shelf software," making it easy to avoid "reinventing the wheel." Thus, you should look for an existing class or interface to use before designing a new one. The advantages of reusing standard software types include the following:

❏   It saves you the expense of building and testing your own software.

❏   You can be fairly confident that the commercial types will work as advertised.

❏   Commercial software is likely to be nearly optimal in its use of time and space.

❏   Your system will be better understood because other programmers will have access to the same kinds of software (classes and interfaces) and thus are likely to be familiar with them.

In this book, we will use Java standard library types whenever possible. In cases where the type itself is our object of study, we may also examine alternative implementations. Moreover, you are encouraged to write your own versions and compare them with the standard classes.

If a suitable existing type cannot be found, then you must design a custom type. If Java is being used, then the type can be specified as a Java interface and its methods can be described using the Javadoc documentation utility that comes with every Java installation.

Listing 1.1 is an example of a design specification for a class to be used to solve the temperature conversion problem.

---

[1] Java 1.4 has 136 packages that define 3,020 types (classes and interfaces) with 32,138 members (fields, constructors, and methods).

LISTING 1.1: A Java Interface for the Temperature Conversion Problem

```
1   /**
2    *   An interface for representing temperatures, with functionality
3    *   for converting their values between Celsius and Fahrenheit.
4    *   @author   John R. Hubbard
5    *   @see      MyTemperature
6    */
7
8   public interface Temperature {
9     /** @return   the Celsius value for this temperature.   */
10    public double getCelsius();
11
12    /** @return   the Fahrenheit value for this temperature.   */
13    public double getFahrenheit();
14
15    /** @param   celsius   the Celsius value for this temperature.   */
16    public void setCelsius(double celsius);
17
18    /** @param   fahrenheit   the Fahrenheit value for this temperature.*/
19    public void setFahrenheit(double fahrenheit);
20  }
```

This Java interface defined in Listing 1.1 specifies four methods: two "getter" methods and two "setter" methods. As an interface, it leaves the decision about how the temperature will be stored to the implementors. An *interface* defines only what the type can do, not how it does it.

The code comments in Listing 1.1 are one of three kinds of comments available in Java. Ordinary *C style comments* are delimited by /* and */, like this:

```
/*  This is a C style comment.   */
```

C++ style comments begin with // and extend only to the end of the line, like this:

```
//  This is a C++ style comment.
```

Javadoc comments are the same as C style comments except that their left delimiter has an extra asterisk, like this:

```
/**  This is a Javadoc comment.   */
```

The comments in Listing 1.1 on page 6 are Javadoc comments. When a Java source code file like the one in Listing 1.1 is processed by the Javadoc utility, it generates a special HTML file that displays information based upon the Javadoc comments in the source code.

The web page shown in Figure 1.6 on page 7 was produced by executing the Javadoc utility with the Windows Command Prompt, like this:

```
A:\>javadoc Temperature.java
```

where `Temperature.java` is the name of the file[2] that contains the source code shown in Listing 1.1. Note that the name of this web page is `Temperature.html`.

---

[2] Be aware that the Javadoc command will generate quite a few files in your current directory.

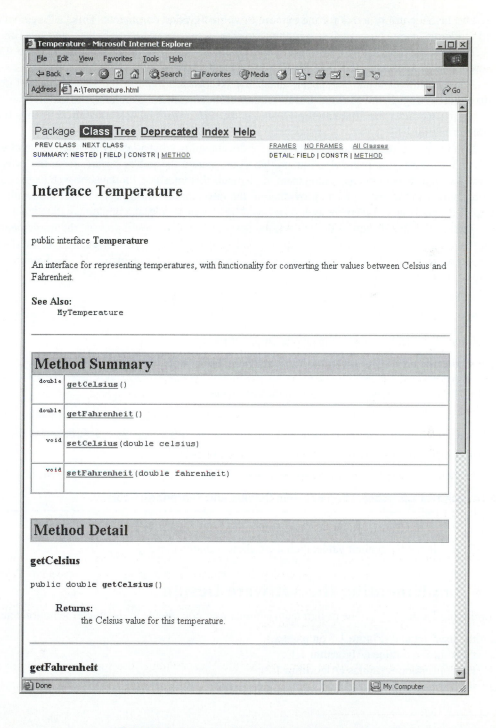

FIGURE 1.6 The Javadoc File Produced from Listing 1.1.

The Javadoc utility looks for the symbol @ within Javadoc comments. This "at" symbol is used to identify parameters such as `@author`, `@param`, `@return`, `@see`, `@throws`, and `@value`.

The text on lines 2–3 in Listing 1.1 appear in the first part of the document. Line 4 is ignored. Line 5 appears as the "**See Also:**" part of the document.

The text in lines 9 and 12 appears under the "**Returns:**" label in the **getCelsius** and **getFahrenheit** listings in the **Method Detail** section of the document. Similarly, the text in lines 15 and 18 appears under the "**Parameters:**" label in the **setCelsius** and **setFahrenheit** listings (not visible in Figure 1.6).

Javadoc web pages are excellent devices for documenting what a Java type (interface or class) can do. The abstraction principle requires that you separate the public "*what*" from the private "*how*." As soon as the implementation team implements this interface, the Javadoc web page could be transmitted to the testing team, providing all the information that it needs to test the resulting class. The actual class implementation code could be kept hidden by the implementation team.

To complete the design of the project, the design team also should provide the implementation team with the algorithms[3] that will be needed to implement the Temperature interface. (See Algorithms 1.1 and 1.2.) The formulas for converting between Celsius, C, and Fahrenheit, F, are as follows:

1. $F = 9C/5 + 32$
2. $C = 5(F - 32)/9$

Algebraically, each function is the inverse of the other.

▲ **ALGORITHM 1.1: Solution to the Temperature Conversion Problem**

1. Read two strings, s_1 and s_2, from the command line.
2. Convert s_1 to a decimal number named `value`, representing a temperature value.
3. Convert s_2 to a character named `scale`, indicating either Celsius or Fahrenheit scale.
4. Create a `Temperature` object from `value` and `scale`.
5. Print the object's data in the form: `<Celsius-value> C = <Fahrenheit-value> F`

▲ **ALGORITHM 1.2: Converting between Celsius and Fahrenheit Scales**

1. If C is the Celsius value, then the Fahrenheit value is $F = 9C/5 + 32$.
2. If F is the Fahrenheit value, then the Celsius value is $C = 5(F - 32)/9$.

1.3 Implementing the Software Design

Continuing Example 1.1: The design team submits four documents to the implementation team:

❑   the user manual (Figure 1.5 on page 5.);
❑   the solution outline (Algorithm 1.1);
❑   the conversion formulas (Algorithm 1.2);
❑   the Temperature interface (Listing 1.1 on page 6).

---

[3] An *algorithm* is a sequence of instructions that solves a problem and can be implemented by other people or machines.

The implementation team is obliged to implement each component of the software project and to assemble it into a solution. For our temperature conversion problem, the temperature interface is implemented as shown in Listing 1.2.

Listing 1.2: An Implementation of the Temperature Interface

```
1   public class MyTemperature implements Temperature {
2     private double celsius;   // stores temperature as a Celsius value
3
4     public MyTemperature(double value, char scale) {
5       if (scale=='C') setCelsius(value);
6       else setFahrenheit(value);
7     }
8
9     public double getCelsius() {
10      return celsius;
11    }
12
13    public double getFahrenheit() {
14      return 9*celsius/5 + 32.0;
15    }
16
17    public void setCelsius(double celsius) {
18      this.celsius = celsius;
19    }
20
21    public void setFahrenheit(double fahrenheit) {
22      this.celsius = 5*(fahrenheit - 32)/9;
23    }
24
25    public String toString() {
26      // Example: "25.0 C = 77.0 F"
27      return round(getCelsius())+ " C = " + round(getFahrenheit())+ " F";
28    }
29
30    private double round(double x) {
31      // returns x, rounded to one digit on the right of the decimal:
32      return Math.round(10*x)/10.0;
33    }
34  }
```

The implementor (declared at line 2) decided to store the data for a Temperature object as a private instance variable of type double whose value is the Celsius value of the temperature being represented. This is a reasonable implementation decision because every temperature has a unique representation in that form. Of course, another implementor could decide to store the Fahrenheit value, or even the Kelvin value, instead. Whatever choice is made here, it would be hidden[4]

----

[4] To say that computer source code is "hidden" means that it is kept in a separate file that should not have to be examined by the client in order to use it effectively. For example, the detailed source code that performs the addition of two integers is hidden.

from anyone outside the Implementation team. Thus, since all three implementations are opera-tionally equivalent, it doesn't really matter which is selected.

To implement the interface, as the class says it does on line 1, it must include complete def-initions of each method specified by the interface. These four methods are defined in lines 9-23. Note that they implement the two formulas listed in Algorithm 1.2 for converting between the Celsius and Fahrenheit scales.

Besides the interface, the implementation team also receives the user manual. In lieu of a complete requirements document, this serves as the blueprint for completing the implementation.

The class also defines a `public` constructor (lines 4–7), a `public` `toString()` method (lines 25–28), and a `private` `round()` method (lines 30–33). The constructor creates a Temper-ature object for a given temperature, which may be in Celsius or Fahrenheit, as indicated by the given character. For example, the expression

```
Temperature t = new MyTemperature(20,'C');
```

creates the `Temperature` object t to represent the temperature 20 degrees Celsius.

The `toString()` method defined in the `MyTemperature` class overrides the corresponding `toString()` method that it automatically inherits from the `Object` class. It returns a `String` representation of the object that can be printed. The string looks like this:

```
20.0 C = 68.0 F
```

It shows both the Celsius and the Fahrenheit values for the temperature that the object represents.

The `toString()` method uses a private `round()` method that rounds a decimal number to an accuracy level one decimal place. For example, `round(12.34)` will return `12.3`, and `round(12.37)` will return `12.4`. It uses the `Math.round()` method, which rounds decimal numbers (type `double`) to whole numbers (type `int`). The expression

```
Math.round(10*x)/10.0;
```

multiplies x by 10, rounds to the nearest whole number, and then divides by 10.0. So, for example, the x value 12.37 produces the value 123.7, which is rounded to the integer 124 and then produces the value 12.4. The denominator 10 is expressed as the `double` type 10.0 to induce floating-point division instead of integer division, which would discard the frac-tional part.

Note how the implementation in Listing 1.2 adheres to fundamental programming principles:

❑ The code is preceded by an identifying comment that explains what it does, who wrote it, and when it was written.

❑ The code is modularized following the maxim that distinct tasks should be carried out by dis-tinct methods.

❑ Variables are named to describe what they represent (`temperature` and `scale`).

❑ In-line comments are added where the code is not clear.

❑ Standard library methods are used where appropriate
(e.g., the `Math.round()` method at line 32).

❏ The input is checked for correctness.

❏ The output is formatted for the user's convenience.

1.4 Testing the Class

The testing stage can be one of the most difficult and important parts of the software development process. It is difficult because, in all but the most trivial cases, only a small fraction of the possible conditions can be tested. It is important because it is usually the only way to find and remove most errors.

Small classes, such as our `MyTemperature` class, can be tested with a test driver program like the one shown in Listing 1.3.

LISTING 1.3: Testing the Solution to the Temperature Problem

```
1   public class Convert {
2     public static void main(String[] args) {
3       if (args.length!=2) exit();
4       double value = Double.parseDouble(args[0]);   // convert string
5       char scale = Character.toUpperCase(args[1].charAt(0));
6       if (scale != 'C' && scale != 'F') exit();
7       Temperature temperature = new MyTemperature(value,scale);
8       System.out.println(temperature);
9     }
10
11    private static void exit() {
12      // prints usage message and then terminates the program:
13      System.out.println(
14        "Usage: java Convert <temperature> <scale>"
15        + "\nwhere:"
16        + "\t<temperature> is the temperature that you want to convert"
17        + "\n\t<scale> is either \"C\" or \"F\"."
18        + "\nExample: java Convert 67 F"
19      );
20      System.exit(0);
21    }
22  }
```

This program reads one pair of inputs from the command line, which requires two string arguments after the `java Convert` command:

```
java Convert 25 C
```

This conforms to the User Manual shown in Figure 1.5 on page 5. So the program first checks on line 3 that the input array `args[]` does indeed have length 2. If the command line is as shown here, then `args[0]` will contain the string `"25"` and `args[1]` will contain the string `"C"`. The statement on line 4 would then apply the `parseDouble()` method of the `Double` class to the string `"25"` to assign the `double` value 25.0 to the local variable `value`. Similarly, the statement on line 5 would extract the first character `'C'` from the string `"C"` and assign it to the local variable `scale`. Note that it applies the `toUpperCase()` method of the `Character` class to ensure that the `scale` variable contains a capital letter. The value of `scale` should be either the character `'C'` (for Celsius) or the character `'F'` (for Fahrenheit), so the statement at line 6 will terminate the program if that condition is not satisfied.

The `Temperature` class is instantiated at line 7 by invoking its two-argument constructor, passing the values of `scale` and `value` to it. Then line 8 invokes the class's `toString()` method by passing the reference `temperature` to the `println()` method. With the input previously shown, this will print

```
25.0 C = 77.0 F
```

The separate `exit()` method on lines 11-21 supports a controlled termination of the program in the case of inadequate input. It prints a "`Usage:`" message that reminds the user what form of input is expected.

When developing a large class, it is helpful to write stubs for the methods initially. A *stub* is a method with a dummy body that has just enough code to compile, deferring its complete implementation until it will be tested. By defining stubs for methods, you can write and run your test driver in stages, each stage testing one more method.

For example, suppose you are building a class whose instances represent points (x, y) in the Cartesian plane. Suppose your class will include the following methods:

```
Point(double, double)          // constructs the point (x,y)
void add(double, double)       // adds the given (dx,dy) displacement
void add(Point)                // adds the given point
double amplitude()             // returns angle radians
boolean equals(Object)         // overrides the Object.equals() method
void expand(double)            // multiplies by the given factor
double x()                     // returns its x-coordinate
double y()                     // returns its y-coordinate
double modulus()               // returns the distance to (0,0)
void moveTo(double, double)    // moves to the given (x,y) position
void moveTo(Point)             // moves to the given point
void rotate(double)            // rotates by the given angle in radians
String toString()              // overrides the Object.toString() method
```

Instead of trying to write and compile the complete class, it is easier to complete just a couple of the methods, and then compile and test them. Next, complete another method, recompile the class, and test it. Repeat this process until all the methods are completed. This makes it much easier to locate and correct errors in the development of the class.

Listing 1.4 illustrates how to implement a class with stubs.

LISTING 1.4: Implementing a `Point` **Class with Stubs**

```
1   public class Point {
2      private double x, y;
3      public static final Point ORIGIN = new Point();
4
5      private Point() {
6      }
7
8      public Point(double x, double y) {
9         this.x = x;
10        this.y = y;
11     }
12
13     public void add(double u, double v)  { }
14     public void add(Point p)  { }
15     public double amplitude()  { return 0.0; }
16     public static double distance(Point p, Point q) { return 0.0; }
17     public boolean equals(Object object)  { return false; }
18     public void expand(double c)  { }
19     public double x()  { return 0.0; }
20     public double y()  { return 0.0; }
21     public double modulus()  { return 0.0; }
22     public void moveTo(double x, double y)  { }
23     public void moveTo(Point p)  { }
24     public void rotate(double t)  { }
25
26     public String toString()  {
27        return "(" + x + "," + y + ")";
28     }
29  }
```

This initial version of the `Point` class contains stubs for every method except the constructor and the `toString()` method. Each of the 12 stubs is a minimal implementation: an empty block for `void` methods and a trivial `return` statement for the non-`void` methods. This incomplete class can be compiled and then tested with a test driver that invokes only the constructor and the `toString()` method. After that initial testing, the development could proceed as follows:

1. Write and test the `x()` and `y()` methods.
2. Write and test the `equals()` method.
3. Write and test the two `add()` methods.
4. Write and test the two `moveTo()` methods.
5. Write and test the `expand()` method.
6. Write and test the `modulus()` method.
7. Write and test the `rotate()` method.
8. Write and test the `amplitude()` method.
9. Write and test the `distance()` method.

This sequence of steps builds the class gradually, from the easier methods to the more difficult methods.

The `Point` class example in Listing 1.4 illustrates the overall testing strategy of incrementally building and testing one method at a time. For testing individual methods, the following strategies are important:

❏ Pick some simple inputs whose correct output is easy to determine.
❏ Check boundary values separately.
❏ Use randomly generated values to test "typical" inputs.

1.5 Implementing and Testing an Algorithm

To illustrate the ideas described in the previous section, suppose you want to implement and test Algorithm 1.3, used to find prime numbers.

▲ **ALGORITHM 1.3: Prime Numbers**

Input: an integer *n*.
Output: *true* if and only if *n* is prime.

  1. If $n < 2$, return *false*.

  2. If $n < 4$, return *true*.

  3. If *n* is even, return *false*.

  4. Repeat step 5 for each odd *d* from 3 to $\sqrt{n}$ inclusive:

  5. If *n* is divisible by *d*, return *false*.

  6. Return *true*.

Recall that a *prime number* is an integer greater than 1 that has no divisors other than itself and 1. So the first 10 primes are: 2, 3, 5, 7, 11, 13, 17, 19, 23, 29.

LISTING 1.5: Finding Prime Numbers

```
1    public static boolean isPrime(int n) {
2       if (n < 2) return false;
3       if (n < 4) return true;
4       if (n%2 == 0) return false;
5       for (int d=3; d*d <= n; d += 2)
6          if (n%d == 0) return false;
7       return true;
8    }
```

Algorithm 1.3 is implemented in Listing 1.5 on page 14. Steps 1–3 are implemented directly at lines 2–4. Note that the condition "*n* is even" in step 3 is translated into (n%2 == 0) at line 4. Recall that the remainder operator % returns the remainder from the indicated division, so the expression n%2 returns the remainder from dividing n by 2. That remainder will be 0 if and only if n is even.

The loop at steps 4–5 in Algorithm 1.3 is translated into the for loop at lines 5–6 in Listing 1.5. To restrict d to odd numbers from 3 to $\sqrt{n}$, we start with d=3, and increment d by 2 (using the expression d += 2, which means "add 2 to d") as long as d*d <= n (*i.e.*, $d \le \sqrt{n}$). The condition "*n* is divisible by d" in step 5 is translated into (n%d == 0) at line 6.

How should the isPrime() method be tested? That is, for which integers n should we evaluate isPrime(n)? Certainly, we should check the 10 values that we already know are prime: 2, 3, 5, 7, 11, 13, 17, 19, 23, 29. We should also check the other numbers in this range (1, 4, 6, 8, 9, 10, *etc.*) because we want to be sure that our method both returns true for numbers that are prime and returns false for numbers that are not prime.[5]

Testing all the integers from 1 to 30 might be a good strategy. That can be done in a simple for loop:

```
for (int n=1; n <= 30; n++)
    if (isPrime(n)) System.out.print(n + " ");
```

This will print

    2 3 5 7 11 13 17 19 23 29

which is correct.

But it is easy to check a wider range. For example, the version

```
for (int n=1; n <= 100; n++)
    if (isPrime(n)) System.out.print(n + " ");
```

will print

    2 3 5 7 11 13 17 19 23 29 31 37 41 43 47 53 59 61 67 71 73 79 83 89 97

which is also correct. Obviously, the more numbers checked, the better off we are. But we cannot check them all, so we have to give some thought to the values we do check.

In choosing a set of inputs to check an algorithm, one should always try to include the boundary values. A *boundary value* is an endpoint or some other special value that is not typical of the others. If an algorithm applies only to a range of numbers, then the minimum and maximum values of that range are boundary values. If we have an algorithm that tests character strings, then the empty string and possibly single character strings would be boundary values. If an algorithm applies to more general objects, then the null reference and references to any specially defined objects would be considered boundary values. It is important to check boundary values because the algorithm's logic is likely to be applied differently to them.

We can see in Algorithm 1.3 that the boundary values are really the special cases that are handled prior to the loop at step 4: integers less than 4 and other even integers. Also, since we are using the integer remainder operator %, which works counterintuitively for negative numbers,[6] we should include some negative inputs in our test driver.

---

[5] In science, a *false positive* is the boolean output true when it should be false, and a *false negative* is the boolean output false when it should be true. In statistics, we call the latter a *type-I error* and the former a *type-II error*.

[6] For example, 8 % –3 evaluates to 2, but -8 % 3 evaluates to –2. In other programming languages, such as C++, the expression -8 % 3 evaluates to 2.

With these ideas in mind, we end up with the test driver shown in Listing 1.6.

LISTING 1.6: Testing the Prime Number Algorithm

```
1  public class TestPrimeAlgorithm {
2    public static void main(String[] args) {
3      for (int n=-10; n <= 100; n++)
4        if (isPrime(n)) System.out.print(n + " ");
5    }
6
7    public static boolean isPrime(int n) {
8      // See Listing 1.5 on page 14.
9    }
10 }
```

The output is

2 3 5 7 11 13 17 19 23 29 31 37 41 43 47 53 59 61 67 71 73 79 83 89 97

One important feature of this test driver is that it does include the inputs whose outputs we already know: the integers from 1 to 30. It also tests the counterintuitive negative inputs, the boundary values 0 and 1, and the larger values from 31 to 100. This seems to be a reasonable test range. The output is small enough to be checked by hand, and it is small enough to fit on one line so as to be easy to view at a glance.

1.6 The Unified Modeling Language

The Unified Modeling Language (UML) is a visual specification language for modeling object-oriented software. It was adopted in 1997 as a standard by the Object Management Group (OMG), which is an international consortium of researchers that promotes object-oriented programming. This section introduces the use of UML in the design of software.

One part of UML is a standardized format for diagrams that specify classes. For example, Figure 1.7 shows a specification for a `Person` class. The information in the box is separated into three compartments: one for the class name, one for its fields, and one for its methods. The class fields and methods are prefixed with a single character to specify their access categories: the plus

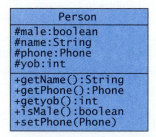

FIGURE 1.7   A UML specification for a `Person` class.

character + for `public`, the minus character – for `private`, and the number sign # for `protected`. Each field type and return type is specified as a suffix following a colon. Parameter types are listed without the parameters' names within the methods' parentheses.

The UML diagram in Figure 1.7 specifies a class named `Person` that has four `protected` fields and five `public` methods. The resulting class definition is shown in Listing 1.7. In addition to the four fields and five methods, the class defines a three-argument constructor. It assumes the existence of a `Phone` class for telephone numbers.

LISTING 1.7: A Person Class

```
1   public class Person {
2      protected boolean male;
3      protected String name;
4      protected Phone phone;
5      protected int yob;
6
7      public Person(String name, boolean male, int yob) {
8         this.name = name;
9         this.male = male;
10        this.yob = yob;
11     }
12
13     public String getName() {
14        return name;
15     }
16
17     public Phone getPhone() {
18        return phone;
19     }
20
21     public int getYob() {
22        return yob;
23     }
24
25     public boolean isMale() {
26        return male;
27     }
28
29     public void setPhone(Phone phone) {
30        this.phone = phone;
31     }
32  }
```

The UML symbol for a class clearly separates the class's fields from its methods. The fields of a class define its *state* (its data), and the methods define its *behavior* (its operations). From the object-oriented point of view, this is a fundamental distinction: the three things that characterize an object are its name, state, and behavior. (See Figure 1.8.) This point of view can be a good way to identify the objects in a solution: Determine which entities have their own state and behavior, and define a class for each of them.

FIGURE 1.8   A UML template.

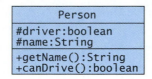
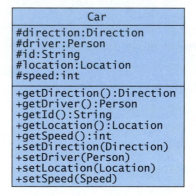

FIGURE 1.9   A Person class and a Car class.

For example, in a simulation involving people riding in cars, we would need a `Person` class and a `Car` class. To decide how to define each class, we should ask what constitutes its state and its behavior. This process can be organized effectively using the UML symbols for the classes, as shown in Figure 1.9.

1.7 Inheritance, Aggregation, and Composition

In object-oriented programming, there are three fundamental ways in which a class can be part of another class: inheritance, aggregation, and composition.

Inheritance is a specialization of another object: A dog is a special type of mammal, a truck is a special type of vehicle, a book is a special type of print media, and a sorted set is a special type of set. This kind of relationship is also called an *is-a* relationship: (e.g., a dog *is a* mammal).

Aggregation is a grouping of other independent objects: A set is a group of its elements; the NATO alliance is a group of member countries. This kind of relationship is also called a *has-a* relationship: The set *has an* element. The member objects are created and destroyed independently of their aggregate container. If the NATO alliance is dismantled, the countries remain.

Relationship	UML Symbol	Meaning	Example
inheritance	———————▷	*is-a*	A book *is a* printed resource.
aggregation	———————◇	*has-a*	A book *has a* publisher.
composition	◆———————	*contains-a*	A book *contains a* chapter.

TABLE 1.1   UML symbols for relationships between classes.

Composition is an inclusion of other objects: A dog includes its heart; a truck includes its engine; a book includes its chapters; a set includes a subset. This kind of relationship is also called a *contains-a* relationship: a set *contains* its subset. If the containing object is destroyed, the objects that it contains are also destroyed.

These three kinds of relationships (also called *associations*) are denoted by the UML symbols shown in Table 1.1.

▼ **EXAMPLE 1.2: Classes for a University Registration System**

Suppose you are designing a software system for a university registrar. Among the various types of objects to be represented are courses, sections of a course, students, and instructors. Students and instructors are special types of persons. To capture these distinctions, we specify the five classes shown in Figure 1.10.

Note that these UML diagrams do not specify any methods (behaviors) for the classes. They also omit the accessibility symbols (+, #, and –). This is acceptable UML; it allows us to focus on the classes themselves and their fields.

The relationships among these classes are illustrated in the UML diagram in Figure 1.11. For simplicity, only the names of the classes are shown.

A course contains sections. This is the *composition* relationship, symbolized by the filled diamond arrow head. The existence of a section depends upon the existence of the course that contains it: if the course is cancelled, then all of its sections must be cancelled as well. A section belongs to only one course.

A section has students enrolled in it, and it has an instructor who teaches it. These are *aggregation* relationships, symbolized by the unfilled diamond arrow head. The student and instructor objects exist independently of the section; they will still exist if the section is cancelled.

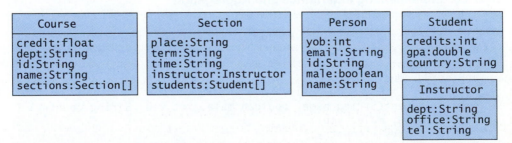

FIGURE 1.10   Five classes for a university registration system.

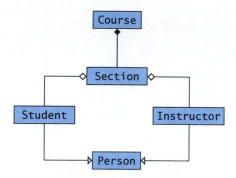

FIGURE 1.11 Relationships among classes.

Students and instructors are special types of persons. These are *inheritance* relationships, symbolized by the unfilled triangle arrow head. Student objects and instructor objects have all the attributes (fields) and operations (methods) that person objects have, as well as some others. In addition to a name, a student also has a grade-point average, and an instructor also has a department.

As a mnemonic to help remember which symbol goes with which relationship, remember that composition is a stronger relationship than aggregation, just as the filled diamond is more solid than the empty diamond.

Among these three kinds of associations described in 1.7, aggregation is probably the one that is most common. Normally, whenever a class *A* has a field of type class *B*, class *A* is an aggregate of class *B*. For example, we see in Figure 1.10 that the `Course` class has three `String` fields: `dept`, `id`, and `name`. Each of these strings exists independently; the `Course` object contains only references to them. If any other references to them exist, then those `String` objects will continue to exist after the `Course` object is destroyed. They need not be bound exclusively to that `Course` object. So these are aggregation associations.

Thus, we see that inheritance and aggregation are easy to implement in Java. Inheritance is implemented by having class B `extend` class A, and aggregation is implemented by declaring a field of type class B within class A.

But how can composition be implemented in Java?

LISTING 1.8: **Implementing Inheritance and Aggregation**

```
1  public class Student extends Person {   // Student inherits Person
2    protected String country;              // Student aggregates String
3    protected int credits;
4    protected double gpa;
5
6    public Student(String name, boolean male, int yob, String country) {
7      super(name, male, yob);
8      this.country = country;
9    }
10 }
```

Composition means exclusive ownership. The component can be part of only one composite, and it must die when the composite dies. This implies that the component object should be completely contained within its composite. In Java, that means that all references to the component must be contained within the composite class.

For our `Student` class, the student's university transcript of grades is a good example of composition. The student is the exclusive owner of the transcript. The university would destroy the transcript if the student dies. Listing 1.9 illustrates how this composition association could be implemented.

LISTING 1.9: Implementing Composition

```
1   public class Student extends Person {   // inheritance
2       private String country;                 // aggregation
3       private int credits;
4       private double gpa;
5       private final Transcript transcript = new Transcript();
6
7       public Student(String name, boolean male, int yob, String country) {
8           super(name, male, yob);
9           this.country = country;
10      }
11
12      public void updateTranscript(Section section, Grade grade) {
13          transcript.add(section, grade);
14      }
15
16      public void printTranscript() {
17          System.out.println(transcript);
18      }
19
20      private class Transcript {               // composition
21          // internal fields...
22          void add(Section section, Grade grade) { //...
23          public String toString() { //...
24      }
25  }
```

Since the `Transcript` class is used only within the `Student` class, we nest it inside as an *inner class* at line 20. Now we can be sure that the `Student` object retains full control over its `Transcript` object. No external object can obtain a reference to any `Transcript` object because the `Transcript` class is a `private` inner class nested in the `Student` class (at line 20), and the `transcript` field is declared `private` (at line 5).

Note that the inner `Transcript` class aggregates the `Section` class and a `Grade` class (Figure 1.12). Instances of these two classes will be used by the `Transcript` classes `add()` method to update the student's `transcript`. This would include updating the student's `credits` and gpa.

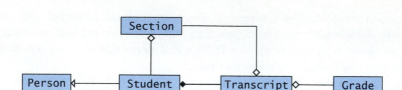

FIGURE 1.12   Relationships among classes

1.8 Mutable and Immutable Objects

Object oriented programming uses the term *immutable* to describe an object whose data cannot be changed; *i.e.*, a constant object. Objects with data that can be changed are called *mutable* objects. Like the notion of composition described in 1.7, immutability is a property that is enforced by the way the class is defined.

In Java, `String` objects are immutable, while `StringBuffer` objects are mutable. Thus, when you execute code such as:

```
String greetings = "Hello";  // immutable object
greetings += ", World!";     // creates new object
```

the system actually creates two distinct `String` objects. First, the `greetings` object is created, containing the string `"Hello"`. Next, a different `String` object is formed by concatenating that string with the literal `", World!"`, and then the resulting new string is assigned to the `greetings` reference. In contrast, the code

```
StringBuffer greetings = new StringBuffer("Hello"); // mutable object
greetings.append(", World!");                       // same object
```

is more efficient because it creates only one object, changing its size with its `append()` method.

Ordinarily, when we define new classes, we make them mutable, even including setter methods to change their fields. For example, the `Person` class defined in Listing 1.7 on page 17 is mutable. Its phone field can be changed with its `setPhone()` method. But suppose we don't want clients to be able to change that field. How can we modify the `Person` class to make it immutable?

An obvious solution is to remove the "setter" method, and then change the constructor so that object's phone field will have to be set when the `Person` object is constructed.

Another essential change would be to declare all the fields `private`. We defined them to be `protected` in Listing 1.7 so that they could be accessed directly by extensions such as a `Student` or `Instructor` subclass. But that means that such a subclass could define setter methods for those fields, thus allowing clients to change them.

Listing 1.10 shows a revised version of our `Person` class from Listing 1.7. To make it immutable, we have specified that all of its fields be `final`. Its UML diagram is shown in Figure 1.13.

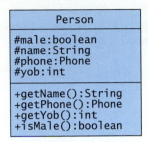

FIGURE 1.13 A revised Person class.

LISTING 1.10: A Revised Person Class

```
1   public class Person {
2     protected final boolean male;
3     protected final String name;
4     protected final Phone phone;
5     protected final int yob;
6
7     public Person(String name, boolean male, int yob, Phone phone) {
8       this.name = name;
9       this.male = male;
10      this.yob = yob;
11      this.phone = phone;
12    }
13
14    public String getName() {
15      return name;
16    }
17
18    public Phone getPhone() {
19      return phone;
20    }
21
22    public int getYob() {
23      return yob;
24    }
25
26    public boolean isMale() {
27      return male;
28    }
29  }
```

But is this revised Person class really immutable?

The answer is "no," unless we ensure that the Phone class is immutable. By using aggregation instead of composition, the Person class becomes just as mutable as any of its aggregated classes.

To see how the `Person` class could be mutable, suppose we define the `Phone` class as shown in Listing 1.11. This includes a "setter" method at line 9 for changing the area code of a telephone number, thereby rendering the class mutable.

LISTING 1.11: A Mutable Phone Class

```
1   class Phone {
2     private String areaCode, number;
3
4     public Phone(String areaCode, String number) {
5       this.areaCode = areaCode;
6       this.number = number;
7     }
8
9     public void setAreaCode(String areaCode) {
10       this.areaCode = areaCode;
11     }
12  }
```

Then, suppose we define the two objects `tel` and `gwb` like this:

```
Phone tel = new Phone("202", "4561414");
Person gwb = new Person("G. W. Bush", true, 1946, tel);
```

The two objects are illustrated in Figure 1.14.

The four fields of the gwb object are declared **final** (*i.e.*, constant), so they cannot be changed. But the phone field is a reference to a mutable object, and `tel` is an independent reference to that same object. So changing the `tel` object with a statement such as `tel.setAreaCode("808")` can change the Phone object, and thereby change the gwb object.

The problem is that the `Person` class is an aggregate of the `Phone` class, instead of being a composite. The `tel` object has an existence that is independent of its gwb object.

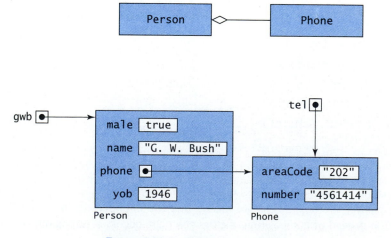

FIGURE 1.14 A mutable Person object.

The solution is to completely encapsulate the `Phone` object within the `Person` object, thus preventing any outside access to it. Declaring the phone field `final` is not good enough. The immutable version is shown in Listing 1.12.

LISTING 1.12: An Immutable `Person` Class

```
1   public class Person {
2       // INVARIANT: all instances are immutable;
3       protected final boolean male;
4       protected final String name;
5       protected final Phone phone;
6       protected final int yob;
7
8       public Person(String name, boolean male, int yob, Phone phone) {
9           this.name = name;
10          this.male = male;
11          this.yob = yob;
12          this.phone = new Phone(phone);
13      }
14
15      // Lines 14-28 from Listing 1.10 on page 23 go here.
16  }
```

The only difference between the mutable version in Listing 1.10 and the immutable version in Listing 1.12 is at line 12 in the constructor. It assumes that the `Phone` class has a *copy constructor* that constructs a duplicate of a specified `Phone` object, like this:

```
public Phone(Phone that) {
    this.areaCode = that.areaCode;
    this.number = that.number;
}
```

With these changes to the `Phone` and `Person` classes, the gwb object will have its own independent copy of the `tel` object, and it will retain complete control over that object, as shown in Figure 1.15. Now `tel` and `gwb.phone` are separate, independent objects, and gwb has exclusive access to the latter. This independent, exclusive access is what makes the association composition instead of aggregation.

Of course, if the `Phone` class were itself immutable, like the `String` class, then the simpler aggregate `Person` class would be immutable. If we define our own `Phone` class, then we can obtain an immutable `Person` class either way: define `Phone` to be immutable, or use composition. But in the frequent situation where we have to use an existing mutable component class, we will have to use composition to obtain an immutable resultant class.

Another advantage of immutable classes is that distinct instances can share the same data. This is seen with the `java.math.BigInteger` class. Its instances represent integer values of (nearly) any size. It stores the integer's digits in an array and uses a separate `int` field for the sign. Its `negate()` method returns a new `BigInteger` object the represents the negative of the integer represented by the default argument. But instead of duplicating the array of digits, it simply uses the same array.

Suppose that we add the constructor shown in Listing 1.13 to the `Person` class defined in Listing 1.12 on page 25.

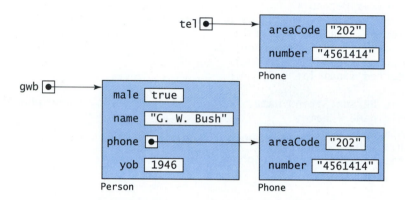

FIGURE 1.15   An immutable Person object.

LISTING 1.13: **Immutable** Person **Objects Sharing the Same** Phone **Object**

```
1  public Person(String name, boolean male, int yob, Person friend) {
2      this.name = name;
3      this.male = male;
4      this.yob = yob;
5      this.phone = friend.phone;
6  }
```

This will allow us to construct a new Person object who shares the same phone as the friend object passed as the fourth argument of the constructor.

Listing 1.14 shows a program to test the constructor defined in Listing 1.13.

LISTING 1.14: **A Test Driver for the Revised** Person **Class**

```
1  public class TestPerson {
2      public static void main(String[] args) {
3          Phone p = new Phone("804", "3790550");
4          Person john = new Person("John Adams", true, 1980, p);
5          System.out.println(john);
6          Person jane = new Person("Jane Adams", false, 1981, john);
7          System.out.println(jane);
8          john = null;
9          System.out.println(jane);
10     }
11 }
```

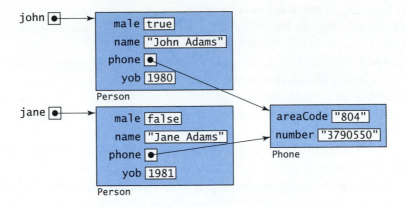

FIGURE 1.16 Two Person objects sharing one Phone object

The output is

```
Mr. John Adams (1980), tel. (804)379-0550
Ms. Jane Adams (1981), tel. (804)379-0550
Ms. Jane Adams (1981), tel. (804)379-0550
```

At lines 3–6, we create and print a Person object named john. At line 7, we create a new Person object named jane, which shares the Phone object that belongs to john. The output from line 7 verifies that the two Person objects have the same phone number.

At line 8, the john object is destroyed (by removing all references to it). But, as the output from line 9 shows, the Phone object still exists. This is illustrated in Figure 1.16.

CHAPTER SUMMARY

❑ Problems are solved by a software development process consisting of a sequence of independent stages: a feasibility study, a requirements Analysis, and project design, implementation, testing, and maintenance.

❑ The feasibility study conducts a cost–benefit analysis before making recommendations on whether to proceed with a project.

❑ The requirements analysis produces an operational definition of the project, defining *what* the software will do, without constraining *how* it will do it. This analysis is also used to produce the user manual.

❑ The project design team defines all the software components that will be used and produces a blueprint for the implementation.

❑ The implementation team writes and compiles the code, implementing the design.

❏ The testing team tests the software.

❏ The maintenance stage covers the rest of the life of the software, including user support and revisions.

❏ UML diagrams are useful for designing and modeling object oriented programs.

❏ UML uses different arrow symbols to distinguish the *inheritance*, *aggregation*, and *composition* relationships between classes.

❏ Inheritance is the specialization of one class by another; it can be implemented in Java by extending the inherited class.

❏ Aggregation is the inclusion of one class instance as part of another; it can be implemented in Java by declaring a class reference as a field of the aggregate class.

❏ Composition is the exclusive ownership of one class uniquely by another; it can be implemented in Java by nesting the component class within the composing class.

❏ A class is immutable if it maintains separate protected copies of all of its object fields that are mutable.

REVIEW QUESTIONS

1.1   Some authors refer to the diagram in Figure 1.2 on page 2 as the "life cycle" of a software solution.

    a. How is this name appropriate?
    b. How is it not appropriate?

1.2   Some authors refer to the diagram in Figure 1.3 on page 3 as a "waterfall" or "cascade."

    a. How are these terms appropriate?
    b. How are they not appropriate?

1.3   How is the Principle of Abstraction used in the software development process?

1.4   What are boundary values in a program?

1.5   What is a stub?

1.6   What are stubs good for?

1.7   Which stage of the software development process produces the user manual, and why is it done at that stage?

1.8   What is the difference between the state of an object and its behavior?

1.9   What is UML?

1.10   What is the difference between aggregation and composition?

1.11   What is the difference between mutable and immutable objects?

1.12   In making the `Person` class immutable (in Section 1.8) why was it not necessary to modify the `name`, `male`, and `father` fields?

1.13   To make a class immutable, why can't we simply declare its fields to be `final`?

EXERCISES

1.1   The Fahrenheit-to-Celsius problem was solved in Section 1.1 with a Java application that outputs the Fahrenheit value for an input Celsius value. Suppose instead that your client wants a conversion table like the one shown in Figure 1.16.

   The user enters three command line arguments: the first Celsius temperature for the table (0), the last Celsius temperature (40), and the Celsius increment (4). For the output shown in Figure 1.17, that command line would be

```
javac CelsiusToFahrenheit 0 40 4
```

1.2   Show another typical cycle, other than the one shown Figure 1.3 on page 3, that is likely to occur in the software development process.

1.3   Draw a UML diagram for a class whose instances represent combination locks. Such a lock stores a sequence of three integers in the range 0 to 36. That sequence is called the lock's "combination." The lock is opened by inputting its combination. The combination is not needed to close the lock. Assume that the combination can be changed if it is inputted.

1.4   In Algorithm 1.3 on page 14, why is it unnecessary to check for divisors of n that are greater than $\sqrt{n}$?

1.5   Modify the UML diagram in Figure 1.11 on page 20 by adding the relationship that an instructor may have as an academic advisor to a student.

1.6   Modify the UML diagram in Figure 1.11 on page 20 by adding a `Department` class for academic departments (*e.g.*, chemistry, mathematics), and add appropriate relationships to the other classes. For example, an instructor may be the chair of a department.

1.7   Modify the UML diagram in Figure 1.11 on page 20 by adding classes for `Undergraduate` and `Graduate` students, and add appropriate relationships to the other classes.

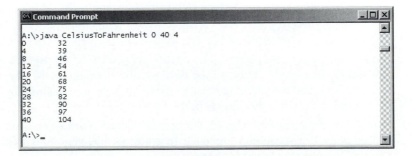

FIGURE 1.17   Output from a temperature conversion solution.

1.8   Draw UML diagrams and show their relationships for the following group of classes:

Bus
Car
Driver
Owner
Person
Truck
Vehicle

1.9   Draw UML diagrams and show their relationships for the following group of classes:

Account
Bank
BankBranch
CheckingAccount
Credit
Customer
Debit
Manager
Person
SavingsAccount
Transaction

1.10   Draw UML diagrams and show their relationships for the following group of classes:

Book
BroadcastMedia
Journal
Magazine
Newspaper
Periodical
PrintMedia
RadioProgram
TelevisionProgrsm
Website

PROGRAMMING PROBLEMS

1.1   Modify the Temperature interface and its implementation by adding functionality for converting to and from the Kelvin scale. Kelvin temperature is computed by adding 273.16 to Celsius temperature. For example, 75.0 F = 23.89 C = 297.05 K.

1.2   Modify the program in Listing 1.2 on page 9 and Listing 1.3 on page 11 so that the user can specify how many digits will be displayed on the right of the decimal point. For example, to round a decimal number to five-digit accuracy, multiply by 10^5, round to the nearest integer, and then divide by 10^5.

1.3   Repeat Programming Problem 1.2, but use the DecimalFormat class (new to Java 1.4) instead of the Math.round(x) method. To get the right pattern for d digits, you can use:

```
String s = "###,###,###,###.###############";
String pattern = new String(s.toCharArray(), 0, 16 + d);
```

1.4   Modify the test driver in Listing 1.6 on page 16 so that it uses inputs that are uniformly distributed throughout the range 0 to `Integer.MAX_VALUE`.

1.5   Write and test complete Java definitions for the five classes shown in Figure 1.10 on page 19.

1.6   Compile and test a `ComboLock` class that implements the UML diagram described in Exercise 1.3.

1.7   Complete and test the `Student` class defined in Listing 1.9 on page 21 to verify that it implements composition.

1.8   Test the `Person` class defined in Listing 1.12 on page 25 to verify that it is immutable.

PROJECTS

1.1   Design, write, and test an interface `Distance` for converting between distances measured in kilometers and distances measured in miles. Then implement it with a `MyDistance` class. Include a user manual like the one in Figure 1.5 on page 5 and Javadoc comments that will generate a Javadoc web page like the one in Figure 1.6 on page 7. *Hint*: Include the constant

```
private static final double K_TO_M = 3280.0/5280;
```

1.2   Carry out the following four stages in the production of a solution that performs like a simple four-function pocket calculator:

a. Write a requirements document that includes the functional objectives, a graphical user interface (GUI), the actions of each button and text field, and the management of user error.

b. Write a design specifications document and a corresponding user manual that meet the requirements set forth the requirements document.

c. Implement the design specifications with a Java class named `Calculator`.

d. Run a test driver named `testCalculator`.

1.3   Here is the U.S. Federal Tax Rate Schedule X for the year 2001:

Schedule X—Use if your filing status is Single

If the amount on Form 1040, line 39, is: *Over—*	*But not Over—*	Enter on Form 1040, line 40	*of the amount over—*
$0	$27,050	—— 15%	$0
27,050	65,550	$4,057.50 + 27.5%	27,050
65,550	136,750	14,645.00 + 30.5%	65,550
136,750	297,350	36,361.00 + 35.5%	136,750
297,350	——	93,374.00 + 39.1%	297,350

Implement this algorithm and test it to compute the tax on various incomes. Pay careful attention to testing boundary values.

1.4   Write and test a Java method that takes a string argument and returns `true` if and only if it is a palindrome. Recall that a *palindrome* is a string whose character sequence is the same when the string is reversed. For example, RADAR is a palindrome. Pay careful attention to testing boundary values.

1.5   Write and test a Java method that solves quadratic equations ($ax^2 + bx + c = 0$). Implement the *quadratic formula*:

$$x = \frac{-b \pm \sqrt{b^2 - 4ac}}{2a}$$

Give serious consideration to what input triples (a, b, c) to use for testing. Be sure to include all boundary values (*i.e.*, special cases).

1.6   Implement and test this algorithm for finding square roots:

▲ **ALGORITHM 1.4: The Bisection Method**

Input: a positive number x.
Output: a positive number y.
Postcondition: y closely approximates $\sqrt{x}$.

1. Let $a = 0$ and $b = (x+1)/2$.
2. Repeat steps 3-4 many times.
3. Let $y = (a+b)/2$.
4. If $y^2 > x$, set $a = y$; otherwise, set $b = y$.
5. Return y.

The number of times to repeat the loop in steps 2-3 depends on the accuracy you want for y. For this exercise, 50 repetitions should suffice.
To determine whether each output y is the square root of its input x, print the values of y^2 and x. They should be nearly equal.
Give serious consideration to what input values of x to use for testing. Be sure to include all boundary values.

1.7   Implement and test this algorithm[7] for finding square roots:

▲ **ALGORITHM 1.5: The Babylonian Algorithm**

Input: a positive number x.
Output: a positive number y.
Postcondition: y closely approximates $\sqrt{x}$.

---

[7] This is probably the oldest algorithm in history, it was used by the ancient Babylonians to lay out the foundations for their buildings.

1. Let $y = (x + 1)/2$.

2. Repeat step 3 many times.

3. Let $y = (y + x/y)/2$.

4. Return y.

The number of times to repeat the loop in steps 2-3 depends on the accuracy you want for y. For this exercise, 20 repetitions should suffice.

To determine whether each output y is the square root of its input x, print the values of y^2 and x. They should be nearly equal.

Give serious consideration to what input values of x to use for testing. Be sure to include all boundary values.

1.8 Implement and test code to represent points and lines in the coordinate plane. First draw UML diagrams for an immutable Point class and a mutable Line class and the relationship between them. Use the fact that every line is determined by two distinct points. Include equals() methods in both classes. Include methods in the Line class to translate (*i.e.*, shift) and rotate lines.

1.9 Implement the *Chance-It game*.[8] In this game, two or more players alternately toss a pair of dice to accumulate a score. The player with the highest cumulative score at the end of the game wins. The game proceeds through a series of rounds. On each round, each player takes a turn in sequence. On each turn, the player tosses the dice repeatedly, attempting to get a high score among the possible range of values 2 to 12. He/she may continue to toss the dice as long as no score matches the score on the first toss. If no such match occurs, then the highest score on that turn gets added to the player's cumulative score. If a toss does match the first toss of that turn, then no score gets added for that player on that round.

Here is a sample run in a four-round game with two players:

```
Round 1:
        Player 1:
                Your first roll is 9    Roll again? (y/n): n
        Player 2:
                Your first roll is 6    Roll again? (y/n): y
                Your next roll is 7     Roll again? (y/n): y
                Your next roll is 6 - A MATCH!
        Player 1 score: 9
        Player 2 score: 0
Round 2:
        Player 1:
                Your first roll is 5    Roll again? (y/n): y
                Your next roll is 7     Roll again? (y/n): n
        Player 2:
                Your first roll is 12   Roll again? (y/n): n
        Player 1 score: 16
        Player 2 score: 12
```

---

[8] Introduced by Joel C. Adams in 1998.

```
Round 3:
      Player 1:
             Your first roll is 8      Roll again? (y/n): n
      Player 2:
             Your first roll is 6      Roll again? (y/n): y
             Your next roll is 8       Roll again? (y/n): n
      Player 1 score: 24
      Player 2 score: 20
Round 4:
      Player 1:
             Your first roll is 5      Roll again? (y/n): y
             Your next roll is 2       Roll again? (y/n): y
             Your next roll is 4       Roll again? (y/n): y
             Your next roll is 12      Roll again? (y/n): n
      Player 2:
             Your first roll is 7      Roll again? (y/n): n
      Player 1 score: 36
      Player 2 score: 27
Player 1 wins.
```

On the first round, Player 2 gets a match on his/her third toss, resulting in a score of 0 for that round. Player 1 ends up winning with a cumulative score of $9 + 7 + 8 + 12 = 36$.

Use the four classes specified in the UML diagrams in Figure 1.18. The main class is Game, whose `main()` method invokes the constructor, passing it the number of rounds to be played. That constructor creates an input object (e.g., see Listing B.16 on page 553), a dice object, and two player objects. The Dice constructor can be invoked as

```
dice = new Dice(new java.util.Random());
```

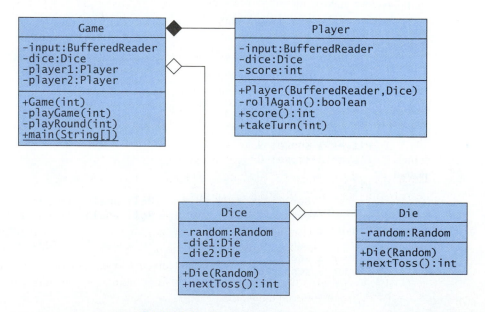

FIGURE 1.18 Classes for the Chance-It game

passing it an anonymous random number object that will be used to simulate the tossing of the dice.

After instantiating its four objects, the Game constructor calls the `playGame()` method, passing it the number of rounds to be played. That method simply repeats calling the `playRound()` method, and then prints the result of the game (who won). The `playRound()` method simply tells each play to take a turn (e.g., `player1.takeTurn(1)`), and then tells each play to report his/her score (e.g., `player1.score()`).

ANSWERS TO REVIEW QUESTIONS

1.1 **a.** The name "life cycle" is appropriate because the actual process usually does include some cycling back.
   b. One reason it is not appropriate is that it suggests that the complete process is a single cycle.

1.2 **a.** The term "waterfall" is appropriate because, like water flowing down a stream, cascading over a sequence of separate waterfalls, a stream of software problems are solved, flowing through the separate stages of the software development process.
   b. The term may not appropriate, because it suggests a single waterfall.

1.3 The principle of abstraction appears in the software development process, where the specification of *what* the software will do is separated from the implementation of *how* it will do it. The *what* is done by the requirements analysis and the project design teams. The *how* is done by the implementation team.

1.4 The *boundary values* of a program are input values that lie on the boundaries of intervals of typical values. For example, if you expect your program to work for double values x in the range $0.0 \le x \le 80.0$, then 0.0 and 80.0 would be boundary values.

1.5 A *stub* is a minimal version of a method that will compile, but is probably incomplete.

1.6 Stubs are used to get a minimal first version of a program to compile. This allows the incremental development of the program by completing one stub at a time and recompiling. This reduces the number of compile errors on each iteration.

1.7 The user manual is produced at the requirements analysis stage because that analysis defines how the user will interface with the system.

1.8 The *state* of an object consists of its data (its fields, in Java). The *behavior* or an object consists of its operations (its methods, in Java).

1.9 UML is the Unified Modeling Language, used to design object-oriented programs.

1.10 Aggregation and composition both refer to the association of an object with its constituent parts. Aggregation when the existence of the parts is independent of the existence of the whole, thereby allowing the constituent objects to be part of more than one whole. Composition is when the whole has exclusive control over the parts, which cannot exist independently from the whole.

1.11 An *immutable object* is an object that cannot be changed.

1.12   To make the Person class immutable, we only have to modify its mutable fields. The name field has type String, which is immutable. The male field has type boolean, which is primitive (so no references exist). And the father field has type Person, which was made immutable.

1.13   Declaring a reference field to be final will not prevent its objects from being changed. It will only make the reference itself constant. An external reference to its object could still change the object.

Chapter 2

Abstract Data Types

An *abstract data type* (ADT) is a generalized description of a concrete data type, such as `int` or `String`. An ADT specifies the operations that can be performed on objects of that type without specifying how those operations are to be implemented. This data abstraction underlies the methodology of object-oriented programming. It facilitates the development of large software projects by encapsulating data and operations into separate modules that can be implemented independently.

This chapter describes the general discipline of data abstraction and shows how it is implemented in Java programs.

2.1 Concrete Data Types

Java is a *strongly typed* programming language: Data to be stored in variables must be declared explicitly to have a specific data type. For example, the declarations

```
int n=44;
String s="Hello!";
```

declare the variable n to have data type `int` and the variable s to have data type `String`. These declarations determine how the variables' data values are stored and what operations can be performed on them. Values for the variable n are stored as 32-bit twos-complement integers to which the arithmetic operations of +, -, *, /, and % can be applied. Values for the variable s are stored using an array of 6 Unicode (16-bit) characters which supports the concatenation operation and many specific methods defined in the `String` class.

The data type `int` is a *primitive data type* in Java. This means that it is built into the language, supplied automatically to the programmer, without any need to import or explain its meaning. Java defines eight primitive data types. The other seven are `boolean`, `char`, `byte`, `short`, `long`, `float`, and `double`.

The data type `String` is a Java class. It is part of the Java Application Program Interface (API). Although we think of these standard classes also as being built in to the language, each class is actually defined in a separate source code file. You can get a summary of all the methods of each class in the API by downloading the Java API Specification or by accessing it online from `java.sun.com`.

Each data type determines the kind of data that its variables can store and the operations that can be performed on that data. For example, `boolean` variables have only two possible values (`true` and `false`) and can be combined using any of the six logical operators &, |, ^, !, &&, and ||. On the other hand, `byte` variables have 256 possible values and can be combined using any of the five arithmetic operators or the six bitwise operators &, |, ^, <<, >>, and >>>.

In Java, a data type is either a primitive data type, an interface, a class, or an array type. For example, these are valid declarations:

```
boolean isOK;            // primitive
float x;                 // primitive
Comparable object;       // interface
java.util.List toDo;     // interface
String name;             // class
java.io.File input;      // class
int[] frequencies;       // array
double[][] matrix;       // array
String[] args;           // array
```

These declare the variables `isOK`, `x`, `object`, `toDo`, `name`, `input`, `frequencies`, `matrix`, and `args`. Other than the names of the variables, there is no indication as to what they represent. The declaration is obliged only to give the type and the name of the variable.

Optionally, a declaration can also include an initialization, like this:

```
boolean isOK = true;
float x = 3.14159;
Comparable object = new Integer(-3);
java.util.List toDo = new ArrayList();
String name = "George Herbert Walker Bush";
java.io.File input = new File("Presidents.dat");
int[] frequencies = new int[100];
double[][] matrix = { {1.0, 2.0}, {3.0, 4.0}, {5.0, 6.0} };
String[] args = {"Sara", "John", "Andy", "Mike"};
```

In general, a variable's data type determines what kind of data it can store, and what kind of operations it can perform. For example, the `isOK` variable in the preceding program has type `boolean`, so it can store only the two values `true` or `false`, and can be operated on by using the six logical operators. Similarly, the `name` variable has type `String`, so it can store strings like `"ABC"` and can respond to method calls such as `name.charAt(2)` and `name.indexOf("B")`.

The data that is stored in an object is called it's *state*, and the operations that can be performed on it are called its *behavior*. Both of these properties are controlled by the object's data type.

2.2 Abstraction

Most programming languages allow programmers to define their own data types. These are called *user-defined types*, or more properly, *programmer-defined types*. In Java, you can define your own classes and interfaces. This gives you a lot of power. However, power without discipline can lead to chaos. The discipline that helps programmers avoid chaos is *abstraction*.

The word "abstract" has several meanings. In ordinary speech, it often suggests something not quite real, something that may be vague and unspecific. In science, the meaning is more precise: An abstraction is a separation of the relevant from the irrelevant, focusing on the general concepts that apply to different but concrete instances.

For example, in arithmetic, we learn that $2 + 3 = 5$, focusing on the abstract ideas of number, separating it from the concrete instances of two people plus three people or two keys plus three keys. (See Figure 2.1.) This is a great efficiency. The fact that the addition rule applies to people and to keys is irrelevant to the rule itself. We learn the abstract rule first, and then we can apply it to situations that we hadn't thought about before learning the rule (*e.g.*, two CDs plus three CDs). One abstraction applies to many instances.

As another example, consider the science of anatomy, in which one studies the human body as an ideal—how it is structured and how it works. From that abstraction, the physician can then study specific pathologies found in actual people. But no one is perfect. The abstraction is an idealization that is not real. Its specific instances are realizations of the ideal.

Of course, deriving the abstraction usually comes after having experienced some of its concrete instances. Most children learn that two fingers plus three fingers comes to five fingers before they learn that $2 + 3 = 5$. Similarly, in science, Galileo rolled balls down inclined planes and perhaps even dropped rocks from towers before he derived his formula $s = ct^2$ that applies to any falling object.

The notion of abstraction goes back to the ancient Greeks. Plato talked about ideals such as Truth and Beauty. Euclidean geometry uses abstractions such as dimensionless points, infinitely straight lines, and perfect circles. These objects do not exist in the real world. Yet, by deriving formulas and properties of these ideals, we can then apply them to real objects and obtain practical results.

The great efficiency comes from applying one idealization to many different objects. The circumference of an imaginary circle is $2\pi r$. This abstraction applies to bicycle tires and to planetary orbits.

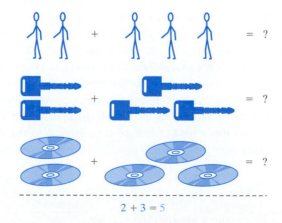

$$2 + 3 = 5$$

FIGURE 2.1 The Concrete and the Abstract.

2.3 Abstract Data Types

Suppose that you have already created the best-selling video game of all time, and you now have a new idea to make it even better. But as you rewrite your code, you discover that the long integer type that you have been using does not work quite the same way with your new code; somehow, the way the long type was implemented depended upon something intrinsic to the previous version of your video game code.

Of course, that wouldn't happen. The way that data types are implemented is independent of how they are used in client programs. Both the implementations and the programs that use them are software. But they are written by different people, at different times, and are always assumed to be completely independent.

The reverse is also true. If you upgrade your computer with a new version of Windows, you expect the programs that you have been using will still work the same way. This will be true even if the actual implementation of a particular data type, such as long or String, has been changed. The reason that the programs are not affected by such changes is that the data type's *operations* are still defined the same way, and that's the part of the data type that your program depends upon. If, for some reason, String objects are now stored using 24-bit characters instead of 16-bit characters, the String operations such as the concatenation operator (+) and the substring() method will still work the same way. So you won't have to make any changes to your program to accommodate the new implementation of the data type.

This is the idea behind data abstraction and *abstract data types* (ADTs). The ADT is the interface between the client programs and the data type's implementation. It tells the client programmer *what* operations he/she can use with the data type, while hiding the details of *how* those operations are actually implemented. (See Figure 2.2) When you use the String type, you know that you can invoke the length() method to get the length of a string, but you don't know how that length is determined. Is it stored in the object, or is it computed on the fly?

This is called *information hiding*. The only information you have about the data type is what you need to know in order to use the data type: its operations. You don't *want* to know how those operations are implemented.

Information hiding is used beneficially in areas other than computer programming. When you are driving a car and you make a left turn, you don't want to have to think about how the car's turning mechanism is actually implemented. All that you need to know is that when you rotate the steering wheel counterclockwise, the car turns to the left. The information on the actual turning mechanisms in the car fortunately is hidden from your attention.

Not only does information hiding help you concentrate on the task at hand; it also relieves you from the distraction of irrelevant details. It also facilitates change. Suppose that you take the car into a shop that completely replace the steering mechanism, installing a better version. But it still works the same way. You don't have to adjust your driving to the new mechanism. The implementation of the turning mechanism is independent from its client driver.

FIGURE 2.2 The ADT is the Interface.

In object-oriented programming (OOP), we focus on the objects that the program will manipulate. These objects will have to be implemented as instances of data types. In Java, the data types are interfaces and classes. But no matter what OOP language we are using, we should be able to write the code that manipulates the objects without first having to write the code that implements their data types. In fact, we should be able to compile our client software, even before those implementations have been written (or, for that matter, formulated). It is the abstraction of the data type that allows us to do that.

In Java and other OOP languages, objects have two parts: their state and their behavior. The *state* of an object is the data that it contains; the *behavior* of an object is the set of operations that it can perform. This dichotomy is emphasized in the UML diagrams that we use for classes. (See Section 1.6 on page 16.) The ADT encapsulates the behavior of the object, without any mention of its state.

We use abstraction to obtain precise definitions of data types before implementing them in a programming language such as Java. The abstract data type is a theoretical construct that serves as an ideal for later implementations. To encapsulate the complete nature of the new data type, the abstraction must specify both the kind of data that it describes and also the operations that may be applied to it. Each realization of the abstract data type will be a concrete data type, implemented in a specific programming language, which can then be used to construct specific objects of that type. The data in the object is called the *state* of the object, and the operations that can be performed upon it are called its *behavior*. In Java, the concrete data type would be a class; its data and operations would be the fields and methods defined in that class.

An ADT is a general specification of a data type and its operations. As an abstraction, the ADT specifies what the operations are, but it gives no details on how those operations are to be executed. They are left for the implementations as concrete data types.

One of the benefits of specifying an ADT before considering how to define it in a programming language is that it focuses our attention on the behavior of the data type. We use that behavior to distinguish the intrinsic differences among data types. Those distinctions are easier to recognize in the absence of programming languages.

To appreciate that point, we consider two similar ADTs: **Bag** and **Set**. (See Figures 2.3 and 2.4.) Intuitively, a "bag" is a container like a shopping bag, which may contain duplicate objects. On the other hand, a "set" is a container that does not allow duplicate elements. That is the only difference between the two data types. They are both unstructured and unordered collections with no other distinguishing features. It is the operations, defined by their ADTs, that show how they differ.

These ADTs specify two *mutator* operations (**add** and **remove**) and four *accessor* operations. You can identify the acccessor operations by their postcondition that the container remain unchanged.

The two **get** operations are meant to be used to access all the elements of the bag, as in Algorithm 2.1.

▲ ALGORITHM 2.1: Printing a *Bag*

Input: a *Bag* b;
Output: a printed copy of all the elements of **b**.
Postcondition: the bag **b** is unchanged.

1. Let *x* object returned by **b.getFirst**().

2. If *x* is **null**, return.

3. Print *x*.

4. Let *x* object returned by **b.getNext**().

5. Go to step 2.

ADT: *Bag*

A **Bag** is a collection of objects.
  void **add**(*Object* object)
     Postcondition: the given object is in this bag.
  boolean **contains**(*Object* object)
     Postcondition: this bag is unchanged.
     Returns: true iff the given object is in this bag.
  Object **getFirst**()
     Returns: an element of this bag.
     Postcondition: this bag is unchanged.
  Object **getNext**()
     Returns: some element of this bag other than those already returned by the
     last call to **getFirst**() and subsequent calls to **getNext**(); if all elements have
     been accesssed by that previous sequence of calls, then **null** is returned.
     Postcondition: this bag is unchanged.
  boolean **remove**(*Object* object)
     Returns: true iff this bag was changed.
  integer **size**()
     Postcondition: this bag is unchanged.
     Returns: the number of elements in this bag.

FIGURE 2.3   An abstract data type for a general bag container.

ADT: *Set*

A **Set** is a collection of unique objects.
  boolean **add**(*Object* object)
     Postcondition: the given object is in this set.
     Returns: true iff this set was changed.
  boolean **contains**(*Object* object)
     Postcondition: this set is unchanged.
     Returns: true iff the given object is in this set.
  Object **getFirst**()
     Returns: an element of this set.
     Postcondition: this set is unchanged.
  Object **getNext**()
     Returns: some element of this set other than those already returned by the
     last call to **getFirst**() and subsequent calls to **getNext**(); if all elements have
     been accesssed by that previous sequence of calls, then **null** is returned.
     Postcondition: this bag is unchanged.
  boolean **remove**(*Object* object)
     Postcondition: the given object is not in this set.
     Returns: true iff this set was changed.
  integer **size**()
     Postcondition: this set is unchanged.
     Returns: the number of elements in this set.

FIGURE 2.4   An abstract data type for a general set container.

This algorithm uses the *getFirst*() operation at step 1 to read a copy *x* of the "first" element in the bag. Of course, we cannot tell which element that will be. The operation is equivalent to looking in a grocery bag and making a note of what and where one of the items is located. The operation neither removes nor duplicates the item; it simply returns a reference *x* to it.

If the bag is empty, then *x* will be *null*, and the algorithm will terminate at step 2. Otherwise, *x* is used at step 3 to print a description of the item. This assumes that some kind of *print*() method has been implemented.

Steps 2–5 constitute a loop that will read each element and print it. The loop terminates at step 2 when all the elements have been accessed.

Both the *Bag* and the *Set* ADTs have these six operations: *add*, *contains*, *getFirst*, *getNext*, *remove*, and *size*. All but the two mutators, *add* and *remove*, are the same for both ADTs.

Since a bag can hold duplicate elements, there is no way that its *add* operation can fail (assuming that overflow is prevented). But the *Set.add* operation should not insert an object that is already in the set. In that case, it returns false, signalling that the insertion failed. The *Bag.add* operation has `void` return type because it has no information to return to its client.

The *remove* operation is different for the two ADTs: We can be sure the deleted object is no longer in the set, but we have no such assurance for the bag. For example, the bag could contain five references to the same object, in which case it would have to delete that object five times before it would no longer be an element of the bag. So the *Set.remove* operation has the postcondition that the object is no longer an element, but the *Bag.remove* operation does not.

Finally, it is worth noting that an abstract data type is not the same as an `abstract` class. In Java, an `abstract` class is a class that has at least one `abstract` method. An `abstract` method is simply a method prototype: the method header without its body block. So an `abstract` class is like a partial interface: Some methods may be implemented, but at least one is not.

2.4 Preconditions and Postconditions

We saw in the previous section how an ADT is defined by its set of operations. The operations themselves are defined in terms of preconditions, postconditions, and return values.

A *precondition* for an operation is a condition that is assumed to be true before the operation begins. A *postcondition* is a condition that is guaranteed to be true after the operation ends, provided that the preconditions were satisfied. The preconditions and postconditions of an operation can be regarded as a contract between the client and the operation: If the client satisfies the preconditions, then the operation is guaranteed to satisfy the postconditions. They can also be regarded as before-and-after snapshots: The preconditions describe the situation just before the operation begins to execute, and the postconditions describe the situation just after it has finished.

The *Bag* and *Set* ADTs had postconditions, but no preconditions. The next example has both. The *Date* ADT shown in Figure 2.7 on page 44 defines a type that represents calendar dates. (The type is summarized in the UML diagram shown in Figure 2.6.) For example, an object that represents July 4, 1776, could be created that stores the three integers 4, 7, and 1776. That implementation would make it easy to implement the six methods required by the ADT.

The first three operations in this ADT have postconditions that simply require those operations to leave the object unchanged.

IntsDate

FIGURE 2.5 An IntsDate object.

```
            Date
+getDay():integer
+getMonth():integer
+getYear():integer
+setDay(integer)
+setMonth(integer)
+setYear(integer)
```

FIGURE 2.6 UML diagram.

ADT: *Date*

A **Date** represents a calendar date, such as July 4, 1776.
  *integer **getDay**()*
      Postcondition: this date is unchanged.
      Returns: the day number of this date.
  *integer **getMonth**()*
      Postcondition: this date is unchanged.
      Returns: the month number of this date.
  *integer **getYear**()*
      Postcondition: this date is unchanged.
      Returns: the year number of this date.
  *void **setDay**(integer day)*
      Precondition: $1 \leq day \leq 31$
      Postcondition: this date's day has the given value.
  *void **setMonth**(integer month)*
      Precondition: $1 \leq month \leq 12$
      Postcondition: this date's month has the given value.
  *void **setYear**(integer year)*
      Precondition: $1700 \leq year \leq 2100$
      Postcondition: this date's year has the given value.

FIGURE 2.7 An abstract data type for a calendar dates.

The last three operations have both preconditions and postconditions. Each of these three operations uses its argument to reset the corresponding data item in the object. Its postcondition guarantees that the data item will be reset to the given value, as long as that value lies within a prescribed range. For example, the **setMonth** operation will reset the month value to the given month, provided that it is a number in the range $1 \leq month \leq 12$. Each range is specified by the operation's precondition.

ADT operations are typically categorized according to whether their execution can change the state of the object. Those which can are called *mutators*; those that cannot are called *accessors*.

In the *Date* ADT shown in Figure 2.7, the accessor methods can be identified by the post-condition that says the object is left unchanged: *getDay*, *getMonth*, and *getYear* are accessors. In the previous *Bag* and *Set* ADTs, the *contains* and *size* accessor method also use that postcondition. Note that accessors typically return information about the state of the object; they allow the client to access information without changing anything. They are *read-only* operations.

The mutator operations among the *Bag*, *Set*, and *Date* ADTs are *add*, *remove*, *setDay*, *setMonth*, and *setYear*. Each of these changes the state of the object, either by adding or removing something from it or by resetting one of its data values. Mutators usually require arguments to obtain the information they need to make the changes to the object.

Note the names of the six operations in the *Date* ADT. The last three have the form *setX*, where *X* is one of the three data fields that the object maintains: *day*, *month*, and *year*. Each of these three operations simply resets the value of the corresponding data field with the value passed by the argument. Operations like that are called *setter* operations. Setter operations are specialized mutators that have a `void` return type, returning nothing. Information flows only one way, from the client to the object. Setter operations are write-only from the client's viewpoint and read-only from the object's viewpoint.

The first three operations in the *Date* ADT have the form *getX*, where *X* is one of the three data fields. Each of these three simply returns the value of the corresponding data field. Operations like that are called *getter* operations. Getter operations are specialized accessors that have no parameters, receiving nothing. Again, information flows only one way, but this time from the object back to the client. Getter operations are write-only from the object's viewpoint, and read-only from the client's viewpoint.

Note that not all mutators are setters, and not all accessors are getters. The *Bag.remove* operation is a mutator that returns a *boolean* value. And the *Bag.contains* operation is an accessor that has an *Object* parameter.

2.5 Using ADTs in Algorithms

An ADT provides an *operational definition* of a data type: The type is defined in terms of its operations. Later implementations of the ADT will define the actual storage structures to be used in the data type. Those are necessary to compile and run client programs that use the data type. But those implementation details are not necessary to use the ADT in algorithms that solve problems. The algorithms need only the operational definition. This was illustrated in Algorithm 2.1 on page 41.

This high-level application of operational definitions is common in mathematics. For example, consider the quadratic formula in algebra:

$$x = \frac{-b \pm \sqrt{b^2 - 4ac}}{2a}$$

This is an algorithm for solving a quadratic equation, $ax^2 + bx + c = 0$. It uses the square root function. But how is that defined? For algebraic purposes, we need only know that the square root of a number d is any number whose square equals d. This is an operational definition; it defines the square root in terms of how it works. To actually obtain a numerical value of, say $\sqrt{5}$, requires more. But to use the square root in the specification of a client algorithm such as the quadratic formula requires only the operational definition.

Algorithm 2.1 on page 41 is an example of a *client algorithm* for our **Bag** ADT: Its only access to the contents of the bag are through the ADTs operations. Algorithm 2.2 provides another example.

▲ **ALGORITHM 2.2: Remove All Instances of an Object from a *Bag***

Input: a **Bag** b; an object x;
Output: the number of objects removed.
Postcondition: the bag b contains no x objects.

1. Let n be the *integer* 0.
2. If *contains*(x) is false for the bag b, then return n.
3. *remove*(x) from b.
4. Add 1 to n.
5. Go to step 2.

This algorithm removes all occurrences of a given object from the bag. For example, if b is a bag that contains five apples, seven oranges, and four lemons, and x is a lemon, then the algorithm would remove the four lemons from the bag and return the number 4. This would require four iterations of the loop defined by steps 2–5 in the algorithm.

The complete specification of the algorithm requires only the ADT *Bag*. Of course, a complete implementation of this algorithm, for example, as a Java method, would require a complete implementation of the data type in Java. But that is not needed to specify and analyze the algorithm.

2.6 Concrete Data Types

An abstraction is not very useful unless it has concrete realizations. Having a blueprint for a jet aircraft is useful to an aircraft manufacturer who plans to build such aircraft. But a blueprint for a warp-drive star ship isn't very useful.

The purpose of an ADT is to facilitate the definition and implementation of concrete data types that can be used to declare objects in a real programming language. If the Java programming language is used, then that realization takes the form of an interface which can then be implemented as a class.

Listing 2.1 is a Java realization of our **Bag** ADT.

LISTING 2.1: An Interface for a *Bag* ADT

```
1   public interface Bag {
2       public void add(Object object);
3       public boolean contains(Object object);
4       public Object getFirst();
5       public Object getNext();
6       public boolean remove(Object object);
7       public int size();
8   }
```

Note that the structure of each operation is replicated in the corresponding method prototype. For example, the *contains* operation takes an *object* for input and returns a *boolean*, so our contains method has a parameter of type Object and a boolean return type.

Translating an ADT into a Java interface is similar to translating an algorithm into a Java method. For example, Listing 2.2 is the Java version of Algorithm 2.2, which removes all occurrences of a given object from a bag.

LISTING 2.2: Removing Elements from a Bag

```
1  public int remove(Object object, Bag bag) {
2      int n=0;
3      while (bag.remove(object))
4          ++n;
5      return n;
6  }
```

This is a *client method*; it is not a member of either the Bag interface or any implementation of it.

This remove method uses the Bag interface as a Java type. As a member of a main class, it will compile as soon as the Bag interface has been compiled. The interface does not have to be implemented as a Java class for this remove method to compile. That implementation can be done later. Of course, no bag object can be created until some bag class has been defined. But we can compile this remove method without it.

Listing 2.3 is a simple implementation of the Bag interface in Listing 2.1.

LISTING 2.3: An ArrayBag Implementation of the Bag Interface

```
1  public class ArrayBag implements Bag {
2      private Object[] objects = new Object[1000];
3      private int size, i;
4
5      public void add(Object object) {
6          objects[size++] = object;
7      }
8
9      public boolean contains(Object object) {
10         for (int i=0; i<size; i++)
11             if (objects[i]==object) return true;
12         return false;
13     }
14
15     public Object getFirst() {
16         i = 0;
17         return objects[i++];
18     }
19
20     public Object getNext() {
21         return objects[i++];
22     }
```

```
23
24    public boolean remove(Object object) {
25      for (int i=0; i<size; i++)
26        if (objects[i]==object) {
27          System.arraycopy(objects, i+1, objects, i, size-i-1);
28          objects[--size] = null;
29          return true;
30        }
31      return false;
32    }
33
34    public int size() {
35      return size;
36    }
37  }
```

This implementation uses an array to store the elements of the bag. Each element that is added to the bag is simply stored in the next free location in the array (at line 6). The size counter keeps track of how many objects are in the bag. Note that the same object may be added several times, as the **Bag** ADT allows. Note also that this implementation provides room for 1,000 elements.

The remove() method searches through the array for the given object. If a match is found (at line 26), then the object is removed by shifting all the array elements that follow back one position and decrementing the size counter. The shifting is done by the System.arraycopy() method at line 27. In general, the call System.arraycopy(a,i,b,j,n) will copy the array segment of n elements that begins at a[i] into the array segment of n elements that begins at b[j]. This works even if b[] is the same array as a[], overwriting elements, if necessary.

Figure 2.8 shows two UML diagrams: one for the ArrayBag class defined in Listing 2.3, and one for the interface that it implements. The interface is identified by the special label «interface». (In the UML world, this is called a *stereotype*.) The implementation arrow is the same as an inheritance arrow except that it has a dashed shaft.

This implementation uses an array to store its elements, which is not very efficient. We would probably want to replace this with a more efficient data structure at some point. But this is adequate for illustrating the progression from ADT to interface to class.

The next step is to instantiate the class by creating an object of that type. For example, suppose we execute these seven statements in a test program:

```
Bag bag = new ArrayBag();
bag.add("CA");
bag.add("US");
bag.add("MX");
bag.add("RU");
bag.add("US");
bag.add("MX");
```

The first line declares a reference named bag to Bag objects, and then initializes it to an instance of the ArrayBag class. Its data type is the interface Bag, which means that it can perform only the operations declared in that interface.

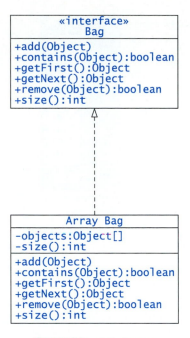

FIGURE 2.8 UML diagram.

The `ArrayBag` object to which the `bag` reference refers is illustrated in Figure 2.9. The six calls to the `add` method would insert six references to `String` objects. At that point, the bag contains six elements; its size is 6.

Now suppose we execute the statement

```
bag.remove("US");
```

This deletes one of the references to the `"US"` object, leaving the bag in the state shown in Figure 2.10, with `size` 5. Note that there are only four `String` objects. The bag contains two references to the same `"MX"` string. They count as two separate but equal elements of the bag.

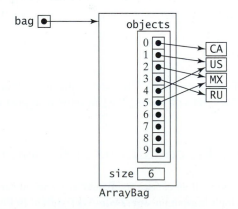

FIGURE 2.9 An ArrayBag object.

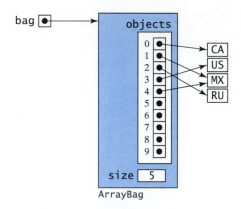

FIGURE 2.10   An ArrayBag object.

FIGURE 2.11   The bag.remove method.

Recall that when two references `object1` and `object2` refer to the same object, the `bool-ean` expression (`object1==object2`) will evaluate to `true`. Conversely, when the two references refer to distinct (separate) objects, that `boolean` expression will evaluate to `false`. Thus, the statement at line 26 in Listing 2.3 will do the right thing: As soon as an element of the `objects[]` array is found that refers to the same object as the one to be deleted, the block in lines 27–29 will execute, shifting the elements that follow back one position in the array, decrementing the `size` field, setting the last reference (which was copied) to `null`, and returning `true`. Hence, the code

        bag.remove("US");

makes the changes shown in Figure 2.11. The call to the `arraycopy` method in line 27 of Listing 2.3 shifts the four references `objects[2:5]` into the four positions `objects[1:4]`.

2.7 Implementing Preconditions and Postconditions

Preconditions can be enforced in Java classes by means of standard run-time exceptions. This is illustrated in Listing 2.4, which implements the ***Date*** ADT shown in Figure 2.7 on page 44. (See Listing 2.5 for the interface definition.)

LISTING 2.4: An `IntsDate` **Class for the** `Date` **Interface**

```java
1   public class IntsDate implements Date {
2     private int day, month, year;
3
4     public IntsDate(int year, int month, int day) {
5       setDay(day);
6       setMonth(month);
7       setYear(year);
8     }
9
10    public int getDay()  {
11      return day;
12    }
13
14    public int getMonth()  {
15      return month;
16    }
17
18    public int getYear()  {
19      return year;
20    }
21
22    public void setDay(int day) {
23      if (day<1 || day>31) throw new IllegalArgumentException();
24      this.day = day;
25    }
26
27    public void setMonth(int month) {
28      if (month<1 || month>12) throw new IllegalArgumentException();
29      this.month = month;
30    }
31
32    public void setYear(int year) {
33      if (year<1700 || year>2100) throw new IllegalArgumentException();
34      this.year = year;
35    }
36  }
```

The `IllegalArgumentException` class is an extension of the `RuntimeException` class. That makes it an *unchecked exception*, so its use does not have to be encapsulated within a `try` bock and no `throws` clause is needed in the method declarations. (See Appendix B.)

For production software, it is also wise to use the Javadoc tool to establish the preconditions and the postconditions. Javadoc is a special form of Java comments that can processed automatically into web pages (HTML code) that serve as formal documentation for your interfaces and classes. This is illustrated in Listing 2.5.

LISTING 2.5: Using Javadoc to Implement Postconditions

```
1   public interface Date {
2      /**
3       * @return the day number of this date.
4       */
5      public int  getDay();
6
7      /**
8       * @return the month number of this date.
9       */
10     public int  getMonth();
11
12     /**
13      * @return the year number of this date.
14      */
15     public int  getYear();
16
17     /**
18      * Sets the day number of this date to the given day value.
19      * @throws IllegalArgumentException if day < 1 or day > 31.
20      */
21     public void setDay(int day);
22
23     /**
24      * Sets the month number of this date to the given month value.
25      * @throws IllegalArgumentException if month < 1 or month > 12.
26      */
27     public void setMonth(int month);
28
29     /**
30      * Sets the year number of this date to the given year value.
31      * @throws IllegalArgumentException if year < 1700 or year > 2100.
32      */
33     public void setYear(int year);
34  }
```

Here, each method is preceded by a Javadoc comment. The special symbol /** signals the beginning of the Javadoc comment, and the usual C-style */ symbol ends the comment. The @ symbol is used to identify special Javadoc words, such as @return and @throws. These words are used by the Javadoc interpreter to format the resulting HTML document.

The web page shown in Figure 2.12 on page 53 was produced by executing the javadoc command at the Command Prompt, like this:

```
javadoc Date.java
```

This conforms nicely to the standard format used for all Java documentation.

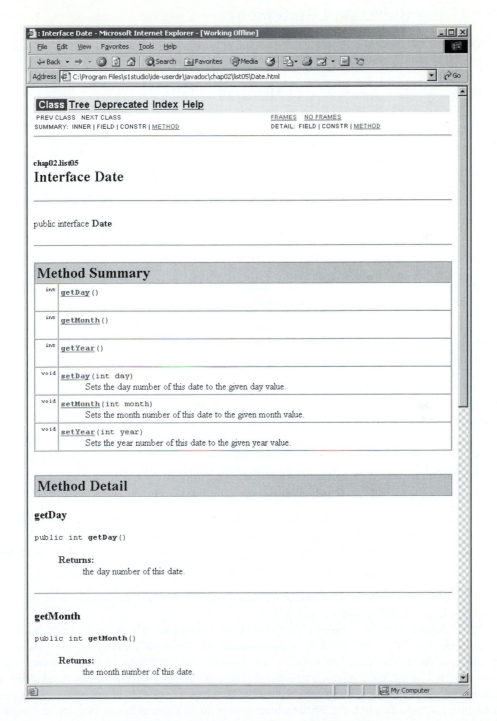

FIGURE 2.12 Web page produced by the javadoc utility.

2.8 Using the assert Statement

With Version 1.4, Java introduced a new statement into the language. The assert statement allows you to test the truth of an assumption, as illustrated in Listing 2.6.

LISTING 2.6: Using a Simple assert Statement

```
1  class TestAssert {
2    public static void main(String[] args) {
3      assert 2 < 4;
4      System.out.println("The assert statement is working.");
5      assert 4 < 4;
6      System.out.println("This line should not execute.");
7    }
8  }
```

The following is the complete output from Listing 2.6 on page 54:

```
The assert statement is working.
Exception in thread "main" java.lang.AssertionError
        at TestAssert.main(TestAssert.java:5)
```

The first assert statement, at line 3, asserts a true condition (2 < 4), so execution continues uninterrupted at line 4, printing the first output string. But the second assert statement, at line 5, asserts a false condition (4 < 4), so an AssertionError is thrown and the program is terminated. The output statement at line 6 is never executed.

To use the assert statement, you must have Java version 1.4.0 (or later). This is downloadable for free from Sun Microsystems at java.sun.com. More information about the new assert statement can be found at java.sun.com/j2se/1.4/docs/guide/lang/assert.html.

If you use the Command Prompt to compile and run your Java code, you will have to use special options for the assert statements (See Appendix B). For example, to compile a program in a file named TestAssert.java, execute the javac command like this:

```
javac -source 1.4 TestAssert.java
```

The -source 1.4 option tells the compiler to accept assert statements. Without it, the program is assumed to be written in pre-1.4 Java, which did not include an assert statement.

To run a program defined by a main class named TestAssert, execute the java command

```
java -ea TestAssert
```

The -ea option tells the Java Runtime Environment (JRE) to "enable assertions." Without it, the assert statements will simply be ignored.

The assert statement throws an Error object when its condition is false. Like the Exception class, the Error class is an extension of the Throwable class. (See Appendix B.) Instances of the Error class are *unchecked exceptions*, which means that their source statement need not be enclosed within a try block. Thus, the assert statement can stand alone, as it does in lines 3 and 5 of Listing 2.6 on page 54. However, by placing it inside a try block, as in Listing 2.7, we can catch the Error object that it throws, thereafter continuing the normal execution of the program.

LISTING 2.7: Using an assert Statement in a try Block

```
1   class TestAssert {
2     public static void main(String[] args) {
3       assert 2 < 4;
4       System.out.println("The assert statement is working.");
5       try {
6         assert 4 < 4;
7         System.out.println("This line should not execute.");
8       } catch (Error error) {
9         System.out.println("Catching the " + error + " object.");
10      }
11      System.out.println("The error was caught.");
12    }
13  }
```

The complete output is

```
The assert statement is working.
Catching the java.lang.AssertionError object.
The error was caught.
```

As in the previous program, the first `assert` statement here, at line 3, asserts a true condition (2 < 4), so execution continues uninterrupted at line 4, printing the first output string. Then the `try` statement, which extends over lines 5–10, executes. The first statement within the try block, at line 6, is an `assert` statement whose condition (4 < 4) is false. So the JRE immediately throws an `AssertionError`. Since the `assert` statement is in a `try` block, program control immediately jumps to the `catch` clause at line 8, ignoring the remaining statement at line 7 in the `try` block. The `catch` block (lines 8–10) contains a single output statement at line 9. This forms the string

```
Catching the java.lang.AssertionError object.
```

and prints it. (The `AssertionError` class's `toString()` method invoked on the error object returns the string `"java.lang.AssertionError"`.) After that, program control continues with the next statement after the `try` statement, which is the output statement at line 11.

The Windows screen capture in Figure 2.13 shows the entire process. The `type` command simply displays the source code in the `TestAssert.java` file. The only difference between this program and the one in Listing 2.7 on page 55 is the alternate form of the `assert` statement at line 6:

```
assert (4 < 4) : "(4 < 4)";
```

This form includes a colon(`:`) after the condition and another expression after that. The second expression, which may be any primitive type or object, is passed to the `AssertionError` object if one is thrown. Here, the string `"(4 < 4)"` is passed to the `AssertionError` object, and consequently appears in the string that is printed at line 9.

The second command executed in Figure 2.13 is the same compile statement described previously:

```
javac -source 1.4 TestAssert.java
```

The `-source 1.4` option tells the compiler to accept `assert` statements.

```
Command Prompt                                                        _ □ ×
A:\>type TestAssert.java
class TestAssert {
  public static void main(String[] args) {
    assert 2 < 4;
    System.out.println("The assert statement is working.");
    try {
      assert (4 < 4) : "(4 < 4)";
      System.out.println("This line should not execute.");
    } catch (Error error) {
      System.out.println("Catching the " + error + " object.");
    }
    System.out.println("The error was caught.");
  }
}
A:\>javac -source 1.4 TestAssert.java

A:\>java -version
java version "1.4.1_02"
Java(TM) 2 Runtime Environment, Standard Edition (build 1.4.1_02-b06)
Java HotSpot(TM) Client VM (build 1.4.1_02-b06, mixed mode)

A:\>java -ea TestAssert
The assert statement is working.
Catching the java.lang.AssertionError: (4 < 4) object.
The error was caught.

A:\>java TestAssert
The assert statement is working.
This line should not execute.
The error was caught.

A:\>
```

FIGURE 2.13   Compiling and Running a Program with Assertions.

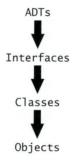

FIGURE 2.14   From the abstract to the concrete.

The third command executed in Figure 2.13 asks for the current version of the JRE:

```
java -version
```

The system reports that we have version 1.4.1_02. This is important information because earlier versions do not recognize assertions.

The fourth command executed in Figure 2.13 runs the program with the -ea option:

```
java -ea TestAssert
```

The output is similar to that of the program in Listing 2.7 on page 55. The only difference is that the second line of output includes the string expression `"(4 < 4)"` passed to the `AssertionError` object at line 6.

The last command executed in Figure 2.13 runs the program without any switch:

```
java TestAssert
```

This causes all the `assert` statements to be ignored. Consequently, the output statement at line 7 is executed, printing

```
This line should not execute.
```

The program executed in Figure 2.13 illustrates both forms of the `assert` statement. Here is the syntax for these two forms:

```
assert ex1 ;
assert ex1 : ex2 ;
```

In the first form, the keyword `assert` is followed by a `boolean` expression *ex1*. The second form contains the keyword `assert`, followed by a `boolean` expression *ex1*, followed by the colon character (`:`), followed by any expression *ex2*. As we see in Figure 2.13, when the `boolean` expression *ex1* evaluates to `true`, the statement execution terminates and control advances immediately to the next statement. When the expression *ex1* evaluates to `false`, the JRE throws an `AssertionError`, which terminates the program unless the error is caught. If the second form of the assert statement is used, then the value of the expression *ex2* is passed to the `AssertionError` object, which includes the string representation of that value in error message that it outputs. In the program in Figure 2.13, that string was `"(4 < 4)"`.

Assertions can be used to check preconditions, postconditions, and class invariants.

2.9 Class Invariants

A *class invariant* is a condition imposed upon the state of a class; i.e., its data fields. The condition typically constrains the range of values that the data fields may assume in the class objects. These constraints can be inforced by the class's constructors and mutator methods, as expressed by their preconditions.

The `IntsDate` class implemented in Listing 2.4 on page 51 enforces these invariants:

```
1 <= day && day <= 31
1 <= month && month <= 12
1700 <= year && year <= 2100
```

We can be sure that the day, month, and year fields of every `IntsDate` object satisfy these constraints. We have that confidence because the setter methods impose those constraints and the constructor uses the setter methods; there is no other way that the field values can be changed.

Class invariants are used to enforce *data integrity*. This is a term used in database systems to describe the state of the data being stored. It means that all the data is in the form that is expected. In large dynamic systems, data integrity is difficult to maintain, so a lot of attention and effort is devoted to mechanisms that enforce data integrity. Defining class invariants when we implement an ADT facilitates that effort.

For the `IntsDate` class, the constraints on the day and month fields have obvious benefits. A `Date` object with a day value of 44 or a month value of –3 would make no sense. The constraints on the year field may be less obvious, because they tend to be a bit arbitrary. The point here is that we should have some limit on the range of values. We probably wouldn't have much use for year values of 1,000,000 or –10,000. The constraint

```
1700 <= year && year <= 2100
```

is a bit tight; it might be appropriate for, say, dates of published newspaper articles. On the other hand, if we were using the `IntsDate` class for biographical information processing, then a constraint such as

```
-2100 <= year && year <= 2100
```

might be more appropriate.

Class invariants can be more complex than those just specified. For example, we know that not all months have 31 days, so we might include these additional constraints on our `IntsDate` class:

```
if (month == 4 || month == 6 || month == 9 || month == 11) day <= 30;
if (month == 2) day <= 29;
```

We could define a special `private` utility method for determining leap years and then use that for the addition constraint:

```
if (month == 2 && !isLeap(year)) day <= 28;
```

If we were to use the wider ranging year constraint, then we might also add these constraints to accommodate the Gregorian calendar:

```
year != 0;
if (year == 1582 && month == 10) day <= 4 || day >= 15;
```

2.10 Inheritance and Polymorphism

Software can be developed by following the progression from defining an ADT to translating it into a Java interface, to implementing it with one or more Java classes, to creating objects by instantiating those classes. But the relationship between interfaces and classes is a bit more general, because in Java, a class may implement several interfaces. This is regarded as a kind of "pseudo-multiple-inheritance." Java does not allow true multiple inheritance of one class from several other classes. But inheritance can be multiple in this sense that a class can inherit behavioral specifications from several interfaces.

As realizations of ADTs, interfaces encapsulate behavior. Some objects have the behavioral capabilities of several distinct types (*i.e.*, they can "wear several hats"). For example, consider the college student who is also employed part time by the college. That individual behaves both like a student and like an employee. This is called *polymorphism*: The object has more than one form, sometimes a student, sometimes an employee.

Figure 2.15 shows a UML diagram of two interfaces and one class that implements them both. A `StudentEmployee` is both a `Student` and an `Employee`, so it implements both kinds of

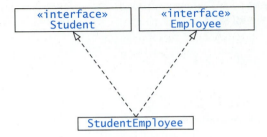

FIGURE 2.15 Multiple implementations.

behaviors. As a student, a student-employee can report his or her grade-point average (gpa), as an employee, his or her weekly pay (wages). This is polymorphism, literally "many forms": The student-employee can act like a student and like an employee.

Polymorphism is illustrated in the example in Listing 2.8 on page 59.

LISTING 2.8: Using Polymorphism

```
1   public class TestPolymorphism {
2     public static void main(String[] args) {
3       StudentEmployee joe = new StudentEmployee(3.29, 6.75);
4       report((Student)joe);
5       report((Employee)joe);
6     }
7
8     static void report(Student student) {
9       System.out.println("This student's gpa is: "
10                      + student.getGpa());
11    }
12
13    static void report(Employee employee) {
14      System.out.println("This employee's wages are: $"
15                     + employee.getWages());
16    }
17  }
18
19  interface Student {
20    double getGpa();
21  }
22
23  interface Employee {
24    double getWages();
25  }
26
27  class StudentEmployee implements Student, Employee {
28    private double gpa, wages;
29
30    public StudentEmployee(double gpa, double wages) {
```

```
31      this.gpa = gpa;
32      this.wages = wages;
33    }
34
35    public double getGpa() {
36      return gpa;
37    }
38
39    public double getWages() {
40      return wages;
41    }
42  }
```

The output is

```
This student's gpa is: 3.29
This employee's wages are: $6.75
```

In addition to the main class, this example defines a Student interface, an Employee interface, and a StudentEmployee class that implements them both. (See Figure 2.16.) Each interface specifies one getter method, and the class implements them both.

The main method instantiates a StudentEmployee object named joe, with gpa 3.29 and wages 6.75. Then it invokes its two (overloaded) report methods, first passing joe cast as a Student, and then passing joe cast as an Employee. The Java run-time system selects the correct method on the basis of the type of argument it receives.

Another form a polymorphism that arises from the use of interfaces is illustrated in Listing 2.9. This is called *parametric polymorphism* because the variables that can assume several forms are parameters of methods.

This program assumes that there are four different implementations of the Bag interface, as shown in Figure 2.17. It instantiates each of the four classes with bag1, bag2, bag3, and bag4. It also assumes that each of the four classes has a constructor that takes an array of strings and loads them as objects into the bag. So if the program is run from the command line

```
java TestBags AR BR CA MX US
```

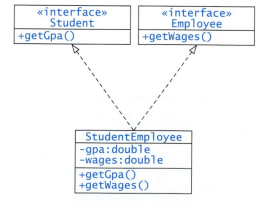

FIGURE 2.16 Multiple implementations.

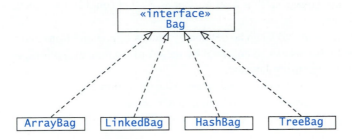

FIGURE 2.17 Multiple implementations.

LISTING 2.9: Parametric Polymorphism

```
1  public static void main(String[] args) {
2      Bag bag1 = new ArrayBag(args);
3      Bag bag2 = new LinkedBag(args);
4      Bag bag3 = new HashBag(args);
5      Bag bag4 = new TreeBag(args);
6      remove(bag1, "MX");
7      remove(bag2, "CA");
8      remove(bag3, "US");
9      remove(bag4, "BR");
10     System.out.println(bag1 + ", " + bag2 + ", " + bag3 + ", " + bag4);
11 }
```

each of the four bags would be initialized with the same five string objects "AR", "BR", "CA", "MX", and "US". Then the client method remove, defined in Listing 2.2 on page 47, is called in lines 6–9, once for each of the four bags. The result should be the removal of "MX" from bag1, "CA" from bag2, "US" from bag3, "BR" from bag4. But it is the same remove method being used on four different types of bags.

The parameter bag at line 1 of Listing 2.2 on page 47 is declared to have type Bag. That is an interface. Consequently, any object of any type that implements that interface can be passed as an argument to that parameter. Hence, the parameter bag is *polymorphic*: At line 6 it assumes the form of an ArrayBag, at line 7 it assumes the form of a LinkedBag, and so on.

CHAPTER SUMMARY

❏ A *data type* is a specification of a range of values together with a set of operations which any variable of that type may have.

❏ An *abstraction* is a generalization that separates the specific details from the common features.

❑ An *abstract data type* (ADT) is a set of operations that could be used on variables of a (concrete) data type.

❑ The operations of an ADT can be defined by means of preconditions and postconditions.

❑ In Java, preconditions can be enforced by means of runtime exceptions, and postconditions can be documented using Javadoc.

❑ ADTs can be used with pseudocode to describe algorithms.

❑ An ADT can be translated directly into a Java interface.

❑ That interface can be implemented by Java classes.

❑ That interface and those classes are concrete data types that the ADT represents.

❑ A class invariant is a condition imposed on the data fields of the class. Class invariants are used to ensure data integrity.

❑ A Java *assertion* is a condition about the state of a program that the programmer believes to be true. Java 1.4 includes an `assert` statement for checking assertions.

❑ Java allows a single class to implement several independent interfaces. This allows polymorphism where a single object may take the form of the different types defined by the interfaces that its class implements.

❑ Polymorphism also occurs when arguments of different types are passed to the same parameter whose type is implemented (or extended) by those arguments' types.

REVIEW QUESTIONS

2.1   What is the difference between a specification and an implementation?

2.2   What is the purpose of data abstraction?

2.3   How can UML help in the development of data types?

2.4   How are ADTs useful in the derivation of algorithms?

2.5   What is the difference between a mutator method and a setter method.

2.6   What is the purpose of specifying preconditions and postconditions for ADTs?

2.7   What is an `abstract` class?

2.8   How can preconditions and postconditions be implemented in Java?

2.9   How can class invariants be implemented?

2.10   What is the purpose of the `assert` statement?

2.11   What kind of multiple inheritance does Java have?

EXERCISES

2.1   Define an ADT for integers, such as 44 and –7, and draw a UML diagram for it. Then translate it into a Java interface.

2.2   Define a *Counter* ADT. An instance of this type would be an object like a hand-held counter device for counting things like cars in a parking lot. The object stores a single non-negative integer (the current count). It can be incremented, it can be reset to zero, and its current value can be read at any time. Draw a UML diagram for it and translate it into a Java interface.

2.3   Modify the *Date* ADT in Figure 2.7 on page 44 so that it includes an operation that adds a given number of days to the date, and one that returns the number of days between the date and a given date. Draw its UML diagram, and translate it into a Java interface.

2.4   Write an algorithm that uses your *Date* ADT from Exercise 2.3 to determine whether a given date is in a leap year. Recall that a leap year is a year that is divisible by 4, but not by 100 unless also by 400. Then translate it into a Java method.

2.5   Write an algorithm that determines whether one given bag contains all the objects that are in another given bag. Then translate your algorithm into a Java method.

2.6   Write an algorithm that returns the number of different objects that are common to two given bags. Then translate your algorithm into a Java method.

2.7   Write an algorithm that removes all the elements from one given bag that are not in another given bag. Then translate your algorithm into a Java method.

2.8   Figure 2.18 shows an abstract data type for a single card out of an ordinary deck of playing cards. Give a UML diagram for this ADT, and then translate it into a Java interface.

2.9   Figure 2.19 shows an abstract data type for a single die. Dice are used in games to produce random integers that are (ideally) uniformly distributed in the range 1 to 6. Give a UML diagram for this ADT, and then translate it into a Java interface.

ADT: *Card*

> A *Card* is a an object that has a *Suit* (*SPADES, HEARTS, DIAMONDS*, or *CLUBS*) and a *rank* (an integer in the range 1 to 13).
>   *Card*(*Suit suit, integer rank*)
>   *Constructs*: a card object with the given suit and rank.
>   *Suit getSuit*()
>   *Returns*: the suit of this card.
>   *integer getRank*()
>   *Returns*: the rank of this card.
>   *String toString*()
>   *Returns*: a string that describes this card.

FIGURE 2.18   An abstract data type for a playing card.

ADT: *Die*

> A *Die* is a an object that displays a random number from 1 to 6.
>   *Die*()
>   *Constructs*: a die object that uses a global Random number generator.
>   *Die*(*Random x*)
>   *Constructs*: a die object that uses the given Random number generator.
>   *integer nextToss*()
>   *Returns*: a random integer in the range 1 to 6.

FIGURE 2.19   An abstract data type for dice.

2.10   Figure 2.20 shows an abstract data type for a pair of dice. (See Exercise 2.9.) Give a UML diagram for this ADT, and then translate it into a Java interface.

2.11   Figure 2.21 is a UML diagram for a data type for representing numbers.

   a. Translate the diagram into an ADT specification, including preconditions and postconditions.

   b. Translate your ADT into a Java interface named `Number`.

2.12   Figure 2.22 is a UML diagram for a data type for representing points.

   a. Translate the diagram into an ADT specification, including preconditions and postconditions.

   b. Translate your ADT into a Java interface named `Point`.

ADT: *Dice*

> A *Dice* is a an object that represents two *Die* objects (a pair of dice).
> **Dice**()
>   *Constructs*: a dice object that uses a global Random number generator.
> **Dice**(*Random x*)
>   *Constructs*: a dice object that uses the given Random number generator.
> *integer* **nextToss**()
>   *Returns*: an integer in the range 2 to 12 that represents the outcome of tossing two fair dice; so the numbers returned are distributed as the (non-uniform) sum of two uniform random numbers in the range 1 to 6.

FIGURE 2.20   An abstract data type for dice.

```
                    Number
+add(Number)
+subtract(Number)
+multiply(Number)
+divide(Number)
+sum(Number):Number
+difference(Number):Number
+product(Number):Number
+quotient(Number):Number
```

FIGURE 2.21   A `Number` type.

```
                     Point
+getX():double
+getY():double
+setX(double)
+setX(double)
+moveTo(double,double)
```

FIGURE 2.22   A `Point` type.

2.13   Figure 2.23 is a UML diagram for a data type for representing vectors.

    a. Translate the diagram into an ADT specification, including preconditions and postconditions.

    b. Translate your ADT into a Java interface named `Vector`.

2.14   Figure 2.24 is a UML diagram for a data type for representing matrices.

    a. Translate the diagram into an ADT specification, including preconditions and postconditions.

    b. Translate your ADT into a Java interface named `Matrix`.

2.15   Figure 2.25 is a UML diagram for a data type for representing polynomials.

    a. Translate the diagram into an ADT specification, including preconditions and postconditions.

    b. Translate your ADT into a Java interface named `Polynomial`.

2.16   Figure 2.26 is a UML diagram for a data type for representing a coin purse, such as one containing 2 pennies, 7 nickels, 3 dimes, and 5 quarters.

    a. Translate the diagram into an ADT specification, including preconditions and postconditions.

    b. Translate your ADT into a Java interface named `Purse`.

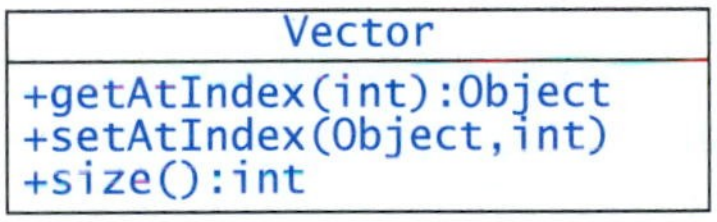

```
                Vector
+getAtIndex(int):Object
+setAtIndex(Object,int)
+size():int
```

FIGURE 2.23   A Vector type.

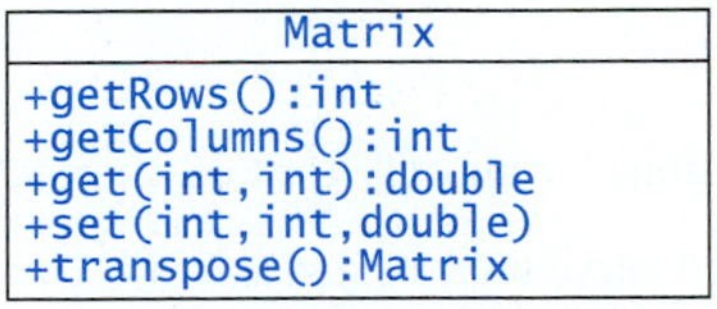

```
                Matrix
+getRows():int
+getColumns():int
+get(int,int):double
+set(int,int,double)
+transpose():Matrix
```

FIGURE 2.24   A Matrix type.

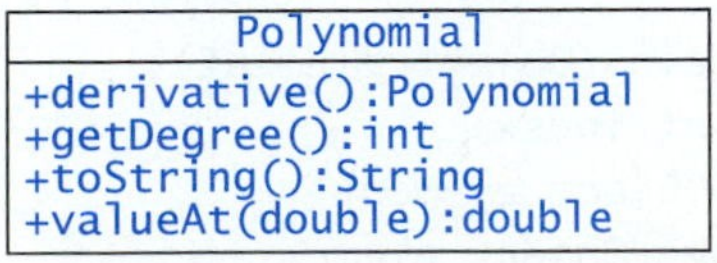

```
              Polynomial
+derivative():Polynomial
+getDegree():int
+toString():String
+valueAt(double):double
```

FIGURE 2.25   A Polynomial type.

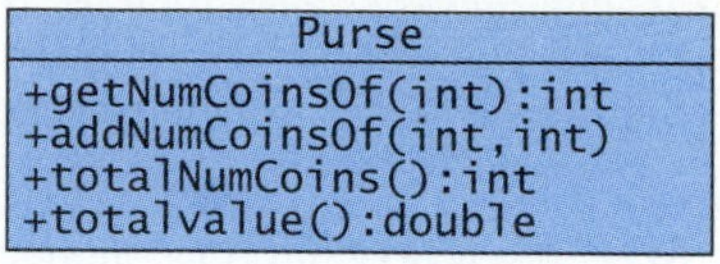

```
           Purse
+getNumCoinsOf(int):int
+addNumCoinsOf(int,int)
+totalNumCoins():int
+totalvalue():double
```

FIGURE 2.26   A Purse type.

2.17   Here is a simplified version of the `java.util.Set` interface:

```java
public interface Set {
  boolean add(Object element);
  void clear();
  boolean contains(Object element);
  boolean equals(Object object);
  boolean remove(Object element);
  int size();
}
```

Give the specifications for an ADT for this interface, and draw its UML diagram.

2.18   Here is a simplified version of the `java.util.Map` interface:

```java
public interface Map {
  void clear();
  boolean containsKey(Object key);
  Object get(Object key);
  Set keySet();
  Object put(Object key, Object value);
  Object remove(Object key);
  int size();
}
```

Give the specifications for an ADT for this interface, and draw its UML diagram.

2.19   Here is a simplified version of the `java.util.List` interface:

```java
public interface List {
  void add(int index, Object element);
  void clear();
  boolean contains(Object element);
  Object get(int index);
  int indexOf(Object element);
  boolean remove(Object element);
  Object set(int index, Object element);
```

```
    int size();
    List subList(int fromIndex, int toIndex);
}
```

Give the specifications for an ADT for this interface, and draw its UML diagram.

PROGRAMMING PROBLEMS

2.1   Translate the *Set* ADT shown in Figure 2.4 on page 42 into a Java interface named `Set` and compile it.

2.2   Implement the `Set` interface in Problem 2.1 as a class named `ArraySet`, using an array, as in Listing 2.3 on page 47.

2.3   Run a test program for the `ArraySet` class in Problem 2.2.

2.4   Run a test program for the `IntsDate` class in Listing 2.4 on page 51.

2.5   Expand the class invariants for `IntsDate` class in Listing 2.4 on page 51 by adding all the constraints described in Section 2.9. This requires the method

```
private static boolean isLeap(int year)
```

The Gregorian rule is that a year is a leap year if it is divisible by 4 but not by 100 unless also by 400. (See `serendipity.magnet.ch/hermetic/cal_stud/cal_art.htm`.)

2.6   Modify the `ComboLock` class from Programming Problem 1.6 on page 31 by enforcing a class invariant that every instance of the class contains a readable, but immutable, unique serial number. Use a `public final long` id field, as in Listing B.17 on page 554 in the appendix. Test your modified class.

PROJECTS

2.1   Define a *Purse* ADT whose instances would represent coin purses that hold pennies, nickels, dimes, and quarters. Then translate your ADT into a Java interface, implement the interface in a class named `ArrayPurse`, and run a test driver on it. (See Exercise 2.16.)

2.2   Implement the `Date` interface in Listing 2.5 on page 52 with a class named `IntDate` that uses a single `int` field to store the number of days that have elapsed since December 31, 1699. For example, the date March 15, 1702, would be stored as the integer 804 (2x365 + 31 + 28 + 15). Run a test driver on your class.

2.3   Define a *Time* ADT whose instances would represent a time of day to the nearest second. Specify appropriate operations for the ADT. Translate your ADT into a Java interface with the name `Time`. Then implement the interface in a class named `IntsTime` that uses `int` fields named `hour`, `minute`, and `second`. Test your class.

2.4   Define a *Polynomial* ADT whose instances would represent mathematical functions of the form $p(x) = a_0 + a_1 x + a_2 x^2 + \cdots + a_n x^n$, where the coefficients $a_0, a_1, a_2, ..., a_n$ are numbers. Then translate your ADT into a Java interface, implement the interface in a class named `ArrayPolynomial`, and run a test driver on it. (See Exercise 2.15.)

2.5   Define a *Counter* ADT that stores a single `long` integer for counting things. Include operations for resetting the counter to zero, incrementing the counter, and getting the current value of the counter. Show the UML diagram for this ADT. Then translate your ADT into a `Counter` class and test your implementation. (See Exercise 2.2.)

2.6   Give a UML diagram for a class named `CyclicCounter` that extends the `Counter` class defined in Project 2.5. Then translate your extension into a Java subclass and test your implementation.

2.7   Figure 2.27 on page 68 shows an ADT for objects that represent ordinary alarm clocks. Draw a UML diagram for this ADT. Then translate it into an `AlarmClock` class and test your implementation.

2.8   Figure 2.28 shows an ADT for rational numbers (*i.e.*, fractions).

a. Compile a Java interface for this ADT. Name it `RatioInterface`.

b. Draw a UML diagram for a `Ratio` class based upon this ADT.

c. Compile and test the `Ratio` class that implements your interface from part **a** and which is represented by your UML diagram from part **b**. Use these two fields:

```
long num, den;   // numerator and denominator
```

d. Add this class invariant to your `Ratio` class from part **c**:

```
den > 0;
num and den have no common factors;
```

ADT: *AlarmClock*

An *AlarmClock* is a device that reports the time and can signal an "alarm". It keeps track of the current time and stores an alarm time.
> *void setCurrentTime(Time time)*
> > *Postcondition*: the stored current time equals the specified time.
> *Time getCurrentTime()*
> > *Returns*: the stored current time.
> *void setAlarmTime(Time time)*
> > *Postcondition*: the stored alarm time equals the specified time.
> *Time getAlarmTime()*
> > *Returns*: the stored alarm time.
> *void advanceCurrentTime()*
> > *Postcondition*: the stored time is advanced by one second.
> *boolean isAlarmTime()*
> > *Returns*: true if current time equals alarm time.

FIGURE 2.27   An abstract data type for alarm clocks.

ADT: *Ratio*

A ***Ratio*** is a numeric fraction.
> ***Ratio***(*integer m*)
>> *Constructs*: the ratio *m*/1, equal to the integer *m*.
> ***Ratio***(*integer m, integer n*)
>> *Constructs*: the ratio *m*/*n*.
> *Ratio* ***plus***(*Ratio x*)
>> *Returns*: the sum of this ratio plus *x*.
> *Ratio* ***minus***(*Ratio x*)
>> *Returns*: the difference of this ratio minus *x*.
> *Ratio* ***times***(*Ratio x*)
>> *Returns*: the product of this ratio times *x*.
> *Ratio* ***dividedBy***(*Ratio x*)
>> *Precondition*: *x* is not zero.
>> *Returns*: the quotient of this ratio divided by *x*.

FIGURE 2.28   An abstract data type for numeric ratios (fractions).

To enforce the second constraint, implement this algorithm:

▲ **ALGORITHM 2.3: Euclidean Algorithm**

Input: two positive integers: *m* and *n*.
Output: the greatest common divisor of *m* and *n*.

1.   Repeat steps 2-4:
2.   If $m < n$, subtract *m* from *n*; otherwise, subtract *n* from *m*.
3.   If $m = 0$, return *n*.
4.   If $n = 0$, return *m*.

To ensure that `num` and `den` have no common factors, simply divide them both by their greatest common divisor.

e. Use Java `assert` statements to check the class invariant from part **d**.

2.9   Figure 2.29 shows an ADT for complex numbers ($x + iy$, where *x* and *y* are real numbers).

a. Compile a Java interface for this ADT. Name it `ComplexInterface`.

b. Draw a UML diagram for a `Complex` class based upon this ADT.

c. Compile and test the `Complex` class that implements your interface from part **a** and which is represented by your UML diagram from part **b**. Use these two fields:

```
double x, y;   // real and imaginary parts
```

Use these algorithms for the four arithmetic methods:

$$(x_1 + i\,y_1) + (x_2 + i\,y_2) = (x_1 + x_2) + i\,(y_1 + y_2)$$

$$(x_1 + i\,y_1) - (x_2 + i\,y_2) = (x_1 - x_2) + i\,(y_1 - y_2)$$

$$(x_1 + i\,y_1)\,(x_2 + i\,y_2) = (x_1 x_2 - y_1 y_2) + i\,(x_1 y_2 - y_1 x_2)$$

$$(x_1 + i\,y_1)\,/\,(x_2 + i\,y_2) = (x_1 x_2 + y_1 y_2)/d + i\,(y_1 x_2 - x_1 y_2)/d_2,$$

where d_2 is the magnitude of $(x_2 + i\,y_2)$.

ADT: *Complex*

A *Compex* is a complex number $x + iy$.
  Complex(*real x*)
    Constructs: the complex number that is equal to x.
  Complex(*real x, real y*)
    Constructs: the complex object that is equal to $x + iy$.
  *real **magnitude**()*
    Returns: the magnitude $\text{sqrt}(x^2 + y^2)$ of this complex number.
  *Complex **plus**(Complex z)*
    Returns: the sum of this plus z.
  *Complex **minus**(Complex z)*
    Returns: the difference of this minus z.
  *Complex **times**(Complex z)*
    Returns: the product of this times z.
  *Complex **dividedBy**(Complex z)*
    Precondition: z is not zero.
    Returns: the quotient of this divided by z.

FIGURE 2.29 An abstract data type for complex numbers.

ANSWERS TO REVIEW QUESTIONS

2.1 A *specification* tells what it is or what it does. An *implementation* provides all the information needed for its creation and use (*i.e.*, how it works). Java interfaces are specifications, and classes are implementations.

2.2 By defining an ADT, we can concentrate on what the objects of that type can do, while postponing decisions about how they will do it.

2.3 Unified Modeling Language (UML) diagrams simplify and neatly summarize the data types and the relationships among them.

2.4 Algorithms are best derived in pseudocode, independent of any specific programming language. ADTs provide a natural way to define the variables used in that pseudocode.

2.5 A *mutator* is any method that can change any data value in the class. A *setter* method is a special mutator method whose only purpose is to set the value of a single field.

2.6 The effect of an operation can be defined by specifying the state of an object before and after the operation is applied to it. These two states are defined by preconditions and postconditions, respectively. Their specification provides a "contract" which the implementor of the ADT is bound to honor.

2.7 An `abstract` class is a class that has at least one abstract method. An `abstract` method is simply the specification of the method, without any block of executable code.

2.8 In Java, preconditions can be enforced by throwing runtime exceptions when they are violated, and postconditions can be expressed using javadoc.

2.9 Class invariants can be implemented by preconditions on constructors and mutators.

2.10   The Java `assert` statement allows the programmer to check the validity of his or her runtime assumptions about the program.

2.11   Formally, multiple inheritance means one class extending several other independent classes. This is not allowed in Java. However, Java does allow one class to implement several independent interfaces.

One must learn by doing the thing,
for though you can think you know it
you have no certainty until you try it.

— Sophocles

Chapter 3

Arrays

An *array* is a sequence of contiguous elements that are accessible by means of a subscript operator. The array is the prototype data structure. It is the simplest kind of container of elements. All of the other data structures that we will study in this book are comparable to the array data structure.

3.1 Arrays in Java

In Java, an array is an object. Its type is *t*[], where *t* is the array's element type. For example, if the element type is int, then the array type is int[].

Array types are one of the four kinds of types in Java, the other three being primitives, classes, and interfaces. An array's element type can be any of these four kinds of types. For example, these are all valid array declarations:

```
int[] a;            // elements have primitive type int
String[] args;      // elements have object type String
List[] lists;       // elements have interface type List
double[][] matrix;  // elements have array type double[]
int[][][] x3d;      // elements have array type int[][]
```

The matrix array is a *two-dimensional array* (an array of arrays), and the x3d array is a *three-dimensional array* (an array of two-dimensional arrays).

The foregoing five declarations simply declare the array objects. Like any object declaration, the reference variable will be null until it has been allocated:

```
int[] a; // declares a null reference to arrays of int elements
Date d;  // declares a null reference to Date objects
```

Also, like any other object reference, an array can be allocated by means of the new operator:

```
a = new int[8];  // allocates an array of 8 int elements
d = new Date();  // allocates a Date object
```

For arrays, the new operator allocates the number of elements indicated in the brackets. For non-array objects, the new operator invokes a class constructor.

If an array of primitive type is allocated with the new operator, then its elements will automatically be initialized to their type's zero value.[1] For example, the 8 int elements of the integer array allocated above will all be initialized to 0, as shown in Figure 3.1.

Arrays can be visualized conveniently this way. The object a has type int[], and it contains a sequence of 8 integers indexed from 0 to 7.

In Java, arrays always use *zero-based indexing*. This means that the index range will always be from 0 to $n-1$, where n is the *length* of the array (its number of elements). For example, the array shown in Figure 3.1 has length $n = 8$, so its elements are indexed from 0 to 7.

You can always access the length of an array by means of its length field, like this:

```
int n = a.length;   // the number of elements in the array a
```

Unlike some other programming languages,[2] Java automatically checks each array index to ensure that it will not be out of range. If the index i is out of bounds (*i.e.*, i<0 or i>=a.length), then the Java Runtime Environment (JRE) will throw an ArrayIndexOutOfBoundsException exception, which will abort the program (unless the exception is caught):

```
int x = a[a.length];   // THIS WILL CRASH!
```

If you know the length of the array and its elements' values at compile time, then you can simultaneously allocate and initialize the array with an *initialization list* in its declaration. For example, the declaration

```
int[] a = {44,77,22,33,66};
```

allocates the array a[] to length 5 with the values specified. This is shown in Figure 3.2.

Note that initialization lists cannot be used in assignment statements:

```
int[] a;                 // OK
a = {44,77,22,33,66};    // ILLEGAL!
```

An attempt to compile this will result in an "illegal start of expression" message from the compiler.

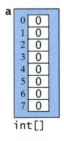

int[]

FIGURE 3.1 An array of 8 ints.

---

[1] The *zero values* for the primitive types are: false for boolean, '\000' for char, 0 for byte, 0 for short, 0 for int, 0L for long, 0.0F for float, 0.0 for double.

[2] Perhaps the biggest complaint among C++ programmers about that language is that it does not prevent array indexes from running out of bounds. But some enthusiasts reply that it is precisely this lack of "hand-holding" that allows C++ code to be so fast.

FIGURE 3.2 initialized.

Initialization lists can also be used in the creation of *anonymous arrays*. For example, the expression

```
new int[] {44,77,22,33,66}
```

defines an anonymous array of five `int` elements with the values indicated. This anonymous array expression could be passed to a method, thus:

```
print(new int[] {44,77,22,33,66});   // OK
```

It could also be used to reallocate an existing array, like this:

```
aa = new int[] {44,77,22,33,66};      // OK
```

Note that the initialization list is being used to initialize a newly allocated anonymous array. Assigning the list to the array reference aa merely copies the memory address of that anonymous array object into the reference variable aa.

Here are some other basic facts about arrays in Java:

❑ Like any object, an array may have several references to it:

```
int[] aa = a;
```

❑ An array parameter is declared in a method's parameter list the same way it is declared elsewhere:

```
public void print(int[] a)
```

❑ An array is passed to a method using only its name:

```
print(a);
```

❑ An array type can be a return type for a method:

```
public int[] randomArray(int n)
```

❑ Assigning one array to another does not duplicate it; it merely gives it another name (*i.e.*, another reference):

```
b = a;   // makes a[] and b[] the same array
```

❑ To copy an array, you can use the `arraycopy()` method defined in the `System` class:

```
System.arraycopy(a, 0, b, 0, a.length);
```

❑ To create a duplicate, you can use the `clone()` method defined in the `Object` class:

```
b = (int[])a.clone();
```

The return type for the `clone()` is `Object`, so it has to be recast as an array.

❑ Arrays are usually processed by **for** loops:

```
for (int i = 0; i < a.length; i++)
    a[i] = random.nextInt(1000);
```

❑ If an array is declared to be **final**, then its reference cannot be reassigned:

```
final int[] a = {22, 44, 66, 88};
a[3] = 99;      // OK
a = new int[8];  // ILLEGAL!
```

The program in Listing 3.1 illustrates some of these properties.

LISTING 3.1: Testing Arrays

```
1   public class Main {
2     private static java.util.Random random = new java.util.Random();
3
4     public static void main(String[] args) {
5       int[] a = randomInts(10,1000);
6       int[] aa = (int[])a.clone();  // creates a duplicate of a in aa
7       print(a);
8       print(aa);
9       a[0] = a[1] = a[2] = 888;
10      print(a);
11      print(aa);
12    }
13
14    public static int[] randomInts(int n, int range) {
15      int[] a = new int[n];
16      for (int i = 0; i < n; i++)
17        a[i] = random.nextInt(range);
18      return a;
19    }
20
21    public static void print(int[] a) {
22      System.out.print("{" + a[0]);
23      for (int i = 1; i < a.length; i++)
24        System.out.print("," + a[i]);
25      System.out.println("}");
26    }
27  }
```

The output is

```
{102,955,717,249,649,596,131,414,849,759}
{102,955,717,249,649,596,131,414,849,759}
{888,888,888,249,649,596,131,414,849,759}
{102,955,717,249,649,596,131,414,849,759}
```

At line 5, the program creates an array a[] of 10 random integers that are in the range 0 to 999 (inclusive). That array is then cloned at line 6, producing the duplicate array aa[]. The two arrays are printed at lines 7 and 8 to show that they have the same elements.

The clone() method produces a copy that is distinct from the original. To verify that, we change the first three elements in a[] to 888, and then print both arrays again at lines 10 and 11. The last two lines of output confirm that the array aa[] is distinct from the array a[].

3.2 Printing an Array in Java

In Java, an object exists only as long as there is at least one reference to it. As soon as all references to it have gone out of scope, the Java garbage collector can destroy the object, returning its storage space to the memory heap so it can be used for other data.

An array is an object. The name of the array is actually the name of a reference variable to it. That variable holds the starting address of the array in memory. As with any reference variable, printing it will display that memory address (in hexadecimal). Java also indicates the element type, preceded by the left bracket character " [" to indicate that the object is an array. This is illustrated in Listing 3.2.

LISTING 3.2: Printing an Array Reference

```
1   public class Print {
2     public static void main(String[] args) {
3       int[] a = {66, 33, 99, 88, 44, 55, 22};
4       System.out.println(a);
5     }
6   }
```

The output is

    [I@73d6a5

The output string [I@73d6a5 has two parts. The first part is [I, which means that the object is an array of type int[]. The [stands for "array", and the I stands for "int". The second part is @73d6a5, which gives the address in memory where the array is stored. The @ stands for "at", and the 73d6a5 is the actual hexadecimal address of the first byte of the array. Since this is an array of seven ints, and each int occupies 4 bytes, this array will occupy 56 contiguous bytes in the computer's main memory (RAM), from hexadecimal address 0x73d6a5 to hexadecimal address 0x73d6a5+0x37 = 0x73d6dd (7,591,589 to 7,591,645, in decimal).

If you want to print the elements of an array, you have to do it one element at a time, as shown in lines 22–27 of Listing 3.1. That method has an output like this:

    {102,955,717,249,649,596,131,414,849,759}

You can easily modify it to space out the elements.

3.3 Some Simple Array Algorithms

Finding the largest element in a sequence (*i.e.*, an array) is a common task that is often required by more substantial algorithms. The solution to this problem is a simple and intuitive algorithm:

Look at each element, and hold the index of the largest element seen. This requires a single loop that looks at one element on each iteration. If that element is larger than the element located by the saved index, then save its index in place of the other. When the loop is finished, we can be sure that the element located by the saved index is the largest.

Algorithm 3.1 is a formalized statement of this solution.

▲ **ALGORITHM 3.1: The Maximum Element**

Input: a sequence $\{a_0, a_1, a_2, ..., a_{n-1}\}$ of comparable elements.
Output: an index value m.
Postconditions: $a_m \geq a_i$, for all i.

1. Let $m = 0$.

2. Repeat Step 3 for $i = 1$ to $n-1$.

3. If $a_i > a_m$, set $m = i$.

4. Return m.

Note that this algorithm returns the first index of the maximum value. For example, if the maximum value is 88 and $a_2 = a_6 = a_9 = 88$, then the algorithm will return the index 2.

Another common task performed on arrays is the swapping of two of its elements, moving each into the other's position. Again, the solution is simple: Copy one element into a temporary location, copy the other element into that element's position, and then copy the temporary into the other element's position. That is how you and your friend would swap positions, standing in line for a movie. This process is formalized in Algorithm 3.2.

▲ **ALGORITHM 3.2: The Swap**

Input: a sequence $\{a_0, a_1, a_2, ..., a_{n-1}\}$ of comparable elements, and index values i and j.
Postconditions: elements a_i and a_j have been interchanged.

1. Let $x = a_i$.

2. Set $a_i = a_j$.

3. Set $a_j = x$.

Note that Algorithm 3.2 will be more efficient if we skip all the steps when the two elements are equal. This can be achieved by preceding step 1 with this step:

1. If $a_i = a_j$, return.

The improved swap algorithm is implemented for arrays of `ints` in Listing 3.3.

LISTING 3.3: The `swap()` Method

```
1   void swap(int[] a, int i, int j) {
2     int ai = a[i], aj = a[j];
3     if (ai == aj) return;
4     a[i] = aj;
5     a[j] = ai;
6   }
```

This version is a little different from a direct translation of Algorithm 3.2. It uses two temporary variables, `ai` and `aj`, instead of only one. This makes the code a little more symmetric. It also is a little more efficient because it uses only four array accesses instead of the six that the improved algorithm would make.[3] That may seem like a negligible improvement. But some sorting algorithms require a very large number of calls to the `swap()` method, so a little improvement here could result in a significant reduction in the total run time.

3.4 Arrays of Objects

Array elements can be any type, primitive or reference. If the element type is primitive, then all the elements must be that same type. However, if the element type is an reference, then the actual elements can be different types, as long as they are all extensions of the array's declared element type. This allows for *heterogeneous arrays* in Java.

Listing 3.4 illustrates a heterogeneous array of objects. The array is declared to have element type `Object` so that any type of object can be stored in it. It is then loaded with a `String` object, a `Float` object, a `java.util.Date` object, and an `int[]` object.

LISTING 3.4: A Heterogeneous Array of Objects

```
1   public class ObjectArray {
2     public static void main(String[] args) {
3       String s="Mercury";
4       Float x = new Float(3.14159);
5       java.util.Date d = new java.util.Date();
6       int[] a = new int[] {11, 33, 55, 77, 99};
7       Object[] objects = {s, x, d, a};
8       print(objects);
9     }
10
11    static void print(Object[] a) {
12      System.out.print("{" + a[0]);
13      for (int i=1; i<a.length; i++)
14        System.out.print("," + a[i]);
15      System.out.println("}");
16      if (a[0] instanceof String)
17        System.out.println(((String)a[0]).charAt(6));
18      if (a[1] instanceof Float)
19        System.out.println(((Float)a[1]).isNaN());
20      if (a[2] instanceof java.util.Date)
21        System.out.println(((java.util.Date)a[2]).getTime());
22      if (a[3] instanceof int[])
23        System.out.println(((int[])a[3]).length);
24    }
25  }
```

---

[3] A good optimizing compiler might make this improvement automatically.

The output is

```
{Mercury,3.14159,Sat May 12 12:41:43 EDT 2001,[I@17d257}
y
false
989685703734
5
```

The print() method first sends each of the element objects to the System.out.print() method, which invokes the toString() method of the array element's class. For example, the toString() method of the java.util.Date class is invoked for a[2].

To recover each element's original type, the corresponding array element a[i] must be recast to that type. The print() method uses the **instanceof** operator to confirm the underlying type before recasting it. Then, for testing purposes, a characteristic method for that type is invoked on the recast object. For example, the isNaN() method ("is not a number") is defined only for objects of type Float and Double. It returns false for ((Float)a[1]) because that object represents the number 3.14159.

3.5 The Sequential Search

The *sequential search algorithm* (also called the linear search and the serial search) searches through a list sequentially from the beginning, searching for a given target value. It returns either the first location of the target that it finds, or a negative number if the target is not found. The details of the algorithm are presented as Algorithm 3.3. Listing 3.5 is its Java implementation.

LISTING 3.5: The Sequential Search

```
1   public class TestSequentialSearch {
2
3     public static void main(String[] args) {
4       int[] a = {66, 44, 99, 33, 55, 22, 88, 77};
5       System.out.println("search(a," + 55 + "): " + search(a,55));
6       System.out.println("search(a," + 50 + "): " + search(a,50));
7     }
8
9     public static int search(int[] a, int target) {
10      for (int i = 0; i < a.length; i++)
11        if (a[i] == target) return i;
12      return -a.length;
13    }
14  }
```

Here is the output:

```
{66,44,99,33,55,22,88,77}
search(a,55): 4
search(a,50): -8
```

On the first call to search(), the target 55 is found at index 4. On the second call, the target 50 is not found, so –8 is returned.

Note that this implementation of the sequential search returns the *first* index that it finds for the target, if it is in the array. (See Programming Problem 3.5 on page 114.)

We present algorithms in a *pseudocode* style that can be translated directly into Java or any other programming language. To facilitate the analysis of the algorithms, their presentations include the following formalisms: input and output specifications, preconditions and postconditions, and invariants. The input and output specifications translate directly into parameter lists and return values for the algorithm's implementation. The preconditions and postconditions form the "contract" for the algorithm: If the preconditions are met, then the algorithm promises to meet the postconditions. The invariants are conditions that are asserted to be true during the execution of the algorithm. These are used to prove that the algorithm is guaranteed to fulfill its contract (*i.e.*, that it is *correct*.).

▲ **ALGORITHM 3.3: Sequential Search**

Input: a sequence $\{a_0, a_1, a_2, ..., a_{n-1}\}$ and a target value x.
Output: an index value i.
Postcondition: Either $a_i = x$, or $i = -n$ and each $a_j \neq x$.

1. For each i from 0 to $n-1$, do step 2.

2. If $a_i = x$, return i.

3. Return $-n$.

It is pretty obvious why this algorithm works. The loop in steps 1–2 compares each element of the sequence with the target x and returns the location of the fist element that equals x. If the loop finishes, then every element has been checked and x has not been found, so $-n$ is returned at step 3.

How fast is the sequential search? The answer is, not very fast. On average, the number of steps executed is proportional to the number n of elements in the sequence. If it averages 3 milliseconds on a sequence of 10,000 elements, then it will average 6 milliseconds on a sequence of 20,000 elements. On average, a sequence twice as long will take twice as long to search. We say that the algorithm runs in *linear time* because the run time is a linear function of the size of the data structure. This is denoted by the symbol $\Theta(n)$.[4]

To see why the sequential search runs in $\Theta(n)$ time, suppose first that the target is not in the array. Then the search loop will iterate n times before returning $-n$. On the other hand, if the target is in the array, then we may assume that it is equally likely to be in any one of the n positions. The search loop will iterate $i + 1$ times, where i is the index of the target. So it is equally likely that the number of iterations will be any of the n values 1, 2, 3, ..., n. The average of these n numbers is $n/2$. Hence, if the target is in the loop, it will iterate, $n/2$ times on average. Thus, whether the target is or is not in the array, the algorithm will take twice as long to run on arrays that are twice as long. That's what "$\Theta(n)$ time" means.

3.6 Complexity Analysis

The analysis of the run time for the sequential search, uses the expression $\Theta(n)$ to describe the fact that the run time is proportional to n, the length of the list: Doubling the size doubles the run

---

[4] Some authors also denote "linear time" with the symbol $O(n)$, which is similar, but not as precise. (See Appendix C.)

time. This expression is one of several generally used to describe the efficiency of algorithms. In this section, we define these expressions and show how they compare.

We restrict our attention to positive functions $f(n)$ that are ascending on the positive integers:

$$0 < f(1) \le f(2) \le f(3) \le \cdots \le f(n) \le \cdots$$

For example, $\lg n$, n, $n \lg n$, n^2, n^3, and 2^n are all such functions[5], as are constant functions such as $f(n) = 1$. These functions are used to categorize algorithms according to their run times.

Two functions are *asymptotically proportional* if their ratio and its reciprocal are both bounded above by some constant. This means that the two functions grow at about the same rate and that they are nearly proportional for large values of n. For example, the two functions $f(n) = 4n - 3$ and $g(n) = n$ are asymptotically proportional because their ratio $f(n)/g(n) = (4n - 3)/(n) = 4 - 3/n$ is bounded above by 4, and its reciprocal $g(n)/f(n) = (n)/(4n - 3) = 1/(4 - 3/n)$ is bounded above by 1. Indeed, if n is very large, then $3/n$ will be very small, and $f(n)/g(n)$ will nearly equal 4, which means that $f(n) \approx 4g(n)$.

The set of all functions that are asymptotically proportional to $g(n) = n$ is denoted by $\Theta(n)$. So $f(n) = 4n - 3$ is a member of the complexity class $\Theta(n)$. This is written as $4n - 3 \in \Theta(n)$, or $4n - 3 = \Theta(n)$. (We can also say that $n = \Theta(4n - 3)$, but the simpler function is usually the one that we want to put with the $\Theta()$.)

Here is a more important, but less obvious example:

▼ **EXAMPLE 3.1: Two Asymptotically Proportional Functions**

Suppose that $f(n) = 2n \ln n + 5n$ and $g(n) = n \lg n$. Here, $\ln n = \log_e n$, the *natural logarithm* of n, and $\lg n = \log_2 n$, the *binary logarithm* of n. Then we have

$$\frac{f(n)}{g(n)} = \frac{2n \ln n + 5n}{n \lg n} = 2\left(\frac{\ln n}{\lg n}\right) + \frac{5}{\lg n} = 2(0.693) + \frac{5}{\lg n} = 1.386 + \frac{5}{\lg n} \le 7$$

and

$$\frac{g(n)}{f(n)} = \frac{n \lg n}{2n \ln n + 5n} = \frac{\lg n}{2 \ln n + 5} \le \frac{\lg n}{2 \ln n} = \frac{1}{2 \ln 2} \le 1$$

Since $f(n)/g(n)$ is bounded above by 7 and $g(n)/f(n)$ is bounded above by 1, we can conclude that $f(n)$ and $g(n)$ are asymptotically proportional: $2n \ln n + 5n = \Theta(n \lg n)$.

One important use of this kind of analysis is that it allows us to represent complicated functions like $2n \ln n + 5n$ with simpler functions like $n \lg n$. When analyzing algorithms, we are interested in how the run time behaves for larger and larger values of n; that is, its *asymptotic behavior*. Example 3.1 shows that an algorithm whose run time is $2n \ln n + 5n$ is essentially the same as one whose run time is $n \lg n$; that is, they have the same asymptotic run-time behavior.

In computing, we try to categorize the algorithms that we use according to their asymptotic run-time functions. It turns out that the run-time behavior of most algorithms falls into one of

---

[5] Actually, $\lg n$ (the binary logarithm of n) is positive only for $n > 1$, but that doesn't affect asymptotic analysis, which deals only with "large" values of n.

only about seven primary categories: $\Theta(1)$, $\Theta(\lg n)$, $\Theta(n)$, $\Theta(n \lg n)$, $\Theta(n^2)$, $\Theta(n^3)$, and $\Theta(2^n)$.[6] We call these categories *complexity classes* or *asymptotic growth classes*. Example 3.1 shows that an algorithm whose run time is $2n \ln n + 5n$ is in the fourth of these classes: $2n \ln n + 5n = \Theta(n \lg n)$.

We saw in Section 3.5 that the sequential search algorithm belongs to the $\Theta(n)$ complexity class. We will see in Section 3.7 that the *binary search* algorithm belongs to the $\Theta(\lg n)$ complexity class.

As an example of a simple algorithm that belongs to the $\Theta(1)$ complexity class, think of the process of retrieving an element from an array, given its index. Since the index provides direct access into the array, the time it takes to complete this task is independent of the length n of the array. We say that algorithms in this class run in *constant time*. This means that the run time is essentially the same, no matter how large the array is.

Algorithms that belong to the $\Theta(n^2)$ class are said to run in *quadratic time*. That means that if you double the size of the problem, then the run time will be quadrupled. Some of the slower sorting algorithms are in this class. The faster sorting algorithms are in the $\Theta(n \lg n)$ class. (See Chapter 15.)

Most algorithms for solving a system of equations for n unknowns run in *cubic time*; that is, their run time functions belong to the $\Theta(n^3)$ class.

We will usually want to find the complexity class $\Theta(g(n))$ to which the algorithm's run time function belongs. But it is not always possible. In some cases, we can draw only less precise conclusions. For these cases we have less specific kinds of complexity classes.

Here are definitions of the five different complexity classes that are used in the analysis of computer algorithms:

$$O(g(n)) = \{ \, f(n) \, | \, f(n)/g(n) \text{ is bounded } \}$$
$$\Omega(g(n)) = \{ \, f(n) \, | \, g(n)/f(n) \text{ is bounded } \}$$
$$\Theta(g(n)) = \{ \, f(n) \, | \, f(n)/g(n) \text{ is bounded and } g(n)/f(n) \text{ is bounded } \}$$
$$o(g(n)) = \{ \, f(n) \, | \, f(n)/g(n) \to 0 \text{ as } n \to \infty \}$$
$$\omega(g(n)) = \{ \, f(n) \, | \, g(n)/f(n) \to 0 \text{ as } n \to \infty \}$$

These symbols are pronounced "big oh of $g(n)$", "big omega of $g(n)$", "big theta of $g(n)$", "little oh of $g(n)$", and "little omega of $g(n)$".

Note that all five complexity classes are defined in terms of the ratios $f(n)/g(n)$ and $g(n)/f(n)$. Some authors instead define these classes using several quantifiers and inequalities. But for positive ascending functions, it can be shown that these definitions are equivalent to their more complex versions.

It helps to think of these five classes like this:

$O(g(n))$ is the set of all functions that are asymptotically slower than or equivalent to g

$\Omega(g(n))$ is the set of all functions that are asymptotically faster than or equivalent to g

$\Theta(g(n))$ is the set of all functions that are asymptotically equivalent to g

$o(g(n))$ is the set of all functions that are asymptotically slower than g

$\omega(g(n))$ is the set of all functions that are asymptotically faster than g

---

[6] That is why logarithms are so important in computing: Two of these classes use logarithms.

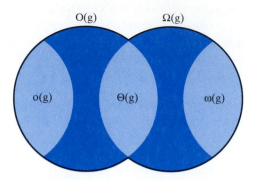

FIGURE 3.3   The five asymptotic growth classes.

The term "asymptotic" refers to the function's behavior for very large values of n (*i.e.*, as n approaches infinity ($n \rightarrow \infty$)).

The Euler–Venn diagram in Figure 3.3 shows the relationships among the five complexity classes for a given test function $g(n)$. These relationships include the following:

$$\Theta(g) = O(g) \cap \Omega(g) \tag{3.1}$$

$$o(g(n)) \subset O(g(n)) - \Theta(g(n)) \tag{3.2}$$

$$\omega(g(n)) \subset \Omega(g(n)) - \Theta(g(n)) \tag{3.3}$$

When we say that $f(n)$ is "asymptotically slower" than $g(n)$, we mean that once n is large enough, $f(n)$ will be less than some multiple of $g(n)$. For example, the function $8n + 600$ is asymptotically slower than the function n^2 because $8n + 600 < n^2$ for all $n > 100$. We express this fact symbolically as $8n + 600 \in O(n^2)$. Thus, in this case, "large enough" means "greater than 100." Once n is greater than 100, the function $8n + 600$ is less than the function n^2. The actual cut-off value for n is not important. The important thing is that there is some cut-off value of n, beyond which the function $8n + 600$ is less than some multiple the function n^2. Finding the cut-off value at $n = 200$ or at $n = 30$ is just as good.

The definition of "big-oh" on page 83 requires us to show that the ratio $f(n)/g(n)$ is bounded. Indeed, that ratio, $(8n + 600)/n^2$, is bounded by 1000:

$$(8n + 600)/n^2 < 1000$$

The actual value of the bound is not important. What is important is that some bound can be found. Discovering a different bound, such as 20,000 or 609 is just as good.

The fact that the ratio $f(n)/g(n)$ is bounded means that the denominator n^2 grows faster than the numerator $8n + 600$. That is why we say that the numerator $8n + 600$ is asymptotically slower than the denominator n^2.

3.7 The Binary Search

If a sequence is sorted, the binary search algorithm (Algorithm 3.4) can be used to search for a target value in much less time than the sequential search. It repeatedly divides the sequence in half, each time focusing on the half whose range includes the target.

For example, if you are searching for the target 66 in a sorted sequence of 100 numbers, you would look first at the middle number a_{50}. Suppose that its value is less than 66. Then, since the sequence is sorted you know that the target cannot be in the lower half of the sequence, so you would focus your search on the subsequence $\{a_{51}, ..., a_{99}\}$. Repeating that process, you would look next at the middle element of that subsequence, a_{75}. Suppose that its value is greater than 66. Then you would focus your search on the subsequence $\{a_{51}, ..., a_{74}\}$.

As the search continues, notice how fast the size of the remaining subsequence decreases: 100 elements, 49 elements, 24 elements, *etc.* Each iteration has about half as many elements to search. So the number of iterations is, at most, the number of times the original size can be divided by 2. That number is $\lceil \lg n \rceil$, the integer binary logarithm of n. That means only seven iterations for searching 100 elements, and only ten iterations for searching 1000 elements.

▲ **ALGORITHM 3.4: Binary Search**

Input: a sequence $\{a_0, a_1, a_2, ..., a_{n-1}\}$ and a target value x.
Output: an index value i.
Precondition: The sequence is sorted: $a_0 \le a_1 \le a_2 \le \cdots \le a_{n-1}$.
Postcondition: Either $a_i = x$; or $i = -p - 1$, where $a_j < x$ for all $j < p$, and $a_j > x$ for all $j \ge p$.

1. Let $p = 0$ and $q = n-1$.

2. Repeat steps 2-5 while $p \le q$.

3. Let $i = (p + q)/2$.

4. If $a_i = x$, return i.

5. If $a_i < x$, let $p = i + 1$; otherwise let $q = i - 1$.

6. Return $-p-1$.

The binary search runs in $\Theta(\lg n)$ time. This means that the run time is roughly proportional to the logarithm[7] of the size of the array. So for example, if it takes 3 milliseconds to search an array of 1,000 elements, then it should take about 6 milliseconds (twice as long) to search an array of 1,000,000 elements.[8] This is very fast—about as fast as algorithms get.

To see why the Binary search "runs in logarithmic time," note that the run time is proportional to the number of iterations made by the loop in steps 2-5. Each iteration either returns or resets one of the two bounds p or q. Each time a bound is reset, the length of the subsequence $\{a_p, a_{p+1}, ..., a_q\}$ is reduced to about half of what it was on the previous iteration. So the total number of iterations is at most the number of times n can be divided in half. That is the binary logarithm.

The binary search algorithm is implemented in the `java.util.Arrays` class. (See Section 3.8.) An equivalent implementation is show in Listing 3.6.

---

[7] The symbol $\lg n$ means the binary logarithm of n. But since all logarithm functions are multiples of each other, the complexity class $\Theta(\lg n)$ is the same as $\Theta(\log n)$ for any logarithm function (*i.e.*, any base).
[8] This is because $\log(1,000,000) = \log(1,000^2) = 2 \log(1,000)$.

LISTING 3.6: The Binary Search

```
1   public class TestBinarySearch {
2
3     public static void main(String[] args) {
4       int[] a = {22, 33, 44, 55, 66, 77, 88, 99};
5       System.out.println("search(a," + 55 + "): " + search(a, 55));
6       System.out.println("search(a," + 50 + "): " + search(a, 50));
7     }
8
9     static int search(int[] a, int x) {
10      int p = 0, q = a.length-1;
11      while (p <= q) {              // search the segment a[p..q]
12        int i = (p+q)/2;            // index of element in the middle
13        if (a[i] == x) return i;
14        if (a[i] < x) p = i+1;      // search upper half
15        else q = i-1;               // search lower half
16      }
17      return -p-1;                  // not found
18    }
19  }
```

The output is

```
search(a,55): 3
search(a,50): -4
```

The program creates an ascending array of integers and then makes the same two `search()` calls that were made in Listing 3.5 on page 80 for the sequential search. The only difference is that the negative output can be used to determine the index where the target should be placed to keep the array sorted. When the output is a negative number k, the correct index for the target will be $i = -k - 1$. In this case, $k = -4$, so $i = -(-4) - 1 = 3$, which means that the target 50 belongs at `a[3]`.

The strategy used by the binary search algorithm is known as *divide and conquer*. It "conquers" (solves) the problem by dividing it up into smaller problems and applying the same strategy on them. This technique is widely used in sorting algorithms. (See Chapter 15.)

3.8 The java.util.Arrays Class

The `java.util.Arrays` class provides some utility methods for manipulating arrays. These methods are all declared `static` (so they are invoked with the prefix "`Arrays.`"). Among them are the following:

```
public static int binarySearch(double[] a, double x)
public static boolean equals(double[] a, double[] b)
public static void fill(double[] a, double x)
public static void fill(double[] a, int lo, int hi, double x)
public static void sort(double[] a)
```

There are nine versions of each of these methods, one for each of the eight primitive types and one for `Object` types. So, for example, the class includes these two distinct methods:

```
public static void sort(int[] a)
public static void sort(Object[] a)
```

Each of the `equals(a,b)` methods tests for equality (not identity) of the two arrays a and b, the same way an `equals()` method would be defined for any class. It returns true if a and b are the same array type, they have the same size, and their corresponding elements are equal.

Each of the `fills(a,lo,hi,x)` methods inserts `hi-lo` copies of x in the array a, starting at `a[lo]`. Note that, consistent with other Java methods, this uses the first index (`lo`) as the starting index and the second index (`hi`) as the stopping index (*i.e.*, only elements `a[lo]..a[hi-1]` are affected). An important consequence of this convention is that the total number of elements affected is the difference `hi-lo` of those two index values.[9]

Each of the `sort()` methods sorts the array into ascending order.

The `binarySearch()` method implements the binary search algorithm (Algorithm 3.4 on page 85). The call `binarySearch(a,x)` searches for x among the elements of the array a. It assumes that the array is sorted. If x is found, the method returns its index in the array. Otherwise, it returns the negative integer i, such that the value $-i-1$ is the index of the correct location to insert x in the array, keeping it sorted. For example, if a is the array $\{22,44,66,88\}$, then `binarySearch(a,50)` would return $i = -3$, since 50 is not in the array; if it were to be inserted, it should be inserted at index $-i-1 = -(-3)-1 = 2$, shifting `a[2..3]` into `a[3..4]`, and resulting in the sorted array $\{22,44,50,66,88\}$.

The program in Listing 3.7 illustrates the `Arrays.sort()` and the `Arrays.binary-Search()` methods. It defines an unsorted array `a[]` of eight integers, prints it, sorts it, prints it again, and then tests the `binarySearch()` method on four different targets:

LISTING 3.7: **Using the `java.util.Arrays` Class**

```
1   public class TestJavaUtilArrays {
2
3      public static void main(String[] args) {
4         int[] a = {77, 44, 55, 22, 99, 66, 33, 88};
5         print(a);
6         java.util.Arrays.sort(a);
7         print(a);
8         test(a,55);
9         test(a,60);
10        test(a,88);
11        test(a,90);
```

---

[9] This convention is standard throughout Java and (C++). It competes with two other conventions that programmers use: (1) make the second integer the number of elements affected; (2) make the second integer the index of the last element affected. The preferred Java/C++ convention has the advantage that the number of elements affected is the difference `hi-lo`, and it is consistent with zero-based indexing where `a.length` is one more than the index of the last element. It is also consistent with the mathematical notion of the left-closed, right-open interval $[3, 7) = \{\, t \mid 3 \le t < 7 \,\}$ that allows for consistent partitioning (disjoint unions) of intervals, like this: $[1, 9) = [1, 3) \cup [3, 7) \cup [7, 9)$.

```
12    }
13    static void test(int[] array, int target) {
14       int i = java.util.Arrays.binarySearch(array,target);
15       System.out.print("target="+target+", i="+i);
16       if (i >= 0) System.out.println("\ta[" + i + "]=" + array[i]);
17       else System.out.println("\tInsert " + target+" at a["+(-i-1)+"]");
18    }
19
20    static void print(int[] a) {
21       // See lines 22-27 in Listing 3.1 on page 76
22    }
23 }
```

The output is

```
a = {77,44,55,22,99,66,33,88}
a = {22,33,44,55,66,77,88,99}
target=55, i=3  a[3]=55
target=60, i=-5 Insert 60 at a[4]
target=88, i=6  a[6]=88
target=90, i=-8 Insert 90 at a[7]
```

The first search target is 55, which is in the array; so the method returns its location: $i = 3$. The second search target is 60, which is not in the array; so the method returns index $i = -5$, which indicates that the target should be inserted at index $-i - 1 = -(-5) - 1 = 4$. The third search target is 88, which is in the array; so the method returns its location: $i = 6$. The fourth search target is 90, which is not in the array, so the method returns index $i = -8$, indicating that the target should be inserted at index $-i - 1 = -(-8) - 1 = 7$.

3.9 A User-Defined IntArrays Class

There are many other utility methods that one could include in an Arrays class. Some of these are illustrated in the "homegrown" IntArrays class for arrays of ints presented in Listing 3.8. Notice that, like the java.util.Arrays class, all the methods here are static, so they are invoked by using the class name IntArrays as a prefix. We included javadoc comments to clarify what these methods do.

The isSorted() method is a boolean method that determines whether the elements in a[] are in ascending order. It uses a for loop to check the order of pairs of adjacent elements. If any pair is out of order, the method returns false immediately. It returns true only if it makes it all the way through the loop without finding any pairs out of order.

The print() and randomInts() methods are the same as in Listing 3.1 on page 76, except that we have added bounds checking on the arguments for the randomInt() method. It uses a random number generator that is seeded by the current time. The swap() method is the same as in Listing 3.3 on page 78.

The resize() method returns a new array that contains the same elements as the specified array a[]. It uses the System.arraycopy() method to copy the elements of a[] into the new array. The new array will have length n, and its extra elements will be 0.

LISTING 3.8: A User-Defined Utility IntArrays Class

```java
public class IntArrays {
    private static java.util.Random random = new java.util.Random();

    /**
     * Determines whether the specified array is in ascending order.
     *
     * @param  a the array.
     * @return true if a[] is in ascending order, otherwise false.
     */
    public static boolean isSorted(int[] a) {
        for (int i = 1; i < a.length; i++)
            if (a[i] < a[i-1]) return false;
        return true;
    }

    /**
     * Prints all the elements in the specified array.
     *
     * @param  a the array.
     */
    public static void print(int[] a) {
        System.out.print("{" + a[0]);
        for (int i = 1; i < a.length; i++)
            System.out.print("," + a[i]);
        System.out.println("}");
    }


    /**
     * Returns a new array of n random integers. If range>0, then
     * the elements will be uniformly distributed in the range
     * 0 <= a[i] < range; otherwise, they will range over all int
     * values.
     *
     * @param  n the length of the new array.
     * @param  range determines the range of the element values.
     * @throws IllegalArgumentException.
     * @return the new array.
     */
    public static int[] randomInts(int n, int range) {
        if (n<0 || range<2) throw new IllegalArgumentException();
        int[] a = new int[n];
        for (int i=0; i<n; i++)
            a[i] = random.nextInt(range);
        return a;
    }

    /**
```

```
48      * Returns a new array of size n that contains the elements of
49      * the specified array a and 0s thereafter.
50      *
51      * @param  a the array to be copied.
52      * @param  n the length of the new array.
53      * @throws IllegalArgumentException.
54      * @return the new array.
55      */
56     public static int[] resize(int[] a, int n) {
57         if (n<a.length) throw new IllegalArgumentException();
58         int[] aa = new int[n];
59         System.arraycopy(a, 0, aa, 0, a.length);
60         return aa;
61     }
62
63     /**
64      * Interchanges element i with element j in the specified array.
65      *
66      * @param  a the array.
67      * @param  i index of one element.
68      * @param  j index of the other element.
69      */
70     public static void swap(int[] a, int i, int j) {
71         int ai = a[i], aj = a[j];
72         if (ai == aj) return;
73         a[i] = aj;
74         a[j] = ai;
75     }
76 }
```

The System.arraycopy() method is the most efficient way to copy elements from one array to another in Java. Its general syntax is

```
System.arraycopy(a, m, aa, mm, k);
```

This copies the k elements $\{a[m], ..., a[m+k-1]\}$ into the n positions $\{aa[mm], ..., aa[mm+k-1]\}$. Here $a[]$ is the source array, $aa[]$ is the target array, m is the starting index in $a[]$, mm is the starting index in $aa[]$, and k is the number of elements copied. The method can also be used to copy a segment of elements from one location to another in the same array, even if those segments overlap. For example,

```
System.arraycopy(a, 5, a, 3, 4);
```

will copy a[5..8] into a[3..6] correctly, shifting the four elements back two positions.

3.10 The java.util.Vector Class

With version 1.1, Java introduced a Vector class in its java.util package. Although it has since been superseded by the java.util.ArrayList class (See Chapters 7–8 and Appendix D.) it still provides an instructive example of resizable arrays.

The term *resizable array* refers to the programming technique of replacing an array by a larger array that contains the same elements. Typically, the new array will have twice the length of the original. This technique is used in the data structures in the java.util package that are implemented with arrays.

Listing 3.9 shows how to resize an array in Java:

LISTING 3.9: Resizing an Integer Array

```
1    int[] resized(int[] a) {
2      int n=a.length;
3      int[] aa = new int[2*n];
4      System.arraycopy(a,0,aa,0,n);
5      return aa;
6    }
```

Since the length of an array is an intrinsic part of its definition, a whole new array must be allocated. If the resized() method is invoked, as in

        a = resized(a);

then the array a[] will end up with its length doubled, but otherwise will appear unchanged. That is because the local array aa[] is renamed a[] by that assignment. Unless some other array reference variable that had previously been assigned to a[] is still in use, the previous shorter array will be deleted by the Java garbage collector. Note that the call resized(a) is equivalent to IntArrays.resize(a, 2*a.length), using the IntArrays class in Listing 3.8 on page 89.

Instances of the java.util.Vector class are direct generalizations of ordinary arrays of objects. A Vector object maintains a sequence of Object references in its own protected Object[] array, which is called its *backing array*. Listing 3.10 defines the java.util.Vector class.

The backing array is declared in line 2. The size field at line 3 keeps track of how many objects are actually stored in the vector; its initial value is 0. Line 4 defines the default capacity (of the backing array) to be 10.

The one-argument constructor defined at line 6 allocates the backing array with the given capacity. (See Figure 3.4.) The no-argument constructor defined at line 11 invokes the one-argument constructor to allocate the backing array with the default capacity. The size() method at line 15 is a simple accessor method for the size field. The comment at line 19 suggests that other class methods would be defined there.

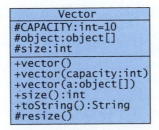

FIGURE 3.4 Our Vector class.

LISTING 3.10: A Simplified Version of the `java.util.Vector` Class

```
1   public class Vector {
2      protected Object[] objects;        // backing array
3      protected int size;                // actual number of Objects stored
4      protected static final int CAPACITY=10;  // default array length
5
6      public Vector(int capacity) {
7         if (capacity<=0) throw new IllegalArgumentException("capacity<=0");
8         objects = new Object[capacity];
9      }
10
11     public Vector() {
12        this(CAPACITY);
13     }
14
15     public int size() {
16        return size;
17     }
18
19     //...
20
21     protected void resize() {
22        int n=objects.length;
23        Object[] temp = new Object[2*n];
24        System.arraycopy(objects, 0, temp, 0, n);
25        objects = temp;
26     }
27  }
```

The `resize()` method at lines 21–26 is a local version of the method in Listing 3.9 on page 91. The only differences are that it resizes an array of objects instead of integers, and the new array is immediately assigned (at line 25) to the `objects` field instead of being returned.

One method that every data structure class should include is a `toString()` method. This method is defined in the `Object` class itself, so every class automatically inherits it. But the string returned by that version merely includes the object's type and its address. To obtain a string that actually lists the individual elements of the data structure, you have to write your own custom version. Listing 3.11 gives a `toString()` method for our `Vector` class.

LISTING 3.11: A `toString()` Method for the `Vector` Class

```
1      public String toString() {
2         if (size == 0) return "()";
3         StringBuffer buf = new StringBuffer("(" + objects[0]);
4         for (int i = 1; i < size; i++)
5            buf.append("," + objects[i]);
6         return buf + ")";
7      }
```

If the vector is empty, then the string `"()"` is returned at line 2. Otherwise, a string is returned at line 6 that lists all the objects in the vector. That string list is delimited by parentheses and is formed by the `for` loop in lines 4-5. To do that, we use a `StringBuffer` instead of a `String` object, for greater efficiency. Since `String` objects are immutable, each time the concatenation operator + is applied to one, a new object is created. The alternative is to use the `append()` method of the `StringBuffer` class, thereby obtaining the same result without a proliferation of objects.

Note that in the argument to the `append()` method at line 5, the string `","` is concatenated with the object `objects[i]`. That result itself is a `String` expression, so the individual object's `toString()` method is implicitly invoked there, and the string that it returns is appended to the string `","`.

Listing 3.12 provides a constructor that can be used to build a new vector out of an existing array.

LISTING 3.12: A Constructor That Loads an Array

```
1    public Vector(Object[] a) {
2       int n = a.length;
3       objects = new Object[2*n];
4       System.arraycopy(a,0,objects,0,n);
5       size = n;
6    }
```

At line 3, it allocates the backing array, setting its length to be twice the length of the given array. At line 4, references to the objects in the given array `a[]` are copied into the backing array and then the `size` field is initialized at line 5.

Listing 3.13 gives a test driver for the `Vector` class, as defined by the last three listings:

LISTING 3.13: Testing the Vector Class

```
1    public static void main(String[] args){
2       Vector v = new Vector(args);
3       System.out.println(v);
4    }
```

The output from running the driver at the command line is

```
A:\>java TestVector alpha beta gamma delta
(alpha,beta,gamma,delta)
```

On this run, we enter the four command line arguments: **alpha beta gamma delta**. These are copied into the `args[]` array when `main()` starts. Then at line 2, references to those four `String` objects are copied into the new vector v. At line 3, the `toString()` method defined in Listing 3.11 on page 92 is invoked implicitly, producing the output `(alpha,beta,gamma,delta)`.

The `Vector` object v in this test driver is depicted in Figure 3.5 on page 94. It contains two fields: the array a and the integer `size`. The array a has eight elements: The first four are references to strings, and the last four are `null`. The integer `size` has the value 4. Note that the actual `String` objects (`"alpha"`, `"beta"`, `"gamma"`, and `"delta"`) are external to the `Vector` object.

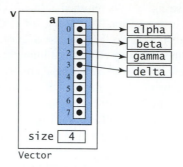

FIGURE 3.5 The vector in Listing 3.13.

The `java.util.Vector` class has many more methods than those described here. The complete class is summarized by the UML diagram in Figure 3.6. Some of these methods are developed in the Programming Problems at the end of the chapter. In Chapter 8 we will review the `java.util.ArrayList` class, which is the preferred alternative to the `java.util.Vector` class. The UML diagram for our simpler Vector class is shown in Figure 3.4 on page 91.

3.11 Multidimensional Arrays

Array elements can be objects of any type. Arrays themselves are objects. Therefore, one can have an array whose elements are arrays. This is called a *two-dimensional array*. (See Listing 3.14.)

LISTING 3.14: Using Two-Dimensional Arrays

```
1   public class TwoDimensionalArrays {
2     public static void main(String[] args) {
3       int[][] a = new int[3][];          // an array of 3 sub-arrays (rows)
4       a[0] = new int[]{22,44,66,88};     // the first row
5       a[2] = new int[]{33,77};           // the third row
6       System.out.println("a: " + a + "\na.length: " + a.length);
7       IntArrays.print(a[0]);
8       IntArrays.print(a[2]);
9       System.out.println("a[2].length: " + a[2].length);
10      int[][] b = { { 22,44,66,88 },     // the first row of b
11                    { 0, 0, 0, 0 },      // the second row of b
12                    { 33,55,77, 0 } };   // the third row of b
13      System.out.println("b: " + b + "\nb.length: " + b.length);
14      IntArrays.print(b[0]);
15      IntArrays.print(b[2]);
16      System.out.println("b[2].length: " + b[2].length);
17    }
18  }
```

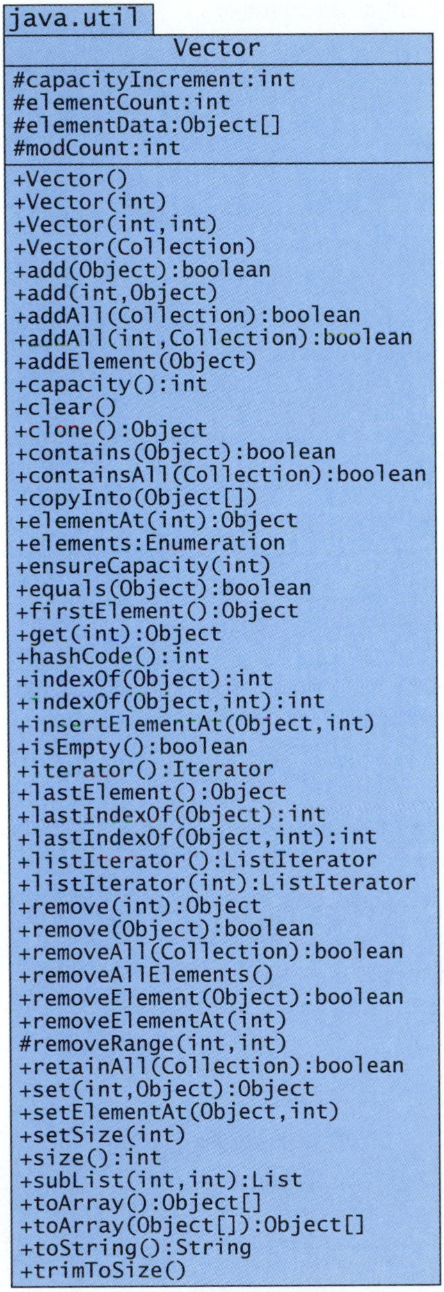

```
java.util

                    Vector

#capacityIncrement:int
#elementCount:int
#elementData:Object[]
#modCount:int

+Vector()
+Vector(int)
+Vector(int,int)
+Vector(Collection)
+add(Object):boolean
+add(int,Object)
+addAll(Collection):boolean
+addAll(int,Collection):boolean
+addElement(Object)
+capacity():int
+clear()
+clone():Object
+contains(Object):boolean
+containsAll(Collection):boolean
+copyInto(Object[])
+elementAt(int):Object
+elements:Enumeration
+ensureCapacity(int)
+equals(Object):boolean
+firstElement():Object
+get(int):Object
+hashCode():int
+indexOf(Object):int
+indexOf(Object,int):int
+insertElementAt(Object,int)
+isEmpty():boolean
+iterator():Iterator
+lastElement():Object
+lastIndexOf(Object):int
+lastIndexOf(Object,int):int
+listIterator():ListIterator
+listIterator(int):ListIterator
+remove(int):Object
+remove(Object):boolean
+removeAll(Collection):boolean
+removeAllElements()
+removeElement(Object):boolean
+removeElementAt(int)
#removeRange(int,int)
+retainAll(Collection):boolean
+set(int,Object):Object
+setElementAt(Object,int)
+setSize(int)
+size():int
+subList(int,int):List
+toArray():Object[]
+toArray(Object[]):Object[]
+toString():String
+trimToSize()
```

FIGURE 3.6 The `java.util.Vector` class.

The output is

```
a: [[I@cac268
a.length: 3
{22,44,66,88}
{33,77}
a[2].length: 2
b: [[I@8d107f
b.length: 3
{22,44,66,88}
{33,55,77,0}
b[2].length: 4
```

This program defines two two-dimensional arrays. The first, `a[][]`, is defined and initialized as an array of separate arrays. This is called a *ragged array* because its component arrays have different sizes. The second two-dimensional array, `b[][]`, is uniform: all three of its component arrays are four-element sub-arrays (rows).

The `IntArrays.print()` calls at lines 7–8 and 13–14 are to the `static print()` method defined in the `IntArrays` class in Listing 3.8 on page 89. Note that it is applied to one-dimensional row arrays of `a[][]` and `b[][]`.

We can visualize the array `a[][]` like the picture in Figure 3.7. The object a is an array of three elements: `a[0]`, `a[1]`, and `a[2]`. The first element `a[0]` is itself an array of four `int`s:

```
4        a[0] = new int[]{22,44,66,88};   // the first row
```

The second element `a[1]` is the `null` value; as an array, it has not been allocated. The third element `a[2]` is an array of two `int`s:

```
5        a[2] = new int[]{33,77};         // the third row
```

The array `b[][]` is uniform, so it can be declared and initialized more simply, in a single statement:

```
9        int [][] b = { { 22,44,66,88 },   // the first row of b
10                       {  0, 0, 0, 0 },   // the second row of b
11                       { 33,55,77, 0 } }; // the third row of b
```

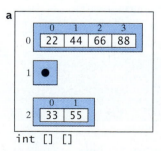

FIGURE 3.7 A ragged array.

Of course, this could be presented all on the same line, like this:

```
int[][] b = { {22,44,66,88}, {0,0,0,0}, {33,55,77,0} };
```

But we usually think of a two-dimensional array as, well, two-dimensional (*i.e.*, with rows and columns). We visualize b[][] as shown in Figure 3.8, with three rows and four columns. This would also be called a three-by-four *matrix*.

The first line of output from the program prints the array reference a. It shows the array type, [[I, and its location in memory, cac268. Note that the two left brackets [[indicate that it is a two-dimensional array, and the I indicates that its elements have type int.

The second line of output confirms that a[][] is indeed an array of three elements. The third and fourth lines of output print two of those elements, each of which is a one-dimensional array. The fifth line of output confirms that a[3] is indeed an array of two elements.

The remaining lines of output provide similar information about the b[][] array. Note that the last line shows that, although a[][] and b[][] are both arrays of three-array elements, they do not have the same shape: The last row of a[][] has length 2, while the last row of b[][] has length 4.

▼ **EXAMPLE 3.2: Pascal's Triangle**

Figure 3.9 is an example of *Pascal's triangle,* a two-dimensional array that has the binomial coefficient c_{ij} for its element at row i and column j (for $j \leq i$). Rows 0–6 are shown in Figure 3.9. The program in Listing 3.15 generates Pascal's triangle using the recurrence relation $c_{ij} = c_{i-1,j-1} + c_{i-1,j}$. This means that each interior number in the triangle is the sum of the number directly above it and the number above and to the left. For example, 15 is the sum of 10 and 5, as indicated in Figure 3.9.

b

	0	1	2	3
0	22	44	66	88
1	0	0	0	0
2	33	55	77	0

int[][]

FIGURE 3.8   A two-dimensional array.

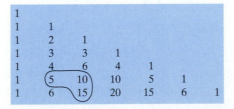

FIGURE 3.9   Pascal's triangle.

LISTING 3.15: Pascal's Triangle

```
1   public class PascalsTriangle {
2     public static void main(String[] args) {
3       int rows = Integer.parseInt(args[0]);
4       int[][] a = init(rows);
5       print(a);
6     }
7
8     static int[][] init(int n) {
9       int[][] a = new int[n][n];
10      for (int i = 0; i < n; i++)
11        for (int j = 0; j <= i; j++)
12          if (j == 0 || j == i) a[i][j] = 1;
13          else a[i][j] = a[i-1][j-1] + a[i-1][j];
14      return a;
15    }
16
17    static void print(int[][] a) {
18      for (int i = 0; i < a.length; i++) {
19        for (int j = 0; j <= i; j++)
20          print(a[i][j], 5);
21        System.out.println();
22      }
23    }
24
25    static void print(int n, int w) {
26      // prints n right-justified in a field on width w:
27      String s = "" + n, blanks = "                        ";
28      int len = s.length();
29      System.out.print(blanks.substring(0, w-len) + s);
30    }
31  }
```

The output from a command line argument of 7 (for `args[0]`) is

```
1
1    1
1    2    1
1    3    3    1
1    4    6    4    1
1    5   10   10    5    1
1    6   15   20   15    6    1
```

3.12 Case Study: Building a Concordance

A *concordance* of a text document is an index of all the words in the document, listing the location (volume, chapter, section, page, paragraph, and/or line number) of each occurrence of each word. Concordances have been used by scholars for centuries to study classical works of literature.

▼ **EXAMPLE 3.3: A Concordance of Mark Antony's Speech**

Figure 3.10 on page 100 shows a concordance of the famous Mark Antony speech from Shakespeare's play *Julius Caesar* (III, ii, 78–79). The 35-line text is shown on the left, and (part of) its 135-line concordance is shown on the right. The third word in the concordance is "ALL," and its line list is "11, 11, 23, 30." This means that the word occurs twice on line 11, once on line 23, and once on line 30 in the text. The words are stored in uppercase to facilitate searching.

To solve the problem of building a concordance, we take an OOP approach. The concordance itself should be an object: an instance of some class whose methods perform all the operations that we need to build and use the concordance. So we begin by formulating an ADT that specifies those operations.

A concordance is a list of entries, where each entry contains a unique word and a list of line numbers where the word appears in the given document.[10] When the concordance is printed, as in Figure 3.10, each entry is printed on a separate line consisting of the word, followed by its line number list:

    BRUTUS: 5,9,10,14,15,21,22,26,28

The concordance is built by scanning the given text document, line by line, and examining each word separately. If the word is not already in the concordance, then it will be added together with its line number. If the word is already in the concordance, then its line number will simply be appended to its existing line number list.

For example, the word "Brutus" is first encountered on line 5. So at that point, the entry

    BRUTUS: 5

is added to the concordance. The word is encountered next at line 9. So then the entry is modified to

    BRUTUS: 5,9

There is still only one entry for the word "Brutus".

Our ADT will need a search operation that determines whether a given word is already in the concordance. We could specify a boolean operation for this purpose. But instead of returning only true or false, it would be better to specify a *get*() operation that returns `null` when the word is not in the concordance, and returns its line number list when it is. This is a "look-up" operation that makes the concordance far more useful when there are thousands of words.

We also need an insert operation for adding word/list pairs to the concordance, and an update operation for appending line numbers to existing word lists. Instead of requiring these two as separate operations, we'll specify a single *put*() operation that can manage both the insert and the update actions. As we shall see later (in Chapter 7), this design decision is consistent with the Java Collections Framework.

---

[10] To keep it simple, we'll ignore paragraphs, page, section, chapter, and volume numbers.

Friends, Romans, countrymen, lend me your ears;
I come to bury Ceasar, not to praise him.
The evil that men do lives after them;
The good is oft interred with their bones;
So let it be with Caesar. The noble Brutus
Hath told you Caesar was ambitious:
If it were so, it was a grievous fault,
And grievously hath Caesar answer'd it.
Here, under leave of Brutus and the rest--
For Brutus is an honourable man;
So are they all, all honourable men--
Come I to speak in Caesar's funeral.
He was my friend, faithful and just to me:
But Brutus says he was ambitious;
And Brutus is an honourable man.
He hath brought many captives home to Rome
Whose ransoms did the general coffers fill:
Did this in Caesar seem ambitious?
When that the poor have cried, Caesar hath wept:
Ambition should be made of sterner stuff:
Yet Brutus says he was ambitious;
And Brutus is an honorable man.
You all did see that on the Lupercal
I thrice presented him a kingly crown,
Which he did thrice refuse: was this ambition?
Yet Brutus says he was ambitious;
And, sure, he is an honourable man.
I speak not to disprove what Brutus spoke,
But here I am to speak what I do know.
You all did love him once, not without cause:
What cause withholds you then, to mourn for him?
O judgment! thou art fled to brutish beasts,
And men have lost their reason. Bear with me;
My heart is in the coffin there with Caesar,
And I must Pause till it come back to me.

A: 7,24
AFTER: 3
ALL: 11,11,23,30
AM: 29
AMBITION: 20,25
AMBITIOUS:6,14,18,21,26
AN: 10,15,22,27
AND:8,9,13,15,22,27,33,35
ANSWER'D: 8
ARE: 11
ART 32
BACK: 35
BE: 5,20
BEAR: 33
BEASTS: 32
BONES: 4
BROUGHT: 16
BRUTISH: 32
BRUTUS: 5,9,10,14,15,21,22,26,28
BURY: 2
BUT: 14,29
CAESAR: 2,5,6,8,18,19,34
CAESAR'S: 12
CAPTIVES: 16
CAUSE: 30,31
COFFERS: 17
COFFIN: 34
COME: 2,12,35
COUNTRYMEN: 1
CRIED: 19
CROWN: 24
DID: 17,18,23,25,30
DISPROVE: 28
-- 106 entries omitted here --
YOU:6,23,30,31
YOUR: 1

FIGURE 3.10 A text document and its concordance.

The ADT is called *map*,[11] because it is used like an input–output device, mapping each input to some output. (See Figure 3.11.) The input is the word, and the output is the list of line numbers where it can be found. It is like a mathematical function $y = f(x)$, where x represents the word to be searched, y is the resulting line number list, and the function f is the mapping itself. The input x is called the *key*, and the output y is called its *value*.

Our ADT specifies four operations: a look-up operation *get*(*String key*), an input operation *put*(*String key, String value*), an accessor operation *size*(), and a *toString*() operation for printing the concordance.

The *get*(*key*) operation searches the map for the given *key*. If found, its *value* is returned. Otherwise, *null* is returned.

The *put*(*key, value*) operation also searches the map for the given *key*. If found, its current value is returned, after replacing it with the new *value* that is passed in the second argument. If the *key* is not found, then the new (*key, value*) pair is added to the map. The **Map** ADT requires all *key* values to be unique and immutable. Consequently, the *put*() operation performs a replace action instead of an add action when the given key is already in the map.

ADT: Map

ADT: *Map*

A **Map** is a collection of entries, where each *entry* is a (*key, value*) pair. The *key* fields must be unique and immutable.

String **get**(*String key*)
    Returns: the current value for the given *key*, or *null* if not found.
    Postcondition: this map is unchanged.

String **put**(*String key, String value*)
    Returns: the old value for the given *key*, or *null* if not found.
    Postcondition: the entry pair (*key, value*) is in the map.

int **size**()
    Returns: the number of entry pairs in the map.
    Postcondition: this map is unchanged.

String **toString**()
    Returns: a string representation of the enire collection.
    Postcondition: this map is unchanged.

FIGURE 3.11   An abstract data type for *Map* types.

---

[11] A map data structure is also called a *dictionary*, an *associative array*, or simply a *look-up table*. The term "dictionary" is used because it works like an ordinary dictionary, where you look up a word (the "key") and find its definition (the "value"). The term "associative array" refers to one possible implementation that uses parallel arrays: an array keys[] of keys, and a parallel array values[] of values. The two arrays are associated by their indexes: the value for key [i] is stored in values[i]. Modern databases use look-up tables that are essentially map data structures.

```
            <<interface>>
                Map
+get(String):String
+put(String,String):String
+size():int
+toString():String
```

FIGURE 3.12   UML diagram for a Map interface

Figure 3.12 shows a UML diagram for a Map interface that satisfies the requirements of the *Map* ADT. The corresponding Java code is given in Listing 3.16.

LISTING 3.16: A Map **Interface**

```
1  public interface Map {
2    public String get(String key);
3    public String put(String key, String value);
4    public int size();
5    public String toString();
6  }
```

The next step is to find a good data structure to implement the interface. We'll use an array for this implementation because arrays are the simplest of all data structures. In later chapters, we'll find more efficient data structures to implement this interface.

So the name of the class that implements the Map interface will be ArrayMap. Its backing store will be an array of Entry objects, each of which will hold a word in its key field and a line number list in its value field. The members of this Entry class will be relevant only within the ArrayMap class; hence, adhering to the principle of information hiding,[12] we should define the Entry class to be a member of the ArrayMap class. This is called a *nested class.*

The UML diagram in Figure 3.13 on page 103 shows the relationships among the Map interface, its ArrayMap class implementation, and its nested Entry class. Note the symbols that are used to denote these relationships. The symbol

represents the implementation of an interface, and the symbol

———————————⊕

represents the nesting of one class within another.

The ArrayMap class implements the Map interface. In addition to the four public methods that the Map interface requires, the ArrayMap class also has three private data fields, a public constructor, and a private method named resize(). The INITIAL_LENGTH constant will be the initial length of the backing array a[], and the size field will be the actual number of entries in the array. The resize() method will be called by the put() method to double the length of the array when it is full.

---

[12] This is a fundamental tenet of software design: access to data and operations should be restricted as much as possible.

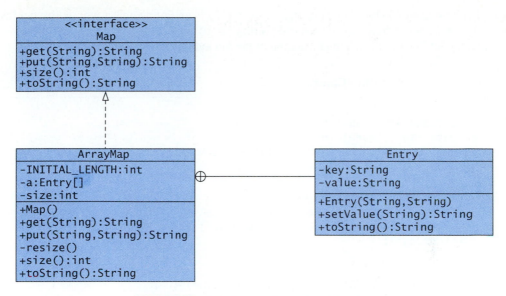

FIGURE 3.13 UML diagrams for the `ArrayMap` class.

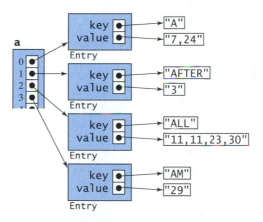

FIGURE 3.14 The concordance data structure.

The nested `Entry` class has two `private` fields, a `public` constructor, and two `public` methods. The `key` field holds one word from the original text document, and the `value` field holds the list of line numbers where the word appears in the document. The constructor creates a new `Entry` object with the specified `key` and `value`. The `setValue()` method replaces the entry's current `value` with the specified `value` passed to it and returns the replaced `value`. This is a utility method that will be used by the `put()` method. Similarly, the `toString()` method in the `Entry` class will be used by the `toString()` method in the `ArrayMap` class. Each returns a string that represents the state of its object.

The picture in Figure 3.14 shows (part of) the underlying data structure for a `Map` object. The array is named `a[]`. Each of its elements is a reference to an `Entry` object that has two string fields: key and value. For example, element a[2] is an Entry object whose key field is the string "ALL" and whose value field is the string "11,11,23,30".

Listing 3.17 gives a Java implementation of the ArrayMap class specified in Figure 3.13.

LISTING 3.17: An ArrayMap Class

```java
1   public class ArrayMap implements Map {
2       private static final int INITIAL_LENGTH=10;
3       private Entry[] a = new Entry[INITIAL_LENGTH];
4       private int size;
5
6       public String get(String key) {
7           for (int i = 0; i < size; i++)
8               if (a[i].key.equals(key)) return a[i].value;
9           return null;
10      }
11
12      public String put(String key, String value) {
13          for (int i = 0; i < size; i++)
14              if (a[i].key.equals(key)) return a[i].setValue(value);
15          if (size == a.length) resize();
16          a[size++] = new Entry(key,value);
17          return null;
18      }
19
20      private void resize() {
21          Entry[] aa = new Entry[2*a.length];
22          System.arraycopy(a, 0, aa, 0, a.length);
23          a = aa;
24      }
25
26      public int size() {
27          return size;
28      }
29
30      public String toString() {
31          StringBuffer buf = new StringBuffer();
32          for (int i = 0; i < size; i++)
33              buf.append(a[i] + "\n");
34          return buf.toString();
35      }
36
37      private static class Entry {
38          String key, value;
39
40          public Entry(String key, String value) {
41              this.key = key;
42              this.value = value;
```

```
43        }
44
45        public String setValue(String value) {
46            String oldValue = this.value;
47            this.value = value;
48            return oldValue;
49        }
50
51        public String toString() {
52            return key + ": " + value;
53        }
54    }
55  }
```

The INITIAL_LENGTH constant is set at 10 at line 2. So as soon as the 11th entry is inserted with the put() method, the call to resize() at line 15 will execute, rebuilding the map in a new backing array of length 20. And each time after that when put() is called on a full array, its length will be redoubled.

The get() method makes a sequential search through the array for the specified key. If it is found, its value is returned at line 8; otherwise, null is returned to report that the key was not found.

Note that the equals() method is used at line 8 (and line 14) to compare the stored key with the specified key. This is necessary because we are comparing two distinct String objects to determine whether they have the same contents. The equality operator == would not work here because it returns true only if the two references refer to the same object.

The put() method takes the same initial action as the get() method: It first searches the array for the given key. If found, it calls the setValue() method of the nested Entry class to replace the entry's current value with the specified value, and then returns the old value. If not found, then it creates a new Entry object for the specified (key, value) pair and inserts it into the array at the next available location.

Note that the size counter is incremented at line 16, after its value is used as an index into the array. This way, size will always equal the index of the next available location in the array, which is always equal to the number of elements before that location. For example, when size equals 4, a[4] is the next available location, because the elements that are already in use are a[0], a[1], a[2], and a[3].

The toString() method uses the Entry.toString() method at line 34. It is invoked automatically by the string expression a[i] + "\n" since a[i] is an Entry object and "\n" is a String literal.

The Main class has these operations to perform:

1. Scan the text document, line by line, parsing each word.

2. If the word is not in the map, then put it and its line number in the map.

3. If the word is already in the map, then append its line number to that word's list.

4. Print the entire map.

This algorithm is implemented in Listing 3.18.

LISTING 3.18: Testing the ArrayMap Class

```java
1   import java.io.*;   // defines the FileReader and BufferedReader classes
2   import java.util.StringTokenizer;
3
4   public class Main {
5
6      public Main(String file) {
7        Map map = new ArrayMap();
8        int lineNumber = 0;
9        try {
10         BufferedReader in = new BufferedReader(new FileReader(file));
11         String line = in.readLine();
12         while(line != null) {
13           ++lineNumber;
14           StringTokenizer parser = new StringTokenizer(line, " ,:;-.?!");
15           while (parser.hasMoreTokens()) {
16             String word = parser.nextToken().toUpperCase();
17             String list = map.get(word);
18             if (list == null) map.put(word, "" + lineNumber);
19             else map.put(word, list + "," + lineNumber);
20           }
21           System.out.println(lineNumber + ":\t" + line);
22           line = in.readLine();
23         }
24         in.close();
25       } catch(IOException e) { System.out.println(e); }
26       System.out.println(map);
27       System.out.println("lines: " + lineNumber);
28       System.out.println("distinct words: " + map.size());
29     }
30
31     public static void main(String[] args) {
32       new Main(args[0]);
33     }
34   }
```

At line 32, the `main()` method passes the command line argument `args[0]` to the class constructor `Main()`. This is assumed to be the name of the file that contains the given text document. It
would be passed to the run-time system when the program is run at the command line, like this:

      java **Main Caesar.txt**

It could alternatively be hard-coded in at line 36, like this:

```
32     new Main("Caesar.txt");
```

Or it could be hard-coded in as a local `String` variable just before line 9, like this:

```
9      String file = "Caesar.txt";
```

The original version is preferred because it makes the solution more flexible, allowing it to be
run on any text document without having to recompile the program.

In Java, an external text file is read as a stream of individual characters, called an *input stream*. Such streams are read by `FileReader` objects. The constructor

> `public FileReader(String file)`

creates a new `FileReader` object and connects it to the external text file that has the specified `file` name. But that object only knows how to read the file one character at a time. To read one line at a time, we use that object to create a `BufferedReader` object with the constructor

> `public BufferedReader(Reader reader)`

These objects have a `readLine()` method.

The construction of a `FileReader` object from the `file` and then a `BufferedReader` object from that can be done in two steps, like this:

```
FileReader reader = new FileReader(file);
BufferedReader in = new BufferedReader(reader);
```

Instead, we used an anonymous `FileReader` object at line 10:

```
10  BufferedReader in = new BufferedReader(new FileReader(file));
```

obtaining the `BufferedReader` object in one step.

Note that these `Reader` classes are defined in the `java.io` package, so the program should include the import statement

```
1  import java.io.*;
```

The setup of our outer `while` loop is a standard way to read an external text file, line by line:

```
11  String line = in.readLine();
12    while(line!=null) {
13      ++lineNumber;
        // process the line
21      System.out.println(lineNumber + ":\t" + line);
22      line = in.readLine();
23    }
24  in.close();
```

The first `line` is read at line 11. If the file is empty, then that call to `readLine()` will return `null`, causing the `while` loop block to be skipped altogether and the file to be closed immediately at line 24. Otherwise, the `line` gets processed inside the `while` loop, and then the next `line` is read at line 22. This continues until the end of the file is reached. Then the call to `readLine()` at line 22 returns `null`, stopping the `while` loop and closing the file at line 24.

The setup of our inner `while` loop is a standard way to parse words in a string:

```
14  StringTokenizer parser = new StringTokenizer(line," ,:;-.?!");
15  while (parser.hasMoreTokens()) {
16    String word = parser.nextToken().toUpperCase();
      // process the word
20  }
```

On each iteration of the loop, another `word` is extracted from the `line` variable. When the end of the line is reached, the `hasMoreTokens()` method returns `false`, causing the loop to terminate.

At line 14, a `StringTokenizer` object is constructed, using the `line` to be parsed and a string literal that contains eight punctuation characters. This `parser` will extract words from the specified `line`, using the specified punctuation characters as delimiters. So for example, on the first iteration of the inner `while` loop, when `line` contains the text

        Friends, Romans, countrymen, lend me your ears;

the code at line 16 will assign the string `"FRIENDS"` to word, discarding the comma or the space. And on the seventh iteration of the inner `while` loop, it will assign the string `"ears"` to word, discarding the semicolon. The `toUpperCase()` method is used to convert the words to upper-case so that scanned words like `"The"` and `"the"` will be considered equal.

Line 17 determines whether the word is already in the map. If not, then the `list` string returned by the `get()` method will be `null`, and then the new word and its `lineNumber` will be added to the map at line 18.[13] Otherwise, the `lineNumber` is appended to the currently stored `list` by this code:

```
19    else map.put(word, list + "," + lineNumber);
```

The expression `list + "," + lineNumber` appends the current `lineNumber` to the `list`.

For example, at the 30th line of the `Caesar.txt` document, the second word is "all." Its uppercase equivalent is already in the map, and at that point its line number `list` is `"11, 11, 23"`. The current value of `lineNumber` is the integer 30. So the expression at line 19 converts that integer to the string `"30"`, concatenates the two strings `"11, 11, 23"` and `","`, and then passes the resulting string `"11, 11, 23, 30"` as the second argument to the `put()` method. It then replaces the old `value` for that word with the string `"11, 11, 23, 30"`.

The `println()` statement at line 26 invokes the map's `toString()` method. As defined in Listing 3.17 on page 104, this will print each map entry in the order that they were inserted into the backing array. Obviously, that will not be the alphabetical order shown in the output in Figure 3.10 on page 100. To achieve that improvement, we have to modify the `put()` method.

The solution in Listing 3.18 on page 106 prints a list of all the words and their line numbers. But the words are printed in the order that they are parsed from the document:

```
FRIENDS: 1
ROMANS: 1
COUNTRYMEN: 1
LEND: 1
ME: 1,33,35
YOUR: 1
EARS: 1
I: 2,12,24,28,29,29,35
COME: 2,12,35
TO: 2,2,12,13,16,28,29,31,32,35
BURY: 2
CAESAR: 2,5,6,8,18,19,34
   :
```

Obviously, they should be printed in alphabetical order.

---

[13] The expression `""+lineNumber` converts the integer to a string.

To solve this problem, we modify the put() method at lines 12–18 in Listing 3.17 on page 104 as shown in Listing 3.19.

LISTING 3.19: **Inserting the Entries in Alphabetical Order**

```
1    public String put(String key, String value) {
2      int i=0;
3      while (i<size) {
4        if (a[i].key.equals(key)) return a[i].setValue(value);
5        if (a[i].key.compareTo(key) > 0) break;
6        ++i;
7      }
8      if (size == a.length) resize();
9      System.arraycopy(a, i, a, i+1, size-i);
10     a[i] = new Entry(key, value);
11     ++size;
12     return null;
13   }
```

The while loop at line 3 acts like the for loop in the previous version: it traverses the array, looking for a key match. If found, it takes the same action at line 4 as before: Invoke the Entry class's setValue() method to replace the current value with the specified value, and return the old value.

If the two keys are not equal, then at line 5 the current key is compared to the specified key to determine whether that is the correct alphabetical location in the array to insert the new Entry object. The call a[i].key.compareTo(key) at line 5 will return a positive value if and only if the string a[i].key is alphabetically greater than the new key.[14] If that happens, the current value of i is the correct alphabetical location to insert the new key into the array.

For example, when the new key is "COFFIN", part of the array looks like the picture in Figure 3.15. The while loop will continue iterating as long as i is less than 28, because each of those words is alphabetically less than "COFFIN". But when i equals 28, the call a[i].key.compareTo(key) at line 5 will return a positive value, because then a[i].key equals the string "COME", and that is alphabetically greater than the string "COFFIN". That triggers the break statement at line 5, terminating the loop with i equal to 28.

If the array is full, it gets copied at line 8 into a new array that is twice as long. Then the System.arraycopy() method is invoked at line 9 to shift up all the entries whose key is alphabetically greater than the specified key. This makes room to insert the new entry at a[i], as shown in Figure 3.16.[15]

---

[14] In general, the call s1.compareTo(s1) will return negative if s1 alphabetically precedes s2, it will return zero if s1 equals s2, and it will return positive if s1 alphabetically follows s2.

[15] Note that the entry for "COME" is actually duplicated by the System.arraycopy() method. When the object is copied into a[29], it is not removed from a[28]. We could set a[28] to null. But that is unnecessary, because the next step sets it to the new entry.

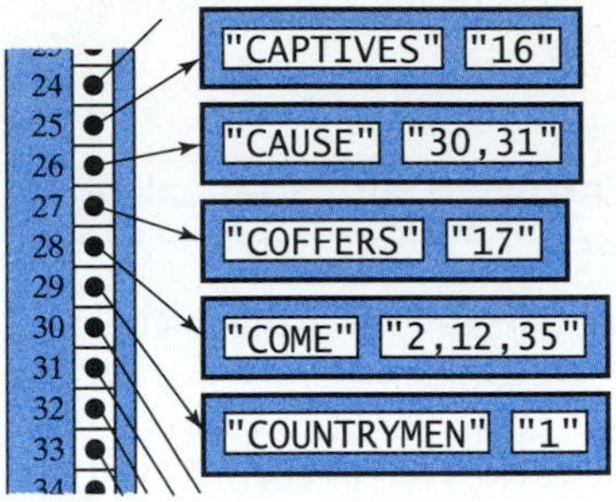

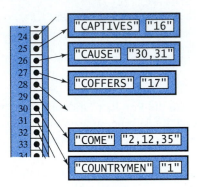

FIGURE 3.15   The concordance data structure.

FIGURE 3.16   The concordance data structure.

With this new version of the put() method, the output from the program in Listing 3.18 on page 106 is the sorted concordance shown in Figure 3.10 on page 100.

CHAPTER SUMMARY

❏   An array is an object with numbered components.

❏   An array type is defined by appending [] to some other type, like this:

```
String[]
```

❏   Arrays have the same general properties as other objects: they can be passed to and returned from methods, and they can be assigned as references to other array references.

❏   Arrays can be duplicated with the clone() method.

❏   Arrays can be copied with the System.arraycopy() method.

❏   If you pass an array object to the System.out.println() method, it will print only the name of the array type and its memory address.

❑ The elements of an array have to be printed individually, usually with a `for` loop.

❑ The `java.util.Arrays` class defines several useful static utility methods, including `binarySearch()` and `sort()` methods.

❑ The Sequential Search algorithm runs in linear time: $\Theta(n)$.

❑ The Binary Search algorithm runs in logarithmic time: $\Theta(\lg n)$.

❑ A resizable array is an imaginary construct implemented by programming the automatic replacement of one array with another that is a different size and contains the same elements.

❑ The `java.util.Vector` class is implemented with a resizable array.

❑ Multidimensional arrays are arrays of arrays.

❑ The rows of a two-dimensional array can be arrays of different lengths.

REVIEW QUESTIONS

3.1 How can you always access the last element of an array?

3.2 What is the difference between an empty array and a `null` array?

3.3 What is a `final` array?

3.4 Under what circumstances must all the elements of an array be the same type in Java?

3.5 If the Binary Search algorithm is so much faster than the Sequential Search algorithm, why would anyone ever want to use the latter?

3.6 What is the difference between an array and a `Vector`?

3.7 What is a heterogeneous array?

3.8 What is a ragged array?

3.9 How many different objects exist in the program in Listing 3.14 on page 94?

EXERCISES

3.1 Write an algorithm, similar to Algorithm 3.1 on page 78, that returns the index of a minimum element of an array.

3.2 Prove that Algorithm 3.1 on page 78 is correct. Formulate your argument like this:

    a. After iteration i of the loop in steps 2–3, m is the index of the largest element in the subsequence $\{a_0, a_1, a_2, ..., a_i\}$.

    b. Since the statement in part **a** is true for every i from 0 to $n-1$, it is true when $i = n-1$.

    The statement in part **a** is called a *loop invariant*. It must be verified inductively: Assume that it was true at the end of the previous iteration, and deduce from that assumption that it must also be true at the end of the *i*th iteration. That deduction will be based upon what happens in step 3 of the algorithm.

3.3   If several elements of an array are equal to the target value, Algorithm 3.3 on page 81 returns the smallest index among them. Modify the algorithm so that it returns the largest index of all elements equal to the target.

3.4   Prove that Algorithm 3.3 on page 81 is correct.

3.5   Write an algorithm that finds the maximum value in an array by comparing the elements pairwise, like an athletic tournament. First copy the array into the second half of a separate temporary array that is twice as long. Then repeatedly copy the larger of each pair into the element $a_{i/2}$, like this:

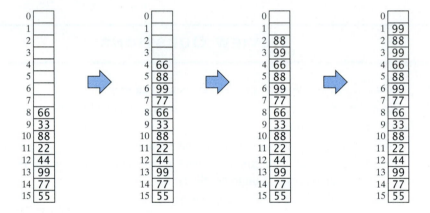

3.6   Derive a formula for an upper bound on how many array accesses the Sieve of Eratosthenes will require for an input of *n*. (See Project 3.3 on page 119.)

3.7   The following method is meant to return a duplicate of the specified array:

```
public static int[] getCopy(int[] a) {
    int[] b = a
    return b;
}
```

Explain why this won't work, and then correct it.

3.8   The following method is meant to swap the *i*th and *j*th elements of the array:

```
public static void swap(double[] a, int i, int j) {
    int temp = i;
    i = j;
    j = temp;
}
```

Explain why this won't work, and then correct it.

3.9 The following method is meant to reverse the specified array.

```java
public static void reverse(int[] a) {
    int n = a.length;
    for (int i = 0; i < n; i++)
        swap(a, i, n-1-i);
}
```

Explain why this won't work, and then correct it. (Assume that the swap() method is correct.)

3.10 Predict the output of the following code:

```java
int[] x = {22,33,11};
System.out.println(x);
int[] y = {22,33,11};
System.out.println(y);
boolean eqeq = (x == y);
System.out.println("eqeq = " + eqeq);
boolean dotEq = java.util.Arrays.equals(x,y);
System.out.println("dotEq = " + dotEq);
y = x;
System.out.println(y);
eqeq = (x == y);
System.out.println("eqeq = " + eqeq);
```

Then run it to check your predictions.

3.11 When the target value occurs more than once in the search array, the sequential search guarantees returning the smallest index among those that locate the target. Explain how the binary search algorithm could be modified to do the same.

3.12 Some authors claim that the binary search algorithm is the method that most people naturally use when looking up a word in a dictionary or a name in a telephone book. But the truth is that most people probably use a modified version where dividing index i is not set at the middle index $(p + q)/2$. Instead, most people would select i proportionally according to where they would expect to find the target in the subsequence. For example, if one is searching for the name Wilson in a telephone book of 1000 pages, one would open it first near the end of the book instead of at page 500. This algorithm is called the *interpolation search*. Modify Algorithm 3.4 on page 85 so that it implements the interpolation search.

3.13 Verify Equation (3.1) on page 84.

3.14 Show that $o(g(n)) \subseteq O(g(n)) - \Theta(g(n))$ (*i.e.*, show that if $f(n)$ is in $o(g)$, then it is also in $O(g)$, but not in $\Theta(g)$). Note that this is not quite the same as Equation (3.2) on page 84, which asserts that $o(g(n)) \subset O(g(n)) - \Theta(g(n))$. That assertion also implies that the subset is proper (*i.e.*, that there is some function in $O(g(n)) - \Theta(g(n))$ that is not in $o(g(n))$).

3.15 Show that $\omega(g(n)) \subseteq \Omega(g(n)) - \Theta(g(n))$.

3.16   Show that $o(g(n)) \neq O(g(n)) - \Theta(g(n))$ by showing that $f(n) \in O(g(n)) - \Theta(g(n)) - o(g(n))$ where $f(1) = 1$ and $f(2k) = f(2k+1) = g(2k-1) = g(2k) = 2^{k(k-1)/2}$ for $k = 1, 2, 3, \dots$

3.17   Show that $f(n) \in O(g(n))$ if and only if $g(n) \in \Omega(g(n))$.

3.18   Show that $f(n) \in \Theta(g(n))$ if and only if $g(n) \in \Theta(g(n))$.

3.19   Show that $f(n) \in o(g(n))$ if and only if $g(n) \in \omega(g(n))$.

PROGRAMMING PROBLEMS

3.1   Modify the program in Listing 3.1 on page 76 so that the two arrays are of type `double[]` instead of `int[]`. You can use the following formatting and print methods:

```
private void print(double[] a) {
    printf(a[0], "{#.###");
    for (int i = 1; i < a.length; i++)
        printf(a[i], "', '#.###");
      System.out.println("}");
}
private void printf(double x, String fs) {
    System.out.print(new java.text.DecimalFormat(fs).format(x));
}
```

3.2   Write a simple program like the one in Listing 3.2 on page 77 that prints the value of the array reference for an array of each of these types: `boolean[]`, `char[]`, `byte[]`, `short[]`, `long[]`, `float[]`, `double[]`, and `Object[]`.

3.3   Write and test a method, similar to the `randomInts(int)` method at line 15 in Listing 3.1 on page 76, that returns a random string of capital letters:

```
private String letters(int n)
// Returns: an object s of type String;
// Postconditions: s.length() == n;
//                  each character of s is a capital letter:
```

3.4   Write and test a method, similar to the `randomInts(int)` method at line 15 in Listing 3.1 on page 76, that returns an array whose sequence is a random permutation of the n integers from 0 to $n-1$:

```
private int[] permutation(int n)
// Returns: an array a[] of type int[];
// Postconditions: a.length == n;
//                  0 <= a[i] < n, for all i;
//                  all n elements of a[] are different;
```

3.5   Modify and test the `search()` method in Listing 3.5 on page 80 so that it returns the last index of the target if it is in the array.

3.6 Run a test driver to test the methods in the `IntArrays` class in Listing 3.8 on page 89.

3.7 Add this method to the `IntArrays` class in Listing 3.8 on page 89:

```
public static int[] truncate(int[] a, int n)
    // returns a new array with the first n elements of a[];
```

3.8 Add this method to the `IntArrays` class in Listing 3.8 on page 89:

```
public static int[] reverse(int[] a)
    // returns a new array with the elements of a[] in reverse order;
```

3.9 Add this method to the `IntArrays` class in Listing 3.8 on page 89:

```
public static int[] uniqueRandomInts(int n, int range)
    // returns a new array of length n with unique nonnegative random
    // integers that are less than the specified range;
```

3.10 Add this method to the `IntArrays` class in Listing 3.8 on page 89:

```
public static int[] permutation(int n)
    // returns a new array of length n whose elements are the n
    // nonnegative integers that are less than n, in random order;
```

3.11 Add the following two methods to the `IntArrays` class in Listing 3.8 on page 89:

```
public static boolean isDescending(int[] a)
public static boolean isSorted(int[] a)
```

The `isSorted()` method should return true if either `isAscending()` or `isDescending()` is true.

3.12 Part of the "contract" of the binary search algorithm is that it should indicate where in the sequence the target element should be inserted if it is not found. This is done by returning a negative integer k with the advice that the index $i = -k - 1$ is the correct location, in the sense that if the subsequence $\{a_i, ..., a_{n-1}\}$ is shifted to the right into $\{a_{i+1}, ..., a_n\}$ and the target is inserted into a_i, then the sequence will still be in ascending order. Check this empirically by running the program in Listing 3.6 on page 86 and printing a_{i-1} and a_i, when the returned value $k < 0$.

3.13 Write and test the following method, which "bubbles up" the largest element in the array to the last position by successively comparing adjacent elements and swapping them if they are out of order, beginning with the first pair `a[0]` and `a[1]`:

```
void bubble(int[] a)
```

3.14 Write and test the following method, which "selects" the largest element in the array and swaps it with the last element:

```
void select(int[] a)
```

3.15 Write and test the following method, which, assuming that all but the last element is sorted in ascending order, "inserts" the last element into the sorted part so that the entire array is sorted:

```
void insert(int[] a)
```

3.16   Write and test the following method, which, assuming that both the first half and the second half of the array are already sorted in ascending order, merges the two halves so that the entire array is sorted:

```
void merge(int[] a)
```

3.17   Write and test this method, which returns the frequency of the given value in the given array a[]:

```
int frequency(int[] a, int value)
```

The *frequency* of a value in a sequence is the number of times that value occurs in the sequence. For example, in the array
$$\{1, 4, 5, 4, 9, 2, 4, 3, 1, 1, 6, 1, 3, 5, 3, 2, 4, 2, 9, 2, 1, 1, 4, 8, 4, 3, 2, 1, 1\}$$
the value 1 has frequency 8, and the value 2 has frequency 5.

3.18   Write and test this method, which returns the number of runs of the given length in the given array a[]:

```
int numRuns(int[] a, int length)
```

A *run* in a sequence is a subsequence of equal elements. For example, in the array
$$\{1, 4, 4, 4, 2, 2, 4, 3, 1, 1, 1, 1, 3, 3, 3, 2, 4, 2, 2, 2, 1, 1, 4, 4, 4, 3, 2, 1, 1\}$$
there are three runs of length 2, four runs of length 3, and one of length 4.

3.19   Write and test the following method:

```
int partition(int[] a)
```

It returns the index j after partitioning the array so that all elements that are less than a[0] have been moved to the left of position j, all elements that are greater than a[0] have been moved to the right of position j, and a[0] itself has been moved to position j. For example, the array {44, 99, 55, 88, 33, 66, 22, 77} would be transformed into the array {33, 22, 44, 88, 55, 66, 99, 77} and 2 would be returned. The initial value of a[0] (44, in this example) is called the *pivot* of the partition. The algorithm uses two indexes i and j; i begins at 1 and increments, while j begins at a.length-1 and decrements; when a[i] is greater than the pivot and a[j] is less than the pivot, a[i] is swapped with a[j]. (Int his example, 99 gets swapped with 22, and 55 gets swapped with 33.) When i and j meet, a[0] is swapped with a[j] (44 with 33, in this example).

3.20   Write and test a program that prints the strings that are read from the command line into the args[] array, printing each on a separate line, in order of their lengths. For example if the command line arguments are

```
    Sol Mercury Venus Earth Luna Mars Jupiter Saturn Uranus Neptune
Pluto  then the output would be
Sol
Luna
Mars
Venus
Earth
Pluto
Saturn
Uranus
```

```
Mercury
Jupiter
Neptune
```

3.21 Add this method to the Vector class defined in Listing 3.10 on page 92, and test it:

```
public void copyInto(Object[] aa)
// Replaces the first n elements of aa[] with the n elements of
// this vector, where n is the size of this vector.
```

3.22 Add this method to the Vector class defined in Listing 3.12 on page 93, and test it:

```
public void trimToSize()
// Resizes the backing array this vector, making its length
// equal to the size of this vector.
```

3.23 Add this method to the Vector class defined in Listing 3.10 on page 92, and test it:

```
public void ensureCapacity(int n)
// Resizes the backing array this vector, making its length
// equal to n.
```

3.24 Add this method to the Vector class defined in Listing 3.10 on page 92, and test it:

```
public int indexOf(Object x)
// Returns the smallest index of any component of this vector
// that equals(x). If not found, -1 is returned.
```

3.25 Add this method to the Vector class defined in Listing 3.10 on page 92, and test it:

```
public boolean contains(Object x)
// Returns true if and only if some component of this vector
// equals(x).
```

3.26 Add these methods to the Vector class defined in Listing 3.10 on page 92, and test them:

a. `public Object elementAt(int i)`
```
// Returns the element at index i in this vector.
```
b. `public Object firstElement()`
```
// Returns the first element in this vector.
```
c. `public Object lastElement()`
```
// Returns the last element in this vector.
```
d. `public void setElementAt(Object x, int i)`
```
// Replaces the element at index i with x.
```

3.27 Add these methods to the Vector class defined in Listing 3.10 on page 92, and test them:

a. `public Object get(int i)`
```
// Returns the element at index i in this vector.
```
b. `public Object set(int i, Object x)`
```
// Replaces the element at index i with x.
```

    c. `public boolean` `add(Object x)`
        `// Appends x to the end of this vector and returns true.`

3.28   Add this method to the `Vector` class defined in Listing 3.10 on page 92, and test it:

```
public boolean remove(Object x)
// Deletes the first occurrence of x from this vector, shifting all
// the elements that follow it back one position. Returns true if
// x is found and removed; otherwise returns false.
```

3.29   Add this method to the `Vector` class defined in Listing 3.10 on page 92, and test it:

```
public void add(int i, Object x)
// Inserts x at index i, shifting all the elements from that
// position to the end forward one position.
```

3.30   Add this method to the `Vector` class defined in Listing 3.10 on page 92, and test it:

```
public Object remove(int i)
// Removes the element at index i, shifting all the elements
// that follow it back one position. Returns the removed object.
```

3.31   Write and test this method:

```
public boolean isHomogeneous(Object[] a)
// Returns true iff every non-null element has the same type.
```

3.32   Write and test this method:

```
public void print(int[][] a)
// Prints the two-dimensional array a[][], one row per line.
```

3.33   Modify the Pascal's triangle program in Listing 3.15 on page 98 so that it uses a ragged (triangular) array that stores no zeros (*i.e.*, row i is defined to be an array of $i+1$ integers).

3.34   Modify the Pascal's triangle program in Listing 3.15 on page 98 so that it computes the numbers directly from the formula $c(n, k) = (n!)/(k!(n-k)!)$. (See Appendix C.)

3.35   Modify the program in Listing 3.15 on page 98 so that it prints the multiplication table instead of Pascal's triangle, like this:

```
1    2    3    4    5    6    7
2    4    6    8   10   12   14
3    6    9   12   15   18   21
4    8   12   16   20   24   28
5   10   15   20   25   30   35
6   12   18   24   30   36   42
7   14   21   28   35   42   49
```

3.36   Modify the program in Listing 3.18 on page 106 so that it prints the total number of words and characters in the specified text document.

PROJECTS

3.1   Write a program that empirically tests the $\Theta(\lg n)$ complexity of the binary search algorithm. For various array sizes n, generate a random array of integers in the range 0 to $2n$. (Thus, about half the numbers in that range will be in the array, with possible duplication.) For each of these arrays, sort the array, and then run the binary search for the target t, for each t from 0 to $2n$. On each of these runs, count the number k of iterations of the algorithm's `while` loop. For each n, print n, the average of the $2n$ values of k, and the value of $\lg n$. (The expression `Math.log(n)/Math.log(2)` returns the binary logarithm of n.) Your output should look something like this:

```
   n    average   lg(n)
-------  -------  -------
      4   2.125     2.0
      8   3.063     3.0
     16   4.031     4.0
     32   4.688     5.0
     64   5.594     6.0
    128   6.543     7.0
    256   7.537     8.0
    512   8.519     9.0
   1024   9.516    10.0
-------  -------  -------
```

3.2   Write a method that implements the *perfect shuffle* of an array. For example, it would change the array {0,1,2,3,4,5,6,7} into {0,4,1,5,2,6,3,7}. Then use your method to determine empirically how many times the perfect shuffle has to be applied before the array is restored to its original order. The answer depends upon the size of the array.

3.3   Write a program that implements the *Sieve of Eratosthenes*. This algorithm, named after the Greek mathematician Eratosthenes[16] of Cyrene, Egypt, is called a "sieve" because, like sifting sand through a sieve, it "catches" the prime numbers, letting all the other numbers fall through the sieve:

▲ **ALGORITHM 3.5: The Sieve of Eratosthenes**

Input: a sequence $\{b_0, b_1, b_2, ..., b_{n-1}\}$ of boolean elements, all initially `false`.
Postcondition: b_i is `true` if and only if i is prime.

1. For each $i = 2$ to $n-1$, set $b_i =$ `true`.
2. Let $p = 2$.
3. Repeat steps 4-5 while $p^2 < n$.
4. Increment p until b_p is `true`.
5. For each $j = 2$ to $(n-1)/p$, set $b_{pj} =$ `false`.

---

[16] Eratosthenes (276-194 BC) is best known for being the first person to estimate accurately the size of the earth. He was brought to Alexandria by Ptolemy III to be head of the great library at the university there.

3.4   Write a program that generates term papers. First create these external files of words or phrases, one per line:

```
Nouns.txt
Pronouns.txt
Adjectives.txt
Verbs.txt
Adverbs.txt
```

For example, your `Nouns.txt` file might contain the words `friend`, `roommate`, `car`, `dog`, `homework`, *etc.*, and your `Verbs.txt` file might contain the words and phrases `wrote`, `fixed`, `kissed`, `yelled at`. Your program should print a random number of paragraphs, each containing a random number of well-formed sentences of the form "My <adjective> <noun> <verb> <adjective> <noun> rather <adverb>."

ANSWERS TO REVIEW QUESTIONS

3.1   The last element of an array is always `a[a.length-1]`.

3.2   An empty array is an allocated array with length 0. A `null` array is unallocated, so it has no `length`. For example,

```
int[] a;              // a is null
int lena = a.length;  // will not compile: a is uninitialized
b = int[0];           // allocates b as an empty array
int lenb = b.length;  // initializes lenb to 0
```

3.3   Since arrays are objects in Java, declaring an array `final` simply prevents its reference variable from being changed. Its elements can still be modified.

3.4   The elements of an array in Java must all be of the same type if the element type is one of the eight primitive types. But if the element type is an interface or class, then the elements can be instances of different classes as long as they all are extensions of the declared type. If that declared type is `Object`, then the elements can be instances of any class.

3.5   The binary search algorithm requires the array to be sorted. Some applications may require the array to remain unchanged.

3.6   An *array* is a data structure based upon an element type. A `Vector` is a class whose instances are indexed collections. The `Vector` class uses an array for its backing store.

3.7   A *heterogeneous array* is an array whose elements have different type.

3.8   A *ragged array* is an array of arrays of different lengths.

3.9   The program in Listing 3.14 on page 94 has three objects: the two-dimensional array a and the two one-dimensional arrays a[0] and a[2]. Note that, as usual, the number of objects equals the number of times the new operator has been invoked.

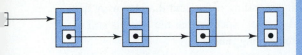

*There's nothing remarkable about it.
All one has to do is hit the right keys at the right time
and the instrument plays itself.*

— Johann Sebastian Bach

Chapter 4

Linked Structures

Arrays work well for unordered sequences, and even for ordered sequences if they don't change much. But if you want to maintain an ordered list that allows quick insertions and deletions, you should use a linked data structure. This chapter shows how to do that.

4.1 Maintaining an Ordered Array

In Section 3.7, we saw how the binary search can find elements very quickly in an array that is sorted. This suggests that we should keep our arrays in sorted order. But inserting new elements in an ordered array is difficult. The main problem is that we have to move all the larger elements over to make room for the new element to be placed in its correct ordered position. This can be done by the insert() method shown in Listing 4.1.

LISTING 4.1: **Listing 4.1 Inserting into an Ordered Array**

```
1   int[] insert(int[] a, int n, int x) {
2      // preconditions: [0] <= ... <= a[n-1], and n < a.length;
3      // postconditions: a[0] <= ... <= a[n], and x is among them;
4      int i = 0;  // find the first index i for which a[i] > x:
5      while (i < n && a[i] <= x)
6         ++i;
7      // shift {a[i],...,a[n-1]} into {a[i+1],...,a[n]}:
8      System.arraycopy(a, i, a, i+1, n-i);
9      // insert x into a[i]:
10     a[i] = x;
11  }
```

The insert() method takes three arguments: the array a[], the number n of elements that are already sorted in the array, and the new element x to be inserted among them. The preconditions at

121

line 2 specify that the first n elements of the array are in ascending order, and that the array has room for at least one more element. The postconditions at line 3 specify that the array is still in ascending order, and that x has been successfully inserted among them.

The code at lines 4–6 searches the array for the correct position for x to be inserted. It should be the smallest index i for which a[i] > x. For example, if x = 50 for the array shown in Figure 4.1, then the correct position for x is at index i = 1, because a[0] <= x < a[1].

After the correct position i has been located for x, the insert() method shifts the elements that are greater than x one position to the right. This is accomplished by the call

```
System.arraycopy(a, i, a, i+1, n-i);
```

at line 8. The arraycopy() method is a static method in the System class. It is usually the most efficient way to copy elements between arrays or within a single array. Its five arguments are: the source array, the index of the first element to be copied from the source array, the destination array, the index in the destination array where the first element is to be copied, and the number of elements to be copied. If n = 4 and i = 1, as shown in Figure 4.1, then the call is

```
System.arraycopy(a, 1, a, 2, 3);
```

This shifts elements {a[1], a[2], a[3]} = {66, 88, 99} into elements {a[2], a[3], a[4]}.
Finally, x is inserted into a[i] at line 10, as show in Figure 4.2.

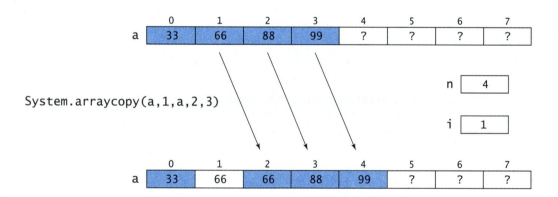

FIGURE 4.1 Making Room for the New Element

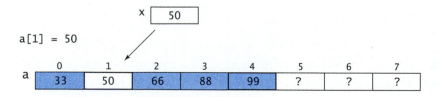

FIGURE 4.2 Copying x into its correct position

The `insert()` method may move a lot of data. For example, if n = 1000, and x is less than all of those elements, then the method will move all 1000 elements. On average, inserting into a sorted array of *n* elements will move *n*/2 elements. So this is a O(n) operation.

Deleting an element is simply the reverse of the insertion process. It too will have to move *n*/2 elements, on average. So deletion is also a O(n) operation.

4.2 Indirect Reference

One solution to the data movement problem that is intrinsic to dynamic ordered arrays is to use an auxiliary index array to keep track of where the elements actually are. This solution requires more space (a second array) and makes the code a bit more complicated, but it eliminates the need to move the elements. It allows the elements to be stored at arbitrary positions in the array, using the auxiliary index array to locate them for ordered access.

The main idea is shown in Figure 4.3. The elements {22, 33, 44, 55, 66} are kept in arbitrary positions in the array a[], and their order is determined by some auxiliary mechanism.

Each element is kept in a numbered component: 22 is in component 3, 33 is in component 5, 44 is in component 1, *etc*. So if we save the order of the index numbers (3, 5, 1, 4, 6), then we can access the elements in order: a[3], followed by a[5], followed by a[1], and so forth.

An *index array* is an array whose elements are index values for another array. By storing the index numbers 3, 5, 1, 4, 6 in an index array, we can use them to access the data elements 22, 33, 44, 55, 66 in order.

Although this may be an improvement, it is not optimal. The reason we wanted to allow the element to be stored in arbitrary positions in the first place was to simplify the insertion and deletion operations. We wanted to avoid having to shift segments of a[] back and forth. But the solution in Figure 4.4 merely transfers that obligation from a[] to k[]. If we had to insert the element 50, we could put it at position a[0] or a[2] or any place after a[6], but we would then have to insert its index into the index array k[] between k[2] and k[3] to keep track of the order of the elements.

A better solution is to use the same array positions in the index array k[] as we are using in the data array a[]. Since the index array is keeping track of the correct order of the index numbers of the data elements, it can be used in the same way for the index numbers themselves. (See Figure 4.5.)

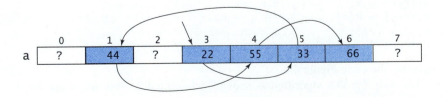

FIGURE 4.3 Referring to the Order of the Array Elements

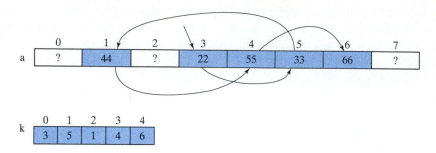

FIGURE 4.4 Using an Index Array

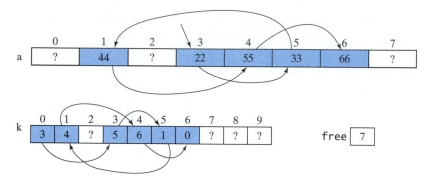

FIGURE 4.5 Using an Index Array

In that figure, the index array k[] keeps track of the order of the elements in a[]. The starting index 3 is stored in k[0]. That begins the chain of indexes: k[0] = 3, k[3] = 5, k[5] = 1, k[1] = 4, k[4] = 6, k[6] = 0. The index 0 signals the end of the ordered sequence. The index sequence 0, 3, 5, 1, 4, 6 gives us the data elements in order: a[3] = 22, a[5] = 33, a[1] = 44, a[4] = 55, a[6] = 66.

The extra variable free in Figure 4.5 saves the index of a free location in both the index array k[] and the data array a[]. The value 7 means that k[7] and a[7] should be used next.

The implementation of an index array solves the problem of having to shift segments of array elements back and forth during deletions and insertions. For example, to insert x = 50 in Figure 4.5, we first traverse the sequence to find the index i of the largest element that is less than x: i = 1. Then just do these four steps:

```
a[free] = x;       // put x into the next free position
k[free] = k[i];    // store the next index in that position in k[]
k[i] = free;       // store the index of x in k[]
++free;            // advance free to the next unused position
```

The changes are shown in Figure 4.6.

The Java code for this algorithm is shown in Listing 4.2. This improves the insert() method shown in Listing 4.1 on page 121, because its only data movement is the actual insertion of x into the array a[] at line 5.

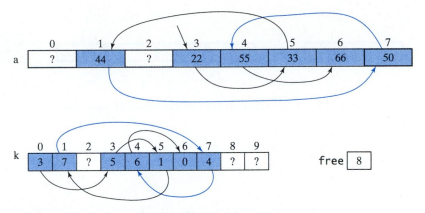

FIGURE 4.6 Inserting an Element

LISTING 4.2: Inserting into an Sorted Array with Indirection

```
1  void insert(int[] a, int[] k, int x, int free) {
2    int i=0;
3    while (k[i]!=0 && a[k[i]]<x)
4      i = k[i];
5    a[free] = x;
6    k[free] = k[i];
7    k[i] = free++;
8  }
```

The `while` loop at lines 3–4 is similar to the `while` loop at lines 5–6 in Listing 4.1 on page 121: it finds the first index i for which `a[k[i]] > x`. At line 5, x is inserted in the next free location in the array `a[]`. At line 6, the index of the next location after x is stored in `k[free]`. At line 7, the index of x is stored in `k[i]`, and then `free` is incremented to the index of the next free location.

Note that this code assumes that the array is large enough to accommodate all elements that might be inserted. In practice, we would probably include a `resize()` call.

4.3 Linked Nodes

The values of the index array `k[]` in Figure 4.6 on page 125 are used as locators, addressing the actual data array `a[]`. We don't really need a separate array for them. Their relative positions in the index array match the positions of the corresponding data elements. Thus, we can combine them into a single array of data-address pairs, as shown in Figure 4.7.

In this version, our array `a[]` would be defined as

```
Node[] a = new Node[size];
```

where Node would be defined as a separate class:

```
class Node {
  int data;
  int next;
}
```

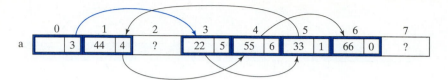

FIGURE 4.7 Storing the Indexes with their Elements in the Same Array

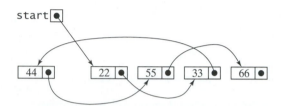

FIGURE 4.8 Using Objects for the Elements and Their References

This makes the array `a[]` a little more complex, but it eliminates the need for an auxiliary array altogether.

Fortunately, Java allows an even better solution, one that allows us to eliminate both arrays! Taking an object-oriented point of view, we see in Figure 4.7 a sequence of `Node` objects. Each object contains a data element and the address of the next object in the sequence. In Java, objects are directly accessed by their addresses. That's what an object reference is: the address of where the object is stored in memory. So by reinterpreting the meaning of "address," as a memory address (*i.e.*, object reference) instead of an array index, we can simplify the structure to the one shown in Figure 4.8. Here, the arrows represent object references (*i.e.*, memory addresses).

Now, instead of an array `a[]`, we need only keep track of the single `start` reference. The Java run-time system does all the rest of the bookkeeping. The code is given in Listing 4.3.

LISTING 4.3: A `Node` Class

```
1   class Node {
2     private int data;
3     private Node next;
4
5     public Node(int data) {
6       this.data = data;
7     }
8   }
```

Notice that the `Node` class is now *self-referential*: Its `next` field is declared to have type `Node`. Each `Node` object contains a field that is a reference to a `Node` object.

The other field in the `Node` class is its `data` field, declared at line 2 here to be an `int`. Of course, in general, we could make this field any type we want—whatever type values we have to store in the list.

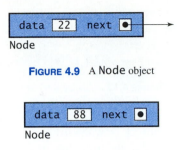

FIGURE 4.9 A **Node** object

FIGURE 4.10 Another **Node** object

The Node class in Listing 4.3 also includes a one-argument constructor, at line 5. Note that, because we have explicitly defined a constructor that takes at least one argument, the compiler will *not* implicitly define a no-argument constructor. Therefore, since we have *not* explicitly defined a no-argument constructor, none will exist. That means that the only way a Node object can be created is with the one-argument constructor (at line 5) (*i.e.*, we must provide a data value for each new Node object that we create).

Figure 4.9 shows a typical Node object. Its data field contains the integer 22, and its next field contains a reference to another Node object (not shown). Although one generally use an arrow like this to represent an object reference, one should also keep in mind that the actual value of the reference is the memory address of the object to which it refers. In other programming languages, such variables are called *pointers*—hence their common depiction as arrows.

Remember that in Java, each reference variable either locates an object or is null. The value null means that the variable does not refer to any object. The memory address that is stored in a null reference variable is 0x0 (the hexadecimal value 0); no object is ever stored at that address. Figure 4.10 shows a Node object whose next field is null.

Listing 4.4 illustrates how our five-element list could be created:

LISTING 4.4: Constructing a Linked List

```
1   Node start = new Node(22);
2   start.next = new Node(33);
3   start.next.next = new Node(44);
4   start.next.next.next = new Node(55);
5   start.next.next.next.next = new Node(66);
```

At line 1, we create a node containing the data value 22 and initialize our start variable to it. The result is shown in Figure 4.11. Note that the start variable is merely a reference to the Node object. Also note that the next reference in the Node object is null, indicated by the black dot with no arrow emanating from it. The node's next field is null because the constructor (defined at line 5 in Listing 4.3 on page 126) does not initialize it. In Java, every class field that is an object reference (*i.e.*, its type is either a class or an interface) is automatically initialized to null, unless it is initialized by its constructor to some existing object.

In the figures that follow we depict each Node object as a box with two parts: The left side contains the integer data, and the right side contains the next reference. This simply abbreviates the versions shown in Figure 4.9.

FIGURE 4.11   Initializing `start`

Continuing the code in Listing 4.4, at line 2, the `start` node's `next` field is assigned to a new `Node` object containing the datum 33. Now the list has two nodes. (See Figure 4.12.)

The next node is added to the end of the list at line 3. To do that, we have to assign it to the `next` field of the node that contains 33. But the only node to which we have external access (*i.e.*, the only node that has a variable name) is the first node. Its name is `start`. So we have to use the expression `start.next.next` to refer to the `next` field of the node that contains 33.

Similarly, the fourth node is added at line 4 using the expression `start.next.next.next`, and the fifth node is added at line 5 using the expression `start.next.next.next.next`. That finally gives us the five-node list shown in Figure 4.13.

The code in Listing 4.4 is clumsy and unsuited for generalization. Obviously, if we wanted to build a linked list of 50 nodes, this approach would be unworkable. The solution is to use a local reference variable that can "walk through" the list, locating one node after the other and thereby giving local access to the nodes. Traditionally, the variable p (for "pointer") is used for this purpose. Since it will refer to individual nodes, it should be declared to be a `Node` reference, like this:

```
Node p;
```

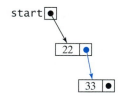

FIGURE 4.12   Adding a node

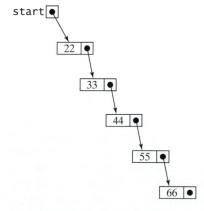

FIGURE 4.13   The five-node list

Since our only access to the nodes is from the `start` node, we should initialize p like this:

```
Node p=start;
```

This is shown in Figure 4.14. Then the assignment

```
p = p.next;
```

will advance the locator variable p to the next node, as shown in Figure 4.15. This same assignment can thus be executed as many times as is needed to advance through the linked list.

Listing 4.5 shows how we could have used this technique to build the linked list in the first place.

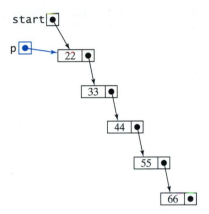

FIGURE 4.14 Initializing p at the `start` node

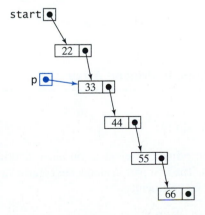

FIGURE 4.15 Advancing p to the second node

LISTING 4.5: **Constructing a Linked List**

```
1   start = new Node(22);
2   Node p=start;
3   p.next = new Node(33);
4   p = p.next;
5   p.next = new Node(44);
6   p = p.next;
7   p.next = new Node(55);
8   p = p.next;
9   p.next = new Node(66);
```

This code may not seem much better than the other version in Listing 4.4. But one big advantage is that it is easily managed within a loop. For example, the same list can be built with the three lines of code in Listing 4.6.

LISTING 4.6: **Using a for Loop**

```
1   Node p = start = new Node(22);
2   for (int i=0; i<4; i++)
3       p = p.next = new Node(33+11*i);
```

Obviously, this form could just as easily build a linked list of 50 nodes. Each step in the execution of this code is shown in Figure 4.16 on page 131.

The reference variable p is analogous to an array index i: It advances through the nodes of a linked list just as i advances through the elements of an array. Consequently, it is natural to use p in a **for** loop, just as we would use the array index i. For example, compare Listings 4.7 and 4.8.

LISTING 4.7: **Using a for Loop to Print a Linked List**

```
1   for (Node p = start; p != null; p = p.next)
2       System.out.println(p.data);
```

LISTING 4.8: **Using a for Loop to Print an Array**

```
1   for (int i=0; i < n; i++)
2       System.out.println(a[i]);
```

In both listings, the **for** loop prints one element on each iteration. The **for** statement has a three-part control mechanism. The first part declares the control variable (p for the list, i for the array) and initializes it to the first element:

```
Node p=start
int i=0
```

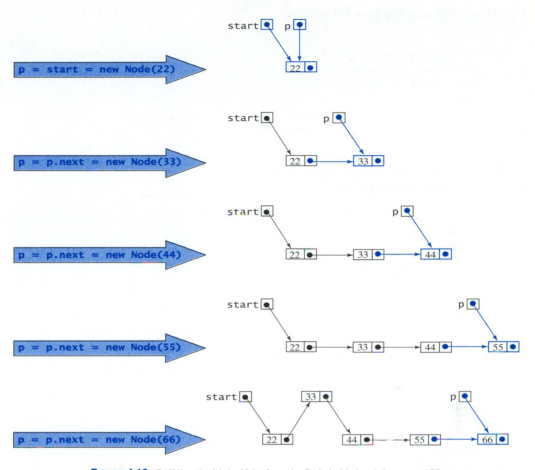

FIGURE 4.16 Building the Linked List from the Code in Listing 4.6 on page 130.

The second part gives the continuation condition, asserting that there are more elements:

```
p != null
i < n
```

The third part gives the update expression, advancing the control variable to the next element:

```
p = p.next
i++
```

In each of these parts, the two versions are analogous.

Listing 4.9 shows a test driver for the Node class. The code is essentially the same as in Listings 4.3, 4.6, and 4.7.

The first node is constructed at line 3. Then the **for** loop at lines 5–6 constructs the other four nodes. The second **for** loop at lines 7–8 prints the node data in the first five lines of output. The third **for** loop at lines 9–10 gives the actual memory addresses of the five Node objects.

```
1   public class TestNode {
2     public static void main(String[] args) {
3       Node start = new Node(22);
4       Node p=start;
5       for (int i = 1; i < 5; i++)
6         p = p.next = new Node(22+11*i);
7       for (p = start; p! = null; p = p.next)
8         System.out.println(p.data);
9       for (p = start; p != null; p = p.next)
10        System.out.println(p);
11    }
12  }
13
14  class Node {
15    // See Listing 4.3 on page 126
16    }
17  }
```

The output is

```
22
33
44
55
66
Node@7182c1
Node@3f5d07
Node@f4a24a
Node@cac268
Node@a16869
```

When you use an object reference like p in a string expression such as

```
System.out.println(p);
```

the system automatically invokes that object's `toString()` method. Unless it has been over-ridden, the version of the `toString()` method that is defined in the `Object` class will execute, as it did in the program in Listing 4.9. The string returned by that version merely contains the object's type (`Node`, in this case) followed by the @ sign and the memory address of the object (*e.g.*, 7182c1). So the last five lines of output report that the five `Node` objects are stored at the (hexadecimal) memory addresses 0x7182c1, 0x3f5d07, 0xf4a24a, 0xcac268, and 0xa16869. These, then, are the actual values stored in the reference variables `start`, `start.next`, `start.next.next`, `start.next.next.next`, and `start.next.next.next.next`.

You can see from Figure 4.17 why we usually draw linked lists using arrows to represent the `Node` references. Showing the actual memory address values instead requires more effort to see which node references which. Moreover, those memory address values are run-time dependent: they will be different on different computers, and maybe even on the same computer at different times.

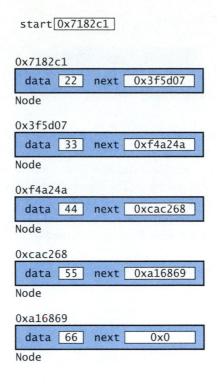

FIGURE 4.17 The five Node objects

One final note: On line 6, we use the chained assignment

```
p = p.next = new Node(22+11*i);
```

It is important to remember the order of operations in such a statement. Here, the first thing that happens is the evaluation of the expression 22+11*i. When i is 1, that evaluates to 33; when i is 4, it evaluates to 66. After the value is obtained, it is passed to the Node class constructor at line 5 of Listing 4.3 on page 126. That class constructs a node with that value in its data field and null in its next field. The constructor returns a reference to the Node object. It is that reference that is assigned first to p.next, and then to p. The key is that the assignments are made from right to left, so we know that p is not updated untial after its next field is. Hence, first the next field is set to point to the new node, and then the loop control variable p is advanced to that next node.

4.4 Inserting an Element into a Linked List

Now let's look again at how a new element can be inserted into the linked list that was built in Figure 4.16 on page 131. To simplify the process, we add a two-argument constructor to our Node class, as shown in Listing 4.10 on page 134. This allows us to create the node and insert it all at once.

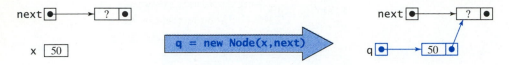

FIGURE 4.18 Invoking the two-argument Node constructor

Figure 4.18 illustrates the invocation of the two-argument Node constructor. It shows next as a reference to a Node object and x as an int with value 50. Passing these two arguments to the constructor creates a new Node object that contains 50 and whose next field points to the same object that the given next pointer points to. The constructor then returns a reference to the new Node object, which is assigned to q.

The code for inserting an element into a nonempty linked list is given in Listing 4.11. To appreciate its simplicity, compare it with the equivalent method in Listing 4.2 on page 125.

LISTING 4.10: A Node **Class with Two Constructors**

```
1   class Node {
2      int data;
3      Node next;
4
5      Node(int data) {
6         this.data = data;
7      }
8
9      Node(int data, Node next) {
10        this.data = data;
11        this.next = next;
12     }
13  }
```

The insertion has two steps: (1) find the list node p that should precede the new node; (2) create and attach the new node.

LISTING 4.11: **Inserting into a Nonempty Sorted Linked List of Integers**

```
1   void insert(Node start, int x) {
2      // PRECONDITIONS: the list is in ascending order, and x > start.data;
3      // POSTCONDITIONS: the list is in ascending order, and it contains x;
4      Node p = start;
5      while (p.next != null) {
6         if (p.next.data > x)   break;
7            p = p.next;
8      }
9      p.next = new Node(x,p.next);
10  }
```

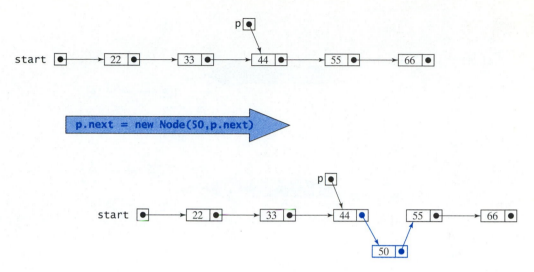

FIGURE 4.19   Inserting into a Nonempty Sorted Linked List

The first step is done by the loop at lines 5–8. The variable p is declared at line 4 to be a reference to Node objects. It is initialized to point to the start node, which contains 22 in Figure 4.19. The loop control condition (p.next != null) at line 5 will allow the loop to iterate until p points to the last element in the list. At that point, p.next will be null, stopping the loop. But inside the loop, at line 6, the condition (p.next.data > x) will stop the loop prematurely, before p reaches any nodes that should come after the new node. This is how the list remains in ascending order: New elements are always inserted between the elements that are less than it and those that are greater than it.

The assignment p = p.next at line 7 is the standard mechanism for traversing a linked list. On each iteration of the while loop, this assignment moves p to point to the next node in the list.

The actual insertion is done by the statement at line 9. The expression new Node(x,p.next) creates the new node and initializes its two fields, as we saw previously in Figure 4.18 on page 134. In that version, it assigned the new node's reference to q. The statement at line 7 assigns it to p.next instead. This changes the next pointer of the p node (the node containing 44): It was pointing to the node containing 55; now it points to the new node that contains 50.

This second stage of the insertion could be done by several separate statements, like this:

```
Node q = new Node(x);
q.next = p.next;
p.next = q;
```

These separate steps are illustrated in Figure 4.20 on page 136. Once we understand this process, however, we might as well use the power of Java and write it in the single statement

```
p.next = new Node(x,p.next);
```

without the clutter of the extra variable q.

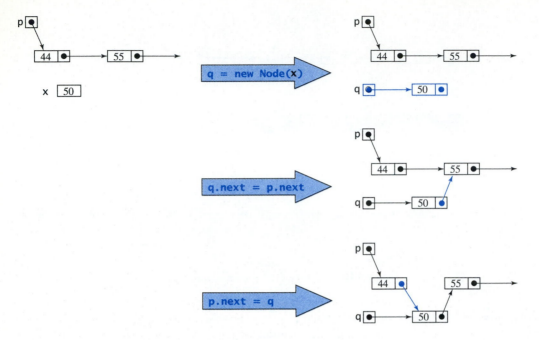

FIGURE 4.20   Inserting the New Node in Three Steps

4.5 Inserting at the Front of the List

The insert() method in Listing 4.11 on page 134 includes the extra precondition that x be greater than the first element in the list (start.data). To see why that precondition is needed, look at what the method would do if x were 20 instead of 50. In that case, the break condition at line 6 would be true on the first iteration of the while loop, leaving p pointing at the start node when the new node gets inserted at line 9. The result, as shown in Figure 4.21, is that 20 gets inserted between 22 and 33, instead of where it belongs at the front of the list. The problem is that we lack a node to precede the new one.

One way to solve this problem is to restructure the linked list itself so that it maintains a "dummy" head node that precedes the first real data node. This uses a little extra space, but it allows the insert() method in Listing 4.11 to work for all cases.

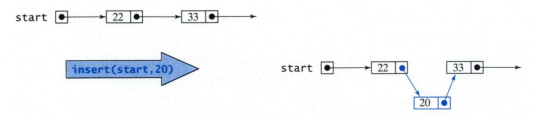

FIGURE 4.21   Inserting 20 Incorrectly

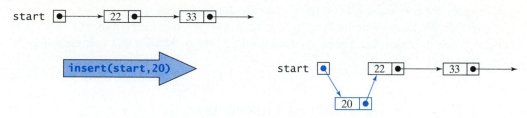

FIGURE 4.22 Inserting 20 Correctly

The other solution is to modify the `insert()` method in Listing 4.11 so that it handles this special case separately. This is done in Listing 4.12 and illustrated in Figure 4.22. There are two situations in which the insert should be done at the front of the list: If the list is empty or if the new element is less than the first element of the list. Both conditions are handled at line 4. In the first case, using the one-argument constructor, we could simply reset `start` to a new node containing x, like this:

```
start = new Node(x);
```

In the second case, we also have to assign the new node to `start`, and we also have to connect it to the rest of the list. But the only reference we have to the beginning of the list is `start` itself, so we would have to hold that reference in a temporary variable before reassigning `start` to the new node.

LISTING 4.12: **Linked List Insertion**

```
1   Node insert(Node start, int x) {
2     // precondition: the list is in ascending order;
3     // postconditions: the list is in ascending order, and it contains x;
4     if (start == null || start.data > x) {
5       start = new Node(x,start);
6       return start;
7     }
8     Node p=start;
9     while (p.next != null) {
10      if (p.next.data > x)  break;
11        p = p.next;
12    }
13    p.next = new Node(x,p.next);
14    return start;
15  }
```

Using the two-argument constructor obviates the need for that extra temporary assignment:

```
start = new Node(x,start);
```

Moreover, it also handles the first case, where the list was empty, because in that case, `start` is `null`, and passing `null` to the second parameter is equivalent to using the one-argument constructor:

```
start = new Node(x, null);  // equivalent
start = new Node(x);        // equivalent
```

So once again, the two-argument constructor provides the best solution.

Note that, unlike the simpler version in Listing 4.11, the complete `insert()` method in Listing 4.12 has to return the `start` `Node` reference. This is because that reference may be changed at line 5.

4.6 Deleting from a Sorted Linked List

Implementing an ordered list with a linked structure makes insertion far more efficient because it eliminates the need to shift elements. The same is true for deletion.

Like the `insert()` method, the `delete()` method has two main parts: (1) find the element; (2) delete it. It also handles the special case at the front of the list separately. Listing 4.13 shows the `delete` method.

LISTING 4.13: **Linked List Deletion**

```
1   Node delete(Node start, int x) {
2      // precondition: the list is in ascending order;
3      // postconditions: the list is in ascending order, and if it did
4      // contains x, then the first occurrence of x has been deleted;
5      if (start == null || start.data > x) // x is not in the list
6        return start;
7      if (start.data==x) // x is the first element in the list
8        return start.next;
9      for (Node p = start; p.next != null; p = p.next) {
10       if (p.next.data > x) break; // x is not in the list
11       if (p.next.data == x) { // x is in the p.next node
12         p.next = p.next.next; // delete it
13         break;
14       }
15     }
16     return start;
17  }
```

If the list is empty, then `start` `==` `null`, and nothing more needs to be done. Also, if the first element is greater than x, then, since the list is sorted, all the elements must be greater than x, so x is not in the list. Both of these cases are handled first at line 5.

If the first element in the list equals x, then it is deleted at line 8. This is done by returning `start.next` to `start`, as shown in Figure 4.23. If no other reference is pointing to the original `start` node, then it will be deleted by the Java "garbage collector."

If the first element of the list is less than x, then the `for` loop at line 9 searches for the first element that is greater than or equal to x. If it finds one greater, then the method breaks at line 10 and returns without changing the list. If it finds an element equal to x, then it deletes it at line 12. This is illustrated in Figure 4.24.

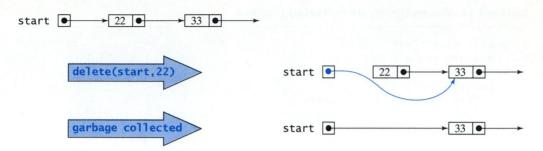

FIGURE 4.23   Deleting the First Element from a Sorted Linked List

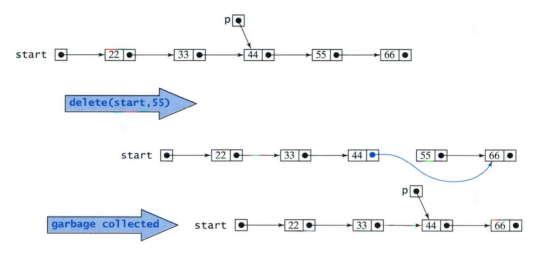

FIGURE 4.24   Deleting an Element from a Sorted Linked List

4.7 Nested Classes

In Java, a class member may be a field, a constructor, a method, an interface, or another class. A class that is a member of another class is called a *nested class*.

If the only place where a class Y will be used is within another class X, then class Y should be nested within class X. This is an important example of the *information hiding* principle that we have discussed in earlier chapters.

If X is any type (class or interface) and Y is any other type nested within X, then every member of X is accessible from Y and every member of Y is accessible from X. This is illustrated in Listing 4.14.

The Main class in Listing 4.14 has a `private` nested class named Nested. Both classes have a `private int` field. Main declares and initializes m at line 2; Nested declares and initializes n at line 15. The Nested class also defines a `private` method f() at line 17.

LISTING 4.14: Accessibility from Nested Classes

```java
1  public class Main {
2     private int m = 22;
3
4     public Main() {
5        Nested nested = new Nested();
6        System.out.println("Outside of Nested; nested.n = " + nested.n);
7        nested.f();
8     }
9
10    public static void main(String[] args) {
11       new Main();
12    }
13
14    private static class Nested {
15       private int n = 44;
16
17       private void f() {
18          System.out.println("Inside of Nested; m = " + m);
19       }
20    }
21 }
```

The output is

```
Outside of Nested; nested.n = 44
Inside of Nested; m = 22
```

The `main()` method invokes the `Main()` constructor at line 11. That instantiates the `Nested` class at line 5. The `private` field n of the `Nested` class is accessed at line 6, and the `private` method `f()` of the `Nested` class is accessed at line 7. This shows that `private` members of a nested class are accessible from its enclosing class. Symmetrically, the `private` members of the enclosing class are accessible from within its nested class, as demonstrated by line 18.

The UML symbol for the nesting of one class inside another uses a circle with a plus sign inside in place of the arrow head, as shown in Figure 4.25.

Since all members of a `private` nested class are still accessible from anywhere else in the enclosing class, those members are usually declared without any access modifier (`private`, `protected`, or `public`), for simplicity.

Normally, a nested class should be declared `static` unless its instances need to access non-`static` members of its enclosing class.[1]

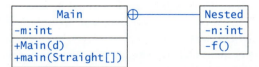

FIGURE 4.25   UML diagrams for a `Nested` classes

---

[1] Non-`static` nested classes are called *inner classes*.

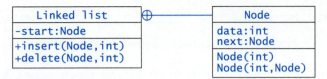

FIGURE 4.26 A Node class nested within a LinkedList class

The Node class defined in Listing 4.10 on page 134 is used only within the context of the linked lists that are being implemented. So it should be nested inside its List class. Moreover, since nodes have no need to access List methods or fields, the Node class should be declared as a **static** nested class. This is done at line 12 in Listing 4.15 and is illustrated in Figure 4.26.

LISTING 4.15: Nesting the Node Class within a LinkedList Class

```
1   public class LinkedList {
2     private Node start;
3
4     public void insert(int x) {
5       // See Listing 4.12 on page 137
6     }
7
8     public void delete(int x) {
9       // See Listing 4.13 on page 138
10    }
11
12    private static class Node {
13      // See Listing 4.10 on page 134
14    }
15  }
```

Hiding the Node class within the LinkedList class encapsulates the LinkedList class, making it self-contained and concealing its implementation details. A developer could change the implementation without having to modify any code outside of that class.

4.8 Case Study: Arbitrarily Long Integers

Like other programming languages, Java includes an int type that allows 2^{32} different integer values, from $-2{,}147{,}483{,}648$ to $2{,}147{,}483{,}647$. It also includes a long type that allows 2^{64} different integer values, from $-9{,}223{,}372{,}036{,}854{,}775{,}808$ to $9{,}223{,}372{,}036{,}854{,}775{,}807$. These are two of the eight primitive types in Java. If you need more than 19 digits for your integers, you can use the java.math.BigInteger class, whose instances allow integers with arbitrarily many digits. In this section, we show how linked lists can be used to build such integer objects.

The idea is to represent each integer as a linked list in which each digit is stored in a separate node. For example, the integer 13,579 would be represented by the linked list shown in Figure 4.27.

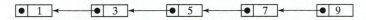

FIGURE 4.27   A linked list that represents the integer 13,579

Notice that the list is drawn from right to left, because we are storing the digits that way. That is necessary to implement the addition algorithm, which begins with the ones' digit and moves left to the tens' digit, then the hundreds' digit, etc.

The two `private` members of our linked lists are shown in Listing 4.16.

LISTING 4.16: The `private` Members of a `BigInt` Class

```
1   public class BigInt {
2     private Node start;
3
4     private static class Node {
5       int digit;
6       Node next;
7       Node(int digit) { this.digit = digit; }
8     }
9   }
```

As in Section 4.3, we define a starting node named `start` and a nested class named `Node`. The `Node` class has two fields, `digit` and `next`, and a one-argument constructor. We don't need the two-argument constructor from Listing 4.10, because each new node in this `BigInt` class will be added to the end of the list.

We define two constructors for our `BigInt` class: one that builds a big integer from of an ordinary `int` like 13579, and one that builds one from a string like `"12345678901234567890"`. These are shown in Listings 4.17 and 4.18, respectively.

LISTING 4.17: The `BigInt` Class Constructor for a Given `int`

```
1   public BigInt(int n) {
2     if (n<0) throw new IllegalArgumentException(n+"<0");
3     start = new Node(n%10);
4     Node p=start;
5     n /= 10;
6     while (n>0) {
7       p = p.next = new Node(n%10);
8       n /= 10;
9     }
10  }
```

To see how this constructor will work, suppose we execute the statement

```
BigInt x = new BigInt(13579);
```

This will invoke the constructor in Listing 4.17, passing the `int` value 13579 to n. At line 3, `start` is assigned a new node containing the value of the expression n%10. That expression returns the ones' digit of n, which is 9 in this case.

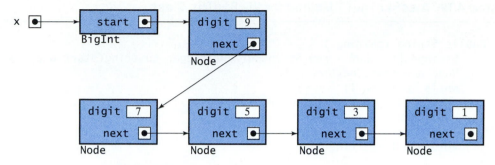

FIGURE 4.28 The `BigInt` that represents the integer 13,579

Next, the local variable p is initialized point to that `start` node at line 4, and n is divided by 10 at line 5, reducing it to 1357. Then the `while` loop begins. At line 7, a new node is constructed with `digit` value 7, `p.next` is assigned to point to that node, and then p is advanced to that node too. At line 8, n is reduced to 135.

The next three iterations of the loop link up three more nodes, containing 5, 3, and 1. The details look like Figure 4.28. This shows six objects: a `BigInt` object and five `Node` objects. The reference variable x holds the address of the `BigInt` object. That object holds the `int` value 9 in its `digit` field and the address of a `Node` object in its next `field`. The chain continues to the last `Node` object, which holds the `int` value 1 in its `digit` field and the `null` address (0x0) in its next `field`.

LISTING 4.18: The `BigInt` Class Constructor for a Given `String`

```
1   public BigInt(String s) {
2     if (s.length() == 0)
3       throw new IllegalArgumentException("empty string");
4     start = new Node(digit(s, s.length()-1));
5     Node p=start;
6     for (int i = s.length()-2; i >= 0; i--)
7       p = p.next = new Node(digit(s, i));
8   }
9
10  private int digit(String s, int i) {
11    String ss = s.substring(i, i+1);
12    return Integer.parseInt(ss);
13  }
```

This second `BigInt` constructor uses a `private` auxiliary `digit()` method that returns the integer digit stored at position i in the given string s. It does that by extracting the single digit as the substring ss, and then uses the `Integer.parseInt()` method to convert it to type `int`.

The constructor has to build the `BigInt` list from the right, extracting the last digit from the given string first. The call `digit(s, s.length()-1)` at line 4 does that, returning the `int` to the Node constructor to build the first node, which is then assigned to `start`. It builds the rest of the nodes the same way, inside the `for` loop at lines 6–8.

Listing 4.19 shows a `toString()` method for printing the `BigInt` objects as integers. It uses a `StringBuffer` object to accumulate the digits.

LISTING 4.19: A `toString()` Method for the `BigInt` Class

```
1   public String toString() {
2       StringBuffer buf = new StringBuffer(Integer.toString(start.digit));
3       Node p = start.next;
4       while (p != null) {
5          buf.insert(0,Integer.toString(p.digit));
6           p = p.next;
7       }
8       return buf.toString();
9   }
```

The `StringBuffer` object `buf` is initialized at line 2 with the first digit. The expression `Integer.toString(start.digit)` returns the `String` equivalent for the `digit` in the `start` node. Then the `while` loop traverses the linked list, extracting each digit and prepending it to the beginning of the buffer. The `insert()` method at line 5 inserts the digit at position 0 in the buffer.

Listing 4.20 shows a method for adding big integers. It adds the `BigInt` y to the `BigInt` object upon which the call is made.

LISTING 4.20: A Method for Adding `BigInt` Objects

```
1   public BigInt plus(BigInt y) {
2     Node p = start, q = y.start;
3     int n = p.digit + q.digit;
4     BigInt z = new BigInt(n%10);
5     Node r=z.start;
6     p = p.next;
7     q = q.next;
8     while (p != null && q != null) {
9        n = n/10 + p.digit + q.digit;
10       r.next = new Node(n%10);
11       p = p.next;
12       q = q.next;
13       r = r.next;
14    }
15    while (p != null) {
16       n = n/10 + p.digit;
17       r.next = new Node(n%10);
18       p = p.next;
19       r = r.next;
20    }
21    while (q != null) {
22       n = n/10 + q.digit;
23       r.next = new Node(n%10);
24       q = q.next;
25       r = r.next;
26    }
27    if (n > 9) r.next = new Node(n/10);
28    return z;
29  }
```

The local `Node` pointer variables p and q are initialized at the `starts` of the two lists at line 2. Then a local `int` variable n is initialized with the sum of the first digits of the two lists. At line 4, the new `BigInt` object z that will return the sum is constructed and initialized with the ones' digit of n. Then a third `Node` pointer variable r is declared at line 5 and initialized to the `start` node of the new list z. Then p and q are advanced to the second nodes of their lists, either of which could be `null`.

Figure 4.29 on page 146 illustrates the situation after line 7 has executed, in adding 628 to 13,579. From there, we can see that, as long as both p and q point to non`null` nodes, we should repeat these steps:

1. Replace n with its tens' digit added to the next digit in each of the two given lists.

2. Append a new `Node` to z, containing the ones' digit of n.

3. Advance all three pointers: p, q, and r.

These are the actions that are taken inside the `while` loop at lines 8–14.

After one of the loops runs out, we continue the same process with the other loop. That will be either lines 15–20 or lines 21–26. After that, all that remains is to add one more node if there was a carry at line 27, and then return z.

Listing 4.21 is a test driver for the `BigInt` class.

LISTING 4.21: Testing the `BigInt` Class by Generating Fibonacci Numbers

```
1   public class TestBigInt {
2     public static void main(String[] args) {
3       BigInt x = new BigInt(0);
4       BigInt y = new BigInt(1);
5       BigInt z = new BigInt(1);
6       for (int i = 0; i < 100; i++) {
7         x = y;
8         y = z;
9         z = x.plus(y);
10        System.out.println(z);
11      }
12    }
13  }
```

This generates the next 100 Fibonacci numbers[2] that follow the first three (0, 1, 1) in the sequence. The first three lines of output are

```
2
3
5
```

---

[2] The Fibonacci number (The sequence is 0, 1, 1, 2, 3, 5, 8, . . .) is discussed in Section 10.3

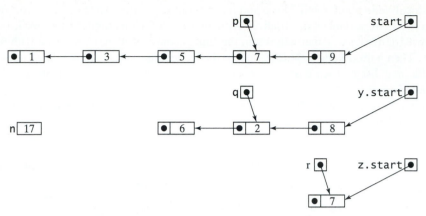

FIGURE 4.29   Adding the `BigInt` 628 to the `BigInt` 13,579

The last three lines of output are

    354224848179261915075
    573147844013817084101
    927372692193078999176

Each number is the sum of its two predecessors.

CHAPTER SUMMARY

❏ An insertion into an ordered array requires shifting all the elements that are greater than the new one.
❏ This can be avoided by using a second index array to locate the elements in the data array.
❏ The same result is achieved more easily by using a linked list instead.
❏ Each link (called a "pointer") in a linked list is simply the memory address of the next element of the list.
❏ List node objects typically have a field for the data field and a `next` field for the link.
❏ Inserting into a linked list only requires changing two pointers.
❏ Inserting into the front of the list requires separate steps unless a dummy head node is used.
❏ Deletion from a linked list only requires changing one pointer.
❏ Arbitrarily long integers can be represented and manipulated using linked lists of digits.

REVIEW QUESTIONS

4.1   Why is an array such an inefficient data structure for a dynamic sorted list?

4.2   What is an index array?

4.3   If linked lists are so much better than arrays, why are arrays used at all?

4.4   Why does insertion at the front of a linked list have to be done differently from insertion elsewhere?

4.5   Why are the lists backwards in the `BigInt` class?

EXERCISES

4.1   Draw pictures that show the insertion of 40 into the sorted list shown in Figure 4.6 on page 125.

4.2   Draw pictures that show the deletion of 55 from the sorted list shown in Figure 4.6 on page 125.

PROGRAMMING PROBLEMS

4.1   Write and test this method, similar to the `insert()` method in Listing 4.1 on page 121:

```
void delete(int[] a, int n, int x)
// precondition: 0 <= n < a.length;
// postconditions: the first occurrence of x among
                   {a[0], ..., a[n-1]} has been deleted;
```

For example, if `a[]` is the array {33, 55, 77, 99, 77, 55, 33, 0}, then `delete(a, 6, 55)` will change `a[]` to {33, 77, 99, 77, 55, 33, 0, 0}.

4.2   Write and test this method:

```
int size(Node list)
// returns: the number of nodes in the specified list;
```

For example, if `list` is {33, 55, 77, 99}, then `size(list)` will return 4.

4.3   Write and test this method:

```
int sum(Node list)
// returns: the sum of the integers in the specified list;
```

For example, if `list` is {25, 45, 65, 85}, then `sum(list)` will return 220.

4.4   Write and test this method:

```
void deleteLast(Node list)
// precondition: the specified list has at least two nodes;
// postconditions: the last node in the list has been deleted;
```

For example, if `list` is {22, 44, 66, 88}, then `deleteLast(list)` will change it to {22, 44, 66}.

4.5   Write and test this method:

```
Node copy(Node list)
// returns: a new list that is a duplicate of the specified list;
```

Note that the new list must be completely independent of the specified list. Changing one list should have no effect upon the other.

4.6   Write and test this method:

```
Node sublist(Node list, int p, int q)
// returns: a new list that contains copies of the q-p nodes of the
//    specified list, starting with node number p (starting with 0);
```

For example, if list is {22, 33, 44, 55, 66, 77 88, 99}, then sublist(list, 2, 7) will return the new list {44, 55, 66, 77, 88}. Note that the two lists must be completely independent of each other. Changing one list should have no effect upon the other.

4.7   Write and test this method:

```
void append(Node lists1, Node list2)
// precondition: list1 has at least one nodes;
// postconditions: list1 has list2 appended to it;
```

For example, if list1 is {22, 33, 44, 55} and list2 is {66, 77, 88, 99}, then append(list1, list2) will change list1 to {22, 33, 44, 55, 44, 55, 66, 77, 88}. Note that no new nodes are created by this method.

4.8   Write and test this method:

```
Node concat(Node list1, Node list2)
// returns: a new list that contains a copy of list1, followed by
//    a copy of list2;
```

For example, if list1 is {22, 33, 44, 55} and list2 is {66, 77, 88, 99}, then concat(list1, list2) will return the new list {22, 33, 44, 55, 44, 55, 66, 77, 88}. Note that the three lists should be completely independent of each other. Changing one list should have no effect upon the others.

4.9   Write and test this method:

```
void replace(Node list, int i, int x)
// replaces the ith element with x;
```

For example, if list is {22, 33, 44, 55, 66, 77, 88, 99}, then replace(list, 2, 50) will change list to {22, 33, 50, 55, 66, 44, 88, 99}.

4.10   Write and test this method:

```
void swap(Node list, int i, int j)
// swaps the ith element with the jth element;
```

For example, if list is {22, 33, 44, 55, 66, 77, 88, 99}, then swap(list, 2, 5) will change list to {22, 33, 77, 55, 66, 44, 88, 99}.

4.11   Write and test this method:

```
Node merged(Node list1, Node list2)
// precondition: list1 and list2 are both in ascending order;
```

```
// returns: a new list that contains all the elements of list1 and
//   list2 in ascending order;
```

For example, if `list1` is {22, 33, 55, 88} and `list2` is {44, 66, 77, 99}, then `merged(list1, list2)` will return the new list {22, 33, 44, 55, 66, 77, 88, 99}. Note that the three lists should be completely independent of each other. Changing one list should have no effect upon the others.

4.12　Write and test this method:

```
void shuffle(Node list)
// performs a perfect shuffle on the specified list;
```

For example, if `list` is (22, 33, 44, 55, 66, 77, 88, 99}. then `shuffle(list)` will change `list` to {22, 66, 33, 77, 44, 88, 55, 99}. Note that no new nodes are created by this method.

PROJECTS

4.1　Complete the `BigInt` class from Section 4.8 by adding these methods:

```
boolean equals (Object object)
int intValue ()
long longValue()
int numdigits
BigInt times(int n)
```

Begin your `equals()` method with these lines:

```
if (!(object instanceof BigInt)
    throw new Illegal ArgumentException();
BigInt x = (BigInt) object;
```

This allows access to the `x.start` field, so you can traverse the linked list that the object maintains.

To implement the `times()` method, use the standard elementary school algorithm, multiplying n by each digit in the `BigInt` object, carrying the excess to the next digit. Note that this method is obliged to return a new `BigInt` object, leaving the operating `BigInt` object (the "this" object) unchanged.

Expand the tester program in Listing 4.21 on page 145 so that it thoroughly tests all the methods in the class.

4.2　Implement the `BigInt` class (See Section 4.8) using an array instead of a linked list. Store each digit in a separate element of a backing array `a[]`. For example, the integer 13579 would be stored as shown in Figure 4.30.

Also include a `private field` named `size` that stores the number of digits in the integer. When `size == a.length`, a `private resize()` method should be invoked to replace `a[]` with a copy that is twice as long.

FIGURE 4.30   Backing array

Implement all the constructors and methods that are described in Section 4.8 and in Project 4.1. Thoroughly test your class with a separate test driver.

ANSWERS TO REVIEW QUESTIONS

4.1   Arrays are inefficient for implementing dynamic sorted lists because the insert and delete operations require moving half the elements, on average.

4.2   An index array is an array whose elements are index values into another array.

4.3   Linked lists provide no direct access. To find the 100th element, you have to move sequentially through the first 99 elements.

4.4   Insertion at the front of a linked list has to be done differently because the link to the new node is the `start` link; it is not `p.next` for any node p (unless you use a dummy head node).

4.5   We had to define the linked lists backwards in the `BigInt` class because the digits of an integer are processed from right to left in the common arithmetic operations.

BANANAS

PICKLES

RAISINS

ORANGES

Embrace simplicity

— Lao-tzu (604 BC – 531 BC)

Chapter 5

Stacks

Imagine that you are the stock manager for a grocery store, and you have a stack of crates of different foods, such as carrots, oranges, etc. Suppose that the top crate is bananas. You can take a banana out of the top crate without changing the stack at all. But if you want to access the crate of oranges, you will have to remove all of the crates above it first. And if you want to add a crate of walnuts to the structure, it has to be put on top of the crate of bananas; you couldn't put it under the crate of bananas without removing that crate first. These access features characterize the data structure known as a stack.

5.1 The Stack ADT

A *stack* is a data structure that implements the last-in-first-out (LIFO) protocol: The only accessible object in the structure is the one that was inserted most recently.

Here is a formal description of a stack as an abstract data type:

ADT: Stack

A *stack* is a collection of elements that maintains the LIFO access protocol.

Operations

1. *Peek*: If the stack is not empty, return its top element.

2. *Pop*: If the stack is not empty, delete and return its top element.

3. *Push*: Add a given element to the top of the stack.

4. *Size*: Return the number of elements in the stack.

The UML diagram for this ADT is shown in Figure 5.1. The ADT is translated into a Java interface in Listing 5.1.

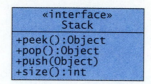

FIGURE 5.1   A Stack interface.

LISTING 5.1: **A** Stack **Interface**

```
1   /**
2    * The <code>Stack</code> inerface specifies the basic operations
3    * of a last-in-first-out (LIFO) containers.
4    */
5   public interface Stack {
6
7       /**
8        * Returns a reference to the top element on this stack, leaving
9        * the stack unchanged.
10       *
11       * @return the element at the top of this stack.
12       * @throws IllegalStateException if this stack is empty
13       */
14      public Object peek();
15
16      /**
17       * Removes and returns the element at the top of this stack.
18       *
19       * @return the element at the top of this stack.
20       * @throws IllegalStateException if this stack is empty
21       */
22      public Object pop();
23
24      /**
25       * Adds the specified element to the top of this stack.
26       *
27       * @param object the element to be pushed onto this stack.
28       */
29      public void push(Object object);
30
31      /**
32       * Returns the number of elements in this stack.
33       *
34       * @return the number of elements in this queue.
35       */
36      public int size();
37  }
```

This interface includes Javadoc comments that will generate the standard Web page API documentation for the interface.

The *Peek*, *Pop*, *Push*, and *Size* operations are translated directly into specifications for methods named peek(), pop(), push(), and size(), respectively. These are traditional names for stack functions.

Each method is defined by specifying its return value, any changes that it makes to the object, and any exceptions that might be thrown. Note that the exception IllegalStateException is thrown when the state of the object prevents it from carrying out the task required by the specifications.[1]

5.2 An Array Implementation

There are several ways to implement the Stack interface. The most obvious and probably the simplest is to use an ordinary array. This is done in Listing 5.2. Its UML diagram is shown in Figure 5.2.

The ArrayStack implementation uses a backing array a[] to store the stack's elements. Its other field is the integer size, which keeps a count of the number of elements in the stack.

In addition to the four methods required by the interface, the class also includes a public isEmpty() method and a private resize() method. The latter is called by push() when the array is full. It rebuilds the array, doubling its size. This is done by declaring a temporary reference aa[] to the array in line 35, redefining a[] as a new array with twice the length in line 36, and then using the arraycopy() method of the System class to copy all the stack's elements from aa[] back to a[] in line 37. (See Section 3.9 on page 88 for a discussion about the System.arraycopy() method.)

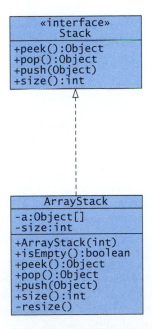

FIGURE 5.2 Implementing the stack interface.

---

[1] We could also use the EmptyStackException class defined in the java.util package.

LISTING 5.2: **An** ArrayStack **Class**

```
1   public class ArrayStack implements Stack {
2       private Object[] a;
3       private int size;
4
5       public ArrayStack(int capacity) {
6           a = new Object[capacity];
7       }
8
9       public boolean isEmpty() {
10          return (size == 0);
11      }
12
13      public Object peek() {
14          if (size == 0) throw new IllegalStateException("stack is empty");
15          return a[size-1];
16      }
17
18      public Object pop() {
19          if (size == 0) throw new IllegalStateException("stack is empty");
20          Object object = a[--size];
21          a[size] = null;
22          return object;
23      }
24
25      public void push(Object object) {
26          if (size == a.length) resize();
27          a[size++] = object;
28      }
29
30      public int size() {
31          return size;
32      }
33
34      private void resize() {
35          Object[] aa = a;
36          a = new Object[2*aa.length];
37          System.arraycopy(aa, 0, a, 0, size);
38      }
39  }
```

The specifications for the peek() and pop() methods in the Stack interface require that the stack be not empty. This constraint is enforced at lines 14 and 19. If the precondition that the stack be nonempty is violated, then an IllegalStateException object is thrown, aborting the execution of any client program that called the method.

Note at line 21 the pop() method resets to null the array element that references the object being removed from the stack. This prevents an unreachable reference from being maintained.

The ArrayStack class is tested in the program in Listing 5.3.

LISTING 5.3: **Testing the** ArrayStack **Class**

```
1   public class TestArrayStack {
2     public static void main(String[] args) {
3       Stack crates = new ArrayStack(4);
4       crates.push("CARROTS");
5       crates.push("ORANGES");
6       crates.push("RAISINS");
7       crates.push("PICKLES");
8       crates.push("BANANAS");
9       System.out.println("crates.size(): " + crates.size()
10                        + "\tcrates.peek(): " + crates.peek());
11      System.out.println("crates.pop(): " + crates.pop());
12      System.out.println("crates.pop(): " + crates.pop());
13      System.out.println("crates.pop(): " + crates.pop());
14      System.out.println("crates.size(): " + crates.size()
15                        + "\tcrates.peek(): " + crates.peek());
16      cratecrates.push("WALNUTS");
17      cratecrates.push("OYSTERS");
18      System.out.println("crates.size(): " + crates.size()
19                        + "\tcrates.peek(): " + crates.peek());
20      System.out.println("crates.pop(): " + crates.pop());
21      System.out.println("crates.pop(): " + crates.pop());
22      System.out.println("crates.pop(): " + crates.pop());
23      System.out.println("crates.pop(): " + crates.pop());
24      System.out.println("crates.pop(): " + crates.pop());
25    }
26  }
```

The output is

```
crates.size(): 5          crates.peek(): BANANAS
crates.pop(): BANANAS
crates.pop(): PICKLES
crates.pop(): RAISINS
crates.size(): 2          crates.peek(): ORANGES
crates.size(): 4          crates.peek(): OYSTERS
crates.pop(): OYSTERS
crates.pop(): WALNUTS
crates.pop(): ORANGES
crates.pop(): CARROTS
java.lang.IllegalStateException: stack is empty
Exception in thread main
```

The program creates a stack named `crates` with a capacity of 4 at line 3. The next five lines push five strings onto the stack. The output from line 9 confirms that the stack now contains five objects and that its top object is the string `"BANANAS"`. This shows that the `resize()` method worked, doubling the capacity of the stack to 8.

The output from lines 11–13 show the effect of the `pop()` method. Each call removes and returns the top element. So at line 14 we see that the stack is down to two elements, with `"ORANGES"` on top. Two more calls to `push()` increase the size to 4. Then, repeated calls to `pop()` finally empty the stack.

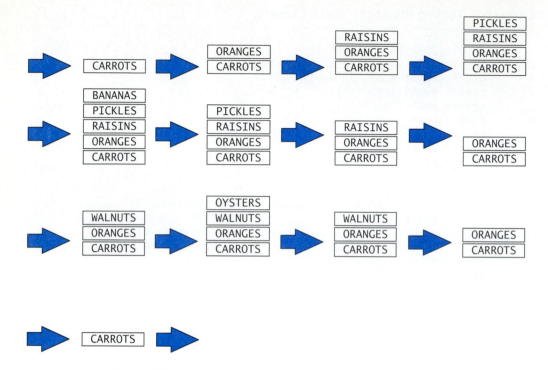

FIGURE 5.3   The client's view of the program in Listing 5.3 on page 155.

The last call to pop() on line 24 throws an IllegalStateException because the stack is empty at that point.

The separation of the ADT specifications from their implementations in a Java class can be interpreted in terms of different audiences viewing the data structure. One point of view is that of the *client*, who uses the data structure without concern for how it is implemented; the client sees only the ADT. On the other side is the *implementor*, who understands all the details of the code in the class that implements the data structure.

The client's view of the execution of the program is shown in Figure 5.3. All of the implementation details are hidden from view. All that the client sees is that the stack of crates grows and shrinks with the *Push* and *Pop* operations.

The implementor's view of the program execution is shown in the two snapshots in Figure 5.4. There, the underlying array data structure is revealed. The structure on the left is the implemented stack after the third call to push(). It shows that the object crates is an instance of the ArrayStack class which has two fields: the integer size and the Object array a[]. At that moment, size has the value 3 and a[] has length 4. The elements of the array are Object references. The first three references point to String objects, and the fourth is null.

The snapshot on the right shows the implementor's view of the data structure after the fifth call to push(). In that call, the condition (size == a.length) at line 26 in the ArrayStack class was true, so resize() was called, replacing the array with one of length 8. That provides enough room to add the fifth string, "BANANAS". Note that the last three elements are null.

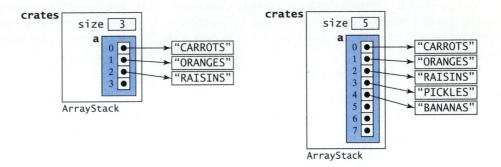

FIGURE 5.4 The implementor's view of the program in Listing 5.3 on page 155.

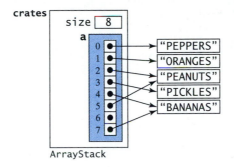

FIGURE 5.5 Possible anomalies with this implementation.

Note that this implementation of the Stack interface is not a perfect representation of a real world stack. As indicated in Figure 5.5 on page 157, such an implementation could allow several elements of the stack to be references to the same object, and it could allow some references to be null. (See Programming Problem 5.19 and Programming Problem 5.20 on page 173 for correcting these anomalies.)

5.3 Application: Evaluating Postfix Expressions

Ordinarily, people write arithmetic expressions like this: (8 – 3)*(5 + 6). This is called *infix notation*. Computers manage such expressions better using *postfix notation* instead. In that form, the operators always follow their operands. So the infix expression "8 – 3" is written "8 3 –", "5 + 6" is written "5 6 +", and "(8 – 3)*(5 + 6)" is written "8 3 – 5 6 + *".

Note that with postfix notation, there is no need for parentheses, because there is no ambiguity. Each operator always operates on the last two values that precede it. So in the postfix expression "8 3 – 5 6 + *", the "–" operator must operate on the 8 and the 3, the "+" operator must operate on the 5 and the 6, and the "*" operator must operate on the values returned by the "+" and the "–".

The program in Listing 5.4 evaluates postfix expressions. (It is called an RPN calculator because postfix notation is also called "reverse Polish notation.") The program reads a postfix expression from the command line and then prints its evaluation. This sample run is executed at the command line as

    java **RPN 7 2 A 5 8 4 D S M**

These nine command line arguments are interpreted as $7\ 2 + 5\ 8\ 4\ /- *$, which is postfix for the infix expression $(7 + 2) * (5 - (8\ /\ 4))$. This evaluates to $(9) * (5 - (2)) = 9 * 3 = 27$.

LISTING 5.4: **An RPN Calculator**

```
1   public class RPN {
2     public RPN(String[] args) {
3       Stack stack = new ArrayStack(args.length);
4       for (int i = 0; i < args.length; i++) {
5         String input = args[i];
6         if (isAnOperator(input)) {
7           double y = Double.parseDouble((String)stack.pop());
8           double x = Double.parseDouble((String)stack.pop());
9           double z = evaluate(x, y, input);
10          stack.push("" + z);
11        }
12        else stack.push(input);
13      }
14    }
15
16    private boolean isAnOperator(String s) {
17      return (s.length() == 1 && "ASMD".indexOf(s) >= 0);
18    }
19
20    private double evaluate(double x, double y, String op) {
21      double z = 0;
22      if      (op.equals("A")) z = x + y;
23      else if (op.equals("S")) z = x - y;
24      else if (op.equals("M")) z = x * y;
25      else                     z = x / y;
26      System.out.println(x + " " + op + " " + y + " = " + z);
27      return z;
28    }
29
30    public static void main(String[] args) {
31      new RPN(args);
32    }
33  }
```

The output is

```
7.0 A 2.0 = 9.0
8.0 D 4.0 = 2.0
5.0 S 2.0 = 3.0
9.0 M 3.0 = 27.0
```

The program uses a stack to evaluate the postfix expressions. As it parses the input, it distinguishes the operators ("A", "S", "M", and "D") from the operands (the numeric values). It pushes the operands on the stack. When it encounters an operator, it assumes that the two operands that belong to that operator are the last two numbers that were pushed on the stack. So it pops them, evaluates the corresponding expression, and then pushes that numeric result back onto the stack. It uses a separate `evaluate()` method to evaluate the expression and to print the evaluation.

To qualify as a valid operator, the `input` string must be either "A", "S", "M", or "D". Line 17 uses the *index string*, "ASMD", to test that requirement:

```
17        return (s.length() == 1 && "ASMD".indexOf(s) >= 0);
```

The expression "ASMD".indexOf(s) returns 0, 1, 2, or 3, if s is "A", "S", "M", or "D", respectively. If s is any other single-character string, then that expression will return -1.[2]

Note that when an element is popped from the stack at lines 7–8, it is returned as an instance of the `Object` class, so it has to be recast as

```
(String)stack.pop()
```

before it can be used as a string. Also, when a numeric value is pushed onto the stack, the expression "" + z is used at line 10 to obtain a string representation of it.

5.4 Case Study: Solving a Maze

Here is another application that illustrates how stacks are used. We are given a maze, like this:

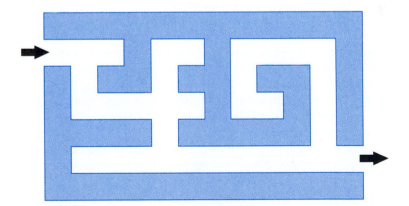

FIGURE 5.6 A maze.

The problem is to find a path through the maze, from the entrance point at the upper left to the exit point on the lower right, as shown in Figure 5.6. Imagine a rat trying to find its way through this maze.

---

[2] Note that we do have to check the length of s too. For example, "ASMD".indexOf("MD") would return 2.

`Maze.txt`

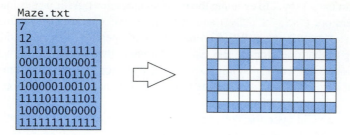

```
7
12
111111111111
000100100001
101101101101
100000100101
111101111101
100000000000
111111111111
```

FIGURE 5.7 Loading the maze from a text file.

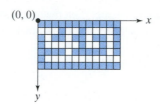

FIGURE 5.8 Coordinates.

We will store the maze in a two-dimensional array of `ints`, the value of each element being either 0 or 1. The value 0 represents part of a corridor, and the value 1 represents part of a wall. We will load the array from an ordinary text file like the one shown Figure 5.7. This `Maze.txt` file would load an array that would represent the maze.

The file first lists the number of rows ($m = 7$) and the number of columns ($n = 12$). Then, starting on the third line, it gives the complete m-by-n array of 0s and 1s that define the maze.

To be consistent with the graphics context of the Java Abstract Window Toolkit (AWT), we use (x, y) coordinates with the origin $(0, 0)$ at the upper left corner, the x-axis running horizontally across the top to the right, and the y-axis running vertically along the left edge downward, as shown in Figure 5.8. So the entrance cell will always be at coordinates $(0,1)$ and the exit cell will always be at coordinates $(n-1, m-2)$. In this example, the exit cell is $(11, 5)$.

For an object-oriented solution to the problem, we first identify the primary objects: the maze itself, and a rat to move about in the maze. These require a `Maze` class and a `Rat` class. We'll use a separate `main()` class named `SolveMaze` to generate the solution, a path through the maze.

To generate the path, we have to move about, from one location to another in the maze. So we'll also define a `Location` class and a `Direction` class. A location is really just a pair of integer coordinates (x, y), and a direction is really just one of four compass directions: north, south, east, or west. Creating separate classes for these entities is consistent with the spirit of object orientation, and it renders the result easier to understand and thus easier to generalize (*e.g.*, to three dimensions). The five classes, each in its own file, are depicted in Figure 5.10.

Listing 5.5 shows the `main()` class. It declares three objects: a `maze`, a `rat`, and a `stack`. The `main()` method simply instantiates the `main()` class, passing to the constructor the command line argument `args[0]` which names the input file that contains the definition of the maze to be solved. We run the program with this command:

> java **SolveMaze Maze.txt**

LISTING 5.5: Solving a Maze

```
1   public class SolveMaze {
2     Maze maze;
3     Rat rat;
4     Stack stack;
5
6     public static void main(String[] args) {
7       new SolveMaze(args[0]);
8     }
9
10    public SolveMaze(String file) {
11      maze = new Maze(file);
12      rat = new Rat(maze);
13      stack = new ArrayStack();
14      maze.print();
15      while (!rat.isOut()) {
16        Location currentLocation = rat.getLocation();
17        // see Programming Problem 5.23 on page 173
18      }
19    }
20  }
```

The output is

```
###########
oo # #    #
# ## ## ## #
#     # # #
#### ##### #
#
###########

###########
oo?#??#????#
#o##?##?##?#
#oooo?#??#?#
####o#####?#
#    oooooooo
###########
```

The output consists of the results from two calls to the `Maze.print()` method: one before, and one after the solution has been found. For this maze, the first seven lines of the output show the maze rendered with `'#'` and `' '` characters for the walls and corridors, respectively. The path of the rat is shown with `'o'` characters. So the "before" picture shows the rat just getting started in the upper left corner at the entrance to the maze. The "after" picture (the last seven lines here) shows the rat's path from entrance to exit. It also shows attempted dead ends, rendered with the `'?'` character.

The main() class constructor invokes the Maze, Rat, and ArrayStack constructors at lines 11–13 to initialize the maze, rat, and stack objects. These are illustrated in Figure 5.9. A Location object is a pair of integers, such as (10, 2). A Maze object is a two-dimensional array of integers, along with its dimensions m and n. The Rat object stores its current location and a reference to the Maze. Besides the Rat object and the Maze object, the main() class also has an ArrayStack object.

After these objects have been instantiated, the program prints the maze and starts the main while loop at line 15. On each iteration of the while loop, the rat makes one move on the grid, from one cell to a neighboring cell. The loop is controlled by an isOut() method in the Rat class that can determine when the rat gets out of the maze. We also assume the Rat class has a getLocation() method that returns the current location of the rat in the maze.

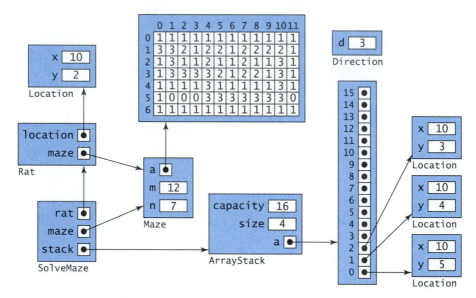

FIGURE 5.9   The data structures for the Maze solution.

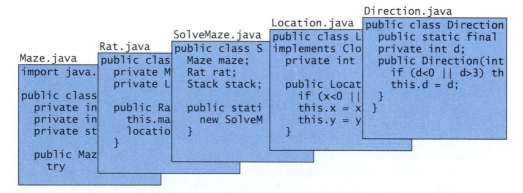

FIGURE 5.10   The classes for the Maze solution.

The states of the data structures shown in Figure 5.9 represent the maze on the iteration where the rat has moved all the way into the spiral and then back-tracked to location (10,2). The back-tracking from the center of that spiral that the rat has already done is marked by the "2" digits at positions the (8,3), (7,3), (7,2), (7,1), (8,1), (9,1), and (10,1). The back-tracking that the rat still has to do is marked by the "3" digits at positions the (10,2), (10,3), (10,4), and (10,5). After that, it will find the exit at (11,5).

LISTING 5.6: **The** Maze **Class**

```java
1   import java.io.*;
2
3   public class Maze {
4      private int m, n;
5      private int[][] a;
6      private static final int OPEN = 0, WALL = 1,  TRIED = 2, PATH = 3;
7
8      public Maze(String file) {
9         // see Programming Problem 5.26 on page 173
10     }
11
12     public boolean isOpen(Location location) {
13        return (a[location.getY()][location.getX()] == OPEN);
14     }
15
16     public void markMoved(Location location) {
17        a[location.getY()][location.getX()] = PATH;
18     }
19
20     public void markTried(Location location) {
21        a[location.getY()][location.getX()] = TRIED;
22     }
23
24     public int getWidth() {
25        return n;
26     }
27
28     public int getHeight() {
29        return m;
30     }
31
32     public void print() {
33        char[] chars = {' ', '+', '?', 'o'};
34        for (int i = 0; i < m; i++) {
35           for (int j = 0; j < n; j++)
36              System.out.print( chars[ a[i][j] ] );
37           System.out.println();
38        }
39     }
40  }
```

We implement the following backtracking algorithm to solve the maze problem:

1. If the rat can move in any one of the four directions (north, east south, west), then push its current location on the stack and move it to the neighboring location in that direction;
2. Otherwise, if the stack is empty, report that there is no solution, and exit;
3. Otherwise, mark the current location in the maze as "tried," pop the last location from the stack, and move the rat back to that previous location.

The Maze class (see Listing 5.6) uses four static named constants: OPEN, WALL, TRIED, and PATH. Each element of the array a[][] stores one of these four values. Initially, they all are either OPEN or WALL, as read from the file. Each iteration of the main loop changes one cell to either TRIED or PATH. When the loop is terminated, the PATH cells show the solution to the maze. For example, the array a[][] for the maze shown in Figure 5.6 will progress as shown Figure 5.11 on page 165. The WALL cells (value 1) are slightly shaded. The cell that changed at each iteration is shown with a darker square boundary. The three dots stand for 35 missing snapshots of the grid before it reaches the final two states shown. The TRIED cells (value 2) indicate *backtracking*.

LISTING 5.7: The Rat Class

```
1   public class Rat {
2      private Maze maze;
3      private Location location;
4
5      public Rat(Maze maze) {
6         this.maze = maze;
7         location = new Location(1,1);
8      }
9
10     public Location getLocation() {
11        return (Location)location.clone();
12     }
13
14     public void setLocation(Location location) {
15        this.location = location;
16     }
17
18     public boolean canMove(int direction) {
19        Location neighbor = location.adjacent(direction);
20        return maze.isOpen(neighbor);
21     }
22
23     public void move(int direction) {
24        location.move(direction);
25        maze.markMoved(location);
26     }
27
28     public boolean isOut() {
29        // See Programming Problem 5.27 on page 174
30     }
31  }
```

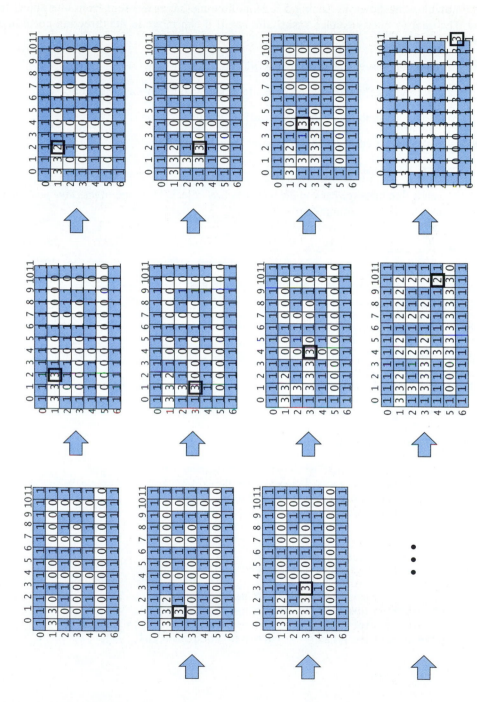

FIGURE 5.11 A trace of the solution to the Maze problem.

The Rat class is shown in Listing 5.7. Note how messages are sent from one object to another. The main() class instance "asks" the rat if it can move in the direction north in a statement:

```
if (rat.canMove(Direction.NORTH)) ...
```

To respond, the rat "asks" its location object to report who its northern neighbor is:

```
Location neighbor = location.adjacent(direction);
```

Then it "asks" the maze object whether that neighbor is open:

```
return maze.isOpen(neighbor);
```

The rat then sends that message back to the main() class object. This kind of *message passing* is central to object-oriented programming.

LISTING 5.8: **The** Location **Class**

```
1   public class Location implements Cloneable {
2      private int x, y;
3
4      public Location(int x, int y)  // See Programming Problem 5.28
5
6      public Object clone()  // See Programming Problem 5.28 on page 174
7
8      public int getX()  // See Programming Problem 5.28
9
10     public int getY()  // See Programming Problem 5.28
11
12     public void move(int direction) {
13        switch (direction) {
14          case Direction.NORTH: --y;  break;
15          case Direction.EAST : ++x;  break;
16          case Direction.SOUTH: ++y;  break;
17          case Direction.WEST : --x;  break;
18        }
19     }
20
21     public Location adjacent(int direction) {
22        switch (direction) {
23          case Direction.NORTH: return new Location(x, y-1);
24          case Direction.EAST : return new Location(x+1, y);
25          case Direction.SOUTH: return new Location(x, y+1);
26          case Direction.WEST : return new Location(x-1, y);
27        }
28        return null;
29     }
30
31     public String toString()  // See Programming Problem 5.28 on page 174
32  }
```

The `Location` class is shown Listing 5.8. Note the use of the `break` statement in the `switch` statement at lines 14–17 to avoid a "fall through."

Finally, the `Direction` class is shown in Listing 5.9. It is really little more than an enumeration type.

LISTING 5.9: The `Direction` Class

```
1   public class Direction {
2     public static final int NORTH = 0, EAST = 1, SOUTH = 2, WEST = 3;
3     private int direction;
4
5     public Direction(int d) {
6       if (d < 0 || d > 3) throw new IllegalArgumentException();
7       direction = d;
8     }
9
10    public int getDirection() {
11      return direction;
12    }
13  }
```

The use of a stack to manage backtracking is a common strategy for game playing and for more general modeling of rational thought. No one knows yet quite how the brain works, but its use of general trial-and-error strategies is clear. Simulating that with a computer usually calls for the stack data structure.

5.5 A Linked Implementation

The `ArrayStack` implementation of our `Stack` interface is a little inefficient, because it requires rebuilding the array when it gets full. Since arrays maintain their elements in contiguous memory locations, they are unable to grow dynamically. The entire array has to be reallocated and copied in order to expand it. We can overcome this problem by using a linked structure instead of an array to store the stack's elements.

A linked implementation of our `Stack` interface is shown in Listing 5.10. It has a `private static` nested class named `Node` with two instance variables: `object` and `next`. The elements of the stack are kept in the `object` fields. The `next` fields are the *links* that connect the nodes. The last node's next field is `null`.

The picture in Figure 5.12 shows how the linked stack looks after running a test driver like the one shown in Listing 5.3 on page 155. After pushing `"CARROTS"`, `"ORANGES"`, and `"RAISINS"` onto the stack, the invocation `stack.push("PICKLES")` executes the line

```
    top = new Node(object,top);
```

This invokes the `Node` constructor, passing the string element `"PICKLES"` and the current value of `top` to it. At that moment, `top` was a reference to the node containing `"RAISINS"`. Since the argument `top` is assigned to the constructor parameter `next`, the new node's `next` field gets that reference to the `"RAISINS"` node. After assigning the string `"PICKLES"` to the new node's `object` field, the constructor returns a reference to that new node. This reference is then assigned to `top`. The result is illustrated in Figure 5.12.

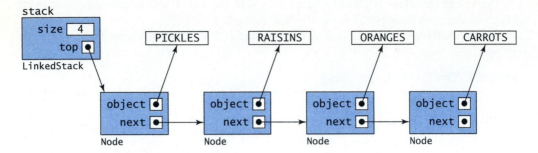

FIGURE 5.12 A linked implementation of the Stack interface.

LISTING 5.10: A LinkedStack **Class**

```
1   public class LinkedStack implements Stack {
2      private Node top;
3      private int size;
4
5      public boolean isEmpty() {
6         return (size == 0);
7      }
8
9      public Object peek() {
10        if (size == 0) throw new java.util.NoSuchElementException();
11        return top.object;
12     }
13
14     public Object pop() {
15        if (size == 0) throw new java.util.NoSuchElementException();
16        Object oldTop = top.object;
17        top = top.next;
18        --size;
19        return oldTop;
20     }
21
22     public void push(Object object) {
23        top = new Node(object,top);
24        ++size;
25     }
26
27     public int size() {
28        return size;
29     }
30
31     private static class Node {
32        Object object;
33        Node next;
34        Node(Object object, Node next) {
```

```
35          this.object = object;
36          this.next = next;
37        }
38     }
39  }
```

Note that the no-argument constructor is created automatically by the constructor, since there is no other constructor defined in the class.

Figure 5.13 shows how the pop() method works. First, assuming that the stack is non-empty, it saves at line 16 the item that is currently on the top of the stack in the local variable oldTop. Then, at line 17, it resets its top field to top.next, which will be the second node in

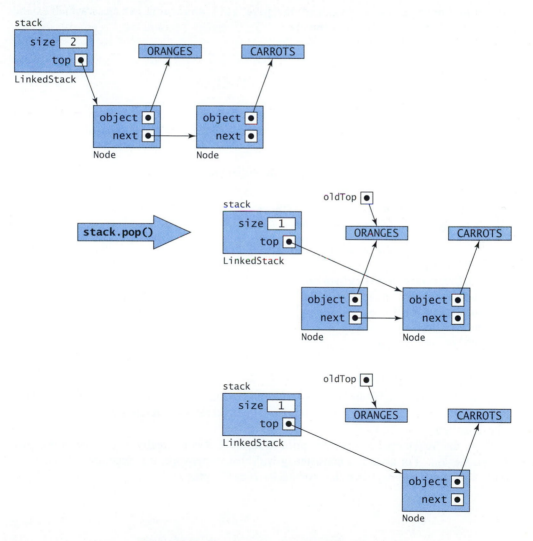

FIGURE 5.13 The effect of a call to the pop() method.

the list—the one that references CARROTS in the figure. Then it decrements the `size` field at line 18 and returns the `oldTop` reference at line 19.

The bottom picture in Figure 5.13 shows the ORANGES node missing. Since there are no more references to that object, it has been "garbage collected."[3] In Java, that means that it no longer exists; the memory space that it was using has been returned to the "general store" (also called the heap) to be used by other objects and variables.

5.6 The `java.util.Stack` Class

Java implements its own `Stack` class in the `java.util` package. It extends the `java.util.Vector` class, which extends the `java.util.AbstractList` class, which extends the `java.util.AbstractCollection` class.

```
Object
   └ AbstractCollection
       └ AbstractList
           └ Vector
               └ Stack
```

Listing 5.11 shows an outline of some of its members.

LISTING 5.11: The `java.util.Stack` Class

```
1   public class Stack extends Vector {
2       public Stack()
3       public boolean empty()
4       public Object peek()
5       public Object pop()
6       public Object push(Object object)
7       public int size()
8   }
```

These match nearly exactly our `Stack` interface in Listing 5.1 on page 152. The only significant difference is that the `java.util.Stack.push()` method returns a reference to the object that it pushes onto the stack.

Since the `Stack` class was written prior to Java 1.2, it is not really part of the Java Collections Framework. For complete consistency with that framework, it is recommended that you use the `java.util.ArrayList` class for stacks. (See Chapter 7.)

---

[3] More accurately, it has been designated as a candidate for garbage collection. We cannot be sure when that will occur.

CHAPTER SUMMARY

❏   Stacks are simple last-in-first-out (LIFO) data structures.

❏   The *Stack* ADT specifies four fundamental operations: *Peek*, *Pop*, *Push*, and *Size*.

❏   That ADT is translated into a Java interface that specifies four methods: `peek()`, `pop()`, `push(Object)`, `size()`.

❏   That Java interface is implemented with an array in the `ArrayStack` class in Listing 5.2 on page 154 and with a linked list in the `LinkedStack` class in Listing 5.10 on page 168.

❏   The `ArrayStack` implementation is applied in Section 5.3 on page 157 to simulate an RPN calculator that takes input in postfix notation.

❏   The `ArrayStack` implementation is applied again in Section 5.4 to solve a maze that takes input in postfix notation.

❏   The java util package includes a stock class that works the same way as our `ArrayStack` and `LinkedStack` classes.

REVIEW QUESTIONS

5.1   What does "LIFO" mean?

5.2   What is the difference between a stack and an array?

5.3   What is the difference between infix and postfix notation?

5.4   Why do computers handle postfix notation more easily than infix notation?

5.5   Why does the `switch` statement require `break` statements in the `move()` method but not in the `adjacent()` method of the `Location` class in Listing 5.8 on page 166?

5.6   What is the difference between the `ArrayStack` implementation and the `LinkedStack` implementation of the `Stack` interface?

5.7   When the exception is thrown at the end of the program in Listing 5.3 on page 155, how many elements are in the stack, and how many objects are in the array a[]?

5.8   Tell what is wrong with this external method to copy a stack:

```
LinkedStack copy(LinkedStack stack)
{ LinkedStack copy = new LinkedStack();
  while (!stack.isEmpty())
    copy.push(stack.pop());
  return copy;
}
```

EXERCISES

5.1   Trace the following code, showing the contents of the stack after each statement:

```
Stack stack = new ArrayStack();
stack.push("Monday");
stack.push("Tuesday");
stack.push("Wednesday");
stack.pop();
stack.pop();
stack.push("Thursday");
stack.push("Friday");
stack.pop();
stack.push("Saturday");
stack.push("Sunday");
stack.pop();
stack.pop();
```

5.2   Translate each of the following infix expressions into postfix:

a. $(x+4)-(y/(8+z))$
b. $x/((6/y)*(5-z))$
c. $(x/(2/y))*(7-z)$

5.3   Translate each of the following postfix expressions into infix:

a. $x\,4+y\,3-/z+$
b. $x\,9\,y+6\,z-*-$
c. $x\,3\,y\,2\,z////$

PROGRAMMING PROBLEMS

5.1   Write and test a class named `IntArrayStack` that is the same as the `ArrayStack` class in Listing 5.2 on page 154, except that it stores `int`s instead of `Object`s.

5.2   Write and test a class named `ArrayListStack` that implements the `Stack` interface in Listing 5.1 on page 152 by using a `java.util.ArrayList` to hold its objects.

5.3   Add and test a `toString()` method to the `ArrayStack` class.

5.4   Add and test a `toString()` method to the `LinkedStack` class.

5.5   Add and test an `equals()` method to the `ArrayStack` class.

5.6   Add and test an `equals()` method to the `LinkedStack` class.

5.7   Add and test a `toArray()` method to the `LinkedStack` class; it returns an array that contains the contents of the stack.

5.8   Add and test the following conversion method to the LinkedStack class; it returns the equivalent ArrayStack:

ArrayStack toArrayStack()

5.9   Add and test the following conversion method to the ArrayStack class; it returns the equivalent LinkedStack:

LinkedStack toLinkedStack()

5.10 Add and test a method for the LinkedStack class that returns a copy of the element that is second from the top, if it exists. Return null if it doesn't exist.

5.11 Add and test a method for the ArrayStack class that removes and returns the element that is second from the top, if it exists.

5.12 Add and test a method for the LinkedStack class that returns a copy of the element that is on the bottom, if it exists. Return null if it doesn't exist.

5.13 Add and test a method for the ArrayStack class that removes and returns the element that is on the bottom, if it exists.

5.14 Add and test a method for the LinkedStack class that reverses the order of the elements in the stack.

5.15 Write and test an external client method that removes and returns the second-from-top element from a given stack. Return null if there is no such element.

5.16 Write and test an external client method that uses local auxiliary stack(s) to remove and return the bottom element from a given stack.

5.17 Write and test an external client method that uses local auxiliary stack(s) to reverse a given stack.

5.18 Write and test an external client method that uses one or more local auxiliary stacks to return a new stack that has the same contents of a given stack, but in the opposite order, leaving the given stack in its original state.

5.19 Modify the ArrayStack implementation in Listing 5.2 on page 154 so that no two elements can be references to the same object. Hint: Change the push method.

5.20 Modify the ArrayStack implementation in Listing 5.2 on page 154 so that no element can be null.

5.21 Write Javadoc comments for the ArrayStack class in Listing 5.2 on page 154, and generate the resulting web page.

5.22 Write Javadoc comments for the LinkedStack class in Listing 5.10 on page 168, and generate the resulting web page.

5.23 Complete the SolveMaze class in Listing 5.5 on page 161.

5.24 Complete the constructor for the Maze class in Listing 5.6 on page 163, and write a test class. It should read all the numbers from the specified file and store them in the instance variables m, n, and a[][].

5.25 Complete the Rat.isOut() method in Listing 5.7 on page 164, and write a test class. It should return true if and only if this rat is in the final path position at $(n-1, m-2)$.

5.26 Complete the Location class in Listing 5.8 on page 166, and write a test class.

5.27   Follow the backtracking algorithm presented just before Listing 5.7, and complete the
SolveMaze class in Listing 5.5 on page 161. Use an `if...else if...` construct with
conditions like

```
if (rat.canMove(Direction.NORTH))  ...
```

5.28   Follow the backtracking algorithm presented just before Listing 5.7, and complete the
SolveMaze class in Listing 5.5 on page 161. Use a `for` loop like this:

```
for (int d=Direction.NORTH; d<=Direction.WEST; d++)
  if (rat.canMove(d))  ...
```

5.29   Generate your own maze, code it into a text file suitable for input into the SolveMaze
program, and then run the program to solve it.

5.30   Add some `println()` statements to the SolveMaze program to produce output that
shows the progress on each iteration of the main `while` loop.

PROJECTS

5.1   Write a program that does an empirical analysis of the run time of a stack's `push()` and
`pop()` methods. Generate n random integers, wrap each in an `Integer` object, and
store them all in a single array a. Then for each object x in the array, do one of the following. If x is positive, push it on the stack. If x is negative, discard it and pop the stack
unless it is empty. Record the time required to process the array (but not the time that it
took to build it). Print n and the time `time(n)`. Then encapsulate your program into a
method `test(n)` and run it for value of n = 1000, 2000, 4000, 8000, *etc.* to obtain
enough data to draw a conclusion.

5.2   Write a program that simulates a simple four-operand calculator by evaluating fully
parenthesized infix expressions that are input at the command line, like this:

```
A:\dswj\Chapter04>java Calculator "(88 - 33)*(44 + (55/7))"
(88 - 55)*(44 + 33/7) = 1607.57142857143
```

Note that to be read as a single string, the command line input must be wrapped in quo-
tation marks.

5.3   Build a graphics component to the solution of the maze problem (Section 5.3). Use the
`java.awt` packages or the `javax.swing` packages to provide graphical images of the
maze. For extra credit, add animation that shows the rat as it moves from cell-to-cell in
the maze.

5.4   Write a program that generates random mazes. Then add and test a predicate method
for the Maze class named `isSolvable()` that returns true if and only if the maze has at
least one solution. Use the SolveMaze program from Section 5.3. For extra credit, add
a method that uses empirical evidence to estimate the percentage of all random mazes
of a given size that are solvable.

5.5   Write a program that takes as input text that contains directions for getting to a friend's house. Each line should contain text in this form

`<direction-to-travel> <route-name>`

For example,

`"north on RT 511"`

indicates that the driver should travel north on Rt 511. Use a stack to produce instructions on how you should get back home from your friend's house. Use a `BufferedReader` object to read the original directions from a text file named `goingThere.txt` Your program should produce another text file named `comingBack.txt`
Here is a possible sample run which includes a printout of the stack containing the reverse trip instructions:

```
F:\chap05\project5>java ReturnTrip
stack containing reverse directions
   top -> east on Rt 150
          south on Rt 511
          east on Robious Rd
bottom -> south on Salisbury Rd
Compare two files:
"goingThere.txt" vs "comingBack.txt"

F:\chap05\project5>type going There.txt
north on Salisbury Rd
west on Robious Rd
north on Rt 511
west on Rt 150

F:\chap05\project5>type comingBack.txt
east on Rt 150
south on Rt 511
east on Robious Rd
south on Salisbury Rd
```

ANSWERS TO REVIEW QUESTIONS

5.1   The acronym "LIFO" stands for "last in, first out." It refers to the access protocol that characterizes stacks.

5.2   A stack is an abstract data type whose only specifications are *what* it can do: push(), pop(), size(), *etc*. An array is a concrete structure that is used to *implement* ADTs, thus defining *how* its operations are to work. The class `ArrayStack` uses an array to implement the `Stack` ADT (interface). A specific stack instance of the `ArrayStack` class (or any other class) could be used to implement other ADTs, but only if that implementation could be achieved using only the operations push(), pop(), size(), *etc*.

5.3   For algebraic expressions, infix notation places the operator in between its operands, like this: 2 + 3. Postfix notation places the operator after its operands, like this: 2 3 +.

5.4   Infix requires parentheses; postfix does not. For example, the average of two numbers x and y in infix is $(x + y)/2$. But in postfix, it's $x\ y + 2\ /$.

5.5   The `switch` statement requires `break`s statements in the `move()` method to avoid a fall through (*i.e.*, a cascade of executions of the succeeding statements in the `switch` block instead of just the one that belongs with the selected `case`). That can't happen in the `adjacent()` method because each `case` statement is a `return` statement.

5.6   The `ArrayStack` implementation uses an array, which has the disadvantage of having to be rebuilt when it gets full. The `LinkedStack` uses a list of linked `Node` objects, one for each element on the stack. This will be more efficient, performing each of its operations in $\Theta(1)$ time. The disadvantage, in general, of the linked structure is that it has no direct (indexed) access: getting to an arbitrary element in the list runs in $\Theta(n)$ time. But that's not an issue when implementing stacks because a stack is only allowed to access its top element anyway.

5.7   When the exception is thrown at the end of the program in Listing 5.3 on page 155, there are no elements in the stack and four objects are in the array a[].

5.8   The `copy()` method does not duplicate the objects that are "on" the given stack, it merely copies the references to them. The return stack object is not independent of the original. Worse, it destroys the original stack in the process.

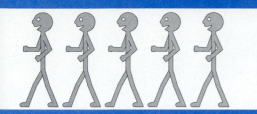

Chapter 6

Queues

The queue data structure is nearly the same as the stack data structure. But instead of inserting and deleting elements at the same end, a queue inserts at one end and deletes at the other. The analysis, implementations, and applications of queues in this chapter are similar to those for stacks in Chapter 5.

6.1 The Queue ADT

A *queue* (pronounced "cue") is a data structure that implements the first-in-first-out (FIFO) protocol. The only access points in the structure are at its ends where elements are inserted and removed. Insertions are always made at the back of the queue, and removals are always made at the front.

The queue data structure abstracts the notion of an ordinary waiting line, such as a line of people waiting to purchase admission tickets or a line of airplanes waiting on an airport runway to take off.

Here is a formal description of a queue as an abstract data type:

ADT: Queue

A *queue* is a collection of elements that maintains the FIFO access protocol.

Operations

1. *Add*: Insert a given element at the back of the queue.
2. *First*: If the queue is not empty, return the element that is at the front of the queue.
3. *Remove*: If the queue is not empty, delete and return the element that is at the front of the queue.
4. *Size*: Return the number of elements in the queue.

Figure 6.1 shows a UML diagram for the ***Queue*** ADT. It is translated into a Java interface in Listing 6.1.

```
<<interface>>
Queue
+add(object)
+first():object
+remove():object
+size():int
```

FIGURE 6.1   A Queue interface.

LISTING 6.1: **A** Queue **Interface**

```
1   /**
2    * The <code>Queue</code> interface specifies the basic operations
3    * of a first-in-first-out (FIFO) containers.
4    */
5   public interface Queue {
6
7       /**
8        * Adds the specified element to the back of this queue.
9        *
10       * @param object the element to be added to this queue.
11       */
12      public void add(Object object);
13
14      /**
15       * Returns the element at the front of this queue.
16       *
17       * @return the element at the front of this queue.
18       * @throws IllegalStateException if this queue is empty
19       */
20      public Object first();
21
22      /**
23       * Removes and returns the element at the front of this queue.
24       *
25       * @return the element at the front of this queue.
26       * @throws IllegalStateException if this queue is empty
27       */
28      public Object remove();
29
30      /**
31       * Returns the number of elements in this queue.
32       *
33       * @return the number of elements in this queue.
34       */
35      public int size();
36  }
```

Note the similarities between these specifications and those of stacks in Listing 5.1 on page 152. The only real difference, besides the names of the operations, is that queues add new elements at the opposite end from which they are accessed, while stacks add them at the same end.

The names add, first, remove, and size are used for most data structures in the Java Collections Framework. (See Chapter 7 and Appendix D.)

6.2 Case Study: Capital Gains Valuation

When a U. S. citizen sells some shares of common stock, he or she must pay federal tax on the net gain from each stock share. That capital gain is defined as the difference between the price at which the investor sells the stock and the price at which the investor bought it. That calculation is trivial if only one share is bought and sold: tax = rate × (priceSold – priceBought).

But a more common situation is one in which the investor buys and sells different amounts of the stock at different times. For example, suppose that an investor has this schedule:

Mar 15: buy 100 shares @$25/share.

Jun 10: sell 60 shares @$30/share.

Aug 20: buy 200 shares @$20/share.

Oct 25: sell 240 shares @$50/share.

How should the capital gains be computed? Which shares are sold at a profit of $5, which at $10, which at $25, and which at $30.

The standard accounting principle for computing capital gains is first-in-first-out (FIFO). Whenever a share is sold from a portfolio of shares that were bought at different times, one should assume that the share is taken from the group of shares that have been held the longest.

Solving the problem by hand is illustrated in Table 6.1. The 60 shares sold at $30 per share on June 10 are taken from the group that were bought at $25 per share on March 15. That leaves 40 shares from that group. So 40 of the 240 shares sold at $50 per share on October 25 were bought at $25 per share and the other 200 shares were bought at $20 per share on August 20. Thus, the capital gains from the 60 shares sold on June 10 are (60)($30–$25) = $300, the capital gains from the first 40 shares sold on October 25 are (40)($50–$25) = $1000, and the capital gains from the last 200 shares sold on October 25 are (200)($50–$20) = $6000.

This is a natural situation in which to use FIFO queues, one for the shares bought, and one for the shares sold. Each element of the "bought" queue is a block of shares that were bought at one time and at one price, and each element of the "sold" queue is a block of shares that were sold at one time.

Date	Shares	Sold at	Bought at	Gain
Jun 10	60	$30	$25	$300
Oct 25	40	$50	$25	$1000
Oct 25	200	$50	$20	$6000

TABLE 6.1   Capital gains valuation.

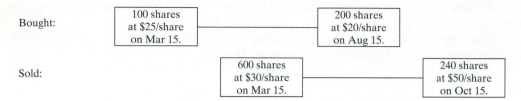

Bought:

| 100 shares at $25/share on Mar 15. | 200 shares at $20/share on Aug 15. |

Sold:

| 600 shares at $30/share on Mar 15. | 240 shares at $50/share on Oct 15. |

FIGURE 6.2   The two queues interleaved.

Thus, the solution to the capital gains problem consists of repeatedly removing equal numbers of shares from the front block of each queue and removing each front block itself when it is empty. The details are described in Algorithm 6.1.

▲ **ALGORITHM 6.1: Solution to the Capital Gains Problem**

1. Create a *Queue* named *bought*.
2. For each block of stocks bought, create a *Transaction* object that contains that data and *add*() it to the *bought* queue. Add these elements in the order in which their transactions occur.
3. Create another *Queue* named *sold*.
4. For each block of stocks sold, create a *Transaction* object that contains that data and *add*() it to the *sold* queue. Add these elements in the order in which their transactions occur.
5. Initialize an *integer* named *gains* to 0.
6. While both queues are nonempty, repeat steps 7–8.
7. Let *buy* = *bought.first*() and *sell* = *sold.first*().
8. If *buy.count* < *sell.count*, do steps 9–11; otherwise, do steps 12–14.
9. Add *buy.count**(sell.price − buy.price*) to *gains*.
10. *remove*() the first element from *bought*.
11. Reduce *sold.first().count* by *buy.count*.
12. Add *sell.count**(sell.price − buy.price*) to *gains*.
13. *remove*() the first element from *sold*.
14. If *buy.count* = *sell.count*, *remove*() the first element from *bought*; otherwise, reduce *bought.first().count* by *sell.count*.
15. Return *gains*.

Figure 6.3 shows a trace of the progress of the algorithm for the example described previously.

On the first iteration of the loop at steps 6–14, *buy.count* = 100 and *sell.count* = 60, so the condition at step 8 is false, and step 12 adds 60($30 − $25) = $300 to *gains*, making it $300. Then step 13 removes that first transaction from the *sold* queue, and step 14 reduces the *count* field of the first *bought* transaction by 60, making it 40.

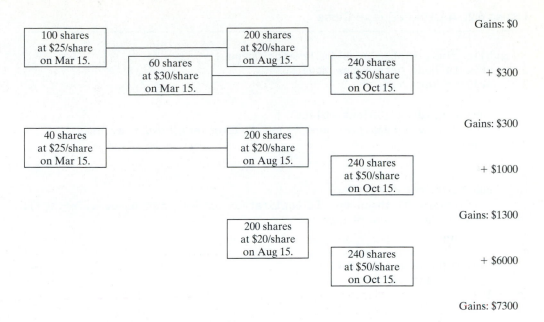

FIGURE 6.3   A trace of Algorithm 6.1.

On the second iteration, **buy.count** = 40 and **sell.count** = 200, so the condition at step 8 is true, and step 9 adds 40($50 − $25) = $1000 to **gains**, making it $1300. Then step 10 removes that first transaction from the **bought** queue, and step 11 reduces the **count** field of the first **sold** transaction by 40, making it 200.

On the third iteration, **buy.count** = 200 and **sell.count** = 200, so the condition at step 8 is false, and step 12 adds 200($50 − $20) = $6000 to **gains**, making it $7300. Then step 13 removes that first transaction from the **sold** queue, and step 14 removes that first transaction from the **bought** queue.

Now both queues are empty, so at step 6, the algorithm returns the **gains** value 7300.

Algorithm 6.1 is implemented in Project 6.1 on page 197.

6.3 A Linked Implementation

There are several ways to implement the Queue interface. One simple way is to use an array, as we did with the ArrayStack implementation of the Stack interface in Listing 5.2 on page 154. (See Programming Problem 6.1 on page 196.)

The simplest alternative to an array implementation is a linked implementation, given in Listing 6.2.

The linked implementation has two important advantages over the array implementation: It is faster, and it wastes no space. It is faster because the locations for insertion and removal are always the same—at the back and at the front. It wastes no space because removed nodes are deleted by the automatic garbage collector process.

LISTING 6.2: A LinkedQueue **Class**

```
1   public class LinkedQueue implements Queue {
2      private Node head = new Node(null);
3      private int size;
4
5      public void add(Object object) {
6         head.prev = head.prev.next = new Node(object,head.prev,head);
7         ++size;
8      }
9
10     public Object first() {
11        if (size==0) throw new IllegalStateException("the queue is empty");
12        return head.next.object;
13     }
14
15     public boolean isEmpty() {
16        return size==0;
17     }
18
19     public Object remove() {
20        if (size==0) throw new IllegalStateException("the queue is empty");
21        Object object=head.next.object;
22        head.next = head.next.next;
23        head.next.prev = head;
24        --size;
25        return object;
26     }
27
28     public int size() {
29        return size;
30     }
31
32     private static class Node {
33        Object object;
34        Node prev=this, next=this;
35
36        Node(Object object) {
37           this.object=object;
38        }
39
40        Node(Object object, Node prev, Node next) {
41           this.object=object;
42           this.prev=prev;
43           this.next=next;
44        }
45     }
46  }
```

Figure 6.4 shows how an instance of the LinkedQueue class looks after inserting the four strings "Sara", "John", "Andy", and "Mike". That is the detailed, implementor's view of the data structure. The simpler, client's view is shown in Figure 6.5.

This structure is actually a circular, doubly linked list with a dummy head node. The circularity eliminates any null link fields; the double links provide bidirectional navigation throughout the list, and the dummy head node allows simpler insertion and deletion algorithms.

The nested Node class in the LinkedQueue class has three fields: object, prev (for "previous"), and next. The object and next fields play the same role as in the LinkedStack class (Listing 5.10 on page 168). The prev field provides the second, reverse link for each node. Note how both link fields are initialized to this, which makes each new node link point to itself by default. This enforces the requirement that no link field be null.

The LinkedQueue class itself has only two fields: head and size. The head link always points to the dummy head node. That node is constructed by the one-argument Node constructor when the queue itself is constructed.

The add() method appends a new node containing the given object at the (right) end of the list. To do so requires setting four link fields: head.prev.next, head.prev, and both the prev and the next fields of the new node. The Node constructor sets both of its link fields: it sets its prev field to head.prev and its next field to head. Before the fourth ("Mike") node was inserted into the queue shown previously, the head.prev field pointed to the "Andy" node, and the head pointed to the "Sara" node. So the Node constructor assigned the new "Mike" node's prev link to the "Andy" node, and its next link to the "Sara" node. The Node constructor returns a reference to the new node. The add() method assigns that reference first to head.prev.next and then to head.prev. (Chained assignments are processed from right to left.)

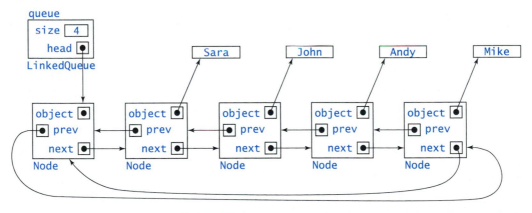

FIGURE 6.4 A linked implementation.

FIGURE 6.5 A client's view.

The `remove()` method removes the first data node from the list. That is the node that `head.next` points to. Its `object` field has to be returned by the method. In the view shown in Figure 6.4, that `object` would be the string `"Sara"`. Deleting the node is simply a matter of redirecting two links: `head.next.next.prev` and `head.next`. By resetting `head.next` to `head.next.next` first, we then need only set `head.next.prev` to `head`, because the first assignment changes the reference `head.next.next.prev` to `head.next.prev`.

The relationships among the queue interface, the `LinkedQueue` class, and the `Node` class are shown in the UML diagram in Figure 6.6.

6.4 Case Study: Simulation with Queues

There are many situations, both in computer systems and in the real world, in which queues are used to manage services performed by one entity for another. The entity performing the service is called the *server*, the entity receiving the service is called the *client*, and the context is called a *client/server system*. For example, when an Internet user clicks on a link, the user's computer is the client, requesting a web page from another computer, which is the server. That computer may immediately forward the request to another computer, in which case its role flips to being the client with respect to the next computer.

Consider the real-world example of cars arriving at a station of toll booths. Here, the clients are the cars and the servers are the toll booths (or their operators). Such a client/server system is pictured in Figure 6.7 with three toll booths, labeled A, B, and C. The cars are numbered. Cars 24, 21, and 22 are being served, while cars 25–28 are waiting in the queue.

A *simulation* is a model of a real-world phenomenon where each significant event has a counterpart in the model. An *object-oriented computer simulation* is a simulation in which the events are managed by objects. To obtain our solution, we have the following tasks:

1. Identify the objects.
2. Identify the events.
3. Derive the algorithms.
4. Implement the algorithms.
5. Define the interfaces for the objects.
6. Define other classes.

The objects are

❑   Clients (the cars).
❑   Servers (the toll booths).
❑   A queue.

The events are

❑   A *client* arrives at the queue.
❑   A *server* begins serving a client.
❑   A *server* finishes serving a client.

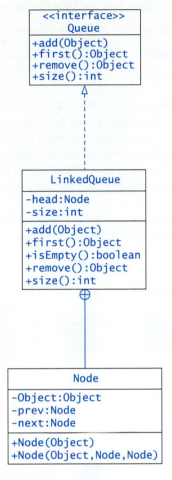

FIGURE 6.6 A queue implementation.

Algorithm 6.2 gives the steps leading up to solution.

▲ **ALGORITHM 6.2: Client/Server Simulation**

1. Repeat steps 2 and 6 for times $t = 0, 1, ...$

2. If t = time for next arrival, do steps 3-5.

3. Create a new **client**.

4. Add the **client** to the queue.

5. Set **time** for next arrival.

6. Repeat steps 7 and 8 for each server.

7. If *t* = *time* for the *server* to finish serving, have it stop.

8. If *server* is idle and the queue is not empty, do steps 9–10.

9. Remove *client* from the queue.

10. Tell *server* to start serving *client*.

This simulation is *time driven*; that is, it is controlled by a main loop (step 1) that iterates once for each tick of the clock. The actual elapsed time Δt represented by one iteration of the main loop is not important. For the toll booth example, it might be one minute; for a bank of computer printers serving a local area network, it might be one millisecond. The essential feature is for Δt to be small enough that nothing occurs between the clock ticks. With that assumption, we can use integer values instead of floating-point values for our time variable *t*. This is called *discrete time simulation*.

To define the interfaces for the objects, we have to determine what actions they have to perform. We do that by implementing Algorithm 6.2 in Listing 6.3.

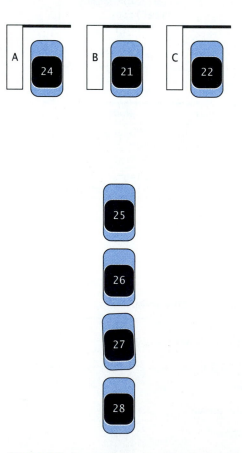

FIGURE 6.7   A queue of cars at a toll booth plaza.

LISTING 6.3: Client/Server Simulation

```
1   for (int t=0; ; t++) {                                    // step  1
2     if (t==nextArrivalTime) {                               // step  2
3       Client client = clients[i++] = new SimClient(i,t);    // step  3
4       queue.add(client);                                    // step  4
5       nextArrivalTime = t + randomArrival.nextInt();        // step  5
6     }
7     for (int j=0; j<numServers; j++) {                      // step  6
8       Server server = servers[j];
9       if (t==server.getStopTime()) server.stopServing(t);   // step  7
10      if (server.isIdle() && !queue.isEmpty()) {            // step  8
11        Client client = (SimClient)queue.remove();          // step  9
12        server.startServing(client,t);                      // step 10
13      }
14    }
15  }
```

We will store all servers in a `servers[]` array and all clients in a `clients[]` array. The number of servers and the number of clients will be read from the command line. The coded algorithm in Listing 6.3 assumes that the names of the server and client classes will be `SimServer` and `SimClient`.

From this implementation of the algorithm, we see that, in addition to client, server, and queue objects, we will need a random number generator. This can be instantiated from an extension of the `java.util.Random` class. Hence, because we already have an `ArrayQueue` class that we can use for the queue object, the only interfaces that we need are for the client objects and the server objects. These are given in Listings 6.4 through 6.6.

LISTING 6.4: An Interface for Servers

```
1   public interface Server {
2     public int getMeanServiceTime();
3     public int getStopTime();
4     public boolean isIdle();
5     public void startServing(Client client, int t);
6     public void stopServing(int t);
7   }
```

LISTING 6.5: An Interface for Clients

```
1   public interface Client {
2     public void setStartTime(int t);
3     public void setStopTime(int t);
4   }
```

```
1   public class SimServer implements Server {
2      private Client client;
3      private int id, meanServiceTime, stopTime=-1;
4      private java.util.Random random;
5
6      public SimServer(int id, int meanServiceTime) {
7         this.id = id;
8         this.meanServiceTime = meanServiceTime;
9         this.random = new ExponentialRandom(meanServiceTime);
10     }
11
12     public int getMeanServiceTime() {
13        return meanServiceTime;
14     }
15
16     public int getStopTime() {
17        return stopTime;
18     }
19
20     public boolean isIdle() {
21        return client==null;
22     }
23
24     public void startServing(Client client, int t) {
25        this.client = client;
26        this.client.setStartTime(t);
27        this.stopTime = t + random.nextInt();
28        System.out.println(this + " started serving " + client
29           + " at time " + t + " and will finish at time " + stopTime);
30     }
31
32     public void stopServing(int t) {
33        client.setStopTime(t);
34        System.out.println(this+ " stopped serving " + client
35           + " at time " + t);
36        client = null;
37     }
38
39     public String toString() {
40        String s="ABCDEFGHIJKLMNOPQRSTUVWXYZ";
41        return "Server " + s.charAt(id);
42     }
43  }
```

The SimServer class (for "simulated server") is implemented in Listing 6.6. An instance of the class is illustrated in Figure 6.8. The id field identifies the object. Its meanServiceTime field is initialized when the object is created. Its value is the average time that this server will spend serving a client. The stopTime field is the time when this server will finish serving its current client. The client and random fields are references to the current client object and the random number generator object that will generate this server's service times.

FIGURE 6.8 A SimServer object.

The SimServer constructor initializes the new object's id and meanServiceTime fields with the given values of its arguments. It then instantiates its random object as an instance of the ExponentialRandom class, passing that meanServiceTime value to is constructor.

The SimServer.startServing() method assigns the given client to be this server's client and passes the time value t to that client's setStartTime() method. That time value will be the current time, so this method assigns t + random.nextInt() to its stopTime field, thus using the random number returned by random.nextInt() as the service time for this current client. This method also prints one line of output, reporting that service has begun.

The SimServer.stopServing() method passes the time value t to its client's setStop-Time() method. Then it prints one line of output, reporting that service has ended, and it sets its client field to null, meaning that this server is now idle.

The other four methods of the SimServer class are self-evident: getter methods for meanServiceTime and stopTime fields, a predicate method reporting whether this server is idle, and a toString() method that reports this server's id as a letter ("A", "B", "C", etc.).

The SimClient class is implemented in Listing 6.7 on page 190. An instance is illustrated in Figure 6.9. The id field identifies the object. Its other three fields store the three transition times of its tenure in the system: when it arrived, when it started getting served, and when it finished.

The constructor and five methods of the SimClient class are self-evident.

Both the main Simulation class and the SimServer class require random numbers. These represent elapsed time intervals: the time between the arrivals of consecutive clients, and the time that a server spends serving a client. Experience and theoretical considerations suggest that, normally, the best distribution for these random time intervals is the *exponential distribution*. Its probability density function is $e^{-\alpha t}$, where the parameter α is the reciprocal of the expected time.

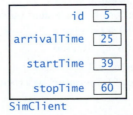

FIGURE 6.9 A SimClient object.

For example, if we specify an expected service time of 30, then the density function is $e^{-t/30}$. This means that the probability that the random number is between $t = a$ and $t = b$ is

$$P\{a \le t < b\} = e^{-a/30} - e^{-b/30}$$

For example, $P\{20 \le t < 40\} = e^{-(20)/30} - e^{-(40)/30} = 0.5134 - 0.2636 = 0.2498$ (*i.e.*, there is about a 25% chance that the time interval will be between 20 and 40).

LISTING 6.7: A Client Class

```
1   public class SimClient implements Client {
2       int id, arrivalTime=-1, startTime=-1, stopTime=-1;
3
4       public SimClient(int id, int t) {
5           this.id = id;
6           arrivalTime = t;
7           System.out.println(this + " arrived at time " + t);
8       }
9
10      public int getStartTime() {
11          return startTime;
12      }
13
14      public int getStopTime() {
15          return stopTime;
16      }
17
18      public void setStartTime(int t) {
19          startTime = t;
20      }
21
22      public void setStopTime(int t) {
23          stopTime = t;
24      }
25
26      public String toString() {
27          return "Client " + id;
28      }
29  }
```

To generate a distribution $F(x) = P\{t < x\}$ on a computer, we assume that u is uniformly distributed over the interval $0 \le u < 1$, where $u = F(x)$. We then solve this equation for $x = F^{-1}(u)$ and apply this inverse function to uniformly distributed random numbers. The exponential distribution is $u = F(t) = P\{t < x\} = P\{0 \le t < x\} = e^{-\alpha(0)} - e^{-\alpha(x)} = 1 - e^{-\alpha x}$. Its inverse is $x = -(1/\alpha)\ln(1 - u)$. So we use the following method:

```
public double nextDouble() {
    return -mean*Math.log(1.0-super.nextDouble());
}
```

This will be in an extension of the `java.util.Random` class, which has a `nextDouble()` method that returns random numbers that are uniformly distributed over the interval $0 \le u < 1$.

The ExponentialRandom class is shown in Listing 6.8. Its constructor uses the statement

```
super(System.currentTimeMillis());
```

to invoke the one-argument java.util.Random constructor, passing the current time that is returned by the System.currentTimeMillis() method. That method returns a long integer that equals the number of milliseconds elapsed since the end of 1969. That number changes every millisecond. The argument that is passed to the one-argument java.util.Random constructor is used to "seed" the random number generator. Passing different arguments ensures that different sequences of numbers will (almost certainly) be generated.

Our Simulation program uses the ExponentialRandom.nextInt() method, which returns the ceiling of (the least integer, not less than) the value returned by the nextDouble() method of the ExponentialRandom class, which returns exponentially distributed random numbers with the given mean value. The ceiling is used because we want only positive integers for our time intervals.

LISTING 6.8: A Random Number Class for Exponential Distributions

```
1   public class ExponentialRandom extends java.util.Random {
2     private double mean;
3
4     public ExponentialRandom(double mean) {
5       super(System.currentTimeMillis());
6       this.mean = mean;
7     }
8
9     public double nextDouble() {
10      return -mean*Math.log(1.0-super.nextDouble());
11    }
12
13    public int nextInt() {
14      return (int)Math.ceil(nextDouble());
15    }
16  }
```

The main class for our simulation program is shown in Listing 6.9 on page 193. It implements Algorithm 6.2 on page 185. Its data structures can be visualized as shown in Figure 6.10. This is the situation for the run shown in Listing 6.7 on page 190, which uses three servers (toll booths) and 20 clients (cars). It assumes that the average service time among all three servers is 30 seconds and that clients arrive, on average, every 5 seconds. That causes the queue to expand: after 75 seconds there are 10 clients waiting to be served.

The run shown in the output after Listing 6.9 can be viewed as shown in Figure 6.11 on page 192. It shows the locations of clients 1–10 during the first 100 seconds. The four possible locations are the queue (Q) and the three servers (A, B, and C). For example, client 5 arrives at time 25. At that time, all three servers are busy and one other client (4) queue is already waiting in the queue. So client 5 waits in the queue too. At time 39, server A finishes serving client 1, and client 5 is at the front of the queue (client 4 left the queue at time 28), so client 5 moves from the queue to server A (shown with a dotted arrow).

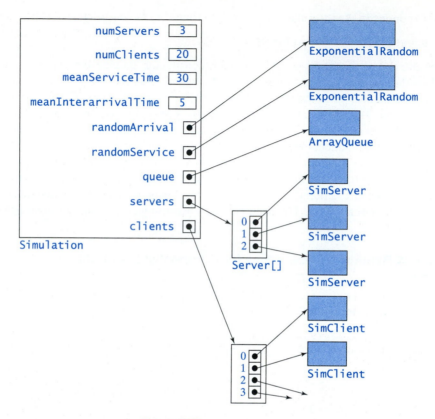

FIGURE 6.10   Simulation objects.

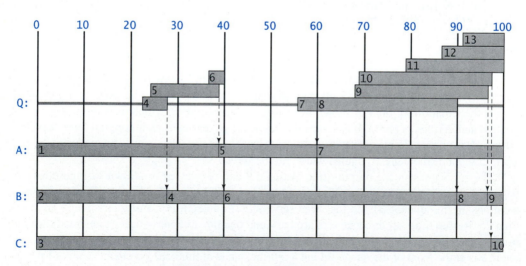

FIGURE 6.11   Arrivals and departures.

LISTING 6.9: A Simulation Class

```
1  public class Simulation {
2    static int numServers;
3    static int numClients;
4    static int meanServiceTime;
5    static int meanInterarrivalTime;
6    static Server[] servers;
7    static Client[] clients;
8    static Queue queue = new ArrayQueue();
9    static java.util.Random randomArrival;
10   static java.util.Random randomService;
11
12   public static void main(String[] args) {
13     init(args);
14     // See Listing 6.3 on page 187
15   }
16
17   static void init(String[] args) {
18     if (args.length<4) {
19       System.out.println("Usage: java Simulation <numServers> "
20         + "<numClients> <meanServiceTime> <meanInterarrivalTime>");
21       System.out.println(" e.g.: java Simulation 3 100 12 4");
22       System.exit(0);
23     }
24     numServers = Integer.parseInt(args[0]);
25     numClients = Integer.parseInt(args[1]);
26     meanServiceTime = Integer.parseInt(args[2]);
27     meanInterarrivalTime = Integer.parseInt(args[3]);
28     servers = new Server[numServers];
29     clients = new Client[numClients];
30     randomService = new ExponentialRandom(meanServiceTime);
31     randomArrival = new ExponentialRandom(meanInterarrivalTime);
32     queue = new ArrayQueue();
33     for (int j=0; j<numServers; j++)
34       servers[j] = new SimServer(j,randomService.nextInt());
35     System.out.println("      Number of servers = " + numServers);
36     System.out.println("      Number of clients = " + numClients);
37     System.out.println("     Mean service time = " + meanServiceTime);
38     System.out.println("Mean interarrival time = "
39       + meanInterarrivalTime);
40     for (int j=0; j<numServers; j++)
41       System.out.println("Mean service time for " + servers[j]
42         + " = "+ servers[j].getMeanServiceTime());
43   }
44 }
```

The output looks like this:

```
Number of servers = 3
Number of clients = 20
Mean service time = 30
```

```
Mean interarrival time = 5
Mean service time for Server A = 34
Mean service time for Server B = 19
Mean service time for Server C = 78
Client 1 arrived at time 0
The queue has 1 clients
The queue has 0 clients
Server A started serving Client 1 at time 0 and will finish at time 39
Client 2 arrived at time 6
The queue has 1 clients
The queue has 0 clients
Server B started serving Client 2 at time 6 and will finish at time 28
Client 3 arrived at time 10
The queue has 1 clients
The queue has 0 clients
Server C started serving Client 3 at time 10 and will finish at time 98
Client 4 arrived at time 23
The queue has 1 clients
Client 5 arrived at time 25
The queue has 2 clients
Server B stopped serving Client 2 at time 28
The queue has 1 clients
Server B started serving Client 4 at time 28 and will finish at time 40
Client 6 arrived at time 37
The queue has 2 clients
Server A stopped serving Client 1 at time 39
The queue has 1 clients
Server A started serving Client 5 at time 39 and will finish at time 60
Server B stopped serving Client 4 at time 40
The queue has 0 clients
Server B started serving Client 6 at time 40 and will finish at time 90
Client 7 arrived at time 56
The queue has 1 clients
Client 8 arrived at time 60
The queue has 2 clients
Server A stopped serving Client 5 at time 60
The queue has 1 clients
Server A started serving Client 7 at time 60 and will finish at time 149
Client 9 arrived at time 68
The queue has 2 clients
Client 10 arrived at time 71
The queue has 3 clients
```

Simulating queueing systems like this can help us understand the system and how it might be made more efficient. For example, this analysis suggests that it might be worthwhile to add a fourth server. Such changes can be simulated before a decision is made about changing the real world system. (See, for example, Project 6.2 on page 198.)

Finally, note how the development of the solution was partitioned into six separate stages. In a larger project, these separate stages could be done by separate teams of developers.

CHAPTER SUMMARY

❏   Queues are simple first-in-first-out (FIFO) data structures.
❏   The *Queue* ADT specifies four fundamental operations: *Add*, *First*, *Remove*, and *Size*.
❏   The Queue ADT is translated into a Java interface that specifies four methods: `add(Object)`,
     `first()`, `remove()`, `size()`.
❏   The Java interface is implemented with a linked list in the `LinkedQueue` class in Listing 6.2
     on page 182.
❏   It can also be implemented as an `ArrayQueue` class (see Programming Problem 6.1 on
     page 196) and by extending the `java.util.ArrayList` class.
❏   The solution to the capital gains problem uses a queue to process interleaved buys and sales
     of stock shares.
❏   A client/server simulation is also implemented using queues.

REVIEW QUESTIONS

6.1   What does "FIFO" mean?

6.2   Would it make sense to call a queue a "LILO" structure?

6.3   What is the difference between a queue and a stack?

6.4   What is the difference between a queue and an array?

6.5   What is the purpose in initializing both `Node` fields as
         `Node prev=this, next=this;`
         in the `LinkedQueue` class in Listing 6.2 on page 182?

EXERCISES

6.1   Trace the following code, showing the contents of the `queue` after each statement:

```
Queue queue = new ArrayQueue();
queue.add("DE");
queue.add("PA");
queue.add("NJ");
queue.remove();
queue.remove();
queue.add("GA");
queue.add("CT");
queue.remove();
queue.add("MA");
queue.add("MD");
```

```
queue.remove();
queue.remove();
```

6.2   Explain why the permuted statement

```
head.prev.next = head.prev = new Node(object,head.prev,head);
```

would not work in place of the first statement in the `add()` method of the `LinkedQueue` class in Listing 6.2 on page 182.

6.3   Do a hand calculation to determine the capital gains that result from this series of transactions:

> Feb 20: buy 200 shares @$20/share.
> Apr 15: sell 100 shares @$22/share.
> Jun 25: buy 150 shares @$25/share.
> Aug 10: buy 250 shares @$24/share.
> Sep 20: sell 300 shares @$28/share.
> Nov 15: sell 200 shares @$32/share.

6.4   Explain how you could implement the `Queue` interface using only two stacks, instead of an array or any other structure. What would be the run-time complexity classes for the `add()` and `remove()` methods?

PROGRAMMING PROBLEMS

6.1   Implement the `Queue` interface (Listing 6.1 on page 178) with a class named `ArrayQueue` that is similar to the `ArrayStack` class defined in Listing 5.2 on page 154. Then write and run a test driver for the class.

6.2   Write Javadoc comments for the `ArrayQueue` class from Problem 6.1, and generate the resulting web page.

6.3   Write Javadoc comments for the `LinkedQueue` class in Listing 6.2 on page 182, and generate the resulting web page.

6.4   Write and test a class named `ArrayListQueue` that implements the `Queue` interface in Listing 6.1 on page 178 by using a `java.util.ArrayList` to hold its objects.

6.5   Use a queue to compute the capital gains that result from the series of transactions given in Exercise 6.3 on page 196.

6.6   Modify the `Simulation` program so that it provides the following statistical information about the simulation: the average time that a client waits in the queue, the average time each server takes to serve a client, the average service time among all servers, and the average total time (waiting + service) that a client spends in the system.

6.7   Add and test a `toString()` method for the `LinkedQueue` class.

6.8   Add and test a `equals()` method for the `LinkedQueue` class.

6.9   Add and test a `clone()` method for the `LinkedQueue` class.

6.10   Add and test a `toArray()` method for the `LinkedQueue` class; it returns an array that contains the contents of the queue.

6.11   Add and test the conversion method

`ArrayQueue toArrayQueue()`

for the `LinkedQueue` class. The method returns the equivalent `ArrayQueue`.

6.12   Add and test a method for the `LinkedQueue` class that returns a copy of the element that is second from the front, if it exists.

6.13   Add and test a method for the `LinkedQueue` class that removes and returns the element that is second from the front, if it exists.

6.14   Add and test a method for the `LinkedQueue` class that returns a copy of the element that is last, if it exists.

6.15   Add and test a method for the `LinkedQueue` class that reverses the order of the elements in the queue.

6.16   Write and test an external method that removes and returns a copy of the second element from a given queue.

6.17   Write and test an external method that uses a local auxiliary stack to remove and return the last element from a given queue.

6.18   Write and test an external method that uses a local auxiliary stack to reverse a given queue.

6.19   Write and test an external method that uses a local auxiliary stack to return a new queue that has the same contents of a given queue, but in the opposite order, leaving the given queue in its original state.

PROJECTS

6.1   Implement and test Algorithm 6.1 on page 180. You can use the `LinkedQueue` class in Listing 6.2 on page 182 or the `ArrayQueue` class from Problem 6.1 on page 196. Alternatively, you can extend the `java.util.ArrayList` to an implementation of the `Queue` interface. Use the `Transaction` class shown in Figure 6.12 to define objects to be stored in the queues. Load your `bought` and `sold` queues from data stored in external files.

Transaction
+count:int
+price:int
+date:Date

FIGURE 6.12   A Transaction class.

6.2   Modify the Simulation program so that it provides strategic data for making decisions about how many servers to provide. The program should allow the user to compare statistical results (see Programming Problem 6.6 on page 196) using various numbers of servers.

6.3   Implement and test a RingQueue class. A *ring* is an array that "wraps around" its ends so that a[0] follows a[n-1], where n == a.length. So the add() method can work when back == a.length without resizing the array as long a front > 1. The resize() method needs to be called only when back-front+1 is a multiple of a.length. Note that after every call to add(), back must still index an unused cell.

6.4   A *deque* (pronounced "deck") is a double-ended queue, allowing insertions and removals from both its front and back. Give an ADT together with a UML diagram for deques. Then define a Deque interface, implement it with a doubly linked structure named LinkedDeque, and write and run a test driver for it.

ANSWERS TO REVIEW QUESTIONS

6.1   The acronym "FIFO" stands for "first in, first out." It refers to the access protocol that characterizes queues.

6.2   Yes; "last in, "last out" is also true of the elements in a queue. But that phrase does not really define the queue property, because it does not specify how to implement the *remove* operation.

6.3   The difference between a queue and a stack is their access points. A stack is a LIFO structure in which both insertion and removal are at the same end. A queue is a FIFO structure with insertion at one end and removal at the other.

6.4   The difference between a queue and an array is really the same as the difference between a stack and an array. (See the answer to Question 5.2 on page 175.) A queue is an abstract data type whose only specifications are *what* it can do: add(), first(), remove(), *etc*. An array is a concrete structure that is used to *implement* ADTs, thus defining *how* its operations are to work. The class ArrayQueue uses an array to implement the Queue ADT (interface).

6.5   Initializing both Node fields to this in the LinkedQueue makes both links point to the node itself by default.

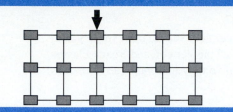

The greatest university of all is a collection of books.

— Thomas Carlyle (1795 - 1881)

Chapter 7

Collections

A *collection* is a general data structure that maintains its elements for efficient access. For example, stacks, queues, lists, sets, and tables are different kinds of collections.

7.1 The Java Collections Framework

The `java.util` package defines a family of interfaces and classes for various types of collections. This family is called the *Java Collections Framework*. Its inheritance hierarchy is shown in Figure 7.1. The classes are shown on the left, and the interfaces that they implement are shown in italics on the right. The implementations are marked by dashed lines. For example, the `TreeMap` class extends the `AbstractMap` class and implements the `SortedMap` interface.

The outline in Figure 7.1 shows the Java Collections Framework as of version 1.4 of Java. More classes and interfaces might be added in the future. The `LinkedHashSet` and `LinkedHashMap` classes were added with version 1.4. The framework itself was added with version 1.2. Prior to that,

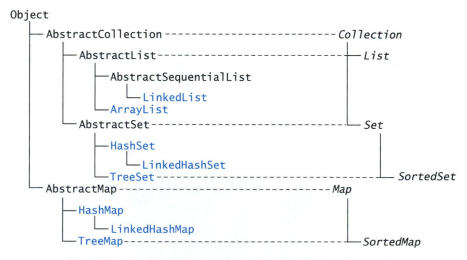

FIGURE 7.1   The inheritance hierarchy for the Java Collections Framework.

developers used four other classes in the java.util package: Vector, Stack, Dictionary, and Hashtable. Those classes are now regarded as "legacy classes," the Vector and Stack classes having been superseded by the ArrayList class, and the Dictionary and Hashtable classes by the HashMap class.

7.2 A Simple Collection Interface

Before examining the complete java.util.Collection interface, we consider the pared-down version shown in Figure 7.2 that specifies only 7 of its 15 methods. Listing 7.1 implements the interface.

LISTING 7.1: A Collection Interface

```
1   public interface Collection {
2      public boolean   add(Object object);
3      public void      clear();
4      public boolean   contains(Object object);
5      public boolean   isEmpty();
6      public Iterator  iterator();
7      public boolean   remove(Object object);
8      public int       size();
9   }
```

The add() method at line 2 has the postcondition that its given object be an element of the collection. If the collection allows duplicate elements, then the given object will be added to it, thus increasing its size. If the collection does not allow duplicate elements (*e.g.*, if it is a set), then the given object will be added only if it is not already an element. In any case, the method returns true if and only if it changes the contents of the collection.

The clear() method at line 3 removes every element from the collection. Its postcondition is that the collection's size is 0.

The contains() method at line 4 returns true to indicate that the referenced object is a member of the collection. More specifically, that means that the collection includes a reference x such that either both object and x are null or x.equals(object) is true.

Keep in mind that a collection's elements are references, some of which may be null, and several of which may refer to the same object. We can visualize a general collection as shown in Figure 7.3. The picture shows a collection c of size 10, containing four null references. Three

```
            <<interface>>
             Collection
  +add(Object):boolean
  +clear()
  +contains(Object):boolean
  +isEmpty():boolean
  +iterator():Iterator
  +remove(Object):boolean
  +size():int
```

FIGURE 7.2 The Collection interface.

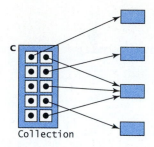

FIGURE 7.3   A collection of size 10.

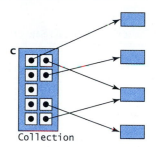

FIGURE 7.4   A collection of size 9.

of its other six references are equal; they refer to the same object. The call `c.contains(object)` would return `true` for only five different values of the given `object` reference: either `null` or one of the four distinct objects indicated.

The `isEmpty()` method at line 5 of Listing 7.1 returns `true` if and only if the collection has size 0.

The `iterator()` method at line 6 returns a `java.util.Iterator` object that is poised to traverse the collection. Iterators are described in detail in the next section.

The `remove(object)` method at line 7 removes one occurrence of the given object if the collection contains it. Like the `add(object)` method, the `remove(object)` returns `true` if and only if it changes the collection. For example, if x refers to the third of the four objects pictured in Figure 7.3, then the call `c.remove(x)` would change c to look like the picture in Figure 7.4, removing one of its references to that object. Note that this collection now has five references to objects and four `null` references. A call to `c.size()` would return 9.

7.3 Iterators

An *iterator* is an object that acts like a cursor or pointer, moving about on a data structure, locating individual elements for access. The `iterator()` method in the `Collection` interface returns an `Iterator` object that "iterates" through the collection, much like the way an index iterates through an array.

We can visualize an iterator named `it` traversing a collection named c as shown in Figure 7.5. At any moment, the iterator locates a unique element of the collection. Its methods then provide access to that element.

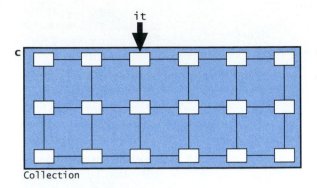

FIGURE 7.5 An iterator locating an element of a collection.

Figure 7.6 shows a simple `Iterator` interface. Its Java code is given in Listing 7.2.

LISTING 7.2: An `Iterator` **Interface**

```
1  public interface Iterator {
2     public boolean hasNext();
3     public Object next();
4     public void remove();
5  }
```

The `hasNext()` method returns `true` if and only if the `next()` method can be invoked successfully. If so, then the next call to the iterator's `next()` method will return the element that it is currently locating.

The `next()` method does two things: It returns a reference to the element that the iterator currently locates, and it advances the iterator to the next element in the collection. The order in which the iterator visits the elements is determined by the iterator itself.

The `remove()` method works only after a separate call to the `next()` method. It removes that element that was returned by the last call to `next()`.

The `Iterator` object is initialized at the beginning of the collection when it is first returned by the `iterator()` method. For example, the code

```
for (Iterator it = c.iterator(); it.hasNext(); ) {
    Object obj=it.next();   // returns current element and advances
    // do something with object
}
```

```
         <<interface>>
           Iterator
+hasNext():boolean
+next():Object
+remove()
```

FIGURE 7.6 An `Iterator` interface.

uses the Iterator object it to traverse the Collection object c. The object is initialized by the call c.iterator() to the first element in the collection. On each iteration of the for loop, it uses its next() method to assign a reference to the next element to the variable obj. The loop continues until the call it.hasNext() returns false, which will be after the last element has been accessed.

That code is analogous to traversing an array with a for loop:

```
for (int i = 0; i < a.length; i++) {
  Object object = a[i];
  // do something with object
}
```

Used this way, the iterator object it is analogous to the array index i. The expression it.hasNext() is analogous to the expression i < a.length, which evaluates to true unless the end of the array has been reached.

Note that the iterator's for loop has no explicit update expression: The third part of the for loop control mechanism is empty. Thus, the following is perhaps a better analogy:

```
for (int i = 0; i < a.length; ) {
  Object object = a[i++];
  // do something with object
}
```

The expression it.next() is analogous to the expression a[i++]. Each does two things: It returns the current element, and it advances to the next element.

Note that "hasNext" really means that the next call to the next() method will return a reference. That reference may be null (if null was added to the collection), but at least it won't throw an exception. The message that the collection "has a next object" is a message to the client that it can access another element from the collection. This is consistent with the use of the word "next" in other classes in the java.util package, such as in the nextInt() and nextToken() methods in the Random and StringTokenizer classes, respectively.

Iterators are similar to array indexes. But there are some important differences. Unlike an array index that provides direct access into the array, an iterator provides only *sequential access*. One can access the 73rd element of an array directly with the expression a[72]. But to access the 73rd element of a collection with an iterator requires a sequence of 72 iterations of a loop like the one previously shown.

7.4 An AbstractCollection Class

One of the primary objectives of object-oriented programming (OOP) is to reduce code redundancy. Less redundancy means simpler, more manageable code that is easier to understand, debug, and maintain. Redundancy is reduced by coalescing similar classes into an abstract superclass whose code replaces its subclasses' redundant code.

You can see from the outline in Figure 7.1 on page 199 that each of the interfaces Collection, List, Set, and Map in the Java Collections Framework is implemented directly by an abstract class. For example, AbstractSet is an abstract class which implements the Set interface. The purpose of each of these abstract classes is to encapsulate all the executable code for a general

```
AbstractSet -----------------Set
     ├─ HashSet
     │      └─ LinkedHashSet
     └─ TreeSet
```

FIGURE 7.7 The Set classes.

implementation of the interface that can be compiled independently of any particular backing data structure.

For example, the Set interface has three different concrete implementations: HashSet, LinkedHashSet, and TreeSet. (See Figure 7.7.) The HashSet class uses a hash table for its backing structure; the TreeSet uses a binary search tree. The common code for these two classes that is independent of their backing structures is inherited from the AbstractSet class. It must be an abstract class because it has to omit the code that depends on the backing structure.

Thus, abstract classes reduce code redundancy, thereby rendering the framework simpler and more manageable. Another advantage is that they provide a substantial foundation for programmers to define their own implementations. For example, you might decide to implement the Set interface with a class named GraphSet that stores its elements in a graph data structure. You could do that by extending the AbstractSet class, leaving relatively little extra code to be added.

Before examining the complete java.util.AbstractCollection class, we first present a simpler version. The UML diagram in Figure 7.8 shows an AbstractCollection class that is an abstract implementation of the Collection interface given in Listing 7.1 on page 200. This class is abstract because it has two abstract methods: iterator() and size().[1] Since it is abstract, it cannot be instantiated directly, and so it has no fields (no data storage). Its Java code is shown in Listing 7.3.

The AbstractCollection defers the iterator() and size() methods by declaring them abstract. It defers the add() method by defining its body to be a block that merely throws an UnsupportedOperationException. The advantage of throwing an exception instead of declaring it abstract is that, as a concrete method, it can be invoked by other concrete methods. But it can still be overridden by subclasses, providing complete code that depends upon the backing data structure.

```
┌─────────────────────────────────┐
│       AbstractCollection        │
├─────────────────────────────────┤
│ +AbstractCollection()           │
│ +add(Object):boolean            │
│ +clear()                        │
│ +contains(Object):boolean       │
│ +isEmpty():boolean              │
│ +iterator():iterator            │
│ +remove(Object):boolean         │
│ +size():int                     │
│ +toString():String              │
└─────────────────────────────────┘
```

FIGURE 7.8 An AbstractCollection class.

---

[1] In UML, abstract methods are shown in italics.

LISTING 7.3: An AbstractCollection **Class**

```
1   public abstract class AbstractCollection implements Collection {
2     protected AbstractCollection() {
3     }
4
5     public boolean add(Object object) {
6       throw new UnsupportedOperationException();
7     }
8
9     public void clear() {
10      for (Iterator it = iterator(); it.hasNext(); ) {
11        it.next();
12        it.remove();
13      }
14    }
15
16    public boolean contains(Object object)
17      // See Problem Listing 7.12 on page 219
18
19    public boolean isEmpty() {
20      return (size() == 0);
21    }
22
23    public abstract Iterator iterator();
24
25    public boolean remove(Object object) {
26      Iterator it=iterator();
27      if (object == null)
28        while (it.hasNext()) {
29          if (it.next() == null) {
30            it.remove();
31            return true;
32          }
33        }
34      else
35        while (it.hasNext())
36          if (object.equals(it.next())) {
37            it.remove();
38            return true;
39          }
40      return false;
41    }
42
43    public abstract int size();
44
45    public String toString() {
46      if (isEmpty()) return "[]";
47      Iterator it = iterator();
```

```
48      StringBuffer buf = new StringBuffer("[" + it.next());
49      while (it.hasNext())
50        buf.append(", " + it.next());
51      return (buf + "]");
52    }
53  }
```

In addition to the seven methods specified by the Collection interface, this class also defines a protected no-argument constructor and a toString() method. The constructor is declared to be protected because it is meant to be used only by extensions (subclasses) of the AbstractCollection class. This is because an abstract class cannot be instantiated, since some of its methods may be abstract and thus would not be executable. But concrete (*i.e.*, nonabstract) extensions would have all the code necessary to execute any of its methods, so they should be allowed to instantiate the class.

Most of the concrete methods use an iterator to do their jobs. Here is the spirit of OOP at work. Without any information about how the iterator() method will be implemented, we are still able to use it in other concrete methods. The clear() method uses an iterator at line 10 to traverse the collection, deleting each element with the iterator's remove() method (yet to be implemented). The contains() method uses an iterator to traverse the collection, searching sequentially for the given object. The remove() method does the same thing, and if it finds the object, it uses the iterator's remove() method to delete it at lines 30 and 37. The toString() method uses an iterator to traverse the collection, accumulating the string to be returned.

7.5 An ArrayCollection Class

The AbstractCollection class leaves only three methods that have to be overridden by its subclasses:

```
add(object)
iterator()
size()
```

These comprise the unfinished part of the implementation of the Collection interface that depends upon the specific data structure used to store the collection's elements. We will implement two concrete extensions of our AbstractCollection class: an ArrayCollection class, and a LinkedCollection class. This hierarchy is shown in Figure 7.9.

The simplest data structure to use to store the collection's elements is an array. So the first concrete implementation that we define is an ArrayCollection class, shown in Listing 7.4. It uses an array data structure to complete the implementation of the Collection interface, similar to the way the ArrayStack class implemented the Stack interface in Chapter 5 and the way

```
AbstractCollection ----------Collection
        ├── ArrayCollection
        └── LinkedCollection
```

FIGURE 7.9 Two different implementations.

the ArrayQueue class implemented the Queue interface in Chapter 6. Instances of the ArrayCollection class are unsorted collections that allow duplicate elements. This kind of data structure is called a *bag* or *multiset*.

LISTING 7.4: An ArrayCollection Class

```
1   public class ArrayCollection extends AbstractCollection {
2       private final int INITIAL_LENGTH = 16;
3       private int size;
4       private Object[] a = new Object[INITIAL_LENGTH];
5
6       public boolean add(Object object) {
7           if (size == a.length) resize();
8           a[size++] = object;
9           return true;   // no object is rejected
10      }
11
12      public Iterator iterator() {
13          return new LocalIterator();
14      }
15
16      public int size() {
17          return size;
18      }
19
20      protected void resize() {
21          Object[] aa = new Object[2*a.length];
22          System.arraycopy(a, 0, aa, 0, size);
23          a = aa;
24      }
25
26      private class LocalIterator implements Iterator {   // inner class
27          private int i = 0;   // index of current element
28          private boolean okToRemove=false;
29
30          public boolean hasNext() {
31              return (i < size);
32          }
33          public Object next() {
34              if (i == size) throw new RuntimeException();
35              okToRemove = true;
36              return a[i++];
37          }
38          public void remove() {
39              if (!okToRemove) throw new IllegalStateException();
40              a[--i] = a[--size];
41              a[size] = null;
42              okToRemove = false;   // must call next() again before remove()
43          }
44      }
45  }
```

The add() method at line 6 first determines whether the backing array is full. If it is, then the resize() method is invoked. It creates a new backing array that is twice as long as the current one, copies all the element references into it, and then assigns it to the backing array a[] at line 23. Then at line 8, the given object is simply added to the end of the sequence of elements that are already in the collection.

The iterator() method at line 12 is required by the AbstractCollection interface to return an Iterator object that can traverse the collection, providing access to its elements. It does this by constructing and returning a LocalIterator object from the inner class defined at lines 26–44. This inner class implements the Iterator interface, defining the following three methods:

```
public boolean hasNext()
public Object next()
public void remove()
```

Since this extension of the AbstractCollection class uses an array to store its elements, it uses an index i for the iterator to locate its current element. The iterator is initialized at the first element of the collection by setting i=0 at line 27. The hasNext() method at line 30 simply returns the boolean expression i<size, because that's precisely the condition that determines whether the iterator has any more elements to visit. The next() method at line 33 returns a[i], which is the current element. Note that it uses the post-increment operation i++ to advance the cursor to the next element. The remove() method at line 38 is required to delete that last element returned by the next() method. That would be a[i-1]. It uses the predecrement operation --i at line 40 to access the preceding element and to set its location as the current one. The actual deletion is achieved by replacing that element with the last element in the list: a[size-1]. The predecrement operation --size provides the right element and resets size to the right value. The element a[size] is set to null at line 41 so that the object to which it referred can be garbage collected if no other references to it exist.

The LocalIterator class also defines a boolean field named okToRemove at line 28. This is used to enforce the requirement that the remove() method be called only immediately after next() has been called. That means that remove() should not be called until after next() has been called at least once. The next() method must be called at least once between any two calls to remove(). This is ensured by the code that controls the okToRemove flag. If remove() is called when the flag is false, an IllegalStateException is thrown, thus aborting the call. The flag is set true only in the next() method, at line 35, and each call to remove() resets it to false. In computer science, such a flag is called a *semaphore*.

Note that the condition (i == size) generates a RuntimeException in the next() method at line 34. That should never happen, because next() should be called only immediately after hasNext() returns true.

The implementation in Listing 7.4 uses the non-static nested class LocalIterator to implement the Iterator interface and construct the Iterator object that the iterator method is required to return. This nested class must be non-static because it has to access the non-static fields (size and a) of its encompassing ArrayCollection class. A non-static nested class is called an *inner class*.

In Java, inner classes like this are usually defined to be *anonymous* (*i.e.*, nameless). To do this, we place the entire body block of the inner class (the highlighted lines 26–44 in Listing 7.4) immediately in front of the semicolon that terminates the `return` statement at line 13. Then we change the name of the `LocalIterator()` constructor to `Iterator()`, using the name of the interface that is being implemented. Listing 7.5 is a revision of Listing 7.4.

LISTING 7.5: Using an Anonymous Inner Class

```
1   public class ArrayCollection extends AbstractCollection {
2     private final int INITIAL_LENGTH = 16;
3     private int size;
4     private Object[] a = new Object[INITIAL_LENGTH];
5
6     public boolean add(Object object) {
7       if (size == a.length) resize();
8       a[size++] = object;
9       return true;  // no object is rejected
10    }
11
12    public Iterator iterator() {
13      return new Iterator() {    // anonymous inner class
14        private int i = 0;   // index of current element
15        private boolean okToRemove = false;
16        public boolean hasNext() {
17          return (i < size);
18        }
19        public Object next() {
20          if (i == size) throw new RuntimeException();
21          okToRemove = true;
22          return a[i++];
23        }
24        public void remove() {
25          if (!okToRemove) throw new IllegalStateException();
26          a[--i] = a[--size];
27          a[size] = null;
28          okToRemove = false;   // must call next() again before remove()
29        }
30      };   // note the required semicolon, ending the return statement
31    }
32
33    public int size() {
34      return size;
35    }
36
37    protected void resize() {
38      Object[] aa = new Object[2*a.length];
39      System.arraycopy(a, 0, aa, 0, size);
40      a = aa;
41    }
42  }
```

The body block of the anonymous inner class is highlighted in lines 13–30. This is the same code that is highlighted in Listing 7.4 on page 207. It is now all part of the `return` statement that begins on line 13, which is why it is followed by the semicolon on line 30.

Note that line 13 now appears to be invoking an "interface constructor":

```
13          return new Iterator() {      // anonymous inner class
```

The identifier "`Iterator`" is the name of an interface, not a class. But we know that interfaces do not have constructors, because they do not have any executable code. In this special Java syntax for anonymous inner classes, the interface name is used this way for two purposes: (1) to indicate which interface is being implemented by the anonymous class; and (2) to show that the anonymous class no-argument constructor is being invoked.

LISTING 7.6: Testing the `ArrayCollection` **Class**

```
1   public class TestArrayCollection {
2     public static void main(String[] args) {
3       String[] strings = {"CH", "JP", "IN", "ID", "AU", "NZ"};
4       Collection bag = new ArrayCollection();
5       for (int i = 0; i < strings.length; i++)
6         bag.add(strings[i]);
7       System.out.println(bag);
8       bag.add("JP");
9       bag.add("TH");
10      System.out.println(bag);
11      for (Iterator it = bag.iterator(); it.hasNext(); )
12        System.out.print(it.next() + " ");
13      System.out.println();
14      if (bag.remove("KR")) System.out.println(bag);
15      else System.out.println("\"KR\" not found");
16      if (bag.remove("JP")) System.out.println(bag);
17      else System.out.println("\"JP\" not found");
18      Iterator it=bag.iterator();
19      it.next();
20      it.next();
21      it.remove();
22      System.out.println(bag);
23      it.next();
24      it.next();
25      it.next();
26      it.remove();
27      System.out.println(bag);
28    }
29  }
```

The output is

```
[CH, JP, IN, ID, AU, NZ]
[CH, JP, IN, ID, AU, NZ, JP, TH]
CH JP IN ID AU NZ JP TH
"KR" not found
[CH, TH, IN, ID, AU, NZ, JP]
```

```
[CH, JP, IN, ID, AU, NZ]
[CH, JP, IN, NZ, AU]
```

The ArrayCollection class is tested in Listing 7.6. We use a for loop at line 5 to load an array of six strings into a collection named bag, shown in Figure 7.10. Then the toString() method is invoked implicitly by the println() method at line 7, checking the contents of bag. Two more string references are added next and then checked. Note the string "JP" now occurs twice in bag.

The iterator() method is tested in a separate for loop at line 11, passing it.next() to the println() method on each iteration. Then the remove() method is tested at line 14 by attempting to remove "KR" which is not in the collection, and "JP" which occurs twice. Note that the first occurrence of "JP" is removed and replaced by the last element "TH".

Finally, the remove() method of the Iterator interface is tested at line 21. The first call removes the second element, "TH", since next() was called twice. The second call at line 26 removes the element, "ID", since next() was called three more times, advancing the iterator past "TH", "IN", and "ID".

7.6 A LinkedCollection Class

Just as with our Stack interface in Chapter 5 and our Queue interface in Chapter 6, our Collection interface can be implemented with a linked data structure as well as with an array. This is done in Listing 7.7. Compare this implementation with the ArrayCollection in Listing 7.5.

The LinkedCollection class is nearly the same as the LinkedQueue class in Listing 6.2 on page 182. It uses doubly linked Node objects that form a circular list with a special dummy head node to simplify the insertion and deletion operations.

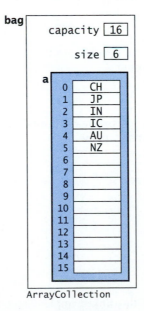

FIGURE 7.10 An ArrayCollection object.

Like the ArrayCollection class, this extension of the AbstractCollection class needs to implement only the three methods add(), iterator(), and size(). The add() method works the same way as the add() method in the LinkedQueue class in Listing 6.2.

LISTING 7.7: A LinkedCollection **Class**

```
 1  public class LinkedCollection extends AbstractCollection {
 2    private static class Node {
 3      Object object;
 4      Node prev, next;
 5      Node() { prev = next = this; }
 6      Node(Object o, Node p, Node n) { object=o; prev=p; next=n; }
 7    }
 8    private int size;
 9    private Node head = new Node();   // dummy head node
10
11    public boolean add(Object object) {
12      head.prev = head.prev.next = new Node(object,head.prev,head);
13      ++size;
14      return true;   // no object is rejected
15    }
16
17    public Iterator iterator() {
18      return new Iterator() {     // anonymous inner class
19        private Node cursor=head.next;   // current element node
20        private boolean okToRemove=false;
21        public boolean hasNext() { return cursor!=head; }
22        public Object next() {
23          if (cursor == head) throw new RuntimeException();
24          okToRemove = true;
25          Object object = cursor.object;
26          cursor = cursor.next;
27          return object;
28        }
29        public void remove() {
30          if (!okToRemove) throw new IllegalStateException();
31          cursor.prev = cursor.prev.prev;
32          cursor.prev.next = cursor;
33          --size;
34          okToRemove = false;   // must call next() again before remove()
35        }
36      };
37    }
38    public int size() {
39      return size;
40    }
41  }
```

The iterator() method for this linked implementation is completely analogous to the iterator() method for the array implementation in Listing 7.5 on page 209. It returns an

Iterator object that can traverse the collection. The object is created by invoking the anonymous constructor that is defined by the anonymous inner class at line 18. That Iterator class maintains an instance variable named cursor that refers to the iterator's current node. This variable serves the same purpose as the variable i in the array implementation's Iterator class. The end of the collection is reached when the cursor has reached the dummy head node, so the hasNext() method simply returns the value of the boolean expression cursor!=head. The next() method advances the cursor to the next node and returns the object in the node that the cursor previously located.

The remove() method at line 29 removes the last element that was returned by next(). It does that by deleting the node that is previous to the cursor. Like the remove() method in the LinkedQueue class, this requires resetting only two links, as shown in the before-and-after picture in Figure 7.11.

The LinkedCollection class is tested in Listing 7.8. This test driver is essentially the same as that in Listing 7.6, which tests the ArrayCollection class.

The remove() method in the LinkedCollection class is implemented differently than the remove() method in the ArrayCollection class. In the array implementation, an element is removed by replacing it with the last element of the array. In the linked implementation, the element is removed by resetting two links, leaving the rest of the collection unchanged, as shown in Figures 7.11 and 7.12. This difference is evident by comparing the output in Listing 7.6 with that in Listing 7.8. In the ArrayCollection, the first occurrence of JP is removed by overwriting it with the last element TH, as shown in Figure 7.13.

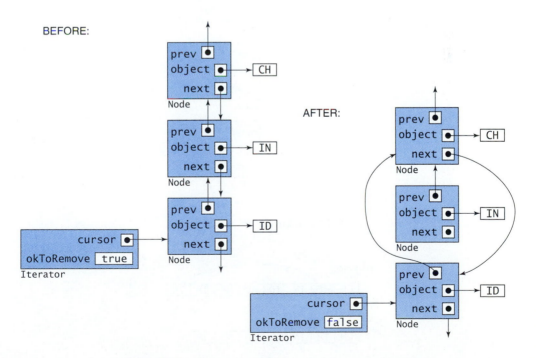

FIGURE 7.11 Removing IN from the LinkedCollection object.

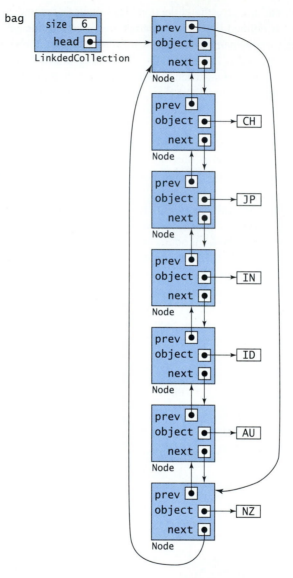

FIGURE 7.12   A LinkedCollection object.

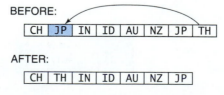

FIGURE 7.13   An ArrayCollection removal.

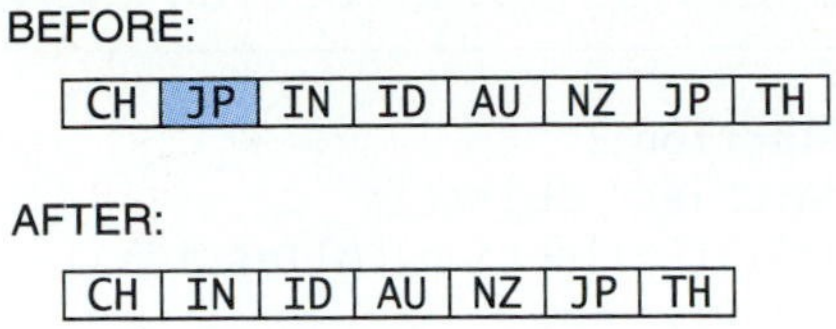

BEFORE:

| CH | JP | IN | ID | AU | NZ | JP | TH |

AFTER:

| CH | IN | ID | AU | NZ | JP | TH |

FIGURE 7.14 A LinkedCollection removal.

In the LinkedCollection, the first occurrence of JP is removed directly by deleting it, as shown in Figure 7.14.

Note that if the collection is empty, then a call to remove() will throw an IllegalStateException at line 30 in Listing 7.7 on page 212 because the okToRemove flag will be false. The only way it can be true is by the next() method setting it true, and that cannot happen when the collection is empty, because the next() method cannot reach line 24 when cursor == head.

LISTING 7.8: Testing the LinkedCollection Class

```
1   public class TestLinkedCollection {
2     public static void main(String[] args) {
3       String[] strings = {"CH", "JP", "IN", "ID", "AU", "NZ"};
4       Collection bag = new LinkedCollection();
5       // insert lines 5-29 of Listing 7.6 on page 210 here
```

The output is

```
[CH, JP, IN, ID, AU, NZ]
[CH, JP, IN, ID, AU, NZ, JP, TH]
CH JP IN ID AU NZ JP TH
"KR" not found
[CH, IN, ID, AU, NZ, JP, TH]
[CH, ID, AU, NZ, JP, TH]
[CH, ID, AU, JP, TH]
```

This test driver has the same effect as the tester in Listing 7.6 on page 210. When bag.remove("KR") is called at line 14, the remove() method of the AbstractCollection class is invoked at line 25 of Listing 7.3 on page 205. Since this bag is instantiated as a Linked-Collection object (at line 4 of Listing 7.8), the it.remove() call at line 30 in Listing 7.3 calls the iterator remove() method of the LinkedCollection class at line 29 of Listing 7.7 on page 212. In the tester in Listing 7.6, the same bag.remove("KR") call invoked the iterator's remove() method at line 24 of Listing 7.5 on page 209 instead, because that bag was an instance of the LinkedCollection class.

7.7 The Complete java.util.Collection Interface

All the methods specified in our Collection interface in Listing 7.1 on page 200 are taken from the Collection interface that is defined in the java.util package, shown in Listing 7.9.

LISTING 7.9: **The Complete** `java.util.Collection` **Interface**

```
1   public interface Collection {
2       public boolean  add(Object object);
3       public boolean  addAll(Collection collection);
4       public void     clear();
5       public boolean  contains(Object object);
6       public boolean  containsAll(Collection collection);
7       public boolean  equals(Object object);
8       public int      hashCode();
9       public boolean  isEmpty();
10      public Iterator iterator();
11      public boolean  remove(Object object);
12      public boolean  removeAll(Collection collection);
13      public boolean  retainAll(Collection collection);
14      public int      size();
15      public Object[] toArray();
16      public Object[] toArray(Object[] objects);
17  }
```

The `equals()` and `hashCode()` methods are listed to suggest that they should be defined differently from the `Object` class versions that they inherit.

The four methods that take a `Collection` argument apply the action to every element in the given `collection`. The call `addAll(y)` will add every element of the collection y, the call `removeAll(y)` will remove every element of the collection y, the call `retainAll(y)` will remove every element except those that are in the collection y, and the call `containsAll(y)` will return true if and only if the collection y is a subset. These four methods implement the fundamental operations for mathematical sets:

Method	Set Operation	Symbolic
`x.addAll(y)`	union	$x = x \cup y$
`x.contains(y)`	subset	$x \supseteq y$
`x.removeAll(y)`	relative complement	$x = x - y$
`x.retainAll(y)`	intersection	$x = x \cap y$

For example, if x represents the set $x = \{A, B, C, D, E\}$ and y represents the set $y = \{A, E, I, O, U\}$, then after the invocation `x.retainAll(y)`, x would represent the set $x \cap y = \{A, E\}$.

Listing 7.10 shows a test program for the `java.util.Collection` interface. It uses the `java.util.ArrayList` implementation.

The two `toArray()` methods return an array of references to the collection's elements. The no-argument version returns a generic array of type `Object[]`. The `toArray(objects)` version returns an array of the same type as the given `objects` array. If that given array is big enough, it returns it after replacing its first *n* elements with references to the collection's elements and setting its *n*th element to null, where *n* is the size of the collection. Otherwise, the method returns a new array of size *n* containing references to the collection's elements.

LISTING 7.10: Testing the java.util.Collection **Interface**

```
1   import java.util.*;   // includes the Collections Framework
2
3   public class TestCollection {
4     public static void main(String[] args) {
5       String[] strings = {"CA", "US", "MX", "AR", "BR", "CH"};
6       println(strings);
7       ArrayList list = new ArrayList(Arrays.asList(strings));
8       System.out.println(list);
9       list.add("VE");                System.out.println(list);
10      ArrayList list2 =
11        new ArrayList(Arrays.asList(new String[] {"MX", "HN", "GT"}));
12      System.out.println(list2);
13      list.addAll(list2);            System.out.println(list);
14      list.remove("MX");             System.out.println(list);
15      System.out.println("list.containsAll(list2) = "
16        + list.containsAll(list2));
17      list.remove("HN");             System.out.println(list);
18      System.out.println("list.containsAll(list2) = "
19        + list.containsAll(list2));
20      list.removeAll(list2);         System.out.println(list);
21      ArrayList list3 =
22        new ArrayList(Arrays.asList(new String[] {"BR", "US", "PE"}));
23      System.out.println(list3);
24      list.retainAll(list3);
25      System.out.println(list);
26      list.toArray(strings);
27      println(strings);
28    }
29
30    public static void println(String[] a) {
31      System.out.print("{" + a[0]);
32      for (int i = 1; i < a.length; i++)
33        System.out.print("," + a[i]);
34      System.out.println("}");
35    }
36  }
```

The output is

```
{CA,US,MX,AR,BR,CH}
[CA, US, MX, AR, BR, CH]
[CA, US, MX, AR, BR, CH, VE]
[MX, HN, GT]
[CA, US, MX, AR, BR, CH, VE, MX, HN, GT]
[CA, US, AR, BR, CH, VE, MX, HN, GT]
list.containsAll(list2) = true
```

```
[CA, US, AR, BR, CH, VE, MX, GT]
list.containsAll(list2) = false
[CA, US, AR, BR, CH, VE]
[BR, US, PE]
[US, BR]
{US,BR,null,AR,BR,CH}
```

7.8 The java.util.AbstractCollection Class

As the outline in Figure 7.1 on page 199 shows, the java.util package defines an AbstractCollection class to implement its Collection interface. As with our smaller AbstractCollection class (Listing 7.3 on page 205), the purpose of this abstract class is to include all the method definitions that are independent of the actual data structure used to store the elements.

LISTING 7.11: **The Complete** java.util.AbstractCollection **Class**

```
1   public abstract class AbstractCollection implements Collection {
2       protected AbstractCollection() { }
3       public boolean add(Object object) {
4           throw new UnsupportedOperationException();
5       }
6       public boolean addAll(Collection collection)  // See Problem 7.11
7       public void clear()  // See Problem 7.12
8       public boolean contains(Object object)  // See Listing 7.12
9       public boolean containsAll(Collection collection)  //See Problem 7.13
10      public boolean isEmpty() { return (size() == 0); }
11      public abstract Iterator iterator();
12      public boolean remove(Object object)  // See Listing 7.3 on page 205
13      public boolean removeAll(Collection collection)  // See Listing 7.13
14      public boolean retainAll(Collection collection)  // See Problem 7.14
15      public abstract int size();
16      public Object[] toArray()  // See Problem 7.15
17      public Object[] toArray(Object[] objects)  // See Listing 7.14
18      public String toString()  // See Listing 7.3 on page 205
19  }
```

This java.util.AbstractCollection class includes the eight methods that we defined in our "home-grown" AbstractCollection class in Listing 7.3 on page 205. But by specifying that it implements Collection, this version is also required to include the other seven methods that are listed in the java.util.Collections interface (Listing 7.9 on page 216).

Note that, like all classes, this class inherits default versions of the equals() and hashCode() methods. Also note that only the iterator() and size() methods are declared abstract. The add() method is meant to be overridden by subclasses. All the other methods can be implemented using the size() and add() methods and the Iterator methods (hasNext(), next(), and remove()). Those are the only methods that depend directly upon the actual storage structures used by the implementation.

LISTING 7.12: The `AbstractCollection.contains(Object)` **Method**

```
1  public boolean contains(Object object) {
2    Iterator it = iterator();
3    if (object == null)
4      while (it.hasNext()) {
5        if (it.next() == null) return true;
6      }
7    else
8      while (it.hasNext())
9        if (object.equals(it.next())) return true;
10   return false;
11 }
```

The `contains(object)` method is shown in Listing 7.12. Since general collections may include `null` elements, we separate that case from the non-`null` case. In both cases, we iterate through the collection and return true as soon as the given `object` equals one of the elements. This is the $\Theta(n)$ sequential search algorithm. We cannot return `false` until every element has been checked (*i.e.*, until the loop has finished iterating).

The `removeAll(collection)` method illustrates the use of an iterator's `remove()` method. It is shown in Listing 7.13. As the iterator traverses `this` collection, the given `collection`'s `contains()` method is invoked on the iterator's current element. If that element is contained in the given `collection`, then the iterator removes it from `this` collection.

LISTING 7.13: The `AbstractCollection.removeAll(Collection)` **Method**

```
1  public boolean removeAll(Collection collection) {
2    boolean modified = false;
3    for (Iterator it = iterator(); it.hasNext(); )
4      if (collection.contains(it.next())) {
5        it.remove();
6        modified = true;
7      }
8    return modified;
9  }
```

A call to the `removeAll(collection)` method can be visualized like the picture shown in Figure 7.15 on page 220. Here, the iterator `it` is locating the element `"MX"` in `this` collection. Since the specified `collection` also contains `"MX"`, it will be removed from `this` collection. Remember that the `Collection` elements are really only references to external objects.

The `toArray(Object[])` method is shown in Listing 7.14. Its actions depend upon whether the given `objects` array is large enough to hold all the references in `this` collection. If not, then the given `objects` array has to be reallocated. But that new array must have the same type as the given `objects` array, so its allocation is managed by the four statements inside the `if` block (lines 4–7).

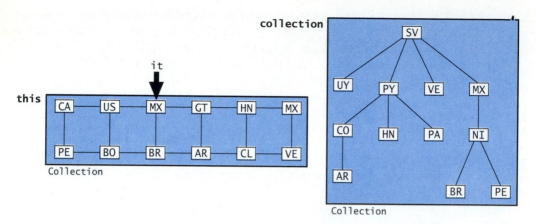

FIGURE 7.15 An iterator implementing the call `removeAll(collection)`.

LISTING 7.14: **The** `AbstractCollection.toArray(Object[])` **Method**

```
1   public Object[] toArray(Object[] objects) {
2     int n = size();
3     if (objects.length<n) {
4       Class objectsType = objects.getClass();
5       Class componentType = objectsType.getComponentType();
6       Object x = java.lang.reflect.Array.newInstance(componentType,n);
7       objects = (Object[])x;
8     }
9     Iterator it=iterator();
10    for (int i = 0; i < n; i++)
11      objects[i] = it.next();
12    if (objects.length>n) objects[n] = null;
13    return objects;
14  }
```

The statement at line 7 assigns to `objects` a new array of length n whose component type is the same as the array that was passed to that method. For example, if that component happens to be `String`, then the effect of line 7 is the same as this:

```
objects = new String[n];
```

However, if the name of the component type is not known at compile time, we have to use some special methods to extract it from the `objects` parameter. These methods are known as *reflection* methods[2] and are defined in the `java.lang.Class` class and the `java.lang.reflect.Array` class.

---

[2] The term "reflection" is used because, the object uses those methods to get information about itself, much as we gain information about ourselves when we look in a mirror.

The statement at line 4 declares a reference named `objectsType` that refers to the unique `Class` object that represents the `objects` array's type.[3] Similarly, the statement at line 5 declares a reference named `componentType` that refers to the unique `Class` object that represents the `objects` components' type. For example, if the given `objects` array happened to have been defined to have type `String[]`, then `objectsType` would refer to the unique `Class` object that represents the type `String[]`, and `componentType` would refer to the unique `Class` object that represents the type `String`.

The statement at line 6 declares x to be an array of length n whose elements have type `componentType`. So as an object, x has the same type as the `objects` object passed to this method, except that x has length n. Thus x is the right type for holding all the elements of this collection. But this method returns an object of type `Object[]`. So `objects` is cast as type `Object[]` at line 7.

After ensuring that the `objects` array is large enough to hold the n references that are in this collection, we use an iterator at lines 10–11 to copy those references into the `objects` array.

Finally, if it exists, the element that follows those n elements is set to `null` to mark the end of the segment that was changed. Note that this marking may be futile if any of the other elements of either array were already `null`.

The `java.util.AbstractCollection` class is a partial implementation of the `java.util.Collection` interface, defining as many methods as possible without specifying the data structure used to store the elements. As the outline in Figure 7.1 on page 199 shows, this `abstract` class has several specific extensions that use various data structures. We shall examine these in the chapters that follow.

CHAPTER SUMMARY

❏ The Java Collections Framework is a family of interfaces and classes defined in the `java.util` package. These allow most data structures to be implemented in a consistent manner by extending them with little extra code.

❏ Our `Collection` interface defined in Listing 7.1 on page 200 is a simplified version of the `java.util.Collection` interface. Its `AbstractCollection` implementation is defined in Listing 7.3 on page 205, with concrete extensions defined as `ArrayCollection` on Listing 7.6 on page 210 and `LinkedCollection` on Listing 7.7 on page 212.

❏ Iterators allow the traversal of a collection, like an index on an array. But unlike an array index, an iterator provides only sequential access.

❏ The `Iterator` interface defined in Listing 7.2 on page 202 is the same as the `java.util.Iterator` interface. It defines the three fundamental iterator methods `hasNext()`, `next()`, and `remove()`.

❏ An `abstract` class is used to consolidate all the code that is independent of the backing structure. It is then extended by concrete subclasses that use specific data structures to hold their data.

---

[3] In Java, each type is represented by a unique object of type `Class`. The `getClass()` method that is defined in the `Object` class can be used on any object x to obtain a reference to the unique `Class` object that represents that x's type. These `Class` objects are constructed automatically by the Java Virtual Machine as classes are loaded.

```
AbstractCollection----------Collection
          ├─ ArrayCollection
          └─ LinkedCollection
```

FIGURE 7.16 Our `Collection` Framework.

❑ Our `AbstractCollection` in Listing 7.3 on page 205 is a partial implementation of our `Collection` interface. It defines all the methods that can be defined without specifying the data structure used to store the elements.

❑ Our `ArrayCollection` in Listing 7.4 on page 207 completes the implementation using an array to store the elements.

❑ Our `LinkedCollection` in Listing 7.7 on page 212 completes the implementation using a linked list to store the elements.

❑ Our `Collection` interface and its `AbstractCollection` implementation, shown in Figure 7.16, are part of the corresponding `Collection` interface and its `AbstractCollection` implementation that are defined in the `java.util` package. That package defines these nine extensions of the `AbstractCollection` class.

❑ The Java Collections Framework defines interfaces for three general kinds of containers: List, Set, and Map. Each of these three has two or three kinds of concrete implementations, as shown in Table 7.1. One kind uses links: either a linked list data structure or a tree data structure. One kind uses contiguous storage: either a simple array or a hash table. The other kind uses a hash table with an embedded linked list.

Data Structure	List	Set	Map
linked	LinkedList	TreeSet	TreeMap
contiguous	ArrayList	HashSet	HashMap
contiguous with links		LinkedHashSet	LinkedHashMap

TABLE 7.1   Concrete `Collection` classes of the JCF.

REVIEW QUESTIONS

7.1   What is a collection?

7.2   What is the Java Collections Framework?

7.3   What is an iterator?

7.4   Can an element of a collection be `null`?

7.5   Can a collection have several distinct elements that are equal?

7.6   True or false: `add(x)` returns `true` if and only if it increases the collection's size by 1.

7.7   True or false: `remove(x)` returns `true` if and only if it decreases the collection's size by 1.

7.8   Why are the `iterator()` and `size()` methods declared to be `abstract` in the definition of the `AbstractCollection` class?

7.9   What is the difference between the `remove(object)` method declared in the `Collection` interface and the `remove()` method declared in the `Iterator` interface?

7.10   If x and y are `Collections`, what is the difference between `x.addAll(y)` and `x.add(y)`?

7.11   Why bother with `abstract` methods? For example, why not simply omit the `iterator()` and `size()` methods altogether from the `AbstractCollection` class?

7.12   Why does the `add()` method in the `AbstractCollection` class throw an exception instead of implementing its code directly?

7.13   Why does the `add()` method in the `AbstractCollection` class throw an exception instead of being declared `abstract` like the `iterator()` and `size()` methods?

7.14   Why does the `AbstractCollection` class define a `protected` constructor?

7.15   Why can't an `abstract` class be instantiated?

7.16   What is an inner class?

7.17   What is an anonymous inner class?

7.18   What is an anonymous constructor?

7.19   How is an iterator's `next()` method constrained by its `hasNext()` method?

7.20   How is an iterator's `remove()` method constrained by its `next()` method?

7.21   What is the purpose of the okToRemove flag in the iterator classes?

7.22   What is a semaphore?

EXERCISES

7.1   In the program in Listing 7.6 on page 210, what would the output be if lines 8–27 were replaced by the following code:

```
Iterator it=bag.iterator();
it.next();
it.remove();
System.out.println(bag);
it.next();
it.next();
it.remove();
System.out.println(bag);
it.next();
it.next();
it.next();
it.remove();
System.out.println(bag);
```

7.2   Predict the output from this program, and then run it to check your prediction:

```java
import java.util.*;
public class TestCollection {
  public static void main(String[] args) {
    String[] data = {"CA", "US", "MX", "AR", "BR", "CH"};
    List list = new ArrayList();
    list.addAll(Arrays.asList(data));
    System.out.println(list);
    List sublist = list.subList(2,5);
    System.out.println(sublist);
    list.set(3, "CO");
    System.out.println(list);
    System.out.println(sublist);
    sublist.set(2, "VE");
    System.out.println(list);
    System.out.println(sublist);
  }
}
```

7.3   Predict the output from this program, and then run it to check your prediction:

```java
import java.util.*;
public class TestCollection {
  public static void main(String[] args) {
    String[] data = {"CA", "US", "MX", "AR", "BR", "CH"};
    List list = new ArrayList();
    list.addAll(Arrays.asList(data));
    System.out.println(list);
    System.out.println(list.remove(3));
    System.out.println(list);
    list.removeAll(Arrays.asList(new String[] {"CA", "AR", "VE"}));
    System.out.println(list);
    list.retainAll(Arrays.asList(new String[] {"BR", "US", "VE"}));
    System.out.println(list);
  }
}
```

7.4   Predict the output from this program, and then run it to check your prediction:

```java
import java.util.*;
public class TestCollection {
  public static void main(String[] args) {
    String[] data = {"CA", "US", "MX", "AR", "BR", "CH"};
    List list = Arrays.asList(data);
    System.out.println(list);
    data[3] = "CO";
    System.out.println(list);
    data[2] = null;
    System.out.println(list);
  }
}
```

7.5   Predict the output from this program, and then run it to check your prediction:

```java
import java.util.*;
public class TestCollection {
  public static void main(String[] args) {
    String[] data = {"CA", "US", "MX", "AR", "BR", "CH"};
    List list = new ArrayList();
    list.addAll(Arrays.asList(data));
    System.out.println(list);
    Iterator it=list.iterator();
    it.next();
    it.next();
    it.remove();
    System.out.println(list);
    it.next();
    it.remove();
    System.out.println(list);
    it.next();
    it.next();
    it.next();
    it.remove();
    System.out.println(list);
  }
}
```

7.6   Hand trace the program shown below.

a. What is the effect of lines 7-8?

b. What will be returned by the call to toStr(list) on line 10?

c. How do lines 11-13 change list?

d. How do lines 16-18 change list?

e. Predict all output from the program.

```java
1  import java.util.*;
2  public class Main {
3    public static void main(String[] args){
4      ArrayList list = new ArrayList() ;
5      System.out.println("initial size is " + list.size());
6      System.out.println( toStr(list) ) ;
7      for ( int i = 0; i < 5 ; i++ )
8        list.add( new Integer( 10*i ) ) ;
9      System.out.println("**current size is " + list.size());
10     System.out.println( toStr(list) ) ;
11     list.add( 0, new Integer( -80 ) ) ;
12     list.add( 2, new Integer( -70 ) ) ;
13     list.add( 4, new Integer( -60 ) ) ;
14     System.out.println("****current size is " + list.size());
15     System.out.println( toStr(list) ) ;
16     System.out.println("removing " + list.remove(1)) ;
17     System.out.println("removing " + list.remove(4)) ;
18     System.out.println("removing " + list.remove(5)) ;
```

```
19       System.out.println("******current size is " + list.size());
20       System.out.println( toStr(list) ) ;
21    }
22    static String toStr( ArrayList a ){
23       int n = a.size() ;
24       if (n == 0) return "empty" ;
25       String str = "[0]" + a.get( 0 );
26       for ( int i = 1 ; i < n ; i++ )
27         str += ", ["+i+"]" + a.get(i);
28       return str ;
29    }
30}
```

7.7   Hand trace the program shown below.

   a. What is the effect of lines 9-10?

   b. How does method printA() differ from method printB()?

   c. What is the effect of lines 14-19?

   d. Give the index and value of the item removed on line 24.

   e. Predict all output from the program.

```
1 import java.util.*;
2 public class Main {
3  public static void main(String[] args){
4     ArrayList dList = new ArrayList() ;
5     double[] vals = {6.6, 5.5, -2.2, -4.4, 9.9} ;
6     ListIterator itr = dList.listIterator() ;
7     System.out.println("testing itr.add()");
8     for ( int i = 0 ; i < 5 ; i++ )
9       itr.add( new Double( vals[i] ) ) ;
10    System.out.println("current size is " + dList.size());
11    System.out.println("calling printB( dList )");
12    printB( dList ) ;
13    System.out.println("testing itr.set()");
14    while ( itr.hasPrevious() ){
15      int ndx = itr.previousIndex() ;
16      double d = -1.0 * ((Double)itr.previous()).doubleValue() ;
17      System.out.println("changing node at index "+ndx+" to "+d);
18      itr.set( new Double( -d ) ) ;
19    }
20    System.out.println("**current size is " + dList.size());
21    System.out.println("calling printA( dList )");
22    printA( dList ) ;
23    System.out.println("testing itr.remove()");
24    itr.remove() ;
25    System.out.println("current size is " + dList.size());
26    System.out.println("calling printA( dList )");
27    printA( dList ) ;
```

```
28    }                   // end main()
29
30    static void printA( ArrayList a ){
31      ListIterator itrA = a.listIterator() ;
32      while ( itrA.hasNext() ){
33        String prefix = "[" + itrA.nextIndex() + "]" ;
34        System.out.println( prefix + itrA.next() ) ;
35      }
36    }                     // end print1()
37
38    static void printB( ArrayList a ){
39      ListIterator itrB = a.listIterator() ;
40      while ( itrB.hasNext() )
41        itrB.next() ;
42      while ( itrB.hasPrevious() ) {
43        String prefix = "[" + itrB.previousIndex() + "]" ;
44        System.out.println( prefix + itrB.previous() ) ;
45      }
46    }
47 }
```

PROGRAMMING PROBLEMS

7.1   Add these three constructors to the `ArrayCollection` class (Listing 7.4 on page 207), and then test them:

a. An explicit no-argument constructor:

```
public ArrayCollection()
```

b. A constructor that sets the capacity with a given value:

```
public ArrayCollection(int capacity)
```

c. A constructor that initializes the array with references to the objects in a given array:

```
public ArrayCollection(Object[] objects)
```

7.2   Add this method to the `ArrayCollection` class (Listing 7.4), and then test the method:

```
public Object getLast()
// returns a reference to the last element of this collection;
// or returns null if this collection is empty;
```

7.3   Using an iterator, write and test the following client method for `Collection` objects:

```
public Object getLast(Collection collection)
// returns a reference to the last element of the collection;
// or returns null if the given collection is empty;
```

7.4   Add the following method to the `ArrayCollection` class (Listing 7.4), and then test the method:

```
public boolean removeLast()
// removes the last element if this collection is not empty;
// returns true if and only if it changes this collection;
```

7.5   Using an iterator, write and test the following client method for `Collection` objects:

```
public boolean removeLast(Collection collection)
// removes the last element if the collection is not empty;
// returns true if and only it changes the given collection;
```

7.6   Add the following method to the `LinkedCollection` class (Listing 7.7), and then test the method:

```
public int frequency(Object object)
// returns the number of occurrences of the given object
// in this collection;
```

7.7   Using an iterator, write and test the following client method for `Collection` objects:

```
public int frequency(Collection collection, Object object)
// returns the number of occurrences of the given object
// in the given collection;
```

7.8   Add the following method to the `LinkedCollection` class (Listing 7.7), and then test the method:

```
public boolean removeOdd()
// removes every other element (the first, the third, etc.) from
// this collection; returns true iff this collection is changed;
```

7.9   Using an iterator, write and test the following client method for `Collection` objects:

```
public boolean removeOdd(Collection collection)
// removes every other element (the first, the third, etc.) from
// the given collection; returns true iff it is changed;
```

7.10   Modify the `LinkedCollection` class (Listing 7.7 on page 212) so that, instead of a circular list, it uses two dummy nodes, named `head` and `tail`, that precede the first element and follow the last element, as shown in Figure 7.17.

7.11   Implement the `addAll()` method for the `java.util.AbstractCollection` class (Listing 7.11 on page 218). Use the `add()` method within an iterator-controlled loop.

7.12   Implement the `clear()` method in the `AbstractCollection` class (Listing 7.11 on page 218). Use an iterator and its `remove()` method.

7.13   Implement the `containsAll()` method in the `AbstractCollection` class (Listing 7.11 on page 218). Use an iterator.

7.14   Implement the `retainAll()` method in the `AbstractCollection` class (Listing 7.11 on page 218). Use an iterator and its `remove()` method.

7.15   Implement the `toArray()` method in the `AbstractCollection` class (Listing 7.11). See Listing 7.14 on page 220.

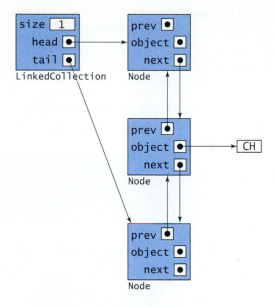

FIGURE 7.17 Using head and tail pointers.

PROJECT

7.1 Recall that a *set* is a collection with no duplicate or null elements. (See Figure 2.4 on page 42.) In this project, we implement a Set interface, first with an AbstractSet class and then with two concrete extensions—an ArraySet class and a LinkedSet class. In the process, we learn how to implement iterators on both arrays and linked lists, and we see how an abstract class can help reduce code duplication. The resulting framework of two interfaces and three classes closely follows the architecture of the *Java Collections Framework*.

```
                                 Iterator
        AbstractSet ----------Set
              |— ArraySet
              |— LinkedSet
```

Begin by translating the Iterator and Set interfaces shown here into Java. Then compile them.

Next, compile an AbstractSet class that implements the Set interface. As an abstract class, it will have no fields nor constructors; only abstract methods and concrete methods. Recall that an *abstract class* is a class that has at least one abstract method, and an *abstract method* is merely a method declaration, with no body. An `abstract` method is just like a method declaration in an interface, except that it includes the keyword `abstract`, like this:

```
public abstract boolean add(Object x);
public abstract Iterator iterator();
public abstract int size();
```

Using iterators, you should be able to write concrete implementations of all of the other nine methods.

```
            <<interface>>
              Iterator
+hasNext():boolean
+next():Object
+remove()
```

```
            <<interface>>
                Set
+add(Object):boolean
+addAll(Set):boolean
+clear()
+contains(Object):boolean
+containsAll(Set):boolean
+equals(Object):boolean
+isEmpty():boolean
+iterator():Iterator
+remove(Object):boolean
+removeAll(Set):boolean
+retainAll(Set):boolean
+size():int
+toArray():Object[]
+toString():String
```

Next, compile an `ArraySet` extension of your `AbstractSet` class. Use an `Object[]` array and a `size` counter. Include a default (no-arg) constructor, a copy constructor, and a constructor that specifies the initial length of the backing array. The `add()` method should enforce the constraint that a set contains no `null` or duplicate elements. For the `iterator()` method, you can use lines 12–35 of Listing 7.5 on page 209. Test each method separately.

Finally, compile a `LinkedSet` extension of your `AbstractSet` class. Use a nested `private static` Node class. Use a dummy head node and a `size` counter. Insert new elements at the front of the list. In your anonymous inner `Iterator` class, use two `Node` references: p, which points to the node whose next pointer points to the node whose data will be returned by the next call to `next()`; and pp, which points to the node whose next pointer points to the node that will be deleted by the next call to `remove()`. The condition (pp != p) is then equivalent to the okToRemove flag. Initialize p to `head` and pp to `null`. Then the `next()` method should set pp to p and then advance p. The `remove()` method should set p to pp after deleting pp.next. It also has to decrement the `size` field of its enclosing `LinkedSet` class, like this:

```
--LinkedSet.this.size;
```

Both the `next()` and the `remove()` method should throw an `IllegalStateException` if its precondition is not satisfied.

ANSWERS TO REVIEW QUESTIONS

7.1 A collection is a general data structure that contains objects and defines operations for accessing them.

7.2 The *Java Collections Framework* is a family of classes and interfaces in the `java.util` package that is used to define data structures.

7.3 An *iterator* is an object that moves about a data structure, providing access to one element at a time. It is used like an array index, but it can be defined on any kind of linear or nonlinear structure.

7.4 Yes.

7.5 Yes.

7.6 True.

7.7 True.

7.8 The `iterator()` and `size()` methods are Abstract in the `AbstractCollection` class because their implementations depend directly upon the implementations of the data storage. For example, the `size()` method returns the value of the `size` variable.

7.9 The `remove(object)` method declared in the `Collection` interface removes the first occurrence of the given `object` from the collection, or returns `false` if it cannot be found. The `remove()` method declared in the `Iterator` interface removes the last object returned by its `next()` method.

7.10 The invocation `x.addAll(y)` will add all the elements of y to x. But the invocation `x.add(y)` will add the `Collection` y itself as a single element to x.

7.11 The `abstract` methods such as `iterator()` and `size()` in the `AbstractCollection` class are required because they are specified in the `Collection` interface that it implements.

7.12 The `add()` method in the `AbstractCollection` class throws an exception instead of implementing its code directly because its implementation depends upon the backing data structure, which is not defined in the `abstract` class.

7.13 The `add()` method in the `AbstractCollection` class throws an exception instead of being declared `abstract` because it has to be called by other concrete methods in its class.

7.14 The `AbstractCollection` class defines a `protected` constructor so that it can be used by its subclasses. It cannot have a `public` constructor because `abstract` classes cannot be instantiated.

7.15 An `abstract` class cannot be instantiated because it has at least one (`abstract`) method that has not been implemented.

7.16 An *inner class* is a non-`static` class that is defined as a member of another class.

7.17   An anonymous inner class is an inner class that has no name. Its entire defining block is listed directly after an invocation of its no-argument constructor, like the one at line 13 in Listing 7.5 on page 209:

```
13    return new Iterator() {  /* anonymous inner class */  };
```

7.18   An *anonymous constructor* is a constructor that is invoked for an anonymous class. It is identified by the name of the interface that the anonymous class is implementing. For example, in the statement at line 13 in Listing 7.5 on page 209, the expression new Iterator() is invoking the anonymous constructor for the anonymous class that is implementing the Iterator interface.

7.19   An iterator's next() method should not be called except after its hasNext() method has returned true.

7.20   An iterator's remove() method should not be called except after a call to its next() method.

7.21   The okToRemove flag is used in the iterator classes to enforce the requirement that the remove() method should not be called except after a call to its next() method. The flag is false initially and is reset false within the remove() method. The add() method resets it true, and the remove() method throws an exception if it isn't true.

7.22   A semaphore is a flag (a boolean variable) that is used to signal that a structure or system is in a required state. The okToRemove flag in the iterator classes is a semaphore.

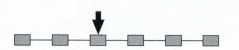

When I write a program,
I should keep in mind that its next reader might be someone
who is totally unfamiliar with it (*such as myself, a year later*).

— Donald E. Knuth, Literate Programming

Chapter 8

Lists

In previous chapters, we used linked lists to implement stacks and queues. In this chapter, we take the Java point of view that a list is an abstract data type defined as an interface. A data structure of this type is a linear collection (*i.e.*, a sequence of elements). In Java, list elements are numbered just as in an array: 0, 1, 2, *etc.* Any integer variable that is used to access list elements by number is called an *index* on that list. Thus, in Java, a list is an indexed collection. As with ordinary arrays, a list may contain duplicate references and `null` references.

8.1 List Classes in the Java Collections Framework

The Java Collections Framework (JCF)[1] is set up to allow the following general strategy to be used for implementing ADTs:

1. Use an interface (*e.g.*, `Collection`, `List`, `Set`, `Map`) to define the structure.

2. Partially implement that interface with an `abstract` class.

3. In that `abstract` class implement all the interface methods that can be written without actually specifying the object's storage structure.

4. Complete the implementation by extending the `abstract` class with various concrete classes that do specify the storage structure.

As we saw in Chapter 7, the JCF supports this strategy by providing substantial interfaces and `abstract` classes to use as building blocks. (See Figure 7.1 on page 199.) Those that are specialized for building list classes are shown in Figure 8.1.

Viewed from the bottom up, the framework provides two concrete list classes: `ArrayList` and `LinkedList`. The `ArrayList` class uses an array to store its elements, so it provides constant time access, but requires linear time for insertions and deletions. The `LinkedList` class uses a linked list

---

[1] For more details, see Appendix D.

233

```
Object
  └ AbstractCollection ------------------------- Collection
      └ AbstractList--------------------------┴ List
            ├ AbstractSequentialList
            │      └ LinkedList
            └ ArrayList
```

FIGURE 8.1 The list classes that implement the `List` interface in the `java.util` package.

to store its elements. As a result, it can perform insertions and deletions in constant time, but locating an element requires linear time.

8.2 Bidirectional List Iterators

Lists are linear structures. So moving backward through a list should be no more complicated than moving forward. This bidirectional motion is embodied in the `java.util.ListIterator` interface summarized by the UML diagram of Figure 8.2. The code for the interface is shown in Listing 8.1.

LISTING 8.1: The `java.util.ListIterator` Interface

```
1   package java.util;
2   public interface ListIterator extends Iterator {
3       public void     add(Object object);
4       public boolean  hasNext();
5       public boolean  hasPrevious();
6       public Object   next();
7       public int      nextIndex();
8       public Object   previous();
9       public int      previousIndex();
10      public void     remove();
11      public void     set(Object object);
12  }
```

The `hasPrevious()` and `previous()` methods are similar to the `hasNext()` and `next()` methods. In addition to moving in opposite directions, there is another distinction between the `next()` and `previous()` methods. The `next()` method works like a postincrement operator (*e.g.*, n++), returning the current element before advancing the cursor forward. The `previous()` method works like a predecrement operator (*e.g.*, --n), returning the current element after moving the cursor backward.

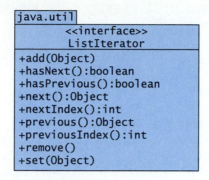

FIGURE 8.2   The java.util.ListIterator interface.

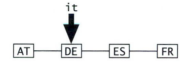

FIGURE 8.3   A list iterator.

For example, Figure 8.3 shows a list iterator that is currently locating the element DE in a list of four strings. At that moment, a call to it.next() would advance the iterator to ES and return the previous element DE. On the other hand, a call to it.previous() would move the iterator back to AT and return that object.

Listing 8.2 shows how the previous() and next() methods work together. A list of four elements is created with the java.util.Arrays.asList() method, and then a list iterator named it is attached to it by its listIterator() method. The list itself is printed, and then a sequence of calls to it.next() and it.previous() is executed. The progress of the iterator through these calls is shown in Figure 8.4. Each call moves the iterator one element either forward or backward. The calls to it.next() return the current element before the move; while the calls to it.previous() return the current element after the move.

The last two lines of output in Listing 8.2 show that when the first element is the iterator's current element, it.hasPrevious() will return false and it.hasNext() will return true.

The other extreme is when the iterator has moved past the end of the list (to the imaginary "end of list" element; see Figure 8.5). That is when it.hasPrevious() will return true and it.hasNext() will return false.

List iterators are richer than ordinary iterators. Besides being bidirectional, they also generate index numbers. Thus, any collection that has a list iterator is like an array, numbering its elements 0, 1, 2, *etc*. These index numbers are returned by the list iterator's nextIndex() and previousIndex() methods.

LISTING 8.2: **Testing the** `java.util.ListIterator` **Interface**

```java
1    import java.util.*;
2    public class TestListIterator2 {
3      public static void main(String[] args) {
4        List list = Arrays.asList( new String[]{"AT", "DE", "ES", "FR"});
5        System.out.println("list: " + list);
6        ListIterator it=list.listIterator();
7        System.out.println("it.next(): " + it.next());
8        System.out.println("it.next(): " + it.next());
9        System.out.println("it.previous(): " + it.previous());
10       System.out.println("it.next(): " + it.next());
11       System.out.println("it.next(): " + it.next());
12       System.out.println("it.previous(): " + it.previous());
13       System.out.println("it.previous(): " + it.previous());
14       System.out.println("it.hasPrevious(): " + it.hasPrevious());
15       System.out.println("it.hasNext(): " + it.hasNext());
16     }
17   }
```

The output is

```
list: [AT, DE, ES, FR]
it.next(): AT
it.next(): DE
it.previous(): DE
it.next(): DE
it.next(): ES
it.previous(): ES
it.previous(): DE
it.previous(): AT
it.hasPrevious(): false
it.hasNext(): true
```

Listing 8.3 shows how the `nextIndex()` and `previousIndex()` methods work. The `nextIndex()` method returns the index of the element that would be returned by the next call to `next()`. For example, the element DE has index 1, so after the iterator has been advanced to DE (by the first call to `it.next()`), the call `it.nextIndex()` returns 1.

The `previousIndex()` method returns the index of the element that would be returned by the next call to `previous()`. So after the iterator has been advanced to FR (by the third call to `it.next()`), the call `it.previousIndex()` returns 2.

These examples use the `Arrays.asList()` method to return a `List` object that contains the strings AT, DE, ES, and FR. This is done in Listing 8.2 on page 236 by passing an anonymous `String` array to the `asList()` method. In Listing 8.3 on page 238, we use a *named* `String` array instead. So this program has two data structures containing the same four strings: a `String`

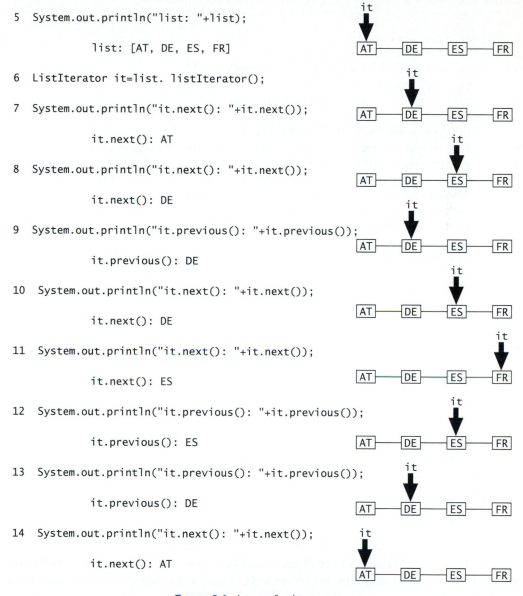

```
5  System.out.println("list: "+list);

        list: [AT, DE, ES, FR]

6  ListIterator it=list. listIterator();

7  System.out.println("it.next(): "+it.next());

        it.next(): AT

8  System.out.println("it.next(): "+it.next());

        it.next(): DE

9  System.out.println("it.previous(): "+it.previous());

        it.previous(): DE

10  System.out.println("it.next(): "+it.next());

        it.next(): DE

11  System.out.println("it.next(): "+it.next());

        it.next(): ES

12  System.out.println("it.previous(): "+it.previous());

        it.previous(): ES

13  System.out.println("it.previous(): "+it.previous());

        it.previous(): DE

14  System.out.println("it.next(): "+it.next());

        it.next(): AT
```

FIGURE 8.4 A trace of an iterator tester.

FIGURE 8.5 An iterator past the end.

LISTING 8.3: **Testing the** `java.util.ListIterator` **Interface**

```
1   import java.util.*;
2   public class TestListIterator {
3     public static void main(String[] args) {
4       String[] countries = {"AT", "DE", "ES", "FR"};
5       List list = Arrays.asList(countries);
6       System.out.println("list: " + list);
7       ListIterator it=list.listIterator();
8       System.out.println("it.nextIndex(): " + it.nextIndex());
9       System.out.println("it.next(): " + it.next());
10      System.out.println("it.nextIndex(): " + it.nextIndex());
11      System.out.println("it.next(): " + it.next());
12      System.out.println("it.nextIndex(): " + it.nextIndex());
13      System.out.println("it.next(): " + it.next());
14      System.out.println("it.previousIndex(): " + it.previousIndex());
15      System.out.println("it.previous(): " + it.previous());
16      System.out.println("it.previousIndex(): " + it.previousIndex());
17      System.out.println("it.previous(): " + it.previous());
18    }
19  }
```

The output is

```
list: [AT, DE, ES, FR]
it.nextIndex(): 0
it.next(): AT
it.nextIndex(): 1
it.next(): DE
it.nextIndex(): 2
it.next(): ES
it.previousIndex(): 2
it.previous(): ES
it.previousIndex(): 1
it.previous(): DE
```

array named `countries`, and a `List` object named `list`. The `asList()` method actually uses the given array as the storage structure for the `List` object, so the individual string elements are not duplicated.

Listing 8.4 shows that the same `String` array is used as the storage structure for the `List` object, as shown in Figure 8.6. The program first calls `it.next()` twice, at lines 8–9, to make DE the *mutable element*. That allows the call `it.set("CZ")` to change it to CZ. Then it prints `countries[1]` at line 12 to show that there was only one DE element, common to both the `countries` array and the `list` object. Next, it assigns "GB" to `countries[3]` to change FR to GB. The final printing of the `list` object shows again that there was only one array referenced by the string and list objects.

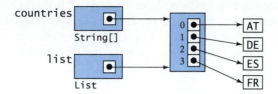

FIGURE 8.6 A list and a string array.

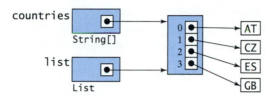

FIGURE 8.7 A modified list.

LISTING 8.4: **Testing the** `java.util.ListIterator` **Interface**

```
1   import java.util.*;
2   public class TestListIterator3 {
3     public static void main(String[] args) {
4       String[] countries = {"AT", "DE", "ES", "FR"};
5       List list = Arrays.asList(countries);
6       System.out.println("list: " + list);
7       ListIterator it=list.listIterator();
8       it.next();
9       it.next();
10      it.set("CZ");                    // change DE to CZ
11      System.out.println("list: " + list);
12      System.out.println("countries[1]: "+countries[1]);
13      countries[3] = "GB";            // change FR to GB
14      System.out.println("list: " + list);
15    }
16  }
```

The output is

```
list: [AT, DE, ES, FR]
list: [AT, CZ, ES, FR]
countries[1]: CZ
list: [AT, CZ, ES, GB]
```

Note that the `set()` method is like the `remove()` method in `Iterator` classes. It must be preceded by a call to `next()` (or `previous()`) to designate the element that it will change. We call that the *mutable element* to distinguish it from the current element that the iterator locates. For example, before any calls to `next()` have executed, the current element is the first element in the list and there is no mutable element. After the first call to next(), the first element is the mutable element and the second element is the current element. Note also that a list produced by the Array.asList() method has a *fixed length*: It does not allow the addition or removal of any elements. That is because it uses the same array that is passed to it for its actual storage structure.

8.3 The java.util.List Interface

The java.util.List interface is shown in Listing 8.5. All but 10 of these methods are inherited from the java.util.Collection interface. (See Listing 7.9 on page 216.) The 10 new methods are specialized operations for sequential collections (lists). They either involve an index or return a ListIterator object.

The interface is summarized by the UML diagram in Figure 8.8, and its Java code is given in Listing 8.5. Note that the only types that are specified are int, boolean, Object, Collection, Iterator, ListIterator, and Object[].

LISTING 8.5: The java.util.List **Interface**

```
1   package java.util;
2   public interface List extends Collection {
3       public boolean      add(Object object);
4       public void         add(int index, Object object);
5       public boolean      addAll(Collection collection);
6       public boolean      addAll(int index, Collection collection);
7       public void         clear();
8       public boolean      contains(Object object);
9       public boolean      containsAll(Collection collection);
10      public boolean      equals(Object object);
11      public Object       get(int index);
12      public int          hashCode();
13      public int          indexOf(Object object);
14      public boolean      isEmpty();
15      public Iterator     iterator();
16      public int          lastIndexOf(Object object);
17      public ListIterator listIterator();
18      public ListIterator listIterator(int index);
19      public Object       remove(int index);
20      public boolean      remove(Object object);
21      public boolean      removeAll(Collection collection);
22      public boolean      retainAll(Collection collection);
23      public Object       set(int index, Object object);
24      public int          size();
25      public List         subList(int index1, int index2);
26      public Object[]     toArray();
27      public Object[]     toArray(Object[] objects);
28  }
```

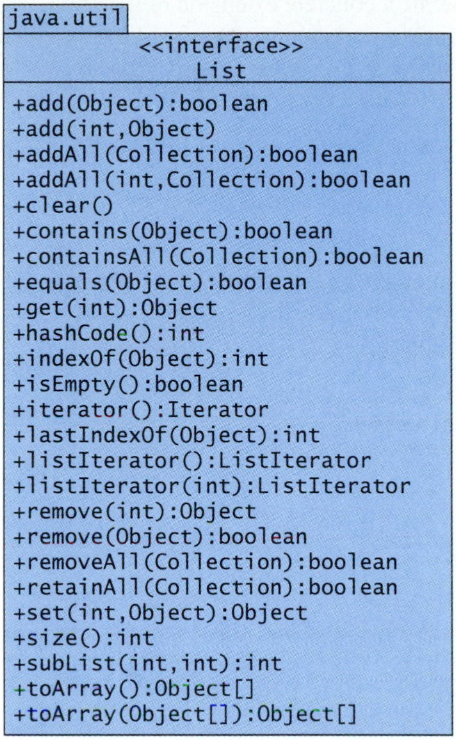

```
java.util
                    <<interface>>
                        List
+add(Object):boolean
+add(int,Object)
+addAll(Collection):boolean
+addAll(int,Collection):boolean
+clear()
+contains(Object):boolean
+containsAll(Collection):boolean
+equals(Object):boolean
+get(int):Object
+hashCode():int
+indexOf(Object):int
+isEmpty():boolean
+iterator():Iterator
+lastIndexOf(Object):int
+listIterator():ListIterator
+listIterator(int):ListIterator
+remove(int):Object
+remove(Object):boolean
+removeAll(Collection):boolean
+retainAll(Collection):boolean
+set(int,Object):Object
+size():int
+subList(int,int):int
+toArray():Object[]
+toArray(Object[]):Object[]
```

FIGURE 8.8 The `java.util.List` interface.

8.4 Implementing the `java.util.List` Interface

We can see from the inheritance diagram in Figure 8.1 on page 234 that the Java Collections Framework defines four implementations of the `java.util.List` interface: two abstract classes and two concrete classes. The two concrete classes, `ArrayList` and `LinkedList`, use the two common data structures to store list elements: The `ArrayList` class uses an array, and the `LinkedList` class uses a linked list. The executable code that is common to both concrete classes is collected in the `AbstractList` class. Then the `ArrayList` class extends that abstract class by adding all the code that is necessary for an array implementation, and the `LinkedList` class extends the abstract class by adding all the code that is necessary for a linked list implementation. This illustrates one important use of abstract classes: They reduce code redundancy.

Another purpose of abstract classes is to provide an outline for user-defined classes. To have a fully usable concrete class, the user needs only to extend the abstract class, defining the fields for the data and implementing the abstract methods. Thus, the Java Collections Framework, makes it easier for the user to define custom classes that are consistent with the rest of the framework.

To illustrate this, we define a concrete extension of the `java.util.AbstractList` class in Listing 8.6. Since this class uses a contiguous array to store the elements, we call it `Contiguous-List`. It is very similar to the `java.util.ArrayList` class.

LISTING 8.6: Extending the `java.util.AbstractList` Class

```java
1   import java.util.*;
2
3   public class ContiguousList extends AbstractList {
4      private static final int INITIAL_LENGTH=100;
5      private Object[] objects;
6      private int size;
7
8      public ContiguousList() {
9         this(INITIAL_LENGTH);
10     }
11
12     public ContiguousList(int capacity) {
13        objects = new Object[capacity];
14     }
15
16     public ContiguousList(Collection collection) {
17        int n = collection.size();
18        objects = new Object[2*n];
19        Object[] a = collection.toArray();
20        System.arraycopy(a,0,objects,0,n);
21     }
22
23     public void add(int i, Object object) {  // optional override
24        if (i<0 || i>size) throw new ArrayIndexOutOfBoundsException();
25        if (size==objects.length) resize();
26        System.arraycopy(objects,i,objects,i+1,size-i);  // shift up
27        objects[i] = object;
28        ++size;
29     }
30
31     public Object get(int i) {  // override required by AbstractList
32        if (i<0 || i>=size) throw new ArrayIndexOutOfBoundsException();
33        return objects[i];
34     }
35
36     public Object remove(int i) {  // optional override
37        if (i<0 || i>=size) throw new ArrayIndexOutOfBoundsException();
38        Object object = objects[i];
39        System.arraycopy(objects,i+1,objects,i,size-i-1);  // shift down
40        objects[--size] = null;
41        return object;
42     }
43
```

```
44    public Object set(int i, Object object) {  // optional override
45      if (i<0 || i>=size) throw new ArrayIndexOutOfBoundsException();
46      Object oldObject = objects[i];
47      objects[i] = object;
48      return oldObject;
49    }
50
51    public int size() {  // override required by AbstractList
52      return size;
53    }
54
55    private void resize() {
56      Object[] temp = new Object[2*objects.length];
57      System.arraycopy(objects,0,temp,0,size);
58      objects = temp;
59    }
60  }
```

The only abstract methods in the AbstractList class are get() and size(). Hence, list objects can be instantiated from any subclass that implements these two required methods. The ArrayList class does that by storing its elements in an array.

The class defines three fields at lines 4–6: the constant named INITIAL_LENGTH, the backing array named objects, and the counter named size.

The no-argument constructor at line 8 passes the INITIAL_LENGTH constant to the constructor defined at line 12, which allocates the objects array at the given capacity. The constructor at line 16 allocates the objects array at a capacity that is twice the size of the referenced collection. Then it uses the temporary array a to copy the n references from collection to the objects array.

The add() method at line 23 adds the given object to this list at the given position i. First it checks at line 24 whether the given index value i is in bounds. Then it checks whether this list is full; if so, then the private resize() method doubles its capacity. Then it uses the System.arraycopy() method to shift the elements from position i through size-1 to the right one position, so that the given object can be inserted at position i at line 27.

The required get() method at line 31 is the simplest of all: We merely use direct access into the backing array to find and return the element at the given position.

The remove() method at line 36 is essentially the reverse of the add() method at line 23. After locating the object at position i, it shifts the elements on the right to close the gap. That leaves the last element duplicated (at positions i-1 and i), so we set the last of those references to null at line 40. This prevents "phantom references" from blocking the garbage collection of deleted elements.

The set() method at line 44 replaces the current element at position i with the referenced object, and returns the old one.

The size() method at line 51 is the other required method.

The inheritance diagram in Figure 8.1 on page 234 shows two abstract list classes: the AbstractList class, and the AbstractSequentialList class. The AbstractSequentialList class makes the assumption that its elements will be stored in a sequential (linked) structure, so it uses its listIterator() method to define its add(), get(), set(), and remove() methods.

Consequently, its only `abstract` methods are `listIterator()` and `size()`. The `LinkedList` class defines these two required methods by storing its elements in a linked list.

The `ArrayList` class was illustrated in Listing 8.2 on page 236. The next example shows how to define your own array-based extension of the `AbstractList` class.

The `ContiguousList` class, defined in Listing 8.6 on page 242, extends the `AbstractList` class by storing its elements contiguously in a `private` array named `objects`. Its UML diagram is shown in Figure 8.9. It defines the required `get()` and `size()` methods, using the array's direct access for `get()` and returning the corresponding stored value for `size()`. It also defines three constructors, a `private` `resize()` method, and optional overrides for the `add()`, `remove()`, and `set()` methods.

The first two constructors allocate the `objects` array with an `INITIAL_LENGTH OF 100`. The third constructor sets the backing array's length at twice the size of the given `collection` and then uses the `toArray()` method to load the `objects` array with references to that collection's elements.

The `resize()` method reconstructs the `objects` array, doubling its capacity. It is called by the `add()` method whenever the array is full.

The `add(i,object)` method inserts the given `object` at index `i` in the `objects` array. To do that, it uses the `System.arraycopy()` method to shift the elements `objects[i..size-1]` up one position into the segment `objects[i+1..size]`. Then it sets a reference to the given `object` at position `objects[i]`.

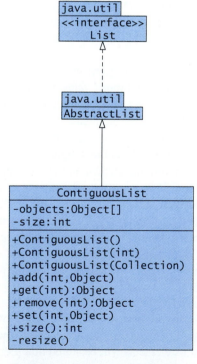

FIGURE 8.9 A `ContiguousList` class.

The remove(i) method reverses the effect of the add(i,object) method. It shifts the elements objects[i+1..size-1] down one position into the segment objects[i..size-2]. Then it sets the element objects[size-1] to null and returns the removed object.

The set(i,object) method simply sets a reference to the given object at position objects[i] and then returns the object that was replaced.

The ContiguousList class is tested in the program shown in Listing 8.7. First it constructs a list named g8 that uses its add() method to insert seven String objects. Then it prints the list, adds the string "JP" at position 6, and prints it again. Finally, it tests the size(), contains(), get(), subList(), remove(), and set() methods.

LISTING 8.7: Testing the ContiguousList **Class**

```
1   public class TestContiguousList {
2     public static void main(String[] args) {
3       java.util.List g8 = new ContiguousList();
4       g8.add("CA");              // Canada
5       g8.add("DE");              // Germany
6       g8.add("FR");              // France
7       g8.add("GB");              // Great Britain
8       g8.add("IT");              // Italy
9       g8.add("RU");              // Russia
10      g8.add("US");              // United States
11      System.out.println(g8);
12      g8.add(5, "JP");           // Japan
13      System.out.println(g8);
14      System.out.println("g8.size(): " + g8.size());
15      System.out.println("g8.contains(\"JP\"): " + g8.contains("JP"));
16      System.out.println("g8.contains(\"CN\"): " + g8.contains("CN"));
17      System.out.println("g8.get(3): " + g8.get(3));
18      System.out.println("g8.subList(3,6): " + g8.subList(3,6));
19      g8.remove(6);
20      System.out.println(g8);
21      System.out.println("g8.set(0,\"CN\"): " + g8.set(0,"CN")); // China
22      System.out.println(g8);
23    }
24  }
```

The output is

```
[CA, DE, FR, GB, IT, RU, US]
[CA, DE, FR, GB, IT, JP, RU, US]
g8.size(): 8
g8.contains("JP"): true
g8.contains("CN"): false
g8.get(3): GB
g8.subList(3,6): [GB, IT, JP]
[CA, DE, FR, GB, IT, JP, US]
g8.set(0,"CN"): CA
[CN, DE, FR, GB, IT, JP, US]
```

LISTING 8.8: Extending the `java.util.AbstractSequentialList` **Class**

```
1   import java.util.*;
2   public class Sequence extends AbstractSequentialList {
3     private Node head = new Node(null, null, null);
4     private int size;
5
6     public Sequence() {
7       head.prev = head.next = head;
8     }
9
10    public Sequence(Collection collection) {
11      this();
12      addAll(collection);
13    }
14
15    public ListIterator listIterator(int index) { // required override
16      return new SequenceIterator(index);
17    }
18
19    public int size() {  // required override
20      return size;
21    }
22
23    private static class Node {
24      Node prev, next;
25      Object object;
26      Node(Node p, Node n, Object o) {
27        this.prev=p; this.next=n; this.object=o;
28      }
29    }
30
31    private class SequenceIterator implements ListIterator {
32      // See Listing 8.9
33    }
34  }
```

The `Java.util.AbstractSequentialList` class has two abstract methods: `listIterator()` and `size()`. These are overridden in the `Sequence` class defined in Listing 8.8. (Its UML diagram is shown in Figure 8.10). The `listIterator()` method has to return a `ListIterator` object that is bound to the list, so the class defines a nested `SequenceIterator` class that extends the `ListIterator` class. (See Listing 8.9.) The test driver for the `ContiguousList` class in Listing 8.7 works the same way for this `Sequence` class.

The `Sequence` class is very similar to the `LinkedCollection` class defined in Listing 7.7 on page 212. It uses a doubly linked list of `Node` objects with a dummy head node.

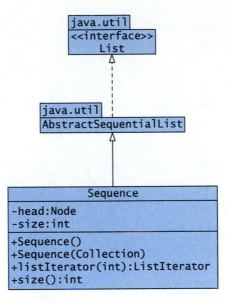

FIGURE 8.10 A Sequence class.

LISTING 8.9: The Nested Sequence.Iterator **Class**

```
1   private class SequenceIterator implements ListIterator {
2     private Node last, next;
3     private int nextIndex;
4
5     public SequenceIterator(int i) {
6       if (i<0 || i>size) throw new IndexOutOfBoundsException();
7       nextIndex = i;
8       next = head.next;
9       for (int j=0; j<i; j++)
10        next = next.next;
11    }
12
13    public void add(Object object) {
14      Node newNode = new Node(next.prev,next,object);
15      newNode.prev.next = next.prev = newNode;
16      ++size;
17      ++nextIndex;
18      last = null;
19    }
20
21    public boolean hasNext() {
22      return nextIndex<size;
23    }
```

```
24
25    public boolean hasPrevious() {
26       return nextIndex>0;
27    }
28
29    public Object next() {
30       if (!hasNext()) throw new NoSuchElementException();
31       last = next;
32       next = next.next;
33       ++nextIndex;
34       return last.object;
35    }
36
37    public int nextIndex() {
38       return nextIndex;
39    }
40
41    public Object previous() {
42       if (!hasPrevious()) throw new NoSuchElementException();
43       next = last = next.prev;
44       --nextIndex;
45       return last.object;
46    }
47
48    public int previousIndex() {
49       return nextIndex-1;
50    }
51
52    public void remove() {
53       if (last == null) throw new IllegalStateException();
54       last.prev.next = last.next;
55       last.next.prev = last.prev;
56       last = null;
57       --size;
58       --nextIndex;
59    }
60
61    public void set(Object object) {
62       if (last == null) throw new IllegalStateException();
63       last.object = object;
64    }
65  }
```

The SequenceIterator class implements the java.util.ListIterator interface
(Listing 8.1 on page 234). It has three fields: last refers to the last node that was returned by a
call to next() or previous(), next refers to the current node, and nextIndex holds its index
number. The last field is used to enforce the constraint that requires each call to remove() or
set() to be immediately preceded by a call to next() or previous().

BEFORE:

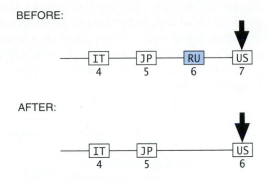

AFTER:

FIGURE 8.11 Removing an element.

BEFORE: AFTER:

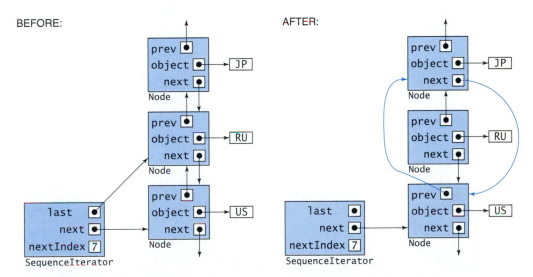

FIGURE 8.12 Removing an element with the linked implementation.

Figure 8.11 shows the effect of the call `g8.remove(6)` at line 19 in the test driver program Listing 8.7 on page 245. The `remove(i)` method, which is inherited from the `AbstractSequentialList` class, uses the `listIterator(i)` method to locate the node at the given index `i`. Then it calls the iterator's `remove()` method to delete the element from the list. Note that the call `listIterator(6)` sets the iterator's next field at the element US, which has index 7 before the deletion.

The details of that `g8.remove(6)` call are shown in Figure 8.12. To delete the RU element, only two links have to be `reset`: `last.prev.next` and `last.next.prev`. It also sets `last` to `null` and decrements `nextIndex` to 6.

8.5 Linked Lists of Primitives and Specialized Objects

Java's Collections Framework provides a rich environment for defining efficient lists with little effort. The only disadvantage is that, like all other data structures derived from the framework, the element type is the general `Object` class. You can have lists of `String` type or any other class, but with the JCF, those elements have to be saved as an `Object` type and then recast to their original type when extracted. If you want a simple list of `int`s or any other primitive type, you have to wrap them as objects. In these cases, you may prefer to define your own simple list class from scratch instead of extending one of the `java.util` classes. This approach is illustrated in the `polynomial` example in Section 8.6.

It is possible to store elements of primitive type (`int`s, `double`s, *etc.*) in a `Collection` object. The solution is to use the corresponding *wrapper class* to wrap each primitive value in an object. Listing 8.10 shows how a list of *int* values can be built using the *integer* wrapper class.

LISTING 8.10: Using the `Integer` Wrapper Class

```
1   import java.util.*;
2
3   public class Main {
4     public static void main(String[] args) {
5       List list = new LinkedList();
6       for (int i=0; i<args.length; i++) {
7         int n = Integer.parseInt(args[i]);
8         System.out.print(n + "\t");
9         Integer x = new Integer(n);
10        list.add(x);
11      }
12      System.out.println();
13      int sum = 0;
14      for (Iterator it=list.iterator(); it.hasNext(); ) {
15        Integer x = (Integer)it.next();
16        int n = x.intValue();
17        sum += n;
18        System.out.print(sum + "\t");
19      }
20      System.out.println();
21    }
22  }
```

The command line input is

```
java Main 11 22 33 44 55 66 77 88
```

The output is

11	22	33	44	55	66
11	33	66	110	165	231

The `main()` method instantiates a linked list object at line 5. Then, at line 6, it iterates the `for` loop once for each input in the `args` array obtained from the command line. For example `args[0]` is the string `"11"`, and `args[1]` is the string `"22"`. Each input string is parsed into an `int n` at line 7 and then printed at line 8. You can see that there are six inputs.

At line 9, an `Integer` object is instantiated, passing the `int n` to the constructor to create a wrapper object that holds that `int` value. That `Integer` object is then added to the list at line 10.

Primitive Type	Wrapper Class
boolean	Boolean
char	Character
byte	Byte
short	Short
int	Integer
long	Long
float	Float
double	Double

TABLE 8.1   Wrapper Classes.

The second for loop at line 14 iterates once for each element in the list. The iterator's next() method returns an Object reference, so that is cast back to an Integer reference at line 15. Then the intValue() method from the Integer class returns the int value to n at line 16. This is added to the sum variable, which is printed at line 18.

Note that the static parseInt() method from the Integer class is used at line 7 to obtain the int value of the corresponding string literal. This is one of many useful static methods found in the wrapper classes. Another example is the one-argument toString() method:

```
String s = Integer.toString(12345);   // s == "12345"
```

This is the inverse of the Integer.parseInt() method.

There are eight wrapper classes in the java.lang package, one for each primitive type. Their names are listed in Table 8.1.

8.6 Case Study: Polynomial Algebra

A *polynomial* is a mathematical function of the form

$$p(x) = a_0 x^n + a_1 x^{n-1} + a_2 x^{n-2} + \cdots + a_{n-1} x + a_n$$

The highest-power exponent, n, is called the *degree* of the polynomial. For example, $p(x) = 7x^4 - 2$ is a polynomial of degree 4. The simplest polynomials are *constant polynomials* such as $p(x) = 6$ (degree 0), *linear polynomials* such as $p(x) = 9x + 6$ (degree 1), and *quadratic polynomials* such as $p(x) = 3x^2 - 2x + 5$ (degree 2). The unique *zero polynomial* $p(x) = 0$ is defined to have degree -1. In this section we present a Polynomial class whose instances represent mathematical polynomials and which supports the usual algebraic operations on them.

A polynomial can be regarded as a sum of distinct terms, where a *term* is a mathematical function of the form $t(x) = cx^e$, in which c is any real number,[2] and e is any nonnegative integer. The number c is called the *coefficient*, and the number e is called the *exponent*.

---

[2] In higher mathematics, polynomial coefficients are allowed to be more general—for example, complex numbers.

FIGURE 8.13 A Term object.

To define a class whose objects represent polynomials, we can use a linked list if we can store each term in a separate node of the list. For example, the polynomial $p(x) = 3x^2 - 2x + 5$ could be represented as a list of three nodes, where the first node represents the term $3x^2$, the second node represents the term $-2x$, and the third node represents the (constant) term 5. To that end, we first define a class whose instances represent terms.

Listing 8.11 shows a Term class whose instances are immutable. The class has two private fields, one for the coefficient (coef) and one for the exponent (exp). Figure 8.13 shows a typical Term object.

LISTING 8.11: A Class for Terms of a Polynomial

```
1   public class Term {
2     // Instances are immutable;
3     // Invariants: ZERO is unique;
4     //              if this != ZERO, then coef != 0.0 and exp >= 0.
5     private double coef;
6     private int exp;
7
8     public static final Term ZERO = new Term();
9
10    private Term() {
11      this.exp = -1;
12    }
13
14    public Term(double coef, int exp) {
15      if (coef == 0.0 || exp < 0) throw new IllegalArgumentException();
16      this.coef = coef;
17      this.exp = exp'
18    }
19
20    public Term(Term term) {   // copy constructor
21      this(that.coef, that.exp);
22    }
23
24    public Term abs() {
25      return new Term(Math.abs(coef),exp);
26    }
27
28    public boolean equals(Object object) {
29      if (object == this) return true;
30      if (! object instanceof Term)) return false;
31      Term that = (Term)object;
32      return (this.coef == that.coef && this.exp == that.exp);
```

```java
33      }
34
35      public double getCoef() {
36          return coef;
37      }
38
39      public int getExp() {
40          return exp;
41      }
42
43      public Term plus(Term that) {
44          if (that.exp != this.exp) throw new IllegalArgumentException();
45          double coef = this.coef + that.coef;
46          if (coef == 0.0) return ZERO;
47          return new Term(coef, this.exp);
48      }
49
50      public Term times(double factor) {
51          if (factor==0.0) return ZERO;
52          return new Term(coef*factor,exp);
53      }
54
55      public Term times(Term term) {
56          if (term.coef==0.0) return ZERO;
57          return new Term(coef*term.coef,exp+term.exp);
58      }
59
60      public String toString() {
61          if (coef==0.0) return "0";
62          if (exp==0.0) return Double.toString(coef);
63          String str;
64          if (coef==1.0) str = "";
65          else if (coef==-1.0) str = "-";
66          else str = "" + (float)coef;
67          if (exp==0) return str;
68          if (exp==1) return str + "x";
69          return str + "x^" + exp;
70      }
71
72      public double valueAt(double x) {
73          return coef*Math.pow(x,exp);
74      }
75  }
```

The class has three constructors, a `private` no-argument constructor at line 10, a constructor with parameters for each of the two fields at line 14, and a copy constructor that duplicates a given `Term` object at line 20. It also has the standard "getter" methods for each of its two fields: `getCoef()` and `getExp()`. It defines the `equals()` and `toString()` methods that override the corresponding methods in the `object` class. It includes five algebraic methods: `abs()`, `plus()`, `times(double)`, `times(Term)`, and `valueAt(double)`. And at line 8, it defines a `static final` object ZERO, which represent the special constant term 0.

The `equals()` method follows the usual three-step Java algorithm: Check its type, recast it, and then check the equality of its fields. Since both of its fields have primitive type, we can simply use the equality operator `==` on them.

The five algebraic methods defined in the `Term` class will be used by the `Polynomial` class. The `abs()` method returns a new term that duplicates the original term, except that the sign of its coefficient is removed. Two terms can be added only if they have the same exponent, like this:

$$5x^4 + 2x^4 = 7x^4$$

In that case, we simply add their coefficients. Multiplying a term by a constant factor, such as

$$(2x^4)(3) = 6x^4$$

simply requires that its coefficient be multiplied by the constant factor. Multiplying a term by another term, such as

$$(2x^4)(3x^5) = 6x^9$$

requires multiplying their coefficients and adding their exponents. The `valueAt()` method uses the power method `Math.pow()` to raise the given argument x to the power of the term's `exp` field to return its value at x.

The `plus(Term)` method at line 39 uses the same logic as the `add(Term)` method. The difference is that the call `t1.add(t2)` modifies the term `t1` by adding the term `t2` to it, whereas the call `t1.plus(t2)` returns the sum of the two terms as a new `Term` object without modifying either of the existing objects. It returns `null` if the two given terms do not have the same exponent.

The `toString()` method returns a string that prints terms like this: `6x^9`. Its special cases make the result look more like the way algebraic terms are printed.

The `Polynomial` class is defined in Listing 8.12 on page 256. It uses a circular singly linked list of `Node` objects. The first node is a dummy header node. Each of the other nodes in the list references a single `Term` object that represents one term of the polynomial. The dummy header node is included to simplify some of the code.

Figure 8.14 shows the linked list for the polynomial

$$p(x) = 1.83x^5 - 9.4x^2 + 6.71$$

This list has four nodes: the header node, and one node for each of the three terms of the polynomial. The `term` field for the dummy node has `coef = 0.0` and `exp = -1`. The `Term` objects for the actual terms of the polynomial are sorted in decreasing order of their `exp` fields.

The *degree* of a polynomial is its largest exponent. Because it is stored in the second `Term` object, we can get it directly from the expression `p.head.next.term.getExp()`. This works even if the polynomial is empty (*i.e.*, it is the *zero polynomial*), because in that case the linked list has only the dummy `Node` object, whose `next` field points to itself, as shown in Figure 8.15. By definition, that polynomial has degree -1.

Note that we are using a *circular linked list* here: the last node points to the first node. This has the advantage of eliminating all `null` references in the data structure. In traversing this list, we continue the `p = p.next` update until `p == head` again.

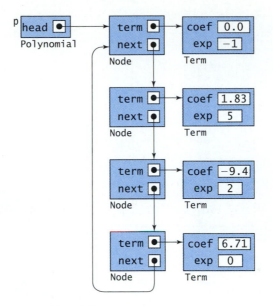

FIGURE 8.14 A `Polynomial` object.

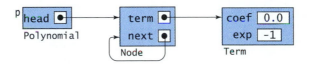

FIGURE 8.15 The `ZERO` `Polynomial` object.

Our `Polynomial` class is an aggregate of its nested `Node` class, which itself is an aggregate of the `Term` class. These class relationships are illustrated by the UML diagram in Figure 8.16 on page 256.

This version of the `Polynomial` class has four constructors: (1) a no-argument constructor at line 10, (2) one that forms a monomial (*i.e.*, a polynomial with one term, like $p(x) = 7x^{22}$) from a given coefficient and a given exponent at line 14, (3) one that forms a monomial from a given term at line 18, and (4) a copy constructor at line 23. All of these use `Node` class and `Term` class constructors.

The `equals()` method at line 37 returns true only if the referenced object is also a `Polynomial` and has the same terms as `this` polynomial. Note that the `Term` class's `equals()` method is used to test for equality of terms.

In addition to its `degree()` method, the `Polynomial` class has six other algebraic methods: `plus(Polynomial)`, `plus(Term)`, `times(double)`, `times(Polynomial)`, `times(Term)`, and `valueAt(double)`. Also, it defines a <code>static final</code> object ZERO, at line 8, which represents the special constant polynomial $p(x) = 0$. Since `Polynomial` objects are immutable, these algebraic methods have to construct new objects.

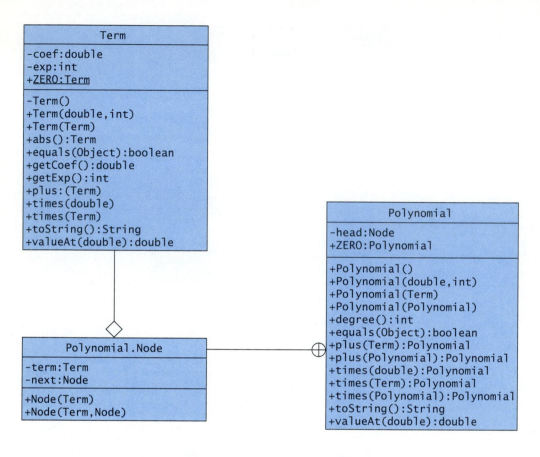

FIGURE 8.16   UML diagrams for the `Polynomial` classes.

LISTING 8.12: **A** Polynomial **Class**

```
1   public class Polynomial {
2       // Invariant: there are no null references; the terms are held in
3       // the nodes of a circular linked list with a dummy header node;
4       // the terms are sorted by decreasing order of their exp fields;
5
6       private Node head = new Node(new Term(0.0,-1));
7
8       public static final Polynomial ZERO = new Polynomial();
9
10      public Polynomial() {
11          head.next = head;
12      }
13
14      public Polynomial(double coef, int exp) {
```

```
15      this(new Term(coef, exp));
16    }
17
18    public Polynomial(Term term) {
19      if (term.equals(Term.ZERO)) head.next = head;
20      else head.next = new Node(term, head);
21    }
22
23    public Polynomial(Polynomial poly) {   // copy constructor
24      if (poly.equals(ZERO)) head.next = head;
25      else {
26        Node pp = head;
27        for (Node p=poly.head.next; p!=poly.head; p=p.next)
28          pp = pp.next = new Node(p.term);
29        pp.next = head;
30      }
31    }
32
33    public int degree() {
34      return head.next.term.getExp();
35    }
36
37    public boolean equals(Object object) {
38      if (!(object instanceof Polynomial)) return false;
39      Polynomial polynomial = (Polynomial)object;
40      Node p=polynomial.head.next, pp=head.next;
41      while (p!=head)
42        if (!(p.term.equals(pp.term))) return false;
43      return true;
44    }
45
46    public Polynomial plus(Polynomial poly) {
47      if (poly.equals(ZERO)) return this;
48      Polynomial result = new Polynomial(this);
49      for (Node p=poly.head.next; p!=poly.head; p=p.next) {
50        result = result.plus(p.term);
51        p = p.next;
52      }
53      return result;
54    }
55
56    public Polynomial plus(Term term) {
57      if (term.equals(Term.ZERO)) return this;
58      Polynomial result = new Polynomial(this);
59      Node p = result.head;
60      while (p.next.term.getExp() > term.getExp())
61        p = p.next;
62      if (p.next.term.getExp()==term.getExp())
63        p.next.term = p.next.term.plus(term);
64      else p.next = new Node(term,p.next);
```

```
65        return result;
66      }
67
68      public Polynomial times(double factor) {
69        if (factor == 0.0) return ZERO;
70        Polynomial result = ZERO;
71        for (Node p = head.next; p != head; p = p.next)
72          result = result.plus(p.term.times(factor));
73        return result;
74      }
75
76      public Polynomial times(Term term) {
77        if (term.equals(Term.ZERO)) return ZERO;
78        Polynomial result = ZERO;
79        for (Node p = head.next; p != head; p = p.next)
80          result = result.plus(p.term.times(term));
81        return result;
82      }
83
84      public Polynomial times(Polynomial polynomial) {
85        if (polynomial.equals(ZERO)) return ZERO;
86        Polynomial result = ZERO;
87        for (Node p = head.next; p != head; p = p.next)
88          result = result.plus(polynomial.times(p.term));
89        return result;
90      }
91
92      public String toString() {
93        if (degree() < 0) return "0";
94        Node p = head.next;
95        StringBuffer buf = new StringBuffer(p.term.toString());
96        for (p = p.next; p != head; p = p.next)
97          buf.append((p.term.getCoef() < 0 ? " - " : " + ") + p.term.abs());
98        return buf.toString();
99      }
100
101     public double valueAt(double x) {
102       if (degree() < 0) return 0.0;
103       double y = head.next.term.getCoef();
104       int e = head.next.term.getExp();
105       for (Node p = head.next.next; p != head; p = p.next) {
106         int ee = e;
107         e=p.term.getExp();
108         y = y*Math.pow(x,ee-e) + p.term.getCoef();
109       }
110       return y;
111     }
112
113   private static class Node {
```

```
114      Term term;
115      Node next;
116      Node(Term term) { this.term = term; }
117      Node(Term term, Node next) { this(term); this.next=next; }
118    }
119 }
```

The plus(Polynomial) method at line 46 simply applies the plus(Term) method for each term in the referenced polynomial. The plus(Term) method at line 56 is not so simple. It has to search this polynomial to find where the referenced term should be placed. If it finds a term with the same exp value, it has to add the referenced term to it. Otherwise, it inserts a new node for the referenced term.

The three times() methods use the corresponding times() methods of the Term class. To multiply a polynomial by a double factor (line 68), it multiplies each of the polynomial's terms by that factor. To multiply a polynomial by a term (line 76), it multiplies each of the polynomial's terms by that term. To multiply a polynomial by another polynomial (line 84), it multiplies each of the polynomial's terms by that polynomial, and returns their sum.

The toString() and valueAt() methods are like the clone() and equals() methods in that they also override Object class methods. The toString() method also uses the corresponding Term class method. The expression

$$(p.term.getCoef() < 0 ? " - " : " + ") + p.term.abs()$$

evaluates to a String object that contains either " - " or " + " followed by the string representation of the absolute value of the term represented by p.term. For example, if the term is $-5.2x^9$, then the string would be " - 5.2x^9". The ternary conditional operator ?: is used here to select the prefix " - " or " + " according to whether the term's coefficient is negative.

The valueAt() method returns the numeric y-value of the polynomial at a given x-value. It uses *Horner's method* for efficient polynomial evaluation. For example, the polynomial

$$p(x) = 1.83x^5 - 9.4x^2 + 6.71$$

would be evaluated in the form

$$p(x) = ((1.83)x^3 - 9.4)x^2 + 6.71$$

More generally, the polynomial

$$p(x) = a_0x^n + a_1 x^{n-1} + a_2 x^{n-2} + \cdots + a_{n-1}x + a_n$$

would be evaluated in the form

$$p(x) = (\cdots (((a_0)x + a_1)x + a_2)x + \cdots + a_{n-1})x + a_n$$

One reason that the polynomial's terms are stored in decreasing order of their exponents is so that Horner's method can be used directly in this way. The advantage is a $\Theta(n)$ run time instead of a $\Theta(n^2)$ run time. (See Exercise 8.4 on page 261.)

CHAPTER SUMMARY

❏ In Java, a list is an indexed collection. Thus, every list in Java has an index like an array.

❏ The `java.util.List` interface (Listing 8.5 on page 240) specifies nine methods that use index numbers: `add()`, `addAll()`, `get()`, `indexOf()`, `lastIndexOf()`, `listIterator()`, `remove()`, `set()`, and `subList()`.

❏ The `java.util.ListIterator` interface (Listing 8.1 on page 234) extends the `java.util.Iterator` interface, specifying six specialized methods for traversing lists. Two of these, `nextIndex()` and `previousIndex()`, return index numbers. List iterators are bound to lists the same way that general iterators are bound to general collections, by calling a `listIterator()` method on the list. Also, the `getNext()` and `getPrevious()` methods must be called before the `nextIndex()` and `previousIndex()` methods.

❏ The Java Collections Framework defines two concrete list classes: `ArrayList` and `LinkedList`.

❏ An `ArrayList` instance stores its elements in an array, so it affords fast random access by index numbers.

❏ A `LinkedList` instance stores its elements in a linked list, so it affords fast insertions and deletions.

REVIEW QUESTIONS

8.1   What is the difference between sequential access and direct access, and how are they provided by our `List` implementations?

8.2   What is the difference between an array and an `ArrayList`?

8.3   How are `abstract` classes different from concrete classes and interfaces?

8.4   In Listing 8.8 on page 246, why is the nested `Node` class declared `static` while the nested `SequenceIterator` class is declared non-`static`?

8.5   How can you use the `java.util.ArrayList` class to create a list of int objects?

8.6   In the `Polynomial` class (Listing 8.12), why is the nested `Node` class declared to be `static`?

EXERCISES

8.1   Suppose that `list1` has size 4 and `list2` is created by cloning `list1` like this:

```
Object list2 = list1.clone();
```

How many new objects will this statement create?

8.2   What would this expression do?

```
list.set(2,list.set(3,list.set(4,list.set(5,list.set(6,"BE")))));
```

8.3   Draw pictures like Figures 8.14 and 8.15 show the effect of the call `p.add(term)` when `term` represents the following terms:

    a. $6.0x^5$

    b. $6.0x^4$

8.4   **a.** Explain why the direct evaluation of a polynomial of the form

$$p(x) = a_0 x^n + a_1 x^{n-1} + a_2 x^{n-2} + \cdots + a_{n-1} x + a_n$$

runs in $\Theta(n^2)$ time.

    b. Explain why Horner's method, evaluating polynomials of the form

$$p(x) = (\cdots (((a_0)x + a_1)x + a_2)x + \cdots + a_{n-1})x + a_n$$

runs in $\Theta(n)$ time.

PROGRAMMING PROBLEMS

8.1   Implement the client method

```
int frequency(java.util.List list, Object object)
// returns the number of occurrences of object in list
```

    a. using the `get(i)` method in a `for` loop;

    b. using an iterator in a `for` loop.

8.2   Run a test driver for the `Sequence` class defined in Listing 8.8 on page 246. Include a test of the `g8.remove(6)` call as shown in Figure 8.11 on page 249.

8.3   Run a test driver for the `Term` class defined in Listing 8.11 on page 252. Test each `public` method and the two `static` field.

8.4   Run a test drive for the `Polynomial` class defined in Listing 8.12 on page 256.

8.5   Add the following constructor to the `Polynomial` class defined in Listing 8.12 on page 256. It constructs the polynomial that has, for each nonzero element $a_k = $ `c[k]`, a term $a_k x^k$:

```
Polynomial(double[] c)
```

For example,

```
double[] c = {0.0, 5.0, 0.0, 4.0, -3.0};
Polynomial p = new Polynomial(c);
```

would construct a `Polynomial` object that represents the polynomial $-3x^4 + 4x^3 + 5x$.

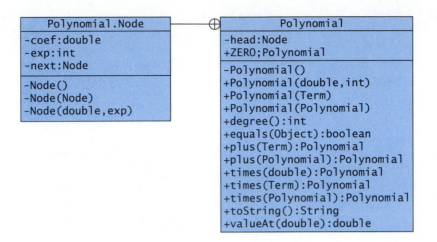

FIGURE 8.17   UML diagrams for `Polynomial` classes.

8.6   Add the following method to the `Polynomial` class defined in Listing 8.12 on page 256. It returns the polynomial's coefficients, including the zero terms, in an array, so that each nonzero element a_k = `c[k]` represents a term $a_k x^k$:

```
double[] toArray()
```

For example, if p represents the polynomial $-3x^4 + 4x^3 + 5x$, then

```
double[] c = p.toArray();
```

would load {`0.0, 5.0, 0.0, 4.0, -3.0`} into the array `c[]`.

8.7   In calculus, the *derivative* of a polynomial is another polynomial obtained by replacing each term $a_k x^k$ with the term $k a_k x^{k-1}$ (and deleting any constant term). For example, the derivative of the polynomial $7x^4 + 2x^3 - 5x + 9$ is the polynomial $28x^3 + 6x^2 - 5$. Add this method to the `Polynomial` class defined in Listing 8.12 on page 256:

```
Polynomial derivative()
```

8.8   Modify the `Polynomial` class defined in Listing 8.12 on page 256 so that its nested `Node` class includes the `coef` and `exp` fields, thus eliminating the need for the `Term` class.

PROJECTS

8.1   Define and test a stack class as an extension of the `ArrayList` class, implementing the `Stack` interface given in Listing 5.1 on page 152. Use the `ArrayList` methods to implement the `Stack` methods. The idea is to use a list as a stack, ignoring all the non-stack features of the list.

8.2 Define and test a queue class as an extension of the `ArrayList` class, implementing the `Queue` interface given in Listing 6.1 on page 178. Use the `ArrayList` methods to implement the `Queue` methods. The idea is to use a list as a queue, ignoring all the non-queue features of the list.

8.3 Define and test a deque class as an extension of the `ArrayList` class, implementing the methods described in Programming Project 6.4 on page 198. The idea is to use a list as a queue, ignoring all the nonqueue features of the list.

8.4 Define and test a `Ring` class as an extension of the `LinkedList` class, overriding its `iterator()` method so that the `Iterator` object that it returns has these modifications to its methods: Its `next()` method wraps around the linked list, returning the first element after the last one (hopping over the dummy head node); its `hasNext()` method always returns `true`. Then use this `Ring` class to solve the *Josephus problem*: Forty soldiers arranged in a circle have made a suicide pact, in which each will slay the (remaining) soldier on his right. Which of them will survive?

8.5 Define and test a `BidirectionalList` class as an extension of the `LinkedList` class, overriding its `iterator()` method so that the `Iterator` object that it returns has a third method, named `previous()`, which returns the current node after moving the iterator back one element. Then use the `BidirectionalList` class to solve this *random walk problem*: How many steps, on average, will an iterator make before it reaches an end of an *n*-element list, if it starts in the middle, and selects its direction (forward or backward) at random on each step?

8.6 Define and test a `Polynomial` class with a doubly linked list, storing the terms in increasing order of their exponents.

ANSWERS TO REVIEW QUESTIONS

8.1 Sequential access locates an element in a list by searching for it, starting with the first element, then the second element, then the third element, and so on., until the target element is found or the end of the list is reached. It is implemented using list iterators. Direct access locates an element in a list by using its index as a relative locator. It is implemented in the `List` interface with the `add(i,object)`, `get(i)`, `remove(i)`, and `set(i,object)` methods, which simulate array subscripts. Direct access is also called "random access," as in "random access memory" (RAM).

8.2 An *array* is a data structure based upon an element type. An `ArrayList` is a class whose instances are indexed collections. The `ArrayList` class uses an array for its backing store.

8.3 Abstract classes lie between interfaces and concrete classes. An interface provides no executable code, an `abstract` class provides some of the executable code, and a concrete class provides all the executable code.

8.4 The nested `SequenceIterator` class has to be declared non-`static` in Listing 8.8 on page 246, because some of its methods have to access the non-`static` `size` field of its enclosing Sequence class. The nested Node class is entirely self-contained, so it can be declared `static`

8.5   Wrap each `int` element in an `integer` object, and add that object to the `ArrayList` object.

8.6   The nested `Node` class is declared `static` because it does not need to access any of the fields of its parent `Polynomial` class.

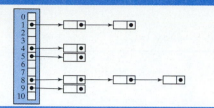

I wish to God these calculations had been executed by steam.

— Charles Babbage, 1812

Chapter 9

Hash Tables

The two general access patterns for data structures are sequential access and direct access. Sequential access is provided by linked lists; direct access is provided by arrays.

With *sequential access*, you find an element by starting at one end of the structure and looking at each element, one after the other, until you find your target or you reach the other end. That search algorithm runs in linear time. Audiotapes and videotapes are examples of data structures that use sequential access.

With *direct access* (also called *random access*), you find an element by using a given index i to go directly to the element a[i]. We think of i as the address of the element a[i]. Direct access is much faster than sequential access, running in constant time. But it requires prior knowledge of the element's index. Audio CDs and video DVDs are examples of data structures that provide direct access.

A *hash table* is a data structure that attempts to provide direct access without requiring prior knowledge of an element's index. This is accomplished by a *hash function* that computes the element's index from its contents. The word "hash" reflects the fact that the elements are all jumbled up, with no order at all. This chapter describes several different kinds of hash tables, including the kind that is implemented in the java.util package.

9.1 Tables and Records

A *record* is a composite data structure with several components. Each component has its own name and type. In some programming languages, records are standard types, like arrays. In Java, records can be implemented as objects.

For example, the class defined in Listing 9.1 can be used to instantiate records of data about countries of the world. We could use it to create these two records:

```
Country france = new Country("France", "French", 211200, 58978172);
Country germany = new Country("Germany", "German", 137800, 82087361);
```

Records are used to hold data on external disks. So the class that we use to define them typically has few (if any) methods. A constructor and a toString() method may be all that we need.

LISTING 9.1: A Country **Class**

```
1   class Country {
2      public String name, language;
3      public int area, population;
4
5      public Country(String n, String l, int a, int p) {
6         name = n; language = l; area = a; population = p;
7      }
8
9      public String toString() {
10        return "(" + name + "," + language + "," + area+","+population+")";
11     }
12  }
```

A *table* is a set of records of the same type. For example, Table 9.1 is a table of six records, using the Country type just defined. Note that tables are unordered data structures.

A *keyed table* is a table whose record type includes one special field, called its *key field*, whose values are unique among all the records in the table. Each key is used to identify its record. Keyed tables are the basic building blocks of computer databases.

Any table that has a column of unique values can be regarded as a keyed table simply by designating that column as the key field. For example, suppose we designate the language field as the key field in Table 9.1. That is not a very good choice, however, because we might want to add the record

> new Country("Austria", "German", 32378, 8139299);

to the table later. Doing so, would violate the uniqueness requirement of key fields, because that record's language would be the same as Germany's. The designation of a table's key field is an intrinsic part of the data structure itself and should not depend upon any particular data set that might currently be populating the structure.

The same problem could arise if we designate area or population as the key field. The only good choice of the key field among the four fields in that table would be the name field.

Key fields are used to look up records. They work best when they are short and simple. Fortunately, the International Standards Organization (ISO) has defined a unique two-letter abbreviation for each of the world's countries, similar to the unique two-letter postal abbreviations that the United States and Canada have for their states and provinces. These make ideal key fields.

name	language	area	population
France	French	211,200	58,978,172
Germany	German	137,800	82,087,361
Greece	Greek	50,900	10,707,135
Italy	Italian	116,300	56,735,130
Portugal	Portuguese	35,672	9,918,040
Sweden	Swedish	173,732	8,911,296

TABLE 9.1   A table of 6 records.

name	iso	language	area	population
Austria	AT	German	32,378	8,139,299
France	FR	French	211,200	58,978,172
Germany	DE	German	137,800	82,087,361
Greece	GR	Greek	50,900	10,707,135
Italy	IT	Italian	116,300	56,735,130
Portugal	PT	Portuguese	35,672	9,918,040
Sweden	SE	Swedish	173,732	8,911,296

TABLE 9.2   A table of 7 records.

The revised Table 9.2 has a new field, named **iso**, which we designate as the key field for the table.

Standardizing authorities have defined similar key fields for other important entities, such as Social Security Numbers (SSN) for Americans, Vehicle Identification Numbers (VIN) for cars and other vehicles, International Standard Book Numbers (ISBN) for books, and Universal Product Codes (UPC) for grocery products.

A keyed table is also called a *map* or a *dictionary*. We will usually use "map."

The term "map" comes from the mathematical idea of a mapping or input/output process: The input is the key, and the output is the rest of the record for that key. The key is "mapped" to the rest of the record:

```
"IT"  →  ("Italy", "Italian", 116300, 56735130)
```

This is analogous to the mathematical idea of a function $y = f(x)$, where x is the input and y is the output:

```
x = key = "IT"
y = value = ("Italy", "Italian", 116300, 56735130)
```

In mathematics, a function or mapping is identified with its graph, which is the set of all ordered pairs (x, y) where $y = f(x)$. Similarly, a keyed table or map is a set of key/value pairs. Moreover, the same functional constraint applies in both cases: No two distinct points (x, y) in a mathematical function can have the same x-coordinate, and no two distinct records in a map data structure can have the same key.

The term "dictionary" is used because keyed tables are used to look up information, much like looking up a word in a dictionary. The input key is the word, and the output value is the word's definition. This analogy isn't quite as good as the mathematical mapping, because the key words in a word dictionary are ordered alphabetically, whereas a keyed table is not ordered. Furthermore, word dictionaries sometimes list the same key word several times, which would violate the uniqueness requirement of keys in a keyed table.

9.2 An ADT for Maps

Maps are collections of keyed records. Thus, in order to provide an abstract data type for maps, we first need one for keyed records.

ADT: Keyed Record

A *keyed record* is an ordered pair of objects named *key* and *value*.

Operations

1. *Initialize*: Create a keyed record having a given key and given value.
2. *Key*: Return the key object in this record.
3. *Value*: Return the value object in this record.
4. *Update*: Replace the value object in this record with a given value object.

Listing 9.2 translates this ADT into a Java interface named `Entry`. Its UML diagram is shown in Figure 9.1. The *Initialize* operation will be implemented as a two-argument constructor, so it does not appear in the interface. The *Key* and *Value* operations are defined as `getKey()` and `getValue()` methods, and the *Update* operation is defined as the `setValue()` method.

LISTING 9.2: An `Entry` Interface

```java
1   public interface Entry {
2      public Object getKey();
3      // RETURN: key;
4      // POST: key is the first object in this ordered pair;
5
6      public Object getValue();
7      // RETURN: value;
8      // POST: value is the second object in this ordered pair;
9
10     public void setValue(Object value);
11     // POST: value is the second object in this ordered pair;
12  }
```

This defines two "getter" methods and one "setter" method. This gives read–write access to the value component, but restricts the key component to read-only access. That is consistent with the constraints of maps, which require their key fields to be immutable.

FIGURE 9.1 An Entry interface.

ADT: Map

A *map* is a collection of keyed records within which the keys are unique.

Operations

1. *Initialize*: Create an empty map.
2. *Search*: For a given key, search the table for a record that has that key. If found, return its value; otherwise, return `null`.
3. *Insert/Update*: For a given record, search the table for a record that has that key. If found, replace the value of the table's record with the value of the given record and return the replaced value; otherwise, insert the given record into the table.
4. *Delete*: For a given key, search the table for a record that has that key. If found, delete it from the table and return its value; otherwise, return `null`.
5. *Count*: Return the number of records in the table.

This ADT specifies only a minimal set of operations. As we shall see later, Java adds more functionality to its `java.util.Map` interface.

The Map ADT is translated directly into a Java interface in Listing 9.3. It's UML diagram is shown in Figure 9.2. The *Initialize* operation will be implemented as a no-argument constructor, so it does not appear in the interface. The *Search* operation is defined as the `get()` method, the *Insert/Update* operation is defined as the `put()` method, the *Delete* operation is defined as the `remove()` method, and the *Count* operation is defined as the `size()` method. As we shall see, these method signatures are the same as those defined in the `java.util.Map` interface. Moreover, the method signatures in the `Entry` interface in Listing 9.2 are the same as those defined in the `java.util.Map.Entry` interface, which is a sub-interface (or *nested interface*) of the `java.util.Map` interface.

Notice how the value returned by `get()`, `put()`, and `remove()` transmits the outcome of the operation. The `null` value signals failure with the `get()` and `remove()` methods. But the `put()` method serves double duty: It is used both to insert new records and to modify existing records. So it returns `null` to signal success at inserting the new record, and non-`null` to signal success at modifying an existing record.

When we think of data structures and abstract data types, we usually imagine them to be implemented in computer memory. But the ADT may apply to much larger structures. For example, the Internet can be regarded as one enormous map. Its keys are the URLs and their values are the web pages that they address. For example, the URL

```
http://www.paris.org/Musees/Louvre/Treasures/gifs/Mona_Lisa.jpg
```

brings up an image of the Mona Lisa from the Louvre in Paris.

FIGURE 9.2 A Map interface.

LISTING 9.3: A Map **Interface**

```
1   public interface Map {
2
3       public Object get(Object key);
4       // RETURN: value;
5       // POST: if value!=null, then (key,value) is in this map;
6       //        if value==null, then no record in this map has the given key;
7
8       public Object put(Object key, Object value);
9       // RETURN: oldValue;
10      // POST: if oldValue==null, then (key,value) is in this map;
11      //        if oldValue!=null, then (key,oldValue) was in this map;
12
13      public Object remove(Object key);
14      // RETURN: oldValue;
15      // POST: if oldValue==null, no record in this map has the given key;
16      //        if oldValue!=null, then (key,oldValue) was in this map;
17
18      public int size();
19      // RETURN: n;
20      // POST: this map contains n records;
21  }
```

9.3 Hash Tables

Without further organization of the data structure, access to a keyed table is sequential. If the table is sorted by its key values and stored in an array, then binary searching could be implemented, improving the access time from $\Theta(n)$ to $\Theta(\lg n)$. With *hashing*, however, we can do better without sorting.

A *hash function* for a keyed table is a function that returns the location (the array index) of the unique record in the able that has the given key value. A *hash table* is a keyed table that has a hash function.

The Java Object class defines a hashCode() method that returns an int for any object. Thus, in Java, every object has its own hash code. The code is computed from the data stored in the object.

For example, the Java hash code for the String object "IT" is 2347. This is $31 \cdot 73 + 84$. Similarly, the hash code for "SE" is 2642, which is $31 \cdot 83 + 69$. So we can see how the Java hash function works, at least for a two-character String object iso: It returns the integer value

```
31*iso.charAt(0) + iso.charAt(1)
```

Table 9.3 shows the Java hashCode() values for the seven ISO strings used in Table 9.2.

In general, the Java hashCode() value for an object can be any int, positive or negative. To use it as an array index, it must be converted into an integer h in the range $0 \le h < m$, where m is the length of the array. A standard technique for doing that is to use the integer

```
int h = (key.hashCode() & 0x7FFFFFFF) % entries.length;
```

key	hashCode(key)
AT	2099
FR	2252
DE	2177
GR	2283
IT	2347
PT	2564
SE	2642

TABLE 9.3   The hashCode() method.

The literal 0x7FFFFFFF is hexadecimal for the bit string 01111111111111111111111111111111 (a"0" followed by 31 "1"s). The operator & is the "bitwise and" operator. When applied to an integer k using the mask 0x7FFFFFFF, it simply changes k's leading bit to 0, which is the same as assigning to k its absolute value $|k|$. The operation x % m gives the remainder from the division of x by m, producing a nonnegative integer less than m. For example, if k is −1836, then the expression

    (k & 0x7FFFFFFF) % m

will evaluate to 7 if m is 41.

A hash function provides nearly constant time access to elements in a hash table. This is seen from the get() and put() methods in the HashTable class shown in Listing 9.4. The array element entries[i] is accessed on lines 6 and 10, where i is the index returned by hash(key). That element, entries[hash(key)], is the value of the key/value pair stored in the hash table.

LISTING 9.4: A Naive Hash Table Class

```
1   public class HashTable implements Map {
2     private Entry[] entries = new Entry[11];
3     private int size;
4
5     public Object get(Object key) {
6       return entries[hash(key)].value;
7     }
8
9     public Object put(Object key, Object value) {
10      entries[hash(key)] = new Entry(key,value);
11      ++size;
12      return null;
13    }
14
15    public Object remove(Object key) {
16      int h = hash(key);
```

```
17        Object value = entries[h].value;
18        entries[h] = null;
19        --size;
20        return value;
21      }
22
23      public int size() {
24        return size;
25      }
26
27      private class Entry {
28        Object key, value;
29        Entry(Object k, Object v) { key = k; value = v; }
30      }
31
32      private int hash(Object key) {
33        return (key.hashCode() & 0x7FFFFFFF) % entries.length;
34      }
35  }
```

The code in Listing 9.4 is consistent with the specifications in the java.util.Map interface, which is discussed later in this chapter. That interface requires the get(), put(), remove(), and size() methods implemented here. This HashTable class defines a private inner class named Entry (at lines 27–30) for its key/value pairs. Its two-argument constructor, defined at line 29, is used by the HashTable constructor at line 10. The data structure for this class is an array of 11 Entry objects, defined at line 2.

This HashTable class is naive because it has no way to handle exceptional situations that are likely to occur. In the example, inserting those seven Country records in a table of length $m = 11$ worked fine because every key hashed to a different location. That will not always happen.

Suppose that the next record to be inserted is the Country record for the United Kingdom. Its ISO key is "GB", which hashes to index 1. The put() method for this naive HashTable class would insert the record at entries[1], overwriting the record for Portugal. This is called a *collision*. Clearly, it should be managed differently.

0	
1	"PT",("Portugal","Portuguese",35672,9918040)
2	"SE",("Sweden","Swedish",173732,8911296)
3	
4	"IT",("Italy","Italian",116300,56735130)
5	
6	"GR",("Greece","Greek",50900,10707135)
7	
8	"FR",("France","French",211200,58978172)
9	"AT",("Austria","German",32378,8139299)
10	"DE",("Germany","German",137800,82087361)

FIGURE 9.3 A hash table of size 7.

9.4 Linear Probing

The simplest way to resolve collisions in a hash table is to put the colliding record in the next available cell in the array. This algorithm is called *linear probing*, because in each "probe" we increment the array index by 1. It is also called *open addressing*, because an element is not always placed in the slot indexed by its hash value; it can end up anywhere in the table.

In the previous example, the call

```
put("GB", new Country("United Kingdom", "English", 94500, 59113439));
```

should resolve the collision by inserting this new record in `entries[3]`, since `"GB"` hashes to index 1 and `entries[1]` and `entries[2]` are occupied. Then the call `get("GB")` would find the record, first by hashing to index 1, and then probing sequentially to `entries[1]`, `entries[2]`, and finally `entries[3]` before finding the record there. This probing is shown in Figure 9.4.

Suppose that the next insertion is

```
put("NL", new Country("Netherlands", "Dutch", 16033, 15807641));
```

The key `"NL"` hashes to index 8, so the linear probing algorithm would search `entries[8]`, `entries[9]`, and `entries[10]`, before finding an empty cell at `entries[0]`. The algorithm "wraps around" the end of the array, like a circular list, as shown in Figure 9.5.

FIGURE 9.4 Linear probing.

FIGURE 9.5 Wrapping around.

The revised code for the put() method would look like this:

```java
public Object put(Object key, Object value) {
    int h = hash(key);
    for (int i = 0; i < entries.length; i++) {
        int j = (h+i)%entries.length;
        Entry entry=entries[j];
        if (entry == null) {
            entries[j] = new Entry(key,value);
            ++size;
            ++used;
            return null;  // insertion success
        }
    }
    throw new IllegalStateException();  // failure: table overflow
    return null;
}
```

The expression (h+i)%entries.length handles the wraparound part of the algorithm. In the "NL" example, h = 8 and i increments in the loop with values 0, 1, 2, and 3, so (h+i) increments through 8, 9, 10, and 11. As long as (h+i) < 11, the value of the expression (h+i)%entries.length will be simply (h+i). When (h+i) = 11, the value of the expression (h+i)%entries.length will be 0 because 11 divided by 11 has remainder 0. In general, the expression (h+i)%entries.length will equal (h+i) or (h+i) − 11, according to whether (h+i) < entries.length or (h+i) ≥ entries.length.

The revision for the get() method is similar.

Revising the remove() method (at line 15) is a bit more complicated. Suppose we remove the "SE" record at entries[2] and then call get("GB"). If remove("SE") sets entries[2] to null, then we will never find "GB" at entries[3], because the search stops when null is encountered. We could just search the entire table, but that would make the algorithm run in linear time, instead of the near-constant time promised by the hash table. A better solution is to replace the deleted Entry object with a special dummy variable that will not stop the linear probing search.

We define a special Entry object named NIL like this:

```java
private final Entry NIL = new Entry(null, null);  // dummy
```

Then the revised remove() method looks like this:

```java
public Object remove(Object key) {
    int h = hash(key);
    for (int i = 0; i < entries.length; i++) {
        int j = (h+i)%entries.length;
        if (entries[j] == null) break;
        if (entries[j].key.equals(key)) {
            Object value = entries[j].value;
            entries[j] = NIL;
            --size;
            return value;
        }
    }
    return null;  // failure: key not found
}
```

Now we can modify the put() method again, interpreting the "next available cell" as being the next entries[j] that is either null or NIL:

```
if (entries[j] == null || entries[j] == NIL) {
    entries[j] = new Entry(key,value);
    ++size;
    return null;
}
```

9.5 Rehashing

The next improvement to make to our HashTable class is to handle the overflow problem. The solution is to rebuild the table using a larger array. This is called *rehashing*.

Here is a rehash() method that creates an array that is more than twice the size of the existing array and moves all the entries from the old array to the new one:

```
private void rehash() {
    Entry[] oldEntries = entries;
    entries = new Entry[2*oldEntries. length+1];
    for (int k = 0; k < oldEntries.length; k++) {
        Entry entry = oldEntries[k];
        if (entry == null || entry == NIL) continue;
        int h = hash(entry.key);
        for (int i = 0; i < entries.length; i++) {
            int j = nextProbe(h,i);
            if (entries[j]==null) {
                entries[j] = entry;
                break;
            }
        }
    }
    used = size;
}
```

First it assigns a new reference, oldEntries[], to the existing array so that the class field name entries[] can be used to reference the new array. The length of the new array is set to $2m+1$, where m is the length of the old array. The "+1" is used to make the length an odd number, thereby reducing its number of divisors. The hash table's performance tends to be better if its array length has fewer divisors.

Note that reallocating the array entries[] automatically redefines the hash() method because it changes the value of entries.length. Also note the rehash() method does not create any new Entry objects. It simply provides new references (in the new array) to the existing objects. The size does not change.

In our solution to the remove() problem described in the previous section, you may have noticed that its creates another problem. As more insertions are deletions are performed, more and more references to the NIL object will be stored in the array. No matter how many remove() operations occur, the probing sequences will never get any shorter. This increases the frequency of collisions, thus making the linear probing sequences longer and degrading the general performance of the data structure.

The rehash() method removes all the NIL references; *i.e.*, it does not copy any of them to the new array. So calling rehash() will generally boost performance. Of course, it is more efficient to initialize the hash table with plenty of space to begin with, rather than to start small and then have to rehash many times.

In any case, experience has shown that calling rehash() before the table becomes full is a good strategy. This is done by setting a threshold size, which triggers a call to rehash(). But instead of storing the threshold value, we specify a maximum ratio $r = n/m$, where n = size and m = entries.length. This ratio is called the *load factor*. Its upper limit is typically set at around 75% or 80%. For example, if we set it at 75% and begin with an array length of 11, then rehash() will be called when the size exceeds 8.25 (*i.e.*, after the 9th record has been inserted). That will rebuild the hash table to a length of 23.

LISTING 9.5:   A Correct Hash Table Class

```
1   public class HashTable implements Map {
2      private Entry[] entries;
3      private int size, used;
4      private float loadFactor;
5      private final Entry NIL = new Entry(null, null);   // dummy
6
7      public HashTable(int capacity, float loadFactor) {
8         entries = new Entry[capacity];
9         this.loadFactor = loadFactor;
10     }
11
12     public HashTable(int capacity) {
13        this(capacity, 0.75F);
14     }
15
16     public HashTable() {
17        this(101);
18     }
19
20     public Object get(Object key) {
21        int h = hash(key);
22        for (int i = 0; i < entries.length; i++) {
23           int j = nextProbe(h,i);
24           Entry entry=entries[j];
25           if (entry == null) break;
26           if (entry == NIL) continue;
27           if (entry.key.equals(key)) return entry.value;   // success
28        }
29        return null;   // failure: key not found
30     }
31
32     public Object put(Object key, Object value) {
33        if (used > loadFactor*entries.length) rehash();
34        int h = hash(key);
35        for (int i = 0; i < entries.length; i++) {
```

```
36        int j = nextProbe(h,i);
37        Entry entry = entries[j];
38        if (entry == null) {
39          entries[j] = new Entry(key, value);
40          ++size;
41          ++used;
42          return null;  // insertion success
43        }
44        if (entry == NIL) continue;
45        if (entry.key.equals(key)) {
46          Object oldValue = entry.value;
47          entries[j].value = value;
48          return oldValue;  // update success
49        }
50      }
51      return null;  // failure: table overflow
52    }
53
54    public Object remove(Object key) {
55      int h = hash(key);
56      for (int i = 0; i < entries.length; i++) {
57        int j = nextProbe(h,i);
58        Entry entry = entries[j];
59        if (entry == null) break;
60        if (entry == NIL) continue;
61        if (entry.key.equals(key)) {
62          Object oldValue = entry.value;
63          entries[j] = NIL;
64          --size;
65          return oldValue;  // success
66        }
67      }
68      return null;  // failure: key not found
69    }
70
71    public int size() {
72      return size;
73    }
74
75    private class Entry {
76      Object key, value;
77      Entry(Object k, Object v) { key = k; value = v; }
78    }
79
80    private int hash(Object key) {
81      if (key == null) throw new IllegalArgumentException();
82      return (key.hashCode() & 0x7FFFFFFF) % entries.length;
83    }
84
85    private int nextProbe(int h, int i) {
```

```
86       return (h + i)%entries.length;        // Linear Probing
87     }
88
89    private void rehash() {
90      Entry[] oldEntries = entries;
91      entries = new Entry[2*oldEntries.length+1];
92      for (int k = 0;  k < oldEntries.length; k++) {
93        Entry entry = oldEntries[k];
94        if (entry == null || entry == NIL) continue;
95        int h = hash(entry.key);
96        for (int i = 0; i < entries.length; i++) {
97          int j = nextProbe(h,i);
98          if (entries[j] == null) {
99            entries[j] = entry;
100           break;
101         }
102       }
103     }
104     used = size;
105   }
106 }
```

The complete corrected HashTable class is shown in Listing 9.5. It includes the loadFactor field and the constant NIL, as well as three constructors and the private rehash() method. The constructors allow the client to set the initial array capacity and the load factor, which otherwise are given the default values of 0.75 and 101, respectively.

The private nextProbe() method generates the indexes for the probing sequence. It is used by the get(), put(), remove(), and rehash() methods as they sequentially search for the next available space or the for a given key. The run time of each of these four methods is proportional to the number of calls that they make to nextProbe().

Note that the put() method now includes code that will update a stored record. When used with a key that is already in the table, it replaces the existing value with a value passed to put() and returns the old value. That is why put() returns null in the other two cases (*i.e.*, inserting a new record or table overflow): to distinguish those outcomes from an update.

9.6 Other Collision Resolution Algorithms

Linear probing is a simple and fairly effective method for resolving collisions. However, if the hash function fails to distribute the records uniformly throughout the table, then linear probing can lead to long chains of records bunched together. This is called *primary clustering*.

For example, suppose we insert these nine countries in an empty table of length $m = 101$:

```
put("FI", new Country("Finland", "Finnish", 130100, 5158372));
put("IQ", new Country("Iraq", "Arabic", 168754, 22427150));
put("IR", new Country("Iran", "Farsi", 636000, 65179752));
put("SK", new Country("Slovakia", "Slovak", 18859, 5396193));
put("CA", new Country("Canada", "English", 3851800, 31006347));
put("LY", new Country("Libya", "Arabic", 679400, 4992838));
```

```
put("IT", new Country("Italy", "Italian", 116300, 56735130));
put("PE", new Country("Peru", "Spanish", 496200, 26624582));
put("IS", new Country("Iceland", "Islenska", 40000, 272512));
```

Their hash() values are shown in Table 9.4. With linear probing, we get 26 collisions when inserting these nine records in that order:

"FI" → 21
"IQ" → 21 → 22
"IR" → 22 → 23
"SK" → 22 → 23 → 24
"CA" → 21 → 22 → 23 → 24 → 25
"LY" → 21 → 22 → 23 → 24 → 25 → 26
"IT" → 24 → 25 → 26 → 27
"PE" → 24 → 25 → 26 → 27 → 28
"IS" → 23 → 24 → 25 → 26 → 27 → 28 → 29

This shows how clustering can degrade performance. The single cluster has no gaps within it. So new records like "PE" and "IS" that hash near the beginning of the cluster have to wade through it one step at a time, causing more collisions and wasting time.

One alternative to linear probing is called *quadratic probing*. That algorithm resolves collisions by incrementing in increasingly greater steps, instead of by 1 each time. To implement it, replace lines 23, 33, 51, and 86 in Listing 9.5 on page 276 with

```
int j = (h + i*i)%entries.length;
```

Instead of adding i to h after each collision, we add i*i. (Quadratic means square the variable.) The increment sequence is 1, 4, 9, 16, 25, · · · . These are the (absolute) increments from the initial hash value h. The successive (relative) increments are 1, 3, 5, 7, 9, · · · .[1]

key	hash(key)
"FI"	21
"IQ"	21
"IR"	22
"SK"	22
"CA"	21
"LY"	21
"IT"	24
"PE"	24
"IS"	23

TABLE 9.4   Hashing Keys.

---

[1] $3 = 4-1; 5 = 9-4; 7 = 16-9; 9 = 25-16$; etc.

With quadratic probing, the same nine-record input sequence results in only 13 collisions:

```
"FI" → 21
"IQ" → 21 → 22
"IR" → 22 → 23
"SK" → 22 → 23 → 26
"CA" → 21 → 22 → 25
"LY" → 21 → 22 → 25 → 30
"IT" → 24
"PE" → 24 → 25 → 28
"IS" → 23 → 24 → 27
```

The probe sequence for "LY" is shown in Figure 9.6.

Quadratic probing produced half as many collisions as linear probing. The improvement results because quadratic probing leaves unused gaps, thereby causing less clustering than linear probing.

But quadratic probing still has problems. For example, suppose we are hashing into a table of length $m = 11$. Suppose also that a key hashes to index $j = 3$ and encounters repeated collisions. The probe sequence will be 3, 4, 7, 1, 8, 6, 6, 8, 1, 7, 4, 3, 4, 7, 1, 8, 6, 6, 8, 1, 7, 4, 3, ···. This is a sparse periodic sequence. It reaches only 6 of the 11 cells. If those six cells are occupied, then put() will fail, even if the other five cells are unoccupied.

The solution is to set the threshold load factor at 50%. It can be shown that the sparse periodic sequences that can result from quadratic probing will always reach more than half of all the cells in the table. In this example, 6 > 11/2. So if no more than half of all cells can be occupied, then those sparse periodic probe sequences will still find empty cells.

Even with limiting the load factor to 50%, double hashing can still suffer from *secondary clustering*. This the same problem that linear probing has: Two different keys that hash to the same value will have the same probe sequence. The solution to that problem is to use a second, independent hash function to determine the probe sequence. That is called *double hashing*.

Like linear probing, double hashing uses a constant increment in its probe sequence. But that increment, determined by the second hash function, is usually greater than 1. So, like quadratic probing, double hashing avoids primary clustering by spreading out its probe sequence.

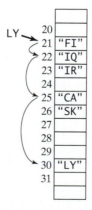

FIGURE 9.6 Quadratic probing.

For double hashing, we need a second hash function, say hash2(). We can use the same code as in lines 85–87 of Listing 9.5, except with this version of line 86:

```
return 1 + (key.hashCode() & 0x7FFFFFFF) % (entries.length - 1);
```

In other words, we use $h = c \% m$ for hash() and $d = 1 + c \% (m - 1)$ for hash2(). This guarantees that the increment d will be in the range $1 \leq d < m$.

The other changes to Listing 9.5 needed for double hashing are to replace lines 21, 34, and 55 with

```
int h=hash(key), d=hash2(key);
```

replace the call to nextProbe(h, i) with nextProbe(h, d, i) at lines 23, 36, and 57, make similar changes in the rehash() method, and add the hash2() method, as described above.

With that implementation, the same nine-record input sequence of Table 9.4 results in only five collisions:

```
"FI" → 21
"IQ" → 21 → 89
"IR" → 22
"SK" → 22 → 97
"CA" → 21 → 85
"LY" → 21 → 91
"IT" → 24
"PE" → 24 → 99
"IS" → 23
```

We have seen that both quadratic probing and double hashing solve the primary clustering problem seen with linear probing. Double hashing also solves the problem of secondary clustering, which occurs with both linear and quadratic probing. Quadratic probing also requires the threshold load factor to be set at 50% to avoid sparse periodic probe sequences.

9.7 Separate Chaining

The hashing algorithms described in the previous section are called *open addressing*, because they seek open positions in the array to resolve collisions. The alternative, called *closed addressing*, avoids collisions altogether by allowing more than one record to be stored at a hash location. This requires a more complex data structure.

Instead of an array of records, we use an array of buckets, where a *bucket* is a collection of records. The simplest data structure to use for a bucket is a linked list. This is called *separate chaining*.

Listing 9.6 shows an implementation of our HashTable class using separate chaining. The only difference in the code for this structure is that the inner Entry class has a next field (at line 62) to implement the singly linked lists.

Although the data structure is more complicated for hash tables with closed addressing, the code is actually a bit shorter. We need no dummy NIL entry, nor any collision resolution algorithms.

The get() method hashes to the target chain (at line 20) and then searches that linked list.

LISTING 9.6: **Closed Addressing by Separate Chaining**

```
1   public class HashTable {
2     private Entry[] entries;
3     private int size;
4     private float loadFactor;
5
6     public HashTable(int capacity, float loadFactor) {
7       entries = new Entry[capacity];
8       this.loadFactor = loadFactor;
9     }
10
11    public HashTable(int capacity) {
12      this(capacity, 0.75F);
13    }
14
15    public HashTable() {
16      this(101);
17    }
18
19    public Object get(Object key) {
20      int h = hash(key);
21      for (Entry e = entries[h]; e != null; e = e.next) {
22        if (e.key.equals(key)) return e.value;   // success
23      }
24      return null;   // failure: key not found
25    }
26
27    public Object put(Object key, Object value) {
28      int h = hash(key);
29      for (Entry e = entries[h]; e != null; e = e.next) {
30        if (e.key.equals(key)) {
31          Object oldValue = e.value;
32          e.value = value;
33          return oldValue;   // successful update
34        }
35      }
36      entries[h] = new Entry(key,value,entries[h]);
37      ++size;
38      if (size > loadFactor*entries.length) rehash();
39      return null;   // successful insertion
40    }
41
42    public Object remove(Object key) {
43      int h = hash(key);
44      for (Entry e = entries[h], prev=null; e!=null; prev=e, e=e.next) {
45        if (e.key.equals(key)) {
46          Object oldValuev=ve.value;
47          if (prev == null) entries[h] = e.next;
48          else prev.next = e.next;
```

```
49          --size;
50          return oldValue;  // success
51        }
52      }
53      return null;  // failure: key not found
54    }
55
56    public int size() {
57      return size;
58    }
59
60    private class Entry {
61      Object key, value;
62      Entry next;
63      Entry(Object k, Object v, Entry n) { key=k; value=v; next=n; }
64      public String toString() {
65        return key + "=" + (Country)value;
66      }
67    }
68
69    private int hash(Object key) {
70      if (key == null) throw new IllegalArgumentException();
71      return (key.hashCode() & 0x7FFFFFFF) % entries.length;
72    }
73
74    private void rehash() {
75      Entry[] oldEntries = entries;
76      entries = new Entry[2*oldEntries.length+1];
77      for (int k = 0; k < oldEntries.length; k++) {
78        for (Entry old = oldEntries[k]; old != null; ) {
79          Entry e = old;
80          old = old.next;
81          int h = hash(e.key);
82          e.next = entries[h];
83          entries[h] = e;
84        }
85      }
86    }
87  }
```

Note that with closed addressing, the load factor may exceed the length of the backing array since there is no limit to the length of the chains. Nevertheless, the hash table's performance will degrade if we allow long chains. So we still include rehashing when the table size exceeds its threshold.

Figure 9.7 shows how the hash table looks after loading the 15 European Union countries, using a capacity of 11 and a load factor of 2.0. This shows only the keys, not the complete records.

Closed addressing has the obvious advantage of preventing collisions: If each bucket can hold arbitrarily many keys, then it won't overflow. The disadvantage is that some chains can become very long. That slows the search because each chain is searched sequentially. A very unbalanced array of bucket chains can destroy the constant time access that hashing is meant to provide.

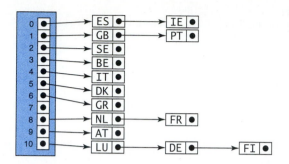

FIGURE 9.7   Closed addressing with chaining.

The risk of nonconstant time sequential searching also exists with open addressing. If most of the keys hash to the same value (a very bad hash function, indeed), then the same kind of long chains can result. Consequently, closed addressing tends to be the choice in many applications.

9.8 The `java.util.HashMap` Class

The standard Java class libraries include a hash table class named `HashMap`, defined in the `java.util` package. It is very similar to the `HashTable` class defined in Listing 9.6 on page 282. It uses closed addressing with a default initial capacity of 101 and a default maximum load factor of 0.75. It implements the `java.util.Map` interface, which is shown in Listing 9.7.

Notice that this interface includes a **public** subinterface named `Entry` to represent key/value pairs. As a subinterface, it can be used as a type name in the form `Map.Entry` (like a **static** member) in classes that implement the `Map` interface.

Listing 9.8 shows a program that tests the `java.util.HashMap` class.

The program first instantiates the `HashMap` class as an object named `map`. It puts eight records into it, prints its `keySet` and its `size`, and uses its `get()` method to retrieve the record for the key `"ES"`. Then it repeats the `get()` call at line 15 and assigns its output value to the `Country` object named `es`. Note that it has to use the expression `(Country)` to cast the object as a `Country` object because the `get()` method returns an object of general `Object` type.

Next, the program at line 16 changes the `population` field of the `es` object to 40,000,000. This assignment is done independently of the hash table. Nevertheless, the next call to `get()` shows that the change was made to the corresponding entry in the table. That is because the hash table stores only references to its `Entry` value objects. Any outside reference to them can change the table's values. This is consistent with the notion that a hash table is a generalized array. Objects stored in an array can be externally modified the same way without using the array.

The call to `remove()` deletes the `"ES"` entry from the table and returns its `Country` object. The next call to `get()` at line 19 returns **null**, confirming that it has been deleted from the table. The last two outputs also verify that the record has been removed.

The `java.util` package also includes a `HashTable` class, but that was superseded by the `HashMap` class in Java 1.2 in 1999. It is more consistent with the general Java Collections Framework.

LISTING 9.7: The `java.util.Map` Interface

```
1   public interface Map {
2     public void        clear();
3     public boolean     containsKey(Object key);
4     public boolean     containsValue(Object value);
5     public Set         entrySet();
6     public boolean     equals(Object object);
7     public Object      get(Object key);
8     public int         hashCode();
9     public boolean     isEmpty();
10    public Set         keySet();
11    public Object      put(Object key, Object value);
12    public void        putAll(Map map);
13    public Object      remove(Object key);
14    public int         size();
15    public Collection values();
16    public interface Entry {
17      public boolean equals(Object object);
18      public Object  getKey();
19      public Object  getValue();
20      public int     hashCode();
21      public Object  setValue(Object value);
22    }
23  }
```

LISTING 9.8: Testing the `java.util.HashMap` Class

```
1   public class TestMap {
2     public static void main(String[] args) {
3       java.util.Map map = new java.util.HashMap();
4       map.put("AT", new Country("Austria", "German", 32378, 8139299));
5       map.put("BE", v Country("Belgium", "Dutch", 11800, 10182034));
6       map.put("DK", new Country("Denmark", "Danish", 16639, 5356845));
7       map.put("FR", new Country("France", "French", 211200, 58978172));
8       map.put("GR", new Country("Greece", "Greek", 50900, 10707135));
9       map.put("IE", new Country("Ireland", "English", 27100, 3632944));
10      map.put("IT", new Country("Italy", "Italian", 116300, 56735130));
11      map.put("ES", new Country("Spain", "Spanish", 194880, 39167744));
12      System.out.println("map.keySet(): " + map.keySet());
13      System.out.println("map.size(): " + map.size());
14      System.out.println("map.get(\"ES\"): " + map.get("ES"));
15      Country es = (Country)map.get("ES");
16      es.population = 40000000;
17      System.out.println("map.get(\"ES\"): " + map.get("ES"));
18      System.out.println("map.remove(\"ES\"): " + map.remove("ES"));
19      System.out.println("map.get(\"ES\"): " + map.get("ES"));
20      System.out.println("map.keySet(): " + map.keySet());
21      System.out.println("map.size(): " + map.size());
22    }
23  }
```

The output is

```
map.keySet(): [AT, FR, GR, DK, IT, BE, ES, IE]
map.size(): 8
map.get("ES"): (Spain,Spanish,194880,39167744)
map.get("ES"): (Spain,Spanish,194880,40000000)
map.remove("ES"): (Spain,Spanish,194880,40000000)
map.get("ES"): null
map.keySet(): [AT, FR, GR, DK, IT, BE, IE]
map.size(): 7
```

9.9 Analysis of Hashing Algorithms

This section presents general formulas for the average run-time complexity of the four hashing algorithms discussed in Sections 9.3–9.7. For each of the four algorithms, a formula is given for the average number of probes in the case where a given key is found and the case where it is not found. For the get() and remove() methods, finding the key would be a success, and not finding it would be a failure. The opposite is true for the put() method. These formulas assume that the length m of the backing array is large and that the hash() method returns index numbers h that are uniformly distributed in the range $0 \le h < m$ for the set of all possible key values.

Recall that the *load factor* for the hash table is the ratio $r = n/m$, where n is the number of records in the table (size) and m is the length of the backing array (entries.length). With open addressing, $r \le 1$. The complexity functions in this table are expressed in terms of the load factor $r = n/m$. For those cases in which $r < 1$, the related quantity q is defined as $q = 1/(1-r) = m/(m-n)$.[2]

		Key is Found	Key is Not Found
Open Addressing ($r < 1$)	Linear Probing	$(1 + q)/2$	$(1 + q^2)/2$
	Quadratic Probing	$1 + \ln q - r/2$	$q + \ln q - r$
	Double Hashing	$(\ln q)/r$	q
Closed Addressing	Separate Chaining	$1 + r/2$	r

These formulas are derived in **[Knuth3]**, listed in Appendix G.

For example, if $r = 75\%$ (so $q = 4.0$ and $\ln q = 1.386$), these formulas evaluate to the numbers shown in the following table:

		Key is Found	Key is Not Found
Open Addressing ($r < 1$)	Linear Probing	2.5	8.5
	Quadratic Probing	2.0	4.6
	Double Hashing	1.8	4.0
Closed Addressing	Separate Chaining	1.375	0.75

---

[2] The variable q is used here merely to simplify the formulas in the tables.

It appears that the average run times for a given load factor get better as we move down the table. This can be verified algebraically. (See Exercise 9.3 on page 294.) In general, closed addressing with separate chaining performs better than the open addressing algorithms. That is why the `java.util.HashMap` class uses that algorithm.

9.10 Perfect Hash Functions

There is one situation in which open addressing does work better than closed addressing. That is when the hash function is one-to-one on the set of all possible keys. This is called a *perfect hash function*. Normally, that specialized situation is very unlikely. However, if one knows the complete key set in advance, then the hash table and its hash function can be tailor-made to fit it.

For example, take our set of 15 European Union countries. If we assume that that number will not change, then we can devise a perfect hash function on it. By trial and error, we can discover that with a capacity of $m = 77$, the standard hash function

```
key.hashCode() % capacity;
```

will be one to one on that set of 15 two-character strings, as shown in Table 9.5. The result is hashing with no collisions and true constant-time $\Theta(1)$ direct access.

So if a perfect hash function is found, then open addressing (with no probing) is best. This data structure is often called a *lookup table* because the hash function provides direct lookup facility.

Of course, this naive approach wastes space. The example here uses an array of length 77 to store 15 records, a load factor of less than 20%. But perhaps with more effort, a one-to-one hash function with a smaller range can be found.

A *minimal perfect hash function* is one that is both one to one and onto (*i.e.*, a perfect hash function with a 100% load factor). These are usually quite difficult to find, but some algorithms exist to aid the search process. One of them was published in 1980 by R. J. Cichelli. It finds a perfect hash function for strings.

Here is an outline of Cichelli's Algorithm:

1. List all the first and last letters of the n keys $\{c_0, c_1, \cdots, c_p\}$ and count their frequencies $f(c_i)$.
2. List the keys $\{k_0, k_1, \cdots, k_{n-1}\}$ in descending order of the sum of their first and last letter frequencies $f(\text{first}(k_j)) + f(\text{last}(k_j))$.
3. For each letter c_i in the first list, assign an integer value $v(c_i)$, choosing these values in the order that they appear in the second list, so that the sum $v(\text{first}(k_j)) + 2v(\text{last}(k_j))$ for each key k_j is unique among the n integers $0, 1, \cdots, n-1$.
4. Define the hash function as $h(k_j) = v(\text{first}(k_j)) + 2v(\text{last}(k_j))$ for each key k_j.

Here are the steps for the set of 15 keys in our European Union example:

1. The list of first and last letters and their frequencies is shown in the first table in Figure 9.8. For example, the letter I has frequency 3 because it is the first letter in IE and IT, and it is the last letter in FI.
2. The list of keys in order of the sum of their first and last letter frequencies is shown in the second table in Figure 9.8. For example, IE is listed first because its sum is $3 + 5 = 8$ (3 for its I and 5 for its E).

Key	Hash
AT	40
BE	56
DE	47
DK	53
ES	21
FI	42
FR	51
GB	66
GR	11
IE	60
IT	4
LU	27
NL	9
PT	8
SE	15

TABLE 9.5   A perfect hash function.

Letter	Freq.
A	1
B	2
D	2
E	5
F	2
G	2
I	3
K	1
L	2
N	1
P	1
R	2
S	2
T	3
U	1

Key	Sum
IE	8
BE	7
DE	7
ES	7
SE	7
IT	6
FI	5
AT	4
FR	4
GB	4
GR	4
PT	4
DK	3
LU	3
NL	3

Letter	Value
A	1
B	4
D	1
E	5
F	4
G	0
I	3
K	3
L	1
N	4
P	2
R	0
S	2
T	0
U	2

Key	Hash
AT	1
BE	14
DE	11
DK	7
ES	9
FI	10
FR	4
GB	8
GR	0
IE	13
IT	3
LU	5
NL	6
PT	2
SE	12

FIGURE 9.8   Encoding for a perfect hash function.

3. This step is the most difficult. It is likely to require some backtracking. It helps to elucidate obvious constraints. For example, E and S must be given different values because ES and SE are both in the key list. Similarly, B, D, I, and S must all be given different values because BE, DE, IE, and SE are all in the key list.

4. Once we have found the code values for the individual letters, we can compute the hash values for the keys from the hash function:

$$h(\text{key}) = v(\text{first}(\text{key})) + 2v(\text{last}(\text{key}))$$

For example, $h(\text{BE}) = v(\text{first}(\text{BE})) + 2v(\text{last}(\text{BE})) = v(\text{B}) + 2v(\text{E}) = 4 + 2(5) = 14$.

The code for this hash function is shown in Listing 9.9.

LISTING 9.9: A Minimal Perfect Hash Function

```
1    private final String LETTERS = "GRTADLPSUIK-BNFE";
2
3    private int v(char ch) {
4       return LETTERS.indexOf(ch)/3;
5    }
6
7    public int hash(Object key) {
8       String s = (String)key;
9       return v(s.charAt(0)) + 2*v(s.charAt(1));
10   }
```

The resulting hash table is shown in Figure 9.9.

Minimal perfect hash functions are useful when the entire key set is known in advance and does not change. Such is the case for tables of programming language reserved words used by a compiler. These are specialized "lookup" tables.

0	"GR",("Greece","Greek",50900,10707135)
1	"AT",("Austria","German",32378,8139299)
2	"PT",("Portugal","Portuguese",35672,9918040)
3	"IT",("Italy","Italian",116300,56735130)
4	"FR",("France","French",211200,58978172)
5	"LU",("Luxembourg","French",998,429080)
6	"NL",("Netherlands","Dutch",16033,15807641)
7	"DK",("Denmark","Danish",16639,5356845)
8	"GB",("United Kingdom","English",94500,59113439)
9	"ES",("Spain","Spanish",194880,39167744)
10	"FI",("Finland","Finnish",130100,5158372)
11	"DE",("Germany","German",137800,82087361)
12	"SE",("Sweden","Swedish",173732,8911296)
13	"IE",("Ireland","English",27100,3632944)
14	"BE",("Belgium","Dutch",11800,10182034)

FIGURE 9.9 The result of perfect hashing.

9.11 Other Hash Functions

If a perfect hash function is not possible, then the best hash functions are those that distribute the records evenly throughout the hash table. With large tables, this can usually be achieved by a function that returns `num(key)%entries.length`, where `num(key)` is a nonnegative integer whose value is equally likely to be any one of a large range of values. In the previous examples, we have been using `key.hashCode() & 0x7FFFFFFF` for `num(key)`. Hash functions of this form are called *division* hash functions because they use the remainder from dividing a large integer by the table's length.

Another common hashing method is called *extraction*. This is really the division method applied to only part of the key. It is used when parts of a key are redundant and thus do not help distinguish the records. For example, hashing the names of the seven days of the week should omit the last three letters of each key word because they are all the same suffix "day".

As a more important example, consider the problem of hashing vehicle identification numbers. A vehicle identification number (VIN) contains 17 alphanumeric characters, like this:

    2HGEH2367NH523465

This is a concatenation of several independent codes that are specified by the International Organization for Standardization (ISO).[3] For example, in this VIN, the first character, 2, indicates that the vehicle was manufactured in Canada, the next two characters, HG, identify the manufacturer as Honda, the next five characters, EH236, identify the body style and engine size, the ninth character, 7, is a check digit that is computed from the other characters, the tenth character, N, indicates that the vehicle was manufactured in 1992, the eleventh character, H, identifies the assembly plant, and the last six characters, 523465, indicate that this was the 523,465th such vehicle produced at that plant in 1992.

A good hash function for a VIN would extract the characters that distinguish the vehicles whose records are stored in the hash table. For example, if the hash table were storing records for a Honda dealer, then the 12 characters shown in bold here might be a good choice for an extraction hash function:

    2**HGEH236**7N**H523465**

The last six characters form a single six-digit integer, so they should be extracted like this:

    h11(key) = Integer.parseInt(key.substring(11,17))

The other six characters are alphanumeric, so they should be extracted, as in previous examples, like this:

    h3(key) = key.charAt(3)

Then the extraction hash function would be

    hash(key) = (h3(key) + h4(key) + ... + h11(key)) % entries.length

---

[3] The standard is identified as ISO-3779. See `http://www.iso.ch/iso/en/ISOOnline.openerpage`.

If the keys can be interpreted is simple integers, then a *folding hash function* provides a simple solution. This method separates the digit string into several parts and then "folds" them together. For example, consider hashing U.S. Social Security numbers. These are nine-digit codes, such as

054-36-1729

This social security number's hash value of 37 is computed by following these steps:

1. Form the corresponding long integer: 054361729
2. Separate it into three parts: 054, 361, 729
3. Reverse the middle part: 054, 163, 729
4. Add the parts: 054 + 163 + 729 = 946
5. Mod by the table length: 946 % 101 = 37

Thus, in a hash table of personnel records with a capacity of 101 records, the record with Social Security number 054-36-1729 would be stored in `table[37]`.

You can see why this method is called *folding* if you imagine the three-part number written on a flexible sheet that is then folded as shown in Figure 9.10. The middle third gets inverted, thus reversing its digits.

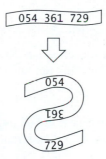

FIGURE 9.10 Folding.

CHAPTER SUMMARY

❑   The two general ways to access data within a data structure are *sequential* access and *direct* access. Sequential access runs in linear time. Direct access runs in constant time. Hash tables provide nearly direct access, running in nearly constant time.

❑   A *record* is a composite data structure whose components are named fields. A *table* is a set of records of the same type. A *keyed table* (*map, dictionary*) is a table whose record type includes a *key field* whose values uniquely identify the records in the table.

❑   A *hash function* returns the array index of the record in a keyed table that has a given key. A *hash table* is a keyed table with a hash function.

❑ The Java hashCode() method, defined in the Object class, can be used to obtain an int hash value for any object. That value is then transformed into a hash value in the range $0 \le h < m$ by the assignment

```
h = (key.hashCode() & 0x7FFFFFFF) % m
```

where *m* is the hash table's *capacity* (*i.e.*, the length of its backing array).

❑ Since most hash functions are not one-to-one, two different records may hash to the same location, causing a *collision*. Collisions are resolved by two different approaches: open addressing and closed addressing.

❑ With *closed addressing*, the hash table's storage cells are defined as multirecord buckets, usually implemented as linked lists. This is called *separate chaining*.

❑ With *open addressing*, a special algorithm is used to locate an open (empty) cell to store the colliding record. The three algorithms presented in this chapter are linear probing, quadratic probing, and double hashing. These are defined in terms of their *probe sequence*, which is the sequence of array indexes that it is following in searching for an open cell.

❑ With *linear probing*, the probe sequence is $h, h+1, h+2, h+3, h+4, \cdots$, increasing with constant incrementing by 1, wrapping around the end of the array. The formula is

```
j = (h + i) % m
```

where h is the collision index and i is the loop index.

❑ With *quadratic probing*, the probe sequence is $h, h+1, h+4, h+9, h+16, \cdots$, increasing with the increasing increments $1, 3, 5, 7, \cdots$. The formula is

```
j = (h + i*i) % m
```

❑ With *double hashing*, the probe sequence is $h, h+d, h+2d, h+3d, h+4d, \cdots$, increasing with the constant increment $d > 0$, obtained a second hash function. The formula is

```
j = (h + i*d) % m
```

where h is the collision index and d is the second hash function value.

❑ The *load factor* of a hash table is the ratio $r = n/m$, where *n* is the number of records in the table and *m* is the hash table's *capacity*; the length of its backing array. To achieve near-constant time access, a hash table should be rebuilt in a larger backing array when its load factor reaches a preset threshold, usually around 75%. This is called *rehashing*.

❑ Rehashing is a way to overcome *primary clustering*, which is when records begin to accumulate in long strings of adjacent positions instead of being uniformly distributed throughout the table. Primary clustering is also reduced by quadratic probing and double hashing.

❑ Both linear and quadratic probing suffer from *secondary clustering*, which occurs when different keys hash to the same index. But that can be overcome with double hashing if the second hash function is independent of the first. For example,

```
h1 = (key.hashCode() & 0x7FFFFFFF) % m
h2 = 1 + (key.hashCode() & 0x7FFFFFFF) % (m - 1)
```

❏   With quadratic probing, the probe sequences are sparsely periodic, requiring the load factor threshold to be set at 50%.

❏   Open addressing is fairly simple and works well for lookup tables (*i.e.*, `static` hash tables that are loaded initially and then not changed). Closed addressing is better for dynamic tables, especially those that have to allow for deletions.

❏   Deletion from a hash table with separate chaining is easy because the chains are disjoint, so deleting a record from one chain has no effect on the search for records in other chains. That is not true with open addressing.

❏   If a hash table that uses open addressing must support deletions, then the best approach is to replace the deleted record with a dummy `NIL` record. In this case, the load factor is the ratio $r = u/m$, where u is the number of cells that are used either by a data record or by the `NIL` record. Consequently, rehashing will be more frequent than with closed addressing.

❏   The `java.util.HashMap` class uses separate chaining with a default capacity of 101 and a load factor threshold of 75%.

❏   The complexity functions for the four algorithms show that hash tables do provide nearly constant time access. With a threshold of 75%, all four algorithms average fewer than three probes for a successful search, and all but linear probing average fewer than five probes for an unsuccessful search.

❏   A *perfect hash function* is one that maps each key to a different location. In that case, there are no collisions, and open addressing is optimal.

REVIEW QUESTIONS

9.1   Which access pattern, sequential or direct, do you use when you use the index of this book to find information about a given term?

9.2   Give an example in which sequential access is required, even though the target's address is known.

9.3   Which hashing algorithm does the `java.util.HashMap` class use, and why?

9.4   Because Social Security numbers are unique, why would the folding hash method be used on them?

EXERCISES

9.1   If the same records are inserted into a hash table in different orders, will they end up in the same locations? Either explain why they will, or give an example to show that they might not.

9.2   Use the complexity formulas in the table on page 286 to compute the average number of keys examined for both cases (found and not found) for the four hashing algorithms for these load factors:

   a. $r = 50\%$

   b. $r = 80\%$

   c. $r = 90\%$

   d. $r = 99\%$

9.3   Use the complexity formulas in the table on page 286 to verify these facts algebraically. You may use this series expansion: $\ln q = r + r^2/2 + r^3/3 + r^4/4 + r^5/5 + \cdots$.

   a. Double hashing is faster than quadratic probing for a key that is in the table.

   b. Separate chaining is faster than double hashing for a key that is in the table.

   c. Separate chaining is faster than double hashing for a key that is not in the table.

   d. With linear probing, searching for a key is faster if it is in the table.

   e. With quadratic probing, searching for a key is faster if it is in the table.

   f. With double probing, searching for a key is faster if it is in the table.

9.4   In our linear probing implementation in Listing 9.5, the search loop at lines 22, 32, and 50 looks like this:

```
for (int i = 0; i < entries.length; i++) {
```

Explain why we could use the shorter loop

```
for (int i = 0; i < size; i++) {
```

Would that simplification also work for quadratic probing? Would it work for double hashing? Explain.

9.5   The complexity formulas on page 286 assume that the keys are uniformly distributed throughout the hash table. What is the worst case if they are not?

9.6   Suppose we use a direct access file to build a hash table with capacity $2^{32} = 2,147,483,648$. That is the number of different values that the Java `hashCode()` method can return. Suppose we use the following hash function:

```
long hash(Object key) {
   long h = key.hashCode();
   return h - Integer.MIN_VALUE;
}
```

This returns long integers in the range 0 to $2^{32} - 1$. Comment on this design. Is this a perfect hash function?

9.7   Explain why the length of an array should be a prime number when the array is used to implement a hash table with open addressing and double hashing. Give an example that shows what can go wrong when the length is not prime.

PROGRAMMING PROBLEMS

9.1 Implement the `HashTable` class with the code given in Listing 9.5 on page 276, and test its methods with a test driver. Use the data given in Table 9.2.

9.2 Implement the `HashTable` class with the code given in Listing 9.6 on page 282, and test its methods with a test driver. Use the data given in Table 9.2.

9.3 Add and test a `toString()` method to the `HashTable` class with the code given in Listing 9.5 on page 276.

9.4 Add and test a `toString()` method to the `HashTable` class with the code given in Listing 9.6 on page 282.

9.5 Modify the `HashTable` class given in Listing 9.5 on page 276 so that it uses quadratic probing instead of linear probing, and test it.

9.6 Modify the `HashTable` class given in Listing 9.5 on page 276 so that it uses double hashing, and test it.

9.7 Run a program that compares linear probing to quadratic probing. Use a hash table of size $m = 17$, and hash these 13 keys: `"AT"`, `"BE"`, `"DE"`, `"DK"`, `"ES"`, `"FR"`, `"GB"`, `"GR"`, `"IE"`, `"IT"`, `"LU"`, `"NL"`, `"SE"` (in that order). Ouput the actual probe sequences and the total number of collisions. Your output should look something like this:

```
Linear Probing:
    1. AT -> 8
    2. BE -> 7
    :
    :
   13. SE -> 7 -> 8 -> 9 -> 10 -> 11 -> 12 -> 13 -> 14
14 collisions.
Quadratic Probing:
    1. AT -> 8
    2. BE -> 7
    :
    :
   13. SE -> 7 -> 8 -> 11 -> 16
8 collisions.
```

9.8 Run a program that compares linear probing to double hashing. Use a hash table of size 17, and hash these 9 keys: `"AT"`, `"BE"`, `"DE"`, `"DK"`, `"ES"`, `"FR"`, `"IT"`, `"LU"`, `"SE"` (in that order). Ouput the actual probe sequences and the total number of collisions. Your output should look something like this:

```
Linear Probing:
    1. AT -> 8
    2. BE -> 7
    :
    :
    9. SE -> 7 -> 8 -> 9 -> 10 -> 11 -> 12 -> 13
```

```
12 collisions.
   Double Hashing:
   1. AT -> 8
   2. BE -> 7
   :
   :
   9. SE -> 7 -> 10 -> 13 -> 16
6 collisions.
```

PROJECTS

9.1   Empirically test the formula $A = (1 + q)/2$ for finding a key in a hash table using linear probing. Use a backing array with capacity $m = 1001$. Do this for each n from 500 to 1000:

1. Insert n (different) random three-letter keys into a data array.
2. Insert all n of those keys into the hash table.
3. Select a random key from your data array and count how many times the get() loop (at line 22 in Listing 9.5 on page 276) iterates.
4. Do step 3 1000 times and print the average count c and also $c \cdot r / \ln q$.

If the formula is correct, then the ratios $2c/(1 + q)$ should remain close to 1.0 as n approaches m.

9.2   Empirically test the formula $A = (\ln q)/r$ for finding a key in a hash table using double hashing. Follow the steps outlined in Project 9.1. If the formula is correct, the ratios $c \cdot r / \ln q$ should remain close to 1.0 as n approaches m.

9.3   Use a java.util.HashMap to implement the concordance from the case study in Section 3.12 on page 98. Test your Concordance class on the Caesar.txt file.

ANSWERS TO REVIEW QUESTIONS

9.1   When you use the index of this book, you use both sequential and direct access. You use direct access to find the page, since the index gives you the page number (the address). You use sequential access when you search the page for the term.

9.2   If you are driving down a street looking for a house with a given street number, then you are using sequential access.

9.3   The java.util.HashMap class uses the separate chaining algorithm because, in general, it runs faster than the open addressing algorithms.

9.4   Hashing is used to produce index numbers that fall in a small range, so that they can be used as array indexes (or record number in a disk file). Folding a nine-digit number into a three-digit number achieves that goal.

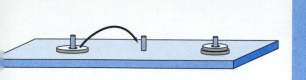

Chapter 10

Recursion

Many operations on data structures—especially those on nonlinear linked structures such as trees and graphs—are easier to implement using the powerful technique of *recursion*. Moreover, many fundamental concepts in computing are more easily understood from a recursive point of view.

10.1 Recursive Functions

A *recursive* function is one that calls itself. This causes automatic repetition, a virtual loop. In fact, most algorithms that use iteration (`for` loops, `while` loops, *etc.*) can be recast, replacing each loop with a recursive call. So recursion can be viewed as an alternative to iteration.

Recursive functions are typically more concise than their iterative alternatives. For example, consider the factorial function. (See Table 10.1) It is defined recursively as

$$n! = \begin{cases} 1, \text{ if } n = 0 \text{ or } 1 \\ n(n-1)!, \text{ if } n > 1 \end{cases}$$

The function $n!$ "recurs" on the right side of the equation

$$n! = n(n-1)!$$

as the expression $(n-1)!$.

Although defining a function in terms of itself this way may seem like circular reasoning, it isn't, because the expression $(n-1)!$ on the right side of the equation is not the same as the expression $n!$ on the left side. The equation defines the factorial of one number in terms of the factorial of a *smaller* number. That single recurrence relation represents an entire sequence of definitions like this:

$$7! = 7(6!)$$
$$6! = 6(5!)$$
$$5! = 5(4!)$$
$$4! = 4(3!)$$
$$3! = 3(2!)$$
$$2! = 2(1!)$$

n	n!
0	1
1	1
2	2
3	6
4	24
5	120
6	720
7	5,040
8	40,320
9	362,880

TABLE 10.1   Factorials.

Of course, the recursion can start with any positive integer, not just 7.

The recursion stops at $n = 1$ because the definition requires that $n > 1$ for the recurrence relation to apply. The value of 1! is given by the non recursive part of the definition. It says that $n! = 1$ if $n = 0$ or 1. So $1! = 1$ by definition. From there, we can run through the sequence of equations in reverse order to obtain the value for 7!:

$$2! = 2\,(1!) = 2\,(1) = 2$$
$$3! = 3\,(2!) = 3\,(2) = 6$$
$$4! = 4\,(3!) = 4\,(6) = 24$$
$$5! = 5\,(4!) = 5\,(24) = 120$$
$$6! = 6\,(5!) = 6\,(120) = 720$$
$$7! = 7\,(6!) = 7\,(720) = 5040$$

This is shown in Figure 10.1.

The process described here for evaluating 7! is the same for all recursive functions. The recursive part of the definition is applied repeatedly until the remaining expression reduces to the case that can be evaluated by the nonrecursive part. That value then allows the other values in the chain to be obtained in a cascade that finally returns the correct value for the original expression. One can imagine climbing down a ladder and picking up the base value ($1! = 1$, in this case).

For recursion to work, it must always include a *base* that provides a direct evaluation that can then be used to climb back up the recursive ladder. A common programming error is to forget the base, resulting in *infinite recursion*, which is a serious run-time error.

For clarity, it sometimes helps to separate the base from the recursion explicitly, like this:

$$n! = 1, \text{ if } n = 0 \text{ or } 1 \quad [\text{base}]$$
$$n! = n\,(n - 1)! \quad [\text{recursion}]$$

The complete definition has two parts: the *base* and the *recursion*.

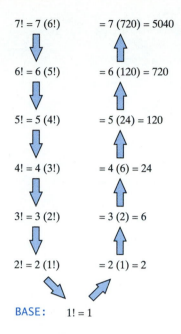

FIGURE 10.1 Computing 7! recursively.

Listing 10.1 tests an implementation of the recursive factorial function. Compare it (lines 7–10) with this iterative version:

```
static long factorial(int n) {
  long m = 1;
  for (int f = 2; f <= n; f++)
    m *= f;
  return m;
}
```

LISTING 10.1: Testing the Recursive Factorial Function

```
1   class TestRecursiveFactorial {
2     public static void main(String[] args) {
3       for (int i = 0; i < 10; i++)
4         System.out.println(i + "\t" + factorial(i));
5     }
6
7     static long factorial(int n) {
8       if (n < 2) return 1;        // base
9       return n*factorial(n-1);   // recursion
10    }
11  }
```

The output is

```
0      1
1      1
2      2
3      6
4      24
5      120
6      720
7      5040
8      40320
9      362880
```

The recursive version is typically more succinct.

10.2 The Towers of Hanoi

Our next example of recursion solves a nonnumeric problem. The problem is called the *Towers of Hanoi*, after a parlor puzzle of that name that was popular near the end of the 19th century.

The puzzle consists of a board with three vertical pegs and a progression of disks of increasing diameter. (See Figure 10.2.) Each disk has a hole in its center. The disks are stacked on one peg so that each disk rests on a larger one. The puzzle is how to transfer all the disks from one peg to another by means of a sequence of individual moves, subject to the restriction that no disk may be placed upon a smaller disk.

The puzzle is defined in terms of n disks, where n is a positive integer. To describe a solution, we label the three pegs A, B, and C, and number the disks from smallest to largest 1, 2, ..., n.

In the simplest, nontrivial case, with $n = 3$ disks, it is easy to see that the solution to the puzzle is the following sequence of seven moves:

1. A → B
2. A → C
3. B → C
4. A → B
5. C → A
6. C → B
7. A → B

These moves are illustrated in Figure 10.3.

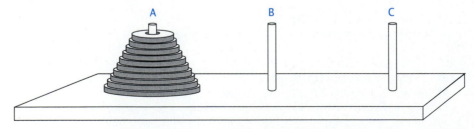

FIGURE 10.2 The Towers of Hanoi game.

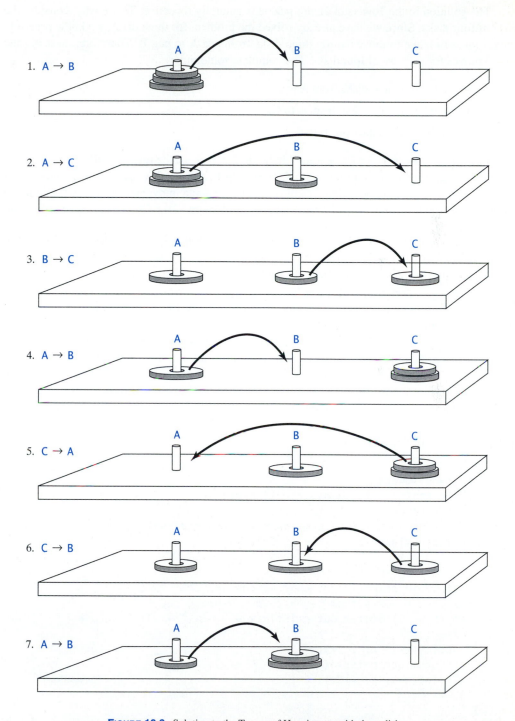

FIGURE 10.3 Solution to the Towers of Hanoi game with three disks.

The solution to the Towers of Hanoi puzzle is naturally recursive. To see why, consider the case of four disks. Since we have already solved the problem for three disks, we know precisely what moves to make to move the top three disks from peg A to peg B. Therefore, these are the first 7 moves for the case of four disks. The complete solution is:

1. Move the top three disks from A to B.

2. Move the remaining disk from A to C.

3. Move the three disks from B to C.

Of course, step 1 and step 3 each require 7 individual moves, so the total is really 15 moves.

The general recursive solution is implemented in Listing 10.2, which reads the number of disks from the command line, using 3 as the default. The actual movement of a disk is simulated by an instruction printed as output. The complete set of instructions for moving three disks from peg A to peg B is shown in the output.

Note that one disk takes one move, two disks take 3 moves, and three disks take seven moves. It is not hard to prove that n disks take $2^n - 1$ moves. (See Exercise 10.5 on page 322.)

The recursive solution to the Towers of Hanoi puzzle demonstrates the power of recursion. (Imagine trying to derive an iterative solution!) It also demonstrates the main idea of *recursive thinking*: To solve a problem of size n, find a solution in terms of solutions to the same problem of sizes less than n.

The solution to the Towers of Hanoi puzzle nicely illustrates the power and intuitive simplicity of recursion: To move n disks from *A* to *B,* move all but the last disk from *A* to *C*; then move the last disk from *A* to *B*; then move all the other disks from *C* to *B*. It also illustrates the inductive nature of recursion: if you know how to solve the problem with $n-1$ disks, then you can use that knowledge to solve the problem with n disks.

LISTING 10.2: The Towers of Hanoi

```
1   class HanoiTowers {
2     public static void main(String[] args) {
3       int numTowers = 3;
4       if (args.length > 0) numTowers = Integer.parseInt(args[0]);
5       print(numTowers, 'A', 'B', 'C');
6     }
7
8     static void print(int n, char x, char y, char z) {
9       // move n disks from peg x to peg y using peg z:
10      if (n == 1) System.out.println(x + " --> " + y);  // base
11      else {
12        print(n-1, x, z, y);                            // recursion
13        System.out.println(x + " --> " + y);
14        print(n-1, z, y, x);                            // recursion
15      }
16    }
17  }
```

The output is

```
A --> B
A --> C
B --> C
A --> B
C --> A
C --> B
A --> B
```

10.3 Fibonacci Numbers

The *Fibonacci numbers* are 0, 1, 1, 2, 3, 5, 8, 13, 21, 34, 55, 89, 144, ... (See Table 10.2.) Each number is the sum of its two predecessors. That is a recursive definition:

$$F_n = \begin{cases} 0, \text{ if } n = 0 \\ 1, \text{ if } n = 1 \\ F_{n-1} + F_{n-2}, \text{ if } n > 1 \end{cases}$$

This definition has two parts to is base: the case $n = 0$ and the case $n = 1$. Its recurrence equation $F_n = F_{n-1} + F_{n-2}$ has two recursive calls.

Listing 10.3 on page 304 tests an implementation of the recursive Fibonacci function. Like the recursive implementation of the factorial function, this method is a direct transliteration from the algebraic formulas into Java.

n	F_n
0	0
1	1
2	1
3	2
4	3
5	5
6	8
7	13
8	21
9	34
10	55
11	89
12	144

TABLE 10.2   Fibonacci Numbers.

LISTING 10.3: Testing the Recursive Fibonacci Function

```
1   class TestRecursiveFibonacci {
2     public static void main(String[] args) {
3       for (int i = 0; i < 13; i++)
4         System.out.println(i + "\t" + f(i));
5     }
6     static long f(int n) {
7       if (n < 1) return 0;      // base
8       if (n < 3) return 1;      // base
9       return f(n-1) + f(n-2);   // recursion
10    }
11  }
```

The output is

0	0
1	1
2	1
3	2
4	3
5	5
6	8
7	13
8	21
9	34
10	55
11	89
12	144

The Fibonacci numbers are useful in quite a few diverse areas of computing. They were discovered by Leonardo Pisano (1170–1250), shown in Figure 10.4. He is best remembered for having written *Liber Abaci*, a textbook on arithmetic which introduced the Hindu–Arabic numerals to Europe. One of the exercises in this book was the famous rabbit problem:

> *A certain man put a pair of rabbits in a place surrounded on all sides by a wall. How many pairs of rabbits can be produced from that pair in a year if it is supposed that every month each pair begets a new pair which from the second month on becomes productive?*

The solution is illustrated in Figure 10.5 on page 305. It assumes that the original newborn pair of rabbits was put in the walled place during January and that it becomes productive during February. So the first new pair is born during March. That new pair then becomes productive during April, giving birth to its first new pair during May. Meanwhile, the original pair continues to produce another new pair during each month after March.

So there are 0 pairs on January 1, one pair on February 1, one pair on March 1, two pairs on April 1, three pairs on May 1, five pairs on June 1, and eight pairs on July 1. These are the Fibonacci numbers: $F_0 = 0$, $F_1 = 1$, $F_2 = 1$, $F_3 = 2$, $F_4 = 3$, $F_5 = 5$, $F_6 = 8$, *etc.*

FIGURE 10.4 Leonardo Pisano.

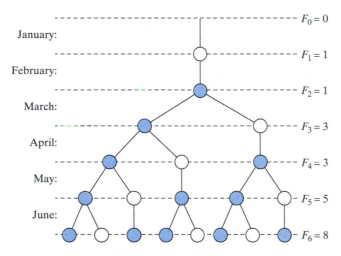

FIGURE 10.5 Fibonacci's rabbit problem.

The preceding numbers follow the Fibonacci recurrence equation

$$F_n = F_{n-1} + F_{n-2}$$

because the number F_n of pairs of rabbits after n months is precisely the number F_{n-1} of pairs that were alive at the end of the previous month (none die) plus the number F_{n-2} that were alive at the end of the month before that (the productive ones).

Now the question in the problem was, how many pairs are produced in a year? The number of pairs produced from the original pair would be the total number after 12 months, minus the original pair:

$$F_{12} - 1 = 144 - 1 = 143$$

So the answer[1] is 143 pairs of new rabbits.

The diagram shown in Figure 10.5 is called a *Fibonacci tree*. Later, we shall see other applications of this particular tree.

10.4 Calling Trees

The program in Listing 10.4 prints the time in milliseconds that elapses during each primary call f(n) to the recursive Fibonacci function, for values of n from 30 to 40. The last line of output shows that it took 8531 milliseconds (8.531 seconds) to compute F_{40} recursively. That data is plotted in Figure 10.6. It shows that the elapsed time grows exponentially. This output shows how inefficient recursive methods can be.

LISTING 10.4: Timing the Recursive Fibonacci Function

```
1   class TimeRecursiveFibonacci {
2     public static void main(String[] args) {
3       for (int n=30; n<=40; n++) {
4         long t0=System.currentTimeMillis();
5         long m=f(n);
6         long t1=System.currentTimeMillis();
7         System.out.println("f(" + n + ") = " + m + "  \ttime: " +(t1-t0));
8       }
9     }
10
11    static long f(int n)   // same as in Listing 10.3 on page 304
12  }
```

The output is

```
f(30) = 832040            time: 78
f(31) = 1346269           time: 125
f(32) = 2178309           time: 188
f(33) = 3524578           time: 297
f(34) = 5702887           time: 468
f(35) = 9227465           time: 782
f(36) = 14930352          time: 1265
f(37) = 24157817          time: 1953
f(38) = 39088169          time: 3219
f(39) = 63245986          time: 5250
f(40) = 102334155         time: 8531
```

This looks like exponential growth, and we shall see that it is.

To see why the recursive Fibonacci function is so slow, we use a tree diagram to analyze the cascade of recursive calls. Figure 10.7 shows the *calling tree* for the call f(6) to the Fibonacci method from main() in the program in Listing 10.3 on page 304. Each call is represented by a

---

[1] Note that the solution, 143, is not one of the Fibonacci numbers, as is often stated.

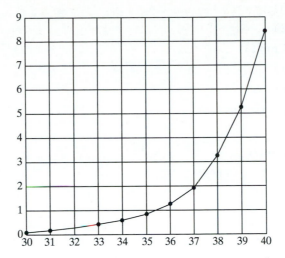

FIGURE 10.6 Exponential growth.

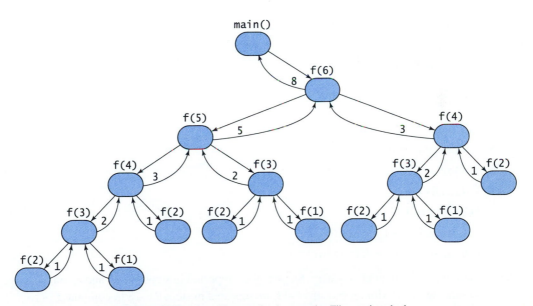

FIGURE 10.7 The calling tree for the recursive Fibonacci method.

shaded oval. The returned values are shown as labels on the arrows that point back up to the oval from where the call was made. The actual sequence of execution is as follows:

1. main() calls f(6)
2. f(6) calls f(5)
3. f(5) calls f(4)

4. f(4) calls f(3)

5. f(3) calls f(2)

6. f(2) returns 1 to f(3)

7. f(3) calls f(1)

8. f(1) returns 1 to f(3)

9. f(3) returns $1 + 1 = 2$ to f(4)

10. f(4) calls f(2)

11. f(2) returns 1 to f(4)

12. f(4) returns $2 + 1 = 3$ to f(5)

13. f(5) calls f(3)

14. f(3) calls f(2)

15. f(2) returns 1 to f(3)

16. f(3) calls f(1)

17. f(1) returns 1 to f(3)

18. f(3) returns $1 + 1 = 2$ to f(5)

19. f(5) returns $3 + 2 = 5$ to f(6)

20. f(6) calls f(4)

21. f(4) calls f(3)

22. f(3) calls f(2)

23. f(2) returns 1 to f(3)

24. f(3) calls f(1)

25. f(1) returns 1 to f(3)

26. f(3) returns $1 + 1 = 2$ to f(4)

27. f(4) calls f(2)

28. f(2) returns 1 to f(4)

29. f(4) returns $2 + 1 = 3$ to f(6)

30. f(6) returns $5 + 3 = 8$ to main()

Clearly there is a lot of redundancy here. Steps 5–8 are repeated in steps 14–17 and again in steps 22–25 to compute f(3). Moreover, steps 4–11 are repeated in steps 21–28 to compute f(4).

The calling tree shows one of the two main reasons that recursion can be inefficient: The same steps to compute the same values may be executed several times. The other main reason is that recursion works by making many method calls. Each call is expensive, in terms of time and space. The calling tree shows that the computation of f(6) required 15 method calls. And as the previous analysis indicated, that number increases exponentially with n.

The program in Listing 10.5 tests an iterative version of the Fibonacci function. Its main() method (lines 2–9) is the same as in Listing 10.4 on page 306. Its output gives the times for computing the same 11 values as with the recursive version. The results speak for themselves.

LISTING 10.5: Timing the Iterative Fibonacci Function

```
1   class TimeIterativeFibonacci {
2     public static void main(String[] args) {
3       for (int n = 30; n <= 40; n++) {
4         long t0=System.currentTimeMillis();
5         long m=f(n);
6         long t1=System.currentTimeMillis();
7         System.out.println("f(" + n + ") = " + m + "  \ttime: " +(t1-t0));
8       }
9     }
10    static long f(int n) {
11      if (n<2) return n;
12      long f0=0, f1=1, f2=1;
13      for (int i=2; i<n; i++) {
14        f0 = f1;
15        f1 = f2;
16        f2 = f1 + f0;
17      }
18      return f2;
19    }
20  }
```

The output is

```
f(30) = 832040           time: 0
f(31) = 1346269          time: 0
f(32) = 2178309          time: 0
f(33) = 3524578          time: 0
f(34) = 5702887          time: 0
f(35) = 9227465          time: 0
f(36) = 14930352         time: 0
f(37) = 24157817         time: 0
f(38) = 39088169         time: 0
f(39) = 63245986         time: 0
f(40) = 102334155        time: 0
```

So if recursion is so inefficient,[2] why bother to study it? The main reason is that for some problems, the simplest solution is the recursive one. This is evident with the Towers of Hanoi problem in Section 10.2 on page 300 and the permutations problem in Section 10.9 on page 315. It will be more evident with our study of tree structures in Chapters 11–13 and sorting in Chapter 15.

10.5 Storing Instead of Recomputing

When an algorithm has both an iterative and a recursive version, typically the iterative version is faster and the recursive version is simpler. The recursive version may be much slower because it recomputes the same values many times. This is certainly true of the recursive Fibonacci method

---

[2] A smart compiler will automatically replace some recursive code with a faster iterative equivalent.

in Listing 10.3 on page 304. The recomputation of the same values can be avoided by storing them the first time they are computed.

The program in Listing 10.6 stores the Fibonacci numbers as they are generated. The output indicates that this is just about as fast as the iterative method.

LISTING 10.6: Using Temporary Storage to Compute Fibonacci Numbers

```
1   class TimeStoredFibonacci {
2     public static void main(String[] args) {
3       for (int n = 30; n <= 40; n++) {
4         long t0 = System.currentTimeMillis();
5         long m = Fibonacci.number(n);
6         long t1 = System.currentTimeMillis();
7         System.out.println("f(" + n + ") = " + m + "  \ttime: " +(t1-t0));
8       }
9     }
10  }
11
12  class Fibonacci {
13    private static long[] fib = new long[100];
14    private static int lastFibIndex = 2;
15
16    static {  // class initializer
17      fib[1] = fib[2] = 1;
18    }
19
20    public static long number(int n) {
21      for (int i = lastFibIndex+1; i <= n; i++)
22        fib[i] = fib[i-1] + fib[i-2];
23      if (n > lastFibIndex) lastFibIndex = n;
24      return fib[n];
25    }
26  }
```

The output is

```
f(30) = 832040        time: 31
f(31) = 1346269       time: 0
f(32) = 2178309       time: 0
f(33) = 3524578       time: 0
f(34) = 5702887       time: 0
f(35) = 9227465       time: 0
f(36) = 14930352      time: 0
f(37) = 24157817      time: 0
f(38) = 39088169      time: 0
f(39) = 63245986      time: 0
f(40) = 102334155     time: 0
```

The program defines a special Fibonacci class (lines 12–26) with two private fields: an array fib[] of 100 long integers, and an index marker named lastFibIndex. It has a public method named number() (lines 20–25) that returns the Fibonacci numbers. The class also has a *static initialization block* (lines 16–18) that initializes the first three elements of the fib[] array. This code is executed only once, when the class is loaded.

The test driver prints the 11 Fibonacci numbers F_{30} through F_{40}. On the first call to Fibonacci.number(n), when n is 30, the number() method computes F_3 through F_{30}, storing each in the fib[] array, resets lastFibIndex to 30, and returns fib[30]. On the second call to Fibonacci.number(n), when n is 31, the number() method computes only F_{31}, storing it in the fib[31] array, resets lastFibIndex to 31, and returns fib[31].

In this approach, the class "remembers" the results that it has already obtained, so it won't have to repeat the work. The only significant time expense is from the initial allocation of the array—in this case, 31 milliseconds.

10.6 De Moivre's Formula

We have seen that the recurrence formula

$$F_n = F_{n-1} + F_{n-2}$$

that defines the Fibonacci numbers is quite inefficient, due to its two recursive calls. The French mathematician Abraham de Moivre (1667–1754), shown in Figure 10.8[3] discovered a closed-form formula for the Fibonacci numbers. It uses the constant φ, which is known as the golden mean.

The golden mean derives from the following ancient Greek geometry problem: find the point C on a segment AB where the ratio AB:AC equals ratio AC:CB. This common ratio is called the *golden mean* (also called the *golden ratio*) and is denoted by φ, the Greek letter *phi*. Its numerical value is φ = $(1 + \sqrt{5})/2$ = 1.618···. (For more details, see Section C.10 on page 576)

Moivre.

FIGURE 10.8 Abraham de Moivre.

---

[3] De Moivre was a French Protestant who emigrated to England when the Huguenots were expelled from France in 1685. He pioneered the development of analytic geometry and probability theory. He is probably best remembered for his formula $e^{i\theta} = \cos \theta + i \sin \theta$.

Formula 10.1 gives the closed-form expression for the Fibonacci numbers. It is truly remarkable because it asserts that a quotient of a difference of powers of irrational numbers evaluates to a positive integer.

◆ **FORMULA 10.1: (De Moivre's Formula)**

The nth Fibonacci number is $F_n = \dfrac{\phi^n - \psi^n}{\sqrt{5}}$, where $\phi = (1 + \sqrt{5})/2$ and $\psi = (1 - \sqrt{5})/2$.

To verify this formula, let f_n be the expression on the right:

$$f_n = \frac{\phi^n - \psi^n}{\sqrt{5}}$$

We show that $f_n = F_n$ for all $n = 0, 1, 2, \ldots$ First show that $f_0 = 0$, $f_1 = 1$, and $f_2 = 1$. Then show that $f_n = f_{n-1} + f_{n-2}$ for all $n > 1$. (See Exercise 10.10 on page 324.) Now, once we know that $f_k = F_k$ for all $k < n$, we can deduce from that recurrence relation that $f_n = f_{n-1} + f_{n-2} = F_{n-1} + F_{n-2} = F_n$, since $n-1 < n$ and $n-2 < n$. This uses the strong principle of mathematical induction.

An important consequence of this formula is that the Fibonacci numbers grow exponentially:

$$F_n = \Theta(\phi^n).$$

This asymptotic formula follows from the fact that $-1 < \psi^n < 1$ for all n. From that we can see that $\Theta(F_n) = \Theta((\phi^n - \psi^n)/\sqrt{5}) = \Theta(\phi^n - \psi^n) = \Theta(\phi^n)$.

De Moivre's formula is tested in Listing 10.7. It computes the first 11 Fibonacci numbers correctly—and of course, the time taken to evaluate the closed-form formula is negligible.

LISTING 10.7: Using De Moivre's Formula to Compute Fibonacci Numbers

```
1   class TestDeMoivre {
2     private static final double SR5=Math.sqrt(5);   //  2.2360679774997896
3     private static final double PHI=(1+SR5)/2;       //  1.6180339887498948
4     private static final double PSI=(1-SR5)/2;       // -0.6180339887498948
5
6     public static void main(String[] args) {
7       for (int n = 0; n <= 10; n++)
8         System.out.println("f(" + n + ") = " + f(n));
9       for (int n = 30; n <= 40; n++) {
10        long t0 = System.currentTimeMillis();
11        long m = f(n);
12        long t1 = System.currentTimeMillis();
13        System.out.println("f(" + n + ") = " + m + "  \ttime: " +(t1-t0));
14      }
15    }
16
17    static long f(int n) {
18      return (long)((Math.pow(PHI,n) - Math.pow(PSI,n))/SR5);
19    }
20 }
```

The output is

```
f(0) = 0
f(1) = 1
f(2) = 1
f(3) = 2
f(4) = 3
f(5) = 5
f(6) = 8
f(7) = 13
f(8) = 21
f(9) = 34
f(10) = 55
f(30) = 832040        time: 0
f(31) = 1346269       time: 0
f(32) = 2178309       time: 0
f(33) = 3524578       time: 0
f(34) = 5702887       time: 0
f(35) = 9227465       time: 0
f(36) = 14930352      time: 0
f(37) = 24157817      time: 0
f(38) = 39088169      time: 0
f(39) = 63245986      time: 0
f(40) = 102334155     time: 0
```

10.7 The Recursive Binary Search Algorithm

The iterative binary search algorithm was presented in Section 3.7 on page 84. The algorithm searches for a given value in a sorted sequence. It uses the divide-and-conquer strategy, each time splitting the sequence in half and then continuing the search on one half. The process is naturally recursive and is given in Algorithm 10.1.

▲ **ALGORITHM 10.1: Recursive Binary Search**

Input: a sequence $\{a_p, a_{p+1}, a_{p+2}, ..., a_{q-1}\}$ and a target value x.
Output: an index value i.
Precondition: The sequence is sorted: $a_p \le a_{p+1} \le a_{p+2} \le \cdots \le a_{q-1}$.
Postcondition: Either $p \le i < q$ and $a_i = x$; or $i < 0$ and $a_j < x$ for all $j < k$, and $a_j > x$ for all $j \ge k$, where $k = -i - 1$.

1. If $q \le p$, return $-p-1$ (base).

2. Let $i = (p + q)/2$ (integer division).

3. If $a_i = x$, return i.

4. If $a_i < x$, return the result from searching the upper subsequence $\{a_{i+1}, a_{i+2}, ..., a_{q-1}\}$.

5. Otherwise, return the result from searching the lower subsequence $\{a_p, a_{p+1}, ..., a_{i-1}\}$.

The postcondition describes the two possible outcomes of the binary search. In the first outcome, the search is successful, and the target x is found at position i in the sequence ($a_i = x$). In the second outcome, the search is unsuccessful; the target x is not in the sequence. So a negative value i is returned to signal that fact. But just as in the nonrecursive version of the binary search

(Algorithm 3.4 on page 85), the returned value can be used to insert the target in the correct position in the sequence to keep it sorted. That position is at the index $k = -i - 1$. If the subsequence $\{a_k, a_{k+1}, a_{k+2}, ..., a_{q-1}\}$ is shifted to the right one position, then the target x can be inserted at a_k, preserving the ascending state of the entire sequence.[4] This is the same postcondition that is implemented in the `java.util.Array.sort()` method.

This recursive algorithm is shorter than Algorithm 3.4 on page 85, and is a little easier to understand. And although its actual run time may be a little longer than that of the iterative version, it does have the same complexity function. (See Formula 10.2.)

◆ **FORMULA 10.2: The Recursive Binary Search**

The recursive binary search runs in $\Theta(\lg n)$ time.

To verify this fact, let $T(n)$ be the run time for a sequence of n elements. Then $T(n)$ equals the time taken to execute steps 1–3 plus (at most) the time taken to make one of the two recursive calls in steps 4 and 5. Since each of those two calls applies the algorithm to a subsequence that is less than half the size of the original, we have

$$T(n) \leq c + T(n/2)$$

where c is a positive constant. Replacing n with $n/2$, this becomes

$$T(n/2) \leq c + T((n/2)/2) = c + T(n/4)$$

Then, substituting the second inequality into the first yields

$$T(n) \leq c + T(n/2) \leq c + [c + T(n/4)] = 2c + T(n/4)$$

Repeating these steps with $n/4$ in place of n results in

$$T(n) \leq 2c + T(n/4) \leq 2c + [c + T(n/8)] = 3c + T(n/8)$$

Then, again substituting $n/8$ in place of n results in

$$T(n) \leq 3c + T(n/8) \leq 3c + [c + T(n/16)] = 4c + T(n/16)$$

In general, we have

$$T(n) \leq kc + T(n/2^k), \text{ for } k = 1, 2, 3, ...$$

When $k = \lg n$, $n = 2^k$ and $n/2^k = 1$, so

$$T(n) \leq (\lg n)c + T(1) = O(\lg n).$$

This argument assumes that n is a power of 2, but that is no loss of generality because, if n is not a power of two, then we can just imagine padding the sequence with copies of the last (and largest) value to obtain a larger sequence whose size n_1 is a power of 2. Then, by the some argument, we have $T(n) \leq T(n_1) = O(\lg n_1) \leq O(\lg(2n)) = O(\lg(n))$.

---

[4] The value $-i-1$ is returned instead of $-i$ to guarantee that it is negative.

10.8 Recursive Exponentiation

In some cases, the recursive version of a function can be faster than its iterative version. This is true of the exponential function.

The algebraic definition of the exponential expression x^n is $x \cdot x \cdots x$ (multiply n factors), so the obvious implementation is

```
double exp(double x, int n) {
    double y = 1.0;
    for (int i = 0; i < n; i++)
        y *= x;
    return y;
}
```

This iterative method runs in $\Theta(n)$ because its `for` loop iterates n times.

The recursive version uses the divide-and-conquer strategy. Consider, for example, computing 2^{100}. Instead of multiplying 1 by 2 one hundred times, we could multiply 1 by 2^2 in half the time. Or multiply 1 by $(2^2)^2$ in one fourth the time. That's the main idea behind the recursive version.

If n is odd, we apply the same idea to x^{n-1} and then multiply the result by x.

Thus, algebraically, we compute x^n in the following way:

$$(x^2)^{n/2}, \text{ if } x \text{ is even;}$$

$$x(x^2)^{(n-1)/2}, \text{ if } x \text{ is odd.}$$

This formulation is naturally recursive:

```
double exp(double x, int n) {
    double factor = (n%2 == 0 ? 1.0 : x);   // 1 if x is even; else x;
    if (n < 2) return factor;                // base
    return factor*exp(x*x, n/2);             // recursion
}
```

Unlike our other examples, here the code is no shorter, but the recursive method is more efficient. By an argument similar to that for Formula 10.2 on page 314, we can see that this recursive method runs in $\Theta(\lg n)$ time. (See Exercise 10.12 on page 323.)

Note that both versions of this exponentiation function work correctly only for nonnegative exponents. (See Programming Problem 10.5 on page 324.)

10.9 Printing Permutations

A *permutation* is a specific arrangement of elements of a sequence. For example, BCAD and CDBA are different permutations of the string ABCD. Permutations can be difficult to work with because there are so many of them. Formula 10.3 tells us exactly how many.

◆ **FORMULA 10.3: Permutations**

There are $n!$ permutations of a sequence of n elements.

To verify this fact, let $p(n)$ be the number of permutations of n elements. Then, clearly, $p(1) = 1$. And $p(2) = 2$ because AB and BA are the only permutations of two elements. In general, $p(n) = n \cdot p(n-1)$ because for each of the $p(n-1)$ permutations of the first $n-1$ elements, there are n positions where the nth element could be placed to make a different permutation of the n elements. Now the recurrence relation $p(n) = n \cdot p(n-1)$, together with the initial values $p(1) = 1$ and $p(2) = 2$, is enough to guarantee that $p(n) = n!$ for all $n > 0$, because the factorial function is defined by that same recurrence relation. We can also see by mathematical induction: If $p(n-1) = (n-1)!$, then $p(n) = n \cdot p(n-1) = n \cdot (n-1)! = n!$.

The program in Listing 10.8 implements a recursive method that prints all $n!$ permutations of a given string of length n. The string s is the default string `"ABC"` unless another is read from the command line. It is passed to a one-argument `print()` method which recasts it as a `StringBuffer` object and passes that to a recursive two-argument `print()` method. This technique of overloading a recursive method with a nonrecursive "wrapper" method is common. Note that the wrapper method is public, while the recursive method is private.

LISTING 10.8: Printing Permutations

```
1   public class Permutations {
2      public static void main(String[] args) {
3         String s = "ABC";
4         if (args.length > 0) s = args[0];
5         print(s);
6      }
7
8      public static void print(String s) {
9         print(new StringBuffer(s), 0);
10     }
11
12     private static void print(StringBuffer s, int k) {
13        // print all permutations of s that leave s[0]..s[k-1] invariant:
14        if (k == s.length()-1) System.out.println(s);   // base
15        else
16           for (int i=k; i<s.length(); i++) {
17              swap(s, k, i);
18              print(s, k+1);   // recursion
19              swap(s, k, i);
20           }
21     }
22     private static void swap(StringBuffer s, int i, int j) {
23        if (i == j) return;
24        char ch = s.charAt(i);
25        s.setCharAt(i, s.charAt(j));
26        s.setCharAt(j, ch);
27     }
28  }
```

The output is

```
ABC
ACB
BAC
BCA
CBA
CAB
```

The recursive `print(s,k)` method prints all permutations of s (including s itself) that leave its substring s[0:k-1] invariant. Suppose s has length 5. Then the call `print(s,4)` prints all permutations of s that leave s[0:3] invariant. That will print just s itself.

The call `print(s,3)` prints all permutations of s that leave s[0:2] invariant, allowing only the 2 characters in s[3:4] to vary. This prints two permutations, by the following four steps:

```
print(s,4);     // prints s as given
swap(s,3,4);    // swaps the last 2 characters
print(s,4);     // prints that permutation
swap(s,3,4);    // swaps the last 2 characters back
```

The call `print(s,2)` prints all permutations of s that leave s[0:1] invariant, allowing the three characters in s[2:4] to vary. This prints six permutations, by the following steps:

```
print(s,3);     // prints 2 permutations s as given
swap(s,2,3);    // swaps s[2] with s[3]
print(s,4);     // prints 2 permutations of that version of s
swap(s,2,3);    // swaps s[2] with s[3] back
swap(s,2,4);    // swaps s[2] with s[4]
print(s,4);     // prints 2 permutations of that version of s
swap(s,2,4);    // swaps s[2] with s[4] back
```

The call `print(s,1)` prints all permutations of s that leave s[0] invariant, allowing the four characters in s[1:4] to vary. This prints 24 permutations, by the following steps:

```
print(s,2);     // prints 6 permutations s as given
swap(s,1,2);    // swaps s[1] with s[2]
print(s,2);     // prints 6 permutations of that version of s
swap(s,1,2);    // swaps s[1] with s[2] back
swap(s,1,3);    // swaps s[1] with s[3]
print(s,2);     // prints 6 permutations of that version of s
swap(s,1,3);    // swaps s[1] with s[3] back
swap(s,1,4);    // swaps s[1] with s[4]
print(s,2);     // prints 6 permutations of that version of s
swap(s,1,4);    // swaps s[1] with s[4] back
```

The call `print(s,0)` prints all permutations of s, allowing all five characters in s[0:4] to vary. This prints 120 permutations, by the following steps:

```
print(s,1);     // prints 24 permutations s as given
swap(s,0,1);    // swaps s[0] with s[1]
print(s,1);     // prints 24 permutations of that version of s
swap(s,0,1);    // swaps s[0] with s[1] back
swap(s,0,2);    // swaps s[0] with s[2]
print(s,1);     // prints 24 permutations of that version of s
swap(s,0,2);    // swaps s[0] with s[2] back
```

```
swap(s,0,3);    // swaps s[0] with s[3]
print(s,1);     // prints 24 permutations of that version of s
swap(s,0,3);    // swaps s[0] with s[3] back
swap(s,0,4);    // swaps s[0] with s[4]
print(s,1);     // prints 24 permutations of that version of s
swap(s,0,4);    // swaps s[0] with s[4] back
```

The calling tree for a string a length 4 is shown in Figure 10.9 on page 319. The initial call is `print("ABCD",0)`. That makes four recursive calls of the form `print(s,1)`, where each s is a permutation of `"ABCD"` obtained by swapping `s[0]` with `s[i]`. Those two characters are underlined. Each of these four calls makes three recursive calls of the form `print(s,2)`, where each s is a permutation of the given string obtained by swapping `s[1]` with `s[i]`. Again, the swapped characters are underlined. Each of these three calls makes two recursive calls of the form `print(s,3)`, illustrated the same way. These 24 calls each print one of the 24 permutations of the original string.

Generating permutations is useful for testing sorting methods. (See Chapter 15.)

10.10 Indirect Recursion

The recursive functions that we have studied so far are examples of *direct recursion*, in which the function calls itself directly. In contrast, in *indirect recursion*, a chain of function calls forms a loop of length greater than one. The simplest kind of indirect recursion is *mutual recursion* in which two functions call each other. More generally, $f()$ could call $g()$, which calls $h()$, which calls $f()$. These types of recursion are illustrated in Figure 10.10.

Listing 10.9 on page 320 illustrates the use of mutual recursion. It tabulates a `sin()` method and a `cos()` method along with the `Math.sin()` and `Math.cos()` methods. The latter are the standard trigonometric functions implemented in Java's `Math` package. The former use mutual recursion to compute their values. As you can see, the match is almost perfect.

The mutually recursive `sin()` and `cos()` methods implement these two trigonometric identities:

$$\sin 2\theta = 2 \sin\theta \cos\theta$$

$$\cos 2\theta = 1 - 2(\sin\theta)^2$$

The sine calls itself and the cosine, and the cosine calls the sine.

By letting $x = 2\theta$, so $\theta = x/2$, we have the equivalent identities

$$\sin x = 2 \sin(x/2) \cos(x/2)$$

and

$$\cos x = 1 - 2(\sin(x/2))^2$$

These are implemented by the methods in Listing 10.9.

Every recursive function must have a base that handles the boundary values. For example, the base for both the factorial function and Fibonacci function covered the cases where $n < 2$. For the continuous trigonometric functions, we define the base to cover the cases for very small

```
print("ABCD",0)
    ├─print("ABCD",1)
    │    ├─print("ABCD",2)
    │    │    ├─print("ABCD",3)
    │    │    └─print("ABDC",3)
    │    ├─print("ACBD",2)
    │    │    ├─print("ACBD",3)
    │    │    └─print("ACDB",3)
    │    └─print("ADCB",2)
    │         ├─print("ADCB",3)
    │         └─print("ADBC",3)
    ├─print("BACD",1)
    │    ├─print("BACD",2)
    │    │    ├─print("BACD",3)
    │    │    └─print("BADC",3)
    │    ├─print("BCAD",2)
    │    │    ├─print("BCAD",3)
    │    │    └─print("BCDA",3)
    │    └─print("BDCA",2)
    │         ├─print("BDCA",3)
    │         └─print("BDAC",3)
    ├─print("CBAD",1)
    │    ├─print("CBAD",2)
    │    │    ├─print("CBAD",3)
    │    │    └─print("CBDA",3)
    │    ├─print("CABD",2)
    │    │    ├─print("CABD",3)
    │    │    └─print("CADB",3)
    │    └─print("CDAB",2)
    │         ├─print("CDAB",3)
    │         └─print("CDBA",3)
    └─print("DBCA",1)
         ├─print("DBCA",2)
         │    ├─print("DBCA",3)
         │    └─print("DBAC",3)
         ├─print("DCBA",2)
         │    ├─print("DCBA",3)
         │    └─print("DCAB",3)
         └─print("DACB",2)
              ├─print("DACB",3)
              └─print("DABC",3)
```

FIGURE 10.9 Calling tree for the recursive permutations method.

values of *x*, in the range $-0.01 < x < 0.01$. This makes sense because these recursive identities compute values for *x* in terms of the smaller values *x*/2, so repeated applications of those identities reduce the size of *x* (which may be positive or negative).

Listing 10.9: Computing Trigonometric Functions with Mutual Recursion

```
1   class TestTrig {
2     public static void main(String[] args) {
3       for (double x = 0.0; x < 1.0; x += 0.1)
4         System.out.println(sin(x) + "\t" + Math.sin(x));
5       for (double x = 0.0; x < 1.0; x += 0.1)
6         System.out.println(cos(x) + "\t" + Math.cos(x));
7     }
8
9     static double sin(double x) {
10      if (-0.01 < x && x < 0.01) return x - x*x*x/6;   // base
11      return 2*sin(x/2)*cos(x/2);                      // recursion
12    }
13
14    static double cos(double x) {
15      if (-0.01 < x && x < 0.01) return 1.0 - x*x/2;   // base
16      return 1 - 2*sin(x/2)*sin(x/2);                  // recursion
17    }
18  }
```

The output is

```
0.0        0.0
0.09983341663923537    0.09983341664682815
0.19866933078010363    0.19866933079506122
0.2955202065505939     0.2955202066613396
0.38941834228053634    0.3894183423086505
0.4794255385224464     0.479425538604203
0.5646424732036842     0.5646424733950354
0.6442176872137436     0.644217687237691
0.7173560908569906     0.7173560908995227
0.783326909559097      0.7833269096274833
0.841470984707226      0.8414709848078964
1.0        1.0
0.9950041652787875     0.9950041652780258
0.9800665778442736     0.9800665778412416
0.9553364891598637     0.955336489125606
0.9210609940147716     0.9210609940028851
0.8775825619350366     0.8775825618903728
0.8253356150405887     0.8253356149096783
0.7648421873046591     0.7648421872844885
0.6967067093909582     0.6967067093471655
0.6216099683568421     0.6216099682706645
0.5403023060249246     0.5403023058681398
```

With the base covering the case where $-0.01 < x < 0.01$, we can see from the output that we get an accuracy of about nine decimal places in Listing 10.9. We can improve that accuracy by

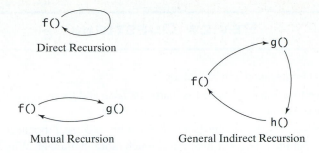

FIGURE 10.10 Different kinds of recursion.

tightening the base range to, say, $-0.0001 < x < 0.0001$. But, of course, that will increase the run time, because it will take much longer for x to reach that range. (See Exercise 10.11 on page 323 and Programming Problem 10.18 on page 325.)

CHAPTER REVIEW

❑ A recursive function is one that calls itself. It is an alternative to iteration for generating repetition.

❑ Recursion can provide a simple solution, but it is usually not as efficient as the iterative version.

❑ The Fibonacci numbers (0, 1, 1, 2, 3, 5, 8, 13, ...) are generated by the recursive formula $F_n = F_{n-1} + F_{n-2}$.

❑ The calling tree for the recursive Fibonacci methods shows that it makes many redundant calls.

❑ Temporarily storing the values overcomes the problem of redundant calls by storing intermediate values.

❑ De Moivre's closed-form formula for the Fibonacci numbers is $F_n = \dfrac{\phi^n - \psi^n}{\sqrt{5}}$, where $\phi = \dfrac{1 + \sqrt{5}}{2} = 1.618$ and $\psi = \dfrac{1 - \sqrt{5}}{2} = -0.618$.

❑ De Moivre's formula shows that $F_n = \Theta(\phi^n)$.

❑ Divide-and-conquer algorithms such as the binary search are naturally recursive: divide the problem in half, and apply the same algorithm to one or both halves.

❑ The recursive algorithm for computing x^n runs in logarithmic time.

❑ The problem of printing all $n!$ permutations of a given sequence of length n can be done fairly easily using recursion.

❑ Indirect recursion is where a sequence of calls cycles back to the original function. An efficient implementation of the sine and cosine functions uses mutual recursion.

❑ The Towers of Hanoi puzzle requires a nonnumerical recursive method.

REVIEW QUESTIONS

10.1   Why is recursion called a "virtual loop"?

10.2   A recursive function must have two parts: its *base* and its *recursive part*. Explain what each of these is and why it is essential to recursion.

10.3   The recursive versions of the factorial function and the Fibonacci function are both inefficient, but the Fibonacci function is much more inefficient. Why?

10.4   What are the advantages and disadvantages of implementing a recursive solution instead of an iterative solution?

10.5   What is the difference between direct recursion and indirect recursion?

10.6   How is the recursive solution to the permutation problem fundamentally different from other recursive solutions presented in this chapter?

10.7   What is the main idea in recursive thinking?

EXERCISES

10.1   How many recursive calls would the call `factorial(8)` generate in the factorial program in Listing 10.1 on page 299?

10.2   Explain why the following alternative solution to the Towers of Hanoi puzzle in Listing 10.2 will not work:

1. Move the top disk from A to B.
2. Recursively move the remaining $n - 1$ disks from A to C.
3. Move the remaining disk from B to C.

10.3   Draw the calling tree for the binary search algorithm on the array

```
int[] a = { 900, 903, 903, 904, 904, 904, 905, 905, 908, 909 };
```

for each of the following calls (see Programming Problem 10.5):

a. `search(a,3,6,905)`
b. `search(a,0,10,905)`
c. `search(a,3,6,910)`

10.4   Draw the calling tree for the Towers of Hanoi program in Listing 10.2 on page 302.

10.5   The Towers of Hanoi program performs seven disk moves for three disks. How many disk moves are performed for:

a. four disks?
b. five disks?
c. *n* disks?

Prove by induction that your formula is correct.

10.6   How many recursive calls would the call f(8) generate in the Fibonacci program in Listing 10.3 on page 304?

10.7   Prove by induction that $n! = \Omega(2^n)$. [Show that $n! > 2^n$ for all $n > 3$.]

10.8   The solution to Fibonacci's rabbit problem in Figure 10.5 on page 305 was 143 pairs of rabbits. This was $F_{12} - 1$. But it should also be the sum of all new pairs produced during those 12 months: $F_1 + F_2 + F_3 + \cdots + F_{10}$. Verify this, and then prove the general formula

$$F_0 + F_1 + F_2 + F_3 + \cdots + F_n = F_{n+2} - 1$$

[*Hint*: sum the equations $F_0 = F_2 - F_1, F_1 = F_3 - F_2, F_2 = F_4 - F_3, ..., F_{10} = F_{12} - F_{11}$.]

10.9   Apply an analysis similar to that in the proof of Algorithm 10.1 on page 313 to conclude that the recursive Fibonacci function runs in exponential time.

10.10   Derive these formulas for $f_n = (\phi^n - \psi^n)/\sqrt{5}$. (See Formula 10.1 on page 312.)

    a. $f_0 = 0, f_1 = f_2 = 1$.
    b. $f_n = f_{n-1} + f_{n-2}$ for all $n > 1$.

10.11   Suppose that we set the base for the sin() and cos() methods in Listing 10.9 on page 320 to be (-t<x && x<t) instead of (-0.01<x && x<0.01), where t is a defined constant. Show that the run time for these two mutually recursive methods is then $\Theta(1/t)$. So using 0.0001 instead of 0.01 for t would double the run time.

10.12   Prove that the recursive version of the exp() method in Section 10.8 on page 315 runs in $\Theta(\lg n)$ time. Let $T(n)$ be the run time for $n > 0$, and explain why $T(n) = c + T(n/2)$ for some constant $c > 0$, and then formulate an argument similar to that for Formula 10.2 on page 314.

10.13   Trace through the call exp(2,100) to the exp() method in Section 10.8 on page 315, showing each recursive call.

10.14   Show that the actual number of multiplications performed by the exp() method in Section 10.8 is $2^n - 1$.

PROGRAMMING PROBLEMS

10.1   Write and test an iterative version of the factorial function.

10.2   Find the largest Fibonacci number of type long.

10.3   Use the java.math.BigInteger class to find the 1000th Fibonacci number F_{1000}. (It has 209 digits!)

10.4   Implement and test the recursive binary search (Algorithm 10.1 on page 313) as

```
int search(int[] a, int p, int q, int x)
```

10.5   Note that the iterative and recursive versions of the exp() method in Section 10.8 on page 315 work correctly only for nonnegative exponents. Modify each method so that it works correctly for negative exponents and then test it.

10.6   Recall Horner's method (Chapter 8) for evaluating a polynomial. Implement this algorithm as a recursive method and test it.

10.7   Write both an iterative and a recursive version of a method that returns a String representation of a given long integer where the string is punctuated (American style) with commas. For example, the call commaString(1234567890) would return "1, 234, 567, 890".

10.8   Write and test a recursive method that returns the maximum value among the n elements $\{a_p, ..., a_{p+n-1}\}$ of a subsequence of integers, using at most lg n recursive calls. [Hint: use the divide-and-conquer strategy.]

10.9   Write and test a recursive method that returns the integer binary logarithm of an integer n (i.e., the number of times n can be divided by 2).

10.10   Write and test a recursive boolean method that determines whether a string is a palindrome. (A *palindrome* is a string of characters that is the same as the string obtained from it by reversing its letters.)

10.11   Write and test a recursive function that returns a string that contains the binary representation of a positive integer.

10.12   Write and test a recursive function that returns a string that contains the hexadecimal representation of a positive integer.

10.13   Write and test a recursive method that reverses a string. For example, reverse("ABCDE") would return "EDCBA".

10.14   The *computable domain* of a numerical method is the set of inputs for which the method will produce correct results. Determine empirically the computable domain of the factorial() in Listing 10.1 on page 299. In other words, write a program that finds the largest n for which $n! <$ Long.MAX_VALUE.

10.15   Determine empirically the computable domain (*c.f.* Exercise 10.17) of the Fibonacci method implemented in Listing 10.3 on page 304. Your result may depend upon how many method calls your computer's operating system will allow.

10.16   Implement and test the Ackermann function $a(m, n)$, defined recursively by

$$a(0, n) = 1$$
$$a(1, 0) = 2$$
$$a(m, 0) = m + 2, \text{ if } m > 1$$
$$a(m, n) = a(a(m-1, n), n-1), \text{ if } m > 0 \text{ and } n > 0$$

Then determine the computable domain (cf. Exercise 10.17) of this method empirically.

10.17   Modify the program in Listing 10.9 on page 320 so that the results are more accurate by narrowing the bases so that recursion continues until $|x| < 0.00005$.

10.18   Modify the program in Listing 10.9 on page 320 so that the results are more accurate by using the more accurate approximations

$$\sin x \approx x - x^3/6 + x^5/120 = x(1 - x^2(1 - x^2/20))$$
$$\cos x \approx 1 - x^2/2 + x^4/24 = 1 - x^2/2 \cdot (1 - x^2/12)$$

10.19   Use mutual recursion to implement the hyperbolic sine and hyperbolic cosine functions. Use these formulas:

$$\sinh 2\theta = 2 \sinh\theta \cosh\theta$$
$$\cosh 2\theta = 1 + 2(\sinh\theta)^2$$
$$\sinh x \approx x + x^3/6$$

and

$$\cosh x \approx 1 + x^2/2$$

Compare your results with the corresponding values of sinh and cosh functions, defined in terms of the exponential function by

$$\sinh x = (e^x - e^{-x})/2$$
$$\cosh x = (e^x + e^{-x})/2$$

10.20   Implement the tangent function recursively using the formulas

$$\tan 2x = \frac{2\tan x}{1 - (\tan x)^2}$$

$$\tan x \approx x + x^3/3$$

10.21   In Exercise 10.11 we see that the with a tolerance t, the run time for the mutually recursive sin() and cos() methods is proportional to $1/t$. Verify this result empirically. Define a class variable tol (for "tolerance") and replace the base conditions in both methods with the condition (-tol<x && x<tol). Define a timing method

```
static double time(double t)
```

that sets tol to t and then returns the time elapsed during the execution of these two loops:

```
for (double x=0.0; x<1.0; x+=0.01)
   sin(x);
for (double x=0.0; x<1.0; x+=0.01)
   cos(x);
```

Use the System.currentTimeMillis() method to get the system time immediately before and immediately after. Run your timing method for tolerances of 1e-2, 1e-3, 1e-4, 1e-5, and 1e-6.

PROJECTS

10.1   The *binomial coefficients* are the coefficients that are generated by the expansion of a binomial expression of the form $(x + 1)^n$. For example, the expansion

$$(x + 1)^6 = x^6 + 6x^5 + 15x^4 + 20x^3 + 15x^2 + 6x + 1$$

generates the seven coefficients 1, 6, 15, 20, 15, 6, and 1.

The French mathematician Blaise Pascal (1623–1662) discovered a recursive relationship among the binomial coefficients. By arranging them in a triangle, he found that each interior number is the sum of the two directly above it. (See Figure 10.11.)

For example, $15 = 5 + 10$.

Let $c(n,k)$ denote the coefficient in row number n and column number k (counting from 0). For example, $c(6,2) = 15$. This is indicated in the figure. The coefficient in row 6 and column 2 is 15. Then Pascal's recurrence relation can be expressed as

$$c(n, k) = c(n-1, k-1) + c(n-1, k), \text{ for } 0 < k < n$$

For example, when $n = 6$ and $k = 2$, $c(6,2) = c(5,1) + c(5,2) = 5 + 10 = 15$.

Note that the base for this recurrence is $c(n, 0) = c(n, n) = 1$, for all $n \geq 0$.

a. Write a program that prints Pascal's triangle down to row 10, using a recursive implementation of the binomial coefficients function $c(n, k)$.

b. Write a second version of the same program that stores the binomial coefficients in a two-dimensional array as they are generated.

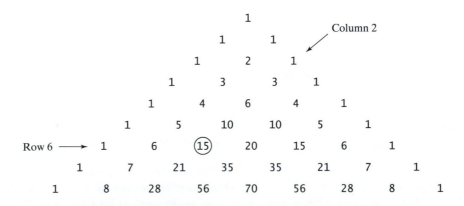

FIGURE 10.11   Pascal's Triangle.

c. Write a timing program that compares the run times of three implementations of the binomial coefficient function $c(n, k)$: (*i*) the recursive version from part (*a*); (*ii*) the stored version from part (*b*); and (*iii*) the following closed-form formula:

$$c(n, k) = \frac{n!}{k!(n - k)!} = \left(\frac{n}{1}\right)\left(\frac{n-1}{2}\right)\left(\frac{n-2}{3}\right)\cdots\left(\frac{n-k+1}{k}\right)$$

Note that this formula is to be evaluated the efficient way, by alternating integer division and multiplication, not by using the factorial function.

10.2   The *Euclidean algorithm* computes the greatest common divisor of two positive integers. Appearing as Proposition 2 in Book VII of Euclid's *Elements* (c. 300 B.C.), it is one of the oldest algorithms in history. As originally formulated by Euclid, it says to subtract repeatedly the smaller number n from the larger number m until the resulting difference d is smaller than n. Then repeat the same steps with d in place of n and with n in place of m. Continue until the two numbers are equal. Then that number will be the greatest common divisor of the original two numbers.

The example shown in Figure 10.12 applies this algorithm to find the greatest common divisor of 494 and 130 to be 26. This is correct because $494 = 26 \cdot 19$ and $130 = 26 \cdot 5$.

a. Write a program that implements and tests the iterative version of the Euclidean Algorithm.

b. Modify your program in part (*a*) so that it uses the following recursive version:

▲ **ALGORITHM 10.2: Recursive Euclidean Algorithm**

Input: two positive integers: m and n.
Output: the greatest common divisor of m and n.

1. If $m = n$, return n.

2. If $m < n$, return the greatest common divisor of m and $n - m$.

3. Return the greatest common divisor of n and $m - n$.

```
  494
 −130
  364
 −130
  234
 −130    130
  104   −104    104
         26    −26
                78
               −26
                52
               −26
                26
```

FIGURE 10.12   The Euclidean algorithm.

c. Modify both your iterative and recursive versions by using the remainder m%n instead of the difference m-n. [*Hint*: The algorithm repeatedly subtracts the smaller from the larger number until the difference is less than the smaller. The remainder operator has the same effect.]

ANSWERS TO REVIEW QUESTIONS

10.1   Recursion is called a "virtual loop" because it produces repetition similar to the iteration produced by a for loop or a while loop.

10.2   The basis of a recursive function is its starting point in its definition and its final step when it is being called recursively; it is what stops the recursion. The recursive part of a recursive function is the assignment that includes the function on the right side of the assignment operator, causing the function to call itself; it is what produces the repetition. For example, in the factorial function, the basis is $n! = 1$ if $n = 0$, and the recursive part is $n! = n(n-1)$ if $n > 0$.

10.3   The recursive Fibonacci function is much more inefficient than the recursive factorial function because it repeats lower level recursive calls. For example, the call f(8) will call f(3) eight times!

10.4   A recursive solution is often easier to understand than its equivalent iterative solution. But recursion usually runs more slowly than iteration.

10.5   Direct recursion is where a function calls itself. Indirect recursion is where a group of functions call each other.

10.6   The number of recursive calls that the solution to the permutation problem makes varies, decreasing from $n - 1$ down to 2. In other solutions considered in this chapter, the number of recursive calls that each call makes is constant (*e.g.*, 1 for the factorial function, 2 for the Fibonacci function, *etc.*).

10.7   The main idea is to assume that you already have solutions to the problem for all sizes less than n and then to find a way to use those solutions to solve the size n version. Then, after finding explicit solutions to the smallest sized versions of the problem, the complete solution can be formulated with recursion.

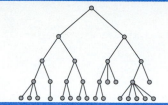

The important thing is not to stop questioning...
One cannot help but be in awe when he contemplates
the mysteries of eternity, of life,
of the marvelous structure of reality.

— Edmund Burke (1729–1797)

Chapter 11

Trees

The sequential data structures that we have considered previously (stacks, queues, lists, tables, and maps) usually are quite suitable for storing unordered collections. But they are not the most efficient structures for ordered collections. Trees provide a better alternative.

11.1 Trees

A *tree* can be defined mathematically in several different (but equivalent) ways. For example, it can be defined as a set of nodes and directed edges that satisfy certain properties. A tree also can be defined as an acyclic graph with one node designated as its root. Or it can be defined recursively. In this book, we will adopt the recursive definition, presented in Section 11.3 on page 336. Prior to that, we take an intuitive approach, to familiarize ourselves with the main properties of trees.

Conceptually, a tree is a hierarchical structure that branches out from various points. Botanical trees (oaks, elms, *etc.*) are not really good analogies because they actually branch out in two directions: upward with their limbs, and downward with their roots. In computer science, we call the starting point the *root* of the tree and usually imagine the branching either downward or to the right.

The Java class inheritance hierarchy is a good example of an abstract tree structure. Each class occupies one *node* of the tree. The `Object` class forms the root node. The diagram in Figure 11.1 shows the Java Collections Framework part of the complete Java inheritance tree of 2367 nodes.[1]

Another good example of an abstract tree is a family tree, like the one in Figure 11.2. Indeed, this kind of tree is the prototype example, because most of the terminology that we use for abstract trees comes from family trees: *parent*, *child*, *ancestor*, and *descendant*. But mixing metaphors, computer scientists also use the botanical terms *root* and *leaf*.

In the tree shown in Figure 11.3, A is the root, C and K are two of the eight leaves, and B is the parent of F and an ancestor of H.

---

[1] Java 1.4 has 2367 classes that define 5136 fields, 3736 constructors, and 23,266 methods. It also specifies 653 interfaces, for a total of 3020 types (classes and interfaces). These are organized in 136 packages.

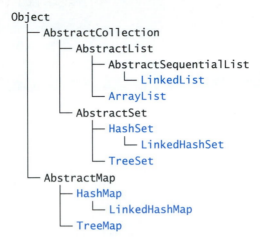

```
Object
    ├── AbstractCollection
    │       ├── AbstractList
    │       │       ├── AbstractSequentialList
    │       │       │       └── LinkedList
    │       │       └── ArrayList
    │       └── AbstractSet
    │               ├── HashSet
    │               │       └── LinkedHashSet
    │               └── TreeSet
    └── AbstractMap
            ├── HashMap
            │       └── LinkedHashMap
            └── TreeMap
```

FIGURE 11.1   The Java Collections Framework classes.

Other terms used with abstract trees are defined in terms of paths. A *path* in a tree is a sequence of adjacent nodes, where two nodes are adjacent if one is the parent of the other. For example, ADGL is a path in this tree.

The *root path* to a node is the unique path from the root to that node. For example, the root path to node E is ABE. A *root-to-leaf path* is a root path to a leaf node. For example, ABEH is a root-to-leaf path.

The *length* of a path is its number of parent-child pairs, which is one less than its number of nodes. For example, the root-to-leaf path ADGK has length 3. Note that a single node can be regarded as a path of length 0.

The *size* of a tree is its number of nodes. The *empty tree* is the unique tree of size 0. A *singleton* is a tree of size 1. The abstract tree shown in Figure 11.3 has size 13.

A tree T_1 is called a *subtree* of a tree T_2 if every node of T_1 is also a node of T_2, and wherever x is the parent of y in T_1, it is also the parent of y in T_2. In this case, T_2 is called a *supertree* of T_1.

11.2 Properties of Trees

The *height* of a tree is the length of its longest root path, which is the same as the length of its longest root-to-leaf path. The abstract tree shown in Figure 11.3 on page 332 has height 3. The tree shown in Figure 11.4 has height 5. A singleton tree has height 0. The empty tree is defined to have height -1.

The *depth* of a node is the length of its root path. For example, in this tree, R has depth 1 and W has depth 4. A tree's root has depth 0. The height of a tree is its greatest depth, which is the depth of its "deepest" leaf.

The nodes of a tree are partitioned into *levels*, each level consisting of all of its nodes at a given depth. For example, in the tree in Figure 11.4, level 1 is the set of two nodes: {Q, R}. In a family tree, levels correspond to generations, and members of the same level are cousins (not necessarily first cousins).

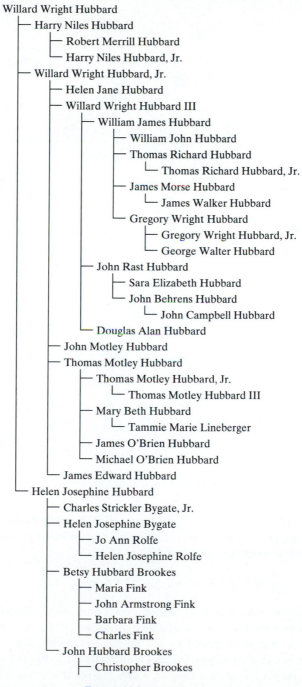

FIGURE 11.2 A family tree.

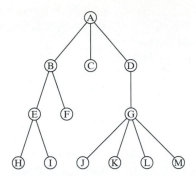

FIGURE 11.3   An abstract tree.

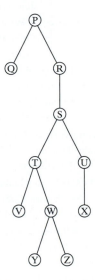

FIGURE 11.4   A tree with path length = 32.

The *path length* of a tree is the sum of the depths of all nodes in the tree. It can be computed as a weighted sum, weighting each level with its number of nodes, or each node by its level. For example, the path length of the tree shown in Figure 11.4 is

$$pl = 0{\cdot}1 + 1{\cdot}2 + 2{\cdot}1 + 3{\cdot}2 + 4{\cdot}3 + 5{\cdot}2 = 32$$

The *width* of a tree is the size of its largest level. For example, the tree in Figure 11.3 has width 6, since its largest level is level 3 containing six nodes: {H, I, J, K, L, M}.

The shape of a tree is measured by its height and width. For example, the tree in Figure 11.3 is wide because its height 3 is less than its width 6. But the tree in Figure 11.4 is narrow because its height 5 is greater than its width 3. Note that a tree of width 1 would be a linear sequence.

The *degree* of a nonempty tree node is its number of children. For example, in the tree in Figure 11.4, node T has degree 2, and node U has degree 1. Obviously, the leaves of a tree are the nodes that have degree 0.

The *degree* of a nonempty tree is the greatest degree of its nodes.[2] For example, the tree in Figure 11.4 has degree 2. The family tree shown in Figure 11.2 has degree 5.

A nonempty tree is said to be *full* if all of its leaves are at the same level and all of its nodes have the same degree. In this case, the degree of each node equals the degree of the tree. These two constraints guarantee that there is only one full tree for each degree and height.

Figure 11.5 on page 333 shows two full trees, one of degree 2 and height 4, and one of degree 5 and height 2. The four characteristic parameters (degree d, height h, width w, size n) are listed for each tree. Note that full trees have maximum possible width and size for given degree and height.

◆ **FORMULA 11.1: The Size of a Full Tree**

The size n of a full tree of degree d and height h is

$$n = \frac{d^{h+1} - 1}{d - 1}.$$

To see why this is true, first consider the case where $h = 0$. In that case, the tree is a singleton, $n = 1$, and the right side of the equation evaluates to

$$(d^{h+1} - 1)/(d - 1) = (d^{(0)+1} - 1)/(d - 1) = (d - 1)/(d - 1) = 1.$$

If $h = 1$, then the tree has $n = 1 + d$ nodes:

$$(d^{h+1} - 1)/(d - 1) = (d^{(1)+1} - 1)/(d - 1) = (d^2 - 1)/(d - 1) = d + 1.$$

If $h > 1$, then as a full tree of degree d, it has 1 node at level 0, d nodes at level 1, d^2 nodes at level 2, *etc.*, so that $n = 1 + d + d^2 + \cdots + d^n$. This is a geometric series, so its sum (see Appendix A) is given by the formula

$$n = \frac{d^{h+1} - 1}{d - 1}$$

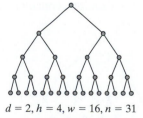

$d = 2, h = 4, w = 16, n = 31$

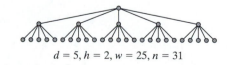

$d = 5, h = 2, w = 25, n = 31$

FIGURE 11.5 Two full trees.

---

[2] Some authors call this the order of the tree.

The data for the two full trees shown in Figure 11.5 agree with the preceding formula:

$$(d^{h+1} - 1)/(d-1) = (2^{(4)+1} - 1)/(2-1) = (2^5 - 1)/(1) = (32-1)/1 = 31$$
$$(d^{h+1} - 1)/(d-1) = (5^{(2)+1} - 1)/(5-1) = (5^3 - 1)/(4) = (125-1)/4 = 124/4 = 31$$

◆ **FORMULA 11.2: The Height of a Full Tree**

The height of a full tree of degree d and size n is $\boldsymbol{h = \log_d(dn - n + 1) - 1}$. This makes $h = \Theta(\lg n)$.

The precise formula follows from Formula 11.1, by solving that equation for h. For the asymptotic version, recall that all logarithms are proportional; that is, $\log_d x = \Theta(\lg x)$, for any base d. (See Formula 3.2.)

◆ **FORMULA 11.3: Bounds on the Size of any Tree**

For any nonempty tree of degree d and height h, the size n satisfies the inequality

$$\boldsymbol{h + d \le n \le \frac{d^{h+1} - 1}{d - 1}}.$$

To see why this is true, first consider the case where $h = 0$. The tree is a singleton, so $d = 0$ and the expression on the right evaluates to 1, which is the correct value for n. Accordingly, consider a tree T of degree d and height $h > 0$. Since T has degree d, it must have at least one node of degree d, say, at level k. Let T_1 be the tree of degree d and height h that has one node of degree d at the same level k, and all other nodes have degree 1. Its size is $n_1 \ge h + d$. Let T_2 be the full tree of degree d and height h. According to the theorem, its size is $n_2 = (d^{h+1} - 1)/(d - 1)$. We can imagine building the given tree T from T_1 by adding more nodes, and building the tree T_2 from the given T by adding more nodes, so $n_1 \le n \le n_2$. (See Figure 11.6 on page 334.)

A node that is not a leaf is called an *internal node*. In some applications, internal nodes are implemented using a different data type than that for leaf nodes. Often the leaf nodes are used only as dummy nodes, containing no data. In this context, leaves are also called *external nodes*. Some applications may even use a single dummy node to represent all external nodes.

In other applications (*e.g.*, B+ trees), all the data is stored in the external nodes, using the internal nodes only as an index to those external data nodes. For example, consider a computer

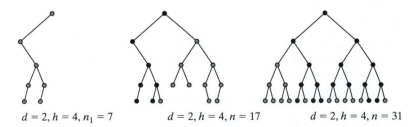

$d = 2, h = 4, n_1 = 7$ $d = 2, h = 4, n = 17$ $d = 2, h = 4, n = 31$

FIGURE 11.6   Trees of degree 2 and height 4.

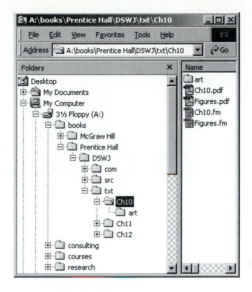

FIGURE 11.7 A File system tree.

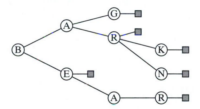

FIGURE 11.8 A spelling tree.

file system that consists of folders and files, like the one shown in Figure 11.7. This file system is a tree hierarchy whose internal nodes are the folders and whose external nodes are the actual files. Folders can contain files and other folders, but files contain neither. So the external nodes have a different type.

As another example, consider the tree in Figure 11.8. This represents the words BAG, BAR, BARK, BARN, BE, and BEAR. The external nodes (drawn as small squares) are dummy nodes. They contain no data (letters), but their existence is necessary to indicate the end of a word. Without them, the words BAR and BE could not be recognized as being stored in the tree.

The tree in Figure 11.9 gives the *Huffman code* for the letters in the message DATA STRUC-TURES. The binary code for each letter is obtained by traversing its root path, marking each left branch with a 0 and each right branch with a 1. For example, the binary code for A would be 011 because the path from the root to the A node goes left-right—right. With this code, the message DATASTRUCTURES is encoded as 1000011000111100010111101010001111011001110.

The Huffman code gives the shortest possible encoding string for the given message. Its tree is an example where all the data is stored in the external nodes, using its internal nodes only to represent the structural relationships among the data.

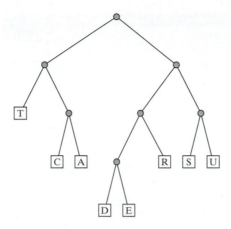

FIGURE 11.9   A Huffman code tree.

In contexts where internal and external nodes are distinguished, the path length usually applies only to the internal nodes and is usually called the *internal path length*. In these cases, the *external path length* is the weighted sum of levels weighted by the number of nodes in the level, except only external nodes are counted. For example, the Huffman code tree shown in Figure 11.9 has internal path length

$$ipl = 0 \cdot 1 + 1 \cdot 2 + 2 \cdot 3 + 3 \cdot 1 = 11$$

and external path length

$$epl = 0 \cdot 0 + 1 \cdot 0 + 2 \cdot 1 + 3 \cdot 5 + 4 \cdot 2 = 25$$

11.3 The Recursive Definition of a Tree

Trees are naturally recursive structures. Moreover, most tree algorithms are more easily understood from a recursive point of view. Thus, we adopt the following recursive definition:

❖ **DEFINITION 11.1**   A *tree* is either the empty set or a pair (r, S), where r is a node and S is a set of disjoint trees, none of which contains r. The node r is called the *root* of the tree, and the trees in S are called its *subtrees*.

We can use this definition to determine whether a given object is a tree. For example, the object T shown in Figure 11.10 can be viewed as a pair (r, S), where r is a node and S is a set of objects $S = \{T_1, T_2\}$. To verify that the elements of S are trees, we examine each element separately. Both T_1 and T_2 can be viewed as pairs: $T_1 = (r_1, S_1)$ and $T_2 = (r_2, S_2)$, where S_1 is the set $S_1 = \{T_3, T_4, T_5\}$ and S_2 is the set $S_2 = \{T_6\}$.

First we verify that the simpler pair $T_2 = (r_2, S_2)$ is a tree. To do that, we have to show that each element of S_2 is a tree. But the only element of S_2 is T_6, and that is a singleton. Every singleton is a tree because it can be viewed as a pair (r, S), where S is the empty set.

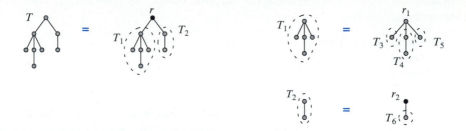

FIGURE 11.10 Verifying the recursive definition of a tree.

Now we know that each of the three elements T_3, T_4, and T_5 is a tree, because T_3 and T_5 are singletons and T_4 has the same structure as T_6. Also note that these three subtrees are disjoint and that none of them contains their root r_1. That allows us to conclude that $T_1 = (r_1, S_1)$ is a tree.

Finally, since T_1 and T_2 are disjoint ad neither contains their root r, we have shown that the given object T satisfies Definition 11.1.

As another example, consider the object shown in Figure 11.11. This is not a tree, because no matter how it is viewed as a pair (r, S), the objects in S will not be disjoint.

Now that we understand that a tree consists of a root node and a set of subtrees, we can redefine all of the properties of trees in terms of this recursive point of view.

A node x is the *parent* of a node y if x is the root of a tree and y is the root of one of its subtrees. In this case we also say that y is a child of x. From there, the definitions of all the other terms (ancestor, descendant, leaf, height, level, *etc.*) arc the same, because they are defined in terms of the basic concepts of parent and child.

The recursive definition of a tree specifies a *set* of subtrees, not a sequence. In other words, the degree of the subtrees is irrelevant. For example, the two sets $\{T_3, T_4, T_5\}$ and $\{T_4, T_5, T_3\}$ are equal, because each is a subset of the other.

Figure 11.12 shows how the equality operator works for unordered trees.

FIGURE 11.11 Not a tree.

FIGURE 11.12 Equal unordered trees.

Implementing recursive definitions is easy in Java. Indeed, we have already done so with Node classes for linked lists:

```java
private class Node {
    Object object;
    Node prev, next;
}
```

This definition is recursive because the class being defined has fields of that type (Node).

The code in Listing 11.1 gives a simple implementation of our recursive definition for unordered trees. This assumes the existence of a Set class. For example, the java.util.TreeSet class could be used.

LISTING 11.1: An UnorderedTree **Class**

```java
1   class UnorderedTree {
2      private Object root;
3      private Set subtrees;
4      private int size;
5      public UnorderedTree() {  // constructs the empty tree
6      }
7
8      public UnorderedTree(Object root) {  // constructs a singleton
9         this.(root);
10        subtrees = new Set();  // constructs the empty set
11        size = 1;
12     }
13
14     public UnorderedTree(Object root, Set trees) {
15        this (root);
16        for (Iterator it=trees.iterator(); it.hasNext(); ) {
17          Object object=it.next();
18          if (object instanceof UnorderedTree) {
19            UnorderedTree tree = (UnorderedTree)object;
20            subtrees.add(tree);
21            size += tree.size();
22          }
23        }
24     }
25
26     public int size() {
27        return size;
28     }
29  }
```

Note that our implementation is a direct translation of the definition of a tree as a pair (r, S), where r is a root node and S is a set of subtrees. We lack only a mechanism for enforcing the constraint that distinct subtrees be disjoint.

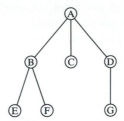

FIGURE 11.13   A tree.

With this implementation, we could build trees from the bottom up, like this:

```
// build leaf nodes:
UnorderedTree treeA, treeB, treeD;
UnorderedTree treeC = new UnorderedTree("C");
UnorderedTree treeE = new UnorderedTree("E");
UnorderedTree treeF = new UnorderedTree("F");
UnorderedTree treeG = new UnorderedTree("G");

// build subtree rooted at B:
Set subtreesOfB = new Set();
subtreesOfB.add(treeE);
subtreesOfB.add(treeF);
treeB = new UnorderedTree("B", subtreesOfB);

// build subtree rooted at D:
Set subtreesOfD = new Set();
subtreesOfD.add(treeG);
treeD = new UnorderedTree("D", subtreesOfD);

// build subtree rooted at A:
Set subtreesOfA = new Set();
subtreesOfA.add(treeB);
subtreesOfA.add(treeC);
subtreesOfA.add(treeD);
treeA = new UnorderedTree("A", subtreesOfA);
```

The result is shown in Figure 11.13.

11.4   Application: Decision Trees

In computer science and other fields, we often have to analyze a sequence of alternatives. Unordered trees are helpful in these tasks. Such a tree is called a *decision tree*. Each internal node represents a stage in the process where a decision is to be made, and its subtrees represent the alternatives for that stage.

For example, suppose a lunch menu has a special that includes three choices of soups, two choices for the main dish, and two choices of beverage, as shown in Figure 11.14. This is a decision tree for that lunch special. The customer's choices are represented by the separate root-to-leaf paths. For example, the root-to-leaf path that terminates at the seventh external node represents the choice sequence (minestrone, salad, cola).

Decision trees can also nicely model more complex situations where some alternatives depend upon others. For example, suppose the lunch special were changed so that the minestrone soup can be selected only with salad, and in that case a third beverage (wine) is possible, as shown in Figure 11.15.

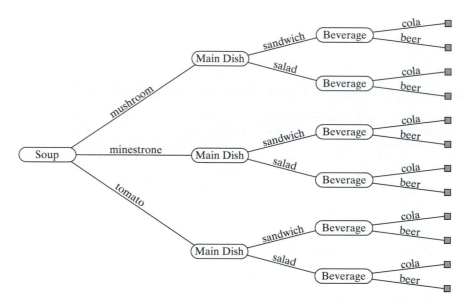

FIGURE 11.14   A decision tree for ordering a meal.

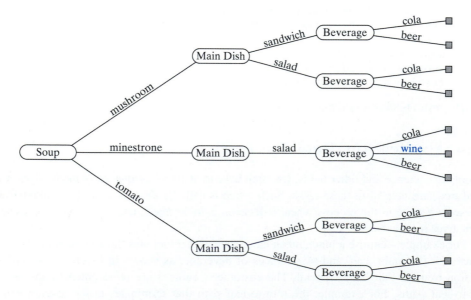

FIGURE 11.15   Another decision tree for ordering a meal.

11.5 Ordered Trees

Most computing applications of trees require that subtrees be ordered. The recursive definition for an ordered tree is nearly the same as that for an unordered tree. The only difference is that each node has a *sequence* of subtrees instead of a set.

❖ **DEFINITION 11.2** An *ordered tree* is either the empty set or a pair (r, S), where r is a node and S is a sequence of disjoint trees, all of which are disjoint from r.

As ordered trees, the trees shown in Figure 11.16 are different. As sets, $\{T_3, T_4, T_5\} = \{T_4, T_5, T_3\}$. As sequences, however, $\{T_3, T_4, T_5\} \neq \{T_4, T_5, T_3\}$.

We have already encountered an important application of ordered trees: the tracing of calls made by recursive methods. For example, the calling tree for the call f(6) to the recursive Fibonacci method in Figure 10.7 on page 307 is shown again here in Figure 11.17. The order is significant because the order of the calls is specified in the method.

Note that an ordered tree is not the same as a sorted tree. The term "ordered" refers to the tree's *structure*, not its contents. Indeed, the actual data stored in the tree nodes has not been relevant to our definitions so far. We will consider sorted trees in the following chapters.

FIGURE 11.16 Unequal ordered trees.

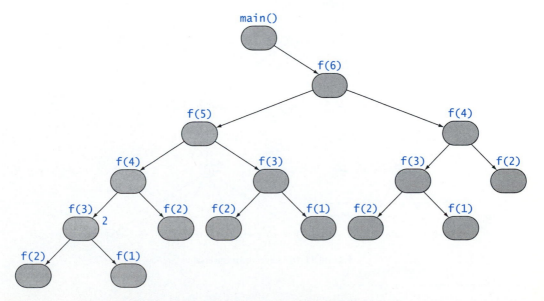

FIGURE 11.17 A calling tree is an ordered tree.

11.6 Traversal Algorithms for Ordered Trees

With the linked list structures that we studied in previous chapters, the concept of a traversal algorithm was not an issue, because there was only one option: start at the beginning and go from each node to its successor node.

For general ordered trees, there are three[3] main traversal algorithms:

❑ level order traversal
❑ preorder traversal (root node first)
❑ postorder traversal (root node last)

The level order traversal algorithm is the simplest to do by hand. It simply "reads" across and down a tree in the same pattern that you use to read this page. For example, Figure 11.18 shows a level order traversal of an ordered tree:

The nodes are visited in this order: A, B, C, D, E, F, G, H, I, J, K, L, M. The traversal is called "level order" because it moves through the levels of the tree in order: level 0 (node A), level 1 (nodes B, C, and D), *etc.*

To implement the algorithm, we use a queue. (See Chapter 5.) This facilitates the move from the end of one level to the beginning of the next level (*e.g.*, from node G to node H in preceding the example). Without the queue, we would have to navigate up to the root and then down the left side of the tree.

▲ **ALGORITHM 11.1: Level Order Traversal of an Ordered Tree**

1. Initialize a queue.

2. Add the root to the queue.

3. Repeat steps 4-6 until the queue is empty.

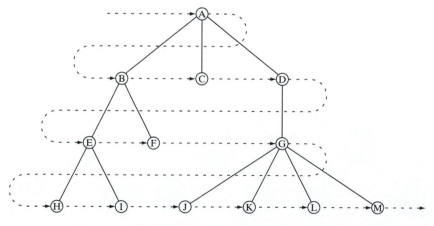

FIGURE 11.18 Level order traversal.

---

[3] When we get to binary trees in Chapter 12, we will have a fourth algorithm, the *inorder traversal*.

4. Remove the first node x from the queue.

5. Visit x.

6. Add all the children of x to the queue, in order.

The preorder traversal algorithm is recursive in its simplest form. To visualize its effect, imagine sailing in a sea where the tree nodes are islands connected by bridges representing parent-child relationships. Sail to the root island. Follow the first bridge to the next island. Then continue visiting the unvisited islands, always sailing so that the bridges and islands are on your port (left) side, as shown in Figure 11.19.

The nodes are visited in this order: A, B, E, H, I, F, C, D, G, J, K, L, M. The traversal is called "preorder" because it visits the root of each subtree before (pre) visiting any of the subtree's nodes.

▲ **ALGORITHM 11.2: Recursive Preorder Traversal of an Ordered Tree**

1. Visit the root.

2. Do a preorder traversal of each subtree in order.

The postorder traversal algorithm is also recursive. Its formulation is just the reverse of the two steps in the preorder traversal.

▲ **ALGORITHM 11.3: Recursive Postorder Traversal of an Ordered Tree**

1. Do a preorder traversal of each subtree in order.

2. Visit the root.

This traversal is called "postorder" because it visits the root of each subtree after (post) visiting all of the subtree's nodes.

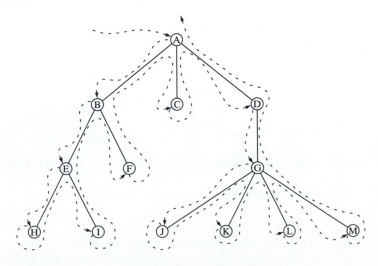

FIGURE 11.19 Preorder traversal.

Applying the postorder traversal to the same tree visits its nodes in this order: H, I, E, F, B, C, J, K, L, M, G, D, A.

All three of the tree traversal algorithms run in $\Theta(n)$ time. This can be seen by observing that each node is processed exactly once.

Both the preorder and postorder algorithms can be implemented iteratively, using a stack very much like the way the level order algorithm uses a queue. (See Programming Problems 10.2 and 10.3.)

11.7 Complete Ordered Trees

To store a tree in memory or on disk it needs to be linearized (*i.e.*, transformed into a node sequence). This process is called *serialization*.[4]

Any one of the three traversal algorithms described in the previous section could be used to linearize a tree. These allow the tree to be stored in an array or a linked list. If the level order traversal is used, the process is sometimes called the *natural mapping* of the tree because we have simple formulas for computing the array indexes of the parent and children of a given node.

The picture in Figure 11.20 shows the serialization of the full ordered tree of degree 3 and height 3. Its nodes are numbered sequentially following a level order traversal of the tree. The numbers are called the *natural index numbers* of the nodes, or simply the *node indexes*. The node indexes at level $l = 2$ in this tree are 4, 5, ..., 12. At level $l = 3$, they are 13, 14, ..., 39.

Consider a general full tree of degree d. There is 1 node above level 1 (the root). There are $1 + d$ nodes above level 2, $1 + d + d^2$ nodes above level 3, $1 + d + d^2 + d^3$ nodes above level 4, *etc.* In general, the number of nodes above level l is $1 + d + d^2 + d^3 + \cdots + d^{l-1}$. This is a geometric series that sums to $(d^l - 1)/(d - 1)$. (See Section C.4 on page 569.) This gives us the result in Formula 11.4.

◆ **FORMULA 11.4: Levels in an Ordered Tree**

At level l in a full ordered tree of degree d, the nodes' natural index numbers are $k, k+1, k+2, \cdots, k+d^l - 1$, where $k = (d^l - 1)/(d - 1)$.

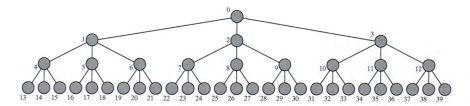

FIGURE 11.20   Serialization of an ordered tree of degree 3.

---

[4] In Java, the term *serialization* refers to the process of converting an object into a byte stream so that it can be stored on disk or transmitted over the Internet. In terms of data structures, it is the same process as discussed here: applying an algorithm that puts the elements of the object into a linear sequence.

For example, in the tree of degree $d = 3$ in Figure 11.20, at level $l = 3$, we have

$$k = (d^l - 1)/(d-1) = (3^3 - 1)/(3-1) = 13$$

so the nodes are numbered $k = 13$, $k + 1 = 14$, $k + 2 = 15 \cdots$, $k + d^l - 1 = 13 + 3^3 - 1 = 39$.

We can use Formula 11.4 to derive Formula 11.5. (See Exercise 11.17 on page 350.)

◆ **FORMULA 11.5: Serialization of an Ordered Tree**

In a full ordered tree of degree d, the parent of node i has index $(i-1)/d$, and the children are numbered $di + 1$, $di + 2$, $\cdots$, $di + d$.

For example, in the tree of degree $d = 3$ in Figure 11.20, the parent of node $i = 8$ is numbered $(i-1)/3 = (8-1)/3 = 2$, and its three children are numbered $3(8) + 1 = 25$, $3(8) + 2 = 26$, $3(8) + 3 = 27$. Note that the division operation is integer division: $7/3 = 2$, not $2.3333\cdots$.

The natural mapping defined in Formula 11.5 gives us a simple way to store an ordered tree in an array: simply store node x in array element a[i], where i is the natural index number of x. This is a very efficient storage algorithm if the tree is full. But if the tree looks like the one in Figure 11.19 on page 343, then the storage will be very inefficient because most of the array will be left unused. That tree has height 2 and degree 4, so by the previous result, the index numbers for the nodes at level 3 are in the range $k = (d^l - 1)/(d-1) = (4^3 - 1)/(4-1) = 21$ to $k + d^l - 1 = 21 + 4^3 - 1 = 84$. But the tree has size $n = 13$. So declaring an array of 85 elements would waste 72 of them.

Clearly, the natural mapping of an ordered tree into an array is efficient only if the tree is full or nearly full. What we want is to avoid gaps of unused elements in the array. For example, the sparse tree of degree 4 in Figure 11.21 would use only 13 of the 57 array elements needed to serialize it with the natural mapping. To that end, we define an ordered tree to be *complete* if it is full except for possibly some missing elements at the right of the bottom level.

Figure 11.22 shows two complete trees. Compare these with the corresponding full trees in Figure 11.5 on page 333.

Each of these trees can be stored in an array without any gaps. The size of the array is equal to the number of nodes in the tree.

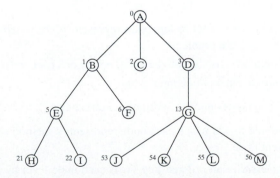

FIGURE 11.21 Node index numbers in a sparsely ordered tree.

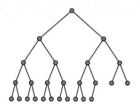

FIGURE 11.22   Two complete trees.

CHAPTER SUMMARY

❏ An abstract *tree* is a nonlinear data structure in which each node is connected to 0 or more child nodes of which it is the parent node.

❏ Each tree node has a unique root path from the tree root to the node. Its length is called the *depth* of the node.

❏ The *height* of a tree is the length of its longest root path.

❏ The *degree* of a node is the number of its children.

❏ The *degree* of a tree is the maximum degree of its nodes.

❏ A *full tree* is one in which all nonleaf nodes have the same degree and all leaf nodes are at the same level

❏ The size n of a full tree of degree d and height h is $n = \dfrac{d^{h+1} - 1}{d - 1}$.

❏ The size n of any nonempty tree of degree d and height h satisfies $h + d \le n \le \dfrac{d^{h+1} - 1}{d - 1}$.

❏ The *path length* of a tree is the sum of all its nodes' depths.

❏ In trees where the leaf nodes serve a special purpose, they are called *external nodes* and the nonleaf nodes are called *internal nodes*.

❏ A *tree* is defined recursively to be either empty or a root and a set of subtrees.

❏ The recursive definition can be implemented as

```
class Tree { Object root; Set subtrees; }
```

❏ A *decision tree* is a tree whose root-to-leaf paths represent all the possible decision sequences that could be made to solve a problem.

❏ An *ordered tree* is defined recursively to be either empty or a root and a sequence of subtrees.

❏ The recursive definition can be implemented as

```
class Tree { Object root; Sequence subtrees; }
```

❏ A *call tree* is an ordered tree in which each node represents a method call by the method represented by its parent node.

❏ The *level order traversal* of an ordered tree visits each node level by level, traversing each level from left to right. It is implemented iteratively with a queue.

❏   The *preorder traversal* of an ordered tree recursively visits the root and then traverses each of its subtrees. It can be implemented iteratively with a stack.

❏   The *postorder traversal* of an ordered tree recursively traverses each of its subtrees and then visits the root. It can be implemented iteratively with a stack.

❏   A *complete tree* is an ordered tree that is full, except possibly for some missing nodes at the right of the bottom level.

❏   There is a natural one-to-one mapping of any complete tree to the elements of an array of the same size.

REVIEW QUESTIONS

11.1   What distinguishes a tree from a more general nonhierarchical structure such as a network?

11.2   What distinguishes a tree from a sequence?

11.3   Why is the degree of a singleton tree equal to 0?

11.4   Why is the height of a singleton tree equal to 0?

11.5   Why is the height of the empty tree defined to be −1?

11.6   How many different words are represented by a word tree that has seven leaves?

11.7   What is the code for the letter E in the Huffman tree shown in Figure 11.9 on page 336?

11.8   Why is a decision tree unordered?

11.9   What is a serialization of a data structure?

11.10 How can an ordered tree be serialized?

11.11 What is the advantage of using the natural mapping of an ordered tree?

EXERCISES

11.1   State whether each of the following is true or false: If true explain why, If false, give a counter example.

   a. The depth of a node in a tree is equal to the number of its ancestors.

   b. The size of a subtree is equal to the number of descendants of the root of the subtree.

   c. If x is a descendant of y in a tree, then the depth of x is greater than the depth of y.

   d. If the depth of x is greater than the depth of y in a tree, then x is a descendant of y.

   e. A tree is a singleton if and only if its root is a leaf.

   f. Every leaf of a subtree is also a leaf of its supertree.

g. The root of a subtree is also the root of its supertree.

h. If *R* is a subtree of *S*, and *S* is a subtree of *T*, then *R* is a subtree of *T*.

i. A node is a leaf if and only if it has degree 0.

j. In any tree, the number of internal nodes must be less than the number of leaf nodes.

k. A tree is full if and only if all of its leaves are at the same level.

l. Every subtree of a full binary tree is full.

m. Every subtree of a complete binary tree is complete.

11.2 For each of the statements in Exercise 11.1 draw a picture that either shows why it is false or illustrates a case in which it is true.

11.3 Figure 11.23 shows a classification tree for Java data types.

a. Should this be regarded as an ordered or an unordered tree?

b. What is the tree's height?

c. What is the tree's degree?

d. What is the tree's width?

e. What is the tree's path length?

11.4 Draw all the different unordered trees of height 2.

11.5 Draw all the different ordered trees of height 2.

11.6 Draw all the different ordered trees of height 3.

11.7 In the Java class inheritance hierarchy, what keyword identifies classes that are at the leaf nodes?

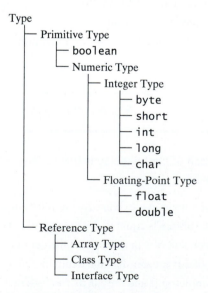

FIGURE 11.23 A classification tree.

11.8   For the tree shown in Figure 11.24, identify each of the following:

   a. the leaf nodes
   b. the children of node D
   c. the depth of node G
   d. the degree of node G
   e. all the ancestors of node G
   f. all the descendants of node G
   g. all the nodes at level 3
   h. the height of the tree
   i. the width of the tree
   j. the degree of the tree

11.9   How many nodes are in the full tree of the following degree and height:

   a. degree 3 and height 4?
   b. degree 4 and height 3?
   c. degree 10 and height 4?
   d. degree 4 and height 10?

11.10   Derive Formula 11.2 on page 334 from Formula 11.1.
11.11   Derive a formula for the width w of a full tree of degree d and height h.
11.12   Derive the formula for the path length of a full tree of degree d and height h.
11.13   Give the order of visitation of the tree in Figure 11.24 using the each of the following:

   a. level order traversal
   b. preorder traversal
   c. postorder traversal

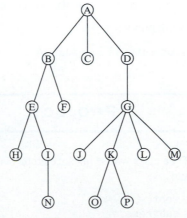

FIGURE 11.24   A tree.

11.14   Which traversals always visit

   a. the root first?

   b. the left-most node first?

   c. the root last?

   d. the right-most node last?

11.15   Using a stack derive an iterative version of the preorder traversal algorithm (Algorithm 11.2 on page 343).

11.16   Using a stack derive an iterative version of the postorder traversal algorithm (Algorithm 11.3 on page 343).

11.17   Derive Formula 11.5 on page 345. [*Hint*: First show that if node x has k nodes on its left at the same level, then the children of x must have between dk and $dk + d - 1$ nodes on their left at their same level.]

PROGRAMMING PROBLEMS

11.1   Implement an `OrderedTree` class similar to the `UnorderedTree` class in Listing 11.1 on page 338. Use the `java.util.LinkedList` type for the sequences of subtrees. Test your class by building the (ordered) tree shown in Figure 11.13.

11.2   Add the method to your `OrderedTree` class of Problem 11.1:

```
public void levelOrderPrint()
```

which implements Algorithm 11.1 on page 342.

11.3   Add the method to your `OrderedTree` class of Problem 11.1:

```
public void preorderPrint()
```

which implements Algorithm 11.2 on page 343.

11.4   Add the method to your `OrderedTree` class of Problem 11.1:

```
public void postorderPrint()
```

which implements Algorithm 11.3 on page 343.

PROJECT

11.1   Define and test a `Tree` class whose instances represent general trees. Use a nested `Node` class with these fields:

```
private Object root;
private Node[] subtrees;
private int size;
```

Include a constructor that allows the user to set the degree of the tree. Also include methods that print the tree using the three traversal algorithms from Section 11.6.

ANSWERS TO REVIEW QUESTIONS

11.1 The connections in a more general nonhierarchical structure may include cycles, like those in Figure 11.25.

11.2 A sequence is linear, with no branching to multiple children.

11.3 A singleton consists of a single node with 0 children.

11.4 The only root path in a singleton is the path of length 0 from the single node to itself.

11.5 The height of the empty tree is defined to be -1 so that the formula

$$n = \frac{d^{h+1} - 1}{d - 1}$$

(and others) will still be correct for the empty tree: $n = 0$ when $h = -1$. (Recall that we defined the degree of the empty tree to be $d = 2$.

11.6 A word tree that has seven leaves represents seven different words.

11.7 The code for the letter E in the Huffman tree in Figure 11.9 on page 336 is 1001.

11.8 A decision tree is unordered because at each point, the set of choices is an unordered set.

11.9 The serialization of a data structure is a transformation of it into a sequence that could be stored in an array or a linked list and later restored.

11.10 An ordered tree can be serialized by the natural mapping that numbers the nodes of the full ordered tree of the same degree and height and assigns each node to the array element indexed by its number.

11.11 The natural mapping of an ordered tree makes it easy to locate the parent and the children of a node in the mapped array: the parent of node i has index $(i-1)/d$, and the children are numbered $di+1, di+2, \cdots, di+d$, where d is the degree of the tree.

FIGURE 11.25 Not a tree.

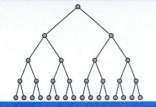

Chapter 12

Binary Trees

In Chapter 11, we studied general trees. This chapter concentrates on the simplest kind of trees: binary trees. After arrays and linked lists, binary trees are probably the most widely used internal data structures in computing.

12.1 Definitions

A *binary tree* is an ordered tree in which every internal node has degree 2. That guarantees that every internal node has two distinguished subtrees, called the *left subtree* and the *right subtree*.

As an ordered tree, a binary tree can be defined recursively, just as we did with general ordered trees in Definition 11.2 on page 341. We take this as our formal definition:

❖ **DEFINITION 12.1**   A *binary tree* is either the empty set or a triple $T = (x, L, R)$, where x is the root and L and R are disjoint binary trees, neither of which contains x. The trees L and R are called the *left subtree* and the *right subtree* of T rooted at x.

The fact that the two subtrees L and R are distinguished by the names "left" and "right" emphasizes that binary trees are ordered trees. Either L or R can be empty, but those two cases result in different binary trees. For example, as unordered trees, the two trees in Figure 12.1 are the same, but as binary trees, they are different.

To conform strictly to our recursive definition, every nonempty node of a binary tree must have both a left subtree and a right subtree. Either of those subtrees may be empty. When drawing binary trees, we often omit the empty trees, as in Figure 12.1, where each node is the root of a nonempty subtree.

For structural clarity, we sometimes also draw in the empty subtrees, as in Figures 12.2 and 12.3. The little squares represent the empty tree and are called NIL nodes. This view of the binary tree is sometimes called the *extended binary tree*. Although the inclusion of the NIL nodes is necessary to satisfy the definition of a binary tree, we do not regard them as ordinary nodes of the tree

FIGURE 12.1 Different binary trees.

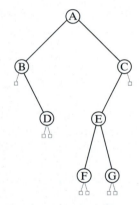

FIGURE 12.2 Equal binary trees.

FIGURE 12.3 A binary tree.

(since they hold no data). Consequently, the leaves of the binary tree are defined to be those nodes whose both left and right children are NIL. For example, the binary tree in Figure 12.3 has three leaves: node D, node F, and node G.

We also ignore the NIL nodes when we compute the size and height of a binary tree. So the tree in Figure 12.3 has size $n = 7$ and height $h = 3$.

12.2 Properties of Binary Trees

Formula 11.1 on page 333 applies to binary trees. With the degree $d = 2$, we have the following formula.

◆ **FORMULA 12.1: Size of a Full Binary Tree**

The size n of the full binary tree of height h is $n = 2^{h+1} - 1$.

Note that this formula applies to "the" full binary tree of height h. That is because there is only one full binary tree for each height. Those with heights less than 5 are shown in Figure 12.4.

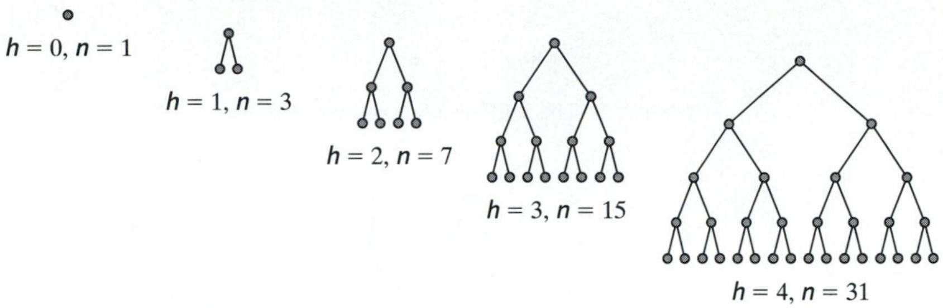

$h = 0, n = 1$

$h = 1, n = 3$

$h = 2, n = 7$

$h = 3, n = 15$

$h = 4, n = 31$

FIGURE 12.4   Full binary trees.

We can regard the empty tree as the full binary tree of height $h = -1$, since that value of h will make $n = 0$ in the formula preceding.

The next two formulas give the relationships between n and h for any binary tree. (See Exercises 12.1 and 12.2 on page 367.)

◆ FORMULA 12.2: Bounds on the Size of a Binary Tree

The size n of any binary tree of height h satisfies $h + 1 \le n \le 2^{h+1} - 1$.

◆ FORMULA 12.3: The Height of a Binary Tree

The height of any nonempty binary tree of size n satisfies $\lfloor \lg n \rfloor \le h$.

Here, the symbol $\lfloor x \rfloor$ means the *floor* of x, which is the greatest integer that is less than or equal to x. (See Section C.1 on page 565.)

12.3 Counting Binary Trees

Counting the number of different binary trees of a given size is a good exercise in recursive thinking.

Table 12.1 gives the number C_n of binary trees of size $n < 6$. The first value, $C_0 = 1$, can be justified by interpreting the unique empty tree as a binary tree. The next value, $C_1 = 1$, follows because there is only one[1] singleton tree.

The two different binary trees of size $n = 2$ are shown in Figure 12.5. The five different binary trees of size $n = 3$ are shown in Figure 12.6.

Table 12.1 asserts that $C_4 = 14$. This can be verified by using Definition 12.1 on page 353. If T is a binary tree of size $n = 4$, then it consists of a root node and three other nodes distributed among its two binary subtrees. Thus, left subtree L must have size 0, 1, 2, or 3, and the corresponding size of its right subtree R must be 3, 2, 1, or 0. Since both of those subtrees are binary trees, we can use our previous values of C_n to count the different possibilities. If $|L| = 0$, then $|R| = 3$. Since there is $C_0 = 1$ possibility for L and $C_3 = 5$ possibilities for R in this case, it follows that there

---

[1] We are counting the number of different structures, without regard to their contents.

FIGURE 12.5 The 2 different binary trees of size 2.

FIGURE 12.6 The 5 different binary trees of size 3.

n	C_n
0	1
1	1
2	2
3	5
4	14
5	42

TABLE 12.1   Catalan numbers.

are $1 \cdot 5 = 5$ different binary trees of size 4 in which the left subtree has size 0. Similarly, there are $C_1 \cdot C_2 = 1 \cdot 2 = 2$ different binary trees of size 4 in which the left subtree has size 1. The complete calculation is thus:

$$C_4 = C_0 \cdot C_3 + C_1 \cdot C_2 + C_2 \cdot C_1 + C_3 \cdot C_0 = 1 \cdot 5 + 1 \cdot 2 + 2 \cdot 1 + 5 \cdot 1 = 5 + 2 + 2 + 5 = 14$$

Similarly,

$$C_5 = C_0 \cdot C_4 + C_1 \cdot C_3 + C_2 \cdot C_2 + C_3 \cdot C_1 + C_4 \cdot C_0$$
$$= 1 \cdot 14 + 1 \cdot 5 + 2 \cdot 2 + 5 \cdot 1 + 14 \cdot 1 = 14 + 5 + 4 + 5 + 14$$
$$= 42$$

The numbers C_0, C_1, C_2, ... are called the *Catalan numbers*. In Section C.11 on page 578, we find the closed-form formula

$$C_n = \frac{(2n)!}{n!(n+1)!}$$

For example, we have

$$C_5 = \frac{(2(5))!}{(5)!((5)+1)!} = \frac{10!}{5!6!} = \frac{10 \cdot 9 \cdot 8 \cdot 7 \cdot 6}{6 \cdot 5 \cdot 4 \cdot 3 \cdot 2} = 42$$

12.4 Binary Tree Traversal Algorithms

In Chapter 11, we studied three traversal algorithms for general ordered trees: the level order traversal (Algorithm 11.1 on page 342), the preorder traversal (Algorithm 11.2 on page 343), and the postorder traversal (Algorithm 11.3 on page 343). Since binary trees are ordered trees, those three algorithms also apply to binary trees. They are restated here in the context of binary trees.

▲ **ALGORITHM 12.1: The Level Order Traversal of a Binary Tree**

1. Initialize a queue.
2. Add the root to the queue.
3. Repeat steps 4–7 until the queue is empty.
4. Remove the first node x from the queue.
5. Visit x.
6. If the left child of x exists, add it to the queue.
7. If the right child of x exists, add it to the queue.

▲ **ALGORITHM 12.2: The Recursive Preorder Traversal of a Binary Tree**

1. Visit the root.
2. If the left subtree is nonempty, perform a preorder traversal on it.
3. If the right subtree is nonempty, perform a preorder traversal on it.

▲ **ALGORITHM 12.3: The Recursive Postorder Traversal of a Binary Tree**

1. If the left subtree is nonempty, perform a postorder traversal on it.
2. If the right subtree is nonempty, perform a postorder traversal on it.
3. Visit the root.

Comparing the preorder and postorder algorithms, we see that the only difference is whether the root is visited before or after the two recursive calls. This suggests another possibility: Visit the root between the two recursive calls. That gives us a fourth traversal algorithm, called the *inorder traversal*, for binary trees:

▲ **ALGORITHM 12.4: The Recursive Inorder Traversal of a Binary Tree**

1. If the left subtree is nonempty, perform an inorder traversal on it.
2. Visit the root.
3. If the right subtree is nonempty, perform an inorder traversal on it.

Note that the prefixes *pre*, *in*, and *post* refer to visiting the root *before*, *between*, or *after* the traversal of the two subtrees.

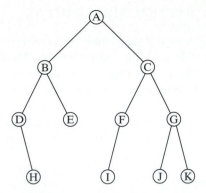

FIGURE 12.7   Traversing a binary tree.

▼ **EXAMPLE 12.1: Traversing a Binary Tree**

Here are the four traversals of the binary tree shown in Figure 12.7:
    Preorder: A, B, D, H, E, C, F, I, G, J, K
    Inorder: D, H, B, E, A, I, F, C, J, G, K
    Postorder: H, D, E, B, I, F, J, K, G, C, A
    Level Order: A, B, C, D, E, F, G, H, I, J, K

12.5 Expression Trees

An arithmetic expression such as

$$(2*x)/(5+3*y)-(4*z-1)$$

is a combination of *arithmetic operators* (+, -, *, and /), *operands* (2, x, 5, 3, *etc.*), and parentheses to override the precedence of the operators. Each expression can be represented by a unique binary tree whose structure is determined by the precedence of the operators in the expression. Such a tree is called an *expression tree*. For example, the expression tree in Figure 12.8 is for the expression $(2*x)/(5+3*y)-(4*z-1)$.
    Algorithm 12.5 builds an expression tree for a given expression.

▲ **ALGORITHM 12.5: Building an Expression Tree**

1. If the expression is a single operand, return the singleton tree that contains it.

2. Formulate the expression as E_1 *op* E_2, where E_1 and E_2 are expressions and *op* is an operator.

3. Apply this algorithm to obtain the expression tree T_1 for expression E_1.

4. Apply this algorithm to obtain the expression tree T_2 for expression E_2.

5. Return the binary tree (*op*, T_1, T_2).

Note how the recursion in Algorithm 12.5 matches the recursion in the Definition 12.1 for a binary tree.

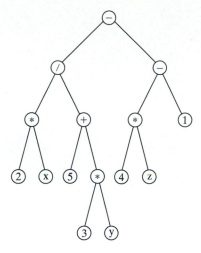

FIGURE 12.8   An expression tree.

Once you have the expression tree for an arithmetic expression, you can reproduce the expression in three different formats, one for each of the three recursive traversal algorithms: preorder, inorder, and postorder. The results are called *prefix*, *infix*, and *postfix* representation, respectively. The postfix representation is also called *reverse Polish notation (RPN)*.

▼ **EXAMPLE 12.2: Prefix, Infix, and Postfix Representations**

Here are the three representations of the expression for the tree in Example 12.1:

Prefix:	− / * 2 x + 5 * 3 y − * 4 z 1
Infix:	2 * x / 5 + 3 * y − 4 * z − 1
Postfix (RPN):	2 x * 5 3 y * + / 4 z * 1 − −

Note that the infix representation is the usual arithmetic representation of the expression with the parentheses removed. Consequently, it can be ambiguous. For example, 9 − 6 − 1 could be interpreted either as $(9 − 6) − 1 = 3 − 1 = 2$ or as $9 − (6 − 1) = 9 − 5 = 4$.

The prefix and postfix representations are unambiguous without any need of parentheses. Each of them generates a unique expression tree, and therefore a unique expression.

▼ **EXAMPLE 12.3: Constructing the Expression Tree from a Given Prefix Representation**

Given the prefix expression + * 3 4 / 8 − 5 1, we can construct the unique expression tree using a preorder traversal, as shown in Figure 12.9. We just have to remember that the operands (in this case, the numbers 8, 4, 8, 5, and 1) form the leaves of the tree.

Constructing the expression tree from a given postfix representation is similar. (See Exercises 12.16–12.18 on page 368.)

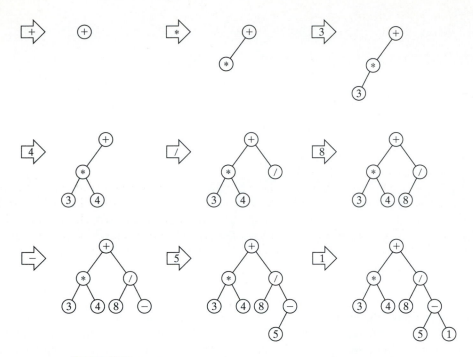

FIGURE 12.9   Building the expression tree from a given prefix representation.

Note that Java methods that represent binary operations actually use the prefix representation. For example, the prefix expression + * 3 4 / 8 - 5 1 in Example 12.3 on page 359 could be evaluated in Java as

```
sum( product( 3, 4 ), quotient( 8, difference( 5, 1 ) ) )
```

if the methods sum(), product(), quotient(), and difference() are defined.

The processes of converting between representations and of evaluating the expression can be automated by building the expression tree and using a stack. (See Chapter 5.) This is illustrated by Algorithm 12.6.

▲ **ALGORITHM 12.6: Evaluating an Expression from Its Postfix Representation**

To evaluate a postfix expression that is input as a sequence of tokens:

1. Create a stack for the operands.
2. Read the next token z from the input.
3. If z is an operand, go to step 7.
4. Pop y from the stack.
5. Pop x from the stack.
6. Evaluate $z = x \, t \, y$.

7. If the stack is empty, return z.

8. Push z onto the stack.

9. Go to step 2.

The next example invokes Algorithm 12.6 to evaluate a given postfix expression.

▼ **EXAMPLE 12.4: Evaluating an Expression from Its Postfix Representation**

Evaluate the postfix expression 5 3 + 7 4 - 1 - /.

The trace is shown in Figure 12.10.

Note that each iteration in Algorithm 12.6 reads one token from the input, so the number of iterations is the same as the number of tokens (nine in this case). Also, each iteration except the last pushes an operand onto the stack. The only difference is that when the token is an operator (+, -, /, *etc.*), two operands are first popped from the stack and then combined with that operator to produce a new operand to be pushed onto the stack (or returned).

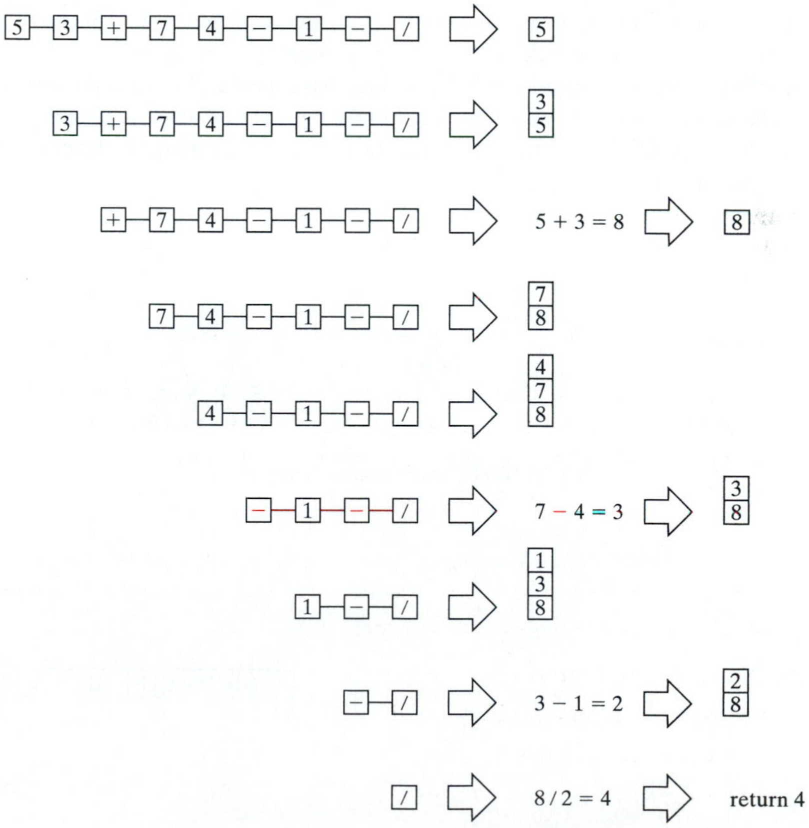

FIGURE 12.10 Evaluating an expression from Its postfix representation.

12.6 Complete Binary Trees

Complete ordered trees were defined in Section 11.7 on page 344 in the previous chapter. We saw that there is a natural mapping of each complete tree into an array of the same size. Since binary trees are ordered trees, the same natural mapping is defined for them. Figure 12.11 shows five complete binary trees. Note that every full binary tree is also complete.

The relationships between the height h and the size n of a complete binary tree are tighter than for a general binary tree. Formulas 12.4 and 12.5 follow from Formula 12.1 on page 354 and are comparable to Formula 12.2 and Formula 12.3 on page 355. (See Exercises 12.1 and 12.2 on page 367.)

◆ **FORMULA 12.4: Bounds on the Size of a Complete Binary Tree**

The size n of a complete binary tree of height h satisfies $2^h \le n \le 2^{h+1} - 1$.

◆ **FORMULA 12.5: The Height of a Complete Binary Tree**

The height of a nonempty complete binary tree of size n is $h = \lfloor \lg n \rfloor$.

For example, the complete binary tree on the right side of Figure 12.11 has size $n = 26$ and height $h = 4$, so $2^h = 2^4 = 16 \le n = 26 \le 2^{h+1} = 2^5 = 32$ and $\lfloor \lg n \rfloor = \lfloor \lg 26 \rfloor = \lfloor 4.7 \rfloor = 4 = h$.

Complete binary trees are important because they have a natural implementation using ordinary arrays. The *natural mapping* of a complete binary tree into an array is obtained by numbering the tree nodes sequentially, starting with 0 at the root and following the level order traversal of the tree, as shown in Figure 12.12.

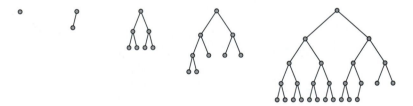

FIGURE 12.11 Some complete binary trees.

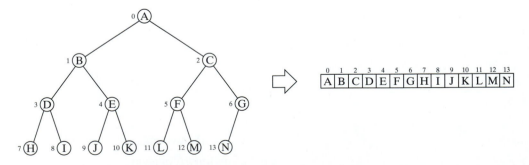

FIGURE 12.12 The natural mapping of a complete binary tree into an array.

One advantage of the natural mapping is that it simplifies the vertical navigation between root and leaf in the tree. Formula 12.6 gives the binary tree version of the general result from page 345.

◆ **FORMULA 12.6: Serialization of a Complete Binary Tree**

In a binary tree, the parent of node i has index $(i-1)/2$, and the children are numbered $2i+1$ and $2i+2$. (Note that this is integer division.)

For example, in the tree in Figure 12.12, the parent of node F at $i = 5$ is node C, numbered $j = 2$, which is computed from the formula $j = (i-1)/2 = (5-1)/2 = 2$. Similarly, the two children of node F are nodes L and M, numbered 11 and 12, which are computed as $2(5)+1 = 11$ and $2(5)+2 = 12$.

By this natural mapping, it is easy to compute the indexes of the nodes on any root path. Moving from any leaf up to the root is done simply by repeatedly replacing the current index i with $(i-1)/2$. For example, the path MFCA in the tree in Figure 12.12 is traversed in the array by the index values

$$12 \rightarrow 5 \rightarrow 2 \rightarrow 1$$

Similarly, moving down the tree from root to leaf is done by repeatedly replacing the current index i with either $2i+1$ or $2i+2$.

Formula 12.7 provides another important fact about complete binary trees that we will use in Chapter 13:

◆ **FORMULA 12.7: Bounds on the Number of Leaves in a Complete Binary Tree**

In a complete binary tree of size n, the leaves are numbered from $n/2$ to $n-1$.

Formula 12.7 can be proved by induction (see Exercise 12.20 on page 368), but it is evident from Figure 12.12 on page 362 that the tree has size $n = 14$ and its leaves are numbered 7 to 13.

Figure 12.13 shows another complete binary tree, with its nodes numbered by the natural mapping. With size $n = 11$, it has five internal nodes and six leaves. This illustrates the next result, Formula 12.8, which can be derived directly from Formula 12.7.

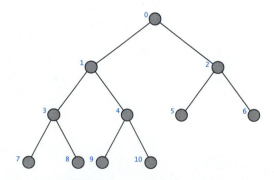

FIGURE 12.13 A complete binary tree.

◆ **FORMULA 12.8: Bounds on the Number of Internal Nodes in a Complete Binary Tree**

A complete binary tree has $n/2$ internal nodes and $(n+1)/2$ leaves.

Of course, the division operator in Formulas 12.7 and 12.8 use integer division, which truncates the fractional part: $11/2 = 5$.

12.7 Forests

A *forest* is a set of trees. An *ordered forest* is a sequence of ordered trees. The picture in Figure 12.14 could be interpreted as being either a forest or an ordered forest. Viewed as an ordered forest, we see that it consists of a sequence of five ordered trees, of heights 3, 4, 0, 5, and 2. The first ordered tree in the sequence has size 16 and degree 5. Note that the individual trees in the forest need not be binary trees.

An ordered forest is a rather complex structure, so it is a bit surprising that it can be uniquely represented by a single binary tree. This fact makes it easy to store ordered forests in a computer.

The natural mapping of an ordered forest into a single binary tree is illustrated in Figure 12.15. To understand the representation, it helps to think of the children of each node in each ordered tree as being listed by decreasing age, the oldest child first, the second oldest child second, *etc.* For example, in the first tree in the forest shown on the left side of Figure 12.15, B is the oldest child of A, C is the next oldest, and D is the youngest. The representation then maps the oldest child of each node into the left child of the corresponding node in the binary tree, and it maps the next sibling of each node into the right child of the corresponding node in the binary tree.

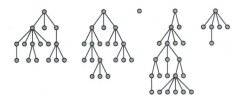

FIGURE 12.14   An ordered forest.

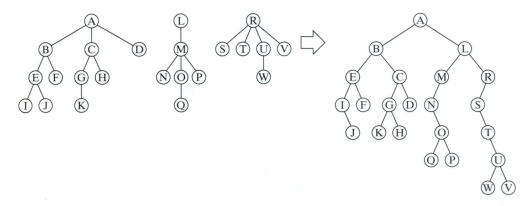

FIGURE 12.15   Representing an ordered forest by a single binary tree.

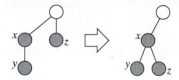

FIGURE 12.16 Steps 2 and 3.

For example, in the representation shown in Figure 12.16, the first child relationship of y to x in the ordered forest on the left is mapped into the left child relationship of y to x in the binary tree on the right. Also, the next sibling relationship of z to y in the ordered forest on the left is mapped into the right child relationship of z to y in the binary tree on the right.

▲ **ALGORITHM 12.7: The Natural Representation of a Forest as a Binary Tree**

1. Map the root of the first tree into the root of the binary tree.
2. If node y is the first child of x and x maps into x', then map y into the left child of x'.
3. If node z is the next sibling of x, then map z into the right child of x'.

In Figure 12.15, the roots of the ordered trees are A, L, and R. They are regarded as siblings, so in the mapped binary tree, L is the right child of A, and R is the right child of L. In the ordered forest, C is the next sibling of B, and D is the next sibling of C, so in the mapped binary tree, C is the right child of B, and D is the right child of C.

Note how each left-most vertical path in the ordered forest gets mapped into a left-most vertical path in the binary tree. For example, the path A → B → E → I is preserved as a left-most path in the mapped binary tree. Similarly, a sequence of siblings gets mapped into a right-most vertical path. For example, the sibling sequence (S, T, U, V) is mapped into the right-most path S → T → U → V in the binary tree.

The binary tree representation of an ordered forest is unique. So the original ordered forest can be recovered from the binary tree. In other words, this natural mapping is one to one.

CHAPTER SUMMARY

❑ A *binary tree* is an ordered tree in which every nonempty node has two subtrees.

❑ A binary tree is *full* if all of its leaves are the same level.

❑ The following formula applies to full binary trees, where n = size and h = height:

$$n = 2^{h+1} - 1$$

❑ The following formulas apply to all binary trees, where n = size and h = height:

$$h + 1 \le n \le 2^{h+1} - 1$$

$$\lfloor \lg n \rfloor \le h$$

❑ The number of distinct binary trees of size n is the nth Catalan number C_n, where $C_0 = C_1 = 1$ and $C_n = \sum_{i=0}^{n} C_i C_{n-i}$.

❑ The general closed-form formula for the Catalan numbers is $C_n = \dfrac{(2n)!}{n!(n+1)!}$.

❑ The four standard traversal algorithms for binary trees are
preorder traversal
inorder traversal
postorder traversal
level order traversal

❑ The three recursive traversal algorithms can be remembered as
preorder: root, left, right
inorder: left, root, right
postorder: left, right, root

❑ An *expression tree* is a binary tree whose nodes contain the operators and operands of an arithmetic expression and whose structure determines the precedence of the operators within the expression. The leaves of the tree contain the operands.

❑ The expression tree for an arithmetic expression in the standard parenthesized format can be built recursively following Algorithm 12.5 on page 358.

❑ Traversing an expression tree produces either the *prefix*, *infix*, or *postfix* representation of the expression, according to whether a preorder, inorder, or postorder traversal is used.

❑ A *complete* binary tree is one that is full except possibly for some missing nodes at the bottom level on the right.

❑ The following formulas apply to complete binary trees, where n = size and h = height:

$$2^h \le n \le 2^{h+1} - 1$$
$$h = \lfloor \lg n \rfloor$$

❑ There is a natural mapping of each complete binary tree into an array $a[]$ of the same size, so that the parent of node $a[i]$ is $a[(i-1)/2]$, and the children of $a[i]$ are $a[2i+1]$ and $a[2i+2]$.

❑ A *forest* is a set of trees.

❑ An *ordered forest* is a sequence of ordered trees.

❑ There is a natural one-to-one mapping between ordered forests and binary trees. (See Algorithm 12.7 on page 365.)

REVIEW QUESTIONS

12.1   How many nodes does the full binary tree of height 5 have?

12.2   If a binary tree has 1000 nodes, what range of values could its height be?

12.3   What is the shape of a binary tree of minimal height for a given number of nodes?

12.4   What is the shape of a binary tree of maximal height for a given number of nodes?

12.5   With which traversal algorithm(s) is the root always visited first?

12.6   With which traversal algorithm(s) is the root always visited last?

12.7   Why is there no inorder traversal algorithm for (general) ordered trees?

12.8   If a binary tree is stored as an array using the natural mapping, what array elements are the ancestors of element `a[i]`?

12.9   What is the difference between a forest and an ordered forest?

EXERCISES

12.1   Prove Formula 12.2 on page 355. [*Hint*: Note that the smallest binary tree for a given height would be a sequence, like the tree in Figure 12.17.]

12.2   Prove Formula 12.3 on page 355. [*Hint*: Solve for h in Formula 12.2.]

12.3   Prove Formula 12.4 on page 362.

12.4   Prove Formula 12.5 on page 362. [*Hint*: solve for h in Formula 12.4.]

12.5   Prove by induction that the number of nodes at level l in a binary tree is between 1 and $2l$.

12.6   Draw the 14 different binary trees of size $n = 4$. Mark those that are complete.

12.7   Draw the 42 different binary trees of size $n = 5$. Mark those that are complete.

12.8   Draw the 21 different binary trees of height $h = 3$. Mark those that are complete, and identify the full tree.

12.9   How many different binary trees are there with height $h = 4$?

12.10 How many different binary trees are there with size $n = 6$?

12.11 How many different binary trees are there with size $n = 7$?

12.12 Use the recursive definition of a binary tree (Definition 12.1 on page 353) to verify that the structure in Figure 12.2 on page 354 is a binary tree.

12.13 True or false? If all of its leaves are at the same level, then the binary tree is full.

12.14 True or false? If every proper subtree of a binary tree is full, then the tree itself must also be full.

12.15 Give the order of visitation for the traversal of the binary tree shown in Figure 12.18, using each of the following traversal algorithms:

   a. level order
   b. preorder
   c. inorder
   d. postorder

FIGURE 12.17 A binary tree.

12.16 Construct the expression tree for the arithmetic expression

2*(8 - 9/3) - 4

Then give the prefix representation, the infix representation, the postfix representation, and the actual numeric value of the expression.

12.17 Construct the expression tree for the expression whose prefix representation is

/ - 8 - 7 5 3

Then give the postfix representation, both the infix representation and the correctly parenthesized infix representation, and the actual numeric value of the expression.

12.18 Construct the expression tree for the expression whose postfix representation is

9 1 - 1 3 + /

Then give the prefix representation, both the infix representation and the correctly parenthesized infix representation, and the actual numeric value of the expression.

12.19 Write an algorithm similar to Algorithm 12.6 on page 360 for evaluating an arithmetic expression from its prefix representation.

12.20 Use mathematical induction to prove Formula 12.7 on page 363.

12.21 Draw the ordered forest that is represented by the binary tree shown in Figure 12.18.

12.22 Draw the binary tree that represents the ordered forest shown in Figure 12.19.

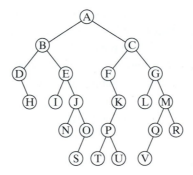

FIGURE 12.18 A binary tree.

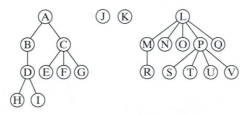

FIGURE 12.19 An ordered forest.

PROGRAMMING PROBLEMS

12.1   Implement the recursive Definition 12.1 on page 353 directly as a `BinaryTree` class with the two fields

```
Object root;
BinaryTree left, right;
```

the three constructors

```
public BinaryTree(Object root)
public BinaryTree(Object root, BinaryTree left, BinaryTree right)
public BinaryTree(BinaryTree that)
```

the three getter methods

```
public Object getRoot()
public BinaryTree getLeft()
public BinaryTree getRight()
```

and the three setter method:

```
public Object setRoot(Object root)
public BinaryTree setLeft(BinaryTree left)
public BinaryTree setRight(BinaryTree right)
```

The first constructor creates a singleton tree. The third constructor is a *copy constructor*, which constructs a tree that has the same structure and whose nodes reference the same objects as that tree. Each setter method returns the old value after replacing it with the given argument.

12.2   Write and test a `toString()` method for the `BinaryTree` class from Problem 12.1. For example, it would return the string `"((B),A,((D),C,(E)))"` for the tree shown in Figure 12.20. That tree could be built as follows:

```
BinaryTree treeB = new BinaryTree("B");
BinaryTree treeD = new BinaryTree("D");
BinaryTree treeE = new BinaryTree("E");
BinaryTree treeC = new BinaryTree("C", treeD, treeE);
BinaryTree treeA = new BinaryTree("A", treeB, treeC);
```

FIGURE 12.20   A binary tree.

12.3   Write and test this method for the `BinaryTree` class from Problem 12.1:

```
/**
 * @return true iff this tree is a leaf.
 */
public boolean isLeaf()
```

For example, in the tree and subtrees in Figure 12.20, `treeA.isLeaf()` would return `false`, and `treeB.isLeaf()` would return `true`.

12.4   Write and test this recursive method for the `BinaryTree` class from Problem 12.1:

```
/**
 * @return the number of elements in this tree.
 */
public int size()
```

For example, in the tree in Figure 12.20, `treeA.size()` would return 5, and `treeC.size()` would return 3.

12.5   Write and test this recursive method for the `BinaryTree` class from Problem 12.1:

```
/**
 * @return the height of this tree.
 */
public int height()
```

For example, in the tree in Figure 12.20, `treeA.height()` would return 2, and `treeC.height()` would return 1.

12.6   Write and test this recursive method for the `BinaryTree` class from Problem 12.1:

```
/**
 * @return true iff the specified object is in this tree.
 */
public boolean contains(Object object)
```

For example, in the tree in Figure 12.20, `treeA.contains("B")` would return `true`, and `treeC.contains("B")` would return `false`.

12.7   Write and test this recursive method for the `BinaryTree` class from Problem 12.1:

```
/**
 * @return the number of leaves in this tree.
 */
public int numLeaves()
```

For example, in the tree in Figure 12.20, `treeA.numLeaves()` would return 3, and `treeC.numLeaves()` would return 2.

12.8   Write and test this recursive method for the `BinaryTree` class from Problem 12.1:

```
/**
 * @return the number of references that this tree has to the
 *   given object x.
 */
public int count(Object x)
```

For example, using the tree in Figure 12.20, if we construct the tree

```
BinaryTree tree = new BinaryTree("E", treeA, new BinaryTree("E"));
```

then `tree.count("E")` would return 3.

12.9   Write and test this recursive method for the `BinaryTree` class from Problem 12.1:

```
/**
 * @return true iff this is a full tree.
 */
public boolean isFull()
```

For example, in the tree in Figure 12.20, `treeA.isFull()` would return `false`, and `treeC.isFull()` would return `true`. (*Hint*: Use the `height()` method from Problem 12.5.)

12.10   A binary tree is said to be *balanced* if at every node the difference between the heights of the two subtrees is less than 2. For example, the tree in Figure 12.20 is balanced because the heights of the two subtrees of node A are 0 and 1, and the heights of the two subtrees of node C are 0 and 0. But the binary tree in Figure 12.18 is not balanced because the heights of the two subtrees of node B are 1 and 3. Write and test this recursive method for the `BinaryTree` class from Problem 12.1:

```
/**
 * @return true iff this tree is balanced.
 */
public boolean isBalanced()
```

[*Hint*: Use the `isLeaf()` method from Problem 12.3 and the `height()` method from Problem 12.5.]

12.11   The *path length* of a binary tree is the sum of the lengths of all the root paths in the tree. For example, the path length of the tree in Figure 12.20 is $0 + 1 + 1 + 2 + 2 = 6$. Note that there is one root path for each node. Write and test this recursive method for the `BinaryTree` class from Problem 12.1:

```
/**
 * @return the path length of this tree.
 */
public int pathLength()
```

[*Hint*: Use the `size()` method from Problem 12.4.]

12.12   The *reverse* of a binary tree is the binary tree that is its mirror image. For example, the tree in Figure 12.21 is the reverse of the binary tree in Figure 12.20 on page 369. Write and test this recursive method for the `BinaryTree` class from Problem 12.1:

```
/**
 * @return the reverse of this tree.
 */
public BinaryTree reverse()
```

FIGURE 12.21   A binary tree.

12.13   Write and test this recursive method for the `BinaryTree` class from Problem 12.1:

```
/**
 * @return the level of the specified object x in this tree;
 *          or -1 if x is not in this tree.
 */
public int level(Object x)
```

For example, in the tree in Figure 12.20, `treeA.level("E")` would return 2, and `treeB.level("E")` would return −1.

12.14   Write and test this recursive method for the `BinaryTree` class from Problem 12.1:

```
/**
 * @return true iff no element in both this tree and that.
 */
public boolean isDisjointFrom(BinaryTree that)
```

12.15   Write and test this recursive method for the `BinaryTree` class from Problem 12.1:

```
/**
 * @return true iff this is a valid binary tree;
 *          i.e., all of its subtrees are disjoint.
 */
public boolean isValid()
```

[*Hint*: Use the `isDisjointFrom()` method from Problem 12.14.]

12.16   Write and test this recursive method for the `BinaryTree` class from Problem 12.1:

```
/**
 * @return true iff the given object is equal to this tree.
 */
public boolean equals(Object object)
```

Note that equality requires that the given `object` be an instance of the `BinaryTree` class, that it have the same structure as `this` tree, and that the `root` of each of its subtrees be `equal()` to the `root` of the corresponding subtree of `this` tree.

12.17   The following recursive `static` methods for the `BinaryTree` class from Problem 12.1 print the tree, using the preorder and the postorder traversal algorithms:

```
static void preOrderPrint(BinaryTree tree)
static void postOrderPrint(BinaryTree tree)
```

For example, the call `postOrderPrint(treeA)` for the tree in Figure 12.20 would print

B D E C A

12.18 Write and test the methods. `static` method for the `BinaryTree` class from Problem 12.1 The following prints the tree, using the level order traversal algorithms:

```
static void levelOrderPrint(BinaryTree tree)
```

For example, the call `levelOrderPrint(treeA)` for the tree in Figure 12.20 would print

A B C D E

Write and test the methods. [*Hint*: consider a queue, implemented as an instance of the `java.util.ArrayList` class, using `add()` and `remove(0)` for insertions and deletions.]

PROJECTS

12.1 Define and test a `BinaryTree` class whose instances represent binary trees. Use an inner `Node` class.

12.2 Use a binary tree to implement the *game of Botticelli*. This a word game played by two or more players. One person, called the *pretender*, assumes the role of a famous person, called the *character*. All the other players, called the *guessers*, try to guess the identity of the character. The game progresses in a sequence of stages. At each stage, a guesser is allowed to ask either a general boolean question (one whose answer is either "yes" or "no") such as "Are you a playwright?" or a direct question such as "Are you William Shakespeare?" The purpose of the general questions is to narrow down the possibilities, as in a binary search. Each guesser may ask only one direct question. The game ends when a direct question identifies the character or when all the guessers have asked their direct questions. The progress of a game of Botticelli can be modeled with a decision tree like the one shown in Figure 12.22.

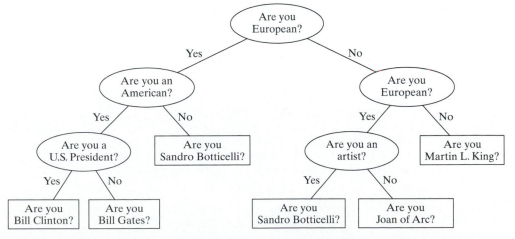

FIGURE 12.22 A Botticelli tree.

ANSWERS TO REVIEW QUESTIONS

12.1   The full binary tree of height 5 has 63 nodes.

12.2   The height of a binary tree with 1000 nodes could be any number from 10 to 999.

12.3   The binary tree of minimal height for a given number of nodes is nearly full.

12.4   The binary tree of maximal height for a given number of nodes is linear.

12.5   The level order and the preorder traversals visit the root first.

12.6   The postorder traversal visits the root last.

12.7   The inorder traversal visits the root between visits to the left and right subtrees. General ordered trees, however, do not have "left" and "right" subtrees.

12.8   If a binary tree is stored as an array using the natural mapping, then the array elements that are the ancestors of element a[i] are those whose indexes arise from reducing i repeatedly by the formula $i \leftarrow (i-1)/2$.

12.9   A forest is a set of trees; an ordered forest is an (ordered) sequence of ordered trees.

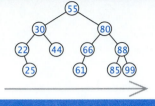

Seek, and ye shall find.

— Matthew v.7

Chapter 13

Search Trees

We saw in Chapter 9 how hash tables can provide nearly constant time access to stored data, as long as you don't need the data retrieved in order. When ordered access is needed, *search trees* are the best data structures to use. They generalize the idea behind the binary search algorithm, providing logarithmic access time, which is almost as good as constant time.

This chapter explores search trees, both binary search trees and the more general B-trees. We use an object-oriented approach that is consistent with the Java Collections Framework.

13.1 Keys and Comparable Types

Search structures are used in computing as indexes to data. Like an index in a book, a search structure contains key "words" that identify the data that you seek and list the locations (*e.g.*, page numbers) where that data can be found. So they require two specialized data types: a key type whose values can be compared (like `int` or `String`), and an address type whose values give data locations (*e.g.*, an array index, a hexadecimal memory address, or an external disk address).

Java provides an elegant solution for key types. It defines an interface, named `Comparable`, that guarantees a method with this signature:

```
public int compareTo(Object object)
```

It returns an integer *c* that is assumed to signal one of three possibilities:

❑ If $c < 0$, then `this` object is less than the given `object`;
❑ If $c = 0$, then `this` object is equal to the given `object`;
❑ If $c > 0$, then `this` object is greater than the given `object`;

This works the same way as the `compareTo()` method in the `String` class. For example,

```
String s1="ACE", s2="ADB";
if (s1.compareTo(s2)<0) System.out.println("s1<s2");
if (s2.compareTo(s1)>0) System.out.println("s2>s1");
```

375

will print

```
s1<s2
s2>s1
```

Objects of any type that `implements` `Comparable` can be tested the same way.

Recall that, in Java, object references and method parameters can be declared by using an interface as well as a class—for example,

```
Comparable[] keys;
int index(Comparable key) { //...
```

Of course, we cannot instantiate objects using interface names, because instantiations invoke constructors and interfaces don't have constructors. We have to use a class to create the objects, like this:

```
Comparable[] keys = new String[200];
int i = index(new Integer(529))
```

Any instance of any class that implements the `Comparable` interface (as do the `String` and `Integer` classes) can be used as a variable declared to have `Comparable` type.

Keys are used to identify data. We saw this with map structures (hash tables) in Chapter 9, where the key served as an input to an operation whose output was the data value. Thus, as in Chapter 9, we will assume that keys are unique: No duplicate keys are allowed.

In addition to unique keys of some `Comparable` type, we will assume that structure also uses some `Address` type whose values locate the data identified by the key. Java makes it easy to formalize this requirement. We simply define an `Address` interface, as in Listing 13.1, and defer its implementation to later applications. For example, if our search tree is an internal red-black tree, then we could store all our data in an array via the code

```
Object[] data = new Object[200];
```

Then we would replace `Address` with `int` and `get(key)` with `data[key]`. On the other hand, if our search tree is an external B-tree, we could define a special `DiskAddress` class like this:

```
class DiskAddress implements Address {
  private String drive;
  private long sector, block;
}
```

Then each call to `get(key)` would execute a disk access, loading the disk block located at the address stored in key. (Red-black trees and B-trees are discussed later in the chapter.)

LISTING 13.1: **An Interface for Disk Addresses**

```
1   interface DiskAddress {
2     public Object get(Comparable key);
3   }
```

In summary, then, we are assuming that each search tree satisfies these three conditions:

❑   The keys within the search tree structure are unique;

❑   Each key is accompanied by the address of the data that it represents;

❏   The keys' type implements the `java.lang.Comparable` interface;

❏   The addresses' type implements the above `Address` interface;

Since our primary interests are the search tree structures themselves, we may not explicitly mention the keys' associated `Address` values. But still assume that they exist. When we refer to a stored key, we really mean a key-address pair.

13.2 Binary Search Trees

A *binary search tree* (BST) is a binary tree that contains a key-address pair in each node which satisfies this *BST property*:

> *For each key in the tree, all the keys in its left subtree are less than it,*
> *and all the keys in its right subtree are greater than it.*

For example, if a node contains the key 55, then all the keys in the left subtree of that node must be less than 55, and all the keys in the right subtree of that node must be greater than 55. This is illustrated in Figures 13.1 and 13.2. Note that the BST property applies at *every* node, not just the root. For example, at node 70 in Figure 13.2, the four keys in its left subtree are less than 70, and the one key in its right subtree is greater than 70.

◆ **FORMULA 13.1: Binary Search Tree Traversal**

An inorder traversal of a binary search tree visits the keys in increasing order.

This fact can be verified by mathematical induction on the tree size n. If $n \leq 1$, then the BST is either empty or is a singleton, so the conclusion is trivially true. Suppose $n > 1$ and assume that the statement is true for all BTSs of size $< n$. The inorder traversal visits the left subtree recursively, then the root, and then the right subtree recursively. By the inductive hypothesis, the two subtree traversals will visit the keys of those subtrees in increasing order. It follows then from the BST property that all n keys will be visited in increasing order because all the keys in the left subtree are less than the root key and all the keys in the right subtree are greater than the root key.

The BST property is used to find elements in the tree according to Algorithm 13.1.

▲ **ALGORITHM 13.1: BST Retrieve**

Input: a binary search tree T and a *key*.
Output: the data address for that *key*, or *null* if that *key* is not in *T*.

   1. If T is empty, return *null*.

   2. If *key* < *root.key* return the value returned by recursively searching *left* for *key*.

   3. If *key* > *root.key* return the value returned by recursively searching *right* for *key*.

   4. Return *root.address*.

For example, to find *key* = 66 in the BST in Figure 13.2 on page 378, we start at the root node (55). Since 66 > 55, we move to the right node (77). Since 66 < 77, we move to its left node (70). Since 66 < 70, we move again to the left to node (60). Since 66 > 60, we move to the right node (66). Now *key* = *x.key*, so we return the address stored in that node x.

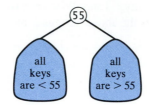

FIGURE 13.1 The BST property.

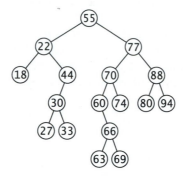

FIGURE 13.2 A binary search tree.

Notice how Algorithm 13.1 uses the recursive divide-and-conquer strategy, just like the Binary Search algorithm. Each time x gets reassigned to one of its children, the subtree of possible nodes that could contain *key* is reduced to one about half as large. That explains why the BST algorithms run in $\Theta(\lg n)$ time when the tree is balanced: A set of elements can be divided in half about $\lg n$ times.

Another way to see why the search algorithm runs in $\Theta(\lg n)$ time is to realize that the search path lies along a single root-to-leaf path in the tree. Hence, the number of comparisons made in searching for a key is never greater than the height of the tree. We know from Formula 12.2 on page 355 that the height of a full binary tree of n elements is $\Theta(\lg n)$, and a balanced binary tree is close to being full. Even when the tree is a little unbalanced, like the one shown in Figure 13.2, the average length of the search paths will be less than $2 \lg n$, as we shall show in Formula 13.4.

The insertion algorithm, Algorithm 13.2 uses the same traversal steps as the search algorithm to locate the position in the tree to insert a new key. New nodes are always inserted at the leaves of the tree.

▲ **ALGORITHM 13.2: BST Insert**

Input: a binary search tree *T* and a *key–address* pair.
Output: *false* if *key* is already in *T*; otherwise *true*.
Postcondition: the *key–address* pair is in *T*.

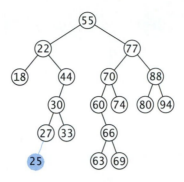

FIGURE 13.3 The BST insert algorithm.

1. If *T* is empty, make it a singleton containing the *key–address* pair, and return *true*.

2. If *key* < *root.key*, return the value returned by recursively inserting the *key–address* pair in the *left* subtree.

3. If *key* > *root.key*, return the value returned by recursively inserting the *key–address* pair in the *right* subtree.

4. Return *false*.

Figure 13.3 illustrates the insertion of the *key* = 25 into the BST from Figure 13.2. We start at the root (55). Since 25 < 55, we move to the left node (22) at step 2. Since 25 > 22, we move to the right node (44). Since 25 < 44, we move to the left node (30). Since 25 < 30, we move again to the left to node (27). Since 25 < 27, we move again to the left node, which is empty. So at step 1 of that recursive call, we add the new node containing the *key–address* pair, and return *true*.

Notice how similar the Insert algorithm is to the Retrieve algorithm. It uses the same conditions to make the recursive calls. Consequently, the Insert algorithm has the same complexity as the Search algorithm: $\Theta(\lg n)$, if the tree is balanced.

Of course, an ordinary BST may become very unbalanced. For example, if you insert the keys 22, 33, 44, 55, 66, 77, 88, 99, in that order, your BST will be a linear linked list. In that case, Retrieve and Insert will take linear, not logarithmic time: $\Theta(n)$, not $\Theta(\lg n)$. Because of that problem, we will develop algorithms for keeping the tree balanced later in this chapter.

▼ **EXAMPLE 13.1: Building a BST**

In general, BSTs are built by repeated calls to the Insert algorithm. For example, Figure 13.4 shows the construction of a BST built by inserting the keys 77, 44, 55, 99, 33, 66, 88, and 22:

The logarithmic run time of the BST algorithms holds in the best case—where the tree is completely balanced—and in the average case as well. However, performance degrades substantially if the tree gets seriously unbalanced. The worst case is when the tree degenerates to a linear list. In that case, obviously the run time is linear. (See Figure 13.5.)

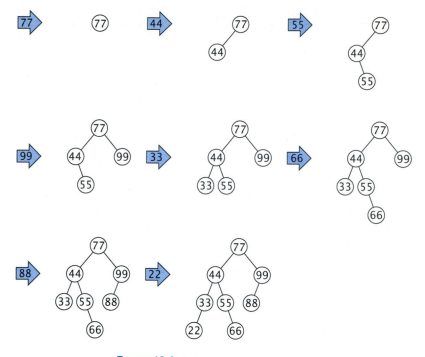

FIGURE 13.4 Building a binary search tree.

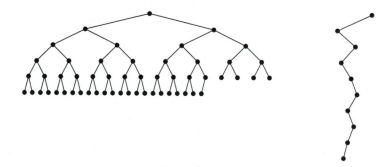

FIGURE 13.5 The best-case and worst-case shapes of a BST.

13.3 BST Deletion

Deleting an element from a binary search tree is more difficult than inserting it because it may be an internal node. For example, simply removing 44 from the 8-node BST in Figure 13.4 would disconnect the tree, as Figure 13.6 shows.

The solution in this case, as shown in Figure 13.7, is to replace the node with its inorder successor node 55.

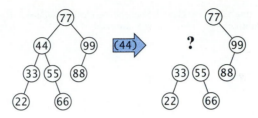

FIGURE 13.6 An incorrect attempt to delete node 44.

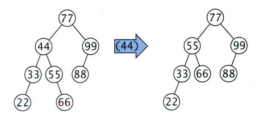

FIGURE 13.7 The correct way to delete a node 44.

So before we can describe the general deletion algorithm, we first have to describe how to find the inorder successor y of a BST node x. There are three possibilities:

1. If x has a right subtree, then y is the left-most node in that subtree.

2. Otherwise, if x has a right ancestor, then y is its closest right ancestor.

3. Otherwise, x is the right-most node in the tree and therefore has no inorder successor.

For example, in Case 1 of Figure 13.8 on page 382, the successor of $x = (55)$ is the minimum node $y = (56)$ of the right subtree of x. In Case 2, the successor of $x = (54)$ is the closest right ancestor $y = (55)$. And in Case 3, $x = (99)$ is the maximum element in the tree, so it has no successor.

The algorithm for finding the minimum of a subtree (see Algorithm 13.3) is to start at the root of the subtree and simply move down its left side.

▲ **ALGORITHM 13.3: BST Minimum**

Input: a nonempty binary search tree T.
Output: the minimum node in T.

1. Let x be the root of T.

2. While $x.left$ is not empty, set $x = x.left$.

3. Return x.

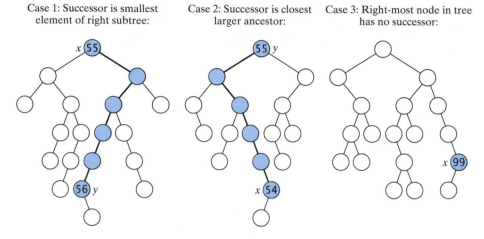

Case 1: Successor is smallest   Case 2: Successor is closest   Case 3: Right-most node in tree
    element of right subtree: larger ancestor: has no successor:

FIGURE 13.8 The inorder successor of a node.

Algorithm 13.4 finds the inorder successor of an element x, covering all three cases described in Figure 13.8.[1]

▲ ALGORITHM 13.4: BST Successor

Input: a nonempty binary search tree T and a node x.
Output: the inorder successor of x, or *nil* if x is the maximum element of T.
Precondition: x is not the maximum node of T.

1. If the right subtree of x is not empty, return its minimum (Algorithm 13.3).

2. While x is a right child, set $x = x.parent$.

3. Return $x.parent$ (which may be NIL).

Note that Algorithm 13.4 requires some mechanism for moving from a node to its parent in the BST. This can be done by maintaining a stack in the algorithm, or by implementing parent links in the data structure itself.

Algorithm 13.5, the deletion algorithm for BSTs, has three separate cases, according to whether the node to be deleted has zero, one, or two children. If it has no children, then it is deleted directly, with no side effects. If it has one child, it is "spliced out" of the tree, as (44) was in Figure 13.7. If it has two children, then it is replaced by its inorder successor (Algorithm 13.4), and then that successor gets spliced out. Note that when we say "replace node x with node y", we mean that both the key and its associated data address in the node x are to be replaced with the corresponding fields from node y.

---

[1] However, we shall see that the first case is the only one that we'll need for the BST Deletion algorithm.

▲ **ALGORITHM 13.5: BST Delete**

Input: a binary search tree *T* and a *key*.
Output: *false* if *key* is not found in *T*; otherwise *true*.
Postcondition: the *key* is not in *T*.

1. If *T* is empty, return *false*.

2. If *key* < *root.key*, return the value returned by recursively deleting the *key* from the *left* subtree.

3. If *key* > *root.key*, return the value returned by recursively deleting the *key* from the *right* subtree.

4. If *T* is a singleton, make it the empty tree and return *true*.

5. If the *left* subtree is empty, copy the *root*, *left*, and *right* fields of the *right* subtree of *T* into *T* itself, and return *true*.

6. If the *right* subtree is empty, copy the *root*, *left*, and *right* fields of the *left* subtree of *T* into *T* itself, and return *true*.

7. Replace the *root* with the node returned by applying *deleteMinimum* to the *right* subtree, and return *true*.

The location of *key* node to be deleted is done by the same recursive steps (steps 1–3) that are used for the **Retrieve** and **Insert** algorithms (on pages 377 and 378). Step 4 handles Case 1 illustrated in Figure 13.9 on page 384, when the node to be deleted is a leaf. Steps 5 and 6 handle Case 2, and Case 3 is handled by step 7, using Algorithm 13.6.

▲ **ALGORITHM 13.6: BST Delete Minimum**

Input: a nonempty binary search tree *T*.
Output: the minimum node *y* in *T*.
Postcondition: *y* has been removed from *T*.

1. If the *left* subtree is empty, return the current node after replacing it with *right*.

2. If the *left* subtree is a leaf, return the current node after replacing it with *left*.

3. Return the node that is returned by applying Delete Minimum to *left*.

This recursive algorithm deletes and returns the minimum node from the tree. Applying it to the *right* subtree of a node *x* replaces *x* with its inorder successor after deleting it from the subtree. This is illustrated by Case 3 in Figure 13.9 on page 384.

13.4 BST Performance

All three BST operations (search, insert, and delete) operate exclusively on one or two root-to-leaf paths of the tree. Hence, the number of comparisons made by any one of them will be proportional to the height of the tree. The height of a completely balanced binary tree is $\Theta(\lg n)$, and

Case 1: x has 0 children:
(No side effects.)

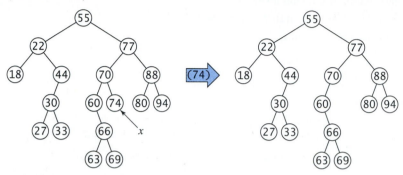

Case 2: x has 1 child:
(Splice it out.)

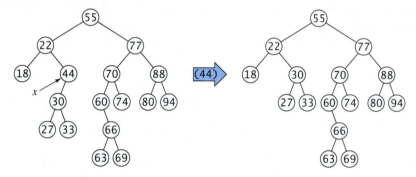

Case 3: x has 2 children:
(Replace x with its successor y, and then splice out y.)

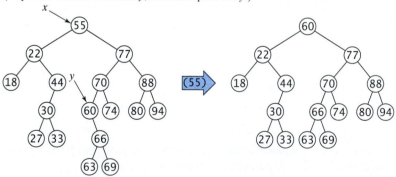

FIGURE 13.9   The three different cases for Algorithm 13.5.

the height of a completely unbalanced binary tree is $\Theta(n)$. So these are the best-case and worst-case complexity functions for all three operations. In that average case, they still run in logarithmic time, about 39% slower (on average) than the best case.

◆ FORMULA 13.2: **Binary Search Tree Insert and Search**

Both the insertion and the search algorithms for a BST have these complexity functions:

$$B(n) = \Theta(1)$$
$$A(n) = \Theta(\lg n)$$
$$W(n) = \Theta(n)$$

The best-case and worst-case examples have already been examined. The derivation for the average case follows from these mathematical results.

◆ FORMULA 13.3: **Average Time Complexity of the BST Search and Insertion Algorithms**

$$A(n) = \frac{2n-2}{n}(H_{n+1} - 1) - 1$$

where H_n is the nth *harmonic number*: $H_n = 1 + 1/2 + 1/3 + ... + 1/n$. (See Section C.8 on page 573.)

From this, we see that for large n, $A(n) \approx 2H_{n+1} - 3$. Now, Formula C.9 states that $H_n \approx \ln n + \gamma$, for large n, where γ is Euler's constant ($\gamma \approx 0.577$). Thus, for large n, $A(n) \approx 2\ln(n+1) + \gamma - 3$.

This gives us the complexity function $A(n) = \Theta(2\ln n) = \Theta(c\lg n)$, where $c = 2\ln 2 = \ln 4 = 1.39$.

◆ FORMULA 13.4: **Average Time Complexity of the BST Search and Insertion Algorithms**

$$A(n) = \Theta(1.39\lg n) = \Theta(\lg n).$$

The average run time of a BST tends to degrade towards $\Theta(n)$ even with random insertions and deletions. This is due to bias in the deletion algorithm. By using the inorder successor, the root of the tree tends to migrate to the right, making the tree larger on the left. This imbalance can be prevented by modifying the deletion algorithm so that on each invocation it makes a random choice between Algorithm 12.5 and its mirror opposite that uses the inorder predecessor instead of the successor.

Even with that improvement, a BST can still degrade towards the worst-case linear structure if the insertions and deletions are not random. This can be overcome by imposing some kind of balancing constraint on the insertion and deletion algorithms. The two most common ways to do that are described in the next two sections.

We conclude this section with a proof of Formula 13.3. This may be omitted by readers who are not so mathematically inclined.

We consider all $n!$ permutations of the n keys $\{0, 1, 2, ..., n-1\}$. For each permutation p, we get a binary search tree T_p by inserting those n keys into T_p in the order specified by the permutation p. For example, if $n = 4$ and $p = (2,0,3,1)$, then the corresponding BST is the one shown here.

To compute the average number $A(n)$ of comparisons made in an unsuccessful search of any BST of size n for an element x, we consider three cases: x is in the root node (N), x is in the left subtree (L), or x is in the right subtree (R). Then the average number of comparisons made will be the sum

$$p_N \cdot a_N + p_L \cdot a_L + p_R \cdot a_R \qquad \text{(13.1)}$$

where p_N is the probability that x is in the root node, a_N is the average number of comparisons made if x is in the root node, p_L is the probability that x is in the left subtree, a_L is the average number of comparisons made if x is in the left subtree, p_R is the probability that x is in the right subtree, and a_R is the average number of comparisons made if x is in the right subtree.

The first two quantities are easy: $p_N = 1/n$, because there is 1 chance in n that x is in the root node if it is equally likely to be in any one of n locations; and $a_N = 1$, because if x is in the root node, then it will be found on the first comparison.

The other four quantities call for a recursive analysis. Suppose that the left subtree has i keys. Then the right subtree must have $n - i - 1$ keys, since there is one key in the root node. Then $p_L = i/n$ and $p_R = (n-i-1)/n$, if x is equally likely to be anywhere in the tree. Moreover, $a_L = 1 + A(i)$ and $a_L = 1 + A(n-i-1)$, because the average number of comparisons made in finding x in either subtree is 1 (the comparison with the root key) plus the average number of comparisons made in that subtree. Thus, the average number of comparisons for this case of i keys in the left subtree is

$$A_i(n) = (1/n)(1) + (i/n)[1 + A(i)] + [(n-i-1)/n][1 + A(n-i-1)] \qquad \text{(13.2)}$$

Now, the actual number of keys in the left subtree can be any i in the range $0 \le i \le n-1$. These n cases correspond to the equally likely n possibilities that the key in the root of the tree is any one of the n values $\{0, 1, 2, ..., n-1\}$. Thus, $A(n)$ must be the average of these n averages $A_i(n)$:

$$A(n) = \frac{1}{n} \sum_{i=0}^{n-1} A_i(n) \qquad \text{(13.3)}$$

Substituting Equation (13.1) into Equation (13.2) and simplifying (see Exercise 13.10 on page 411) yields

$$A(n) = 1 + \frac{2}{n^2} \sum_{i=1}^{n-1} iA(i) \qquad \text{(13.4)}$$

This can be reduced (see Exercise 13.11 on page 411) to the recurrence relation

$$\left(\frac{n+1}{n+2}\right)A(n+1) = \left(\frac{n}{n+1}\right)A(n) + \frac{2n+1}{(n+1)(n+2)} \qquad \text{(13.5)}$$

with $A(1) = 1$.

Now let $f(m)$ be the function

$$f(m) = \left(\frac{m}{m+1}\right)A(m) \qquad \text{(13.6)}$$

With $f(m)$ so defined for any integer $m > 0$, we can transform Equation (13.5) into the simpler recurrence, by direct substitution of Equation (13.6) with n and $n+1$ in place of m:

$$f(n+1) = f(n) + \frac{2n+1}{(n+1)(n+2)} \qquad \text{(13.7)}$$

This equation is solved fairly easily (see Exercise 13.12 on page 411) to obtain

$$f(n) = \sum_{k=1}^{n} \frac{2k-1}{k(k+1)} \tag{13.8}$$

This result can be simplified (see Exercise 13.13 on page 411) to

$$f(n) = 2H_{n+1} - 3 + \frac{1}{n+1} \tag{13.9}$$

Combining this equation with Equation (13.6) yields the final result in Formula 13.3 on page 385.

13.5 AVL Trees

An AVL tree[2] is a binary search tree that maintains its balance by forcing the two subtrees at any node to have nearly the same height. This is done by rotating subtrees whenever an imbalance occurs.

For example, suppose we build a BST by inserting the keys 20, 30, 40, 50, 60, and 70, in that order. Without any extra balancing, the resulting BST would be a linear list. But instead, suppose that we perform a rotation about a node whenever an insertion causes one of that node's subtrees to be more than one level deeper than the other subtree. With this input sequence, that will first happen after 40 is inserted. (See Figure 13.10.)

Before the rotation, node x has a (NIL) left subtree of height -1 and a right subtree of height 1. After the rotation, both subtrees have height 0.

Continuing the insertions, we have another correctable imbalance after 60 is inserted. (See Figure 13.11.)

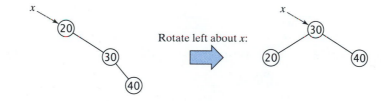

FIGURE 13.10   The AVL Rotate Left algorithm.

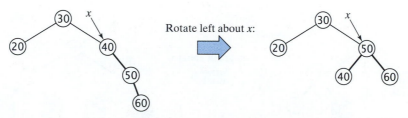

FIGURE 13.11   The AVL Rotate Left algorithm.

---

[2] The name comes from the two inventors of this data structure: G. M. Adel'son-Velskii and Y. M. Landis.

Again, we rotate a three-generation node triple (node–parent–grandparent), pivoting this time about the grandparent $x = (40)$. The path that connects the triple is marked by darker lines.

Inserting 70 requires another rotation, as shown in Figure 13.12.

On this third rotation, the pivot node x is the root again: Before the rotation, x's left subtree has height 0 and its right subtree has height 2; afterwards, both have height 1.

On that third rotation, notice how the node (40) shifts from being the left child of the right child of x to being the right child of the left child of x. This is necessary to maintain the required *BST property* that an inorder traversal will visit the keys in ascending order: Node (40) must remain between (30) and (50).

Figure 13.13 shows the general action of the *rotate left* operation.

The subtree B gets shifted from node (b) to node (a). Notice that the rotation will reduce the height of the subtree rooted at x, as long as the heights of subtrees A and B are no greater than those of C and D.

Continuing our example, suppose that 66 is inserted next, as in Figure 13.14.

The imbalance occurs at node $x = [60]$. Since the parity (left or right) of the child $y = [70]$ is the opposite of that of its new child [66], a double rotation is required. First, a right, two-node mini-rotation is made at y to restore the parity (both right). Then a left rotation is made about node x.

The general action of the compound *rotate right–left* operation is shown in Figure 13.15.

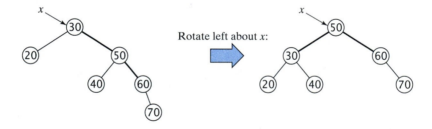

FIGURE 13.12   The AVL Rotate Left algorithm.

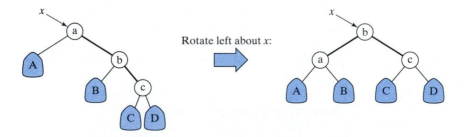

FIGURE 13.13   The AVL Rotate Left algorithm.

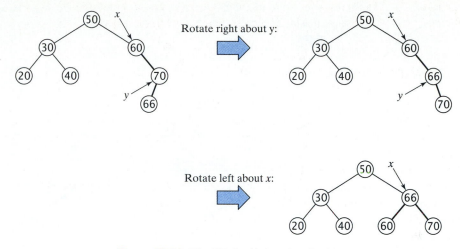

Rotate right about y:

Rotate left about x:

FIGURE 13.14 The AVL Double Rotation algorithm.

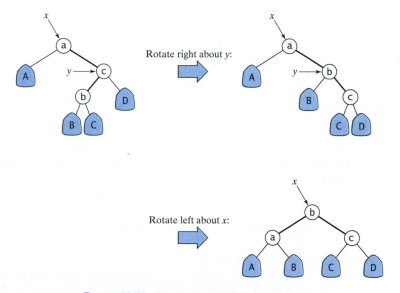

Rotate right about y:

Rotate left about x:

FIGURE 13.15 The AVL Double Rotation algorithm.

The decision on whether to make a simple rotation or a compound rotation is based upon which pattern is causing the imbalance. The four possible patterns are shown in Figure 13.16 on page 390.

Balance control is maintained in AVL trees by enforcing the *AVL criterion*: At each node, the heights of the two subtrees cannot differ by more than 1. If we denote those two heights by h_L and h_R, then the AVL criterion states that $|h_L - h_R| < 2$, which means that the difference can be only -1, 0, or 1. Since this criterion is defined entirely in terms of the subtree heights, an AVL tree is also called a *height-balanced tree*.

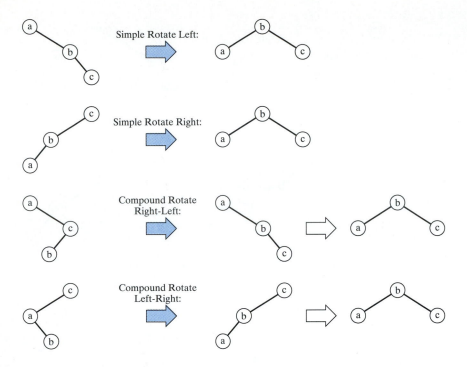

FIGURE 13.16   The four AVL Rotation patterns.

Figure 13.17 shows two binary search trees. The number above each node is the height of the subtree rooted at that node. The tree on the top is not an AVL tree because it has some nodes where the AVL criterion fails. For example, at node (22), the left subtree has height 0 and the right subtree has height 2.

13.6 Implementing AVL Trees

Listing 13.2 presents a Java class for AVL trees:

The class defines a `static` object named `NIL` (line 5) which represents the unique (`final`) empty tree. This uniqueness constraint is enforced by defining the no-argument constructor to be `private`; it is used only once, within the class, to define `NIL`, and cannot be used anywhere else. This constant `NIL` tree object has key = 0, height = −1, and both child pointers pointing to the object itself. A node is a leaf if and only if both of its children are `NIL`. The `NIL` is used in place of the `null` reference. This use allows AVL trees to be built and processed with no occurrences of the `null` reference, and thus no chance of generating a `NullPointerException`.

The class also defines a `private` three-argument constructor at line 45. It is used exclusively by the two rotate methods. It should not be allowed to be used outside the class, because a client could inadvertently use it to build an instance of the `AVLTree` class that is not an AVL tree.

LISTING 13.2: An AVLTree **Class**

```
1   public class AVLTree {
2     private int key, height;
3     private AVLTree left, right;
4
5     public static final AVLTree NIL = new AVLTree();
6
7     public AVLTree(int key){
8       this.key = key;
9       left = right = NIL;
10    }
11
12    public boolean add(int key) {
13      int oldSize = size();
14      grow(key);
15      return size()>oldSize;
16    }
17
18    public AVLTree grow(int key) {
19      if (this == NIL) return new AVLTree(key);
20      if (key == this.key) return this;  // prevent key duplication
21      if (key < this.key) left = left.grow(key);
22      else right = right.grow(key);
23      rebalance();
24      height = 1 + Math.max(left.height,right.height);
25      return this;
26    }
27
28    public int size() {
29      if (this == NIL) return 0;
30      return 1 + left.size() + right.size();
31    }
32
33    public String toString() {
34      if (this == NIL) return "";
35      return left + " " + key + " " + right;
36    }
37
38    private AVLTree() {  // constructs the empty tree
39      left = right = this;
40      height = -1;
41    }
42
43    private AVLTree(int key, AVLTree left, AVLTree right) {
44      this.key = key;
45      this.left = left;
46      this.right = right;
47      height = 1 + Math.max(left.height,right.height);
48    }
49
```

```
50    private void rebalance() {
51      if (right.height > left.height+1) {
52        if (right.left.height > right.right.height) right.rotateRight();
53        rotateLeft();
54      }
55      else if (left.height > right.height+1) {
56        if (left.right.height > left.left.height) left.rotateLeft();
57        rotateRight();
58      }
59    }
60
61    private void rotateLeft() {
62      left = new AVLTree(key,left,right.left);
63      key = right.key;
64      right = right.right;
65    }
66
67    private void rotateRight() {
68      right = new AVLTree(key,left.right,right);
69      key = left.key;
70      left = left.left;
71    }
72  }
```

This is not an AVL tree:

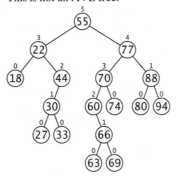

This is an AVL tree:

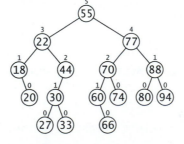

FIGURE 13.17 The AVL criterion.

The only `public` constructor is the one-argument version (line 7) that builds singleton AVL trees. It is used, along with the `add()` method to build trees, like this:

```
AVLTree tree = new AVLTree(20);
tree.add(30);
tree.add(40);
tree.add(50);
```

The `add()` method returns true if it succeeds in adding the given key. That will always happen unless the key is already in the table. The method calls the recursive `grow()` method to do its work.

The `grow()` method uses the BST property to locate where to insert the new key. This is the same algorithm that the BST ADT uses. Since only AVL trees that already have at least one element can call `add()`, we know that the condition `(this==NIL)` at line 19 will be true only on recursive calls, in which case the new subtree will be attached either to a `left` or `right` field (at line 21 or line 22). After that, the subtree is rebalanced, if necessary, and its `height` field is recomputed.

The other two `public` methods, `size()` and `toString()`, are also recursive.

The `rebalance()` method implements the algorithms described in Section 13.5. The four cases described on page 390 are handled by the four `if` statements in this method. For example, if the condition `(right.height>left.height+1)` at line 51 is true, then the height of the right subtree is at least 2 more than that of the left subtree, so `rotateLeft()` is called to rebalance. Whether a simple or a compound rotation is performed depends upon the condition `(right.left.height>right.right.height)` at line 52. This is illustrated in Figure 13.18. When the key 35 is inserted, the subtree rooted at (33) becomes imbalanced: Its left subtree has height 1, while its right subtree has height 3. Moreover, this is a "dog leg" imbalance: The right subtree of (33) is the larger `(right.height>left.height+1)`, but the left subtree of its child (44) is the larger `(right.left.height>right.right.height)`. So the call `right.rotateRight()` at line 52 executes before the call `rotateLeft()` at line 53.

The `rotateLeft()` and `rotateRight()` methods are short and efficient. To avoid losing the current node (located by the immutable "`this`" reference), the contents of that node's child is copied into it, after reproducing that node's contents in a new `AVLTree` object. The third step deletes the only reference to that child node, which results in it being "garbage collected" by the run-time system.

For example, consider the final `rotateLeft()` action, pivoting about node (40), as shown in Figure 13.18. Figure 13.19 illustrates the execution of lines 62–64 of Listing 13.2. Line 62 invokes the `private` three-argument constructor (defined at line 43) to create a subtree rooted at a duplicate copy of node (33) using the existing subtrees A and B as its left and right subtrees. This new subtree is then used to replace the existing left subtree A as the subtree of the old node (33) referenced by "`this`". Line 63 copies the key 40 from the "`this.right`" node to the "`this`" node. Line 64 slides the subtree rooted at (44) up to becoming the "`this.right`" node, replacing the redundant node (40) there. Since `this.right` was the only reference to that node, it will now be deleted by the system's "garbage collector." So there is no net change in the number of nodes. we have

```
62      left = new AVLTree(key,left,right.left);
63      key = right.key;
64      right = right.right;
```

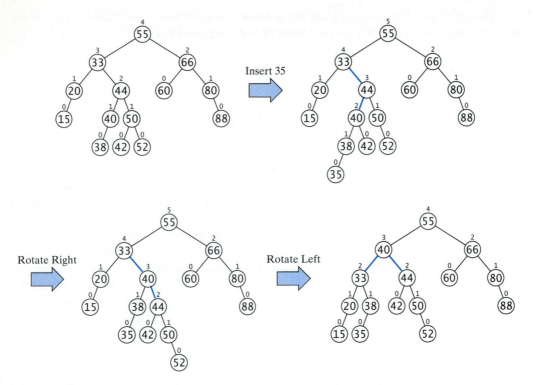

FIGURE 13.18   AVL Insert with rotations.

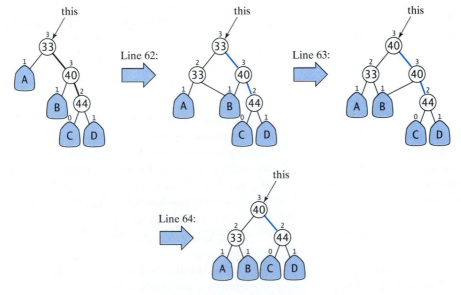

FIGURE 13.19   AVL rotation.

Note that the height of the new node created by the three-argument constructor at line 62 has its height set automatically by that constructor at line 47. And the height of the "this" node is then reset by the grow() method at line 24:

```
height = 1 + Math.max(left.height,right.height);
```

13.7 Fibonacci Trees

Since AVL trees are balanced binary search trees, we know that they will be at least as efficient as unconstrained binary search trees:

$$B(n) = \Theta(\lg n)$$
$$A(n) = \Theta(\lg n)$$
$$W(n) = \Theta(n)$$

But the whole point of balancing them is to reduce that worst-case time. How much better is this improvement?

The answer comes from a special kind of AVL tree, called a *Fibonacci tree*. These are built using the same recursive idea that generates the Fibonacci numbers. (See Appendix C.) We shall see that these trees are the worst-case AVL trees and that their analysis proves that general AVL trees perform in logarithmic time, even in the worst case:

$$W(n) = \Theta(\lg n)$$

To understand the definition of the Fibonacci trees, imagine trying to build worst-case AVL trees. That means that, for each height h, we want to find the binary tree structures that have the fewest elements and still could be AVL trees.

At height $h = 0$, there is no choice: The singleton tree is the only possibility. Call it T_0.

At height $h = 1$, there are three binary trees, all of which could be AVL trees. (See Figure 13.20.) Two of these have size $n = 2$, and one has size $n = 3$. Since we want the ones with the smallest sizes, we have a choice of two trees. They are mirror opposites, so it doesn't matter which one we choose. We therefore choose the first one and define it as the Fibonacci tree of height $h = 1$. and call it T_1.

There are 21 binary trees of height $h = 2$. (See Exercise 13.6 on page 411.) Among them, all but six be AVL trees. These 15 trees have size n in the range $4 \leq n \leq 7$. So the minimal AVL trees of height $h = 2$ have size $n = 4$. The four of those are shown in Figure 13.21 on page 396. We could define any one of these to be "the" Fibonacci tree of height $h = 2$. We choose the first one and call it T_2, as shown in Figure 13.22 on page 396.

We could define any one of the trees in Figure 13.21 as the Fibonacci tree of height $h = 2$. We choose the first one and call it T_2.

Note that T_2 can be built by attaching T_1 and T_0 to a root node as its left and right subtrees. Similarly, we define T_3 to be the binary tree obtained by attaching T_2 and T_1 to a root node as its left and right subtrees.

FIGURE 13.20 Binary trees of height 1.

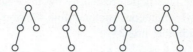

FIGURE 13.21   The four Fibonacci trees of height $h = 2$.

In general, then, we define the *Fibonacci tree T_h* of height $h > 1$ recursively to be the binary tree obtained by attaching T_{h-1} and T_{h-2} to a root node as its left and right subtrees. The first four of these are shown in Figure 13.22.

◆ **FORMULA 13.5: Fibonacci Trees**

Fibonacci trees satisfy the AVL criterion, and they are the minimal size among all binary trees of a given height that satisfy the AVL criterion.

First note that h is the height of the Fibonacci tree T_h. This is true, inductively, because T_h is defined to be a root node with subtrees T_{h-1} and T_{h-2}.

The AVL criterion requires that the two subtrees of any node in the tree differ in height by no more than 1. This is obviously true for the first two Fibonacci trees T_0 and T_1. It also is then inductively true, because every other Fibonacci tree is defined to be a root with subtrees of height $h - 1$ and $h - 2$.

To see that each Fibonacci tree is minimal, we again argue inductively. T_0 and T_1 are both minimal, because there are no smaller binary trees of their heights. Next, suppose that T is some AVL tree of height $h > 1$ and size $n < n_h$, where n_h is the size of the Fibonacci tree T_h of height h. Let L and R be the left and right subtrees of T, and let h_L and h_R be their respective heights, and let n_L and n_R be their respective sizes. Then, either $h_L = h - 1$, or $h_R = h - 1$. (Otherwise, the height of T would be less than h.) Without loss of generality, we may assume that $h_L = h - 1$. Then L is an AVL tree of height $h - 1$. Now, by the inductive hypothesis, any AVL tree of height less than h must have at least as many elements as the Fibonacci tree of the same height, so $n_L \geq |T_{h-1}|$ (the size of T_{h-1}).

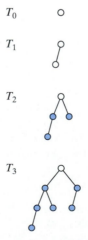

T_0

T_1

T_2

T_3

FIGURE 13.22   Fibonacci trees.

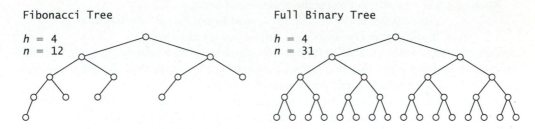

FIGURE 13.23   The smallest and largest AVL trees of height $h = 4$.

Now, since T is an AVL tree, the heights of its two subtrees cannot differ by more than 1. Hence, L is an AVL tree of height either $h - 1$ or $h - 2$. Therefore, again by the inductive hypothesis, $n_R \geq |T_{h-2}|$. Thus, the size of T, $|T| = 1 + n_L + n_R \geq 1 + |T_{h-1}| + |T_{h-2}| = |T_h|$. This verifies that T_h is minimal.

Before we can obtain the main result, we first have to estimate the sizes of Fibonacci trees.

◆ **FORMULA 13.6: Bounds on the Size of a Fibonacci Tree**

The Fibonacci tree of height h has size n in the range $1.5^h < n < 2^h$. This is verified inductively. (See Exercise 13.9 on page 411.)

This result is not surprising when we compare the recursive formula

$$|T_h| = 1 + |T_{h-1}| + |T_{h-2}|$$

with the formula for the Fibonacci numbers, namely,

$$F_j = F_{j-1} + F_{j-2}$$

Evidently, the size of the jth Fibonacci tree should be larger than the jth Fibonacci number—and we know (see Formula 3.9) that the Fibonacci numbers are exponential: $F_n = \Theta(\phi^n)$.

◆ **FORMULA 13.7: The Worst-Case Performance for AVL Trees**

Searching and inserting into an AVL tree runs in $\Theta(\lg n)$ in the worst case.

The time it takes to access, insert, or delete an element in an AVL tree is proportional to its height h. And by Formula 13.6, $1.5^h < n < 2^h$, so $\lg n < h < c \lg n$. Thus, the worst-case run time is $W(n) = \Theta(h) = \Theta(\lg n)$.

We have seen that AVL trees solve the worst-case linear run-time problem that ordinary BSTs often encounter. In fact, the worst-case run time for AVL trees is not much worse at all than the best case. For a given height, the two extremes are exemplified by the Fibonacci tree and the full tree; as shown in Figure 13.23. Every other AVL tree falls somewhere in between these two extremes.

13.8 Multiway Search Trees

So far, this chapter has studied *binary* search trees. We now extend the definitions and operations of binary search trees to *multiway* search trees.

Recall the *BST property*, defined at the beginning of Section 13.2:

> *For each key in the tree, all the keys in its left subtree are less than*
> *it, and all the keys in its right subtree are greater than it.*

Each key separates the keys in the left subtree from those in the right subtree. To apply this property to nodes that have more than two subtrees, we have to allow more than one key per node. In general, we need $d - 1$ keys in a node to separate d subtrees.

To simplify the definition of a multiway search tree, we first define its nodes. A *multiway search node of degree d* is a node that contains a sequence of $d - 1$ keys $(k_0, k_1, k_2, ..., k_{d-2})$, a sequence of $d - 1$ addresses $(a_0, a_1, a_2, ..., a_{d-2})$, and a sequence of d disjoint subtrees $(T_0, T_1, T_2, ..., T_{d-1})$ that satisfy the *MST property*:

> *If $x_0, x_1, x_2, ..., x_{d-1}$ are keys in the subtrees such that each x_i is in*
> *T_i, then: $x_0 < k_0 < x_1 < k_1 < x_2 < k_2 < \cdots < k_{d-2} < x_{d-1}$.*

The property says that each key k_i separates all the keys in subtree T_i from those in subtree T_{i+1}, for each $i = 0, 1, ..., d - 2$. Notice that when $d = 2$, the MST property is simply the BST property: the single key k_0 separates all the keys in the left subtree T_0 from those in the right subtree T_1.

Figure 13.24 shows a multiway search node of degree 7. It contains six keys, six addresses, and seven subtrees. The subtree pointers are shown as black dots positioned at the boundaries of the keys and addresses to suggest the MST property.

A *multiway search tree (MST) of degree m* is an ordered tree of degree m whose nodes are multiway search nodes with degree $\leq m$. Its *size* is the number of keys it contains.

Figure 13.25 shows an MST of degree $m = 5$ and size $n = 20$. It has nine nodes, whose degrees range from 2 to 5. Note that an MST of degree 2 is a BST.

FIGURE 13.24 A multiway search node of degree 7.

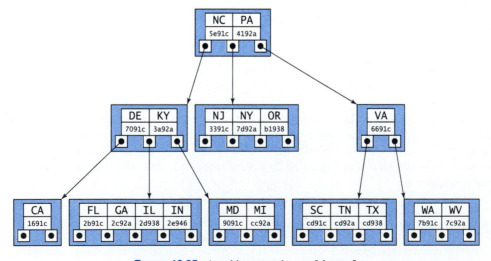

FIGURE 13.25 A multiway search tree of degree 5.

Listing 13.3 on page 399 shows one way to define an MST in Java. It assumes that a DiskAddress class has been defined as in the discussion just prior to Listing 13.1. The MST class defines an inner Node class, which implements MST nodes. It includes a constructor that allocates all three of its arrays using the degree m that is passed to it. Note that the actual number of non-null elements that each array will have will depend upon the value of the degree field specific to that node. The sizes m-1 and m are the maximum numbers.

LISTING 13.3: Java Definitions for a Multiway Search Tree

```
1   public class MST {
2
3      private class Node {
4         int degree;
5         Comparable[] keys;
6         DiskAddress[] locs;
7         Node[] kids;
8
9         Node(int m) {
10           keys = new String[m-1];
11           locs = new DiskAddress[m-1];
12           kids = new Node[m];
13        }
14     }
15
16     private int degree;
17     private Node root;
18
19     public MST(int m) {
20        degree = m;
21        root = new Node(m);
22     }
23  }
```

Figure 13.26 shows a picture of a Java object of type MST.Node. It represents one of the leaf nodes of the MST shown in Figure 13.25 on page 398.

The algorithms for MSTs are similar to those for BSTs.

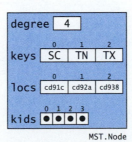

MST.Node

FIGURE 13.26 A Java MST.Node object.

13.9 B-Trees

Just like BSTs, MSTs can become very unbalanced, causing substantial degradation in their access time. AVL trees provides one solution to the problem for BSTs. That is a top-down solution, controlled by rotations to keep the subtree heights nearly equal. The best solution for keeping MSTs balanced is a bottom-up approach. It implements split and join operations on the nodes to keep all leaves at the same level. These structures are called B-trees. Note that the MST shown in Figure 13.25 on page 398 does not satisfy that requirement: It has one leaf at level 1 and four at level 2.

A *B-tree*[3] *of degree m* is a multiway search tree of degree m such that

❏ all leaf nodes are at the same level;
❏ every internal nonroot node has degree at least $\lceil m/2 \rceil$.

We shall see that the second condition is a direct result of the insert and delete operations on B-trees.

Figure 13.27 shows a B-tree of degree $m = 4$, size $n = 20$, and height $h = 2$. Note that all of its leaves are at level 2, and all of its nodes except the root have degree 3 or 4, exceeding the $\lceil m/2 \rceil$ minimum. Also note that from now on, we will avoid showing the address fields from the nodes.

How many keys could a B-tree of degree 5 have? The definition requires all internal nodes except the root to have at least $\lceil m/2 \rceil$ subtrees. With $m = 5$, that means at least three subtrees. So the root can have from two to five subtrees, and all other internal nodes must have from three to five subtrees. Thus the root can have from one to four keys, and all other internal nodes must have from two to four keys. (Remember that the number of keys in any internal node is always one less than the number of subtrees.)

Table 13.1 shows the calculations for the minimum and maximum number of keys per node for a B-tree of degree 5.

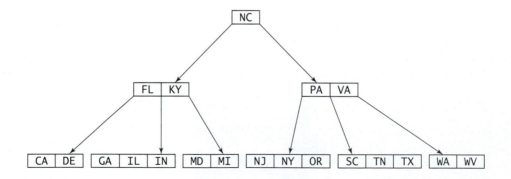

FIGURE 13.27   A B-Tree of degree 4.

---

[3] Invented by R. Bayer and E. McCreight in 1972.

Level	Minimum	Maximum
0	1	4
1	$2 \cdot 2$	$5 \cdot 4$
2	$2 \cdot 3 \cdot 2$	$5 \cdot 5 \cdot 4$
3	$2 \cdot 3 \cdot 3 \cdot 2$	$5^3 \cdot 4$
4	$2 \cdot 3^3 \cdot 2$	$5^4 \cdot 4$
5	$2 \cdot 3^4 \cdot 2$	$5^5 \cdot 4$
6	$2 \cdot 3^5 \cdot 2$	$5^6 \cdot 4$

TABLE 13.1 The size of a B-Tree of degree 5.

At level 0, the root has at least one key and at most four keys. At level 1, there are at least two nodes and at most five nodes, and each one has at least two keys and at most four keys. At every successive level, the minimum increases by a factor of 3, because each node has at least three subtrees. Similarly, the maximum increases by a factor of 5, because each node has at most five subtrees.

If the height of the B-tree is m, then the minimum is

$$1 + 2 \cdot 2 + 2 \cdot 3 \cdot 2 + 2 \cdot 3^2 \cdot 2 + \ldots + 2 \cdot 3^{m-1} \cdot 2 = 1 + 2(3^m - 1)$$

and the maximum is

$$4 + 5 \cdot 4 + 5 \cdot 5 \cdot 4 + 5^3 \cdot 4 + \ldots + 5^m \cdot 4 = 5^{m+1} - 1$$

More generally, we can derive the following bounds. (See Exercise 13.14 on page 411.)

◆ **FORMULA 13.8: Bounds on the Size of a B-Tree**

The number n of keys in a B-tree of degree m and height h is bounded by

$$2\lceil m/2 \rceil^h - 1 \leq n \leq m^{h+1} - 1$$

◆ **FORMULA 13.9: Bounds on the Height of a B-Tree**

The height h of a B-tree of size n and degree m is bounded above by

$$h \leq \log_{m/2} n = \Theta(\lg n)$$

This means that B-trees have logarithmic access time.

B-trees are standard data structures used for implementing external indexes for database tables. Each key is accompanied by the disk address of the key's record. The degree of the B-tree is chosen so that each node can be stored in a single disk block. Then the number of disk reads required to access any record is never more than $h + 2$.

Algorithms 13.7 through 13.10, the algorithms for B-tree operations, are similar to those for BSTs.

▲ ALGORITHM 13.7: B-Tree Insert

Input: a B-tree T and a key–address pair (x, y).
Postcondition: the key–address pair (x, y) is in the tree T.
Output: `true`, if T was changed; otherwise, `false`.

1. If T is empty, replace it by the singleton containing the key–address pair (x, y) and return `true`.

2. Apply the Multiway Search Algorithm to find the leaf node p that should contain x.

3. If x is in p and its address is y, return `false`.

4. If x is in p and its address is not y, replace that address with y and return `true`.

5. If x is not in p, insert the key–address pair (x, y).

6. If p overflowed, split it.

7. Return `true`.

▲ ALGORITHM 13.8: B-Tree Delete

Input: a B-tree T and a key x.
Postcondition: the key x is not in the tree T.
Output: `true`, if T was changed; otherwise, `false`.

1. Apply the Multiway Search Algorithm to find the node p that contains x.

2. If x is not found, return `false`.

3. If p is not a leaf, replace x with is inorder successor; then let x be that successor and p be its node.

4. If p is not minimal, delete x and return `true`.

5. If either of p's siblings is not minimal, rotate from it into x and return `true`.

6. Join p with one of its siblings and their parent, delete x and return `true`.

▼ EXAMPLE 13.2: Example

Figure 13.28 shows a B-tree of height $h = 2$ and degree $d = 4$.

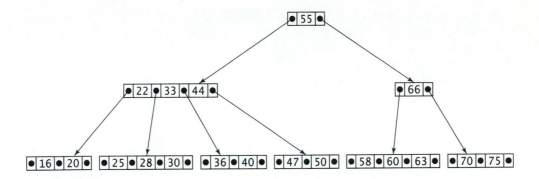

FIGURE 13.28 B-tree.

Here, the NIL trees are shown as `null` references.

▲ **ALGORITHM 13.9: B-Tree Retrieve**

Input: a multiway search tree T and a key x.
Output: whether x is in T.

1. If T is NIL, return false.
2. Binary search the key sequence in the root of T; let i be the index for which $k_{i-1} < x \le k_i$.
3. If $x = k_i$, return true.
4. Let T be the subtree T_i.
5. Return the value returned by searching T_i for x.
6. If $x = k_i$, return false.
7. If T_i is NIL, insert x between k_{i-1} and k_i.
8. Return the value returned by inserting x in T_i.

▲ **ALGORITHM 13.10: B-Tree Split**

The full node is replaced by a singleton node A and its two half-full nodes, B and C, which are its two children. (See Figure 13.29.) The single element in A is the median of the keys in the original node.

13.10 Red-Black Trees

Since B-trees generally are used to implement indexes for database tables, they typically are external data structures, stored permanently on disk instead of temporarily in memory. However, one variety of B-tree is used as a common internal container: the B-tree of degree 4, which can be represented by a special kind of binary search tree.

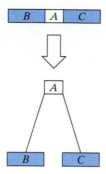

FIGURE 13.29 The B-tree split operation.

A B-tree of degree 4 is also called a *2-3-4-tree* because each internal node has either 2, 3, or 4 children. A node with three children is called a *3-node*, and a node with four children called a *4-node*. The idea behind storing a 2-3-4-tree as a binary tree is to represent each 3-node with a binary tree of size 2, and to represent each 4-node with a binary tree of size 3. These representations are shown in Figure 13.30.

Here, the 3-node containing keys R and S can be represented by two different binary trees of size 2: either the node S node with the left child R, or the node R node with right child S. The 4-node containing keys B, C, and E is represented by the binary tree that has root C at the root and children B and E.

The binary subtrees that we use to represent 3-nodes and 4-nodes are "colored" read and black, as shown in Figure 13.30. In all three cases, the root is black and the children are red. This is how we convert a 2-3-4-tree into a red-black tree: color all singleton nodes black, and replace the 3-nodes and 4-nodes with the red-black subtrees as shown in Figure 13.30.

Figure 13.31 on page 405 shows a complete representation of a 2-3-4-tree by a red-black tree. Note that the number of black nodes in the red-black tree is the actual size, 8, of the 2-3-4-tree that it represents. That will always be true, because the red nodes are used only to represent the "extra" keys of 3-nodes and 4-nodes. Each red node is the child of a black node where both keys are in the same 2-3-4-tree node that they represent. You can think of the red nodes as children who are still living with their parents.

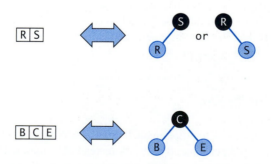

FIGURE 13.30 Red-black tree nodes representing B-Tree Nodes.

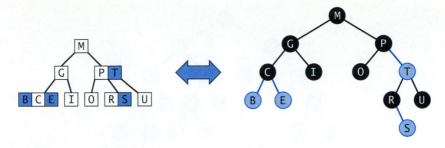

FIGURE 13.31 A red-black tree representing a B-tree.

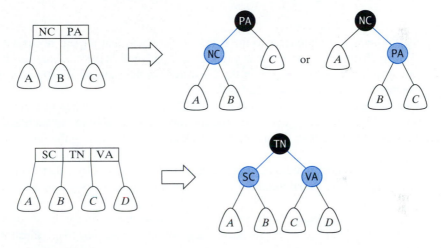

FIGURE 13.32 Subtrees in a 2-3-4-tree remain in order after conversion to a red-black tree.

Figure 13.32 shows why this conversion from 2-3-4-tree to red-black tree will always work. It shows how the subtrees of 3-nodes and 4-nodes will remain in their correct relative positions after the conversion.

Any binary search tree that satisfies these *red-black-tree properties* represents a 2-3-4-tree:

1. Each node is either red or black.
2. The root and NIL nodes[4] are black.
3. Both children of each red node are black.
4. Every root-to-leaf path contains the same number of black nodes.

The 2-3-4-tree that it represents can be obtained simply by merging its red nodes with their parents.

---

[4] A NIL node is a dummy node that represents the empty tree.

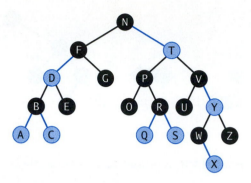

FIGURE 13.33   A red-black tree with black height 2.

Note that Property 4 is equivalent to the B-tree requirement that all leaf nodes are at the same level. The number of black nodes on any root-to-leaf path equals the total number of nodes along the corresponding root-to-leaf path in the 2-3-4-tree. In the example illustrated in Figure 13.31, that number is 3 for every root-to-leaf path.

The number of nodes on any root-to-leaf path in a B-tree is one more than its height, which is 2 in the example illustrated in Figure 13.31. The corresponding number in the red-black tree is called the *black height* of the tree: the number of black nodes, not counting the root or the NIL nodes.

Figure 13.33 shows another red-black tree that has black height 2. Notice that in a red-black tree with black height h, the actual number of nodes (of either color) along a root-to-leaf path can vary from $h + 1$ to $2h$.

Red-black trees are popular data structures[5] because their fundamental operations (retrieve, insert, and delete) are relatively simple algorithms. Algorithm 13.11 illustrates the insert operations.

▲ **ALGORITHM 13.11: Red-Black Tree Insert**

Input: a red-black tree T and a *key–address* pair.
Output: *false* if *key* is already in T; otherwise *true*.
Postcondition: the *key–address* pair is in T.

1. If T is empty, make it a singleton containing *key* as a black node, and return *true*.

2. Let r be the *root* of T.

3. While r is not a leaf, repeat steps 4–8.

4. If r is black and its two children are red, *recolor* all three nodes.

5. If r and its parent are red, *rotate* r, its parent, and its grandparent.

---

[5] Java uses them to implement the `TreeSet` and `TreeMap` classes in its `java.util` package.

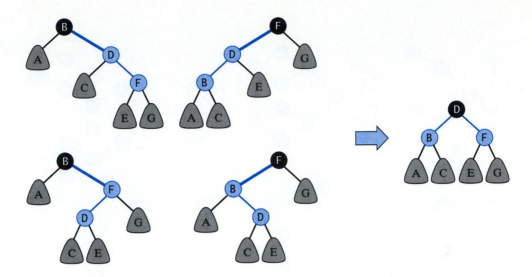

FIGURE 13.34 The four rotations for red-black trees.

6. If *key* < *r.key*, set *r* = *r.left*.

7. Otherwise, if *key* > *r.key*, set *r* = *r.right*.

8. Otherwise, return *false* (because *key* = *r.key*).

9. If *key* < *r.key*, set *r.left* to a new red node containing the *key–address* pair.

10. Otherwise, if *key* > *r.key*, set *r.right* to a new red node containing the *key–address* pair.

11. Otherwise, return *false* (because *key* = *r.key*).

12. If *r* is red, rotate *r*, its parent, and the new node.

13. Return *true*.

The recoloring in step 4 is equivalent to the split operation for the B-tree that the red-black tree represents. The rotation in steps 5 and 12 is equivalent to the insertion in ascending order within the B-tree node.

The rotation algorithm is best understood by viewing the four possible cases shown Figure 13.34 on page 407. In each case, the two outside nodes, (B) and (F), end up being red children of the middle node (D), which is colored black.

▼ **EXAMPLE 13.3: Insertion into a Red-Black Tree**

To see how the Insert algorithm works, and to see the equivalent operations on the B-tree that the red-black tree represents, Figure 13.35 on page 408 shows both data structures after each insertion of the 12 keys B I G C O M P U T E R S, starting with an empty tree.

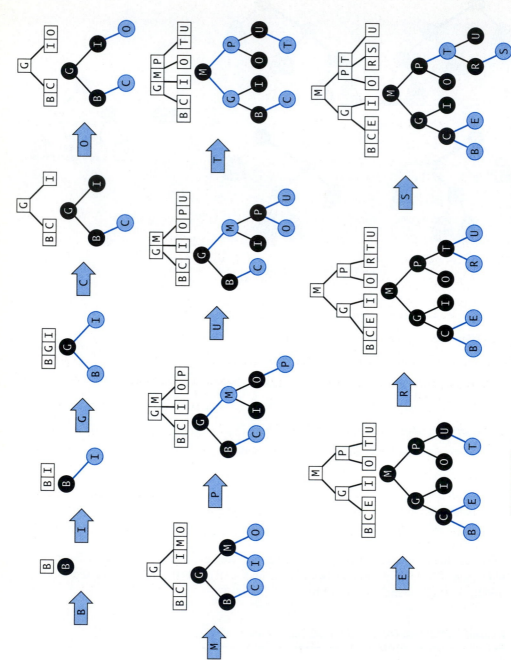

FIGURE 13.35 Insertions into a red-black tree and the B-tree that it represents.

CHAPTER SUMMARY

❏ Keys are used in a storage structure to identify data.

❏ Each key is associated with an address that locates the data.

❏ In a search tree, keys are unique.

❏ In Java, keys can be declared to have the `Comparable` interface type, thereby guaranteeing that a `compareTo()` method is defined for them.

❏ A binary search tree (BST) is a binary tree in which the key in each node is greater than all the keys in the left subtree and less than all the keys in the right subtree.

❏ The BST search is analogous to the Binary Search Algorithm 3.4 on page 85.

❏ BSTs can become very unbalanced, resulting in slow linear time access.

❏ AVL trees are BSTs that use rotation operations to maintain their balance.

❏ Fibonacci trees are AVL trees that have the smallest size for a given height.

❏ A multiway search node contains $d-1$ keys interleaved among d subtrees.

❏ A multiway search tree (MST) is an ordered tree of multiway search nodes.

❏ A B-tree is an MST of degree m, all of whose leaves are at the same level, and in which every internal node except the root has degree $d \geq m/2$.

❏ B-tree retrieval, insertion, and deletion all run in logarithmic time.

❏ A red-black tree is a BST in which each node is colored red or black, the root and nil nodes are black, both children of each red node are black, and all root-to-leaf paths have the same number of black nodes.

❏ The height of a red-black tree of size n is at most $2\lg n$. Consequently, searches, insertions, and deletions run in logarithmic time.

REVIEW QUESTIONS

13.1 How are BSTs different from other binary trees?

13.2 How is searching for a key in a binary search tree similar to the binary search algorithm?

13.3 What's the main problem with BSTs?

13.4 What is an AVL tree?

13.5 How are AVL trees better than BSTs?

13.6 What is a Fibonacci tree?

13.7 What do Fibonacci trees have to do with AVL trees?

13.8 What is an MST?

13.9   What is a B-tree?

13.10   What is a 2-3-4 tree?

13.11   What is a red-black tree?

13.12   How are red-black trees better than 2-3-4-trees?

13.13   What kind of tree does Java use to implement its `TreeSet` and `TreeMap` classes?

EXERCISES

13.1   Show the tree in Figure 13.36 after each insertion of this sequence of keys in this BST: 50, 20, 90.

13.2   Show the tree in Figure 13.36 after each deletion of this sequence of keys in this BST: 18, 22, 70, 77.

13.3   Show the BST built by these insertions: 44, 88, 55, 77, 33, 99, 66, 22, 25, 75.

13.4   Derive a condition on nodes x and y in a BST that would guarantee the order in which their keys are deleted would have no effect on the resulting tree. Explain why your condition is valid.

13.5   For each of the following statements, either explain why it is true, or give an example to show that it is false:

   a. Every subtree of a BST is another BST.

   b. If both the left and right subtrees of a binary tree T are BSTs, then T must be a BST.

   c. If the same keys are inserted in a different order to build a BST, the resulting BST will be the same.

   d. Every subtree of an AVL tree is another AVL tree.

   e. If T is a BST and both the left and right subtrees of T are AVL trees, then T must be an AVL tree.

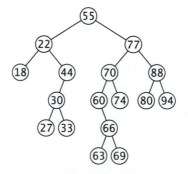

FIGURE 13.36 A BST.

13.6   Draw the 21 binary trees of height $h = 2$. Mark those that could be AVL trees, and identify the full tree and the Fibonacci tree.

13.7   How many different binary trees are there with height $h = 4$ that could be AVL trees?

13.8   Draw the Fibonacci trees T_4 and T_5.

13.9   Use mathematical induction to verify Formula 13.6 on page 397.

13.10   Derive Equation (13.5) on page 386 from Equations (13.3) and (13.4).

13.11   Derive Equation (13.6) on page 386 from Equation (13.5). [*Hint*: (1) Multiply both
sides of Equation (13.5) by n^2; (2) obtain a second equation by substituting $n + 1$ for n
throughout your step–1 equation; (3) subtract your step–1 equation from your step–2
equation and simplify; (4) divide both sides of your step–3 result by $(n + 1)(n + 2)$ and
simplify.]

13.12   Derive Equation (13.9) on page 387 from Equation (13.8).

13.13   Derive Equation (13.10) from Equation (13.9).

13.14   Derive Formula 13.8 on page 401.

13.15   Derive Formula 13.9 on page 401. [*Hint*: Since m is constant, so is $(\lg m)/(\lg m - 2)$.]

PROGRAMMING PROBLEMS

13.1   Add and test this method for the `BinaryTree` class (from Problem 12.1):

```
public boolean isBST()
```

13.2   Add and test this method for the `BinaryTree` class (from Problem 12.1):

```
public boolean isAVLTree()
```

13.3   Add and test these accessor methods for the `AVLTree` class:

```
public int getHeight()
public AVLTree getLeft()
public AVLTree getRight()
public int getRoot()
```

13.4   Add and test this method for the `AVLTree` class:

```
public boolean contains(int x)
```

13.5   Add and test this method for the `AVLTree` class:

```
public AVLTree get(int x)
```

13.6   Add and test this method for the `AVLTree` class:

```
public boolean equals(Object object)
```

13.7   Add and test this constructor for the `AVLTree` class:

```
public AVLTree(int[] a)
```

PROJECTS

13.1   Implement and test a BST class. Use the algorithms given in Sections 13.2 and 13.3. Define the tree class recursively, like this (omitting the `Address` field):

```
public class BST {
    private Comparable key;
    private BST left, right;
}
```

Include a `height()` method and a `size()` method. Use recursion wherever convenient.

13.2   Add and test this method for the `AVLTree` class:

```
public boolean remove(int key)
```

Use the same algorithm as described for the more general BST: Replace the key to be deleted with its inorder successor, if necessary, and then restore balance with a rotation.

13.3   Implement and test a `MultiwayTree` class.

13.4   Implement and test a `RedBlackTree` class.

ANSWERS TO REVIEW QUESTIONS

13.1   A binary search tree is a binary tree that satisfies the BST property that each key is greater than all keys in the left subtree and less than all keys in the right subtree.

13.2   Searching for a key in a binary search tree uses the divide-and-conquer strategy the same as the binary search algorithm. Comparing the search key with the root key is equivalent to comparing it with the middle element of a sequence.

13.3   The main problem with BSTs is that they can become so unbalanced that searches degrade to linear time.

13.4   An AVL tree is a BST that is kept balanced by rotation algorithms.

13.5   By remaining balanced, AVL trees can guarantee logarithmic run time for searching, inserting, and deleting.

13.6   A Fibonacci tree of height $h > 1$ is a binary tree whose two subtrees are Fibonacci trees of height $h-1$ and $h-2$.

13.7   Fibonacci trees are worst-case AVL trees. A Fibonacci tree of height h has the minimum size possible among all AVL trees of that height.

13.8   An MST (multiway search tree) is a tree in which each internal node contains an ascending sequence of keys, with the MST property that for each key x, the condition $y \le x \le z$ holds for all keys y in all subtrees on the left of x, and for all keys z in all subtrees on the right of x.

13.9   A B-tree of degree d is an MST in which all internal nodes except the root have degree between $\lceil d/2 \rceil$ and d, inclusive.

13.10   A 2-3-4-tree is a B-tree of degree 4.

13.11   A red-black tree is a BST that represents a 2-3-4 tree.

13.12   As binary trees, red-black trees are simpler than 2-3-4-trees.

13.13   The `TreeSet` and `TreeMap` classes in `java.util` are implemented with red-black trees.

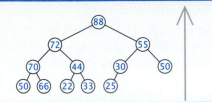

Chapter 14

Heaps and Priority Queues

Binary search trees are ordered from left to right, so that an inorder traversal will visit the keys in ascending order. Heaps are binary trees that are ordered from bottom to top, so that a traversal along any leaf-to-root path will visit the keys in ascending order.[1]

In a data structures course, the heaps usually are studied for two different purposes: (1) to implement priority queues, and (2) to implement the Heap Sort algorithm. This chapter includes the implementation of priority queues. Chapter 15 includes the Heap Sort.

14.1 Heaps

Recall from Section 12.6 on page 362 that a *complete binary tree* is a binary tree that is full except possibly for some missing nodes on the right of the bottom level. Complete binary trees have a natural mapping of their nodes into an array of the same size as the tree, leaving no gaps in the array. This natural mapping numbers the tree nodes according to a level order traversal of the tree. It makes the vertical traversal along root-to-leaf paths simple: the parent of node number i is numbered $(i-1)/2$, and its two children are numbered $2i+1$ and $2i+2$.[2] This is useful for heaps because all their operations are along root-to-leaf paths.

A *heap* is a complete binary tree in which the keys along any leaf-to-root path are ascending. This ordering requirement is equivalent to saying that no key is greater than its parent. It makes a heap partially ordered by the $\leq$ relation on its keys.[3]

---

[1] Technically, such trees are called "max heaps." There is an equivalent definition for "min heaps," which are ordered from top to bottom instead.

[2] Note that if 1-based indexing is used instead of 0-based indexing (*i.e.*, we start numbering with 1 at the root), then the parent and children formulas are even simpler: the parent of node i is numbered $i/2$, and the children are numbered $2i$ and $2i+1$.

[3] A binary relation ρ is called a *partial order* on a set S if it is reflexive ($x\rho x$), antisymmetric ($x\rho y \wedge y\rho x \Rightarrow x=y$), and transitive ($x\rho y \wedge y\rho z \Rightarrow x\rho z$).

415

The tree shown at the beginning of this chapter is a heap. For example, 44 is less that its parent 72 and greater than its children 22 and 33. Note that there is no horizontal relationship among the keys. For example, 44 is less than its left sibling 70, and 22 is less than its right sibling 33.

The natural mapping for complete binary trees makes an array the simplest way to implement a heap. Therefore, although we often will illustrate heaps as binary trees, henceforth we will store and access them as arrays. So, logically, a heap is a sequence with the *heap property*: $a_i \le a_{(i-1)/2}$ for all $i > 0$.

14.2 Heap Algorithms

The main heap operation is to rearrange the elements of the sequence so that they satisfy the heap property. This is done by performing a "heapify" operation on each internal node from the bottom up, as illustrated in Figure 14.1.

The heapify operation rotates two or more elements that are adjacent along a leaf-to-root path in the tree. In the example illustrated in Figure 14.2 on page 417, it is applied to each of these four subsequences:

$$\{a_3, a_7\}$$
$$\{a_2, a_6\}$$
$$\{a_1, a_3, a_7\}$$
$$\{a_0, a_1, a_4\}$$

In general, the heapify operation is applied to each internal node, in reverse order. In the example in Figure 14.1, it was applied to the internal nodes a_3, a_2, a_1, and a_0, in that order.

▼ **EXAMPLE 14.1: Illustrating the Heapify Operation**

Figure 14.1 shows part of a heap. Suppose that the heapify operation is applied to node 44. It is less that its larger child 99, so 99 will replace 44. Its larger child is 88, which is also greater than 44, so 88 will move up to its parent's position. Its larger child is 55, which is also greater than 44, so 55 will move up to its parent's position. Its larger child is 22, however, which is not greater than 44, so 44 is copied into the node vacated by 55, thereby completing the rotation.

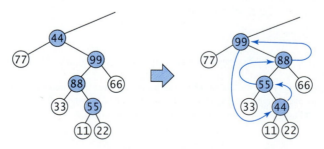

FIGURE 14.1 A Heapify Path.

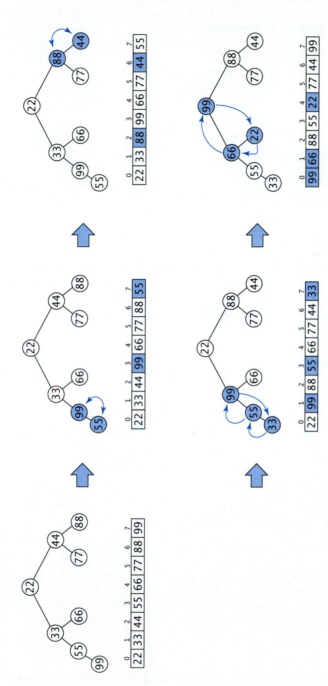

FIGURE 14.2 The heapify operation applied at each of the four internal nodes of the tree.

Algorithm 14.1 implements the heapify operation.

▲ ALGORITHM 14.1: The Heapify Algorithm

Input: a node x in a complete binary tree.
Precondition: the two subtrees of x are heaps.
Postcondition: the subtree rooted at x is a heap.

1. Let *temp* = x.

2. While x is not a leaf, do steps 3-4.

3. Let y be the larger child of x.

4. If $y.key > x.key$, do steps 5-6.

5. Copy y into x.

6. Set $x = y$.

7. Copy *temp* into x.

The run time of Algorithm 14.1 is easy to evaluate. It makes one comparison at step 3 and another at step 4, so each iteration of the loop (steps 2–7) makes two comparisons. The algorithm progresses down the tree from node x toward a leaf, so the total number of iterations cannot exceed the height of the tree. Since the tree is complete, that height is $\lg n$. Thus, the total number of comparisons is at most $2 \lg n$.

◆ FORMULA 14.1: Heapify

The Heapify algorithm makes no more than $2 \lg n$ comparisons.

This means that **the Heapify algorithm runs in logarithmic time**.

Algorithm 14.1 is implemented in Listing 14.1. The loop in steps 2–6 is implemented as a `while` loop at lines 3–8.

LISTING 14.1: The `heapify()` Method

```
1   void heapify(int[] a, int i, int n) {
2     int ai = a[i];
3     while (i < n/2) {                        // a[i] is not a leaf
4       int j = 2*i + 1;                       // a[j] is ai's left child
5       if (j+1 < n && a[j+1] > a[j]) ++j;     // a[j] is ai's larger child
6       if (a[j] <= ai) break;                 // a[j] is not out of order
7       a[i] = a[j];                           // promote a[j]
8       i = j;                                 // move down to next level
9     a[i] = ai;
10  }
```

The condition that x not be a leaf, at step 2, translates into the condition `(i < n/2)` at line 3. (See Formula 12.7 on page 363.) In the loop, $x.key$ translates into `ai`, and $y.key$ translates into `a[j]`.

Lines 4–5 implement Step 3, making j the index of the larger child of a[i]. The condition j+1 < n at line 5 is necessary to ensure that a[j+1] exists in the comparison a[j+1] > a[j].

Steps 4–7 translate directly into lines 6–9 of the listing.

The Heapify algorithm establishes the heap property for the subtree rooted at x. By repeating that operation for each x, starting with the last internal node and working back up to the root, we can heapify the entire tree. This process is called *Build Heap*. (See Algorithm 14.2.)

▲ ALGORITHM 14.2: The Build Heap Algorithm

Input: a complete binary tree T.
Postcondition: T is a heap.

1. If T is a singleton, return.

2. Apply Build Heap to the left subtree.

3. Apply Build Heap to the right subtree.

4. Apply Heapify to the root.

This is a typical recursive algorithm for binary trees. It is analogous to a post-order traversal: first process the two subtrees, and then process the root.

All the work is done by the Heapify algorithm at step 4. But it doesn't "kick in" until T has height 1, because only then will steps 2 and 3 return immediately without further recursion. So first, all the subtrees rooted at level $h-1$ are heapified, then all the subtrees rooted at level $h-2$ are heapified, *and so on*, until we get to the two subtrees rooted at level 1. After they are heapified, step 4 applies Heapify to the root of the original tree T, and the algorithm terminates.

The algorithm is illustrated by Figure 14.2 on page 417.

To analyze the run time of the Build Heap algorithm, let $W(n)$ be the number of comparisons that it makes in the worst case on a tree of size n. Then step 2 and step 3 each will make $W(n/2)$ comparisons and, by step 4, will make at most $2\lg n$ comparisons. This gives us the recurrence relation:

$$W(n) = 2W(n/2) + 2\lg n$$

When $n = 1$, step 1 returns immediately, so $W(1) = 1$. Then, applying the recurrence relation, we have

$$
\begin{aligned}
W(2) &= 2W(1) + 2\lg 2 &&= 2(1) + 2(1) &&= 4 \\
W(4) &= 2W(2) + 2\lg 4 &&= 2(4) + 2(2) &&= 12 \\
W(8) &= 2W(4) + 2\lg 8 &&= 2(12) + 2(3) &&= 30 \\
W(16) &= 2W(8) + 2\lg 16 &&= 2(30) + 2(4) &&= 68 \\
W(32) &= 2W(16) + 2\lg 32 &&= 2(68) + 2(5) &&= 146 \\
W(64) &= 2W(32) + 2\lg 89 &&= 2(146) + 2(6) &&= 304 \\
&\quad\vdots &&\quad\vdots &&\quad\vdots
\end{aligned}
$$

These values are near $5n$, and in fact the difference is $2\lg n + 4$. So the solution is

$$W(n) = 5n - 2\lg n - 4$$

This solution can be verified by direct substitution back into the recurrence relation. If $W(n)$ is indeed that function, $5n - 2\lg n - 4$, then

$$W(n/2) = 5(n/2) - 2\lg(n/2) - 4 = 5n/2 - 2(\lg n - \lg 2) - 4 = 5n/2 - 2(\lg n - 1) - 4 = 5n/2 - 2\lg n - 2$$

so the right-hand side of the recurrence relation is

$$2W(n/2) + 2\lg n = 2(5n/2 - 2\lg n - 2) + 2\lg n = 5n - 4\lg n - 4 + 2\lg n = 5n - 2\lg n - 4$$

which is the same as the right-hand side of the recurrence relation.

This solution is linear: $W(n) = 5n - 2\lg n - 4 = \Theta(n)$.

◆ **FORMULA 14.2: Build Heap**

The Build Heap algorithm makes no more than $5n$ comparisons.

This means that **the Build Heap algorithm runs in linear time**.

The implementation of Algorithm 14.2 is a line-for-line translation, resulting in the recursive method shown in Listing 14.2

LISTING 14.2: The `buildHeap()` **Method**

```
1   void buildHeap(int[] a, int i, int n) {
2     if (i >= n/2) return;
3     buildHeap(a, 2*i+1, n);
4     buildHeap(a, 2*i+2, n);
5     heapify(a, i, n);
6   }
```

Here, n is the number of elements in the heap, and i is the index of the last internal node.

14.3 Priority Queues

A *priority queue* is a queue whose *remove* operation depends upon the priority rankings of its elements. It assumes that the elements can be compared to determine which have higher priority. If we think of an ordinary queue as a first-in, first-out data structure (FIFO), then we can think of a priority queue as a best-in, first-out data structure (BIFO).

Priority queues are widely used in computing. For example, if a processor has to process randomly occurring jobs of different sizes, it can work more efficiently by assigning higher priority to the smaller jobs and then using a priority queue to determine the order in which the jobs get processed. That is how a shared printer is usually managed.

Here is an ADT for priority queues that is similar to the ADT we defined for queues in Section 6.1 on page 177.

ADT: PriorityQueue

A *priority queue* is a collection of elements that maintains the BIFO access protocol.

Operations

1. *Add*: Insert a given element into the queue.
2. *Best*: If the queue is not empty, return the element that has the highest priority.
3. *RemoveBest*: If the queue is not empty, delete and return the element that has the highest priority.
4. *Size*: Return the number of elements in the queue.

Listing 14.3 gives an interface for the ***PriorityQueue*** ADT:

```
«interface»
PriorityQueue

+add(Object)
+best():Object
+removeBest():Object
+size():int
```

LISTING 14.3: A `PriorityQueue` **Interface**

```
1  public interface PriorityQueue {
2     public void add(Object object);
3     // POSTCONDITION: the given object is in this queue;
4
5     public Object best();
6     // RETURN: the highest priority element in this queue;
7     // PRECONDITION: this queue is not empty;
8
9     public Object removeBest();
10    // RETURN: the highest priority element in this queue;
11    // PRECONDITION: this queue is not empty;
12    // POSTCONDITION: the returned object is not in this queue;
13
14    public int size();
15    // RETURN: the number of elements in this queue;
16 }
```

To implement this interface as a collection of objects, we have to have some mechanism for comparing the objects. If the objects' type includes a numeric `priority` field, then we can use that to compare elements. But there is nothing in the interface that requires the objects to be specialized that way.

Another solution is to assume that the objects' class includes this instance method:

```
public int compareTo(Object object)
```

FIGURE 14.3 Inserting 80 into the priority queue.

The `String` class has this. If `s1` and `s2` are strings, and n is the value returned by `s1.compareTo(s2)`, then `s1 < s2` (*i.e.*, `s1` precedes `s2` alphabetically) when $n < 0$, `s1 == s2` when $n = 0$, and `s1 > s2` when $n > 0$. We can have the compiler check whether the objects' class includes this method by requiring that class to implement the `Comparable` interface.

A third solution is to define a separate class that includes this instance method:

```
public int compare(Object object1, Object object2)
```

Its return value is interpreted the same way as that of a `compareTo()` method. If x is an instance of this class and n is the value returned by `x.compare(y1,y2)`, then `y1 < s2` is $n < 0$, `y1 == y2` when $n = 0$, and `y1 > y2` when $n > 0$. We can have the compiler check whether a class includes this method by requiring it to implement the `java.util.Comparator` interface. Then the object `x` is called a *comparator*, capable of comparing objects like `y1` and `y2`.

A fourth alternative for implementing a priority queue is to define it for primitive type instead of for objects. For example, in a priority queue of `int`s, the integer elements can be compared directly.

The `add()` method for the `PriorityQueue` interface uses an algorithm that is essentially the inverse of the Heapify algorithm. (See Algorithm 14.1 on page 418.) Instead of traversing down the tree from root to leaf, it traverses up the tree from leaf to root. Like all insert algorithms for trees, it first inserts the element as a new leaf node. Then it performs a rotation among that node and all of its smaller ancestors. (See Algorithm 14.3.)

Figure 14.3 illustrates the *add()* method. It shows the action on an existing *heap* produced by the call *heap.add(80)*. The key 80 is first inserted as a new leaf, next to 33. Then it is rotated with its parent 55 and its grandparent 66 to restore the heap property.

▲ ALGORITHM 14.3: The Insert Algorithm for Priority Queues

Input: a complete binary tree T and a new node x.
Postcondition: x has been added to T.

1. If T is empty, reassign T to be the singleton containing x, and return.

2. Append a new node to the end T.

3. Let $y = z.parent$.

4. While $y.key < x.key$, do steps 5–6.

5. Set $z.key = y.key$.

6. If y is not the root, do steps 7–8

7. Set *z* = *y*.

8. Set *y* = *y.parent*.

9. Set *y.key* = *x.key*, and return.

14.4 A HeapPriorityQueue Class

In this section, we use the heap algorithms described previously to implement the `PriorityQueue` interface for objects. We require the objects to implement the Comparable interface for comparing their priorities. That is, object x will have a higher priority than object y if x.compareTo(y) > 0. We therefore use a backing array of type `Comparable[]` to store the objects. The code is shown in Listing 14.4.

LISTING 14.4: A HeapPriorityQueue Class

```
1    public class HeapPriorityQueue implements PriorityQueue {
2        private static final int CAPACITY = 100;
3        private Comparable[] a;
4        private int size;
5
6        public HeapPriorityQueue() {
7            this(CAPACITY);
8        }
9
10       public HeapPriorityQueue(int capacity) {
11           a = new Comparable[capacity];
12       }
13
14       public void add(Object object) {
15           if (!(object instanceof Comparable))
16               throw new IllegalArgumentException();
17           Comparable x = (Comparable)object;
18           if (size == a.length) resize();
19           int i = size++;
20           while (i > 0) {
21               int j = i;
22               i = (i-1)/2;
23               if (a[i].compareTo(x) >= 0) {
24                   a[j] = x;
25                   return;
26               }
27               a[j] = a[i];
28           }
29           a[i] = x;
30       }
31
32       public Object best() {
33           if (size == 0) throw new java.util.NoSuchElementException();
34           return a[0];
```

```
35      }
36
37      public Object remove() {
38          Object best = best();
39          a[0] = a[--size];
40          heapify(0, size);
41          return best;
42      }
43
44      public int size() {
45          return size;
46      }
47
48      public String toString() {
49          if (size == 0) return "{}";
50          StringBuffer buf = new StringBuffer("{" + a[0]);
51          for (int i = 1; i < size; i++)
52              buf.append("," + a[i]);
53          return buf + "}";
54      }
55
56      private void heapify(int i, int n) {
57          Comparable ai = a[i];
58          while (i < n/2) {
59              int j = 2*i+1;
60              if (j+1 < n && a[j+1].compareTo(a[j]) > 0) ++j;
61              if (a[j].compareTo(ai) <= 0) break;
62              a[i] = a[j];
63              i = j;
64          }
65          a[i] = ai;
66      }
67
68      private void resize() {
69          Comparable[] aa = new Comparable[2*a.length];
70          System.arraycopy(a, 0, aa, 0, a.length);
71          a = aa;
72      }
73  }
```

The add() method works much like Algorithm 14.3 on page 422, except that we don't insert x into the array until we have determined where it should be placed to maintain the heap property. The best() method returns the element at position a[0] because that is always where the highest-priority element is stored. The removeBest() method removes the element at position a[0], replacing it with the last element in the array, and then applies the heapify() method to restore the heap property to the array.

To test our priority queue class, we simulate a print queue that accepts print jobs and processes them in ascending order of the page size. That is, the small jobs get printed before the larger ones.

The code appears in Listing 14.5.

LISTING 14.5: Testing the HeapPriorityQueue Class

```java
1   public class TestHeapPriorityQueue {
2
3       public TestHeapPriorityQueue() {
4           PriorityQueue queue = new HeapPriorityQueue();
5           int[] pages = {7,3,2,8,3,4,1,3};
6           for (int i = 0; i < pages.length; i++) {
7               queue.add(new PrintJob(null, pages[i]));
8               System.out.println("queue: " + queue);
9           }
10          while (queue.size() > 0) {
11              System.out.println("queue.remove(): " + queue.remove());
12              System.out.println("q: " + queue);
13          }
14      }
15
16      public static void main(String[] args) {
17          new TestHeapPriorityQueue();
18      }
19  }
20
21  class PrintJob implements Comparable {
22      private java.io.File file;
23      private int pages;
24      private String id;
25      private static int n = 100;
26
27      public PrintJob(java.io.File file, int pages) {
28          this.file = file;
29          this.pages = pages;
30          this.id = "ID" + n++;
31      }
32
33      public int compareTo(Object object) {
34          if (!(object instanceof PrintJob))
35              throw new IllegalArgumentException();
36          PrintJob that = (PrintJob)object;
37          return that.pages - this.pages;
38      }
39
40      public String toString() {
41          return id + "(" + pages + ")";
42      }
43  }
```

The output is

```
q: {ID100(7)}
q: {ID101(3),ID100(7)}
q: {ID102(2),ID100(7),ID101(3)}
q: {ID102(2),ID100(7),ID101(3),ID103(8)}
```

```
q: {ID102(2),ID104(3),ID101(3),ID103(8),ID100(7)}
q: {ID102(2),ID104(3),ID101(3),ID103(8),ID100(7),ID105(4)}
q: {ID106(1),ID104(3),ID102(2),ID103(8),ID100(7),ID105(4),ID101(3)}
q:
{ID106(1),ID104(3),ID102(2),ID107(3),ID100(7),ID105(4),ID101(3),ID103(8)}
queue.remove(): ID106(1)
q: {ID102(2),ID104(3),ID101(3),ID107(3),ID100(7),ID105(4),ID103(8)}
queue.remove(): ID102(2)
q: {ID104(3),ID107(3),ID101(3),ID103(8),ID100(7),ID105(4)}
queue.remove(): ID104(3)
q: {ID107(3),ID105(4),ID101(3),ID103(8),ID100(7)}
queue.remove(): ID107(3)
q: {ID101(3),ID105(4),ID100(7),ID103(8)}
queue.remove(): ID101(3)
q: {ID105(4),ID103(8),ID100(7)}
queue.remove(): ID105(4)
q: {ID100(7),ID103(8)}
queue.remove(): ID100(7)
q: {ID103(8)}
queue.remove(): ID103(8)
q: {}
```

We use a separate `PrintJob` class to simulate print jobs, assuming that each job has a file reference, a page count, and a unique identifier ID. That class's `toString()` method returns a string such as `ID105(4)`, which would be a four-page job with identifier ID105. Note how the `static` counter n is used to assign a unique integer to each job id.

The required `compareTo()` method returns the difference

```
    that.pages - this.pages
```

For example, if `this` job has four pages and `that` job has seven pages, then `this.comp-areTo(that)` will return $7 - 4 = 3 > 0$, indicating that `this` job had "higher" priority.

14.5 Case Study: Huffman Codes

In 1952, David Huffman discovered an optimal algorithm for encoding documents. This algorithm assigns binary codes to letters so that the most frequently occurring letters have the shortest codes. This results in a minimal length encoding of a text document. Huffman codes are used in a wide variety of practical applications, including fax machines, modems, computer networks, and high-definition television.

A *Huffman code* for a document is generated from a priority queue that has one leaf for each different character in the document. The code for each character is then determined by the root-to-leaf path to that character. The left branches are labeled "0" and the right branches are labeled "1". So a root-to-leaf path that goes right-left-right determines the code 101.

The Huffman tree shown in Figure 14.4 assigns 00 to C, 01 to A, 100 to B, 101 to D, and 11 to E. This is a correct Huffman code for any document that contains only these five characters, and in which the relative frequencies of those characters determine this particular Huffman tree. We shall see how those relative frequencies are used to build the tree.

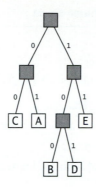

FIGURE 14.4 A Huffman Code.

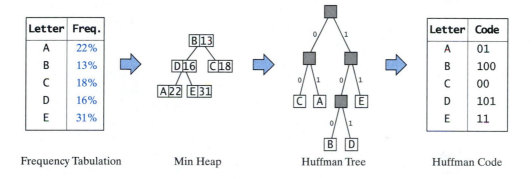

FIGURE 14.5 The Huffman Algorithm.

Once the Huffman tree has been derived, the document can be encoded and decoded uniquely. For example, with the code from the Huffman tree in Figure 14.4, the word ACCEDE would be encoded as 0100001110111. By repeatedly moving down the Huffman tree, it is easy to see that decoding is unique. The first digit is 0, so, starting at the root, we move to the left child of the root. The second digit is 1, so we move to the right child and reach leaf A. So we output A and start up at the root again. The next two digits are 00, so we move left twice and reach the leaf C. We therefore output C again and return to the root. This continues until ACCEDE has been output and we reach the end of the encoded text.

It is significant that, by using a Huffman tree, no character's code is a prefix of any other character's code. This *unique prefix property* guarantees the uniqueness of the decoding.

The Huffman tree is a priority queue in which the priority of each leaf is the relative frequency of the character that it represents, and the priority of each internal node is the sum of the two priorities of its children. The Huffman tree shown in Figure 14.4 was generated from the frequency data shown in Figure 14.5.

The figure shows the four stages of the Huffman algorithm (Algorithm 14.4 on page 428) for encoding a document.

▲ ALGORITHM 14.4: Generating a Huffman Code

Input: a sequence of characters.
Output: a bit code for the input characters.
Postconditions: the bit code has the unique prefix property and is optimal.

1. Tally the frequencies of the input characters.

2. Load the letter-frequency pairs into a min priority queue.

3. *Coalesce* the pairs into a Huffman tree.

4. Encode the character at each leaf with the bit sequence along its root-to-leaf path, as in Figure 14.5.

Step 3 uses the separate Coalesce Algorithm 14.5 that is illustrated by Figure 14.6. This critical step generates a special kind of tree. A *Huffman tree* is a binary tree of integers with these two properties:

1. Each internal node is the sum of its children.

2. Its weighted external path length is minimal.

The *weighted external path length* of a binary tree of integers is the sum of the products of each leaf and its level. For example, Figure 14.6 shows two different binary trees with the same five integers in their leaves. The weighted external path length (WEPL) of the tree on the left is $2(18) + 2(22) + 3(13) + 3(16) + 2(31) = 2(18+22+31) + 3(13+16) = 2(71) + 3(29) = 229$, and the WEPL of the tree on the right is 238. The one on the left is a Huffman tree.

The one on the right is the same except that 22 and 13 have been swapped. Since the larger number has been moved down, it obviously will have a larger WEPL. In fact, the difference is precisely $(1)(22-13) = 9$, because the swap moved the two numbers each a distance of 1 level. This shows, in general, that the Huffman trees will have the smallest numbers at the lowest levels. That is the basis for Algorithm 14.5.

▲ ALGORITHM 14.5: Coalescing a Huffman Tree

Input: a min heap Q of integers.
Output: a Huffman tree H of integers.
Postconditions: the elements of Q are the leaves of H.

1. Restructure Q by interpreting each element as itself a singleton tree.

2. Repeat steps 3-5 while Q has more than one element.

3. Remove the two highest-priority trees x and y from Q.

4. Form the Huffman tree z with children x and y.

5. Add z to Q.

6. Return the remaining element of Q.

Figure 14.7 shows a trace of this Coalescing algorithm on the min heap from Figure 14.5. The resulting tree defines the Huffman tree that gives the Huffman code.

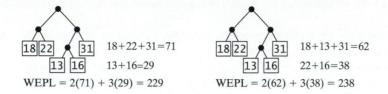

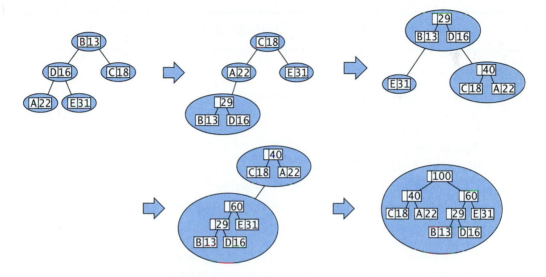

FIGURE 14.6 Huffman Heaps Have Minimal Weighted External Path Length.

FIGURE 14.7 Coalescing a Priority Forest of Huffman Trees.

CHAPTER SUMMARY

❑ A *heap* is a complete binary tree in which the keys along every root-to-leaf path are descending.

❑ A binary tree can be transformed into a heap in $\Theta(n \lg n)$ steps by applying the $\Theta(\lg n)$ Heapify Algorithm to each of its internal nodes.

❑ A *min heap* is the same as a (max) heap, except that the keys along every root-to-leaf path are ascending.

❑ A *priority queue* is a container for prioritized items, from which the item with highest priority is removed first.

❑ A priority queue can be implemented with a heap, since the largest key is always at the root (the front) of the container.

❏ With the heap implementation, the priority queue insert and delete operations run in $\Theta(\lg n)$ time.

❏ A *Huffman code* for a text document is an optimal encoding of its characters so that more frequent characters have shorter codes.

❏ The algorithm for creating Huffman code for a document first tabulates the frequencies of the characters in the document, and inserts those character/frequency pairs into a min heap. From that, it applies the Coalescing Algorithm to produce the Huffman Tree for the data. Then the binary code for each character is read from the root-to-leaf path to the character in the Huffman Tree.

REVIEW QUESTIONS

14.1   What is a heap?

14.2   What is a priority queue?

14.3   Why does the natural mapping of a heap array into its binary tree begin with element a[1] instead of a[0]?

14.4   What are the two main applications of heaps?

14.5   How efficient are insertions into and removals from a heap?

14.6   Why is a priority queue called a "BIFO" container?

14.7   What is the difference between a queue and a priority queue?

14.8   Why are heaps used to implement priority queues?

14.9   Ordered data structures such as priority queues require some mechanism for comparing their elements. Primitive types (int, double, *etc.*) have the six relational operators for that purpose. What ordering mechanisms are possible for Java classes?

14.10   Can the order in which elements are inserted into a priority queue have any effect upon the order in which they are removed?

14.11   How is a Huffman tree different from an ordinary binary tree?

EXERCISES

14.1   In Java, an "infinity" value is often stored in element a[0] of a heap array of primitive type. That should be Integer.MAX_VALUE (2,147,483,647) for arrays of type int. What should it be for arrays of each of the following types:

   a. byte

   b. short

   c. long

   d. float

   e. double

14.2   For each of the heap index numbers m listed in a–d, give its subsequence of index numbers along the leaf-to-root path from m to 1. For example, the leaf-to-root path from index $m = 25$ is (25, 12, 5, 2, 0). Check your path by showing that its length equals $\lfloor \lg m \rfloor$.

   a. $m = 51$

   b. $m = 333$

   c. $m = 1000$

   d. $m = 1024$

14.3   Determine which of the following binary trees is a heap:

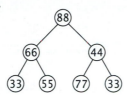

a.

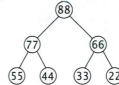

b.

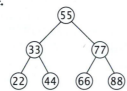

c.

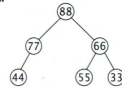

d.

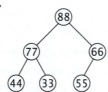

e.

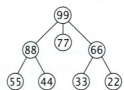

f.

14.4   Determine which of the following arrays have the heap property:

   a.

0	1	2	3	4	5	6	7
99	88	66	44	33	55	77	33

   b.

0	1	2	3	4	5	6	7
99	88	77	66	55	44	33	22

   c.

0	1	2	3	4	5	6	7
99	88	44	77	22	33	55	66

   d.

0	1	2	3	4	5	6	7
99	88	66	77	22	33	44	55

14.5   Verify the following theorem, used to translate Algorithm 14.1 into Listing 14.1 on page 418:

If i and n are positive integers, then the following two conditions are equivalent, regardless of whether n is even or odd:

$$i < n/2$$

$$2i + 1 < n$$

Here, $n/2$ means integer division.

14.6   For each of the following values of n, determine how many steps it would take to traverse a leaf-to-root path in a heap of that size:

    a. $n = 10$

    b. $n = 1000$

    c. $n = 1024$

    d. $n = 1,000,000$

14.7   Show the priority queue after inserting each of these keys in this order: 44, 66, 33, 88, 77, 55, 22.

14.8   Show the array obtained from the natural map of each of the heaps obtained in Problem 14.7.

14.9   The implementation of heaps in this chapter uses the natural mapping which assigns the root of the binary tree to element `a[1]` in the array. Consequently, the parent of `a[i]` is `a[i/2]`, and its two children are `a[2*i]` and `a[2*i+1]`. If we use the alternate protocol of assigning the root to `a[0]`, thereby using `a[0..n-1]` instead of `a[1..n]`, where will the parent and children of `a[i]` be?

14.10   If we map a heap into an array, starting the root at `a[0]` instead of at `a[0]`, thereby using `a[1..n]` instead of `a[0..n-1]`, where will the parent and children of `a[i]` be?

14.11   Define an *m-way heap* to be a tree in which every non-leaf node has m children. If we map an *m*-way heap onto an array starting with the root at `a[0]`, where will the parent and children of `a[i]` be?

14.12   Determine the complexity of the `add()` and `remove()` methods.

14.13   Give an example of a sequence of insertions into the heap implementation of the `PriorityQueue` class that includes two elements of the same priority which are removed

    a.   in the same order in which they were inserted.

    b.   in the opposite order from which they were inserted.

14.14   Prove that the `heapify()` method (defined in Listing 14.1 on page 418) is correct.

14.15   Prove that every subtree of a heap is itself a heap.

14.16   Prove Formula 14.2 on page 420.

14.17   Prove that the largest element in a heap is always at its root.

14.18   Derive formulas for each of the following in a heap array:

    a. $l(i) =$ the index of the left child of `a[i]`.

    b. $r(i) =$ the index of the right child of `a[i]`.

    c. $i(i, k) =$ the index of the left-most descendant of `a[i]` after k generations.

    d. $r(i, k) =$ the index of the right-most descendant of `a[i]` after k generations.

    e. $a(i, k) =$ the index of the ancestor of `a[i]`, k generations above.

PROGRAMMING PROBLEMS

14.1   Write and test the following method as a recursive method:

```
public boolean isHeap(int[] a, int size)
```

14.2   Write and test the following method as a nonrecursive method:

```
public boolean isHeap(int[] a, int size)
```

14.3   Revise the client/server simulation in Section 6.4 on page 184 using a priority queue instead of an ordinary queue. Define a `Comparator` class for the `Client` class so that shorter print jobs will have higher priority.

14.4   Implement a `PriorityQueue` class that uses an unsorted list instead of a heap to store its elements.

14.5   Implement a `PriorityQueue` class that uses a sorted list instead of a heap to store its elements.

14.6   Implement a `PriorityQueue` class that uses an array of queues instead of a heap to store its elements. Assume that all priority values are integers in the range 0..*m*, where the value of *m* is passed to the constructor which then builds *m* queues. An element with priority *i* is inserted into queue *i*.

14.7   Rewrite the `heapify()` method in Listing 14.1 on page 418 as a recursive method.

14.8   Write and test the following predicate method:

```
/**
 * Returns true if no descendant of a[i] is greater than its parent
 * in the binary tree embedded in {a[0], a[1], ..., a[n-1]}.
 */
boolean isHeap(int[] a, int i, int n)
```

[*Hint:* Use recursion.]

14.9   Write and test the `buildHeap()` method defined in Listing 14.2 on page 420. Use the `isHeap()` method from Programming Problem 14.8 to test your heaps.

14.10   Use an ordinary array to implement a priority queue in integers; test your class.

14.11   Use a linked list to implement a priority queue in integers; test your class.

PROJECTS

14.1   Write a program that empirically tests in Formula 14.2 on page 420. Test priority queues of sizes $n_k = 1000(2^k)$ for $k = 0, 1, 2, 3, 4, 5$, and 6. For data, use `Integer` objects that represent randomly generated `int`s that are uniformly distributed in the range 0 to 999,999. Use the `java.util.Random` class to generate the random integers.

For each *k*,

a. Build a priority queue of n_k Integer objects that represent randomly generated, uniformly distributed integers.

b. Insert 20 objects, computing the time each insertion takes. Use the java.util.Date class to generate the random integers. Use the code

```
Date start = new Date();
add(x);
Date stop = new Date();
double time = stop.getTime()-start.getTime();
```

c. Print the average (ave) of the 20 times, the value of lg*n*, and the ratio ave/lg*n*.

d. Remove 20 objects, computing the time each removal takes.

e. Print the average (ave) of the 20 times, the value of lg*n*, and the ratio ave/lg*n*.

If the theorem is correct, then the ratios should be nearly constant.

14.2   Write and test an implementation of the PriorityQueue interface that is based upon a complete *ternary* tree (order 3). If a[0] is the root of the heap (instead of a[1]), then the parent of a[i] is a[(i-1)/3], and its three children are a[3*i-2], a[3*i-1], and a[3*i]. Determine the complexity of the add() and remove() methods.

14.3   Implement Huffman encoding. Use these classes:

HCode
-table:HashMap
+HCode(HPQueue)
+encode(HTree,String)
+toString():String

HTree
-root:Pair
-left:HTree
-right:HTree
+HTree(char,int)
+HTree(HTree,HTree)
+compareTo(Object):int
+getFrequency():Integer
+getLeft():HTree
+getLetter():Character
+getRight():HTree
+isLeaf():boolean
+toString():String

HPQueue
-a:Comparable[]
-size:int
-capacity:int
+HPQueue(Map)
+add(Comparable)
+best():Comparable
+coalesce():HTree
+remove():Comparable
+size():int
+toString():String
-buildHeap(Comparable,int)
-heapify(Comparable,int)
-insert(Comparable)

ANSWERS TO REVIEW QUESTIONS

14.1   A *heap* is a sequence $(x_1, x_2, ..., x_n)$ in which every root-to-leaf subsequence is descending, where a root-to-leaf subsequence is a subsequence $(x_{i_1}, x_{i_2}, ..., x_{i_k})$ in which $i_1 = 1$ and $i_{j-1} = 1$ and $i_j/2$ for all $j > 1$.

14.2   A *priority queue* is a container all of whose elements have priority ranks that determine the order of removal from the container: Higher priority elements are removed ahead of lower priority elements.

14.3   The natural mapping of a heap array begins with element a[1] instead of a[0] so that the index of the parent of any element i will be i/2. If it began with element a[0], then parent index would have to be computed from the slightly more complicated expression (i-1)/2.

14.4   The two main applications of heaps are the implementation of priority queues and the Heap Sort.

14.5   Both the insertion operation and the removal operation for heaps run in O(lg$n$) time. This is very efficient.

14.6   A priority queue can be called a "BIFO" container ("best-in, first-out") because the first item to be removed is always the one with the highest priority.

14.7   A queue is a FIFO ("first-in, first-out") container with no priorities assigned to its elements. So if element x is inserted into a queue that already contains 10 elements, x cannot be removed before those other 10 elements have been removed. But if x is inserted into a priority queue that already contains 10 elements, x will be removed before any of those other 10 elements if it has a higher priority.

14.8   Heaps are used to implement priority queues because the element with the highest priority is always in the first position and because the heap's insertion and removal operations are so efficient.

14.9   The complexity of the first() method is O(1).

14.10   There are two ways that a Java class X can provide an ordering mechanism. It can implement the java.lang.Comparable interface, which requires the definition of a comparesTo() method in the class itself. Or the class X can be packaged with one or more independent comparator classes, each of which implements the java.util.Comparator interface by defining its own compares() method. In that case, an ordered data structure that stores X objects can use a constructor to specify which comparator class is to be used to compare them.

14.11   The order in which two elements are inserted into a priority queue can effect the order in which they are removed only if they have the same priority.

14.12   In a Huffman tree, each internal node is the sum of its children, and the weighted external path length is minimal.

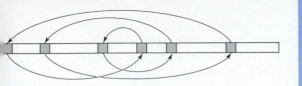

By what course of calculation can these results be arrived at
by the machine in the shortest time?

— Charles Babbage, 1864

Chapter 15

Sorting

We saw in Chapter 3 that searching through an array is far more efficient if its elements are sorted. Anyone who has looked up a word in a dictionary or a number in a phone book knows that.

The algorithms in Chapter 13 sort keys by the manner in which they are inserted into the search trees. This leads to efficient indexing structures that run in logarithmic time.

This chapter presents 10 different algorithms for sorting an existing linear structure such as an array a[]. Unless otherwise noted, "sorting" will always mean rearranging the elements of the array to put them in ascending order: $a[0] \le a[1] \le \cdots \le a[n-1]$, where $n = a.length$.

For simplicity, we assume that the array's element type is int, although the algorithms apply just as well to arrays of any ordinal type. We could use any of the primitive numeric types (long, double, etc.) or any class whose elements implement the Comparable interface (e.g., String).

Most of the sorting algorithms in this chapter are *comparison sorts*. That means that the reordering decisions that they make are based on pairwise comparisons made among the array elements. We shall see that the fastest sorting algorithms known are comparison sorts. Paradoxically, however, we also shall see that comparison sorts cannot break the $\Theta(n \lg n)$ speed limit, even though there are some noncomparison sorts that run in linear time.

Many comparison sorts require the pairwise swapping of elements in the array. For that operation, we will use the optimized swap() method defined in Listing 3.3 on page 78.

Our goal for each of the sorting algorithms is to

❏ state the procedure algorithmically, for a sequence $\{a_0, ..., a_{n-1}\}$;
❏ implement the algorithm as a Java method in the form: void sort(int[] a);
❏ trace the algorithm on a sample array of integers;
❏ derive the best-case, average-case, and worst-case complexity functions;

Although we will not always achieve all of these goals for all of the algorithms, we will come close in most cases.

Some sorting algorithms use auxiliary methods that operate on subarrays. In those cases, we will adhere to the "left-continuous" protocol that delineates the subarray with parameters p and q, where p is the index of the first element of the subarray and q-1 is the index of the last element of the

437

subarray. The notation a[p...q) will be used to denote this subarray {a[p], ..., a[q-1]}. For example, a[5...8) denotes the subarray of three elements {a[5],a[6],a[7]}. Note that, with this protocol, the number of elements in the subarray a[p...q) is q-p. In some cases we will also use the notation a[p...r] to denote the subarray of p-r+1 elements that includes the element a[r].

For simplicity, we will present each algorithm in the form that sorts the entire array a[0,n), where n = a.length. It is an easy matter to modify the algorithm to apply to a subarray a[p...q).

15.1 The Bubble Sort

The *bubble sort* is the simplest of the standard sorting algorithms. It works by comparing adjacent elements in the array and swapping them whenever they are out of order.

The idea is to make the pairwise comparisons sequentially, from the first pair to the last. The largest element will "bubble up" to the end of the array, because after each comparison it gets shifted forward one element. You can imagine each comparison as a collision of two bubbles in a glass of some carbonated beverage, the larger bubbles bouncing ahead of the others.

One complete pass through the array will move the largest element to the end of the array, where it belongs when the array is in ascending order. Repeating that process on the subarray of $n-1$ unsorted elements will move the second-largest element to where it belongs. Repeating the process on each successive subarray eventually moves all the elements to where they belong.

▲ **ALGORITHM 15.1: The Bubble Sort**

---

1. Repeat steps 2–3 for $i = n-1$ down to 1.
2. Repeat step 3 for $j = 0$ up to $i-1$.
3. If $a_j > a_{j+1}$, swap them.

Algorithm 15.1 is implemented, nearly word-for-word, in Listing 15.1.

LISTING 15.1: **The Bubble Sort**

```
1  void sort(int[] a) {
2    for (int i = a.length-1; i > 0; i--)
3      for (int j = 0; j < i; j++)
4        if (a[j] > a[j+1]) swap(a, j, j+1);
5  }
```

The inner loop in lines 3–4 moves the largest element among a[0...i] into position a[i]. The outer loop at line 2 repeats this for i=n-1 down to 1. Since the last iteration moves the largest element among a[0...1] into position a[1], it automatically leaves the smallest element at a[0].

▼ **EXAMPLE 15.1: Tracing the Bubble Sort**

Here is a complete trace of the bubble sort on the array {66,33,99,88,44,55,22,77}:

	a[0]	a[1]	a[2]	a[3]	a[4]	a[5]	a[6]	a[7]
0	66	33	99	88	44	55	22	77
1	33	66						
2			88	99				
3				44	99			
4					55	99		
5						22	99	
6							77	99
7			44	88				
8				55	88			
9					22	88		
10						77	88	
11		44	66					
12			55	66				
13				22	66			
14			22	55				
15		22	44					
16	22	33						

The Bubble Sort.

Lines 1–6 cover the first iteration of the main loop, where i=7. At line 1 of the trace, j=0 and a[0]>a[1], so a[0] and a[1] get swapped. At line 2, j=2, and a[2]>a[3], so a[2] and a[3] get swapped. No swap occurred when j=1 because at that point a[1]<a[2].

At the end of the first iteration at line 6 of the trace, the largest element, 99, has bubbled up from a[2] to a[7]. During the second iteration (lines 7–10), the second-largest element, 88, bubbles up from a[3] to a[6]. Since the third-largest element, 77, was above 88, it lands in its correct location on the same step as did 88 (step 11). During the next iteration (lines 11–13), the fourth-largest element, 66, bubbles up from a[0] to a[4].

Listing 15.2 shows a simple Java program that tests the bubble sort.

LISTING 15.2: Testing the Bubble Sort

```
1   public class TestBubbleSort {
2       public TestBubbleSort() {
3           public[] a = {88, 55, 22, 77, 11, 44, 33, 99, 66};
4           IntArrays.print(a);
5           sort(a);
6           IntArrays.print(a);
7       }
8
9       void sort(int[] a) {
10          for (int i = a.length-1; i > 0; i--)
11              for (int j = 0; j < i; j++)
12                  if (a[j] > a[j+1]) IntArrays.swap(a, j, j+1);
13      }
14
15  public static void main(String[] args) {
16      new TestBubbleSort();
17  }
18 }
```

The output is

```
{66,33,99,88,44,55,22,77}
{22,33,44,55,66,77,88,99}
```

This test program uses the print() and swap() methods that are defined in the IntArrays class in Listing 3.8 on page 89.

The complexity analysis of the bubble sort can be derived directly from its source code in Listing 15.1 on page 439. The outer loop at line 2 iterates $n-1$ times as i runs from $n-1$ down to 1. The number of iterations of the inner loop (lines 2-4) is equal to the value of i, because j runs from 0 up to $i-1$. Each of those iteration makes one comparison, so the total number of comparisons is

$$(n-1) + (n-2) + (n-3) + \cdots + 3 + 2 + 1$$

By Formula 3.6, this sum is $n(n-1)/2$. For large values of n, that expression is nearly $n^2/2$, which is proportional to n^2. This gives us the following general result:

◆ FORMULA 15.1: **Bubble Sort**

The bubble sort makes $\Theta(n^2)$ comparisons. It runs in quadratic time.

This means that if you double the size of the array, the run time will be nearly quadrupled. Of course, this is an approximate statement. It assumes that n is large and that the overhead (*i.e.*, the time that the neglected tasks take) is negligible.

The bubble sort is the slowest of the standard sorting algorithms. This is mainly because the data movements (the swaps) are all done only between adjacent elements. For example, in the trace in Example 15.1 on page 439, element 99 makes five separate swaps to move from a[2] to a[7]. This is highly inefficient.

The only difference between the best case and the worst case for the Bubble Sort is in the actual number of swaps carried out. The best case is when the array is already in ascending order. The method will still make $n(n-1)/2$ comparisons. However, the condition in line 4 will never be true, so swap() will never be called. This obviously will run faster than the average or worst cases, even though the same number of comparisons is made in all cases.

One way to improve the efficiency of the bubble sort is to make it "smart" by having it detect when the array is sorted. (See Programming Problem 15.6 on page 475.)

We can use loop invariants to prove that the bubble sort will always work. A *loop invariant* is a condition that describes the state of the data at every iteration of a loop. These conditions are usually expressed as in-line comments, as in Listing 15.3.

LISTING 15.3: **The Bubble Sort with Loop Invariants**

```
1   void sort(int[] a) {
2     for (int i = a.length-1; i > 0; i--) {
3       for (int j = 0; j < i; j++) {
4         if (a[j] > a[j+1]) swap(a, j, j+1);
5         // INVARIANT: a[j+1] = max{a[0...j+1]};
6       }
7       // INVARIANTS: a[i] = max{a[0...i]};
8       //             a[i...n) is in ascending order;
9   }
```

The invariant at line 5 means that all the elements on the left of a[j+1] are less than or equal to it. That can be verified by induction. (See Exercise 15.3 on page 470.) The invariant at line 7 is the same as the one at line 5, with j = i-1, its last value in the inner loop.

The invariant at line 8 follows from the invariant at line 7. For example, after the first iteration of the outer loop, the invariant at line 7 guarantees that a[n-1] is the largest of all the elements. Since one of those other elements ends up at a[n-2], we know that a[n-2] <= a[n-1]. Similarly, after each iteration of the outer loop, a[i] <= a[i+1], since a[i+1] was the largest among all the unsorted elements including a[i]. So a[i] <= a[i+1] <= a[i+2] <= ... <= a[n-1].

On the last iteration of the outer loop, i = 1. In that case, the loop invariant at line 7 says that a[1] = max{a[0...1]}, and the loop invariant at line 8 says that a[1...n) is in ascending order. This means that a[0] <= a[i], and that a[1] <= a[2] <= ... <= a[n-1]. Thus, the validity of those two loop invariants proves that the bubble sort is correct.

15.2 The Selection Sort

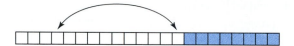

Like the bubble sort, the *selection sort* (Algorithm 15.2) makes the $n-1$ passes through a sequence of n elements, each time moving the largest among the remaining unsorted elements into its correct position. But it is quite a bit more efficient than the bubble sort because it makes only one swap on each pass. It's called the "selection" sort because each pass selects the largest among the remaining unsorted elements and moves it into its correct position.

▲ **ALGORITHM 15.2: The Selection Sort**

1. Repeat Steps 2 for $i = n-1$ down to 1.
2. Swap a_i with $\max\{a_0 \mathinner{.\,.} a_i\}$.

This algorithm is implemented in Listing 15.4. It uses Algorithm 3.1 on page 78 to find the maximum element of the subarray $\{a_0 \mathinner{.\,.} a_i\}$ in step 2.

LISTING 15.4: The Selection Sort

```
1   void sort(int[] a) {
2     for (int i = a.length-1; i > 0; i--) {
3       int m=0;
4       for (int j = 1; j <= i; j++)
5         if (a[j] > a[m]) m = j;
6       swap(a, i, m);
7     }
8   }
```

Here is a trace of the selection sort on the same array that we traced the bubble sort in Example 15.1 on page 439.

Since there are $n = 8$ elements, the selection sort makes $n-1 = 7$ passes. On each pass there is one swap, moving the next largest element into place. The first pass swaps 99 at a[2] with 77 at a[7], moving 99 into its correct position at a[7]. The second pass swaps 88 at a[3] with 22 at a[6], moving 88 into its correct position at a[6]. This process continues to the sixth pass, which swaps 44 at a[0] with 22 at a[2], moving 44 into its correct position at a[2]. The last pass moves no more data because 22 and 33 are already in their correct positions.

The fourth pass is illustrated in Figure 15.1 on page 443. Before the swap, the segment a[5...7] is sorted; after the swap, the segment a[4...7] is sorted. The pass swaps 66 at a[0] with 44 at a[4] because 66 is the maximum among the unsorted segment a[0...4].

▼ **EXAMPLE 15.2: Tracing the Selection Sort**

	a[0]	a[1]	a[2]	a[3]	a[4]	a[5]	a[6]	a[7]
0	66	33	99	88	44	55	22	77
1			77					99
2				22			88	
3			55			77		
4	44				66			
5			22	55				
6	22		44					
7	22	33						

The Selection Sort.

The selection sort can be tested with the program in Listing 15.2 on page 440. The output is the same as for the bubble sort.

◆ **FORMULA 15.2: Selection Sort**

The selection sort makes $\Theta(n^2)$ comparisons. It runs in quadratic time.

Although it has the same $\Theta(n^2)$ complexity function as the bubble sort, the selection sort does run faster, because it makes only $\Theta(n)$ movements of data. On each pass, the selection sort makes only one swap, but the bubble sort makes $\Theta(n)$ swaps. This can be seen from the traces shown in Figure 15.1.

Comparing the traces in the first two examples, we see that the bubble sort and the selection sort both make 21 comparisons (6+5+4+3+2+1). But the bubble sort makes 16 swaps, while the selection sort makes only 7 swaps.

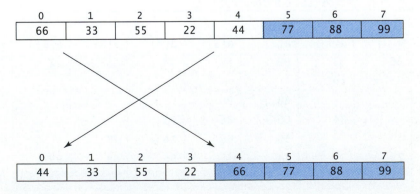

FIGURE 15.1 The Fourth Pass in the Selection Sort.

15.3 The Insertion Sort

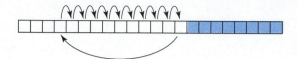

Like the two previous algorithms, the *Insertion Sort* (Algorithm 15.3) makes $n-1$ passes through a sequence of n elements. On each pass it inserts the next element into the subarray on its left, thereby leaving that subarray sorted. When the last element is "inserted" this way, the entire array is sorted. Listing 15.5 gives code for the insertion sort.

▲ **ALGORITHM 15.3: The Insertion Sort**

1. Do Steps 2–5 for $i=1$ up to $n-1$.
2. Hold the element a_i in a temporary space.
3. Locate the least index $j \leq i$ for which $a_j \geq a_i$.
4. Shift the subsequence $\{a_j...a_{i-1}\}$ up one position, into $\{a_{j+1}...a_i\}$.
5. Copy the held value of a_i into a_j.

LISTING 15.5: The Insertion Sort

```
1   void sort(int[] a) {
2     for (int i = 1; i < a.length; i++) {
3       int ai = a[i], j = i;
4       for (j = i; j > 0 && a[j-1] > ai; j--)
5         a[j] = a[j-1];
6       a[j] = ai;
7     }
8   }
```

▼ **EXAMPLE 15.3: Tracing the Insertion Sort**

	a[0]	a[1]	a[2]	a[3]	a[4]	a[5]	a[6]	a[7]
0	66	33	99	88	44	55	22	77
1	33	66						
2			88	99				
3		44	66	88	99			
4			55	66	88	99		
5	22	33	44	55	66	88	99	
6						77	88	99

The Insertion Sort.

On the first pass, $ai = a[1] = 33$ and $j = 1$ at line 3. Since $a[j-1] = a[0] = 66 > ai$, that value 66 is copied into $a[j] = a[1]$ at line 5, and then j is decremented to 0. That stops the inner loop at line 4, which requires $j>0$. Then $ai = 33$ is copied into $a[j] = a[0]$ at line 6. This leaves the segment $a[0...1]$ sorted, as shown at trace line 1.

On the second pass, $ai = a[2] = 99$ and $j = 2$. Since $a[j-1] = a[1] = 66 \le ai$, the inner loop does not iterate at all. Execution jumps immediately to line 6, where the value 99 is (unnecessarily) copied back into $a[2]$. This leaves the segment $a[0...2]$ sorted, as it already was at trace line 1.

On the third pass, $ai = a[3] = 88$ and $j = 3$. Since $a[j-1] = a[2] = 99 > ai$, that value 99 is copied into $a[j] = a[3]$ at line 5, and then j is decremented to 2. That stops the inner loop, because it requires $a[j-1]>ai$ (at line 4) and $a[j-1] = a[1] = 66 \le 88$. Then, at line 6, the value 88 is copied into $a[j] = a[2]$. This leaves the segment $a[0...3]$ sorted, as shown at trace line 2.

On the fourth pass, $ai = a[4] = 44$ and $j = 4$. Since $a[j-1] = a[3] = 99 > ai$, that value 99 is copied into $a[j] = a[4]$ at line 5, and then j is decremented to 3. Now, $a[j-1] = a[2] = 88 > ai$, so the value 88 is copied into $a[j] = a[3]$ at line 5, and j is decremented to 2. Then, $a[j-1] = a[1] = 66 > ai$, so that value 66 is copied into $a[j] = a[2]$ at line 5, and j is decremented to 1. Finally then, $a[j-1] = a[0] = 22 \le 44$, so the inner loop stops, and 44 is copied into $a[1]$ at line 6. This leaves the segment $a[0...4]$ sorted, as shown at trace line 3.

On pass number i, element $a[i]$ is inserted into the sorted segment $a[0...i-1]$ at the location that leaves the segment $a[0...i]$ sorted. Consequently, the last pass leaves the entire array $a[0...7]$ sorted.

The fourth pass is illustrated in Figure 15.2 on page 445.

The resulting action on each pass of the insertion sort is actually a right rotation of a segment of the array. For example, on the fourth pass, the segment $a[1...4]$ is rotated to the right one slot, as illustrated in Figure 15.3. The complete sorting process is a sequence of $n-1$ rotations.

Like the bubble sort and the selection sort, the insertion sort makes $n-1$ passes through the array. On each pass, it rotates a segment within the array. Each rotation moves between 1 and n elements. Moreover, each rotation makes the same number of comparisons as the number of elements it rotates. On average, that number is going to be half the length of the previously sorted segment. The average length of those segments is $n/2$, so the average number of comparisons will be $n/4$. Thus, on average, we'll have $(n/4)(n-1)$ comparisons, and in the worst case fewer than $(n/2)(n-1)$ comparisons.

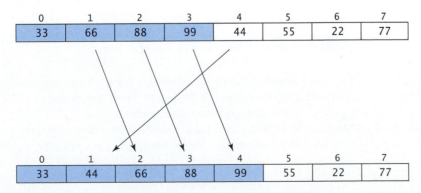

FIGURE 15.2 The Fourth Pass in the Insertion Sort.

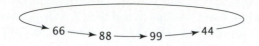

FIGURE 15.3 The Segment is Rotated.

In comparing data movements, we have to count more carefully for the insertion sort because it does not make swaps like the other two sorts. We can count movements of array elements. For example, a rotation of four elements makes four data movements. Comparing the three traces on the same input array, we see that the bubble sort made 32 data movements (16 swaps), the selection sort made 14 data movements (7 swaps), and the insertion sort made 22 data movements (rotations of length 2, 2, 4, 4, 7, and 3).

So, is the insertion sort slower than the selection sort? Not usually, because the selection sort always has to make $(n/2)(n-1)$ comparisons—twice as many as the insertion sort average.

◆ **FORMULA 15.3: Insertion Sort**

The insertion sort makes $\Theta(n)$ comparisons in the best case, and it makes $\Theta(n^2)$ comparisons in both the average and worst cases. On average, then, it runs in quadratic time.

In the best case, however, the insertion sort runs in linear time. What is that best case? It is when only one comparison is made on each pass. That requires `a[j-1]` $\leq$ `ai`, at line 4 in Listing 15.5 on page 444, as it was in the second pass of the trace in Example 15.3 on page 444. But at that point, $j = i$, so `a[j-i]` = `a[i-1]` and `ai` = `a[i]`. So the best case is when `a[i-1]` $\leq$ `a[i]` for each value of `i`; in other words, when the array is already in ascending order before the sort begins!

Note that step 3 of Algorithm 15.3 on page 444 says to locate the correct position for a_i relative to the segment $a_{0...i-1}$ without specifying how that is to be done. Our implementation in Listing 15.5 used a reverse sequential search, decrementing j from $i-1$ until $a_j \leq a_i$. This implementation is called the *straight insertion sort* to distinguish it from the *binary insertion sort*, which uses a binary search instead. (See Exercise 15.26 on page 473.)

15.4 The Shell Sort

The insertion sort runs in linear time on arrays that are already sorted. More importantly, it runs in near linear time on arrays that are nearly sorted. Donald L. Shell discovered in 1959[1] how to exploit that fact to sort general arrays in much better than quadratic time.

The *Shell sort* (Algorithm 15.4), also called the *diminishing increment sort* sorts a sequence by applying the insertion sort to subsequences. The subsequences are selected in a way that

---

[1] Communications of the A.C.M. 2, 7 (July 1959), 30–32.

renders them nearly sorted before the insertion sort is applied to them. Thus, we have a number of runs of them insertion sort, each running in nearly linear time.

The subsequences are defined using *skip number* increments. For example, if the skip number is $d = 4$, then these four subsequences will be sorted independently:

$$\{s_0, s_4, s_8, s_{12}, \ldots\}$$
$$\{s_1, s_5, s_9, s_{13}, \ldots\}$$
$$\{s_2, s_6, s_{10}, s_{14}, \ldots\}$$
$$\{s_3, s_7, s_{11}, s_{15}, \ldots\}$$

Note that each of these four processes could be done independently by separate processors. This makes the algorithm *parallelizable*.

▲ **ALGORITHM 15.4: The Shell Sort**

1. Let $d = n/2$ (the skip number).

2. Repeat steps 3–4 while $d > 0$.

3. Apply the Insertion Sort to each of the d subsequences
$$\{a_0, a_d, a_{2d}, a_{3d}, \ldots\}$$
$$\{a_1, a_{d+1}, a_{2d+1}, a_{3d+1}, \ldots\}$$
$$\{a_2, a_{d+2}, a_{2d+2}, a_{3d+2}, \ldots\}$$
$$\vdots$$
$$\{a_{d-1}, a_{2d-1}, a_{3d-1}, a_{4d-1}, \ldots\}$$

4. Set $d = d/2$;

Step 3 requires an adaptation of the insertion sort to a skip sequence. This is implemented by the iSort() method defined in Listing 15.6. The call iSort(a,c,d) applies the insertion sort to the subsequence $\{a_c, a_{d+c}, a_{2d+c}, a_{3d+c}, \ldots\}$. For example, call iSort(a,3,4) would sort subsequence $\{a_3, a_7, a_{11}, a_{15}, \ldots\}$. This implementation is the same as the ordinary Insertion Sort, implemented in Listing 15.5 on page 444, except that i starts at c+d and increments by d in line 2, a[j-d] is used instead of a[j-1] in lines 4–5, and j is explicitly decremented by d in line 6. Also, the loop control condition j>0 is replaced by j>d in line 4 to prevent j from going out of range.

Algorithm 15.4 is implemented in Listing 15.7. It calls the isort() method at line.

LISTING 15.6: The iSort() Method

```
1   void iSort(int[] a, int c, int d) {
2     for (int i = c+d; i < a.length; i+=d) {
3       int ai = a[i], j = i;
4       while (j > c && a[j-d] > ai) {
5         a[j] = a[j-d];
6         j -= d;
7       }
8       a[j] = ai;
9     }
10  }
```

LISTING 15.7: The Shell Sort

```
1   void sort(int[] a) {
2     for (int d = a.length/2; d > 0; d /= 2)
3       for (int c = 0; c < d; c++)
4         iSort(a, c, d);  // applies Insertion Sort to the skip sequence
5   }
```

Example 15.4 is a trace of the algorithm on the same input array that we used for the previous three sorting algorithms.

▼ **EXAMPLE 15.4: Tracing the Shell Sort**

	a[0]	a[1]	a[2]	a[3]	a[4]	a[5]	a[6]	a[7]
0	66	33	99	88	44	55	22	77
1	44				66			
2			22				99	
3				77				88
4	22		44					
5				55		77		
6							88	99

The Shell Sort.

First, the four subsequences $\{a_0, a_4\}$, $\{a_1, a_5\}$, $\{a_2, a_6\}$, and $\{a_3, a_7\}$ are sorted in lines 1–3. Then, the two subsequences $\{a_0, a_2, a_4, a_6\}$ and $\{a_1, a_3, a_5, a_7\}$ are sorted in lines 4-5. Finally, the entire sequence is sorted at line 6. Notice that each subsequence sort makes only two data movements in this trace.

In general, any subsequence of size m need make no more than $m/2$ comparisons, because half of its elements were sorted on the previous pass. For example, in sorting a sequence of $n = 128$ elements, the first pass would sort 64 subsequences of size 2, the second pass would sort 32 subsequences of size 4, and the third pass would sort 16 subsequences of size 8. In each of those subsequences of size 8, four of the elements were sorted as one of the 32 subsequences in the second pass. So the condition `a[j-d]>ai` in line 4 could be true for only those `a[j-d]` that were not in the 4-element subsequence as `ai`.

Although its proof is beyond the scope of this book, the preceding analysis leads to the following result:

◆ **FORMULA 15.4: Shell Sort**

The Shell sort runs, on average, in $O(n^{1.5})$ time.

This is significantly faster than the $\Theta(n^2)$ sorts, which make $\sqrt{n}$ times as many comparisons. For example, on array of size $n = 10,000$, the slower sorts make 100 times as many comparisons.

15.5 The Speed Limit for Comparison Sorts

The Shell sort is faster than the bubble sort, selection sort, and the insertion sort. What about other possible sorting algorithms? How much better can we do?

For comparison sorts, the speed limit is $\Theta(n \lg n)$. A *comparison sort* is an algorithm that sorts a sequence by permuting its elements based upon how their values compare with each other. To see how comparison sorts are distinguished from other sorts, let's look at a sorting algorithm that is not a comparison sort.

The *counting sort* (also called the *tally sort*) works by counting how many elements there are of each value and then rearranging them in ordered blocks by those values. For example, imagine sorting the personnel records of every student at a university, ordered only by their country of birth. We would simply tabulate all the records, counting how many are Andorran (AD), how many are Afghan (AF), how many are Albanian (AL), etc. Suppose the first part of the tally looks like Figure 15.4. Then we would move the two Andorran records into elements a[0...1], the seven Afghan records into elements a[2...8], the four Albanian records into elements a[9...12], the one Armenian record into element a[13], etc.

Note that even though the values of the keys (AD, AF, AL, *etc.*) must be in order, the counting sort is not a comparison sort, because its individual elements are not compared with each other; they simply are counted.

The counting sort actually runs in linear time! That means that, all other things being equal, if you double the number of elements, it should take about twice as long to sort them. For example, if the university used this algorithm to sort its student records every year, the run time would be proportional to the number of records. The only actions that depend upon the number of records are the counting and moving, and each record is counted once and moved once.

There are other common sorting algorithms that run in linear time. (See Sections 15.9 and 15.11.) But, like the counting sort, these are also not comparison sorts.

◆ **FORMULA 15.5: The Speed Limit for Comparison Sorts**

No comparison sort has a worst-case run time better than $\Theta(n \lg n)$.

Country	Tally
AD	2
AF	7
AL	4
AM	1
AR	23
AT	11

FIGURE 15.4 A tally for the counting sort.

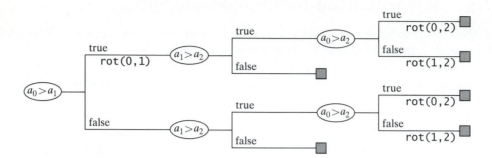

FIGURE 15.5   Decision Tree for the Insertion Sort on Three Elements.

The proof of this "speed limit" theorem is based upon the decision tree of an arbitrary comparison sort. To follow the argument, imagine that you work for the U.S. Patent Office and someone has submitted a new comparison sorting algorithm to be patented. Suppose the person claims that it runs in linear time in the worst case. To verify this claim, you require the decision tree that maps the execution of the algorithm for an arbitrary array of n integers to be submitted.

Since the algorithm is a comparison sort, all of its decisions must be made by comparing the elements of the array, for example, Figure 15.5 shows the decision tree for the Insertion Sort on e elements. If $a_0 > a_1$, then the segment $a_{0...1}$ is rotated to make $a_0 \leq a_1$. Next, if $a_1 > a_2$ and if $a_0 > a_2$, then the segment $a_{0...2}$ is rotated to make $a_0 \leq a_1 \leq a_2$. But, if $a_1 > a_2$ and $a_0 \leq a_2$, then the segment $a_{1...2}$ is rotated to make $a_0 \leq a_1 \leq a_2$. The other cases are analyzed similarly.

The decision tree shown in Figure 15.5 has six leaves, one for each possible initial arrangement of the sequence. In general, a sequence of n elements has $n!$ different arrangements (permutations), so the decision tree for the Insertion Sort on n elements has $n!$ leaves. That must be true for any comparison sort, because the algorithm must be able to distinguish each of the different arrangements that the array could be in.

Now the decision tree is a binary tree, so, by Formula 12.3 on page 355, its height h must be at least $\lg m$, where m is the number of nodes in the tree. Since the tree has $n!$ leaf nodes, it must have more than $n!$ nodes altogether, so we also know that $h > \lg(n!)$. Now, by Formula C.12 $\lg(n!) = \Theta(n \lg n)$. Thus, the height h of the decision tree is at least $\Theta(n \lg n)$, and that is precisely the worst-case number of comparisons that the algorithm can make.

15.6 The Merge Sort

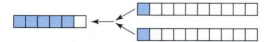

Now that we know (by Formula 15.5) that no comparison sort can run faster than $\Theta(n \lg n)$, the next question is whether there are any that can do that well. The $\Theta(n^2)$ performance of the bubble sort, the selection sort, and the insertion sort is much worse than $\Theta(n \lg n)$. For example, on an array of 1000 elements, they would make about 100 times as many comparisons as an optimal

$\Theta(n \lg n)$ algorithm. The clever Shell sort isn't so bad: It would make only about 3 times as many comparisons.

Fortunately, there are several standard sorting algorithms that do run in the optimal $\Theta(n \lg n)$ time. One of them is the merge sort (Algorithm 15.5).

▲ **ALGORITHM 15.5: The Merge Sort**

1. If the sequence has fewer than two elements, return.

2. Let a_m be the middle element of the sequence.

3. Sort the subsequence of elements that precede a_m.

4. Sort the subsequence of all the other elements.

5. Merge the two sorted subsequences.

Note that this algorithm is recursive: Both steps 3 and 4 invoke the algorithm itself. Note also that it requires a subalgorithm for merging two sorted subsequences. This is done by comparing the elements pairwise, one from each subsequence, as shown in the picture above, and moving the smaller element each time into the output sequence. For this operation, it is best to think of all three sequences as queues.

Since the algorithm is implemented as a recursive method, it probably would be called by a nonrecursive driver method, like this:

```
void sort(int[] a) {
   sort(a, 0, a.length);
}
```

Listing 15.8 is a direct implementation of Algorithm 15.5.

LISTING 15.8: The Merge Sort

```
1   void sort(int[] a, int p, int q) {
2      //  PRECONDITION: 0 < p < q <= a.length
3      //  POSTCONDITION: a[p...q-1] is in ascending order
4      if (q-p < 2) return;
5      int m = (p+q)/2;
6      sort(a, p, m);
7      sort(a, m, q);
8      merge(a, p, m, q);
9   }
```

Steps 6–7 repeatedly divide the array into smaller subarrays until they get down to size 0 or 1. Then the pieces repeatedly are merged until, at step 8, the original size is obtained. Since each merge produces a sorted subarray, when the whole array is finally reassembled, it is in ascending order.

The call `merge(a,p,m,q)` merges the two segments `a[p...m-1]` and `a[m...q-1]`, resulting in the complete segment `a[p...q-1]` being sorted.

LISTING 15.9: **The** merge() **Method**

```
1   void merge(int[] a, int p, int m, int q) {
2       // PRECONDITIONS: a[p...m-1] and a[m...q-1] are in ascending order;
3       // POSTCONDITION: a[p...q-1] is in ascending order;
4       if (a[m-1] <= a[m]) return;   // a[p...q-1] is already sorted
5       int i = p, j = m, k = 0;
6       int[] aa = new int[q-p];
7       while (i < m && j < q)
8          if (a[i]<a[j]) aa[k++] = a[i++];
9          else aa[k++] = a[j++];
10      if (i < m) System.arraycopy(a, i, a, p+k, m-i);   // shift a[i...m-1]
11      System.arraycopy(aa, 0, a, p, k);   // copy aa[0...k-1] to a[p...p+k-1];
12  }
```

The merge() method (Listing 15.9) uses a temporary array aa[] to assemble the merged pieces. The array is initialized at line 5 with size q-p, which is the total number of elements among the two segments a[p...m-1] and a[m...q-1]. On each iteration of the main loop at lines 6-8, one element is copied into aa[] from one of the two segments. Note that the postincrement operators automatically increment only the index of the element copied (a[i] or a[j]) and the index of the location aa[k] where that element is copied. Also note that on every iteration, the value of k is the number of elements merged.

When the main loop terminates, all of the elements of one of the two segments and some of the elements of the other will have been copied to aa[]. If i<m, then the main loop will have terminated because j==q, as shown in Figure 15.6. In that case, we copy the segment of unmerged elements a[i...m-1] into a[p+k,q-1], shifting it to the end of a[]. Then the segment of merged elements aa[0...k-1] can be copied back into a[p...p+k-1]. On the other hand, if the main loop terminates because i==m, then the copy statement at line 11 is precisely all that remains to be done.

Note that the method returns immediately at line 4 if the complete segment is already sorted. That will be true if a[m-1]<=a[m], because a[p...m-1] and a[m...q-1] are in ascending order when the method begins.

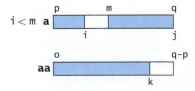

FIGURE 15.6 The merge() Method.

▼ **EXAMPLE 15.5: Tracing the Merge Sort**

	a[0]	a[1]	a[2]	a[3]	a[4]	a[5]	a[6]	a[7]
0	66	33	99	55	88	22	44	77
1	33	66						
2			55	99				
3	33	55	66	99				
4					22	88		
5					22	44	77	88
6	22	33	44	55	66	77	88	99

The Merge Sort.

The Merge Sort is traced in Example 15.5. The first changes to a[] occur in step 1 where a[0] is merged with a[1] into a[0...1]. Then a[2] is merged with a[3] into a[2...3] in step 2, and then a[0...1] is merged with a[2...3] into a[0...3] in step 3. The second half is processed in the same way, ending in step 5 with the subarray a[4...7] in ascending order. Finally, a[0...3] is merged with a[4...7] into a[0...7] in step 6.

In this trace, each horizontal line indicates a call to the merge() method.

The general split-and-merge process can be visualized from the picture in Figure 15.7. It shows the progress of the algorithm for $n = 16$ elements: four levels of splitting, followed by for levels of merging. The total number of levels, 8 in this case, is twice the number of times that n can be divided by 2. That number is the binary logarithm of n: $\lg n$. So in general, there will be $2\lg n$ levels in the progress of the sorting. At each level, all n elements are compared. Thus, the total number of comparisons is at most $(2\lg n)(n) = 2n\lg n$.

◆ **FORMULA 15.6: Merge Sort**

The Merge Sort makes $\Theta(n\lg n)$ comparisons in the worst case.

Note that we refer to the progress of the algorithm through "levels" instead of stages. That is because the individual parts of each stage are actually interleaved in time, due to the recursive nature of the algorithm. This is evident in the trace in Example 15.5 then a[0...1] and a[2...3] are merged into a[0...3] in step 3 before a[4] is merged with a[5].

The Merge Sort seems to require that the size n be a power of 2; otherwise the segment sizes will be imbalanced. However, this is not a requirement. The implementation in Listing 15.9 will work correctly on any size. (See 15.15 on page 476.)

The Merge Sort uses the *divide-and-conquer* strategy: it sorts the entire array by dividing it up into pieces and sorting them by merging. This is the same strategy that the Binary Search uses. (See 3.7 on page 84.)

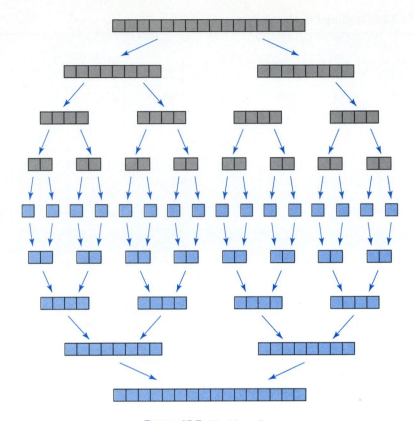

FIGURE 15.7 The Merge Sort.

15.7 The Quick Sort

The *Quick Sort* is another recursive divide-and-conquer algorithm that runs on average in $\Theta(n \lg n)$ time. It was discovered by Anthony Hoare in 1962. Like the Merge Sort, it also has two stages. The first stage, called the *partition*, divides the sequence into two segments separated by a single element a_k, so that $a_i \le a_k$ for all $i < k$, and $a_j \ge a_k$ for all $j > k$. The element a_k is called the *pivot* for the partition. The second stage recursively sorts each of the two segments.

▲ ALGORITHM 15.6: The Quick Sort

1. If the sequence has fewer than two elements, return.

2. Using the first element a_p as the pivot, partition the sequence into $\{a_p, \ldots, a_{q-1}\}$, into three subsequences $\{X, Y, Z\}$, where every element in the subsequence X is bounded above by a_p, every element in the sebsequence Z is bounded below by a_p, and Y is singleton subsequence $Y = \{a_p\}$.

3. Sort the subsequence *X*.

4. Sort the subsequence *Z*.

Note that, since this algorithm is recursive, we assume that it is being applied to a subsequence $a_{p...q-1}$ of size $q-p$. The quick sort algorithm is coded in Listing 15.10.

LISTING 15.10: The Quick Sort

```
1   void sort(int[] a, int p, int q) {
2       //  PRECONDITION: 0<= p < q <= a.length
3       //  POSTCONDITION: a[p...q-1] is in ascending order
4       if (q-p < 2) return;
5       int j = partition(a, p, q);
6       sort(a, p, j);
7       sort(a, j+1, q);
8   }
```

As with the Merge Sort, this implementation uses a separate method to do most of the work. (See Listing 15.11.)

LISTING 15.11: The `partition()` Method

```
1    int partition(int[] a, int p, int q) {
2        // RETURNS: index j of pivot element a[j];
3        // POSTCONDITION: a[i] <= a[j] <= a[k] for p <= i <= j <= k < q;
4        int pivot=a[p], i = p, j = q;
5        while (i < j) {
6          while (j > i && a[--j] >= pivot)
7            ;  // empty loop
8          if (j > i) a[i] = a[j];
9          while (i < j && a[++i] <= pivot)
10           ;  // empty loop
11         if (i < j) a[j] = a[i];
12       }
13       a[j] = pivot;
14       return j;
15   }
```

The partitioning process begins by assigning the first element a[p] to the variable pivot at line 4. The main loop (lines 5–12) separates the rest of the elements into two segments a[p...j] and a[j+1...q-1] so that a[i] <= pivot <= a[k] for i <= j <= k. Then, after a[j] is assigned the pivot value at line 13, the partition is complete. The separation actually is achieved by a rotation of elements that moves the small ones to the left and the large ones to the right.

The elements to be moved are located using two index variables i and j, initialized at line 4 to p and q, respectively. Each iteration of the main loop does four things:

1. It decrements j to the index of the next element that is greater than the pivot (lines 6–7).

2. It copies a[j] into the last vacant position (line 8).

3. It increments i to the index of the next element that is less than the pivot (lines 9–10).

4. It copies a[i] into the last vacant position (line 11).

(The first vacant position is a[p], whose value was saved in the pivot.) The loop stops when i and j together have scanned the entire array. That happens when they cross over, making j<=i. Note the use of *empty loops* at lines 6–7 and 9–10. The only purpose of those loops is to decrement j and increment i, and that is done within their control clauses.

The elements that get moved during the partition process form a "threaded" rotation, as illustrated in Figure 15.8.

The figure shows six elements being moved. The leftmost element is the pivot, which is held in the temporary variable pivot to allow space for the rotation. The last shaded element on the right is the rightmost element a[j] that is less than pivot. It is moved into position a[p]. Then the leftmost element a[i] that is greater than the pivot is moved into that position. This continues until every element that is less than pivot lies to the left of every element that is greater than pivot. Finally, the value of pivot is copied into the last vacated position, completing the rotation circuit. That element is now in its correct position and will not move again throughout the rest of the sort.

Note that in each recursive call to sort, the pivot element plays the same role as the root of each subtree in a binary search tree. (See Section 13.2.)

Example 15.6 shows a trace of the Quick Sort on the same array that was used in Example 15.5 on page 453.

▼ **EXAMPLE 15.6: Tracing the Quick Sort**

	a[0]	a[1]	a[2]	a[3]	a[4]	a[5]	a[6]	a[7]
0	66	33	99	55	88	22	44	77
1	44		22		66	88	99	
2	44	33	22	55				
3	22		44					
4	22	33		55		88	99	77
5						77	88	99
6						77	88	

The Quick Sort.

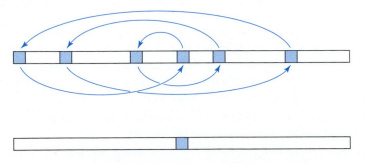

FIGURE 15.8 The partition() Method.

In this trace, each horizontal line indicates the completion of a call to the `partition()` method. As usual, the shaded regions show elements that have reached their correct positions. The elements shown in boldface are the pivot elements.

The first pivot is 66 at `a[0]`. Step 1 shows the result of the first partition:

```
a[0] ← 44
a[6] ← 99
a[2] ← 22
a[5] ← 88
a[4] ← 66
```

Thus, the threaded rotation here is `a[0]` ← `a[6]` ← `a[2]` ← `a[5]` ← `a[0]` ← `a[0]`. This is illustrated in Figure 15.9.

The quick sort is similar to the merge sort in several ways: They both use the divide-and-conquer strategy, they are both recursive, they both use a separate nonrecursive method to do most of the work, and they both have an average $\Theta(n \lg n)$ run time. However, the general run-time analysis of the quick sort is more difficult than that of the merge sort. Except for the "accelerator" step at line 4 in Listing 15.9 on page 452, the merge sort goes through the same $2n \lg n$ steps, regardless of the actual initial arrangement of the sequence; in other words, it is pretty "insensitive to input." But the run time of the quick sort can vary substantially on the same set of data, depending upon their initial arrangement.

In the worst case, the quick sort runs in $\Theta(n^2)$ time. This is when the sequence is initially already in ascending order or in descending order. If it is already in ascending order, then the partition method does no work at all, each time leaving the pivot unmoved. Consequently, the partition $\{a_{p...j-1}, a_j, a_{j+1...q-1}\}$ that is produced by step 2 of Algorithm 15.6 on page 454 is really $\{\emptyset, a_p, a_{p+1...q-1}\}$. The left segment is empty, and the right segment contains every element except the pivot. So each call to the partition() method reduces the size of the unsorted part by only one element. Consequently, $n-1$ calls will be made to the partition() method, and each call compares $\Theta(n)$ elements, resulting in a total of $\Theta(n^2)$ comparisons.

So why is it called the "quick" sort? Because, on average, it really is faster than any of the other sorting algorithms. It can be shown that, in the average case, the quick sort makes only about 38% more comparisons than in the best case, and we can see by an examination of Figure 15.10 that, in the best case the Quick Sort makes only $n \lg n$ comparisons, which is not unlike the performance of merge sort.

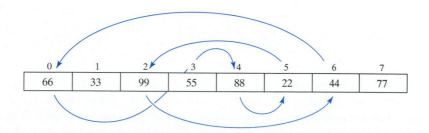

FIGURE 15.9 The First Partition in the Quick Sort.

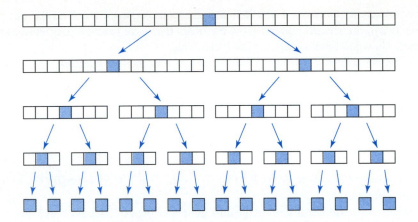

FIGURE 15.10 The Quick Sort in the Best Case.

Also, the best-case quick sort (like the merge sort) repeatedly divides the sequence into two equal segments (plus the single pivot element). This can be done $\Theta(\lg n)$ times, and at each stage, $\Theta(n)$ elements will be compared. So the result is $\Theta(n \lg n)$ comparisons.

◆ **FORMULA 15.7: Quick Sort**

The quick sort makes $\Theta(n \lg n)$ comparisons in the average and best cases and $\Theta(n^2)$ comparisons in the worst case.

The main reason that the quick sort is faster than the merge sort is that it works *in situ* (*i.e.*, "in place"). All the data movements are done by the rotations made by the partition process, which uses only one temporary storage location (for the pivot). The Merge Sort uses a whole array of temporary storage and has to take time to copy the arrays back and forth.

15.8 The Heap Sort

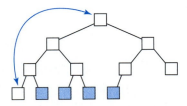

The $\Theta(n \lg n)$ run time of both the merge sort and the quick sort is substantially better than the $\Theta(n^2)$ run time of the selection sort and of the insertion sort. Those two faster algorithms achieve their superior performance by comparing each of the n elements only $\Theta(\lg n)$ times instead of $\Theta(n)$ times. The logarithm arises from the divide-and-conquer strategy that they both employ.

A different process that also runs in logarithmic time is the traversal up or down a root-to-leaf path in a complete binary tree on n elements. If an algorithm can sort the elements by repeating that process once for each element, it will achieve $\Theta(n \lg n)$ run time. This is the idea behind the heap sort. (See Algorithm 15.7.)

The heap sort, as its name implies, is based upon the heap data structure that we studied in Chapter 14. That is a complete binary tree in which the key at each node is not greater than its parent's key. Since heaps are typically stored as arrays, we can apply the heap operations to an array of integers. Throughout this section, therefore, we illustrate the operations as though they are being performed on binary trees, while they are really defined for the arrays that represent them by the natural mapping. (See Figure 12.12 on page 362.)

The main idea of the heap sort is the same as that of the selection sort: Select the maximum element from among the remaining unsorted segment, and swap it into its correct position. This has to be done $n-1$ times. The heap sort improves on the selection sort by managing to do each selection in logarithmic time instead of in linear time. It maintains the unsorted segment as a heap, so its maximum is at position a[0]. Each selection then swaps out a[0] and then restores the heap among the remaining unsorted segment. That takes only $\Theta(\lg n)$ steps, because that restoration is simply the Heapify operation. (Recall Algorithm 14.1 on page 418.)

▲ ALGORITHM 15.7: The Heap Sort

1. Apply Build Heap (Algorithm 14.2 on page 419) to the sequence.
2. Repeat steps 3–4 for $i = n-1$ down to 1.
3. Swap a_i with a_0.
4. Heapify (Algorithm 14.1 on page 418) the subsequence $\{a_0, ..., a_i\}$.

We found in Algorithm 14.2 on page 419 that step 1 makes about $5n$ comparisons. By Algorithm 14.2 on page 419, step 4 makes about $2 \lg n$ comparisons. This gives the following results:

◆ FORMULA 15.8: Heap Sort

The heap sort makes about $5n + 2n \lg n$ comparisons in the worst case. Thus, the heap sort runs in $\Theta(n \lg n)$ time.

The expression $5n + 2n \lg n$ is significant, because the term $5n$ shows that the heap sort is a bit slower than the merge sort and the quick sort. In the worst case, the merge sort makes about $2 \lg n$ comparisons, and the quick sort makes about $1.4 \lg n$ comparisons. But the merge sort requires extra space for duplicating the array, and the quick sort degrades to quadratic time in the worst case.

The Build Heap operation applies the Heapify operation at a[3] at line 1, at a[2] and a[1] at line 2, and at a[0] at line 3. Line 4 swaps a[0] with a[7], and then line 5 rebuilds the heap on the segment a[0...6]. Line 6 swaps a[0] with a[6], and then line 7 rebuilds the heap on the segment a[0...5]. Line 8 swaps a[0] with a[5], and then line 9 rebuilds the heap on the segment a[0...4]. This swap–heapify operation repeats until a[0] with a[2] at line 14, rendering the array sorted.

▼ **EXAMPLE 15.7: Tracing the Heap Sort**

	a[0]	a[1]	a[2]	a[3]	a[4]	a[5]	a[6]	a[7]
0	66	33	99	55	88	22	44	77
1				77				55
2		88			33			
3	99		66					
4	55							99
5	88	77		55				
6	44						88	
7	77	55		44				
8	22					77		
9	66		22					
10	33				66			
11	55	44		33				
12	33			55				
13	44	33						
14	22	33	44	55	66	77	88	99

Tracing the Heap Sort.

Each line of this trace is illustrated in Figure 15.11 on page 461.
Listing 15.12 is a direct implementation of Algorithm 15.7.

LISTING 15.12: The Heap Sort

```
1  void sort(int[] a) {
2    for (int i = (a.length-1)/2; i >= 0; i--)
3      heapify(a, i, a.length);
4    for (int j = a.length-1; j > 0; j--) {
5      swap(a, 0, j);
6      heapify(a, 0, j);
7    }
8  }
```

This implementation uses the heapify() method defined in Listing 14.1 on page 418. Lines 2–3 in this implementation are equivalent to the recursive buildHeap() method defined in Listing 14.2 on page 420.

The heap sort seems like a modified selection sort because both algorithms move the next largest key into its correct position on each iteration of the main loop. But the heap sort is better viewed algorithmically as a combination of the selection sort and the insertion sort. This is easier to see if you think of the insertion sort as an algorithm designed to sort upon insertion into a

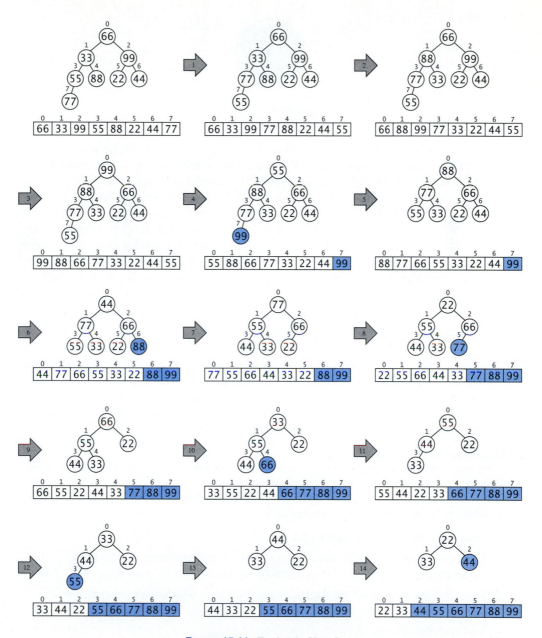

FIGURE 15.11 Tracing the Heap Sort.

linked list, and the selection sort as an algorithm designed to sort upon removal from a linked list. The insertion sort inserts each new arrival into its correct position relative to the other keys already inserted. After they are all inserted, the sequence is in ascending order. On the other hand, the main idea behind the selection sort can be applied to extract the elements of an

FIGURE 15.12   Yin-Yang.

unsorted sequence so that they are removed in ascending order: On each iteration, select the smallest of the remaining elements next. This would be a "min" selection sort, instead of the "max" selection sort that we studied in Section 15.2, but it's the same principle.

The heap sort does its work in two stages: first build the heap, and then sort upon removal from the heap. Between the two stages, the heap is *partially ordered*. So the algorithm does a partial sort upon insertion, followed by a partial sort upon removal. It applies the main ideas behind the two $\Theta(n^2)$ algorithms to obtain a $\Theta(n \lg n)$ algorithm. Combining the best ideas of the two slow algorithms produces a fast algorithm. The heap sort is a "mean between extremes."[2] This is akin to the chinese philosophy that seeks a balance between opposing forces, signified by the Yin-Yang, in Figure 15.12.

15.9 The Bucket Sort

We have studied three $\Theta(n^2)$ sorts (bubble, selection, and insertion), one $O(n^{1.5})$ sort (Shell), and three $\Theta(n \lg n^2)$ sorts (merge, quick, and heap). We now turn to the $O(n)$ sorts.

The *bucket sort* (Algorithm 15.8) uses an array of containers called "buckets" to hold the keys temporarily. It is an example of a *distribution sort*, which begins by distributing the keys among the buckets. The idea is to use n buckets to sort n elements.

▲ **ALGORITHM 15.8: The Bucket Sort**

Input: a sequence of n numeric keys $\{a_0, a_1, a_2, ..., a_{n-1}\}$.
Precondition: the keys are uniformly distributed within the interval $I = [a,b) = \{x \mid a \le x < b\}$.
Postcondition: the sequence is in ascending order.

1. Allocate a sequence of n buckets $\{B_0, B_1, B_2, ..., B_{n-1}\}$.

2. Partition the interval $[a,b)$ into a sequence of n equal subintervals $\{I_0, I_1, I_2, ..., I_{n-1}\}$, where each $I_j = [x_j, x_{j+1})$ has length $\Delta x = (b-a)/n$; so $x_0 = a$, $x_1 = a + \Delta x$, $x_2 = a + 2\Delta x$, *etc.*

3. Distribute the keys a_i among the buckets according to which subinterval a_i is in:
   $a_i \in I_j \Rightarrow a_i$ is put into bucket B_j.

4. Sort each bucket.

5. Copy the keys back from the buckets to the sequence in order of the buckets, B_0, B_1, B_2, ..., keeping the order within each bucket.

---

[2] An example of the ancient chinese philosophy Yin-Yang, represented by the circle of opposing forces shown in Figure 15.12.

If the keys are uniformly distributed, then there will be only one key per bucket, on aver-ages, so each call to selection sort in step 4 runs in constant time. Thus, each of the five steps runs in linear time.

◆ **FORMULA 15.9: Bucket Sort**

The bucket sort runs in linear time in the average case.

Of course, we should not expect to "get something for nothing." The real cost of the bucket sort is the allocation of n buckets. That overhead tends to make this algorithm impractical for most situations.

There are, however, some exceptions. Suppose, for example, you have a 40-volume ency-clopedia on a bookshelf and the 40 numbered books are all out of order. If the shelf below is vacant, the Bucket Sort is an easy way to put the books in order.

As another example, suppose you run a bus company and you have 50 buses on your lot, each with a four-digit license number. Suppose you want to sort the buses by those numbers. In this case, the intervals defined in step 2 would be $I_0 = [0, 199]$, $I_1 = [200, 399]$, $I_2 = [400, 599]$, ..., $I_{49} = [9998, 9999]$, because $\Delta x = 10,000/50 = 200$. So you would set up 50 parking lanes (buckets), and move each bus into the correct lane according to the subintervals. For example, a bus numbered 0483 would be moved into lane 2, because $483 \in I_2$ (*i.e.*, $400 \leq 483 < 600$). If more than one bus goes into the same lane, you could implement step 4 by sorting upon insertion (the Insertion Sort), or by sorting upon removal (the selection sort). This would be a practical solution, especially because of the cost of moving the data.

Algorithmically, the bucket sort is essentially the same as hashing with closed addressing (*i.e.*, separate chaining) into a hash table with size m equal to the number n of keys, where the hash function is $h(a_i) = j$, $a_i \in I_j$, as defined in Algorithm 15.8, and where the chains are main-tained in ascending order. Each bucket corresponds to one component of the hash table and can be implemented as a linked list, sorting upon insertion.

▼ **EXAMPLE 15.8: Applying the Bucket Sort**

For example, to sort the 11 keys 66, 96, 22, 80, 14, 83, 77, 44, 25, 88, 33, the subintervals would be 12-19, 20-27, 28-35, ..., 92-99, because $\Delta x = 88/11 = 8$. Then the keys would be distributed into the 11 buckets as shown in Figure 15.13, inserting each key in order into its bucket. Then the sorted sequence is obtained simply by concatenating the 11 buckets in order.

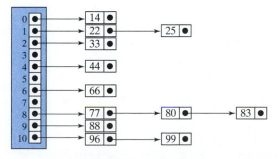

FIGURE 15.13 The Bucket Sort.

15.10 The Counting Sort

The *counting sort* (Algorithm 15.9) was already mentioned earlier. It is another distribution sort. Like the bucket sort, it distributes the keys according to their values. It works well when the number values are much less than the number of keys.

For example, suppose you have 5000 undergraduate student records, and you want to sort them according to academic discipline of major study: accounting (ACC), biology (BIO), chemistry (CHE), *etc.* The method is to tally the records, counting how many are in each discipline. For example, suppose that 914 are in ACC, 729 are in BIO, 485 are in CHE, etc. Then you would insert the ACC records into the segment $a_{0...913}$, insert the BIO records into the segment $a_{914...1642}$, insert the CHE records into the segment $a_{1643...2128}$, *etc.*

▲ ALGORITHM 15.9: The Counting Sort

Input: a sequence of keys $a = \{a_0, a_1, a_2, ..., a_{n-1}\}$.
Precondition: the number m of distinct values in the sequence is much smaller than its length n, and those values are the integers $0, 1, ..., m-1$.
Postcondition: the sequence is in ascending order.

1. Allocate a tally sequence $c = \{c_0, c_1, c_2, ..., c_{m-1}\}$, with each element initialized to 0.
2. Tally the keys in c, so that each c_k is the number of keys that are equal to k.
3. Reprocess c into a cumulative distribution, so that each c_k is the number of keys that are less than or equal to k.
4. Allocate a temporary sequence $b = \{b_0, b_1, b_2, ..., b_{n-1}\}$.
5. For $i = n-1$ down to 0, copy a_i into b_j, and decrement c_k, where $j = c_k$, and $k = a_i$.
6. Copy b to a.

Each of these steps runs in $\Theta(n)$ or $\Theta(mn)$ time, and m is constant. Thus, we have the following formula:

◆ FORMULA 15.10: Counting Sort

The counting sort, coded in Listing 15.13, runs in linear time in the average case.

LISTING 15.13: The Counting Sort

```
1   void sort(int[] a) {
2       int n = a.length;
3       int m = size(a);                    // the number of distinct values of a[]
4       int[] c = new int[m];               // step 1
5       for (int i = 0; i < n; i++)         // step 2
6           ++c[ a[i] ];
7       for (int k = 1; k < m; k++)         // step 3
8           c[k] += c[k-1];
9       int[] b = new int[n];               // step 4
10      for (int i = n-1; i >= 0; i--)      // step 5
11          b[ --c[ a[i] ] ] = a[i];
12      System.arraycopy(b, 0, a, 0, n);    // step 6
13  }
```

Note the expression $b[--c[a[i]]] = a[i]$ in line 11. If the value of $a[i]$ is 2, and the value of $c[2]$ is 7, then this would decrement $c[2]$ to 6, and then assign 2 to $b[6]$. This means that there are 6 keys in $a[]$ that come ahead of $a[i]$ and should remain ahead of $a[i]$ after $a[]$ is sorted.

▼ **EXAMPLE 15.9: Tracing the Counting Sort**

To trace Algorithm 15.9, suppose $a = \{2, 1, 2, 0, 1, 1, 0, 2, 1, 1\}$. Then $n = 10$ and $m = 3$. The tally array is $c = \{2, 5, 3\}$, because there are two 0s, five 1s, and three 2s. In step 3, the tally array is accumulated, becoming $c = \{2, 7, 10\}$, which means that there are 2 keys ≤ 0, 7 keys ≤ 1, and 10 keys (all of them) ≤ 2.

We should end up with the original array sorted as $a = \{0, 0, 1, 1, 1, 1, 1, 2, 2\}$. So the keys should be shifted as shown in Figure 15.14:

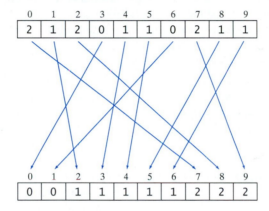

FIGURE 15.14 The counting sort.

	i	k = a_i	c_0	c_1	c_2	j = c_k	b_j
0			2	7	10		
1	9	1		6		6	1
2	8	1		5		5	1
3	7	2			9	9	2
4	6	0	1			1	0
5	5	1		4		4	1
6	4	1		3		3	1
7	3	0	0			0	0
8	2	2			8	8	2
9	1	1		2		2	1
10	0	2			7	7	2

Tracing the Heap Sort.

Step 5 distributes the 10 keys this way, using the array c, which starts out at as $c = \{2, 7, 10\}$ at line 0. At line 1, $i = 9$, and $k = a_9 = 1$, so c_1 is decremented to $j = 6$, and $a_9 = 1$ is copied into b_6. On the next iteration, at line 2, $i = 8$, and $k = a_8 = 1$, so c_1 is decremented to $j = 5$, and $a_8 = 1$ is copied into b_5. On the next iteration, at line 3, $i = 7$, and $k = a_7 = 2$, so c_2 is decremented to $j = 9$, and $a_7 = 1$ is copied into b_9. This process continues for 10 iterations, each time copying the next a_i into b. On the last iteration, at line 10, $i = 0$, and $k = a_0 = 2$, so c_2 is decremented to $j = 7$, and $a_0 = 2$ is copied into b_7.

The main loop at step 5 in the algorithm runs in reverse order, from $n - 1$ down to 0, to preserve the order of equal keys. For example, there are two 0s, originally at a_3 and a_6. These are copied into b_0 and b_1, respectively (*i.e.*, the 0 on the left stays on the left). This order-preserving property is important for the Counting Sort, because it is used by the radix sort (in Section 15.11), which requires that property. In general, sorting algorithms that do not permute equal keys are said to be *stable*. The Counting Sort is a stable sorting algorithm.

Note that the precondition that the keys all be in the set $\{0, 1, ..., m - 1\}$ can be relaxed. For example, in the previous example of sorting the 5000 student records by academic major, the keys were the strings ACC, BIO, CHE, *etc.* To make this situation conform to the algorithm, we would have to devise a one-to-one function $h()$ that assigns $h(\text{ACC}) = 0$, $h(\text{BIO}) = 1$, $h(\text{CHE}) = 2$, *etc.*

One important application of the counting sort is *multidimensional sorting*. For example, suppose the registrar at the university with 5000 undergraduates wants the student records sorted first according to major field of study, then second by the categorization of year of graduation, and third by the categorization of home state or country. Since the counting sort is stable, it can be applied to all three stages, but in reverse order: first by state, second by year, and third by major.

This method of multidimensional sorting by applying the counting sort to each categorization in reverse order also works on a single sequence of d-digit strings, if we regard each string as a point in d-dimensional space. This algorithm is called the radix sort.

15.11 The Radix Sort

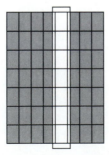

Our last sorting algorithm is another $\Theta(n)$ sort. So, according to Formula 15.5 on page 449, it, too, must do its job by some mechanism other than comparing the keys. In fact, it amounts to a multidimensional application of the counting sort, as mentioned in the last section.

The *radix sort* (Algorithm 15.10) assumes that all the keys are strings of the same length d and that all the characters in the strings range over the set of integers $\{0, 1, ..., r-1\}$. The constant r is called the *radix* of the strings. Here are some examples:

1. U.S. Social Security numbers (*e.g.*, 055-36-8161): $d = 9$ and $r = 10$.

2. Vehicle identification numbers (*e.g.*, 1HGCG1659YA065987): $d = 17$ and $r = 36$.

3. Books by their ISBNs (*e.g.*, 3-89028-941-X): $d = 10$ and $r = 11$.

4. Airport codes (*e.g.*, RIC): $d = 3$, $r = 26$.

▲ **ALGORITHM 15.10: The Radix Sort**

Input: a sequence of d-digit strings of characters of radix r.
Postcondition: the sequence is in ascending order.

1. Do step 2 for each digit j, starting with the least significant $j = 0$.

2. Apply the counting sort, keying on digit j.

Each of the d passes runs the counting sort on n keys in $\Theta(n)$ time, Thus, we have the complete algorithms runs in $\Theta(dn)$ time, and d is constant. Thus, we have:

◆ **FORMULA 15.11: Radix Sort**

The radix sort runs in linear time in the average case.

▼ **EXAMPLE 15.10: Tracing the Radix Sort**

Apply the radix sort to the six keys $\{27586, 47913, 40916, 27983, 40583, 20513\}$. Here, $n = 6$, $d = 5$, and $r = 10$. So the algorithm makes six passes through the set of 6 keys:

On the first pass, it applies the counting sort to the left-most digit (zeros digit): There are four 3s and two 6s, so the keys with the 3s are shifted up above the others. On the second pass, the keys are sorted on their tens digit: there are three 1s and three 8s, so the keys with the 1s are shifted up above the others. Notice now that the two left most digits are sorted: 13, 13, 16, 83, 83, 86. On the third pass, the keys are sorted on their hundreds digit: There are three 5s and three 9s, so the keys with the 5s are shifted up above the others. Now, the three leftmost digits (highlighted in white) are sorted: 513, 583, 586, 913, 916, 983.

On each pass, one more column is added to the sorted part of the strings. After the last pass, the keys are completely sorted. This is illustrated in Figure 15.15.

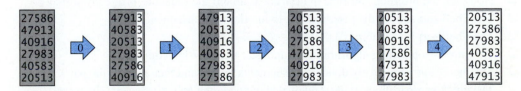

FIGURE 15.15 The Radix Sort.

15.12 The `java.util.Arrays.sort()` Method

We conclude the chapter with a brief description of how the sorting methods defined in the Java class libraries work.

The `java.util` package includes a class named `Arrays`, which contains several **static** utility methods for processing arrays. It includes a `sort()` method for an array of each of the primitive types except **boolean**, and another for arrays of elements of type `Object`. The `Arrays.sort()` method for arrays of primitive types uses a modified quick sort, and the version for arrays of `Objects` uses a modified Merge Sort.

As a recursive algorithm, the quick sort becomes rather inefficient when the recursive calls get down to small subarrays. The algorithm runs faster if the recursive calls to sort the subarrays switch to a nonrecursive algorithm when the length falls below a certain threshold. The `java.util.Arrays.sort()` method for primitive types sets this threshold at 7. For subarrays smaller than 7, it calls the Insertion Sort.

Another acceleration technique used is to make a more "robust" choice of the pivot element. Instead of setting the pivot to be the first element of each subarray, the `java.util.Arrays.sort()` method chooses the median of the first, the last, and the middle elements. This will run faster for arrays that are nearly sorted, either in ascending or in descending order. It makes the degenerative worst-case time of $\Theta(n^2)$ time less likely to occur.

The `Arrays` class methods for sorting `Objects` uses a modified version of the Merge Sort. For the same reason as mentioned earlier, the methods switch to the insertion sort when the segments are shorter than the threshold number 7. They also implement a mechanism for avoiding unnecessary merging. The call to merge checks whether the last element of the first segment is greater than the first element of the second segment. If not, then instead of a linear time merge, it simply performs a constant time concatenation.

CHAPTER SUMMARY

❑ Sequences are sorted so that they can be searched in logarithmic time.

❑ The bubble sort swaps adjacent elements, gradually "bubbling" the larger ones up.

❑ The selection sort selects the largest among the unsorted elements and moves it into its correct position.

❑ The insertion sort inserts each element among the unsorted elements below it.

❑   The bubble, selection and algorithms run in $\Theta(n^2)$ time, insertion sort on average.

❑ However, the insertion sort runs in near linear time if the sequence is already sorted.

❑ The Shell sort applies the insertion sort to interleaved subsequences.

❑ The Shell sort runs in $O(n^{1.5})$ time.

❑ No comparison sorting algorithm can run faster than $\Theta(n \lg n)$ time.

❑ The merge sort recursively divides the segments in half and then merges the pairs.

❑ The quick sort partitions about a pivot element and then recursively sorts the parts.

❑ The heap sort uses the Heapify algorithm to accelerate the Selection Sort.

- ❏ The merge, quick and heap sort algorithms run in $\Theta(n \lg n)$ time, on average.
- ❏ However, the quick sort degrades to $\Theta(n^2)$ time if the sequence is already nearly sorted.
- ❏ The bucket sort distributes the n elements among n buckets and then concatenates.
- ❏ The counting sort shifts equal keys into their positions determined by a tally.
- ❏ The radix sort applies the counting sort to each digit place in the key strings.
- ❏ Those three algorithms run in $\Theta(n)$ time, but the carry substantial overhead.
- ❏ Those three linear sorts also have restrictions on they type of arrays they sort.
- ❏ The `java.util.Arrays` class includes `sort()` methods that implement improved versions of the quick sort and merge sort.

REVIEW QUESTIONS

15.1   Why is the bubble sort so slow?

15.2   We say that an algorithm is *insensitive to input* if its running time is independent of the initial state of its input. For sorting algorithms, that means that the run time depends only on the number of elements to be sorted, not on their initial arrangement. Which sorting algorithms are insensitive to input?

15.3   The insertion sort runs in linear time in the best case and quadratic time in the worst case. What is the best case, and what is the worst case?

15.4   Why are the O(n) sorting algorithms (bucket sort, counting sort, and radix sort) usually slower than the O($n \lg n$) sorting algorithms (merge sort, quick sort, and heap sort)?

15.5   Which sorting algorithms use the divide-and-conquer strategy?

15.6   Which sorting algorithms work as well on linked lists as on arrays?

15.7   Which sorting algorithms have a different worst-case complexity than their average case?

15.8   Which sorting algorithms have a different best-case complexity than their average case?

15.9   Why is the nonrecursive version of a recursive sorting algorithm usually more efficient?

EXERCISES

15.1   Trace the indicated sorting algorithm on the sequence {'C', 'O', 'M', 'P', 'U', 'T', 'E', 'R'}:

    a. bubble sort

    b. selection sort

    c. insertion sort

    d. Shell sort

    e. merge sort

    f. quick sort

    g. heap sort

    h. bucket sort

    i. radix sort

15.2   Trace the indicated sorting algorithm on the sequence {'B', 'I', 'G', 'C', 'O', 'M', 'P', 'U', 'T', 'E', 'R', 'S'}:

    a. bubble sort

    b. selection sort

    c. insertion sort

    d. Shell sort

    e. merge sort

    f. quick sort

    g. heap sort

    h. bucket sort

    i. radix sort

15.3   Trace the indicated sorting algorithm on the sequence {77, 44, 22, 88, 99, 55, 33, 66}:

    a. bubble sort

    b. selection sort

    c. insertion sort

    d. Shell sort

    e. merge sort

    f. quick sort

    g. heap sort

    h. bucket sort

    i. radix sort

15.4   Trace the indicated sorting algorithm on the sequence {66, 88, 33, 55, 99, 44, 22, 77}:

    a. bubble sort

    b. selection sort

    c. insertion sort

    d. Shell sort

    e. merge sort

    f. quick sort

    g. heap sort

    h. bucket sort

    i. radix sort

15.5   Trace the indicated sorting algorithms on the sequence {22, 44, 66, 88, 33, 55, 77, 99}:

    a. bubble sort

    b. selection sort

    c. insertion sort

    d. Shell sort

    e. merge sort

    f. quick sort

    g. heap sort

    h. bucket sort

    i. radix sort

15.6   Trace the indicated sorting algorithms on the sequence {99, 88, 77, 66, 55, 44, 33, 22}:

    a. bubble sort

    b. selection sort

    c. insertion sort

    d. Shell sort

    e. merge sort

    f. quick sort

    g. heap sort

    h. bucket sort

    i. radix sort

15.7   Trace the indicated sorting algorithms on the sequence {0, 1, 0, 0, 1, 1, 0, 1, 0, 0,1,1,1,1.1,0}:

    a. selection sort

    b. insertion sort

    c. merge sort

    d. quick sort

    e. counting sort

15.8   Trace the indicated sorting algorithms on the sequence {"US", "CA", "CN", "US", "GB", "JA", "FR", "CN", "US", "DE", "JA", "GB", "US", "CN", "US", "IT", "AU", "ES", "US", "US"}:

    a. selection sort

    b. insertion sort

    c. merge sort

    d. quick sort

    e. counting sort

15.9   If a computer takes 5 ms to run the selection sort on an array of size 10,000 integers, how long would you expect it to take to run on an array of:

    a. 20,000 integers?
    b. 40,000 integers?
    c. 80,000 integers?
    d. 160,000 integers?

15.10   If a computer takes 3 ms to run the merge sort on an array of 200 integers, how long would you expect it to take to run on an array of size:

    a. 40,000 integers?
    b. 8,000,000 integers?

15.11   If a computer takes 7 ms to run the radix sort on an array of 1,000 20-character names, how long would you expect it to take to run on an array of:

    a. 2,000 20-character names?
    b. 4,000 20-character names?
    c. 8,000 20-character names?
    d. 16,000 20-character names?

15.12   Draw a diagram like the one in Trace 15.1 that traces the execution of the merge sort on the array in Exercise 15.1.

15.13   Use Mathematical Induction to verify the loop invariant at line 5 in Listing 15.3 on page 441.

15.14   Use Mathematical Induction to verify the loop invariant at line 8 in Listing 15.3 on page 441.

15.15   Modify the bubble sort so that it sorts the array in decreasing order.

15.16   Modify the bubble sort so that it terminates as soon as the array is sorted. Then determine how this improvement affects the efficiency of the bubble sort in the best case and in the worst case.

15.17   Modify the selection sort (Algorithm 15.2 on page 442) so that it uses the smallest element of $\{s_i...s_{n-1}\}$ in Step 2.

15.18   Modify the selection sort so that it sorts an external file that has one name on each line.

15.19   Modify the insertion sort so that it sorts the array indirectly. This requires a separate *index array* whose values are the indexes of the actual data elements. The indirect sort rearranges the index array, leaving the data array unchanged.

15.20   Modify the merge sort so that it sorts a linked list.

15.21   Modify the quick sort so that it sorts only a subarray:

```
public void sort(int[] a, int p, int n)
   // PRECONDITIONS: 0 <= p < p+n <= a.length;
   // POSTCONDITION: a[p] <= a[p+1] <= ... <= a[n-1];
```

15.22 For each step in the heap sort trace in Figure 15.11 on page 461, mark which line of the code in the Figure 15.11 on page 461 is executing, and show the current value of the index i.

15.23 Modify the shell sort algorithm (Algorithm 15.4 on page 447) so that it uses the merge sort instead of the insertion sort to sort the subsequences.

15.24 Imagine defining a subclass named `Sorter` for the following `abstract` class:

```
abstract class AbstractSorter {
  private int[] a;
  Sorter(int n) { a = new int[n]; }
  abstract void setNext(int x);    // inputs one element
  abstract int getNext();          // outputs one element
}
```

The only requirement is that the `getNext()` method outputs the element in increasing order, thereby sorting the input.

a. Which sorting algorithm is obtained if the input method `setNext()` inserts the elements in ascending order, keeping the array sorted on input, so that the `getNext()` method need only traverse the array to output the elements in order?

b. Which sorting algorithm is obtained if the input method inserts the elements in the order in which that they arrive, thereby requiring the output method to do all the sorting?

c. Which sorting algorithm is obtained if the input method partially sorts the elements as they arrive, and the output method does the rest of the work?

d. Which of the three methods of allocating the work between input and output is most efficient?

15.25 The *shaker sort* is the same as the bubble sort, except that it alternates "bubbling" up and down the array. Write the shaker sort algorithm, and determine whether it is more efficient than the straight insertion sort.

15.26 The *parity transport sort*, like the bubble sort, compares adjacent elements and swaps them if they are out of order. However, it does this only to disjoint pairs, alternating even and odd indexes on alternate passes. So for example, on the first pass, it compares s_0 with s_1, then s_2 with s_3, then s_4 with s_5, *etc.*, and on the second pass, it compares s_1 with s_2, then s_3 with s_4, then s_5 with s_6, *etc.* Write the parity transport sort algorithm, and compare its efficiency with the bubble sort.

15.27 The *exchange sort*, like the bubble sort and the selection sort, places the next largest element in its correct position on each iteration of the main loop. It does that by comparing each of the unsorted elements with s_i and swaps it with s_i whenever it is larger. Write the exchange sort algorithm, and compare its efficiency with the bubble sort and the selection sort.

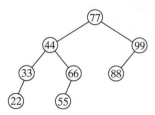

15.28   The *binary insertion sort* is the same as the straight insertion sort, except that it uses the binary search algorithm to do Step 3 in Algorithm 15.4 on page 447. Write the binary insertion sort algorithm, and explain why it is more efficient than the straight insertion sort.

15.29   The *binary tree sort* is similar to the heap sort, except that it uses a binary search tree instead of a heap data structure. It inserts the elements into the binary search tree and then uses the inorder traversal algorithm to copy them back into the array. Write the binary tree sort algorithm, and compare its efficiency with the heap sort.

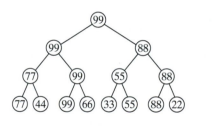
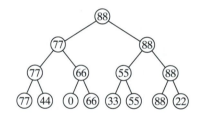

15.30   The *exhaustion sort* checks each permutation of the elements until it finds the right one. What is the complexity of this algorithm?

15.31   The *tournament sort* uses ideas from the selection sort and the heap sort. It sets up a complete binary tree and copies the *n* keys from the given array a[] to its leaves. Then it proceeds like a sports elimination tournament, copying the larger of each pair of sibling element into their parent node until the largest is copied into the root. Then it copies that largest element back to a[n-1], and replaces each occurrence of it in the tree with the smallest possible value (*e.g.*, 0, or Integer.MIN_VALUE). Then it repeats that same process for each of the other *n*−1 elements, copying each back into the array at its correct position. Write the tournament sort algorithm, and compare its efficiency with the bubble sort and the selection sort algorithms.

15.32   A sorting algorithm is said to be *stable* if it leaves the relative positions of equal keys unchanged. We have seen that the counting sort is stable. Determine which of the other 10 sorting algorithms are stable.

15.33   A sorting algorithm is said to be *parallelizable* if it can be modified to be more efficient by doing some of its tasks simultaneously. Determine which of the sorting algorithms in this chapter are parallelizable. Describe how those that are might be modified.

15.34 Two students write programs to test the speed of the quick sort. Both programs print the time that it takes to sort an array of 100,000 random integers. The only difference between the programs is that Ann's program loads the array with random three-digit integers, while Bob's uses five-digit integers. One of the programs runs as expected, while the other crashes with a system stack overflow. Which program fails, and why?

15.35 Verify Formula 15.2 on page 443.

PROGRAMMING PROBLEMS

15.1 Modify and test the program in Listing 15.2 on page 440 so that it calls the `print()` method after each call to `swap()`. This should produce the trace shown in Example 15.1 on page 439

15.2 Modify and test the program in Listing 15.2 on page 440 so that the inner j loop is handled by a separate method:

```
void bubble(int[] a, int i)
// moves the maximum elemenet of a[0...i] into a[i];
```

15.3 Modify and test the program in Listing 15.2 on page 440 so that the inner loop of the bubble sort is performed by a separate method:

```
void bubbleUp(int[] a, int i)
// moves max{a[0...i]} into a[i];
```

(Lines 3–4 in Listing 15.1 on page 439 are replaced by the call `bubbleUp(a,i)`).

15.4 Modify and test the program in Listing 15.2 on page 440 so that, instead of printing the array, it verifies the sort by calling this predicate method:

```
public boolean isSorted(int[] a)
```

15.5 Modify and test the program in Listing 15.2 on page 440 so that it tests the bubble sort on an array of 64,000 random integers. Use the `java.util.Random` class to create a random number generator, like this:

```
java.util.Random random = new java.util.Random();
```

Then you can use that object to produce random 5-digit integers like this:

```
a[i] = random.nextInt(100000);
```

15.6 Write and test a smart bubble sort algorithm that works the same way as Algorithm 15.1 on page 438, except that it detects when the elements are all sorted. Use an extra `boolean` variable that is initialized to `true` at the beginning of the inner j loop and then is reset to `false` whenever a swap is made. If it is still `true` at the end of the inner loop, then the array is sorted and the method can `return`.

15.7   Modify and test your program from Problem 15.5 on page 475 so that it compares the actual run times of the bubble sort in Listing 15.1 on page 439 and your improved algorithm from Problem 15.6.

15.8   Modify and test the program in Listing 15.2 on page 440 so that it implements the bubble sort recursively.

15.9   Modify and test the program in Listing 15.3 on page 441, replacing each of the loop invariants with code that will throw an appropriate exception if the invariant is false.

15.10   Implement and test the selection sort. Include loop invariant similar to those in Listing 15.3 on page 441.

15.11   Modify and test the method in Listing 15.4 on page 442 so that the body of the main loop (lines 3–6) is performed by a separate method:

```
void select(int[] a, int i)
// moves max{a[0...i]} into a[i];
```

15.12   Modify and test the method in Listing 15.4 on page 442 so that it implements the Selection Sort recursively.

15.13   Modify and test the method in Listing 15.5 on page 444 so that the body of the main loop (lines 3–6) is performed by a separate method:

```
void insert(int[] a, int i)
// inserts a[i] into a[0...i] leaving it in ascending order;
```

15.14   Modify and test the method in Listing 15.5 on page 444 so that it implements the Insertion Sort recursively.

15.15   Test the merge sort (Listing 15.8 on page 451) on arrays of random integers of sizes 10 through 20.

15.16   For each of the sorting algorithms a–c, modify the source code so that the method sorts only a subarray from a[p] to a[q-1]:

```
void sort(int[] a, int p, int q)
// Postcondition: a[p] <= a[p+1] <= ... <= a[q-1]
```

   a. Bubble Sort (Listing 15.1 on page 439)

   b. Selection Sort (Listing 15.4 on page 442)

   c. Insertion Sort (Listing 15.5 on page 444)

15.17   Implement the following abstract class to testing the sorting algorithms:

```
abstract class AbstractTester {
   private int[] a;
   private java.util.Random random;
   AbstractTester();              // initializes a[] and random
   public void randomize();       // randomly permutes a[]
   public void reverse();         // reverses the order of a[]
   public void sort();            // sorts a[]
   public boolean isSorted();
```

Have the constructor generate an array of 100 integers that are randomly distributed in the range 100...999.

PROJECTS

15.1   Implement the following **abstract** class for testing the sorting algorithms:

```
public abstract class SortTester {
    private int[] a;
    private java.util.Random random;
    AbstractTester();          // initializes a[] and random
    public boolean isSorted() { /*  ADD CODE HERE  */ }
    public void randomize() { /*  ADD CODE HERE  */ }
    public void reverse() { /*  ADD CODE HERE  */ }
    public abstract void sort();
```

The constructor should instantiate the array `a[]` and the object `random`, and then it should initialize `a[]` with 100 integers that are randomly distributed in the range 100...999. The `isSorted()` method should return `true` if and only if the elements of `a[]` are sorted in nondecreasing order. The `randomize()` method should randomly permute the elements of `a[]`. The `reverse()` method should swap `a[0]` with `a[99]`, `a[1]` with `a[98]`, *etc*. Finally, implement subclasses for each sorting algorithm. For example:

```
class MergeSortTester extends SortTester {
    public void sort() { /*  ADD Merge Sort CODE HERE  */ }
}
```

15.2   Write a program that performs a statistical analysis of the running times of the $O(n^2)$ and $O(n \lg n)$ sorting algorithms. Run each algorithm 10 times on randomly generated arrays and report the average running time t for each. Do this for arrays of size n equal to 10,000, 20,000, 40,000, 80,000, 160,000, 320,000, and 640,000. For the $O(n^2)$ algorithms, print the values of n^2/t. For the $O(n \lg n)$ algorithms, print the values of $(n \lg n)/t$. These ratios should be nearly constant for the larger values of n.

15.3   Repeat Project 15.2, but measure efficiency by counting comparisons made instead of time elapsed. Under what circumstances would you think that this is a better way to measure the efficiency of algorithms?

15.4   For small sequences, the merge sort becomes inefficient due to the overhead of copying the arrays into temporary arrays. So it can be accelerated by applying the Insertion Sort when the array size reaches a certain minimum threshold size. Write a program that allows you empirically to determine that threshold size.

15.5   Do Project 15.4 for the quick sort instead of the merge sort.

15.6   Implement the following interface:

```
public interface Permutation
{ Permutation(int n);
    int[] next();
}
```

The constructor creates a `Permutation` object that can generate permutations on the integers 0, 1, ..., $n-1$. The `next()` method returns a permutation of those n integers, and $n!$ calls to that function will cycle through all n! permutations.

15.7   Perform an empirical study to compare the performance of the quick sort using these different versions of its `partition()` method:

a. Pivot about the middle element in the array;

b. Pivot about the last element in the array;

c. Pivot about the median of the three elements `a[lo]`, `a[mid]`, and `a[hi]`;

d. Select the pivot at random.

Use randomly generated test arrays.

15.8   Perform an empirical study of the skip-subsequence increment for the Shell Sort. Compare running times for the following skip sequences:

a. $(2*d + 1)$: 1, 3, 7, 15, 31, 63, 127, ...;

b. $(3*d + 1)$: 1, 4, 13, 40, 121, ...;

c. $(5*d + 1)$: 1, 6, 31, 156, ...;

d. 1, 3, 7, 21, 48, 112, 336, 861, 1968, 4592, 13776, 33936, 86961, 198768;

The sequence in **d** is described in of [**Knuth3**].[3]

ANSWERS TO REVIEW QUESTIONS

15.1   The bubble sort is so slow because it never moves an element more than one position at a time.

15.2   The bubble sort, selection sort, merge sort, counting sort, and radix sort are insensitive to input.

15.3   The best case for the insertion sort is when the array is already sorted in ascending order. The worst case is when the array is in descending order.

15.4   The $O(n)$ sorting algorithms (bucket sort, counting sort, and radix sort) are slower than the $O(n \lg n)$ sorting algorithms because of the substantial overhead they incur in creating many buckets, repeating the counting sort for d places.

15.5   The merge sort and the quick sort use the divide-and-conquer strategy.

15.6   The bubble sort, the insertion sort, and the merge sort work well on linked lists.

15.7   All of these algorithms except the bubble sort and the merge sort are slower in the worst case.

15.8   The insertion sort and the quick sort have different best case complexity classes.

15.9   Recursion is usually slower because it carries the overhead of repeated method calls.

---

[3] He reports that Janet Incerpi and Robert Sedgewick [*J. Comp Sci.* **31** (1985), 210–224; see also *Lecture Notes in Comp. Sci.* **1136** (1996), 1–11] found that with this sequence, the Shell sort runs in time $O(c^{\sqrt{\ln n}})$, where $c = e^{\sqrt{8 \ln 2.5}} = 14.9911114$.

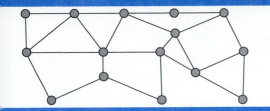

Chapter 16

Graphs

Many storage problems can be solved using the simple linear data structures described in Chapters 3–7: arrays, stacks, queues, and lists. More complex problems require the nonlinear tree structures described in Chapters 10–12. But even those are inadequate for some problems. For example, consider a communication network such as the Internet or a transportation network such as a highway or rail system. Such structures are called *graphs*, which are the topic of this last chapter.

16.1 Graphs

Intuitively, a graph is a structure that consists of disjoint nodes connected by links. Mathematically, the nodes are called *vertices* and the links are called *edges*. For example, the graph in Figure 16.1 has eight vertices and nine edges. The vertices represent the United Kingdom, Sweden, France, Germany, the Czech Republic, Austria, Switzerland, and Italy. The edges represent the high speed (10 gigabytes/second) Internet connections among main cities in these countries. This part of the Internet is called a *backbone* because the slower parts emanate from it.

A graph is also called a *topology* because the geometric locations of the nodes are not important. For example, the essential features of the European Internet backbone shown in Figure 16.1 can be represented more simply by the equivalent graph shown in Figure 16.2. The first graph is drawn to scale, but that scale is irrelevant to the Internet. This, of course, is the essence of mathematics: to disregard all the inessential features of the problem, abstracting it so that its analysis can be applied to all problems that are essentially equivalent.

Formally, a *graph* is a pair $G = (V, E)$, where V and E are sets and every element of E is a two-element subset of V.[1] The elements of V are called *vertices*, and the elements of E are called *edges*. For the graph in Figure 16.1, $V = \{UK, SE, FR, DE, CZ, AT, CH, IT\}$ and $E = \{e_1, e_2, e_3, e_4, e_5, e_6, e_7, e_8, e_9\}$, where each e_i is a two-element subset of V. For example, $e_1 = \{UK, SE\}$, representing the

---

[1] Technically, this defines a *simple graph*, because it precludes loop edges that link a vertex to itself and multiple edges linking the same pair of vertices.

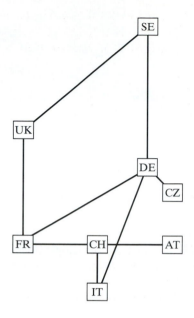

FIGURE 16.1 European Internet Topology.

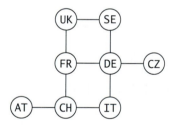

FIGURE 16.2 An Equivalent Graph.

connection between the United Kingdom and Sweden. Two vertices are said to be *adjacent* if there is an edge connecting them.

The *size* of a graph is the number of its vertices. The graph in Figure 16.1 has size 8.

If $G = (V, E)$ is a graph and $G' = (V', E')$ where $V' \subseteq V$ and $E' \subseteq E$, then G' is a *subgraph* of G. For example, the graph G' in Figure 16.3 is a subgraph of the graph G. One vertex and four edges have been removed.

Note that every graph is a subgraph of itself.

A *path from vertex v_0 to vertex v_k* is a sequence of vertices $(v_0, v_1, v_2, ..., v_k)$, where each consecutive pair is connected by an edge: $\{v_{i-1}v_i\} \in E$ for $i = 1, 2, ..., k$. The *length* of a path is the number k of edges. For example, in the graph in Figure 16.2, $p_1 = $ (SE, UK, FR, DE, CZ) is a path of length 4, and $p_2 = $ (AT, CH, IT, DE, SE, UK, FR, DE, CZ) is a path of length 8.

A path p is *simple* if all of its vertices are distinct. Of the two paths mentioned previously, p_1 is a simple path, but p_2 is not because it includes the vertex DE twice.

When a path $(v_0, v_1, v_2, ..., v_k)$ exists, we say that vertex v_k is *reachable* from vertex v_0. A graph is *connected* if when vertex is reachable from every other vertex. The graph in Figure 16.2 on page 480 is connected. But the graph G' in Figure 16.3 is not connected because its left-most vertex is not reachable from any of the other vertices.

A *connected component* G' of a graph G is a maximal connected subgraph. That means that G' is a nonempty subgraph of G, but no other subgraph G'' of G that contains G' is connected. In other words, if any more vertices or edges of G were added to G', it would be disconnected. The graph shown in Figure 16.4 has four components; their sizes are 5, 1, 2, and 4.

A *cycle* is a path from a node back to itself. A *simple cycle* is a cycle in which only the end vertices coincide. For example, in the graph in Figure 16.2 on page 480, p_3 = (SE, UK, FR, DE, CZ, SE) and p_4 = (CH, IT, DE, CZ, DE, FR, CH) are both cycles, but only p_3 is simple.

A graph is *acyclic* if it has no cycles. For example, the disconnected graph G' in Figure 16.3 on page 481 is acyclic.

A connected acyclic graph is called a *free tree*. For example, the graph Figure 16.5 is a free tree that represents the chemical compound ethanol.

The trees that we studied in Chapter 10 are called *rooted trees* to distinguish them from free trees. Mathematically, the only difference is that a rooted tree has a unique vertex that is designated as its root. Thus, we see that trees are special kinds of graphs.

G G'

FIGURE 16.3   Graph G with subgraph G'.

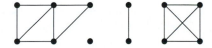

FIGURE 16.4   A Graph with 4 Components.

$$H \quad\quad H$$
$$| \quad\quad |$$
$$H\text{——}C\text{——}C\text{——}O\text{——}H$$
$$| \quad\quad |$$
$$H \quad\quad H$$

FIGURE 16.5   A Free Tree Representing Ethanol.

16.2 The Adjacency Matrix Implementation

There are two common methods used to store a graph: an adjacency matrix, and an adjacency list. The adjacency matrix method is simpler, so we examine that first.

An *adjacency matrix* for a graph is a two-dimensional array of `boolean` elements (see Figure 16.6). It has one row and one column for each vertex in the graph. Its `boolean` entry at row i and column j is `true` if vertex v_i is adjacent to vertex v_j, and `false` otherwise.
Note that the number of entries that are `true` is 12, twice the number of edges in the graph. That is because each edge is counted twice: If v is adjacent to w, then w is also adjacent to v. Note also that, for the same reason, the matrix is symmetric about its main diagonal.

Instead of an array of type `boolean`, we could use an integer array, storing 1 for `true` and 0 for `false`. This is an equivalent form of the adjacency matrix. It may be a little less efficient than the boolean array,[2] but it generalizes easily for weighted graphs. (See Section 16.7 on page 492.)

	A	B	C	D	E
A	0	1	1	0	0
B	1	0	1	1	0
C	1	1	0	1	0
D	0	1	1	0	1
E	0	0	0	1	0

The Java implementation in Listing 16.1 shows how a graph can be stored with an adjacency matrix. It uses the one-dimensional array `vertices[]` to store the vertex labels as strings, and the two-dimensional array `a[][]` to store the edges. The constructor at line 6 loads the vertex array with a given string array `args[]` after assigning its size to the `size` field. Then allocates the adjacency matrix `a[][]` as an *n*-by-*n* array, where $n = $ `size`, the number of vertices.

This implementation requires the size of the graph (the number of vertices) to be known when the graph is constructed, but then allows the edges to be added later by means of the `add()` method. That method (at line 13) takes two vertex labels, v and w, as arguments and then adds the edge{v,w} to the graph by setting the corresponding adjacency matrix elements to `true` (at line 15). To do that, it has to find the array index numbers i and j for the given vertices, v and w. This is done by a separate `index()` method at line 26. That method performs a sequential search through the `vertices[]` array to locate the given vertex.

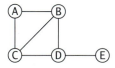

	A	B	C	D	E
A	false	true	true	false	false
B	true	false	true	true	false
C	true	true	false	true	false
D	false	true	true	false	true
E	false	false	false	true	false

FIGURE 16.6   A Graph and Its Adjacency Matrix.

---

[2] An `int` uses four bytes, while a `boolean` uses only one.

LISTING 16.1: **Storing a Graph with an Adjacency Matrix**

```
1   class Graph {
2     int size;
3     String[] vertices;
4     boolean[][] a;   // adjacency matrix
5
6     public Graph(String[] args) {
7       size = args.length;
8       vertices = new String[size];
9       System.arraycopy(args, 0, vertices, 0, size);
10      a = new boolean[size][size];
11    }
12
13    public void add(String v, String w) {
14      int i = index(v), j = index(w);
15      a[i][j] = a[j][i] = true;
16    }
17
18    public String toString() {
19      if (size == 0) return "{}";
20      StringBuffer buf = new StringBuffer("{" + vertex(0));
21      for (int i = 1; i < size; i++)
22        buf.append("," + vertex(i));
23      return buf + "}";
24    }
25
26    private int index(String v) {
27      for (int i = 0; i < size; i++)
28        if (vertices[i].equals(v)) return i;
29      return a.length;
30    }
31
32    private String vertex(int i) {
33      StringBuffer buf = new StringBuffer(vertices[i] + ":");
34      for (int j = 0; j < size; j++)
35        if (a[i][j]) buf.append(vertices[j]);
36      return buf + "";
37    }
38  }
```

Note that the add() method takes $O(2n)$ steps, since it has to perform a sequential search twice. For large graphs (*e.g.*, $n > 1000$), it would be prudent to modify the class so that its constructor stores the vertex labels in alphanumeric order and then implements the index() method with a binary search. (See Programming Problem 16.1 on page 504.) This reduces the complexity of the add() method to $\Theta(\lg n)$.

The adjacency matrix implementation in Listing 16.1 includes a toString() method that returns a string representation of the graph. For example, the graph shown in Figure 16.6 on page 482 would be represented by the string {A:BC,B:ACD,C:ABD,D:BCE,E:D}. This lists each vertex, followed by a list of the vertices to which it is adjacent: A is adjacent to B and C; B is adjacent to A, C, and D; *etc.*

The `toString()` method uses an auxiliary `vertex()` method to build its string representation. For each index *i*, this auxiliary method returns the corresponding vertex label followed by a list of all the adjacent vertices. That list is read directly from row *i* of the adjacency matrix `a[][]`: A vertex *j* is adjacent if and only if `a[i][j]` is `true`.

Listing 16.2 presents a little test driver for the `Graph` class.

LISTING 16.2: Testing the Graph Class

```
1   class TestGraph {
2     public static void main(String[] args) {
3       Graph g = new Graph(new String[]{"A", "B", "C", "D", "E"});
4       System.out.println(g);
5       g.add("A", "B");
6       g.add("A", "C");
7       g.add("B", "C");
8       g.add("B", "D");
9       g.add("C", "D");
10      g.add("D", "E");
11      System.out.println(g);
12    }
13  }
```

The output is

```
{A:,B:,C:,D:,E:}
{A:BC,B:ACD,C:ABD,D:BCE,E:D}
```

The graph g created at line 3 is the same graph as that shown in Figure 16.6 on page 482. It passes an anonymous `String` array containing the five vertex labels to the `Graph()` constructor. The first line of output, produced by the call to the `toString()` method at line 4, shows a graph with five vertices and no edges. After adding the six edges at lines 5-10, the output shows the resulting graph on the second line of output.

16.3 The Adjacency List Implementation

An *adjacency list* for a graph is an array of linked lists, one list for each vertex. The list for a vertex *v* contains one node for each vertex that is adjacent to *v*. Figure 16.7 shows the adjacency list for the graph in Figure 16.6. It is an array `a[]` of five lists. Each element contains the name of a vertex *v* and a linked list of nodes that correspond to the vertices that are adjacent to *v*. For example, `a[0]` contains the name A and a list of two nodes that contain the array indexes of nodes C and B, the two neighbors of A.

Note that the total number of nodes in the adjacency list is 12, twice the number of edges in the graph. That is the same as the number of `true` entries in the adjacency matrix: one for each edge *incidence*. Each edge is incident upon two vertices.

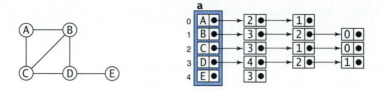

FIGURE 16.7 A Graph and Its Adjacency List.

LISTING 16.3: **Storing a Graph with an Adjacency List**

```
1   class Graph {
2     int size;
3     List[] a;   // adjacency list
4
5     public Graph(String[] args) {
6       size = args.length;
7       a = new List[size];
8       for (int i=0; i<size; i++)
9         a[i] = new List(args[i]);
10    }
11
12    public void add(String v, String w) {
13      a[index(v)].add(index(w));
14      a[index(w)].add(index(v));
15    }
16
17    public String toString() {
18      if (size == 0) return "{}";
19      StringBuffer buf = new StringBuffer("{" + a[0]);
20      for (int i = 1; i < size; i++)
21        buf.append("," + a[i]);
22      return buf + "}";
23    }
24
25    private int index(String v) {
26      for (int i = 0; i < size; i++)
27        if (a[i].vertex.equals(v)) return i;
28      return a.length;
29    }
30
31    private class List {
32      String vertex;
33      Node edges;
34
35      List(String vertex) {
36        this.vertex = vertex;
37      }
38
```

```
39      public void add(int j) {
40          edges = new Node(j, edges);
41      }
42
43      public String toString() {
44          StringBuffer buf = new StringBuffer(vertex);
45          if (edges != null) buf.append(":");
46          for (Node p = edges; p != null; p = p.next)
47              buf.append(Graph.this.a[p.to].vertex);
48          return buf + "";
49      }
50
51      private class Node {
52          int to;
53          Node next;
54          Node(int to, Node next) {
55              this.to = to;
56              this.next = next;
57          }
58      }
59   }
60 }
```

The adjacency list implementation in Listing 16.3 is more complex than the adjacency matrix implementation because the data structure itself is more complex. To implement an array of linked lists, we use a nested List class (line 31), which itself has a nested Node class (line 51). We can then define a[] to be an array of List objects (line 3), as shown in Figure 16.7 on page 485.

The Graph class in Listing 16.3 defines the same three operations as the Graph class in Listing 16.1 on page 483: a constructor, an add() method, and a toString() method. The constructor allocates the array a[] and uses the List constructor (line 35) to load its vertex components with the String labels passed in the args[] array.

The add() method at line 12 adds edge {v,w} to the graph if the two vertices v and w are passed to it. Like the add() method in Listing 16.1 on page 483, this also uses an index() method to obtain the a[] indexes for the two vertices v and w. For example, for the graph shown in Figure 16.6 on page 482, index("D") would return 3, since "D" is stored in a[3]. The expression

```
13      a[index(v)].add(index(w));
```

first obtains the List object a[index(v)] for the given vertex label v, and then calls add(j) on that List object, passing the index j for vertex w to the add() method that is defined in the nested List class at line 39. This in turn passes j to the Node constructor in the expression

```
40      edges = new Node(j,edges);
```

which inserts the new node at the beginning of the list.

The toString() method at line 17 also works the same was as its counterpart in the adjacency matrix implementation in Listing 16.1. At lines 19 and 21, it invokes the toString()

method of the `List` class, which adds the vertex label to the output string at line 44 and then all the adjacent vertices in the loop at line 47.[3] So, for example, the substring `D:BCE` is produced at line 48, contributing to the complete string `{A:BC,B:ACD,C:ABD,D:BCE,E:D}` that is produced at line 22.

The test driver in Listing 16.2 on page 484 produces the same output for adjacency list implementation as for the adjacency matrix implementation.

16.4 Breadth-First Search

Traversing a graph is like traversing a tree. (See Section 11.6.) Indeed, since trees are special types of graphs, any graph traversal algorithm can be specialized to a tree. But what if we try it the other way around, generalizing a tree traversal algorithm to a graph?

Imagine applying a level-order traversal (Algorithm 11.1 on page 342) to the graph in Figure 16.8, starting at vertex A. The two vertices that are adjacent to A (B and E) would be the children of A if the graph were a tree with root A. So in a level-order traversal, the first three vertices to be visited would be A, B, and E.[4] Then the children of the first child B would be visited. Who would those children be, if this graph were a tree? They would have to be adjacent to B, but also farther from the root A than B is. That would be vertices C and F. And that leaves vertex E childless. So after visiting C and F, we go to the children D and H of C, and then finally the child G of F. Thus, the level-order traversal would visit the vertices in this order: A, B, E, C, F, D, H, G.

The traversal just described is called a "greedy algorithm" because it always acts locally. At each stage in the process, it takes the most immediate, short-sighted step toward the complete solution. This is not a good strategy in real life, but it does work well as a graph traversal algorithm.

When applied to a graph, this generalization of the level-order traversal algorithm is called the *breadth-first search* (BFS). It is one of two standard methods for traversing a graph. The other method is called the depth-first search (DFS) and is considered in Section 16.6.

The most common version of this algorithm (Algorithm 16.1) uses a queue. It also assumes that each vertex has an extra `boolean` field, used to mark whether the vertex has been "visited" yet during the execution of the algorithm. Initially, each `visited` field is `false`.

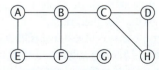

FIGURE 16.8 A Graph to Traverse.

---

[3] Note the Java construct `Graph.this.a[]`, used at line 47 to gain access to the enclosing Graph class's array field `a[]`.
[4] We will assume that the vertices are stored in the order of their labels: A, B, C, *etc.*

▲ **ALGORITHM 16.1: The Breadth-First Search (BFS) Algorithm**

Input: a graph $G = (V, E)$ and an initial vertex $v \in V$.
Output: a list L of all the vertices, in BFS order.

1. Initialize a local queue Q and an output list L of vertices.

2. Mark v visited, and add it to Q.

3. Remove x from Q and add it to L.

4. Repeat step 5 for each vertex y that is adjacent to x.

5. If y has not been visited, mark it visited and add it to Q.

6. If Q is not empty, go to step 3.

▼ **EXAMPLE 16.1: Tracing the Breadth-First Search**

Here is a trace of Algorithm 16.1 on the graph shown in Figure 16.8, starting at vertex A. The vertices are visited in the same order as described before: A, B, E, C, F, D, H, G. That is the order in which they are inserted into the output list L.

The term "breadth-first" is used because the set of visited vertices expands broadly. This is evident from Figure 16.10 on page 490, which illustrates the trace of Example 16.1. It progresses through a series of stages, each of which visits those vertices (shown in red) that are on the boundary of the set of visited vertices (shown in green). Note that the last vertices to be visited are those that are the farthest from the starting vertex A.

◆ **FORMULA 16.1: Breadth-First Search**

The BFS runs in $\Theta(m)$ time, where m is the number of edges or the number of vertices, whichever is greater.

16.5 Spanning Trees

As we saw in Chapter 10, a traversal algorithm linearizes a data structure, either implicitly, as with the tree traversals, or explicitly with a list, as in Algorithm 16.1. But the graph traversal algorithms do more. They also identify an intrinsic skeletal structure embedded within the graph. That structure is a minimal spanning tree for the graph.

A *subtree* of a graph is a subgraph that is also a tree (*i.e.*, a connected acyclic subgraph). For example, the subtree shown in Figure 16.9 is a subtree of the graph shown in Figure 16.8.

A *spanning tree* for a graph is a subtree that connects every vertex of the graph. Obviously, the graph must be connected to have a spanning tree. It is easy to see that a connected cyclic graph will have several spanning trees. The subtree shown in Figure 16.10 is a spanning tree for the graph shown in Figure 16.8.

The usefulness of a spanning tree is pretty obvious in most cases. For example, in the European Internet Topology graph shown in Figure 16.1 on page 480, a spanning tree would define a unique line of communication from any node to any other node.

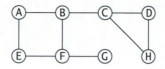

Q	x	L	y
A			
∅	A	A	B
B			E
BE			
E	B	AB	C
EC			
C	E	ABE	F
CF			
F	C	ABEC	D
FD			H
FDH			
DH	F	ABECF	G
DHG			
HG	D	ABECFD	
G	H	ABECFDH	
∅	G	ABECFDHG	

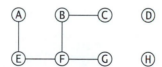

FIGURE 16.9 A Subtree.

Algorithm 16.2, a minor modification of the breadth-first search (Algorithm 16.1 on page 488,) will generate a spanning tree for any connected graph:

▲ **ALGORITHM 16.2: The BFS Spanning Tree**

Input: a graph $G = (V, E)$ and an initial vertex $v \in V$.
Output: a spanning tree T for G.

1. Initialize a local queue Q and an output tree T of vertices.
2. Mark v visited, add it to Q, and insert it as the root of T.
3. Remove x from Q.
4. For each vertex y that is adjacent to x, repeat step 5.
5. If y has not been visited, mark it visited, add it to Q, and to T as the next child of x.
6. If Q is not empty, go to step 3.

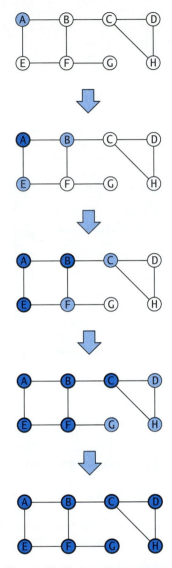

FIGURE 16.10   Breadth-First Search.

The spanning tree that results from applying Algorithm 16.2 to the graph in Figure 16.8 on page 487 is shown in Figure 16.11. It is called the *BFS spanning tree* because the algorithm actually performs a breadth-first search.

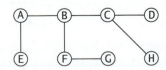

FIGURE 16.11   The BFS Spanning Tree.

16.6 The Depth-First Search

In Section 16.4, we derived the breadth-first search by applying the level-order tree traversal algorithm to a graph. What would we get if we applied the preorder traversal (Section 11.2) instead?

Starting at vertex A, the first "child" would be vertex B, its first child would be vertex C, its first child would be vertex D, and its first child would be vertex H. After that, the next vertex to visit would be the next child of the last visited parent that has any more children. That backtracks all the way back to parent B, whose next child would be vertex F. And its first child would be vertex G. Finally, vertex E would be visited as the second "child" of A. So the complete traversal visits the vertices in the order: A, B, C, D, H, F, G, E.

Now, for technical reasons, apply the same process, except as a "reverse" preorder traversal; that is, process the children of each node in reverse (right-to-left) order. This version of the traversal visits the vertices in the following order: A, E, F, G, B, C, H, D. That is exactly what happens when we apply Algorithm 16.1 on page 488, using a stack instead of a queue. It is called a *depth-first search*. (See Algorithm 16.3.)

▲ ALGORITHM 16.3: The Depth-First Search (DFS) Algorithm

Input: a graph $G = (V, E)$ and an initial vertex $v \in V$.
Output: a list L of all the vertices, in DFS order.

1. Initialize a local stack S and an output list L of vertices.
2. Mark v visited, and add it to S.
3. Remove x from S and add it to L.
4. Repeat step 5 for each vertex y that is adjacent to x.
5. If y has not been visited, mark it visited and add it to S.
6. If S is not empty, go to step 3.

▼ EXAMPLE 16.2: Tracing the Depth-First Search

Figure 16.12 shows a trace of Algorithm 16.3 on the same graph as before. The resulting output list is the same as what we got from the reverse preorder traversal just discussed: A, E, F, G, B, C, H, D.

The name "depth-first" reflects the fact that the traversal follows a single sequence of vertices as deep as it can go before backtracking to follow another sequence. This is evident in the trace in Example 16.2; the first sequence is {A, E, F, G}, followed by the sequence {B, C, H, D}.

◆ FORMULA 16.2: Depth-First Search

The DFS runs in $\Theta(m)$ time, where m is the number of edges or the number of vertices, whichever is greater.

We can make the same modification to Algorithm 16.3 that we made to Algorithm 16.1 on page 488 to obtain an algorithm that generates the *depth-first spanning tree* for a graph. The result for the trace in Exercise Figure 16.12 on page 492 is shown in Figure 16.13 on page 492.

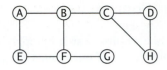

S	x	L	y
A			
Ø	A	A	B
B			E
BE			
B	E	AE	F
BF			
B	F	AEF	G
BG			
B	G	AEFG	
Ø	B	AEFGB	C
C	C	AEFGBC	D
D	F		H
DH			
D	H	AEFGBCH	
Ø	D	AEFGBCHD	

FIGURE 16.12   Depth-First Search.

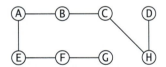

FIGURE 16.13   The DFS Spanning Tree.

Since it uses a stack, Algorithm 16.3 has a simpler recursive version, given as Algorithm 16.4.

▲ ALGORITHM 16.4: The Recursive Depth-First Search (DFS) Algorithm

Input: a graph $G = (V, E)$, an initial vertex $v \in V$.
Output: a list L of all vertices in G, in DFS order.

1. Mark v visited and add it to L.

2. Repeat step 3 for each vertex y that is adjacent to v.

3. If y has not been visited, let $L = depthFirstSearch(G, y, L)$.

16.7 Weighted Graphs

A *weighted graph* is a triple $G = (V, E, w)$, where (V, E) is a graph and $w: E \to R$ is a function that assigns a number $w(e)$ to each edge $e \in E$, called the *weight* (or *cost*, or *length*) of the edge.

If $p = (v_0, v_1, v_2, ..., v_k)$ is a path in a weighted graph, then the *weight* (or *cost*, or *length*) of the path $w(p)$ is defined to be the sum of the weights of all the edges in the path:

$$w(p) = \sum_{i=1}^{k} w(v_{i-1}v_i)$$

▼ **EXAMPLE 16.3: Air Mileages**

The weighted graph in Figure 16.14 shows the air distance in miles between several major airports in South America. The sequence $p = (EZE, LIM, BOG, CCS)$ is a flight path from Buenos Aires to Caracas via Lima and Bogota. Its length is $w(p) = w(EZE,LIM) + w(LIM,BOG) + w(BOG,CCS) = 1955 + 1168 + 636 = 3759$.

The data structures used to store weighted graphs are nearly the same as those used to store (unweighted) graphs. For the adjacency matrix implementation, the array element type is numeric (`long`, `int`, or `double`) instead of `boolean`, to hold the edge weight. (See Figure 16.15.)

Here, the infinity symbol ∞ represents the maximum value possible for the element type (e.g. `Long.MAX_VALUE` = 9,223,372,036,854,775,807).

For the adjacency list, we simply add a `weight` field to the `List.Node` class, as in Figure 16.16.

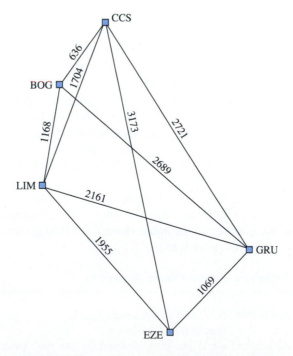

FIGURE 16.14 Air Mileage among South American Cities.

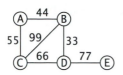

	A	B	C	D	E
A	0	44	55	∞	∞
B	44	0	99	33	∞
C	55	99	0	66	∞
D	∞	33	66	0	77
E	∞	∞	∞	77	0

FIGURE 16.15 The Adjacency matrix for a Weighted Graph.

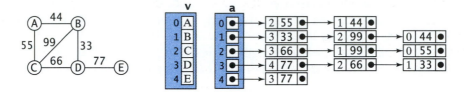

FIGURE 16.16 The Adjacency List for a Weighted Graph.

16.8 Dijkstra's Algorithm

Large weighted graphs are likely to have many comparable paths from one vertex to another. Being able to compute the shortest path is very useful. One way to do that would be to list all the paths with their lengths, and then find the minimum of that list. But that naive algorithm requires exponential time, so it is impractical except for very small graphs.

In 1959, Edsger Dijkstra discovered an algorithm that finds the shortest path from one vertex to each of the others in $O(e \lg n)$ time, where e is the number of edges and n is the number of vertices in the graph. It requires two more fields, in addition to the `boolean` `visited` field, for each vertex: a `prev` field and a `dist` field. The `prev` field points to the previous vertex in the shortest path from the start vertex, and the `dist` field holds the length of that shortest path. The algorithm also uses a priority queue (see Chapter 14) of vertices, where the highest priority is the least `dist` among them.

Dijkstra's algorithm (Algorithm 16.5) is the prototypical "greedy" algorithm. It uses a modified breadth-first search, controlled by the edges' weight function. On each iteration, it visits the next unvisited vertex x that is closest to the initial vertex v and then updates the *y.prev* and *y.dist* fields of all the vertices y that are adjacent to x.

▲ ALGORITHM 16.5: Dijkstra's Shortest Paths Algorithm

Input: a weighted graph $G = (V, E, w)$ and a start vertex $v_0 \in V$.
Output: the vertex set V with its prev and dist fields set.
Postconditions: For each vertex $v \in V$, the path defined by the *prev* pointers is the shortest path from v_0 to v, and $v.dist$ is its length.

1. Set $v.dist = \infty$ for all vertices $v \neq v_0$.[5]

2. Repeat steps 3–6 until all vertices have been visited.

3. Let x be the unvisited vertex with minimal $dist$, and mark x visited.

4. Repeat steps 5–6 for each unvisited vertex y that is adjacent to x.

5. Let $d_y = x.dist + w(x,y)$.

6. If $d_y < y.dist$, set $y.dist = d_y$ and $y.prev = x$. (A shorter path has been found.)

▼ EXAMPLE 16.4: Tracing Dijkstra's Algorithm

Figure 16.17 on page 496 shows a trace of Dijkstra's algorithm on a graph with eight vertices. On each iteration, one more vertex is marked as visited. The vertices that are still in the priority queue are shaded and vertex x is labeled. The distance fields for each vertex are shown adjacent to the vertex, and the back pointers are drawn as arrows.

On the first iteration, the highest priority vertex is $x = A$, because its distance field is 0 and all the others are infinity. Steps 7–10 iterate three times, once for each of A's neighbors $y = B$, C, and D. The values of s computed for these are $0 + 4 = 4$, $0 + 6 = 6$, and $0 + 1 = 1$. Each of these is less than the current (infinite) value of the corresponding distance field, so all three of those values are assigned and the back pointers for all three neighbors are set to point to A.

On the second iteration, the highest priority vertex among those still in the priority queue is $x = D$ with distance field 1. Steps 7–10 iterate three times again, once for each of D's unvisited neighbors $y = B$, F, and G. The values of s computed for these are $1 + 4 = 5$, $1 + 2 = 3$, and $1 + 6 = 7$. Each of these is less than the current value of the corresponding distance field, so all of those values are assigned and the back pointers are set to D. Note how this changes the distance field and point in vertex B.

On the third iteration, the highest priority vertex among those still in the priority queue is $x = F$ with distance field 3. Steps 7–10 iterate three times again, once for each of F's unvisited neighbors $y = C$, G, and H. The values of s computed for these are $3 + 1 = 4$, $3 + 3 = 6$, and $3 + 5 = 8$. Each of these is less than the current value, so all of them are assigned and the back pointers are set to F. Note how this changes the distance field and point in vertex B again.

On the fourth iteration, the highest priority vertex among those still in the priority queue is $x = B$ with distance field 4. Steps 7–10 iterate twice, for $y = C$ and E. The values of s computed for these are $4 + 3 = 7$ and $4 + 5 = 9$. The second of these is less than the current (infinite) value at E, so its distance field assigned the value 9 and its back pointer is set to B. But the s value 7 is not less than the current distance field for C, so its fields do not change.

The algorithm progresses through its remaining iterations, for $x = C$, E, G, and finally H the same way. The final result shows, for example, that the shortest path from A to E is ADFCE with length 6.

In this implementation, we have used a simple search method `closestVertex()` instead of a priority queue. This is less efficient, running in $O(n)$ time instead of the $O(\lg n)$ time that a priority queue would use. (See Project 16.2.)

---

[5] We assume that all instance fields are automatically initialized to their null states, as the Java compiler will do.

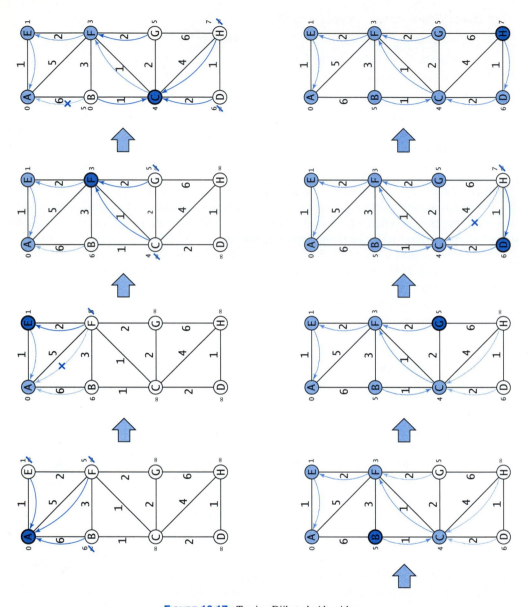

FIGURE 16.17   Tracing Dijkstra's Algorithm.

LISTING 16.4: **Dijkstra's Algorithm**

```
1   public class WeightedGraph {
2       Vertex start;
3
4       private static class Vertex {
5       private Object object;
```

```
6            Edge edges;
7            Vertex nextVertex;
8            boolean done;
9            int dist;
10           Vertex back;
11
12           Vertex(Object object) {
13               this.object = object;
14           }
15
16           public String toString() {
17               return "(" + object + ":" + edges + "\n";
18           }
19
20           void printPath() {
21               if (back == null) return;
22               back.printPath();
23               System.out.print("->" + object + "(" + dist + ")");
24           }
25       }
26
27       private static class Edge {
28           Vertex to;
29           int weight;
30           Edge nextEdge;
31
32           Edge(Vertex to, int weight, Edge nextEdge) {
33               this.to = to;
34               this.weight = weight;
35               this.nextEdge = nextEdge;
36           }
37
38           public String toString() {
39               return weight + "->" + to.object
40                             + ( nextEdge==null ? ")" : "," + nextEdge );
41           }
42       }
43
44       public WeightedGraph(String[] args) {
45           Vertex v = start = new Vertex(args[0]);
46           for (int i=1; i<args.length; i++) {
47               v = v.nextVertex = new Vertex(args[i]);
48               v.dist = Integer.MAX_VALUE;    // infinity
49           }
50       }
51
52       public void addEdge(String vString, String wString, int weight) {
53           Vertex v = find(vString);
54           Vertex w = find(wString);
55           v.edges = new Edge(w, weight, v.edges);
```

```
56                  w.edges = new Edge(v, weight, w.edges);
57          }
58
59      public void findShortestPaths() {
60          // implements Dijkstra's Algorithm:
61          for (Vertex v = start; v != null; v = closestVertex()) {
62              v.done = true;
63              for (Edge e = v.edges; e != null; e = e.nextEdge) {
64                  Vertex w = e.to;
65                  if (!w.done && v.dist+e.weight < w.dist) {
66                      w.dist = v.dist+e.weight;
67                      w.back = v;
68                  }
69              }
70          }
71      }
72
73      public void printPaths() {
74          for (Vertex v = start.nextVertex; v != null; v = v.nextVertex) {
75              System.out.print("\n" + start.object);
76              v.printPath();
77          }
78          System.out.println();
79      }
80
81      public String toString() {
82          StringBuffer buf = new StringBuffer();
83          for (Vertex v = start; v != null; v = v.nextVertex)
84              buf.append(v.toString());
85          return buf + "";
86      }
87
88      private Vertex find(Object object) {
89          // returns the vertex that contains the specified object:
90          for (Vertex v = start; v != null; v = v.nextVertex)
91              if (v.object.equals(object)) return v;
92          return null;
93      }
94
95      private Vertex closestVertex() {
96          // returns the undone vertex with smallest dist field:
97          Vertex v = null;
98          int minDist = Integer.MAX_VALUE;
99          for (Vertex w = start; w != null; w = w.nextVertex)
100             if (!w.done && w.dist < minDist) {
101                 v = w;
102                 minDist = w.dist;
103             }
104         return v;
105     }
106 }
```

Note that the `WeightedGraph` class in Listing 16.4 is incomplete. To be useful, we need other methods, such as constructors, accessor and mutator methods, and perhaps a `toString()` method. (See Project 16.1.)

16.9 Digraphs

A *digraph* (for "directed graph") is the same as a graph, except that its edges are one way. So the formal definition defines an edge as a sequence of two vertices instead of an unordered set of two vertices. The other definitions for graphs apply to digraphs the same way. In particular, a *weighted digraph* is a digraph with a weight function that assigns a number to each directed edge. A weighted digraph is also called a *network*.

Given a weighted digraph, we can imagine three other kinds of graphs embedded within it: a unweighted digraph (ignoring the weights), a weighted graph (interpreting the edges to be two way), and just the graph itself. This point of view allows us to extend algorithms defined for graphs and weighted graphs to digraphs and networks.

▼ **EXAMPLE 16.5: A Weighted Digraph and Its Embedded Structures**

Figure 16.18 shows a weighted digraph together with its embedded weighted graph, its embedded digraph, and its embedded graph. The weights are shown on the edges.

Note that the shortest path between two vertices may not be the same in the four different versions.

The data structures used to store digraphs and networks are the same as those used to store graphs and weighted graphs: adjacency matrices and adjacency lists. The only differences are that with a digraph, the adjacency matrix need not be symmetric, and the adjacency list uses only one list node per edge instead of two. This can be seen from the examples illustrated in Figure 16.19. The graph has six directed edges, so its adjacency matrix has only six positive finite entries, and its adjacency list has only six nodes.

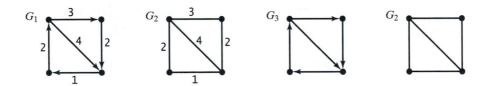

FIGURE 16.18 The Embedded Structures within a Weighted Digraph.

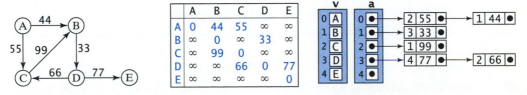

FIGURE 16.19 The Adjacency Matrix and Adjacency List for a Weighted Digraph.

CHAPTER SUMMARY

- ❏ A *graph* is a set of vertices together with a set of edges between them.
- ❏ A *path* in a graph is a sequence of adjacent vertices.
- ❏ The *length* of a path is the number of edges that it spans.
- ❏ A graph is *connected* if every vertex has a path to every other vertex.
- ❏ A *cycle* is a path that ends at the same vertex where it begins.
- ❏ A graph is *acyclic* if it contains no cycles.
- ❏ An *adjacency matrix* for a graph is a two-dimensional matrix that has one row and one column for each vertex and whose entry a_{ij} is 1 or 0 according to whether there is an edge from vertex i to vertex j or not.
- ❏ An *adjacency list* is an array of linked lists, one for each vertex. List i includes a node that references vertex j if and only if there is an edge from vertex i to vertex j.
- ❏ The *Breadth-First Search* (*BFS*) traverses a graph by visiting the neighbors of the start vertex, then visiting its neighbors, and so on. It uses a queue.
- ❏ The *Depth-First Search* (*DFS*) traverses a graph by sequentially visiting one vertex after another until it has to backtrack to find unvisited vertices. It uses recursion or a queue.
- ❏ A *spanning tree* for a (connected) graph is an acyclic subgraph that includes all the vertices. It defines a unique path from each vertex to every other vertex.
- ❏ Both the BFS and the DFS algorithms generate spanning trees.
- ❏ A *weighted graph* is a graph together with a function that assigns a positive number to each edge.
- ❏ In a weighted graph, the *length* of a path is the sum of the weights of the edges that the path spans.
- ❏ Dijkstra's Algorithm finds the shortest path from one vertex to each of the other vertices in a weighted graph.
- ❏ A *digraph* is a set of vertices together with a set of direct edges between them.
- ❏ Every digraph has an embedded graph, obtained by ignoring the edge directions.
- ❏ The BFS and DFS algorithms can be applied to digraphs.
- ❏ A *weighted digraph* is a digraph together with a function that assigns a positive number to each directed edge.
- ❏ Dijkstra's Algorithm can be applied to a weighted digraph.

REVIEW QUESTIONS

16.1   How many connected components does a connect graph have?

16.2   How many different paths are there between two vertices that are in the same cycle?

16.3   How many edges could a connected graph with *n* vertices have?

16.4   For what kind of graphs is the adjacency matrix representation generally more efficient than the adjacency list representation?

16.5   Why is the BFS called a "greedy" algorithm?

16.6   Is the BFS spanning tree usually different from the DFS spanning tree for a graph?

16.7   Why is the symbol ∞ (for "infinity") used in the adjacency matrix of a weighted graph?

16.8   Why is Dijkstra's algorithm called a "greedy" algorithm?

16.9   How is a graph "embedded" within a digraph?

16.10   Why is the adjacency list representation more efficient for a digraph than for a graph?

16.11   How would you define a "directed path" within a digraph?

16.12   What are the two different kinds of connectivity in a digraph?

EXERCISES

16.1   Prove that the number of 1s in the adjacency matrix of a graph is equal to twice its number of edges.

16.2   Prove that the number of nodes in the adjacency list of a graph is equal to twice its number of edges.

16.3   Find each of the following properties for the graph in Figure 16.20.

  a. its size n

  b. its vertex set V

  c. its edge set E

  d. the degree $d(x)$ of each vertex x

  e. a path of length 3

  f. a path of length 5

  g. a cycle of length 4

  h. a spanning tree

  i. its adjacency matrix

  j. its adjacency list

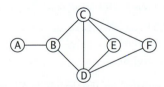

FIGURE 16.20 A Graph.

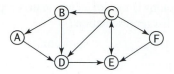

FIGURE 16.21   A Digraph.

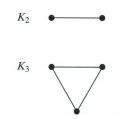

FIGURE 16.22   Complete Graphs.

16.4   Find each of the following properties for the digraph shown in Figure 16.21.

   a. its size n
   b. its vertex set V
   c. its edge set E
   d. the degree $d(x)$ of each vertex x
   e. a path of length 3
   f. a path of length 5
   g. a cycle of length 4
   h. a spanning tree
   i. its adjacency matrix
   j. its adjacency list

16.5   A *complete graph* is a graph that has an edge from each edge to every other edge. For each $n > 1$, there is only one complete graph of size n; it is denoted by K_n. The complete graphs K_2 and K_3 are shown in Figure 16.22.

   a. Draw K_4, K_5, and K_6.
   b. Prove that K_n has $n(n-1)/2$ edges.
   c. Describe the adjacency matrix for K_n.
   d. Describe the adjacency list for K_n.
   e. Draw a BFS traversal of K_6.
   f. Draw a DFS traversal of K_6.

16.6   Trace Dijkstra's algorithm on the graph *in* Figure 16.23 on page 503, showing the shortest path and its distance from node A to every other node.

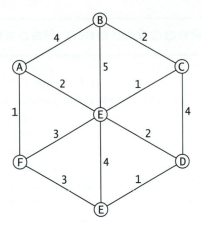

FIGURE 16.23 A Graph.

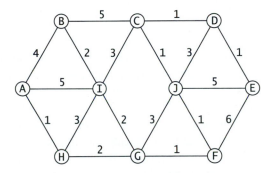

FIGURE 16.24 A Graph.

16.7 Trace Dijkstra's algorithm on the graph *in* Figure 16.24 on page 503, showing the shortest path and its distance from node A to every other node.

16.8 There are four standard algorithms for traversing binary trees: the preorder traversal, the inorder traversal, the postorder traversal. and the level-order traversal. If a binary tree is regarded as a connected acyclic graph, which tree traversal results from a

    a. depth-first search

    b. breadth-first search

16.9 For the graph in Figure 16.23,

    a. Draw the adjacency matrix.

    b. Draw the incidence matrix.

    c. Draw the adjacency list.

PROGRAMMING PROBLEMS

16.1   Modify the Graph class in Listing 16.1 on page 483 so that it stores the vertex labels in (alphanumeric) order and then uses a binary search to implement its `index()` method.

16.2   Add an `equals()` method to the Graph class in Listing 16.1 on page 483 that tests for content equivalence, not isomorphism. This requires checking permutations of the given graph's `vertices[]` array to see if the two graphs have the same vertices, and then comparing their adjacency matrices if they do.

16.3   Add an `equals()` method to the Graph class in Listing 16.1 on page 483 that tests for structural equivalence (isomorphism), not content equivalence. This requires checking permutations of the rows and columns of the given graph's adjacency matrix `a[][]` to look for a match.

16.4   Modify the Graph class in Listing 16.3 on page 485 so that it uses two parallel arrays: the adjacency list `a[]` and a separate `v[]` array for storing the vertex labels, like the `vertices[]` array in Listing 16.1 on page 483. The data structures should look like those shown in Figure 16.25.

16.5   Modify the Graph class in Listing 16.1 on page 483 so that it stores the vertex labels in (alphanumeric) order and then uses a binary search to implement its `index()` method.

16.6   Add an `equals()` method to the Graph class in Listing 16.1 on page 483 that tests for content equivalence, not isomorphism. This requires checking permutations of the given graph's `vertices[]` array to see if the two graphs have the same vertices, and then comparing their adjacency matrices if they do.

16.7   Add an `equals()` method to the Graph class in Listing 16.1 on page 483 that tests for structural equivalence (isomorphism), not content equivalence. This requires checking permutations of the rows and columns of given graph's adjacency matrix `a[][]` to look for a match.

16.8   Add the following method to the Graph class in Listing 16.1 on page 483. Using the breadth-first search (Algorithm 16.1 on page 488):

`public boolean contains(String vertex)`

16.9   Add the following method to the Graph class in Listing 16.3 on page 485. Using the breadth-first search (Algorithm 16.1 on page 488):

`public boolean contains(String vertex)`

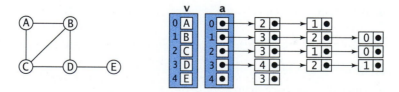

FIGURE 16.25   A Graph and Its Adjacency List.

16.10   Add the following method to the `Graph` class in Listing 16.1 on page 483. Using the breadth-first search (Algorithm 16.1 on page 488):

`public boolean contains(String vertex)`

16.11   Add the following method to the `Graph` class in Listing 16.3 on page 485. Using the breadth-first search (Algorithm 16.1 on page 488):

`public boolean contains(String vertex)`

PROJECTS

16.1   Modify the `WeightedGraph` class in Listing 16.4 on page 496. Store the vertices in a priority queue. (See Section 14.4 on page 423.) Test your resulting class.

16.2   Write and test a program that generates random weighted graphs on a given number of vertices n, and then applies Dijkstra's algorithm. Use an improved version of the `WeightedGraph` class in Listing 16.4 on page 496.

ANSWERS TO REVIEW QUESTIONS

16.1   A connected graph has only one connected component.

16.2   On the same cycle, two different vertices will have at least two different paths connecting them. If the cycle intersects itself, then there will be more than two.

16.3   A graph with n vertices has between $n-1$ and $n(n-1)/2$ vertices (assuming no loops).

16.4   The adjacency matrix will generally be more for graphs that are highly connected (*i.e.*, graphs in which most vertices have edges to most of the other vertices.

16.5   The BFS is called a "greedy" algorithm because its acts locally, processing all neighboring vertices, before branching out globally.

16.6   Yes.

16.7   The ∞ symbol is used in the adjacency matrix of a weighted graph to indicate that no direct edge exists between the two vertices.

16.8   Dijkstra's algorithms called a "greedy" algorithm for the same reason as the BFS: It acts locally, each time finding the next closest vertex to those already visited.

16.9   To see the embedded graph within a digraph, simply ignore the directions of the edges.

16.10   The adjacency list representation is more efficient for a digraph because it has only one node (instead of two) for each edge.

16.11   A *directed path* in a digraph is a sequence of vertices $(v_0, v_1, v_2, ..., v_k)$, where each consecutive pair is connected by a direct edge: $(v_{i-1} v_i)$.

16.12   If every vertex is connected to every other vertex by a directed path, then the digraph is *strongly connected*. If every vertex is connected to every other vertex by an undirected path within its embedded graph, then the digraph is *weakly connected*.

Appendix A

Answers and Hints

This appendix contains answers to some of the exercises and hints to some of the programming problems and projects.

CHAPTER 1 EXERCISES

1.2 Another likely cycle is shown here. This is the common debug cycle, consisting of repeated two-part test-and-correct steps (See Figure A.1).

1.4 If d is a divisor of n that is greater than $\sqrt{n}$, then $m = n/d$ must be a whole number (*i.e.*, an integer), and therefore another divisor of n. But since $d > \sqrt{n}$, we have $m = n/d < n/\sqrt{n} = \sqrt{n}$. So by checking for divisors only among those integers that are less than $\sqrt{n}$, the existence of the divisor $d > \sqrt{n}$ will be found indirectly from $m = n/d < \sqrt{n}$.

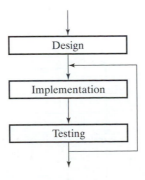

FIGURE A.1 The debug cycle (for Exercise 1.2).

507

1.6   The UML diagram for this exercise is shown in Figure A.2. The `Department` class is an aggregate of the `Course` class and of the `Chair` class. All instances of those component classes would be deleted if their department were deleted. The chair is a specialized instructor, so the `Chair` class inherits from the `Instructor` class. The department is a composite of its instructors; they would not cease to exist if the department were abolished; they could be reassigned to other departments, just as a book could be republished by another publisher.

1.8   The UML diagram for this exercise is shown in Figure A.3. The Bus, Car, and Truck classes are specializations of the `Vehicle` class, just as the `Driver` and `Owner` classes are specializations of the `Person` class. So those five relationships are all inheritance relationships. The roles of `Driver` and `Owner` of buses, cars, and trucks cease to exist when those vehicles cease to exist, so those relationships are all composition relationships.

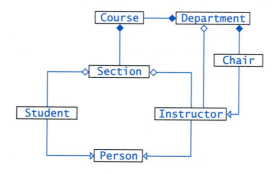

FIGURE A.2   UML diagram for Exercise 1.6.

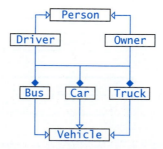

FIGURE A.3   UML diagram for Exercise 1.8.

CHAPTER 2 EXERCISES

2.13   **a.** ADT : *Vector*

> A **Vector** is a sequence of objects.
>   *Object* **getAt**(*int* i)
>   *Precondition*: i is a valid (in range) index value.
>   *Returns*: the vector component at index i.
>   *void* **setAt**(*Object* object, *int* i)
>   *Precondition*: i is a valid (in range) index value.
>   *Postcondition*: the component at index i contains the given object.
>   *integer* **size**()
>   *Postcondition*: this vector is unchanged.
>   *Returns*: the number of elements in this vector.

b.
```java
public class Vector {
   private Object[] a;
   private int size;

   public Vector(int n) {
      size = n;
      a = new Object[n];
   }

   public Object getAt(int i) {
      if (i<0 || i>=a.length) throw new IllegalArgumentException();
      return a[i];
   }

   public void setAt(Object object, int i) {
      if (i<0 || i>=a.length) throw new IllegalArgumentException();
      a[i] = object;
   }

   public int size() {
      return size;
   }
}
```

CHAPTER 3 PROJECTS

3.1   To verify the equation $\Theta(g) = O(g) \cap \Omega(g)$, we have to show that $\Theta(g) \subseteq O(g) \cap \Omega(g)$ and that $\Theta(g) \supseteq O(g) \cap \Omega(g)$. To verify that $\Theta(g) \subseteq O(g) \cap \Omega(g)$, we have to show that every function $f(n)$ that is in $\Theta(g)$ is also in $O(g) \cap \Omega(g)$. So assume that $f(n)$ is in $\Theta(g)$.

Then, by definition (on page 83), $f(n)/g(n)$ is bounded and $g(n)/f(n)$ is bounded. But that means that $f(n)$ is in $O(g)$ and $f(n)$ is in $\Omega(g)$, again by definition. And that means that $f(n)$ is in $O(g) \cap \Omega(g)$. The proof that $\Theta(g) \supseteq O(g) \cap \Omega(g)$ is similar.

3.3   The general outline of the Sieve of Eratosthenes is:

```
for (int p=2; n<n; p++)
  // one array access
for (int p=2; n<n; p++)
  // one array access
  for (int k=2; k*p<n; k++)
    // one array access
```

The first `for` loop iterates $n - 2$ times. The second outside `for` loop also iterates $n - 2$ times. For each of its iterations, an inner `for` loop iterates n/p times. An upper bound for that would be $n/2$ times. So an upper bound for the entire algorithm would be

$$(n - 2) + (n - 2)(n/2) = (n - 2)(1 + n/2) < (n)(n) = n^2$$

CHAPTER 4 PROGRAMMING PROBLEMS

4.11
```
Node merge(Node list1, Node list2) {
    if (list1 == null && list2 == null) return null;
    Node list = null, p1=list1, p2=list2;
    if (p1 == null) {
        list = new Node(p2.data);
        p2 = p2.next;
    } else if (p2 == null) {
        list = new Node(p1.data);
        p1 = p1.next;
    }
    if (p1.data < p2.data) {
        list = new Node(p1.data);
        p1 = p1.next;
    } else {
        list = new Node(p2.data);
        p2 = p2.next;
    }
    Node p=list;
    while (p1 != null && p2 != null)
        if (p1.data < p2.data) {
            p = p.next = new Node(p1.data);
            p1 = p1.next;
        } else {
            p = p.next = new Node(p2.data);
            p2 = p2.next;
        }
```

```
while (p1 != null) {
    p = p.next = new Node(p1.data);
    p1 = p1.next;
}
p.next = p2;
return list;
}
```

CHAPTER 5 EXERCISES

5.1   The trace is shown in Figure A.4.

5.2   The postfix versions are

    a. $x\,4 + y\,8\,z + / -$

    b. $x\,6\,y\,/\,5\,z - * /$

    c. $x\,2\,y\,/\,/\,7\,z - *$

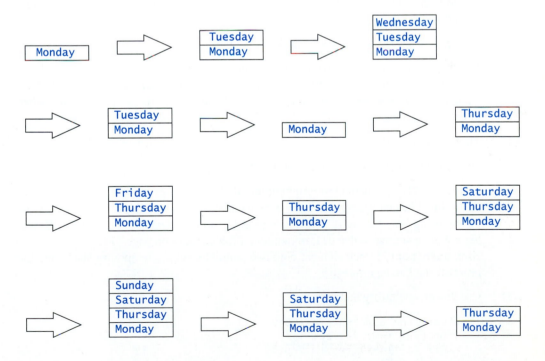

FIGURE A.4   Trace for Exercise 5.1.

5.3   Translate each of the following postfix expressions into infix:

a. $(x+4)/(y-3)+z$

b. $x-(9+y)*(6-z)$

c. $x/(3/(y/(2/z)))$

CHAPTER 5 PROGRAMMING PROBLEMS

5.15   The method that you write should be a `public` member of the `LinkedStack` class. Its purpose is to reverse `this` stack. Its header should be

```
public void reverse() {
```

Hint: `pop()` the elements into an array and then `push()` them back.

5.17   Use a `Main` class with a no-arg constructor, the `main()` method, and the `bottom()` method that has to be written. Have `main()` instantiate the `Main()` constructor, within which you instantiate a `LinkedStack` (or an `ArrayStack`), `push()` some strings onto it, and then print the object returned by a call to your `bottom()` method, whose header should be

```
public Object bottom(Stack stack)
```

Hint: `push(pop())` the elements onto a temporary stack, grab the top element of that temp stack (which was the bottom of the referenced stack), and then `push(pop())` the elements back onto the referenced stack (which should be in its original state when your method returns).

5.19   The header should be

```
public Stack reversed(Stack stack)
```

Like the `bottom()` method in Programming Problem 5.17 on page 173, this is a client method that has no access to the `private` members of the `stack`'s class. It must do its job by using only the `public` methods `peek()`, `pop()`, `push()`, and `size()`. But its logic will be similar to that of Programming Problem 5.15 on page 173.
Hint: `push(pop())` each element onto two parallel stacks: a temporary stack, and the reversed stack to be returned.

5.21   Use this private utility method:

```
private boolean contains(Object x) {
    for (int i=0; i<size; i++)
        if (a[i]==x) return true;
    return false;
}
```

CHAPTER 6 EXERCISES

6.1   The trace is shown in Figure A.5.

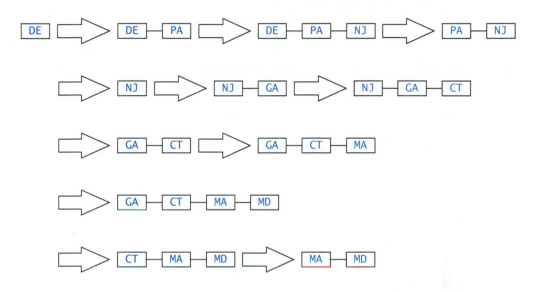

FIGURE A.5   Trace for Exercise 6.1.

6.2   This permuted statement

```
head.prev.next = head.prev = new Node(object,head.prev,head);
```

would not work in place of the first statement in the add() method of the LinkedQueue class in Listing 6.2 on page 182 because it would change the value of head.prev before trying to reset head.prev.next. (Chained assignments are always processed from right to left.)

6.4   Call the two stacks a and b. Include a boolean field named aIsIt. When aIsIt is true, the add() method would simply push the new object onto stack a. When aIsIt is false, the add() method would first dump stack b into stack a (thus reversing the order of the elements), and then push the new object onto stack a. When aIsIt is true, the remove() method would first dump stack a into stack b (thus reversing the order of the elements), and then pop the top object off of stack b and return it. When aIsIt is false, the remove() method would simply pop the top object off of stack b and return it. The run time of each method is $\Theta(n)$.

CHAPTER 7 PROGRAMMING PROBLEMS

7.2
```java
public Object getLast() {
    public Object getLast() {
        // returns a reference to the last element of this collection;
        // or returns null if this collection is empty;
        for (int i = a.length-1; i >= 0; i--)
            if (a[i] != null) return a[i];
        return null;
    }
}
```

7.5
```java
public boolean removeLast(Collection collection) {
    // removes the last element if the collection is not empty;
    // returns true if and only it changes the given collection;
    Iterator it = collection.iterator();
    Object object = null;
    if (!it.hasNext()) return false;
    while (it.hasNext())
        object = it.next();
    it.remove();
    return true;
}
```

7.8
```java
public boolean removeOdd() {
    // removes every other element (the first, the third, etc.) from
    // this collection; returns true iff this collection is changed;
    boolean isOdd = false;
    if (size == 0) return false;
    for (Node p=head; p.next!=head; p = p.next) {
        isOdd = (isOdd ? false : true);  // reverse its truth value
        if (isOdd) {
            p.next = p.next.next;
            p.next.prev = p;
            --size;
        }
    }
    return true;
}
```

CHAPTER 8 EXERCISES

8.1   The clone() statement will create only one new object: list2. Its four elements are references to the same objects to which the corresponding list1 elements refer.

8.2   The expression would shift the elements at positions 3-6 down to positions 2–5 and it would replace the object at position 6 with "BE".

CHAPTER 8 PROGRAMMING PROBLEM

8.1   **a.**
```
int frequency(List list, Object object) {
    // returns the number of occurrences of object in list
        int f = 0;
        for (Iterator it = list.iterator(); it.hasNext(); )
            if (it.next().equals(object)) ++f;
        return f;
}
```

CHAPTER 9 EXERCISES

9.2   **c.**

	Key is Found	Key is Not Found
Linear Probing	5.5	50.1
Quadratic Probing	2.85	11.4
Double Hashing	2.56	10
Separate Chaining	1.9	1.9

9.5   The worst case would be when all keys hash to the same location. In that case, both successful and unsuccessful searches will run in linear time.

9.6   This huge hash table would work if a file that large could be managed. However, 2^{32} records of size 100 KB, for example, would use 400 gigabytes. Probably most of that space would be wasted. Moreover, the hash function is not perfect; (*i.e.*, it is not one to one.) The standard Java `hashCode()` method promises only that it "usually differs for different objects."

9.7   With double hashing, the probe sequence for resolving a collision is h, $h+d$, $h+2d$, $h+3d$, ..., where h is the primary hash value and d is the secondary (rehashed) value. If d is a divisor of the array length, then the probe sequence will include only length/d different index values. Thus, a nearly empty table could reject some insertions. For example, suppose the table length is 100, $h = 63$, and $d = 25$. Then, the probe sequence would be 63, 88, 13, 38, 63, 88, 13, 38, 63, 88, 13, ..., hitting only 4% of the array elements.

CHAPTER 10 EXERCISES

10.1   The call `factorial(8)` will generate eight recursive calls.

10.2   This method violates the rule that no larger disk may be placed upon a smaller disk.

10.3   **a.** The call returns –6; the calling tree has height 4.

b. The call returns 7; the calling tree has height 3.

c. The call returns –10; the calling tree has height 4.

10.6   The call `f(8)` to the Fibonacci function will generate 20 recursive calls.

10.7   When $n = 4$, $n! = 4! = 24 > 16 = 2^4 = 2^n$. In general, if the inequality is true for all values less than some $n > 3$, then $n! = n \cdot (n-1)! > n \cdot (2^{n-1}) > 2 \cdot (2^{n-1}) = 2^n$, because $n-1$ is less than n.

CHAPTER 10 PROGRAMMING PROBLEM

10.11
```
int max(int[] a) {
    return max(a, 0, a.length-1);
}

int max(int[] a, int p, int n) {
    if (n < 2) return a[p];
    int lo = max(a, p, n/2);
    int hi = max(a, p+n/2, n/2);
    return (lo > hi ? lo : hi);
}
```

CHAPTER 11 EXERCISES

11.1   **a.** True

b. False

c. True

d. False

e. True

f. True

g. False

h. True

i. True

j. False

k. False

l. False

m. False

11.7   Classes at the leaf nodes of the Java inheritance hierarchy are identified as `final` classes, meaning that they cannot be extended.

11.8   **a.** H, N, F, C, J, O, P, L, M
   b. G
   c. 2
   d. 4
   e. A, D
   f. J, K, L, M, O, P
   g. E, F, G
   h. 4
   i. 6
   j. 4

11.9   **a.** $(3^5 - 1)/2 = 121$ nodes
   b. $(4^4 - 1)/3 = 85$ nodes
   c. $(10^5 - 1)/9 = 11{,}111$ nodes
   d. $(4^{11} - 1)/3 = 1{,}398{,}101$ nodes

11.11 $w(T) = \max\{ \text{sum}\{ \deg(n) : n \text{ is a node at level } k \} : k \text{ is a level in the tree } T \}$

11.12   The path length of a full tree of order d and height h is
$$\frac{d}{(d-1)^2}[hd^{h+1} - (h+1)d + 1].$$

11.13   **a.** A, B, C, D, E, F, G, H, I, J, K, L, M, N, O, P
   b. A, B, E, H, I, N, F, C, D, G, J, K, O, P, L, M
   c. H, N, I, E, F, B, C, J, O, P, K, L, M, G, D, A

11.14   **a.** The level-order and the preorder traversals always visit the root first.
   b. The postorder traversal always visits the leftmost node first.
   c. The postorder traversal always visits the root last.
   d. The preorder traversal always visits the rightmost node last.

CHAPTER 12 PROGRAMMING PROBLEMS

12.2
```
public String toString() {
    StringBuffer buf = new StringBuffer("[");
    if (left != null) buf.append(left + ",");
    buf.append(root);
    if (right != null) buf.append("," + right);
    return buf + "]";
}
```

12.4
```
public int size() {
    if (left == null && right == null) return 1;
    if (left == null) return 1 + right.size();
    if (right == null) return 1 + left.size();
    return 1 + left.size() + right.size();
}
```

12.8
```
public int count(Object x) {
    int count = ( x.equals(root) ? 1 : 0 );
    if (left != null) count += left.count(x);
    if (right != null) count += right.count(x);
    return count;
}
```

12.10
```
public boolean isBalanced() {
    if (left == null && right == null) return true;
    if (left == null) return right.isLeaf();
    if (right == null) return left.isLeaf();
    int balance = left.height() - right.height();
    return balance > -2 && balance < 2;
}
```

12.13
```
public int level(Object object) {
    if (this.root == object) return 0;
    int levelInLeft = ( left == null ? -1 : left.level(object) );
    if (levelInLeft > -1) return 1 + levelInLeft;
    int levelInRight = ( right == null ? -1 : right.level(object) );
    if (levelInRight > -1) return 1 + levelInRight;
    return -1;
}
```

CHAPTER 13 EXERCISES

13.4   If x is neither an ancestor nor a descendant of y, then the resulting BST will be independent of the order in which they are deleted. This is because the deletion algorithm affects only those nodes that are ancestors or descendants of the node being deleted. If x has fewer than two children (Cases 1 and 2), then no other nodes are affected when x is deleted. If x has two children, then x is replaced by its successor y, which is then spliced out. That successor is either in the right subtree of x (descendants), or it is an ancestor of x.

13.5   If the same keys are inserted in different orders, different BSTs will result. For example, consider the result of building a BST by inserting 22 followed by 33, and then repeat the process in the reverse order:

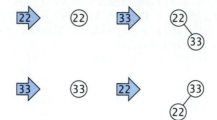

CHAPTER 14 EXERCISES

14.3 **a.** This is not a heap.
  b. This is a heap.
  c. This is not a heap.
  d. This is not a heap.
  e. This is a heap.
  f. This is not a heap.

14.4 **a.** This is not a heap.
  g. This is a heap.
  h. This is not a heap.
  i. This is a heap.

CHAPTER 15 EXERCISES

15.2 **a.** 40 ms.
  b. 160 ms.
  c. 2560 ms.

15.21 The *Exhaustion Sort* has complexity $\Theta(n\,n!) = \omega(2^n)$ (*i.e.*, it runs in exponential time).

CHAPTER 15 PROGRAMMING PROBLEM

15.9
```
public void sort(int[] a) {
    void sort(int[] a) {
```

```
        for (int i = a.length-1; i > 0; i--) {
            for (int j = 0; j < i; j++) {
                if (a[j] > a[j+1]) IntArrays.swap(a, j, j+1);
            if (!invar1(a, j))
                throw new RuntimeException("INVARIANT 1 VIOLATED");
            }
            if (!invar2(a, i))
                throw new RuntimeException("INVARIANT 2 VIOLATED");
        }
    }
```

CHAPTER 16 EXERCISE

16.2   **a.** 6
       e. ABCD
       f. ABCEDF
       g. BCEDF
       i.

	A	B	C	D	E	F
A	0	1	0	0	0	0
B	1	0	1	1	0	0
C	0	1	0	1	1	1
D	0	1	1	0	1	1
E	0	0	1	1	0	0
F	0	0	1	1	0	0

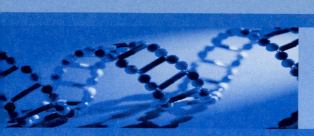

Appendix B

Java Review

This appendix reviews elementary Java programming concepts. It assumes that you have completed an introductory course in programming with Java. If your first course was in another language, such as C++, then the outline book **[Hubbard1]** listed in Appendix E together with this appendix will help you get up to speed with Java.

B.1 Java Programs

A Java program consists of a *main class* together with other classes and interfaces that it uses. The main class is identified by a *main method* that looks like this:

```java
public static void main(String[] args) {
  // executable statements go here
}
```

The method is `public`, which means that it is accessible from outside the class. It is `static`, which means that it belongs to the class itself instead of being bound to individual instances of the class. Its return type is `void`, which means that it doesn't return anything. Its single parameter `args` (for "arguments") is an array of character strings that is initialized at the command line when the program is run.

Listing B.1 shows a simple Java program. It has only one executable statement: the output statement at line 3 that prints "Hello, world!".

LISTING B.1: The Hello World Program

```java
1  class Hello {
2    public static void main(String[] args) {
3      System.out.println("Hello, world!");
4    }
5  }
```

The main class for this program is named Hello. It is defined on line 1. Its scope extends over lines 1–5, beginning with the left brace at the end of line 1 and ending with the right brace on line 5. Its main method, defined on line 2, is enclosed within those braces.

The scope of the main method extends over lines 2–4, beginning with the left brace at the end of line 2 and ending with the right brace on line 4. The output statement at line 3 is enclosed within those braces.

Simple character string output usually is performed in Java with the println() method. When done as

```
3        System.out.println("Hello, world!");
```

the println() method is bound to the out object that is defined in the System class. As a static member of its class, the out object is referenced by the name System.out. The out object itself has type PrintStream, so it can perform the methods of the PrintStream class. One of those methods is println().

The PrintStream class actually defines 10 different *overloaded* versions of the println() method. These versions are distinguished by their parameter types. The version used here on line 3 takes a single String type argument. It is then passed to the string literal "Hello, world!". If we replace line 3 with

```
3        System.out.println(3.14159);
```

then the version of the println() method that takes a single number of type double will be invoked, and it will print the numeric value 3.14159. If we replace line 3 with

```
3        System.out.println();
```

then the version of the println() method that takes no arguments will be invoked, and it will print a blank line.

The PrintStream class also defines nine overloaded versions of a separate print() method. They work the same way as the println() methods except that the "print head" does not advance to the beginning of the next line at the end of the printing. So the next call to print() or to println() will continue on the same line. If we replace line 3 in Listing B.1 on page 521 with

```
3        System.out.print("Hello, ");  System.out.println("world!");
```

we'll get the same output.

Both the print() and the println() methods have a version for an argument of each of the six Java primitive types (boolean, char, double, float, int, long), a version for an argument of type char[], a version for an argument of type String, and a version for an argument of type Object.

B.2 Compiling and Running a Java Program

This assuming that your computer is running Microsoft Windows and that you have a floppy disk in your A: drive, follow these steps to compile and run a simple Java program.

1. Launch Programs > Accessories > NotePad from the Start key.
2. Copy the five lines of code from Listing B.1 on page 521 into your NotePad window.

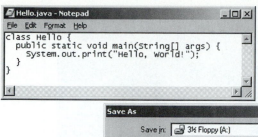

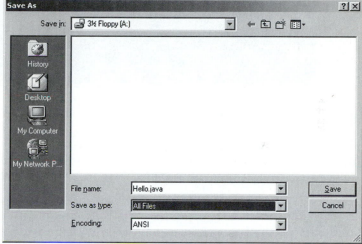

FIGURE B.1   Saving a Java program on a diskette.

3. Save the program by the name `Hello.java` on your floppy disk. To prevent NotePad from appending the `.txt` extension to the file name, select **All Files** in the **Save as type** option:

4. Launch **Programs > Accessories > Command Prompt** from the **Start** key.

5. Enter A: to switch to your floppy drive.

6. Enter `dir` to see that your program is saved on your floppy disk.

7. Enter `javac Hello.java` to compile your program. If that doesn't work, then either your computer does not have Java loaded, its **PATH** variable is not set correctly, or you have an error in your program. Remedies to the first two of these problems are given shortly. If you have an error in your program, you can correct it with the editor.

8. Enter `java Hello` to run your program. The output should look like the screen capture shown in Figure B.2. If that doesn't work, then your computer's **CLASSPATH** variable probably is not set correctly.

To see if your computer has Java loaded on it, launch **Programs > Accessories > Windows Explorer** from the **Start** key, and look for a folder with a name containing j2sdk (for "Java 2 Software Development Kit"). The folder for version 1.4.0 should be named j2sdk1.4.0, and it is most likely installed on your C: drive. To search through your C: drive, right-click on its icon, select **Search**, and enter j2sdk:

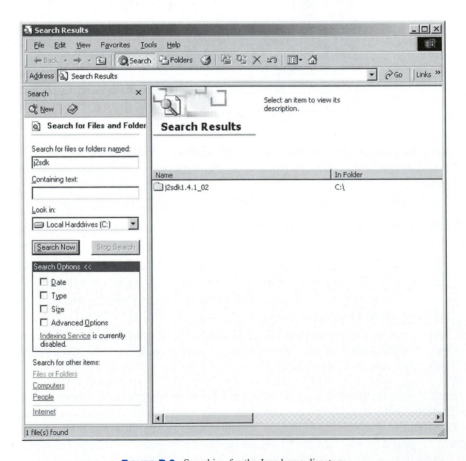

FIGURE B.2   The `dir`, `javac`, and `java` commands.

FIGURE B.3   Searching for the Java home directory.

If it is not found, then you'll have to download it and install it on your computer.

To download Java, go to `http://java.sun.com` in your web browser. This is the home website for Java technology. From it, you can download the Java 2 SDK for free. Just follow the instructions that you find there.

Java uses your computer's two environment variables, PATH and CLASSPATH, to compile and run your programs. The PATH variable lists the directory (folder) paths where your operating system looks for the files that run to execute commands that you enter at the command line. For example, the `javac` and `java` commands work by running the `javac.exe` and the `java.exe` programs that you should have in your Java's `bin` folder (for "binary"); for version 4.0.1, those two files should be in your `C:\j2sdk1.4.0\bin\` folder. To see how your PATH variable is defined, at the command prompt, enter

    echo %path%

The echo command tells the system to display the value of the specified symbol. The percent signs (%) before and after the variable name tell the system to evaluate the PATH variable. In the screen, shown in Figure B.4, that variable had the value `C:\WINNT\system32;C:\WINNT`.

Since that did not include the `C:\j2sdk1.4.0\bin` path, the preceding attempt to execute the `javac` command failed. To include that path, at the command prompt, enter

    set path=C:\j2sdk1.4.0\bin;%path%

Be sure to include all the punctuation.[1] Note that the semicolon (;) is used to separate the paths listed in the variable. This command replaces the current contents of the `C:\j2sdk1.4.0\bin` path.

The echo command tells the system to display the value of your PATH variable with the string

    C:\j2sdk1.4.0\bin;%path%

which is evaluated here as

    C:\j2sdk1.4.0\bin;C:\WINNT\system32;C:\WINNT

as the subsequent `echo` command shows in Figure B.4. Then the `javac` command works.

FIGURE B.4   The echo and set path commands.

---

[1] Note that there are no blank spaces in the PATH variable.

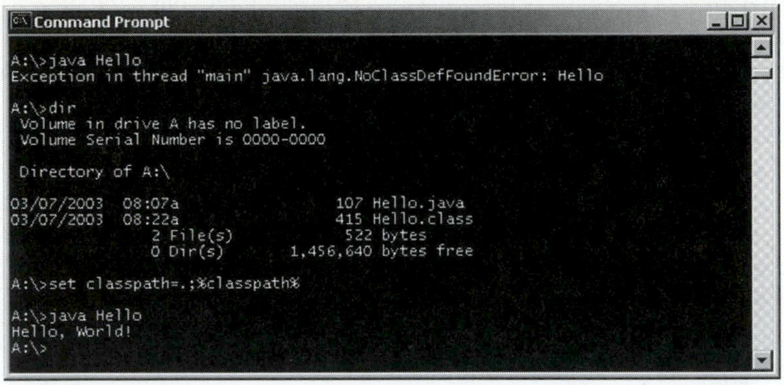

FIGURE B.5   Setting the classpath to run a Java program.

When you compile your program with the `javac` command, the compiler produces a separate *class file* for each class in your program. For example, compiling the `Hello.java` program should result in a new file named `Hello.class` being placed in your same folder. That's the file that actually gets executed when you run the `java Hello` command.

If you get the error message

```
Exception in thread "main" java.lang.NoClassDefFoundError
```

when you run the `java Hello` command, it is because the java command program could not find your class file. The `dir` command should show the class file `Hello.class` in your folder:, as shown in Figure B.5.

If so, then the problem is most likely with your computer system's **CLASSPATH** environment variable. If it does not include the path to the current directory, signified by the single dot (`.`) character, then that error will occur. To fix it, temporarily, amend your **CLASSPATH** variable like this:

```
set classpath=.;%classpath%
```

That puts the dot path first among whatever other paths are already in your **CLASSPATH** variable. Thereafter, the `java` command will look first in the current directory for class files. That should solve the "`NoClassDefFoundError`" problem.

Changing the **PATH** and **CLASSPATH** variables at the command line is only a temporary fix. The changes apply only within the Command Prompt window where they were changed. To change them permanently, you have to use the Windows Control Panel; as shown in Figure B.6. Follow these steps:

1. Select **Settings > Control Panel** from the **Start** key.

2. Double-click on the **System** icon in the Control Panel.

3. Click on the **Advanced** tab in the **System Properties** window.

4. Click on the button labeled Environment Variables.

5. If you have Administrator privileges on your system, you can change the System variables. Otherwise, you will have to create your own User variables named PATH and CLASSPATH. To change an existing variable, select it and click on the Edit button. To create a new variable, click on the New button.

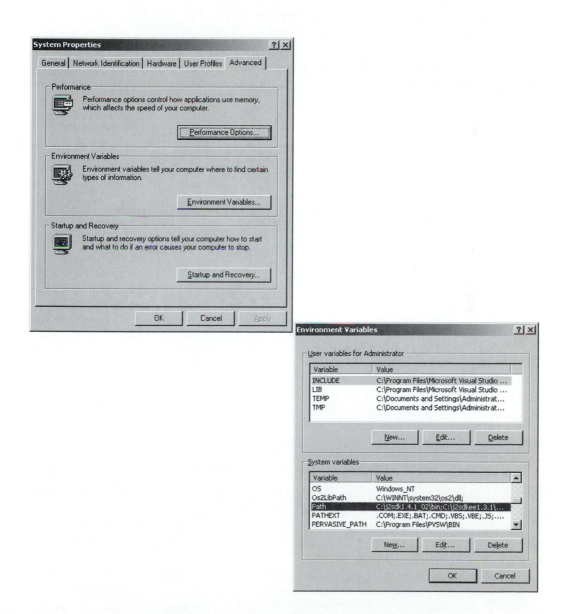

FIGURE B.6 Setting the Path environment variable in windows.

B.3 Java Types

In Java, all variables must be declared by specifying a type for the variable. Java has four kinds of types: primitive types, classes, interfaces, and arrays. For example, the following are valid declarations in Java:

```
double temperature;   // double is a primitive type
String name;          // String is a class
Set friends;          // Set is an interface
String[] args;        // String[] is an array type
```

Java has three kinds of variables: class fields, method parameters, and local variables. Class fields (data members) and local variables (declared inside methods) can be initialized explicitly when they are declared, like this:

```
double temperature = 66.6;      // temperature has the value 66.6
String name = "George";         // name has the value "George"
Set friends = new TreeSet();    // friends references a new TreeSet
Set enemies = null;             // enemies has the value null
int[] aa = new int[8];          // aa has 8 int elements
int n = name.length();          // n has the value returned by length()
```

Method parameters are initialized by the arguments that are passed to them when their methods are invoked. Note that variables that are declared to have an interface type can be initialized only by setting the variable to `null` or by using the `new` operator to invoke a constructor of a class that implements the interface. For example, `TreeSet` is a class that implements the `Set` interface, so `friends` can be initialized by invoking the no-arg constructor `TreeSet()`, as shown previously.

In Java, each class field is automatically initialized to its zero state. For example, if a Student class is defined as

```
class Student {
    String name;
    int credits;
    double gpa;
}
```

and a `Student` object named `ann` is created with

```
Student ann = new Student();   // ann references a new Student object
```

then `ann.name` will be `null`, `ann.credits` will be 0, and `ann.gpa` will be 0.0. Local variables are not initialized automatically, so they should always be initialized explicitly.

Java's eight primitive types are summarized in Table B.1. Note that literals for integers of type `long` must include the suffix L, and literals for decimals of type `float` must include the suffix F.

The Java 16-bit `char` type is more general than the older 8-bit `char` type used previously by languages such as C++ and Pascal. It implements the Unicode character set, which includes the old ASCII character set as a subset. The same character literals such as `'G'` and `'e'` are still valid, in addition to the special *escape sequences* listed in Table B.2.

Name	Data	Bits	Literal Range
boolean	logical	8	false or true
char	Unicode character	16	See http://www.unicode.org/
byte	integer	8	-128 to 127
short	integer	16	-32768 to 32767
int	integer	32	-2147483648 to 2147483647
long	integer	64	-9223372036854775808L to 9223372036854775807L
float	floating-point decimal	32	1.4e-45F to 3.4e38F (positive or negative)
double	floating-point decimal	64	4.9e-324 to 1.8e308 (positive or negative)

TABLE B.1   Java Primitive Types.

Literal	Name	Meaning
'\b'	backspace	Allows overprinting
'\f'	formfeed	Starts a new printed page
'\n'	newline	Starts a new line
'\r'	return	Moves to the left margin
'\t'	horizontal tab	Moves to the next tab stop
'\''	single quote	The apostrophe: '
'\"'	double quote	The quotation mark: "
'\\'	backslash	The back slash: \
'\nnn'		The character whose octal Unicode is $0nnn$.
'\u00nn'		The character whose hexadecimal Unicode is $0x00nn$.

TABLE B.2   Special Escape Sequence Character Literals.

For example, the statement

```
System.out.println("\110\145\154\154\157\041");
```

will print Hello!, since 0110 is the octal code for 'H', 0145 is the octal code for 'e', *etc.*

Variables of numeric type are subject to overflow. That is what happens when an arithmetic operation results in a value that exceeds the maximum value for the type. This is illustrated by the program in Listing B.2. The variable n is initialized to 2^{27} (134,217,728) and then repeatedly doubled as long as its value remains positive. But when n equals 2^{30} (1,073,741,824), that value is more than half the maximum value of $2^{31} - 1$ (2,147,483,647) for int variables, so doubling it causes overflow.

LISTING B.2: Integer Overflow

```
1   public class Overflow {
2     public static void main(String[] args) {
3       int n = 512*512*512;   // (2^9)^3 = 2^27
4       while (n > 0) {
5         System.out.println(n);
6         n *= 2;
7       }
8       System.out.println(n);
9     }
10  }
```

The output is

```
134217728
268435456
536870912
1073741824
-2147483648
```

Floating-point overflow is similar to integer overflow, except that instead of "wrapping around" to negative values, the overflowed variable takes on the special value `Float.POSITIVE_INFINITY`. (See Programming Problem B.1 on page 563.)

B.4 Classes and Members

In Java, all executable statements are placed within classes. A *class* is a blueprint for producing objects. Classes encapsulate three kinds of members: fields, methods, and constructors. Its fields hold its data (its *state*), its methods define its operations (its *behavior*), and its constructors create the objects (its *instances*) and initialize their fields.

A Java program is executed by the system's invocation of the program's `main()` method. When the command

```
java Hello
```

is executed, the system begins executing the statements in the `main()` method of the `Hello` class. These statements may invoke other methods of the `Hello` class and they may manipulate its data. They may also instantiate other classes and use their constructors, fields, and methods.

So the design of a Java program begins with the choice of classes that will constitute it. These will include predefined classes such as those provided by the Java Class Libraries as well as user-defined classes. Listing B.3 shows a simple user-defined class whose instances represent points (x, y) in two-dimensional space.

This class has nine members: three fields, two constructors, and four methods. The two fields x and y represent the x and y coordinates of a point. The **static** field ORIGIN represents the unique point $(0, 0)$. Recall that **static** means that the member is unique to the class itself, independent of any instance of the class. Thus, we may have many `Point` objects, each with their coordinates x and y, but there is only one ORIGIN object. As a **static** member, it is accessed by the name `Point.ORIGIN`, with the prefix using the class name `Point` instead of the name of some instance of the class.

LISTING B.3: A `Point` Class

```
1    public class Point {
2        private double x, y;
3        public static final Point ORIGIN = new Point();
4
5        private Point() {
6        }
7
8        public Point(double x, double y) {
9            this.x = x;
10           this.y = y;
11       }
12
13       public static double distance(Point p, Point q) {
14           double dx=q.x-p.x, dy=q.y-p.y;
15           return Math.sqrt(dx*dx + dy*dy);
16       }
17
18       public double x() {
19           return x;
20       }
21
22       public double y() {
23           return y;
24       }
25
26       public String toString() {
27           return "(" + x + "," + y + ")";
28       }
29   }
```

Note that the fields x and y are declared to be **private**. That prevents any client program from changing the coordinates of a `Point` object. This makes `Point` objects *immutable*. This is similar to the standard Java `String` class: Once an instance of the class has been created, it cannot be changed.

The constructor defined at line 5 is called a "no-arg constructor" because it has no arguments.[2] This is the simplest constructor that a class can have. In general, if there are no explicit constructor definitions in a class, then the compiler will automatically define a **public** no-arg constructor for the class. In this class, however, we have another constructor defined at line 8, so we must also explicitly define the no-arg constructor unless we don't want the class to have one.

Note that this no-arg constructor is declared to be **private**. That makes it like the x and y fields, accessible only from within the class itself. We use it at line 3 to construct the unique

---

[2] In other programming languages, such as C++, the no-arg constructor is called the *default constructor*.

ORIGIN object, but the only way that a client program can create a `Point` object is to invoke the `public` two-arg constructor defined at line 8. This guarantees that all `Point` objects must have their coordinates determined when they are created.

The `distance()` method returns the distance between two points p and q. It uses the formula $\sqrt{(x_2-x_1)^2+(y_2-y_1)^2}$, derived from the Pythagorean Theorem. This requires the use of the `static` square root method, `sqrt()`, defined in the standard Java `Math` class.

Note that the `distance()` method is declared to be **static**, so it would be invoked with

```
double d = Point.distance(p,q);
```

This gives both points equal footing, requiring them both to be passed as arguments. If we made the `distance()` method non-**static** instead, then it would be invoked as `p.distance(q)` or `q.distance(p)`, requiring the method invocation to be bound to one of the points and passing the other as an argument. That might be preferable if we wanted to represent the directed distance from one point to the other. But as an undirected distance, the roles of the two points should be equivalent, so the method should be as symmetric as possible: `distance(p,q)` should return the same value as `distance(q,p)`.

The `x()` and `y()` methods are *accessor methods*. They provide **public** read-only access to the `private` fields x and y.

The `toString()` method overrides the corresponding method defined in the `Object` class. Since every class extends the `Object` class, every class inherits that class's `toString()` method, unless it overrides it with its own version. Either way, the class's **public** `toString()` method is automatically implicitly invoked whenever an object is used in a `String` expression. Each object is "evaluated" this way by the `String` value that the `toString()` method returns.

For example, the code

```
Point p = new Point(5,-4);
System.out.println("The point is " + p);
```

would print

```
The point is (5.0,-4.0)
```

Placing the reference p in the string expression[3] `"The point is "` + p causes the `Point` class's `toString()` method to execute, replacing that reference p with the string (5,-4) that the method returns.

Class fields and methods are either **static** or non-**static**. A *static* field or method, declared with the **static** keyword, is bound to the class itself and is invoked using the class name. For example, in our `Point` class in Listing B.3 on page 531, the ORIGIN field and the `distance()` method are **static**, while the x field and the `toString()` method are non-**static**. Thus, the ORIGIN field and the `distance()` method are used with the class name `Point` as a prefix, like this:

```
if (p == Point.ORIGIN) then System.out.println("Home.");
double d = Point.distance(p,q);
```

---

[3] The expression `""The point is " + p"` is recognized as a string expression because it contains the string literal `"The point is "`, which causes the plus sign (+) to be interpreted as the string concatenation operator.

At the same time, the x field and the `toString()` method are used with the name of some instance of the class as a prefix, like this:

```
double dx=q.x-p.x;
String pLiteral = p.toString();
```

Static methods are appropriate when the action performed is independent of any distinct object of the class. If we think of a class as an environment that encapsulates related objects and actions, then it is reasonable to define a class merely to house related utility methods and fields. That is the purpose of the `System` class, the `Math` class, the `Arrays` class, and wrapper classes such as `Integer` and `Double`. The following commonly used methods and constants are all declared `static`:

```
System.out
System.exit()
System.arraycopy()
Math.sqrt()
Math.PI
Arrays.binarySearch()
Arrays.sort()
Integer.parseInt()
Integer.MAX_VALUE
```

Static methods are also called *class methods*, and non-`static` methods are also called *instance methods*.

B.5 Access Modifiers

Every member of every class and object is defined to have one of four possible access categories: *private*, *protected*, *public,* or *package*. The keywords `private`, `protected`, and `public` are used to distinguish these four categories. These are called *access modifiers*. If no access modifier is specified, then the member is defined to have *package access*.

The four categories are defined as follows:

❑   *private*: accessible only from within the member's own class.
❑   *protected*: accessible only from with the member's class and its extensions.
❑   *package*: accessible from any class in the member's package.
❑   *public*: accessible from any class.

Listing B.3 on page 531 shows our `Point` class with its members' access modifiers appropriately specified. The instance fields x and y are `private`. This adheres to the object-oriented programming principle of *information hiding*, protecting the object's state from being improperly changed. In contrast, the three methods and the two-argument constructor are `public`, allowing them to be used by any client.

The no-argument constructor is `private`, preventing any client from creating a `Point` object with unspecified coordinates. It is invoked to initialize the `public` class field ORIGIN representing the point (0,0). This object is unique (`static`) and constant (`final`).

B.6 The this Keyword

In Java, when an instance method is invoked in an expression like

```
x.doSomething(y,z)
```

the statements in the doSomething() method will execute. During that execution, those statements can use the objects x, y, and z. The y and z objects are called *explicit arguments*, and the x object is called the *implicit argument* for that call.

The code that defines the method may look something like this:

```
public void doSomething(ClassY yy, ClassZ zz) {
    // executable statements...
}
```

When the invocation occurs, the parameters are assigned to their corresponding explicit arguments: The reference yy is assigned to the object y, and the reference zz is assigned to the object z.

But what about the object x? It has no parameter to represent it. The method's executable statements, however, are defined within some ClassX to which the object x belongs. In most cases, therefore the method can access the fields of the implicit parameter x without even mentioning the class name, as shown in Listing B.4.

LISTING B.4: Accessing Class Fields

```
1  class ClassX {
2      private int n;
3      private String s;
4
5      public void doSomething(ClassY yy, ClassZ zz) {
6          if (n == 33) System.out.println(s);
7          // do something with yy and zz...
8      }
9  }
```

At line 6, the doSomething() method accesses the n and s fields of the implicit parameter. Unlike the explicit parameters yy and zz, the implicit parameter has no name inside its own class. But in cases like this, it doesn't need a name; its field names n and s are used without any prefix.

In cases in which a prefix is needed to distinguish the fields of the implicit argument from other variables, the keyword this is used. When used as the name of an object, the keyword this represents the implicit argument.

For example, the previous method definition is equivalent to this form:

```
5   public void doSomething(ClassY yy, ClassZ zz) {
10      if (this.n == 33) System.out.println(this.s);
11      // do something with yy and zz...
12  }
```

The expressions this.n and this.s at line 6 are equivalent to the simpler forms, s and n.

The keyword this may also be used to invoke constructors, as shown in Listing B.5.

LISTING B.5: Using the this Keyword to Invoke Constructors

```
1   class ClassX {
2       private int m, n;
3       private String s;
4
5       public ClassX() {
6           s = "ABC";
7       }
8
9       public ClassX(int m) {
10          this();
11          this.m = m;
12      }
13
14      public ClassX(int m, int n) {
15          this(m);
16          this.n = n;
17      }
18  }
```

The expression this() at line 10 invokes the no-argument constructor at line 5, and the expression this(m) at line 15 invokes the one-argument constructor at line 10.

In Listing B.5, the this keyword is also used to represent the implicit argument at lines 11 and 16. For example, at line 11, it is needed to distincuish the class field m from the parameter m. (See Listing B.19 on page 555 for another example.)

If a constructor is invoked by a this() expression, it must be the first statement. For example, the following code is invalid because line 11 is the second statement of that constructor:

```
9    public ClassX(int m) {
19       this.m = m;
20       this();       // ILLEGAL: must be the first statement
21   }
```

B.7 Packages

Names for variables, methods, classes, etc. should be simple and descriptive. This makes your programs easier to understand and manage. But it also increases the likelihood of a *name clash*: trying to use the same name for different things. For example, the List class that you define is different from the List interface defined in the Java Class Libraries.

Java uses packages to resolve name clashes. A *package* is simply a way to compartmentalize or localize a group of related classes and interfaces.[4] For example, all the data structure classes and interfaces in the Java Collections Framework are defined in the standard Java

---

[4] An *interface* is essentially a class with no executable statements. (See Section B.16 on page 556.)

package named `java.util` (for "utilities"). Thus, the complete name for the standard Java `List` interface is `java.util.List`. This allows you to define your own `List` class without any name conflicts.

You can define your own package by using the **package** keyword at the beginning of your source code file.

▼ EXAMPLE B.1: Using Packages

Figure B.7 shows two different `Date` classes, each in its own package. The only difference is that the `package1.Date` class declares its `year`, `month`, and day fields to have type `String`, while the `package2.Date` class declares them to have type `int`:

Here we are using an editor named Araneae[5] instead of the NotePad editor. Among other advantages, this editor allows several files to be open at once and it displays the current file's path in the title bar.

You can see that the `package1.Date` source code file is saved in the folder `A:\package1\`, while the `package2.Date` source code file is saved in the folder `A:\package2\`. Obviously they must be saved in different folders because Java requires them to have the same file name, `Date.java`. Java source code files that define packages should always be stored this way, mapping the package name into the folder name.

The program shown in Figure B.8 is a simple test driver for testing the two `Date` classes. Note that it is stored in the root folder `A:\`. The two `Date` classes are referred to using their package prefixes: `package1.Date` and `package2.Date`. This tells the Java compiler to look for their class files in the respective folders `package1\` and `package2\`. The separate packages resolve the name clash: two different `Date` classes used in the same program.

The Command Prompt window[6] in Figure B.9 shows how the classes are compiled and how the program is run.

The Windows `dir/b/s` command displays in brief format the files in the current folder and all of its subfolders. The symbols `/b` (for "brief") and `/s` (for "subfolders") are *command switches* for the `dir` (for "directory") command.[7]

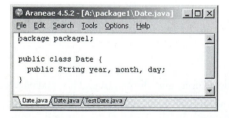
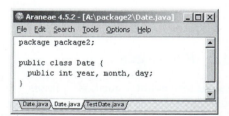

FIGURE B.7   Different Date classes in different packages.

---

[5] You can download this powerful editor for free from `http://www.tucows.com`

[6] You can right-click on the title bar and select Properties to change the background from black to white.

[7] For information on all the switches available for the dir command, enter `help dir` at the command prompt.

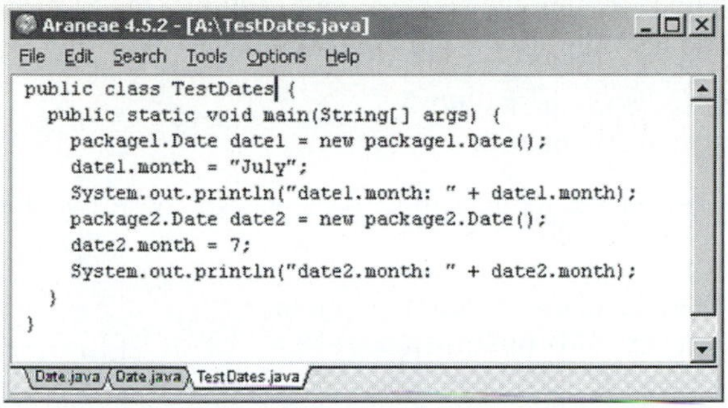

FIGURE B.8 Testing different Date classes.

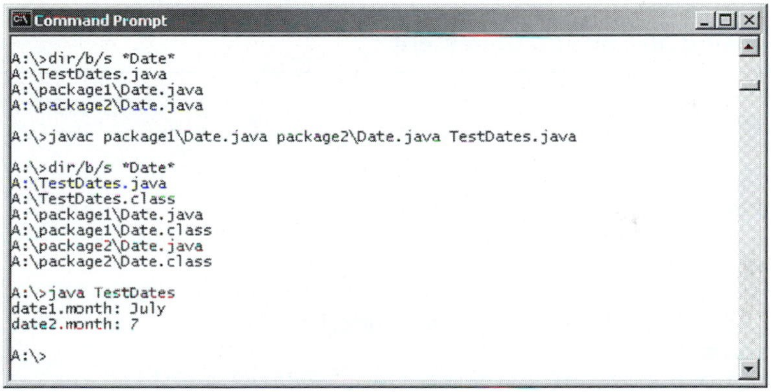

FIGURE B.9 Compiling and running the test program.

The test driver creates two objects: `date1` and `date2`. Since `date1` had type `package1.Date`, its fields are strings, and so date1.month is assigned the string `"July"`. Also, since `date2` had type `package3.Date`, its fields are integers, so `date2.month` is assigned the integer 7.

Note that the class files for the two `Date` classes are both named Date.class and they are kept in their respective subfolders `package1\` and `package2\`. As long as the dot symbol, signifying the current folder, is listed in the **CLASSPATH** environment variable, programs like `TestDate` can be run from that folder. The system automatically follows the path to the subfolders indicated by the package definitions. More generally, you could have a program located in a folder `A:\xx\yy\zz\`, and it could use a class defined in a package named `pp.qq` as long as the class file is in the folder `A:\xx\yy\zz\pp\qq\`.

Every one of the classes defined in the Java Class Libraries belongs to some package. For example, there is a `Date` class defined in the `java.util` package and another `Date` class defined in the `java.sql` package. The fundamental package is named `java.lang` (for "language"). Its classes can be used without naming the package. For example, the `String` and `System` classes belong to the `java.lang` package, so we can use them like this:

```
String name = "George Bush";
System.out.println(name);
```

Their complete, qualified names include their package, so those two lines are equivalent to these:

```
java.lang.String name = "George Bush";
java.lang.System.out.println(name);
```

If a class's package is not `java.lang`, then the package name must be specified explicitly wherever the class is used. There are two ways to do that: Either the package name is used as a prefix to the class name, or the package is specified in an `import` statement.

The `TestDate` program shown in Figure B.9 illustrates how package names are used as prefixes on class names. Listing B.6 shows an equivalent version of that program.

LISTING B.6: Using an `import` Statement

```
1   import package1.Date;
2
3   public class TestDate {
4     public static void main(String[] args) {
5       Date date1 = new Date();
6       date1.month = "July";
7       System.out.println("date1.month: " + date1.month);
8       package2.Date date2 = new package2.Date();
9       date2.month = 7;
10      System.out.println("date2.month: " + date2.month);
11    }
12  }
```

The `import` statement on line 1 tells the compiler to use `package1.Date` whenever it sees an unqualified `Date` class. Thus, line 5 is equivalent to

```
5       package1.Date date1 = new package1.Date();
```

We could have imported `package2.Date` instead of `package1.Date` in Listing B.6 the same way. But we cannot import both because the two distinct classes have the same name `Date`.

Importing packages from the standard Java Class Libraries works the same as from any other source. As long as the class file[8] is in the **CLASSPATH**, you can use its classes either way: by prefixing the class name with the package name or by using an `import` statement.

---

[8] Alternatively, the class's jar file may be listed in the CLASSPATH variable. The standard Java Class Libraries are all compressed in jar (for "Java archive") files. You can see what's in a jar file by using the `jar` command at the Command Prompt. For example, if you are using Java version 1.4.0, execute the command `jar tf rt.jar` from your `C:\j2sdk1.4.0\jre\lib` folder.

If you are using more than one class from the same package, you can use the *wildcard* symbol * to stand for all the classes in the package. For example, a program could begin[9] with the `import` statements

```
import java.awt.*;
import java.awt.event.*;

import java.io.*;
import java.util.Arrays;
import java.util.Random;
import package1.Date;
```

This would allow your program to use all the classes in the `java.awt` package, the `java.awt.event` package, the `java.io` package, in addition to the `java.util.Arrays` class, the `java.util.Random` class, and our own `package1.Date` class, without having to prefix the class names with their package names. Note that we could not use the code

```
import java.util.*;
```

here to import all the classes in the `java.util` package because the `Date` class in that package would then clash with our `package1.Date` class.

B.8 The Scope of a Class

The *scope* of a Java class determines where it can be accessed. There are two possibilities: A class that is defined with the `public` keyword has *public scope*, which means that any other class can use it; and a class that is defined without the `public` keyword has *package scope*, which means that only the other classes in its package can use it.[10] The `Hello` class in Listing B.1 on page 521 has *package scope*.

▼ **EXAMPLE B.2: Public Scope and Package Scope**

The Command Prompt window shown in Figure B.10 contains the compilation and execution of a program that uses four classes. The main class, named `Greetings`, has public scope, hence, the file is named `Greetings.java`. The other three classes, named `English`, `French`, and German, all have package scope. That allows these secondary classes to be defined in a file that has a different name.

Each of the three secondary classes has a single `static` method named `greetings()`. As `static` methods, they are invoked by the class itself (*e.g.*, `English.greetings()`) without having to instantiate the class.

Notice that the compiler generates four class files from the single source code file, one for each class: `Greetings.class`, `English.class`, `French.class`, and `German.class`. But only the `Greetings.class` file is executable because it is the only class that has a `main()` method.

---

[9] When you have several `import` statements, it is recommended that you alphabetize them for easy (human) reference.

[10] If no package is specified at the beginning of the source code file that defines the class, then its package scope consists of only those other class files that are in the same folder.

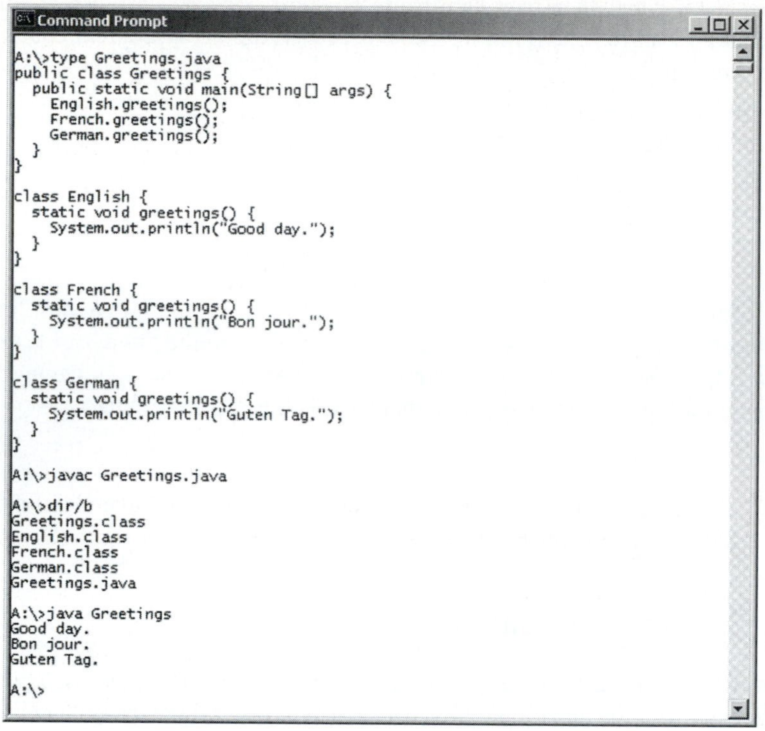

```
Command Prompt                                                    _ □ X
A:\>type Greetings.java
public class Greetings {
  public static void main(String[] args) {
    English.greetings();
    French.greetings();
    German.greetings();
  }
}

class English {
  static void greetings() {
    System.out.println("Good day.");
  }
}

class French {
  static void greetings() {
    System.out.println("Bon jour.");
  }
}

class German {
  static void greetings() {
    System.out.println("Guten Tag.");
  }
}

A:\>javac Greetings.java

A:\>dir/b
Greetings.class
English.class
French.class
German.class
Greetings.java

A:\>java Greetings
Good day.
Bon jour.
Guten Tag.

A:\>
```

FIGURE B.10 A Greetings class.

B.9 The new and instanceof Operators

Java defines two special operators: new and instanceof. The new operator invokes class constructors. The instanceof operator determines whether a given object is an instance of a given class.

The new operator is illustrated on line 5 of the program in Listing B.6 on page 538:

5   Date date1 = new Date();

This invokes the Date class's constructor, creating a new Date object to be referenced by the
variable date1.

The new operator defines an expression that can be used wherever an object reference could
be used, including as an argument to a method. For example,

        double d = Point.distance(p, new Point(25,62));

creates an *anonymous object* representing the point (25,62) and then computes the distance
between it and the Point object p. This is equivalent to the code

        Point q = new Point(25,62);
        double d = Point.distance(p,q);

except that the shorter version does not create the extra object q.

The new operator is also used to create arrays:

```
double[] x = new double[400];      // creates a 4000-element array
String[] names = new String[8];    // creates an 8-element array
int[][] a = new int[4][6];         // creates a 4-by-6 matrix
```

The instanceof operator tests the class of an object. It is typically used in situations like the equals() method shown in Listing B.7.

LISTING B.7: An equals() Method for the Point Class

```
1  public boolean equals(Object object) {
2     if (!(object instanceof Point)) return false;
3     Point point = (Point)object;
4     return (point.x == x && point.y == y);
5  }
```

The purpose of the equals() method is to determine whether the object passed to it represents the same thing as the object to which the call is bound. For example,

```
if (p.equals(q)) q.shift(3,1);
```

would shift q only if it represented the same point as p, and

```
if (q.equals(ORIGIN)) q = null;
```

would set q to null if it represented the origin point (0,0).

Line 2 in Listing B.7 returns false if the given object's type is not Point. Thus, the expression p.equals("George") would evaluate to false because the object "George" has type String, not Point.

Note that the parameter object is declared to have type Object in line 1. That merely means that it could be any type, since every class is an extension of the Object class. If the equals() method does not return at line 2, then the object really is a Point object. However, since its declared type is Object, it cannot be used as a Point object until it is explicitly identified as such. The expression (Point)object does that on line 3. This is known as *typecasting* or *type conversion*. It doesn't really change the type, since the object was really a Point object all along. This is checked at run time. If you try to cast an object to a type that it never was, then the run-time system will throw a ClassCastException.

Typecasting is necessary for the compiler to know what class members apply to the object being cast. By casting object to point in line 3, we can use its Point fields point.x and point.y in line 4.

B.10 Using Command Line Arguments

One way to provide input to a Java program is through the command line. When you execute a program from the command line, such as

```
java Hello
```

FIGURE B.11 Using command line arguments.

you can append strings that will be copied into the `args` array that is declared as a parameter in the `main()` method. For example, if you enter

```
java Hello George Bush
```

then `args[0]` will have the `String` value `"George"` and `args[1]` will have the `String` value `"Bush"`. More generally, if you follow the name of your main class with *n* strings (separated by white space), then the `args[]` array will have length *n* and will contain those *n* strings as its elements. These strings can then be used in your program, as illustrated in Listing B.8

LISTING B.8: Using Command Line Arguments

```
1   class Hello {
2     public static void main(String[] args) {
3       System.out.print("Hello, ");
4       int n = args.length;
5       for (int i = 0; i < n; i++)
6         System.out.print(" " + args[i]);
7       if (n == 0) System.out.println("World!");
8       else System.out.println("\nYour last name is " + args[n-1]);
9     }
10  }
```

The number of command line arguments is copied into the variable n at line 4. That number is 0 on the first run, 2 on the second run, and 4 on the third run shown. (See Figure B.11.)

Generally, when using the command line for input, it is wise to include a check that the user entered the expected arguments and to abort with a corrective error message if not. This is illustrated by the revised program in Listing B.9.

This program prints an error message at line 4 and aborts at line 5 if the user does not enter 2 arguments at the command line. (See Figure B.12.) The message follows the classic "Usage" format,[11] which explains how the program should be run. Not only does it show that

---

[11] For example, if you enter `javac Hello` (instead of `javac Hello.java`) at the command line, you will see the "Usage" statement for the `javac` program.

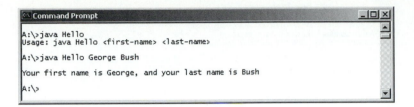

Command Prompt

A:\>java Hello
Usage: java Hello <first-name> <last-name>

A:\>java Hello George Bush

Your first name is George, and your last name is Bush

A:\>

FIGURE B.12   Checking the number of command line arguments.

two arguments are expected, but it also uses the <...> notation to indicate what those arguments should represent.

LISTING B.9: Checking the Number of Command Line Arguments

```
1  class Hello {
2    public static void main(String[] args) {
3      if (args.length != 2) {
4        System.err.println("Usage: java Hello <first-name> <last-name>");
5        System.exit(1);
6      }
7      System.out.print("\nYour first name is " + args[0]);
8      System.out.println(", and your last name is " + args[1]);
9    }
10 }
```

The command line can also be used to enter numeric data. You simply convert the numeric literal stored in the string args[i] to the appropriate numeric type using a parse method. (See Listing B.10.)

LISTING B.10: Numeric Input at the Command Line

```
1  class CommandLineInput {
2    public static void main(String[] args) {
3      int n = Integer.parseInt(args[0]);
4      double x = Double.parseDouble(args[1]);
5      System.out.print("The integer is " + n);
6      System.out.println(", and the decimal is " + args[1]);
7    }
8  }
```

This uses the static parseInt() method defined in the Integer class to convert the String literal "44" to the int value 44 at line 3. (See Figure B.13.) It uses the static parseDouble() method defined in the Double class to convert the String literal "3.14159" to the double value 3.14159 at line 4.

FIGURE B.13   Numeric input at the command line.

B.11 Wrapper Classes

The CommandLineInput program in Listing B.10 uses the two *wrapper classes*, Integer and Double. The java.lang package defines a wrapper class for each of the eight primitive types. They are named Boolean, Character, Byte, Short, Integer, Long, Float, and Double. These classes provide parse methods like those illustrated in Listing B.10, as well as **static** fields and utility methods. For example, the Float and Double classes define constants NaN (for "not a number"), MAX_VALUE, MIN_VALUE, NEGATIVE_INFINITY, and POSIIVE_INFINITY. The NaN value is used to signal an invalid floating-point value. These are illustrated in the program in Listing B.11:

LISTING B.11: Numeric Input at the Command Line

```
1   class CommandLineInput {
2     public static void main(String[] args) {
3       double x = 0.0;
4       System.out.println("x: " + x);
5       System.out.println("(x==0.0): " + (x==0.0));
6       System.out.println("Double.isNaN(x): " + Double.isNaN(x));
7       x /= x;
8       System.out.println("x: " + x);
9       System.out.println("(x==Double.NaN): " + (x==Double.NaN));
10      System.out.println("Double.isNaN(x): " + Double.isNaN(x));
11    }
12  }
```

```
A:\>java TestNaN
x: 0.0
(x==0.0): true
Double.isNaN(x): false
x: NaN
(x==Double.NaN): false
Double.isNaN(x): true

A:\>
```

FIGURE B.14   The NaN value.

The output is:

```
x: 0.0
(x==0.0): true
Double.isNaN(x): false
x: NaN
(x==Double.NaN): false
Double.isNaN(x): true
```

The double value NaN is assigned to x automatically when 0/0 is evaluated. Since that value does not qualify as any number (finite or infinite), the boolean expression (x==Double.NaN) evaluates to false. We have to use the boolean method Double.isNaN(x) to confirm that x has that non-number value.

B.12 Exception Handling

A Java *exception* is an instance of the Throwable class or of one of its extensions. Such an object can be instantiated by a running program in two ways: either explicitly by a throw statement in the program, or implicitly by the Java runtime system when it is unable to execute a statement in the program. When an exception is thrown, it can be caught by a catch clause of a try block. If it is not caught, then it will be rethrown by the method that called the current method, unless it is thrown in the main() method causing the program to terminate. Using a try block to catch an exception is called *exception handling*. That is the preferred solution because it allows the program to continue under program control.

The class inheritance hierarchy in Figure B.15 shows a few of the many standard exception types in Java. Two of the most common are listed last here: ArrayIndexOutOfBoundsException and NullPointerException.

There are two kinds of exceptions: the kind that you can prevent by better coding, and the kind that you can't. The first kind are called *unchecked exceptions*. They are instances of the Error class, the RuntimeException class, and their extensions. For example, if the division of an integer by zero is attempted, the system will generate an ArithmeticException.

Exceptions of the second kind are called *checked exceptions* because they are "checked" at compile time. Statements that throw them must either be placed within a try block or be declared in their method's header. Checked exceptions are the kind that should be expected and therefore managed by an exception handler.

The program in Listing B.12 illustrates an unchecked exception that is thrown by the Java runtime system. The attempt to divide by 0 in line 3 causes an ArithmeticException to be thrown.

LISTING B.12: Throwing an Unchecked Exception Implicitly

```
1  class Main {
2    public static void main(String[] args) {
3      int n = 4/0;
4      System.out.println("OK");
5    }
6  }
```

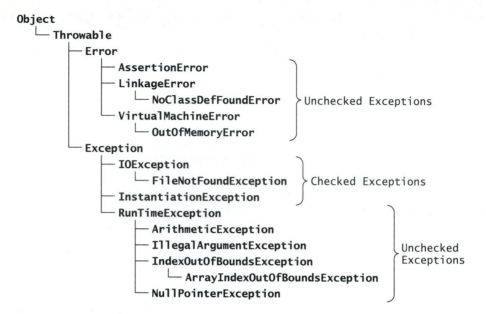

FIGURE B.15   The inheritance hierarchy of some unchecked and checked exceptions.

The output is

```
Exception in thread "main" java.lang.ArithmeticException: / by zero
        at Main.main(TestImplicitUncheckedException.java:3)
```

The program in Listing B.12 illustrates an unchecked exception that is thrown implicitly by the Java run-time system. The program in Listing B.13 illustrates an unchecked exception that is thrown by an explicit throw statement.

LISTING B.13: Throwing an Unchecked Exception Explicitly

```
1   class Main {
2     static double sqrt(double x) {
3       if (x<0) throw new IllegalArgumentException();
4       return Math.sqrt(x);
5     }
6     public static void main(String[] args) {
7       System.out.println(sqrt(-25));
8     }
9   }
```

The output is

```
Exception in thread "main" java.lang.IllegalArgumentException
        at Main.sqrt(TestExplicitUncheckedException.java:3)
        at Main.main(TestExplicitUncheckedException.java:7)
```

Note that the output shows that the exception was thrown at line 3 from the `sqrt()` method that was called at line 9 from `main()`.

Unchecked exceptions generally should not occur, and code that causes them should be corrected. On the other hand, checked exceptions generally cannot be avoided. Instead of being prevented, they are managed by `try...catch` statements.

A method that throws a checked exception must declare the exception with a `throws` clause in its header. A method that calls such a method must either rethrow the exception or encapsulate the call within a `try` block. The `try` block includes a `catch` clause whose block constitutes the exception handler. Listing B.14 illustrates rethrowing an exception. Listing B.15 on page 548 illustrates the alternative of using an exception handler.

LISTING B.14: Rethrowing a Checked Exception

```
1    import java.io.*;
2
3    class CopyFile {
4      public static void main(String[] args) throws IOException {
5        FileInputStream in = new FileInputStream(args[0]);
6        long bytes=0;
7        FileOutputStream out = new FileOutputStream(args[1]);
8        byte[] buf = new byte[512];
9        for (int count = in.read(buf); count > 0; count = in.read(buf)) {
10         out.write(buf,0,count);
11         bytes += count;
12       }
13       System.out.println(bytes + " bytes were copied.");
14     }
15   }
```

The first run copied the file `Contract.html` successfully. (See Figure B.16.) But on the second run, the file name was misspelled, so the program threw a `FileNotFoundException` exception at line 5. Instead of handling the exception, `main()` rethrows it, causing the program to crash.

FIGURE B.16 Throwing a `FileNotFoundException` object.

Note that the `throws` clause at line 4 specifies the `IOException` class, even though the actual exception thrown is a `FileNotFoundException` object. This is a valid use of *polymorphism*; the `FileNotFoundException` class is an extension of the `IOException` class, so any exception of type `FileNotFoundException` also may be regarded as having type `IOException`.

LISTING B.15: Handling a Checked Exception

```
1    import java.io.*;
2
3    class CopyFile {
4      public static void main(String[] args) {
5        int bytes=0;
6        try {
7          FileInputStream in = new FileInputStream(args[0]);
8          FileOutputStream out = new FileOutputStream(args[1]);
9          byte[] buf = new byte[512];
10         for (int count=in.read(buf); count>0; count=in.read(buf)) {
11           out.write(buf,0,count);
12           bytes += count;
13         }
14       } catch (IOException e) { e.printStackTrace(); }
15       System.out.println(bytes + " bytes were copied.");
16     }
17   }
```

The program in Listing B.15 is nearly the same as the program in Listing B.14. The difference is that in Listing B.15 `main()` does not rethrow the I/O exceptions. Instead, it encapsulates the exception-throwing code in a `try` block whose `catch` clause handles the exceptions. The exception is thrown, the same as in Listing B.14. But since it is caught, the program is allowed to continue executing after the `catch` clause, executing the statement at line 15.

B.13 Java I/O

All input and output in Java is managed by stream objects. A *stream* is a flow of information between a program and some external data repository, such as a file, a socket, or an array. An *input stream* flows from the external source into the program, and an *output stream* flows from the program to the external destination.

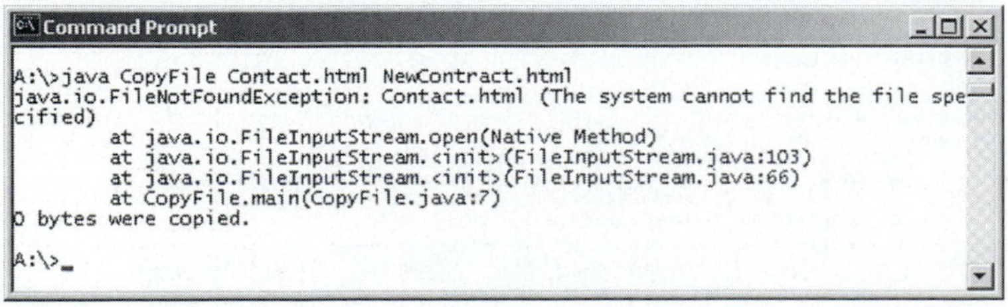

FIGURE B.17 Catching a `FileNotFoundException` object.

Java recognizes two kinds of external data: text and binary. Text information is readable by humans and consists of individual 16-bit characters. Binary information is used mostly for images and sound and it consists of individual bits grouped into 8-bit bytes. Java uses the terms `Reader` and `Writer` for its text streams, and the terms `InputStream` and `OutputStream` for its binary streams, thus defining four `abstract` classes:

	Input	Output
Text	Reader	Writer
Binary	InputStream	OutputStream

This two-dimensional categorization applies to all 34 Java stream classes, summarized in the tables that follow.

The four file processing classes are

Files:	Input	Output
Text	FileReader	FileWriter
Binary	FileInputStream	FileOutputStream

For pipes to and from sockets, the classes are

Pipes:	Input	Output
Text	PipedReader	PipedWriter
Binary	PipedInputStream	PipedOutputStream

For "in-memory" array processing, the classes are

Arrays:	Input	Output
Text	CharArrayReader	CharArrayWriter
Binary	ByteArrayInputStream	ByteArrayOutputStream

Java even has I/O classes for using `String` objects as streams:

Strings:	Input	Output
Text	StringReader	StringWriter

The I/O classes for serializing general objects are

Objects:	Input	Output
Binary	ObjectInputStream	ObjectOutputStream

Similarly, the I/O classes for serializing variables of primitive type (`int`, `double`, *etc.*) are

Primitive Data:	Input	Output
Binary	DataInputStream	DataOutputStream

Some I/O classes are used with others to modify the data in the stream:

Buffering:	Input	Output
Text	BufferedReader	BufferedWriter
Binary	BufferedInputStream	BufferedOutputStream

Filtering:	Input	Output
Text	FilterReader	FilterWriter
Binary	FilterInputStream	FilterOutputStream

There are also specialized input classes for "peeking ahead" and counting line numbers:

Peeking:	Input
Text	PushBackReader
Binary	PushBackInputStream

Counting:	Input
Text	LineNumberReader

In addition, there are special output classes for printing, and there is even one for concatenating a sequence of output streams:

Printing:	Output
Text	PrintWriter
Binary	PrintStream

Concatenation:	Output
Binary	SequenceOutputStream

Finally, there are two specialized classes for using characters with byte streams:

Converting:	Input	Output
Binary	InputStreamReader	OutputStreamWriter

The class hierarchy for these 34 classes and the 4 `abstract` classes that they extend is shown in Figure B.18. It also includes the `File` class and the `RandomAccessFile` class.

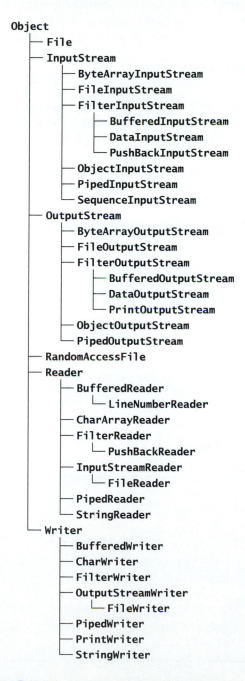

```
Object
    ├── File
    ├── InputStream
    │       ├── ByteArrayInputStream
    │       ├── FileInputStream
    │       ├── FilterInputStream
    │       │       ├── BufferedInputStream
    │       │       ├── DataInputStream
    │       │       └── PushBackInputStream
    │       ├── ObjectInputStream
    │       ├── PipedInputStream
    │       └── SequenceInputStream
    ├── OutputStream
    │       ├── ByteArrayOutputStream
    │       ├── FileOutputStream
    │       ├── FilterOutputStream
    │       │       ├── BufferedOutputStream
    │       │       ├── DataOutputStream
    │       │       └── PrintOutputStream
    │       ├── ObjectOutputStream
    │       └── PipedOutputStream
    ├── RandomAccessFile
    ├── Reader
    │       ├── BufferedReader
    │       │       └── LineNumberReader
    │       ├── CharArrayReader
    │       ├── FilterReader
    │       │       └── PushBackReader
    │       ├── InputStreamReader
    │       │       └── FileReader
    │       ├── PipedReader
    │       └── StringReader
    └── Writer
            ├── BufferedWriter
            ├── CharWriter
            ├── FilterWriter
            ├── OutputStreamWriter
            │       └── FileWriter
            ├── PipedWriter
            ├── PrintWriter
            └── StringWriter
```

FIGURE B.18 The inheritance hierarchy of input/output classes.

Instances of the `File` class represent file names. The file class includes methods for creating and manipulating files.

Instances of the `RandomAccessFile` class represent random access files. These objects include a read/write pointer, set by the `seek()` method, which locates the next byte in the file to be read or overwritten. This random access allows the file to be used like an external array.

▼ **EXAMPLE B.3: Random Access to a File**

The Command Prompt transcript in Figure B.19 illustrates random access of a file.

The file is created by the `Test1` program. It uses a `FileOutputStream` to write 320 bytes to the file. Each byte is the bit string `00101111`, whose decimal value is 47. The `type` command interprets that byte as the character `'/'` (slash), and thus prints that character 320 times.

The `Test2` program uses random access on the file. The call `raf.seek(100)` positions the read-write pointer at byte number 100. The call to the `writeBytes()` method then overwrites

FIGURE B.19   Random access into a file.

bytes 100-129 with the 30-character string `"This overwrites bytes 100-129."`. Next, the read-write pointer is moved to byte number 155, and the call to the `writeByte()` method then overwrites the 155th byte with a newline character `'\n'`. Next, the read-write pointer is moved to byte number 115, and the call to the `readLine()` method reads from that byte to the end of the line, which is identified by the newline character at byte 155. Consequently, the "line" read is the 40-character string `" bytes 100-129.//////////////////////////"`. When the file is typed again at the end of the transcript, the new-line character is identified at byte 155 by the start of a new line there.

B.14 Interactive Input

Interactive input in Java is not quite as simple as it is in some other languages such as C++. As a pure object-oriented language, Java requires some input "reader" objects to be instantiated, and that is best done in a `try` block.

Just as output is done by the `System.out` object, input is done by the `System.in` object. These two objects represent the *standard output* (usually the video display) and the *standard input* (usually the keyboard). By itself, the `System.in` object is capable of reading only 8-bit bytes (raw bit strings). To use more powerful methods on it, we attach an `InputStreamReader` object to it, and then attach a `BufferedReader` object to that. The `BufferedReader` class, like the `RandomAccessFile` class (see Example B.3 on page 552), has a `readLine()` method that returns a `String` object. This allows primitive types (`int`, `double`, *etc.*) as well as ordinary strings to be read from the keyboard by reading them as strings first and them parsing then into numeric values as in the program in Listing B.16 on page 553.

LISTING B.16: Interactive Input

```
1   import java.io.*;
2
3   class Main {
4     public static void main(String[] args) {
5       try {
6         Reader reader = new InputStreamReader(System.in);
7         BufferedReader input = new BufferedReader(reader);
8         System.out.print("Enter your name: ");
9         String string = input.readLine();
10        System.out.println("You entered " + string);
11        System.out.print("Enter an integer: ");
12        int n = Integer.parseInt(input.readLine());
13        System.out.println("You entered " + n);
14        System.out.print("Enter a decimal number: ");
15        double x = Double.parseDouble(input.readLine());
16        System.out.println("You entered " + x);
17      } catch (IOException e) { e.printStackTrace(); }
18    }
19  }
```

The output is

```
Enter your name: Bill Gates
You entered Bill Gates
Enter an integer: 491
You entered 491
Enter a decimal number: 2.71828
You entered 2.71828
```

The input object defined on line 7 reads strings from the keyboard. On line 12 the string "491" is converted to the integer 491, and on line 15 the string "2.71828" is converted to the decimal 2.71828.

B.15 Initialization

An *initialization block* is like an anonymous constructor that is automatically invoked by every other constructor before it executes any of its own statements. It is simply a block of code with no name or label.

LISTING B.17: An Initialization Block to Number Objects

```
1   class Thing {
2      public final long id;
3      public String name;
4      private static long nextId=1000;
5
6      { id = nextId++;
7      }
8
9      public Thing(String name) {
10        this.name = name;
11     }
12
13     // other members included here
14  }
```

The `Thing` class defined in Listing B.17 has an initialization block at lines 6–7. Its single statement has the effect of numbering each object when it is created, beginning with `id` number 1000. That statement could be placed within the constructor, (at line 10 instead,) with the same effect. The advantage is that, with several constructors, the common statements need only be included once, in the initialization block, instead of explicitly within each constructor.

Static fields can be initialized directly, as the `nextId` field is at line 4 in Listing B.17. They can also be initialized with more complex code in a separate *static initializer*. Also called a *static initialization block*, a static initializer is simply an anonymous block of code that is preceded by the `static` keyword:

LISTING B.18: A Static Initializers

```
1   class Primes {
2       public static final int COUNT=1000;
3       public static final int[] prime = new int[COUNT];
4
5       static {
6           prime[0] = 2;
7           prime[1] = 3;
8           for (int i = 2; i < COUNT; i++) {
9               int n = prime[i-1] + 2;
10              for (int j = 1; j < i; j++)
11                  if (n % prime[j] == 0) {
12                      n += 2;
13                      j = 0;
14                  }
15              prime[i] = n;
16          }
17      }
18  }
```

The Primes class defined in Listing B.18 contains a public static array prime[] of the first 1000 prime numbers. The array is initilized by the static initializer at lines 5-17. Its code executes automatically when the class is loaded. That allows the array prime[] to be declared final (*i.e.*, constant).

Note that we cannot use a constructor to set the value of COUNT (even if it isn't declared final) because constructors execute after static initializers.

In addition to initialization blocks and static initializers, a third way to execute statements before a constructor executes its own code is to have the constructor invoke another constructor. This is done by using the this keyword as though it were the name of a method. The Student class in Listing B.19 illustrates this technique.

LISTING B.19: Constructors Invoking Other Constructors

```
1   class Student {
2       public String name;
3       public int credits;
4       public double gpa;
5
6       public Student(String name) {
7           this.name = name;
8       }
9
10      public Student(String name, int credits) {
11          this(name);
12          this.credits = credits;
13      }
14
```

```
15    public Student(String name, int credits, double gpa) {
16       this(name, credits);
17       this.gpa = gpa;
18    }
19 }
```

At line 11, the expression `this`(name) invokes the one-argument constructor defined at line 6, passing the argument name, which then gets assigned to the field name (which is identified by the expression `this`.name to distinguish it from the argument). At line 16, the expression `this`(name, credits) invokes the two-argument constructor defined at line 10, passing the arguments name and credits, which then get assigned to the fields name and credits.

B.16 Interfaces

An *interface* in Java can be regarded as a class with no executable statements. Instead of complete methods, it contains only their signatures (headers). Interfaces can also have fields, but they must be `public`, `static`, and `final`. Since they are `final` (constants), they must also be initialized. By convention, the modifier keywords can be omitted. Interfaces may also have inner (nested) interfaces and classes.

In object-oriented programming, an *abstract data type* (ADT) is a specification for a data type that defers its implementations to concrete data types. Thus, ADTs can be described by interfaces. They act as contracts between the designers and the implementors of the software. They guarantee *what* the data type is able do without defining *how* it is done.

Listing B.20 shows the `Comparable` interface that is defined in the standard `java.lang` package.

LISTING B.20: The `Comparable` Interface

```
1    public interface Comparable {
2       public int compareTo(Object object);
3    }
```

This interface specifies a single method, named `compareTo()`, which returns an `int`. It is meant to be used like this:

```
int c = p.compareTo(q);
if (c < 0) System.out.println("p < q");
else if (c > 0) System.out.println("p > q");
else System.out.println("p == q");   // c==0
```

The actual numeric value of c is irrelevant; only its sign matters. The three possibilities (negative, zero, or positive) indicate whether p is less than q, p equals q, or p is greater than q. Thus, when a class implements the `Comparable` interface, it is announcing that its elements can be totally ordered.

The LatticePoint class shown in Listing B.21 implements the Comparable interface. It does so by including the clause "implements Comparable" in its header and by including a complete definition of the required compareTo() method.

LISTING B.21: A LatticePoint Class that Implements the Comparable Interface

```
1   public class LatticePoint implements Comparable {
2       private int x, y;
3
4       public LatticePoint(int x, int y) {
5           this.x = x;
6           this.y = y;
7       }
8
9       public int compareTo(Object object) {
10          LatticePoint q = (LatticePoint)object;
11          if (x < q.x) return -1;
12          if (x > q.x) return 1;
13          if (y < q.y) return -1;
14          if (y > q.y) return 1;
15          return 0;
16      }
17
18      public String toString() {
19          return "(" + x + "," + y + ")";
20      }
21  }
```

Note that this implementation defines the *lexicographic ordering* for two-dimensional points. For example, (6,2) > (5,4) because 6 > 5, and (6,2) < (8,1) because 6 < 8, but (6,2) > (6,1) because 2 > 1.

An interface need not specify any methods at all. An empty interface like that is used to mark classes.

The Cloneable interface that is defined in the standard java.lang package is an example of a *marker interface*. A class implements Cloneable to indicate that its objects can be cloned (duplicated). The Object class defines a clone() method that performs a field-by-field copy of the original object. But this method has protected scope, so it can be used directly only with an object's own class. Thus, to allow its instances to be cloned, a class must define its own clone() method–And, instead of "reinventing the wheel," the local clone() method should simply invoke the Object class's clone() method, like this:

```
return super.clone();
```

The clone() method in the Object class throws a CloneNotSupportedException. This is a checked exception, so it should be rethrown by the local class's clone() method, as shown in Listing B.22

LISTING B.22: Implementing the `Cloneable` **Interface**

```
1    public class LatticePoint implements Cloneable, Comparable {
2      private int x, y;
3
4      public LatticePoint(int x, int y) {
5        this.x = x;
6        this.y = y;
7      }
8
9      public Object clone() throws CloneNotSupportedException {
10       return super.clone();
11     }
12
13     public int compareTo(Object object) {
14     // The remaining lines are the same as in Listing B.21.
```

This is the standard way for a class to implement the `Cloneable` interface.

Note that a class may implement several interfaces.

B.17 Types and Polymorphism

A *type* in Java is either a class, an interface, an array, or one of the eight primitive types. Types are used to declare class fields, local variables, method parameters, and return types, like this:

```
Person person;
Cloneable line;
LatticePoint[] points;
double x;
```

The word *polymorphic* means "many forms." In computing, it means the ability of an object of one class to have the form of an object of another class; (*i.e.*, the object can be used where objects of another class are expected). In Java, that is always possible as long as the other class is an ancestor class.

If an object is declared to have an interface for its type, then its instantiation must be made by a constructor for a class or extension of a class that implements that interface or one of its extensions:

```
Comparable p = new LatticePoint(6,2);   // OK
Comparable object = new Object();        // ERROR
```

Arrays in Java are also polymorphic. Suppose class B extends class A. We would then have

```
B[] bb = { new B(), new B(), new B() };   // an array of three Bs
A[] aa = bb;   // OK: now aa and bb both refer to the same array
```

B.18 Abstract Methods and Abstract Classes

Interfaces are very useful for specifying what some classes should be able to do, allowing the definitions of how it should be done to be deferred to the class definitions. But in some cases, interfaces are too restrictive. They do not allow any (nonfinal) variable definitions nor any executable statements. Some situations call for a partial class implementation with some methods deferred. That is done with abstract classes and methods.

An *abstract method* is a method heading, with no body of executable statements. An *abstract class* is a class that has at least one abstract method. These are illustrated in Listing B.23. The Shape class must be declared abstract because it has three abstract methods: getArea(), getDiameter(), and getPerimeter(). These methods cannot be implemented until the actual dimensions of the shape are known. And those dimensions depend upon the kind of shape one has. On the other hand, the constructor and the getColor() method can be defined here, so it could not be defined as an interface.

Note that we define the constructor to be private, so it can only be invoked from extensions of this class. This prevents any public instantiation of the abstract class, since it has no other constructors.

Listing B.24 shows a concrete extension of the Shape class. Note that this Circle class has no abstract methods.

LISTING B.23: An Abstract Class

```
1   public abstract class Shape {
2      protected String color = "black";
3
4      protected Shape(String color) {
5         this.color = color;
6      }
7
8      public abstract double getArea();
9
10     public String getColor() {
11        return color;
12     }
13
14     public abstract double getDiameter();
15
16     public abstract double getPermeter();
17  }
```

LISTING B.24: A Concrete Subclass

```
1   public class Circle extends Shape {
2      protected double radius;
3
4      public Circle() {
5         this(1.0, "black");
6      }
7
8      public Circle(double radius, String color) {
```

```
9        super(color);
10        this.radius = radius;
11    }
12
13    public double getArea() {
14        return Math.PI*radius*radius;
15    }
16
17    public double getDiameter() {
18        return 2*radius;
19    }
20
21    public double getPermeter() {
22        return 2*Math.PI*radius;
23    }
24 }
```

B.19   From C++ to Java

We conclude this appendix with some summary information for C++ programmers who are learning Java.

The following are some important distinctions:

❑   In Java, every executable statement must be in some class.
❑   In Java, every class is (directly or indirectly) a subclass of the `Object` class.
❑   In Java, `main()` must defined as

```
public static void main(String[] args)
```

❑   Java uses `Object` elements in lieu of `template` classes.
❑   Java allows no external functions or variables.
❑   Java uses references instead of pointers.
❑   All arguments are passed by value.
❑   The C++ definition

```
string* s = new string;
```

❑   is equivalent to the Java definition

```
String s = new String();
```

❑   Java uses automatic garbage collection instead of the `delete` operator.

Here is a list of correspondences between C++ and Java:

```
bool ........................................ boolean
char ........................................ char
wchar_t ..................................... char
short ....................................... short
int ......................................... int
```

```
long. . . . . . . . . . . . . . . . . . . . . . . . . . . . . . . . . .long
unsigned char . . . . . . . . . . . . . . . . . . . . . . . . .byte
unsigned short . . . . . . . . . . . . . . . . . . . . . . .N/A
unsigned int . . . . . . . . . . . . . . . . . . . . . . . .N/A
unsigned long . . . . . . . . . . . . . . . . . . . . . . .N/A
float . . . . . . . . . . . . . . . . . . . . . . . . . . . . . . .float
double . . . . . . . . . . . . . . . . . . . . . . . . . . . . .double
enum. . . . . . . . . . . . . . . . . . . . . . . . . . . . . . .N/A
string . . . . . . . . . . . . . . . . . . . . . . . . . . . . .String
const . . . . . . . . . . . . . . . . . . . . . . . . . . . . . .final
goto. . . . . . . . . . . . . . . . . . . . . . . . . . . . . . . .N/A
pointer . . . . . . . . . . . . . . . . . . . . . . . . . . . . .N/A
reference . . . . . . . . . . . . . . . . . . . . . . . . . . .N/A
pass by value . . . . . . . . . . . . . . . . . . . . . . . .pass
pass by reference. . . . . . . . . . . . . . . . . . . . .N/A
inline . . . . . . . . . . . . . . . . . . . . . . . . . . . . . .N/A
register . . . . . . . . . . . . . . . . . . . . . . . . . . . .N/A
namespace . . . . . . . . . . . . . . . . . . . . . . . . . .package
printf() . . . . . . . . . . . . . . . . . . . . System.out.println()
scanf() . . . . . . . . . . . . . . . . . . . . .System.in.readln()
class . . . . . . . . . . . . . . . . . . . . . . . . . . . . . .class
struct . . . . . . . . . . . . . . . . . . . . . . . . . . . . .class
data member . . . . . . . . . . . . . . . . . . . . .field, instance variable
member function . . . . . . . . . . . . . . . . . . . . .method
public . . . . . . . . . . . . . . . . . . . . . . . . . . . . .public
protected . . . . . . . . . . . . . . . . . . . . . . . . . .protected
private . . . . . . . . . . . . . . . . . . . . . . . . . . . .private
static . . . . . . . . . . . . . . . . . . . . . . . . . . . . .static
this. . . . . . . . . . . . . . . . . . . . . . . . . . . . . . . .this
new. . . . . . . . . . . . . . . . . . . . . . . . . . . . . . . .new
delete . . . . . . . . . . . . . . . . . . . . . . . . . . . . .N/A
template . . . . . . . . . . . . . . . . . . . . . . . . . . .N/A
operator . . . . . . . . . . . . . . . . . . . . . . . . . . .N/A
friend . . . . . . . . . . . . . . . . . . . . . . . . . . . . .N/A
sizeof . . . . . . . . . . . . . . . . . . . . . . . . . . . . .N/A
typedef . . . . . . . . . . . . . . . . . . . . . . . . . . . .N/A
typeid . . . . . . . . . . . . . . . . . . . . . . . . . . . . .getClass()
assert . . . . . . . . . . . . . . . . . . . . . . . . . . . . .assert
virtual . . . . . . . . . . . . . . . . . . . . . . . . . . . . .abstract
virtual class . . . . . . . . . . . . . . . . . . . . . . . .abstract class
virtual function . . . . . . . . . . . . . . . . . . . . . .abstract method
pure virtual class . . . . . . . . . . . . . . . . . . . . .interface
```

```
header file. . . . . . . . . . . . . . . . . . . . . . . . . . . . . . . . package
#include . . . . . . . . . . . . . . . . . . . . . . . . . . . . . . . . . import
vector . . . . . . . . . . . . . . . . . . . . . . . . . . . . . . . . . . Vector
stack . . . . . . . . . . . . . . . . . . . . . . . . . . . . . . . . . . . Stack
queue . . . . . . . . . . . . . . . . . . . . . . . . . . . . . . . . . . . ArrayList
deque . . . . . . . . . . . . . . . . . . . . . . . . . . . . . . . . . . . ArrayList
priority_queue . . . . . . . . . . . . . . . . . . . . . . . . . . . . . . N/A
list . . . . . . . . . . . . . . . . . . . . . . . . . . . . . . . . . . . . LinkedList
map . . . . . . . . . . . . . . . . . . . . . . . . . . . . . . . . . . . . HashMap, TreeMap
set . . . . . . . . . . . . . . . . . . . . . . . . . . . . . . . . . . . . HashSet, TreeSet
```

APPENDIX REVIEW

❏ Java can be downloaded for free from `http://java.sun.com`.
❏ A Java program is a collection of classes, one of which has a `main()` method.
❏ A class named `MyClass` can be compiled with the command `javac MyClass`.
❏ The program can be executed with the command `java Main`, where `Main` is the name of the class that contains the `main()` method.
❏ The PATH environment variable must include the path to the `javac` the `java` commands.
❏ The CLASSPATH environment variable must include the paths to the class files used by the program.
❏ Java has eight primitive types: `boolean`, `char`, `byte`, short, int, long, `float`, and `double`.
❏ The `char` type uses 2-byte Unicode characters.
❏ The `byte` type uses 1-byte bit strings.
❏ Every executable statement in Java must be in some class.
❏ Classes have three kinds of members: fields, constructors, and methods.

REVIEW QUESTIONS

B.1   What is the difference between a primitive type and a reference type?

B.2   What is an immutable object?

B.3   What is the purpose of a constructor?

B.4   What happens if no constructor is defined explicitly in a class.

B.5   What is the effect of defining a single `private` constructor in a class?

B.6   What does the keyword "`this`" represent?

B.7   In the `Point` class in Listing B.3 on page 531, why make the x and y fields `private` if we are going to allow `public` access to them through their accessor methods x() and y()?

PROGRAMMING PROBLEMS

B.1   Modify the program in Listing B.2 on page 530 so that it tests floating-point overflow for variables of type `float`. Have it repeatedly multiply n by 10 until `Float.isInfinite(n)` returns true.

B.2   Modify the `Point` class in Listing B.3 on page 531 so that `Point` objects can be moved by specified horizontal and vertical increments. Add the method

```
public void moveBy(double dx, double dy)
```

and then test it.

B.3   Modify the `Point` class in Listing B.3 on page 531 so that `Point` objects can be moved to a specified location. Add the method

```
public void moveTo(double x, double y)
```

and then test it.

B.4   Add this *copy constructor* to the `Point` class in Listing B.3 on page 531,

```
public Point(Point p)
```

and then test it.

B.5   Modify the program in Listing B.11 on page 544 by testing 1/0 instead of 0/0. Initialize x to be 1.0, and then use POSITIVE_INFINITY in place of NaN, and use `isInfinite(x)` in place of `isNaN(x)`.

B.6   Modify the program in Listing B.13 on page 546 so that it attempts to print the square root of a `double` value that is read from the command line. Use

```
System.out.println(sqrt(Double.parseDouble(args[0]));
```

Test your program with positive and negative values.

B.7   Consider the expression `"8"` + 3. What type and value will this expression evaluate to in Java? Check your answer by passing the expression to `System.out.println()`.

B.8   Consider the expression `'8'` + 3. What type and value will this expression evaluate to in Java? Check your answer by passing the expression to `System.out.println()`.

ANSWERS TO REVIEW QUESTIONS

B.1   A *primitive type* is one of the eight built-in types: `boolean`, `char`, `byte`, `short`, `int`, `long`, `float`, and `double`. A *reference type* is either a class or an interface.

B.2   An *immutable object* is an object whose fields cannot be changed.

B.3   A constructor implicitly creates an instance of the class to which it belongs. Its explicit obligation is to initialize the fields of the class.

B.4   If no constructor is explicitly defined in a class, then the compiler automatically defines a no-argument constructor.

B.5   If a class has a single `private` constructor defined, then the class will not be able to be instantiated except from within the class itself.

B.6   The keyword `this` is a reference to the current object. It is also used to invoke a class's constructors from within the class.

B.7   If the x and y fields were made `public`, the client programs could change their values. The accessor methods x() and y() provide read-only access to them.

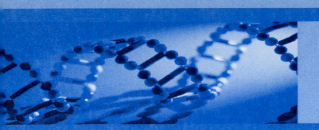

There was more imagination in the head of Archimedes than in that of Homer.

—Voltaire

Appendix C

Essential Mathematics

As a science, computer science depends upon fundamental theoretical principles that are derived and applied using mathematics. This appendix summarizes the mathematical topics that are needed for the study of data structures.

C.1 The Floor and Ceiling Functions

The floor and ceiling functions return the nearest integer for a given real number. The *floor* of x, denoted by $\lfloor x \rfloor$, is the greatest integer that is not greater than x. The *ceiling* of x, denoted by $\lceil x \rceil$, is the smallest integer that is not smaller than x. Another way to put it is that the floor and ceiling of x are the nearest integers on, respectively, the left and on the right of x. (See Figure C.1.)

For example, if $x = 2.71828$, then $\lfloor x \rfloor = 2$ and $\lceil x \rceil = 3$.

◆ **FORMULA C.1: The Floor and Ceiling Functions**

In the following formulas, $\mathbf{Z}$ stands for the set of all integers, and x is any real (decimal) number:

1. $\lfloor x \rfloor = \max\{m \in \mathbf{Z} \mid m \leq x\}$, and $\lceil x \rceil = \min\{n \in \mathbf{Z} \mid n \geq x\}$.
2. $\lfloor x \rfloor \leq x < \lfloor x \rfloor + 1$, and $\lceil x \rceil - 1 < x \leq \lceil x \rceil$.
3. $x - 1 < \lfloor x \rfloor \leq x \leq \lceil x \rceil < x + 1$.
4. If $n \in \mathbf{Z}$ and $n \leq x < n + 1$, then $n = \lfloor x \rfloor$. If $n \in \mathbf{Z}$ and $n - 1 < x \leq n$, then $n = \lceil x \rceil$.
5. If $x \in \mathbf{Z}$, then $\lfloor x \rfloor = x = \lceil x \rceil$.
6. If $x \notin \mathbf{Z}$, then $\lfloor x \rfloor < x < \lceil x \rceil$.
7. $\lfloor -x \rfloor = -\lceil x \rceil$ and $\lceil -x \rceil = -\lfloor x \rfloor$.
8. $\lfloor x + 1 \rfloor = \lfloor x \rfloor + 1$ and $\lceil x + 1 \rceil = \lceil x \rceil + 1$.

565

$$x - 1 < \lfloor x \rfloor \ \le \ x \le \lceil x \rceil < x + 1$$

1   2   3   4

FIGURE C.1 The floor and ceiling functions.

C.2 Logarithms

The *logarithm with base b* of a number x is the exponent y on b for which $b^y = x$. For example, with base 10 the logarithm of 1000 is 3 because $10^3 = 1000$. This is written $\log_{10} 1000 = 3$.

Social scientists usually use base 10 and write $\log x$ for $\log_{10} x$, called the *common logarithm*. Physical scientists and mathematicians usually use base $e = 2.71828$ and write $\ln x$ for $\log_e x$, called the *natural logarithm*. Computer scientists usually use base 2 and write $\lg x$ for $\log_2 x$, called the *binary logarithm*.

As mathematical functions, logarithms are the inverses of exponential functions:

$$y = \log_b x \Leftrightarrow b^y = x$$

For example, $\log_2 256 = 8$ because $2^8 = 256$. This equivalence is the definition of the logarithm. The following properties of logarithms follow directly from the definition of logarithms:

◆ **FORMULA C.2: The Laws of Logarithms**

1. $\log_b(b^y) = y$
2. $b^{\log_b x} = x$
3. $\log_b uv = \log_b u + \log_b v$
4. $\log_b u/v = \log_b u - \log_b v$
5. $\log_b u^v = v \log_b u$
6. $\log_b x = (\log_c x)/(\log_c b) = (\log_b c)(\log_c x)$
7. For a positive integer n, $\lceil \lg(n + 1) \rceil = \lfloor \lg n \rfloor + 1$.

Here are some examples of how these laws can be applied:

$$\log_2 256 = \log_2 (2^8) = 8$$

$$\log_2 1{,}000{,}000{,}000{,}000 = \log_2 1000^4 = 4(\log_2 1000) = 4(9.966) = 39.86$$

$$\log_2 1000 = (\log_{10} 1000)/(\log_{10} 2) = 3/0.30103 = 9.966$$

$$(\ln n)/(\lg n) = (\log_e n)/(\log_2 n) = \log_e 2 = 0.693, \text{ for any } n > 1$$

◆ **FORMULA C.3: Logarithms**

If n and p are integers with $2^p < n < 2^{p+1}$, then $p = \lfloor \lg n \rfloor$ and $p + 1 = \lceil \lg n \rceil$.

The integer $\lfloor \lg n \rfloor$ is called the *integral binary logarithm* of n. This is the number of times that n can be divided by 2 before reaching 1. For example, the integral binary logarithm of 1000 is 9 because 1000 can be split in half nine times: 500, 250, 125, 62, 31, 15, 7, 3, 1.

The program in Listing C.1 illustrates the binary logarithm, implemented as a `static` method named `iLg()`.

LISTING C.1: Testing the Integral Binary Logarithm

```
1   public class TestBinaryLogarithm {
2     public static void main(String[] args) {
3       System.out.println("iLg(1) = " + iLg(1));
4       System.out.println("iLg(2) = " + iLg(2));
5       System.out.println("iLg(3) = " + iLg(3));
6       System.out.println("iLg(4) = " + iLg(4));
7       System.out.println("iLg(10) = " + iLg(10));
8       System.out.println("iLg(100) = " + iLg(100));
9       System.out.println("iLg(1000) = " + iLg(1000));
10    }
11
12    public static int iLg(int n) {
13      int count=0;
14      for ( ; n > 1; n /= 2)
15        ++count;
16      return count;
17    }
18  }
```

The output is

```
iLg(1) = 0
iLg(2) = 1
iLg(3) = 1
iLg(4) = 2
iLg(10) = 3
iLg(100) = 6
iLg(1000) = 9
```

C.3 Asymptotic Complexity Classes

In computer science, algorithms are classified by their complexity functions. These are functions that describe the algorithms' running times relative to the sizes of the problems that they solve. For example, the Bubble Sort has complexity $\Theta(n^2)$. This means that if you double the size of the array, it will take four times as long to sort it.

The symbol $\Theta()$ is one of five symbols used to describe complexity functions. (See Figure C.2.) They all can be defined in terms of the ratios of $f(n)$ and $g(n)$, where $f(n)$ is the

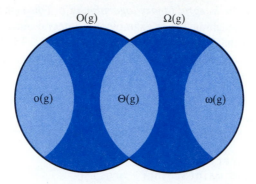

FIGURE C.2   The five asymptotic growth classes.

algorithm's timing function and $g(n)$ is a characterizing function such as $\lg n$ or n^2. For a given function $g(n)$, the five asymptotic complexity classes are

$$O(g(n)) = \{ \, f(n) \mid f(n)/g(n) \text{ is bounded } \}$$
$$\Omega(g(n)) = \{ \, f(n) \mid g(n)/f(n) \text{ is bounded } \}$$
$$\Theta(g(n)) = \{ \, f(n) \mid f(n)/g(n) \text{ is bounded and } g(n)/f(n) \text{ is bounded } \}$$
$$o(g(n)) = \{ \, f(n) \mid f(n)/g(n) \rightarrow 0 \text{ as } n \rightarrow \infty \}$$
$$\omega(g(n)) = \{ \, f(n) \mid g(n)/f(n) \rightarrow 0 \text{ as } n \rightarrow \infty \}$$

Here, we are assuming that all $f(n)$ and $g(n)$ functions are ascending (monotonically increasing).
   Here are some examples:

❏   For every $k > 0$, $(\lg n)^k = o(n)$, because $(\lg n)^k/n \rightarrow 0$.
❏   For every $k > 0$, $n^k = o(2^n)$, because $n^k/2^n \rightarrow 0$.
❏   For every base $b > 1$, $\log_b n = \Theta(\lg n)$, because $\log_b n = (\log_b 2)\,(\lg n)$.
❏   The factorial numbers $n! = \omega(2^n)$, because $n!/2^n$ is unbounded.

The five complexity classes can be imprecisely described by these phrases:

$f(n) = o(g(n))$ means that $f(n)$ grows more slowly than $g(n)$
$f(n) = O(g(n))$ means that $f(n)$ grows more slowly or at the same rate as $g(n)$
$f(n) = \Theta(g(n))$ means that $f(n)$ grows at the same rate $g(n)$
$f(n) = \Omega(g(n))$ means that $f(n)$ grows faster or at the same rate as $g(n)$
$f(n) = \omega(g(n))$ means that $f(n)$ grows faster than $g(n)$

For example, we might have

$$85 \lg n = o(n)$$
$$n \lg n = \omega(n)$$

Keep in mind that these functions $f(n)$, $g(n)$, etc, are usually used to describe how long it takes to run an algorithm. So, if $f(n)$ grows more slowly than $g(n)$, then the algorithm described by $f(n)$ is generally better than the algorithm described by $g(n)$. Less time generally is better.

C.4 The First Principle of Mathematical Induction

The first principle of mathematical induction, also called "weak induction," is often used to prove formulas about positive integers.

Theorem C.1 The First Principle of Mathematical Induction
If $\{P_1, P_2, P_3, \ldots\}$ is a sequence of statements for which the following two properties are true, then all of the statements must be true:

1. P_1 is true.

2. Each statement P_n can be deduced from its predecessor P_{n-1}, for $n > 1$.

Here is an example of how weak induction is used. Suppose we want to prove that the inequality $2^n \leq (n+1)!$ is true for every $n \geq 1$. The sequence of statements is

$$P_1: \quad 2^1 \leq 2!$$

$$P_2: \quad 2^2 \leq 3!$$

$$P_3: \quad 2^3 \leq 4!$$

etc.

The first few statements can be verified explicitly:

$$2^1 = 2 \leq 2 = 2!$$

$$2^2 = 4 \leq 6 = 3!$$

$$2^3 = 8 \leq 24 = 4!$$

In particular, P_1 is true, satisfying the first of the two requirements for weak induction. This is called the *base* of the induction.

To verify the second requirement, we have to show that each statement P_n can be deduced from its predecessor P_{n-1}. So we examine the two general statements P_{n-1} and P_n, and look for a connection:

$$P_{n-1}: \quad 2^{n-1} \leq n!$$

$$P_n: \quad \quad 2^n \leq (n+1)!$$

To derive P_n from P_{n-1} we note that $2^n = (2)(2^{n-1})$ and $(n+1)! = (n+1)(n!)$. Thus, if we assume that P_{n-1} is true, then we have $2^n = (2)(2^{n-1}) \leq (2)(n!) \leq (n+1)(n!) = (n+1)!$, because $n + 1 > 2$.

Verifying the second requirement of mathematical induction is called the *inductive step*.

C.5 The Second Principle of Mathematical Induction

The second principle of mathematical induction, also called "strong induction," is nearly the same as the first principle. The only difference is in the inductive step.

Theorem C.2 The Second Principle of Mathematical Induction

If $\{P_1, P_2, P_3, \ldots\}$ is a sequence of statements for which the following two properties are true, then all of the statements must be true:

1. P_1 is true.
2. Each statement P_n can be deduced from $\{P_1, P_2, P_3, \ldots, P_{n-1}\}$.

Thus, to verify the inductive step with strong induction, we may assume that all $n-1$ statements $P_1, P_2, P_3, \ldots, P_{n-1}$ are true.

As an example, we use strong induction to prove that the Fibonacci numbers 0, 1, 1, 2, 3, 5, 8, 13, 21, ... are asymptotically exponential. More precisely, we prove that $F_n = O(2^n)$, where the Fibonacci numbers F_n are defined as $F_0 = 0$, $F_1 = 1$, and $F_n = F_{n-1} + F_{n-2}$. So our sequence of statements is

$$P_1: \quad F_1 \leq 2^1$$

$$P_2: \quad F_2 \leq 2^2$$

$$P_3: \quad F_3 \leq 2^3$$

etc.

These first few are true because of the following relationships:

$$P_1: \quad F_1 = 1 \leq 2$$

$$P_2: \quad F_2 = 2 \leq 4$$

$$P_3: \quad F_3 = 3 \leq 8$$

For the inductive step, we assume that $n-1$ statements $P_1, P_2, P_3, \ldots, P_{n-1}$ are true and compare them with the nth statement P_n:

$$P_1: \quad F_1 \leq 2^1$$

$$P_2: \quad F_2 \leq 2^2$$

$$P_3: \quad F_3 \leq 2^3$$

$$\vdots \quad \vdots$$

$$P_{n-2}: \quad F_{n-2} \leq 2^{n-2}$$

$$P_{n-1}: \quad F_{n-1} \leq 2^{n-1}$$

$$P_n: \quad F_n \leq 2^n$$

Comparing the nth statement with the two that precede it, we see that

$$F_n = F_{n-1} + F_{n-2}$$

$$2^n = (2)(2^{n-1}) = 2^{n-1} + 2^{n-1} > 2^{n-1} + 2^{n-2}$$

So we can derive P_n from P_{n-1} and P_{n-2} like this:

$$F_n = F_{n-1} + F_{n-2} \leq 2^{n-1} + 2^{n-2} < 2^n$$

This proves that all the statements are true (*i.e.*, $F_n \leq 2^n$ for all n).

C.6 Geometric Series

A *geometric series* is a sum in which each term is the same multiple of its predecessor. For example, $20 + 60 + 180 + 540 + 1620 + 4860 + \cdots$ is a geometric series because each term is 3 times the size of its predecessor. The multiplier 3 is called the *common ratio* of the series.

◆ **FORMULA C.4: Sum of a Finite Geometric Series**

$$a + ar + ar^2 + ar^3 + \cdots + ar^{n-1} = \frac{a(1 - r^n)}{1 - r}$$

Here, a is the first term in the series, r is the common ratio, and n is the number of terms in the series.

For example, the three parameters for the sum $20 + 60 + 180 + 540 + 1620 + 4860$ are $a = 20$, $r = 3$, and $n = 6$. So the sum is

$$a(1 - r^n)/(1 - r) = 20(1 - 3^6)/(1 - 3) = 20(1 - 729)/(-2) = 20(-728)/(-2) = 7280$$

◆ **FORMULA C.5: Sum of an Infinite Geometric Series**

If $-1 < r < 1$, then

$$a + ar + ar^2 + ar^3 + \cdots = \frac{a}{1 - r}$$

For example, consider the infinite series

$$0.42 + 0.0042 + 0.000042 + 0.00000042 + 0.0000000042 + \cdots$$

This, of course, is just the repeating decimal $0.4242424242\cdots$. As a series, its parameters are $a = 0.42$ and $r = 0.01$. So the sum is

$$a/(1 - r) = 0.42/(1 - 0.01) = 0.42/0.99 = 42/99 = 14/33$$

C.7 Other Summation Formulas

Formulas C.6 and C.7 are often used in the analysis of algorithms:

◆ FORMULA C.6: Sum of the First *n* Positive Integers

$$1 + 2 + 3 + \cdots + n = \frac{n(n + 1)}{2}$$

Note that the parameter *n* equals the number of terms in the sum.

An easy way to remember this useful formula is to remember the picture in Figure C.3. It shows two triangles of dots, one white and one gray. The two triangles have the same number of dots, namely $S = 1 + 2 + 3 + \ldots + n$. Together, they form a rectangle *n* dots wide and $(n + 1)$ dots high. So the total number of dots is $n(n + 1)$, which is twice the size of the sum *S*.

For example, $1 + 2 + 3 + 4 + 5 + 6 + 7 + 8 + 9 = 9(10)/2 = 45$.

◆ FORMULA C.7: Sum of the First *n* Square Integers

$$1^2 + 2^2 + 3^2 + \cdots + n^2 = \frac{n(n + 1)(2n + 1)}{6}$$

The expression on the right appears to be a fraction. But it will always turn out to be an integer because it equals a sum of integers.

For example, $1^2 + 2^2 + 3^2 + 4^2 + 5^2 + 6^2 = 6(7)(13)/6 = 546/6 = 91$.

Here is a proof of Formula C.7. The base case ($n = 1$) is true because $1^2 = 1 = 1(2)(3)/6$. To establish the inductive step, assume that the formula is true for $n - 1$:

$$1^2 + 2^2 + 3^2 + \cdots + (n - 1)^2 = \frac{(n - 1)((n - 1) + 1)(2(n - 1) + 1)}{6}$$

This comes from replacing *n* with $(n - 1)$ in the formula that we want to prove. Then simplify the right-hand side:

$$1^2 + 2^2 + 3^2 + \cdots + (n - 1)^2 = \frac{(n - 1)(n)(2n - 1)}{6}$$

FIGURE C.3 The sum $1 + 2 + \cdots + 16$.

Now add n^2 to both sides of that equation, and then simplify the right-hand side again:

$$1^2 + 2^2 + 3^2 + \cdots + (n-1)^2 + n^2 = \frac{(n-1)(n)(2n-1)}{6} + n^2$$

$$= \frac{2n^3 - 3n^2 + n}{6} + \frac{6n^2}{6}$$

$$= \frac{2n^3 + 3n^2 + n}{6}$$

$$= \frac{n(n+1)(2n+1)}{6}$$

By the First Principle of Mathematical Induction, this proves that the general formula is correct.

C.8 Harmonic Numbers

The *harmonic numbers* are simply the partial sums of the reciprocals of the positive integers:

$$H_n = \sum_{k=1}^{n} \frac{1}{k} = 1 + \frac{1}{2} + \frac{1}{3} + \frac{1}{4} + \frac{1}{5} + \cdots + \frac{1}{n}$$

The first seven of these are shown in the table in Figure C.4.

The harmonic sequence grows very slowly — about the same rate as a logarithm, which is slower than any power n^p.

◆ **FORMULA C.8: Harmonic Numbers**

The Harmonic Sequence is asymptotically logarithmic, because $\lim_{n \to \infty} (H_n - \ln n)$ is a positive constant.

Note that the logarithm in Formula C.8 is the natural logarithm, base e.

n	H_n
1	1.000000
2	1.500000
3	1.833333
4	2.083333
5	2.283333
6	2.450000
7	2.592857

FIGURE C.4 The harmonic numbers.

The positive constant that the difference $(H_n - \ln n)$ approaches is called *Euler's constant* and is denoted by the Greek letter gamma:

$$\gamma = \lim_{n \to \infty} (H_n - \ln n) = 0.5772157\cdots$$

This limit is verified empirically by the program in Listing C.2. The next formula is a direct consequence.

◆ **FORMULA C.9: Harmonic Numbers**

For large n, $H_n \approx \ln n + \gamma = \Theta(\ln n) = \Theta(\lg n)$.

This follows from the fact that the limit of the ratio $H_n/\lg n$ is $\ln 2 = 0.693$.

Nobody knows whether γ is a rational number. It appears to be irrational, but no one has been able to prove that yet.

LISTING C.2: Empirical Validation that the Harmonic Numbers are Logarithmic

```
1   public class Euler {
2     public static void main(String[] args) {
3       double h = 0.0;                              // harmonic numbers
4       int pow2 = 1;                                // = 2^0
5       for (int n = 1; n < 1E7; n++) {
6         h += 1.0/n;                                // the nth harmonic number
7         if (n == pow2) {                           // print only for powers of 2
8           double ln = Math.log(n);                 // natural logarithm of n
9           double d = h - ln;                       // approaches Euler's constant
10          System.out.println(n + "\t" + h + "\t" + ln + "\t" + d);
11          pow2 *= 2;                               // = 2^n
12        }
13      }
14    }
15  }
```

The output is

```
1       1.0       0.0       1.0
2       1.5       0.6931471805599453       0.8068528194400547
4       2.083333333333333       1.3862943611198906       0.6970389722134425
8       2.7178571428571425       2.0794415416798357       0.6384156011773068
16      3.3807289932289937       2.772588722239781       0.6081402709892125
32      4.05849519543652       3.4657359027997265       0.5927592926367935
64      4.7438909037057675       4.1588830833596715       0.585007820346096
128     5.433147092589174       4.852030263919617       0.5811168286695567
256     6.124344962817281       5.545177444479562       0.5791675183377185
512     6.81651653454972       6.238324625039508       0.5781919095102124
1024    7.509175672278132       6.931471805599453       0.5777038666786787
2048    8.202078771817716       7.6246189861593985       0.5774597856583172
4096    8.89510389696629       8.317766166719343       0.5773377302469473
8192    9.588190046095265       9.010913347279288       0.577276698815977
```

16384	10.281306710008463	9.704060527839234	0.5772461821692296
32768	10.974438632012168	10.39720770839918	0.5772309236129889
65536	11.667578183235785	11.090354888959125	0.57722329427666
131072	12.360721549112862	11.78350206951907	0.5772194795937917
262144	13.053866822328144	12.476649250079015	0.5772175722491291
524288	13.747013049214582	13.16979643063896	0.5772166185756209
1048576	14.440159752936799	13.862943611198906	0.5772161417378925
2097152	15.133306695078193	14.556090791758852	0.5772159033193418
4194304	15.826453756428641	15.249237972318797	0.5772157841098444
8388608	16.51960087738358	15.942385152878742	0.577215724504839

C.9   Stirling's Formula

The *factorial numbers* frequently appear in the analysis of algorithms:

$$n! = \prod_{k=1}^{n} k = (1)(2)(3)(4) \cdots (n)$$

The first eight factorials are shown in the table in Figure C.5.

Just the opposite of the harmonic sequence, the factorial sequence grows exponentially. This fact is a consequence of Stirling's[1] formula.

n	n!
0	1
1	1
2	2
3	6
4	24
5	120
6	720
7	5040

FIGURE C.5   The factorial numbers.

---

[1] Actually discovered by the French mathematician Abraham De Moivre (1667–1754) .

◆ **FORMULA C.10: Stirling's Formula**

$$n! = \sqrt{2n\pi}\left(\frac{n}{e}\right)^n e^{\theta/12n}, \text{ where } 0 < \theta < 1$$

The value of the variable θ depends upon n, but in any case it is bounded between 0 and 1. Thus, for large n, the exponent $\theta/12n$ will be very close to 0, making the factor $e^{\theta/12n}$ very close to 1. As a result, Stirling's formula is often expressed in its simpler approximate form, $n! \approx \sqrt{2n\pi}\left(\frac{n}{e}\right)^n$.

◆ **FORMULA C.11: Factorial Numbers**

The factorial numbers grow exponentially: $n! = \Omega(2^n)$.

The proof of this formula follows directly from the observation that the ratio $n!/2^n$ is unbounded, which is a consequence of Stirling's formula:

$$\frac{n!}{2^n} = \frac{\sqrt{2n\pi}\left(\frac{n}{e}\right)^n e^{\theta/12n}}{2^n} = \sqrt{2n\pi}\left(\frac{n}{2e}\right)^n e^{\theta/12n} \to \infty$$

Another consequence of Stirling's formula is the following asymptotic formula for the expression $\lg(n!)$. This is useful in analyzing sorting algorithms.

◆ **FORMULA C.12: Logarithms of Factorials**

$$\lg(n!) = \Theta(n\lg n)$$

C.10 Fibonacci Numbers

The *Fibonacci numbers* also frequently appear in the analysis of algorithms:

$$F_n = \begin{cases} 0, \text{ if } n = 0 \\ 1, \text{ if } n = 1 \\ F_{n-1} + F_{n-2}, \text{ if } n > 1 \end{cases}$$

The first thirteen Fibonacci numbers are shown in the table on the right.

Like the factorial sequence, the Fibonacci sequence grows exponentially, as is verified by De Moivre's formula:

◆ **FORMULA C.13: Fibonacci Numbers**

$$F_n = \frac{\phi^n - \psi^n}{\sqrt{5}}, \text{ where } \phi = \frac{1 + \sqrt{5}}{2}, \text{ and } \psi = \frac{1 - \sqrt{5}}{2}$$

n	F_n
0	0
1	1
2	1
3	2
4	3
5	5
6	8
7	13
8	21
9	34
10	55
11	89
12	144

FIGURE C.6 Fibonacci numbers.

Here, $\phi = 1.618034$ and $\psi = -0.618034$, known as the *golden mean* and its *conjugate*. These two number are the solutions to the quadratic equation $x^2 = x + 1$. (See page 307.)

The golden mean is the solution to the ancient problem: at what point C should you cut a segment AB, so that the ratio AB/AC is equal to the ratio AC/CB? The solution can be obtained algebraically by letting $x = AC$ and assuming without loss of generality that $CB = 1$. Then the defining condition for the golden mean,

$$\phi = AB/AC = AC/CB$$

becomes

$$\phi = (x + 1)/x = x/1.$$

This gives us two equations:

$$(x + 1)/x = x/1.$$

$$\phi = x/1$$

The first becomes the quadratic equation $x^2 = x + 1$, whose solutions are $x = \dfrac{1 \pm \sqrt{5}}{2}$, and the second simply states that $\phi = x$. Since ϕ is a ratio of lengths, it must be positive. Thus:

$$\phi = \frac{1 + \sqrt{5}}{2} = 1.618033988749894848204586834365$$

This mathematical constant has many interesting properties. (See Exercises 4-12.)

In addition to the golden mean $\phi = \dfrac{1 + \sqrt{5}}{2}$, de Moivre's formula also uses the constant ψ

(the Greek letter psi) defined to be $\psi = \dfrac{1 - \sqrt{5}}{2}$. This is called the *conjugate* of ϕ because it is

actually the smaller of the two roots $\dfrac{1 \pm \sqrt{5}}{2}$. The decimal value for ψ is

$$\psi = \frac{1 - \sqrt{5}}{2} = -0.6180339887498948482045868343656$$

Here are just a few of the many remarkable properties of these two constants:

$$\phi + \psi = 1$$
$$\phi\,\psi = -1$$
$$\phi^2 = 1 + \phi$$
$$\psi^2 = 1 + \psi$$

These identities follow easily from the defining equations of ϕ and ψ. (See Exercise C.14.)

C.11 Binomial Coefficients

The *binomial coefficients* are the numbers that occur when a binomial expression such as $(1 + x)$ is raised to a power:

$$(1+x)^0 = 1$$
$$(1+x)^1 = 1 + 1x$$
$$(1+x)^2 = 1 + 2x + 1x^2$$
$$(1+x)^3 = 1 + 3x + 3x^2 + 1x^3$$
$$(1+x)^4 = 1 + 4x + 6x^2 + 4x^3 + 1x^4$$
$$(1+x)^5 = 1 + 5x + 10x^2 + 10x^3 + 5x^4 + 1x^5$$
$$(1+x)^6 = 1 + 6x + 15x^2 + 20x^3 + 15x^4 + 6x^5 + 1x^6$$
$$(1+x)^7 = 1 + 7x + 21x^2 + 35x^3 + 35x^4 + 21x^5 + 7x^6 + 1x^7$$
$$(1+x)^8 = 1 + 8x + 28x^2 + 56x^3 + 70x^4 + 56x^5 + 28x^6 + 8x^7 + 1x^8$$

The coefficients (the numbers that multiply the powers of x) reveal some interesting patterns.

Obviously, the leftmost column and the diagonal contain only 1s. In between, we see that the sum of any pair of adjacent numbers is the number directly below the second one. For example, $5 + 10 = 15$ and $35 + 21 = 56$. This pattern was discovered by the French mathematician Blaise Pascal (1623–1662) in 1653[2] and has since been known as *Pascal's Triangle*.

---

[2] The arithmetic triangle was known to Chinese mathematicians several centuries earlier.

```
1
1  1
1  2  1
1  3  3  1
1  4  6  4  1
1  5  10 10 5  1
1  6  15 20 15 6  1
1  7  21 35 35 21 7  1
1  8  28 56 70 56 28 8  1
```

FIGURE C.7 Pascal's triangle.

The pattern that Pascal discovered can be expressed recursively by:

$$c(n, k) = \begin{cases} 1, \text{ if k=0 or k=n} \\ c(n-1, k-1) + c(n-1, k) \end{cases}$$

Here, $c(n, k)$ denotes the coefficient that is in row number n and column number k, where we number the rows and columns beginning with 0. For example, with $n = 6$ and $k = 2$, we have

$$5 + 10 = c(5, 1) + c(5, 2) = c(n-1, k-1) + c(n-1, k) = c(n, k) = c(6, 2) = 15$$

There is also a closed form formula for the binomial coefficients:

$$c(n, k) = \frac{n!}{k!(n-k)!} = \left(\frac{n}{1}\right)\left(\frac{n-1}{2}\right)\left(\frac{n-2}{3}\right)\cdots\left(\frac{n-k+1}{k}\right)$$

The two forms here are equal algebraically. But the second form is much better for computing for large values of n. For example, $c(100,4) = (100/1)(99/2)(98/3)(97/4) = (100/2)(99/3)(98/4)(97) = (50)(33)(49)(97) = 7{,}842{,}450$. This gives the exact integer value. If you try to compute $c(100,4)$ by the factorial formula, the computation will probably ail due to integer overflow (100! has 158 digits), or it will suffer roundoff error due to floating-point conversion.

C.12 Catalan Numbers

The *Catalan numbers* are defined recursively by:

$$C(n) = \begin{cases} 1, \text{ if } n = 0 \\ C(0)C(n-1) + C(1)C(n-2) + C(2)C(n-3) + \cdots + C(n-1)C(0), \text{ if } n > 0 \end{cases}$$

The first 10 Catalan numbers are shown in the accompanying table. This sequence is similar to the Fibonacci sequence: It is defined recursively and it grows exponentially.

n	C(n)
0	1
1	1
2	2
3	5
4	14
5	42
6	132
7	429
8	1430
9	4862

▼ **EXAMPLE C.1: Implementation of the Catalan Function**

```
public static long cat(int n) {
   if (n < 2) return 1;
   long sum = cat(n-1);
   for (int i = 1; i < n-1; i++)
      sum += cat(i)*cat(n-1-i);
   return sum;
}
```

The Catalan sequence was discovered by applying the second principle of mathematical induction to the following problem:

▼ **EXAMPLE C.2: Counting the Triangulations of a Polygon**

A *polygon* is a plane region bounded by noncrossing line segments. A *convex polygon* is a polygon any two points of which have their connecting line segment contained within the polygon, so its boundary has no dents. (See Figure C.8.)

A *triangulation* of a convex polygon is a subdivision of the polygon into triangles, all of whose corners are also corners of the polygon. A triangulation of an s-sided polygon is simply a set a $s-3$ nonintersecting diagonals. Figure C.9 shows four different triangulations of the hexagon.

Figure C.10 on page 581 shows that there are 2 triangulations of a quadrilateral, 5 triangulations of a pentagon, and 14 triangulations of a hexagon. From these data, we can infer Formula C.14.

◆ **FORMULA C.14: Triangulations of a Polygon**

The number of triangulations of a polygon with $n+2$ sides is the nth Catalan number $C(n)$.

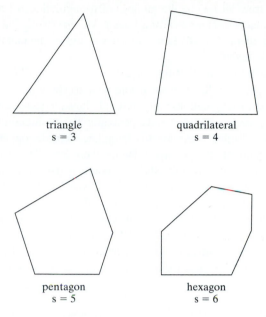

FIGURE C.8   Convex Polygons.

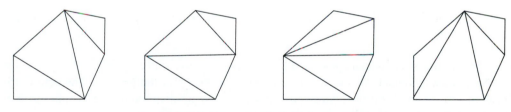

FIGURE C.9   Four Triangulations of the Same Polygon.

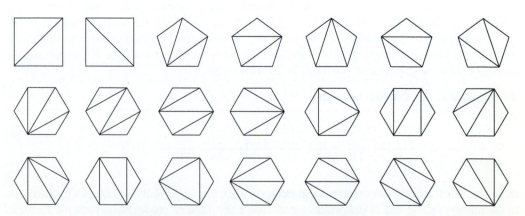

FIGURE C.10   All the Triangulations of the Polygons of Sizes 4, 5, and 6.

To see why this is true, let $f(s)$ be the number of triangulations of a polygon with s sides. Then we have to prove that $f(n+2) = C(n)$ for all $n \geq 1$. We use strong induction.

The basis is the statement $f(3) = C(1) = 1$; this is verified by the fact that there is exactly one triangulation of a triangle: itself.

For the inductive step, assume that for some $n > 1$, $f(k+2) = C(k)$ for all $k < n$. We don't know what n is, but suppose $n = 8$. Then we would have to show that $f(10) = C(8)$; (i.e., that a decagon has 1430 different triangulations). Figure C.11 shows a decagon with one triangle partitioning it into two other pieces: a hexagon and a pentagon. By our inductive hypothesis, we know that there are $f(6) = C(4) = 14$ different ways to triangulate the hexagon, and there are $f(5) = C(3) = 5$ different ways to triangulate the pentagon. Hence there are $C(4) \cdot X(3) = 14 \cdot 5 = 70$ different ways to triangulate this decagon so that the shaded triangle is part of the triangulation. Similarly, the second figure shows that there are $f(8) \cdot \phi(5) = C(4) \cdot X(3) = 132 \cdot 1 = 132$ different ways to triangulate the decagon so that that shaded triangle is part of the triangulation. And the bottom figure shows that there are $f(9) = C(7) = 429$ different ways to triangulate the decagon so that that shaded triangle is part of the triangulation. All $f(10)$ triangulations are partitioned into distinct cases like these three, each determined by the special triangle that has the same base as the decagon. There are eight of these cases, one for each of the vertices A–H. So the total number of triangulations of the decagon is

$$f(10) = f(9) + f(3) \cdot \phi(8) + f(4) \cdot \phi(7) + f(5) \cdot \phi(6) + f(6) \cdot \phi(5) + f(7) \cdot \phi(4) + f(8) \cdot \phi(3) + f(9)$$

Since $f(s) = C(n-2)$ and $C(0) = 1$,

$$f(10) = C(7) + C(1) \cdot X(6) + C(2) \cdot X(5) + C(3) \cdot X(4) + C(4) \cdot X(3) + C(5) \cdot X(2) + C(6) \cdot X(1) + C(7)$$
$$= C(8).$$

The same argument shows that $f(n+2) = C(n)$ for any n.

Note the employment of the *divide-and-conquer* strategy in the proof of Theorem C.15. Recall that the main idea is that, once you have analyzed a problem for all sizes smaller than n, you can analyze the problem for size n by splitting it into two parts and applying your previous analysis to each part. Then the analysis of the complete problem reduces to an analysis of how it relates to the two smaller problems. The divide and conquer strategy is also used in the Binary Search (Algorithm 3.4), the Merge Sort (Algorithm 15.5), and the Quick Sort (Algorithm 15.6).

The formula that defines the Catalan numbers is *recursive*: you cannot use it to obtain the value of $C(n)$ unless you already have obtained the values of $C(k)$ for all $k < n$. In contrast, the next formula is more practical, providing an explicit formula.

◆ **FORMULA C.15: Catalan Numbers**

$$C(n) = \frac{(2n)!}{n!(n+1)!} = \frac{(2n)(2n-1)(2n-2)\cdots(n+2)}{(n)(n-1)(n-2)\cdots(2)}$$

In words, this formula says to form the fraction $(2n)/(n)$; then repeatedly add factors in pairs, one in the numerator and one in the denominator, each 1 less than its predecessor, until the factor in the denominator is 2.

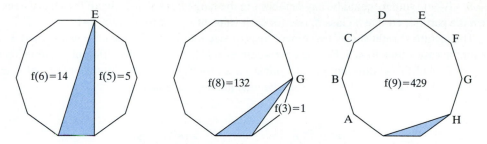

FIGURE C.11 Proof of Formula C.14.

▼ EXAMPLE C.3: Computing Catalan Numbers Directly

The following application of Theorem C.15 confirms the value 4862 given in the table on page 580:

$$C(9) = \frac{(18)(17)(16)(15)(14)(13)(12)(11)}{(9)(8)(7)(6)(5)(4)(3)(2)} = (17)(13)(11)(2) = 4862$$

Since $n = 9$ here, there are 8 factors in the numerator and 8 in the denominator.

Note that all the factors in the denominator cancel.

◆ FORMULA C.16: The Number of Binary Trees

The number of distinct binary trees of size n is the nth Catalan number $C(n)$.

To see why this us true, let $f(n)$ be the number of distinct binary trees of size n. Then $f(0) = 1 = C(0)$ because there is exactly 1 binary tree of size 0: the empty tree. The pictures at right shows that $f(1) = 1 = C(1), f(2) = 2 = C(2)$, and $f(3) = 5 = C(3)$. This verifies the basis of a proof by strong induction (Theorem C.2).

f(1)=1:   •

f(2)=2:

f(3)=5:

Now assume that for some $n > 0, f(k) = C(k)$ for all $k < n$. Let T be a binary tree of size n. As in the proof of Theorem C.15, we apply the divide and conquer strategy. Let T_L and T_R be the left and right subtrees of T. Let n_L and n_R be the sizes of T_L and T_R respectively. Then since n_L and n_R are both less than n, we can apply the inductive hypothesis: $f(n_L) = C(n_L)$ and $f(n_R) = C(n_R)$. Now $n = 1 + n_L + n_R$ because each node in T must be either the root or in T_L or in T_R. So

$n_R = n - 1 - n_L$. And n_L could be any number k in the range $0 \le k \le n{-}1$. So all the binary trees of size n are partitioned into n classes, one for each value of $n_L = k$ for $0 \le k \le n{-}1$.

The picture at right shows two binary trees of size $n = 8$, one for the case where $n_L = 3$ and one for the case where $n_L = 5$. For the case where $n_L = k$ there are $C(n_L)$ different possible binary trees for T_L and $C(n_R)$ different possible binary trees for T_R, so the total number for that case is $C(n_L){\cdot}X(n_R) = C(k){\cdot}X(n - 1 - n)$. Hence the total number of binary trees is

$$f(n) = C(0){\cdot}X(n{-}1) + C(1){\cdot}X(n{-}2) + C(2){\cdot}X(n{-}3) + \ \cdots\ + C(n{-}1){\cdot}X(0) = C(n).$$

This shows that $f(n) = C(n)$ for all n.

REVIEW QUESTIONS

C.1   What is a logarithm?

C.2   What is the difference between the weak induction and strong induction?

C.3   How can you decide when to use strong induction?

C.4   What is Euler's constant?

C.5   How is Stirling's formula useful?

C.6   What is the difference between the recursive formula and the closed-form formula for the Fibonacci numbers? Which is more useful?

EXERCISES

C.1   A function $f()$ is called *idempotent* if $f(f(x)) = f(x)$ for all x in the domain of $f()$. Explain why the floor and ceiling functions are idempotent.

C.2   Sketch the graphs of the following:

    a. $y = \lfloor x \rfloor$
    b. $y = \lceil x \rceil$
    c. $y = \lceil x \rceil - x$
    d. $y = \lceil x \rceil - \lfloor x \rfloor$

C.3   Prove Formula C.1 on page 565.

C.4   Prove Formula C.2 on page 566.

C.5 Prove Formula C.3 on page 566.

C.6 Determine whether each of the following is true or false:

    a. $f = o(g) \Leftrightarrow g = \omega(f)$

    b. $f = O(g) \Leftrightarrow g = \Omega(f)$

    c. $f = \Theta(g) \Leftrightarrow g = \Theta(f)$

    d. $f = O(g) \Rightarrow f = \Theta(g)$

    e. $f = \Theta(g) \Rightarrow f = \Omega(g)$

    f. $f = \Theta(h)$ and $g = \Theta(h) \Rightarrow f + g = \Theta(h)$

    g. $f = \Theta(h)$ and $g = \Theta(h) \Rightarrow fg = \Theta(h)$

    h. $n^2 = O(n \lg n)$

    i. $n^2 = \Theta(n \lg n)$

    j. $n^2 = \Omega(n \lg n)$

    k. $\lg n = \omega(n)$

    l. $\lg n = o(n)$

C.7 Verify the following relationships among the five asymptotic complexity classes:

    a. $o(g) = O(g) - \Theta(g)$;

    b. $\omega(g) = \Omega(g) - \Theta(g)$;

    c. $O(g) = o(g) \cup \Theta(g)$;

    d. $\Omega(g) = \omega(g) \cup \Theta(g)$;

    e. $O(g) \cap \Omega(g) = \Theta(g)$;

C.8 Prove Formula C.4 on page 571. by induction.

C.9 Prove Formula C.6 on page 572. by induction.

C.10 Prove Formula C.7 on page 572. by induction.

C.11 Use Stirling's formula (Formula C.10) to derive this logarithmic version:

$$\ln(n!) = \tfrac{1}{2}\ln(2\pi) + (n + \tfrac{1}{2})\ln n - n + \frac{\theta}{12n}$$

C.12 Derive these formulas from the definitions $\phi = (1 + \sqrt{5})/2$ and $\psi = (1 - \sqrt{5})/2$.

    a. $\phi + \psi = 1$

    b. $\phi \psi = -1$

    c. $\phi^2 = 1 + \phi$

    d. $\psi^2 = 1 - \psi$

C.13 Prove Formula C.13 on page 576 by induction.

C.14 Prove Formula C.15 on page 582 by induction.

PROGRAMMING PROBLEMS

C.1   Run a program similar to that in Listing C.2 on page 574 that empirically verifies Stirling s formula (Formula C.10 on page 576).

C.2   Run a program similar to that in Listing C.2 on page 574 that empirically verifies the closed-form formula for the Fibonacci numbers (Formula C.13 on page 576).

ANSWERS TO REVIEW QUESTIONS

C.1   A *logarithm* is an exponent; the logarithm of x is the exponent y on the base b for which $b^y = x$.

C.2   Weak induction allows you to assume only the single statement P_{n-1} to deduce P_n. Strong induction allows you to assume all the statements $P_1, P_2, P_3, \cdots, P_{n-2}, P_{n-1}$ to deduce P_n.

C.3   Use strong induction when the proposition to be proved for a given n depends upon corresponding propositions farther back in the sequence than just $n - 1$. For example, the Fibonacci numbers F_n are defined in terms of both F_{n-1} and F_{n-2}.

C.4   *Euler's constant* is the limit of the difference $(1 + 1/2 + 1/3 + \ldots + 1/n) - \ln n$. Its value is approximately 0.5772.

C.5   Stirling's formula is a useful method for approximating $n!$ for large n (e.g., $n > 20$).

C.6   The recursive formula for the Fibonacci numbers is $F_n = F_{n-1} + F_{n-2}$. It is not very useful for large values of n, because the number of recursive calls grows exponentially. The closed-form formula is

$$F_n = \frac{\phi^n - \psi^n}{\sqrt{5}}$$

This can be useful for approximating F_n for large values of n. For example, for $n = 100$, ψ^n is nearly 0, so $F_{100} = \phi^{100}/\sqrt{5} = 792{,}070{,}839{,}848{,}372{,}253{,}127/\sqrt{5} = 354{,}224{,}848{,}179{,}261{,}915{,}075$.

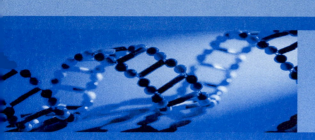

Appendix D

The Java Collections Framework

The Java Collections Framework (JCF) was introduced in Chapter 7. It consists of a group of related interfaces and classes that are defined in the `java.util` package. Its main purpose is to provide a unified framework for implementing common data structures so that the resulting classes can be used in a consistent, efficient, and intuitive manner. This appendix summarizes the JCF.

D.1 The Inheritance Hierarchy

The inheritance hierarchy shown in Figure D.1 is the same as in Figure 7.1 on page 199. The interfaces are on the right, and the classes that implement them are on the left. The dashed lines indicate direct implementation. The eight concrete classes are shown in cyan.

FIGURE D.1 The inheritance hierarchy for the Java Collections Framework.

587

The JCF is described at the website `java.sun.com/j2se/1.4/docs/guide/collections/`. The advantages of using the JCF are that it

❏ reduces programming effort by providing useful data structures and algorithms so you don't have to write them yourself.

❏ increases performance by providing high-performance implementations of useful data structures and algorithms. (Because the various implementations of each interface are interchangeable, programs can be easily tuned by switching implementations.)

❏ provides interoperability between unrelated APIs by establishing a common language to pass collections back and forth.

❏ reduces the effort required to learn APIs by eliminating the need to learn multiple ad hoc collection APIs.

❏ reduces the effort required to design and implement APIs by eliminating the need to produce ad hoc collection APIs.

❏ fosters software reuse by providing a standard interface for collections and algorithms to manipulate them.

Table D.1 shows the eight concrete JCF classes and the data structures that are used to implement them.

The `LinkedList`, `TreeSet`, and `TreeMap` classes are implemented with structures of linked nodes; (*i.e.*, linked lists and trees). The `ArrayList`, `HashSet`, and `HashMap` classes are implemented with structures of indexed elements; (*i.e.*, arrays). The `LinkedHashSet` and `LinkedHashMap` classes are implemented with arrays that are threaded with links that give the order in which the elements were inserted.

D.2 The Collection Interface

The `Object` class is the root of all Java inheritance hierarchies. As Figure D.1 shows, it is directly extended by the `AbstractCollection` and `AbstractMap` classes. The `AbstractCollection` class implements the `Collection` interface. Figure D.2 shows UML diagrams for these types and their relationships. Note that the `Object` class is defined in the `java.lang` package, and all the JCF types (classes and interfaces) are defined in the `java.util` package.

Data Structure	List	Set	Map
linked	LinkedList	TreeSet	TreeMap
indexed	ArrayList	HashSet	HashMap
indexed with links		LinkedHashSet	LinkedHashMap

TABLE D.1   Concentrate Collection classes of the JCF.

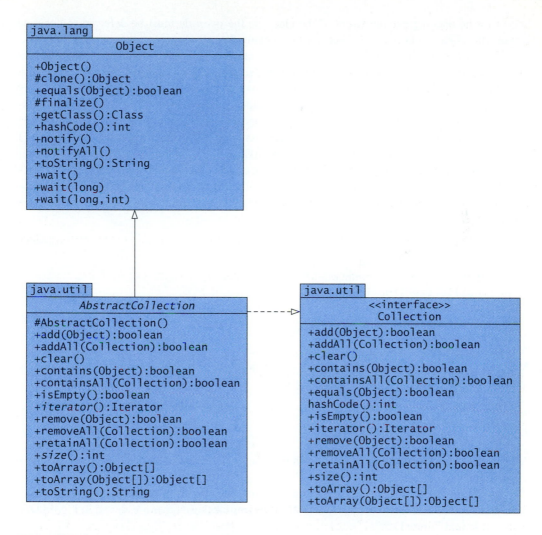

FIGURE D.2 The AbstractCollection class extends the Object class and implements the Collection interface.

The Object class contains three methods that are meant to be overridden by its subclasses: the equals() method, the hashCode() method, and the toString() method. Each of these has default behavior that is defined by the Object class. If x and y are any objects, then x.equals(y) returns true only if x==y (*i.e.*, x and y refer to the same object), x.hashCode() returns an integer that is computed from the contents of x, and x.toString() returns a string that merely identifies x's type and its location in memory.

The Collection interface explicitly specifies the equals() and hashCode() methods. This is done to remind developers that those methods should be overridden by concrete classes. The equals() method should be redefined by the implementing class so that x.equals(y) returns true whenever x and y have the same contents. That determination, of course, requires access to the backing data structure of the class, so the override must be deferred to concrete classes; the abstract classes do not specify the backing data structures.

The purpose of the `hashCode()` method is to return an integer that almost uniquely identifies the object. These numbers should be uniformly distributed among the 4,294,967,296 different values available for an `int` (from –2,147,483,648 to 2,147,483,647). It should be unlikely that any two different objects have the same `hashCode()` value. However, if x and y are two different objects for which `x.equals(y)` returns true, then `x.hashCode()` and `y.hashCode()` should return the same integer. Therefore, any concrete class that overrides the `equals()` method should also override the `hashCode()` method.

The `AbstractCollection` class is abstract because it has two abstract methods: `iterator()` and `size()`. Moreover, the `add()` method only throws an `UnsupportedOperationException` exception. Consequently, concrete collection classes are obliged to override these six methods:

```
public boolean  add(Object object)
public boolean  equals(Oject)
public int      hashCode()
public Iterator iterator()
public int      size();
public String   toString()
```

All the other methods required by the `Collection` interface are implemented by the `AbstractCollection` class. That is its purpose: to implement as many methods as possible without having access to the backing data structure.

D.3 The List Classes

A *list* is a sequence of elements which may or may not be accessible by means of an index variable.

As Figure D.1 shows, the JCF defines a `List` interface that is implemented by two abstract list classes and two concrete list classes. UML diagrams for these types are shown in Figure D.3, Figure D.4, and Figure D.5.

Figure D.3 shows the `AbstractList` and `AbstractSequentialList` classes. Note that both classes define a no-argument constructor that has `protected` access.[1] This allows instantiation only from within the class itself and its extensions, which makes sense, because the class cannot be instantiated until all of its executable code has been provided. Its `abstract` methods can be completed only by extensions.

As Figure D.3 indicates, only the `get()` and `size()` methods are `abstract`. All other functionality has been implemented here. The operations that depend upon the backing data structures are managed by calls to `get()` and `size()`.

---

[1] Recall that in UML, `protected` is indicated by the hash character #.

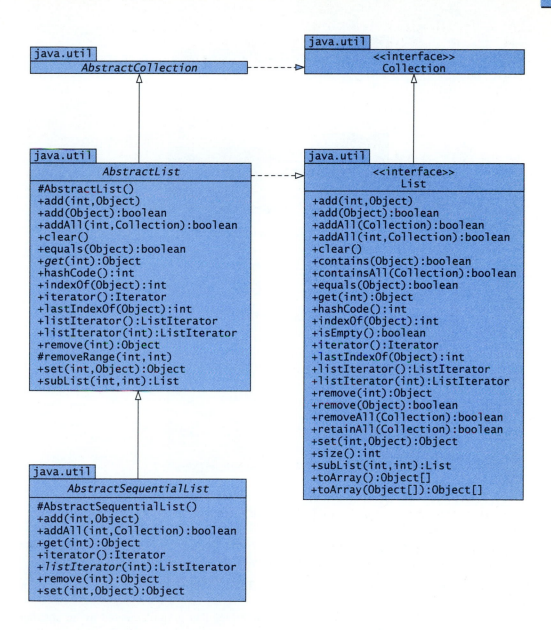

The AbstractSequentialList class, the AbstractList class, and the List interface.

The concrete LinkedList class is a direct extension of the AbstractSequentialList class, as shown in Figure D.4, and the concrete ArrayList class is a direct extension of the AbstractList class, as shown in Figure D.5.

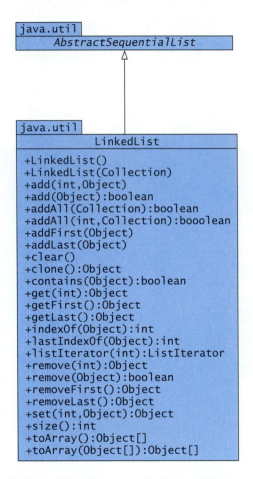

FIGURE D.4   The LinkedList class extends the AbstractSequentialList class.

D.4 The Set Classes

A *set* is an unordered collection of unique elements. The JCF defines a Set interface to represent this abstract data type.

As Figure D.1 shows, the JCF defines a Set interface that is implemented by an abstract class and three concrete classes, one of which also implements a SortedSet interface. UML diagrams for these types are shown in Figure D.6 and Figure D.7.

The TreeSet class uses a red-black tree to store the elements. This gives $\Theta(\lg n)$ performance for the add(), contains(), and remove() methods. It also allows the iterator to access the elements in sorted order, thus implementing the SortedSet interface.

The HashSet class uses a chained hash table to store its elements. This gives nearly $\Theta(1)$ performance for the add(), contains(), and remove() methods, but, of course, the elements are stored in a randomized order.

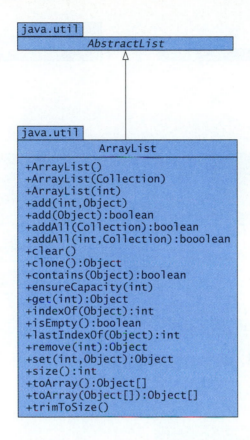

FIGURE D.5 The ArrayList class extends the AbstractList class.

The LinkedHashSet class, adds links to keep track of the order in which the elements are added to the set. The set's iterators will traverse the set in that order.

D.5 The Map Classes

A *map* is a set of key-value pairs, where the keys are unique. The JCF defines a Set interface to represent this abstract data type.

As Figure D.1 shows, the JCF defines a Map interface that is implemented by an abstract class and three concrete classes. UML diagrams for these types are shown in Figure D.8 and Figure D.9.

The TreeMap, HashMap, and LinkedHashMap classes are analogous to the TreeSet, HashSet, and LinkedHashSet classes, using a red-black tree, a hash table, and a threaded hash table, respectively, to store the key-value pairs.

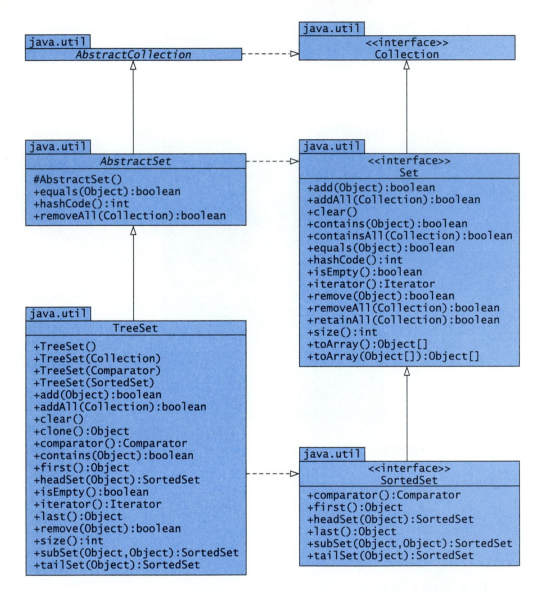

FIGURE D.6   The AbstractSet class, the TreeSet class, the Set interface, and the SortedSet interface.

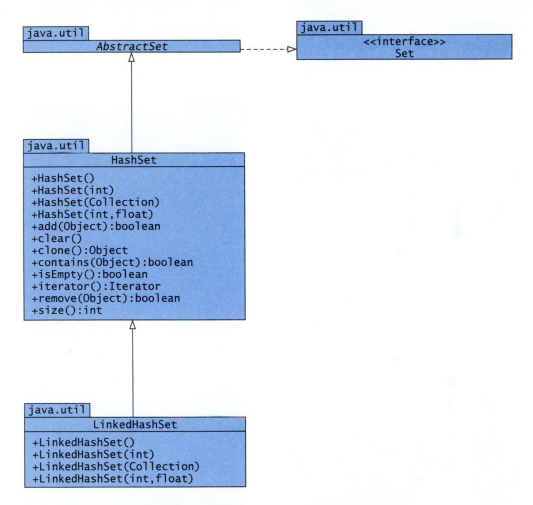

java.util

AbstractSet

java.util

<<interface>>
Set

java.util

HashSet

+HashSet()
+HashSet(int)
+HashSet(Collection)
+HashSet(int,float)
+add(Object):boolean
+clear()
+clone():Object
+contains(Object):boolean
+isEmpty():boolean
+iterator():Iterator
+remove(Object):boolean
+size():int

java.util

LinkedHashSet

+LinkedHashSet()
+LinkedHashSet(int)
+LinkedHashSet(Collection)
+LinkedHashSet(int,float)

FIGURE D.7 The HashSet class and the LinkedHashSet class.

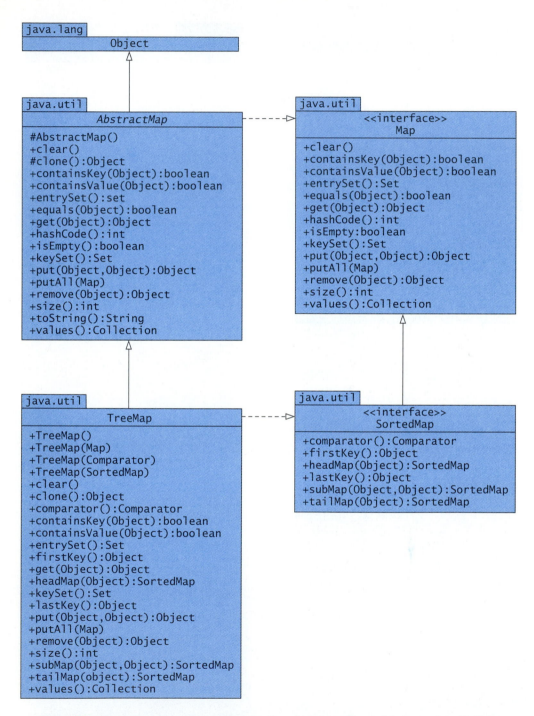

FIGURE D.8 The AbstractMap class, the TreeMap class, the Map interface, and the SortedMap interface.

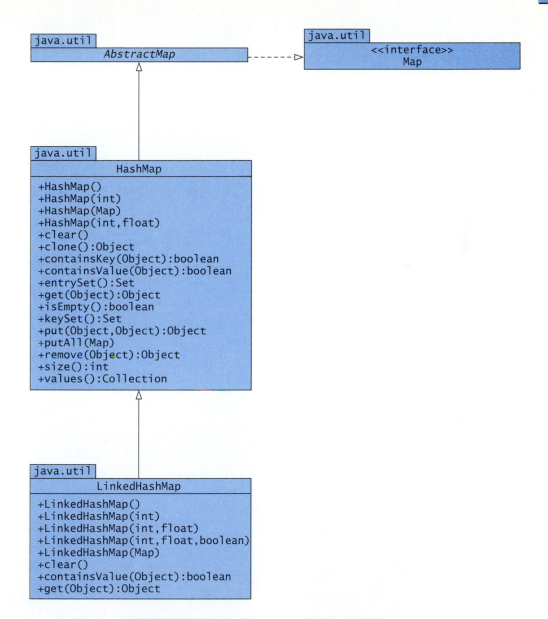

FIGURE D.9 The HashMap class and the LinkedHashMap class.

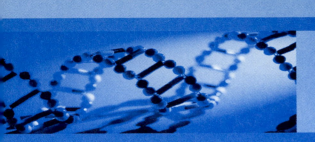

Appendix E

References

E.1 Books

[Aho] Aho, Alfred V., John E. Hopcroft, and Jeffrey D. Ullman. *Data Structures and Algorithms*. Addison-Wesley, Boston, 1983 ISBN: 0201000237.

[Arnold] Arnold, Ken, James Gosling, and David Holmes. *The Java Programming Language, Third Edition*. Addison-Wesley, Boston, 2000 ISBN: 0201704331.

[Baase] Baase, Sara and Allen Van Gelder. *Computer Algorithms, Third Edition*. Addison-Wesley, Boston, 2000. ISBN: 0201612445.

[Bloch] Bloch, Joshua. *Effective Java Programming Language Guide*. Addison-Wesley, Boston, 2001. ISBN: 0201310058.

[Boone] Boone, Barry. *Java Essentials for C and C++ Programmers*. Addison-Wesley, Boston, 1998. ISBN: 020147946X.

[Budd] Budd, Timothy. *Classic Data Structures*. Addison-Wesley, Boston, 2001. ISBN: 0201700026.

[Campione] Campione, Mary, Kathy Walrath. *The Java Tutorial*. Addison-Wesley, Boston, 1998. ISBN: 0201634546.

[Carrano] Carrano, Frank Janet Prichard. *Data Abstraction and Problem Solving with Java*. Addison-Wesley, Boston, 2001. ISBN: 0201702207.

[Chan1] Chan, Patrick, Rosanna Lee, Douglas Kramer. *The Java Class Libraries,* 2d ed., vol. 1. Addison-Wesley, Boston, 1998. ISBN: 0201310023.

[Chan2] Chan, Patrick, Rosanna Lee, Douglas Kramer. *The Java Class Libraries,* 2d ed., vol. 2. Addison-Wesley, Boston, 1998. ISBN: 0201310031.

[Chan3]   Chan, Patrick, Rosanna Lee, Douglas Kramer. *The Java Class Libraries,* 2d ed., vol. 1*, Supplement for the Java 2 Platform Standard Edition, v 1.2*, Addison-Wesley, Boston, 1999. ISBN: 0201485524.

[Chan4]   Chan, Patrick. *The Java Developers ALMANAC 1.4, Volume 1: Examples and Quick Reference*. Addison-Wesley, Boston, 2002. ISBN: 0201722808.

[Cormen]   Cormen, Thomas H., Charles E. Leiserson, Ronald L. Rivest, and Clifford Stein. *Introduction to Algorithms,* 2d ed. MIT Press, Cambridge, MA, 2001. ISBN: 0070131511.

[Drozdek]   Drozdek, Adam. *Data Structures and Algorithms in Java*. Brooks/Cole, Pacific Grove, CA, 2001. ISBN: 0534376681.

[Gosling]   Gosling, James, Bill Joy, Guy Steele, and Gilad Bracha. *The Java Language Specification,* 2d ed. Addison-Wesley, Boston, 2000. ISBN: 0201310082.

[Harary]   Harary, Frank. *Graph Theory.* Perseus Books, Reading, MA, 1969. ISBN: 0201410338.

[Hubbard1]   Hubbard, John R. *Schaum's Outline of Programming with Java,* 2d ed., McGraw-Hill, New York, 2004. ISBN: 0071420401.

[Hubbard2]   Hubbard, John R. *Schaum's Outline of Data Structures with Java*. McGraw-Hill, New York, 2001. ISBN: 0071361286.

[Kanerva]   Kanerva, Jonni. *The Java FAQ*. Addison-Wesley, Boston, 1997. ISBN: 0201634562.

[Knuth1]   Knuth, Donald E. *The Art of Computer Programming, Vol. 1: Fundamental Algorithms,* 3d ed. Addison-Wesley, Boston, 1997. ISBN: 0201896834.

[Knuth2]   Knuth, Donald E. *The Art of Computer Programming, Vol. 3: Seminumerical Algorithms,* 3d ed. Addison-Wesley, Boston, 1998. ISBN: 0201896842.

[Knuth3]   Knuth, Donald E. *The Art of Computer Programming, Vol. 3: Sorting and Searching,* 2d ed. Addison-Wesley, Boston, 1998. ISBN: 0201896850.

[Sahni]   Sahni, Sartaj. *Data Structures, Algorithms, and Applications in Java*. McGraw-Hill, New York, 2000. ISBN: 007109217X.

[Stevens]   Stevens, Perdita, and Rob Pooley. *Using UML*. Addison-Wesley, Boston, 2000. ISBN: 0201648601.

[Unicode1]   The Unicode Consortium. *The Unicode Standard, Version 2.0*. Addison-Wesley, Boston, 1996. ISBN: 0201483459.

[Vermeulen] Vermeulen, Allan, et al. *The Elements of Java Style*. Cambridge University Press, Cambridge, 2001, ISBN: 0521777682.

[Wilson]   Wilson, Robin J., and John J. Watkins. *Graphs: An Introductory Approach*. John Wiley & Sons, New York, 1990, ISBN: 0471615544.

[Wirth]   Wirth, Nicklaus. *Algorithms + Data Structures = Programs*. Prentice Hall, Upper Saddle River, NJ, 1976. ISBN: 0130224189.

E.2 Papers

[Hoare1]   Hoare, Charles A. R., "Algorithm 63: Quicksort," *Communications of the ACM* 4 (1961), 321.

[Hoare2]   Hoare, Charles A. R., "Quicksort," *Computer Journal* 2 (1962), 10–15.

[Knuth4]   Knuth, Donald E., "Von Neumann's First Computer Program," *Computing Surveys* 2 (1970), 247–260.

[Moret]   Moret, B. M. E., "Decision Trees and Algorithms," *Computing Surveys* 14 (1982), 593–623.

[Motzkin]   Motzkin, Dalia, "Meansort," *Communications of the ACM* 26 (1983), 250–251.

[Parnas]   Parnas, D. L., "On the Criteria to Be Used in Decomposing Systems into Modules," *Communications of the ACM* 15 (1972), 1053–1058.

[Shell]   Shell, Donald L., "A High-Speed Sorting Procedure," *Communications of the ACM* 2 (1959), 30–32.

[Williams]   Williams, John W. J., "Algorithm 232: Heapsort," *Communications of the ACM* 7 (1964), 347–348.

E.3 URLs

[AVL]   Animated applets that demonstrate the insertion and deletion algorithms for AVL trees:

```
www.csi.uottawa.ca/~stan/csi2514/applets/avl/BT.html
www.compapp.dcu.ie/~aileen/balance/
www.seanet.com/users/arsen/avltree.html
```

[Hubbard4]   Author's Website of resources for this book:

```
www.mathcs.richmond.edu/~hubbard/PHDSWJ/src/
```

[Java1]   The Java home website, containing the most current information on the Java programming language, including downloads:

```
java.sun.com
```

[Java2]   The complete Java Application Programming Interface (API) documentation:

```
java.sun.com/j2se/1.4/docs/api/
```

[Java3]   The Java Collections Framework:

```
java.sun.com/j2se/1.4/docs/guide/collections/
```

[Java4]   All the examples from **[Chan1]**:

`java.sun.com/docs/books/chanlee/second_edition/vol1/`
`    examples.htm`

[Java5]   Brief tutorials on various Java topics:

`java.sun.com/docs/books/tutorial/`

[Java6]   The Java Developers Connection; subscribe, and receive a biweekly email with two minitutorials on current Java topics:

`developer.java.sun.com/developer/`

[RBT]   Animated applets that demonstrate the insertion and deletion algorithms for red-black trees:

`www.ececs.uc.edu/~franco/C321/html/RedBlack/redblack.html`

[Sorting]   Animated applets that demonstrate the main sorting algorithms:

`www.cs.rit.edu/~atk/Java/Sorting/sorting.html`
`www.cs.ubc.ca/spider/harrison/Java/sorting-demo.html`
`www.scs.carleton.ca/~morin/misc/sortalg/`

[UML]   Information on the Unified Modeling Language:

`www.platinum.com/corp/uml/uml.htm`
`www.rational.com/uml/`
`www.uml.org/`

[Unicode2]   Information on the 16-bit Unicode characters used in Java:

`www.unicode.org`

Index

C